SAME-SEX DESIRE IN EARLY MODERN ENGLAND,
1550–1735

Same-Sex Desire in Early Modern England, 1550–1735

An anthology of literary texts and contexts

Edited by
Marie Helena Loughlin

Manchester University Press
Manchester and New York
distributed in the United States exclusively by Palgrave Macmillan

Published by Manchester University Press
Oxford Road, Manchester M13 9NR, UK
and Room 400, 175 Fifth Avenue, New York, NY 10010, USA
www.manchesteruniversitypress.co.uk

Distributed in the United States exclusively by
Palgrave Macmillan, 175 Fifth Avenue, New York,
NY 10010, USA

Distributed in Canada exclusively by
UBC Press, University of British Columbia, 2029 West Mall,
Vancouver, BC, Canada V6T 1Z2

British Library Cataloguing-in-Publication Data
A catalogue record for this book is available from the British Library

Library of Congress Cataloging-in-Publication Data applied for

ISBN 978 0 7190 8207 8 hardback

ISBN 978 0 7190 8208 5 paperback

First published 2014

Typeset
by Carnegie Book Production, Lancaster
Printed in Great Britain
by Bell & Bain Ltd, Glasgow

For Oliver and Mark

Contents

Illustrations

Images 1–3, 6, 9–10 are reproduced by permission of the Huntington Library Collections; 4 and 5 by permission of the Bodleian Library, University of Oxford; 7 and 8 by permission of the Folger Shakespeare Library.

Preface

Editorial Procedures

I have limited my selections to works that appeared in English between approximately 1550 and 1735, to concentrate on the representations available to the greatest number of literate English men and women. For modern translations of a far wider range of material, including texts in Latin not translated in the period and those in other European vernaculars, see Kenneth Borris's *Same-Sex Desire in the English Renaissance: A Sourcebook of Texts, 1470–1650* (Routledge, 2004). I have modernized each of the texts selected below, normalizing spelling, capitalization, and punctuation, except in particular cases; thus, original spelling has been maintained in poetry, for example, when rhyme or scansion demanded it; dialect forms have also been maintained as far as possible. I have not maintained the originals' use of italics. Readers interested in facsimile editions of some of the works selected for this anthology should examine Alexander Pettit and Patrick Spedding's excellent ten-volume collection *Eighteenth-Century British Erotica, Parts I and II*, particularly part 2, volume 5 (on homosexuality edited by Rictor Norton) and part 1, volume 2 (edited by Kevin L. Cope). For a wealth of material on homosexuality in the eighteenth century, readers should consult Rictor Norton's online *Homosexuality in Eighteenth-Century England: A Sourcebook* (see Works Cited). For the more obscure works selected below, I include a list of available editions.

Annotations and Glossary

Proper names that occur frequently throughout the anthology have been gathered together in a glossary: these include figures from classical mythology and literature (such as Apollo, Achilles, Danae, Elysium, the Furies, etc.), and historical figures from classical antiquity (such as Socrates, Plato, and Heliogabalus), as well as biblical figures (such as David and Jonathan). All other people, places, and things, as well as early modern historical and literary figures are identified in the footnotes.

Cross-References

Each selection has been assigned a number to make cross-references easier to use. Thus, Sappho's poem 'Hymn to Venus' is cross-referenced as follows: **7.5.2**, where '**7**' refers to 'Chapter 7: The Classical Tradition in Translation'; '**5**' refers to the fifth selection in this chapter 'John Addison's *Works of Anacreon* [...] *and Sappho*'; and '**2**' refers to the second poem in this selection, 'Hymn to Venus'. Cross-references within a particular selection will simply refer the reader, for example, to **n3**.

Reference Works

Unless otherwise noted, headnotes and annotations rely on the following.

1. Definitions of words and phrases: *Oxford English Dictionary* (second online edn; accessed 2010); E. Knowles's *Oxford Dictionary of Phrase and Fable* (online edn, 2006); E. Partridge's *Dictionary of Slang* (ed. P. Beale, eighth edn, 2002); G. Williams's *Dictionary of Sexual Language and Imagery in Shakespearean and Stuart Literature*, 2 vols (1994).

2. Classical, literary, and historical figures: *Oxford Classical Dictionary* (third edn, 1999); G. Speake's *Penguin Dictionary of Ancient History* (1994); *Oxford Companion to Classical Literature* (1984); B. Radice's *Penguin Who's Who in the Ancient World* (1973); J. Lemprière's *Classical Dictionary* (1788; rept, 1994).

3. The Bible and Christianity: *HarperCollins' Bible Dictionary* (gen. ed. P.J. Achtemeier, rev. edn, 1996); W.R.F. Browning's *Oxford Dictionary of the Bible* (1996); *Harper's Bible Commentary* (gen. ed. J.L. Mays, 1988); *Oxford Dictionary of the Christian Church* (ed. F.L. Cross and E.A. Livingstone, second rev. edn, 1983).

4. Same-sex lovers in history: J.G. Younger's *Sex in the Ancient World, from A–Z* (2005); *Who's Who in Gay & Lesbian History: From Antiquity to World War II* (ed. R. Aldrich and G. Wotherspoon, 2002).

5. Early modern England's society, history, and culture: Marcel De

Cleene and Marie Claire Lejeune's *Compendium of Symbolic and Ritual Plants in Europe*, 2 vols (1999–2003); L.W. Cowrie's *Wordsworth Dictionary of British Social History* (1996); M.B. Picken's *Dictionary of Costume and Fashion: Historic and Modern* (1985; rept, 1998); *The Diary of Samuel Pepys, Vol. X, Companion* (ed. R.C. Latham and W. Matthews, 1971); M.P Tilley's *Dictionary of the Proverbs in England in the Sixteenth and Seventeenth Centuries* (1966); C.W. Cunnington's *Dictionary of English Costume* (1960); *Calendar of State Papers, Domestic series [of the Commonwealth] 1649–1660* (ed. M.A.E. Green, 1875–1886); Pliny's *Natural History*, 2 vols (trans. P. Holland, 1601).

6. Biographical information on early modern figures: *Oxford Dictionary of National Biography* (*DNB*: online edn, accessed 2011); *Burke's Peerage, Baronetage & Knightage* (ed. C. Mosley, 107th edn, 3 vols, 2003); *Alumni Cantabrigiensis*, 4 vols (ed. J. Venn, 1922–7); *The Eton College Register, 1441–1698* (ed. W. Sterry, 1943).

Unless otherwise noted, references to Greek and Latin texts are to the standard Loeb editions.

Online Companion

Reducing an anthology that once stood at approximately 500,000 words to its present length was a challenge. There are far more texts concerning early modern same-sex erotic relationships and desires than can be contained within a relatively brief anthology. Interested readers may consult the *Online Companion* for additional texts and brief interpretative essays at: http://hdl.handle.net/2429/43470.

Acknowledgements

The editor sincerely thanks all who helped with this project, particularly the following: my insightful and painstaking graduate research assistants, Jannik Eikenaar and Kelly Doyle, my equally conscientious undergraduate research assistant, Richard Benade, and the Work Study Program as well as the Department of Critical Studies (Faculty of Creative and Critical Studies, University of British Columbia-Okanagan) for jointly funding their positions; the helpful librarians and staff at the Bodleian Library, British Library, Folger Shakespeare Library, Wellesley College Library, and Huntington Library; Professors Rictor Norton and Rosalind Ballaster (Mansfield College, Oxford

University) for their kind encouragement; Professor W.R. Jones (University of Leicester) for his information about Lucian's translator, Thomas Brown; Professors Peter Sabor (McGill University) and Thomas Keymer (University of Toronto) for their assistance with *The Sappho-An*; Professor Michael Treschow (UBC-Okanagan) for his generous assistance with Ovid's Latin; my Manchester editors, Matthew Frost, Kim Walker, and Lianne Slavin for their patience and support; John Banks for his painstaking copyediting; and finally my family, without whose forbearance this book would still be unfinished.

General Introduction

The History of the History of 'Homosexuality': Debating Sexual Identity

Same-Sex Desire in Early Modern England, 1550–1735 is an anthology of selections from works dealing with same-sex love, desire, sexual acts, and relationships, in a period when the representation and meanings attached to these realities underwent enormous changes. These selections aim at allowing the reader to consider in detail some of the critical and methodological issues that have been involved in charting the developing representations and realities attached to what we now term 'homosexuality' and 'lesbianism'.[1] These very

[1] I am following North American usage here, where 'homosexuality' and 'homosexual' are generally terms applied to men, since 'lesbianism' and 'lesbian' are terms reserved for women. This usage is both a popular and an informal one in North America, but it is also one that appears in a number of academic works, where the focus is exclusively, or almost exclusively upon men, such that the phrase 'male homosexuality' comes to seem redundant, such as Alan Bray's *Homosexuality in Renaissance England* (New York, 1982; rev. edn, 1995) and Bruce R. Smith's *Homosexual Desire in Shakespeare's England* (Chicago, 1991). Generally, since these modern terms are fraught for reasons I discuss later in the introduction, and in 'Terminology', recent critics generally tend to avoid them altogether, although this is by no means always the case. In the introduction to their recent collection of essays *The Sciences of Homosexuality in Early Modern Europe* (London and New York, 2008), Kenneth Borris and George Rousseau describe their use of the word 'homosexuality' and 'homosexual' as wholly deliberate, and part of an attempt to explore the differences, correlations, and continuities between these terms' 'accumulated connotations in the nineteenth century and beyond' and their 'root meaning of "same-sexual"' ('Introduction' 1). To banish from an exploration of early modern same-sex relationships, acts, and desires the terms 'homosexual' and 'homosexuality' as well as 'lesbian' and 'lesbianism' is to accept a radical division between modern and early modern sexualities, rather than to engage in a mapping of their disjunctions as well as continuities. Borris, Rousseau, and their contributors, however, also employ,

terms, however, have been and continue to be controversial in terms of early modern men's and women's experiences and inscriptions of same-sex erotic love and relationships, and this controversy directs us to the most dominant of those issues that have defined critical analysis for the last twenty years: sexual identity. Historians of homosexuality in the Western tradition are usually presented as committed to one of two models of sexual identity. The essentialist model sees homosexual identity as having existed in a largely unchanged and recognizable form across time, culture, and geographic space, and thus has no difficulty labelling same-sex erotic realities in other historical periods and cultures with modern terms, such as 'homosexual', 'lesbian', 'gay', and 'queer'. In contrast, the social-constructionist model sees homosexual identity as comprising a number of historically specific roles that vary across time, culture, and geographic space, and thus resists modern labels as anachronistic. In practice most explorations on both sides of the essentialist/social-constructionist divide are more nuanced. While the early, influential critics Alan Bray, Rictor Norton, and Randolph Trumbach have all been 'accused' of essentialism, all three conceive of 'homosexuality' as comprising a number of historically and culturally specific roles, with Bray famously noting that 'to talk of an individual in this period as being or not being "a homosexual" is an anachronism and ruinously misleading', since 'the terms in which we now speak of homosexuality cannot be readily translated into those of the sixteenth and seventeenth centuries' (*Homosexuality* 16–17). However critics or readers position themselves, the distance between early modern and modern understandings of sexual identity clearly requires the marshalling of all our imaginative resources to map out the different ways of being in the world that are involved in the early modern textual inscription and lived experience of same-sex desire, love, sexual acts, and relationships.

One of the most vexed issues in the history of 'homosexuality' and 'lesbianism' has been the relationship between the early modern discourses of sodomy and tribadism and notions of early modern sexual identity. Sodomy constitutes the single most prevalent early modern discourse concerning male same-sex sexual acts, and tribadism the single most prevalent concerning female same-sex sexual acts.[2] As a result, until very recently sodomy and

as I do, more 'neutral' descriptors, such as 'female and male same-sex relationships', and are as careful as possible when delimiting the meanings of such vexed terms as 'sodomy' ('Introduction' 4–5). For Borris's introduction of the wider term 'same-sexual', see 'Introduction', p. 5 and p. 31, n2. My own discussion of terminology can be found in 'Terminology', as well as throughout the General Introduction and chapter introductions (especially Chapters 1 and 3).

[2] As the discussion below of the changing representations and valences of sodomy and the sodomite suggests, these words and concepts are over-determined in the period;

tribadism have been accorded a privileged place in an examination of early modern discourses concerning same-sex relationships and acts, and much critical energy has gone into their analysis: Alan Bray offered in 1982 a formative consideration of the profound chasm between the discourse of sodomy and what we can gather of the realities of male same-sex desires and practices, arguing that there was an ubiquitous, virulent condemnation of sodomy (on the one hand) and a quiet institutionalization of homoerotic relationships and same-sex acts (on the other). He and other influential critics, such as Rictor Norton, Jonathan Goldberg, Randolph Trumbach, Harriette Andreadis, Mario DiGangi, Emma Donoghue, and Valerie Traub, have explored how sodomy and the sodomite, as well as tribadism and the tribade, came to function in a wide variety of ways: as the 'other' that helps define a nascent and shifting concept of 'Englishness'; as a reflection of various social and cultural disruptions; as an index of changing attitudes towards sex and sexuality, the body, gender, and human relationships, as well as the anxieties, fears and fantasies related to these issues; and, most recently, as simply one among a number of intersecting discourses that allow us access to early modern conceptions of same-sex love, sexual acts, relationships, and desires.

There has been a move, in short, to contextualize rather than privilege the discourses of sodomy and tribadism in analyses of 'homosexuality' and 'lesbianism' in early modern England. Critics and readers have become acutely aware that the textual contexts in which the sodomite and the tribade appear are almost always proscriptive (satires, legal manuals, criminal pamphlets, religious polemics, etc.) and xeno-homophobic (i.e., they employ the ubiquitous trope of sodomy and tribadism as foreign 'diseases') (Zorach, qtd in Schleiner 247–8). In short, while such texts and tropes may reveal the fantasies, fears, and desires that accompanied the tribade and the sodomite, they alone do not comprise a sufficient context to examine homoerotic love, desire, sexual acts, and relationships in early modern England. Focusing on the discourse of sodomy has led modern critics to sometimes assume that it is the *sine qua non* of discourses when it comes to discussing the representation of male same-sex passionate love, erotic relationships and sexual acts, to the detriment of other, more homophilic contexts, such as *amicitia*

they can mean and imply, in short, radically different things depending on the context, and so answering the question 'what did "sodomy" and "sodomite" mean in early modern England?' becomes a project of marking the shifting meanings attached to these terms, and the often ideologically interested ways in which they were employed. For the varying use of 'sodomy' in legal discourses, for example, see the Introduction to Chapter 3. For an account of tribadic sexual acts, sodomitical sexual acts, and the meanings that attached to them, see Andreadis, *Sappho*, pp. 39–45; Traub, *Renaissance*, pp. 43–8, 193–215; Bray, *Homosexuality*, pp. 13–32; Goldberg, *Sodometries*, pp. 1–25; and Borris, *Same-Sex Desire*, pp. 23–35.

– an idealized, Neoplatonic, classically based conception of male friendship, which sees a pair of friends as 'one soul in bodies twain' – or voluntary kinship – a kind of sworn brotherhood achieved through a ritual or promise, which served as an overarching social institution and set of practices to establish and manage the intimate bonds between men (Bray, *Friend* 104, 110–11). In addition to *amicitia*, critics have turned to discourses describing other intimate relationships between men, such as those between students and tutors, patrons and clients, as well as a variety of homophilic literary conventions, discourses and tropes, such as the imitation of the classical homoerotic relationship between the beloved boy and the older man in the period's elegy, pastoral, and lyric, and the imitation of classical homoerotic martial friendships in the period's drama and narrative. These varying homophilic discourses allow modern critics to balance out the influence of the homophobic discourse of sodomy.

In contrast, tribadism was relatively insignificant as a discourse in the period – it was by no means the social, cultural, and discursive equivalent of sodomy in terms of these discourses' development, deployment, pervasiveness, and influence. As Traub notes, in the hundred and fifty years between Thomas Beard's moral compendium of human vice, *The Theatre of God's Judgements* (1597) (see **1.2**) and Giles Jacob's *New Law Dictionary* and John Disney's *A View of the Ancient Laws Against Immorality and Profaneness* (both 1729), there is only very sporadic recognition of 'the possibility of female-female sex', even though such a recognition was a part of medieval theology, biblical commentary, and penitential manuals. For Traub, trying to place women within the legal and theological discourses of same-sex sexual acts results in frustration; we 'find only absence, hear mostly silence', since female–female sex is only rarely defined as sodomy or buggery (*Renaissance* 167–9). Ironically, the relative absence of the tribade and tribadism in a wide range of texts and discourses at least until the very late seventeenth century has meant that modern analyses of female same-sex erotic relationships have always turned to other ways of accessing such relationships, and have rarely employed the tribade and tribadism as the same privileged point of access to same-sex relationships as has often been the case with sodomy and the sodomite. Critics have focused instead on women's appropriation of *amicitia* and voluntary kinship, as well as a variety of literary discourses and tropes, such as the representation of the transvestite heroine (on stage and in prose romance); the representation of the loving relationships between women on the pre-Restoration and post-Restoration stage (e.g., Catharine Trotter's *Agnes de Castro*: see **9.24**), and in the late seventeenth-century poetry of female friendship; as well as the elegiac and pastoral modes used to express these relationships and contain any challenges they might pose to patriarchal norms (Traub, *Renaissance* 170–5). In short, the discourses of sodomy and tribadism cannot help us recover the *affective* range of men's and women's homoerotic relationships in the period. As George Haggerty so memorably cautions, '[l]ove has often been ignored in histories of sexuality, in part because it is the most elusive of the four-letter words and in part because it has not been understood as central to the question of sexuality itself' ('Male Love' 71). To recover these meanings we need to also recover the ability to distinguish between sodomy and tribadism as offering the signs of disorderly homoerotic relations, and other discourses as offering 'the signs of orderly [...] homoerotic relations', the signs of same-sex love and affect (DiGangi 71).

Interestingly, as critics have widened the contexts within which they analyse male and female homoerotic relationships, they have also returned to the whole issue of sexual identity in the early modern period. Taking on the essentialist/social-constructionist divide, readers and critics have begun to question the notion that 'sexual identity' *per se* is always an anachronistic, essentialist, and misleading category when applied to early modern individuals. Moreover, they have begun to question the notion that idealized same-sex love and friendship (classical *amicitia*) and same-sex sexual and erotic acts and desires are always mutually exclusive, compartmentalized, and set up in binary opposition to each other. That is, recognizing that speaking of sexual identity does not necessarily involve a naive assumption of the equivalence between modern and early modern conceptions of identity, or a jettisoning of careful historical and cultural contextualization, has allowed critics to focus on *early modern* sexual identities and the role of sexual desires and acts in their construction. As Kenneth Borris, David Halperin, and Joseph Cady have pointed out, the fact that early modern sexual identities do not correspond to present-day ones does not mean that early modern individuals had no notion of an identity informed, shaped, and perhaps even made distinct by a person's particular sexual desires and acts.[3] Kenneth Borris and others have demonstrated that something approximating 'sexual identity' can indeed be discerned in early modern cultures, and that same-sex sexual acts are linked, for example, in many early modern scientific discourses 'with apparently distinctive sexual affinities, affiliations, classifications, morphologies, and physiologies' (*Sciences* 4).

Modern critics and readers, then, must be cautious about assuming that an early modern person's engagement in particular same-sex erotic desires and sexual acts indicates his or her possession of a 'homosexual' or 'lesbian' identity *identical* to that which exists in the modern Western world, though nascent concepts of sexual identity do indeed exist in the period; about employing those discourses – sodomy and tribadism – to unproblematically historicize their understanding of this identity and its expression

[3] See Halperin, *How*, pp. 40–4.

in early modern literature; and about expecting to see representations of same-sex sexual acts kept rigidly separate from representations of same-sex passionate love and erotic desire. For the modern reader, sodomy and tribadism have as often occluded the nature of same-sex homoerotic love, desire, sexual acts, and relationships as they have illuminated them. It has been especially difficult to read simultaneously both sexual desire and acts as well as passionate emotional attachment in representations of same-sex relationships, since sodomy and tribadism are drenched in a rhetoric of abhorrence, while idealized, classical *amicitia* is shaped in a rhetoric of celebration. A reader need only turn, however, to Shakespeare's 'Sonnet 20' ('A woman's face with Nature's own hand painted': see **8.10.1**) and to Katherine Philips's 'Friendship in Emblem, or The Seal, to My Dearest Lucasia' (see **9.14.2**) to realize that even the long-assumed, rigid division between the early modern textual representation of homoerotic love and same-sex sexual acts is untenable, but also that the integration of same-sex sexual acts into the poetry of same-sex erotic devotion and love had very different valences for male and female homoeroticism.

While space prevents a detailed analysis here, Shakespeare's 'Sonnet 20' offers the older male speaker's witty engagement with the figure of his beloved young man's penis and implies the possibility of their joining in same-sex intercourse. The tonal register of this sonnet – witty, daring, and risky – relies upon the stigmatization of male same-sex sexual acts for its transgressive *frisson*, at the same time that it inscribes these acts as an imaginative possibility within a deeply affective love relationship. Moreover, Shakespeare's deliberative play upon the transgressive nature of sodomitical acts, and the apparently inviolable division between representations of male same-sex erotic love and *amicitia* (on the one hand) and male same-sex sexual acts (on the other), inflects and shapes not simply the loving, homoerotic relationship between the male speaker and his male beloved but the other relationships that the couple partake in: between poet and patron, between subordinate and superior, between servant and master. In comparison, Katherine Philips's 'Friendship in Emblem, or The Seal, to My Dearest Lucasia' (publ., 1667), partially a reworking of the highly heteroerotic poem by John Donne, 'A Valediction: Forbidding Mourning', likewise employs strategies that suggest that female same-sex sexual acts and desires were not rigidly separated from women's appropriation of the discourse of *amicitia*, nor automatically stigmatized as tribadic. In Philips's hands, Donne's image of himself and his beloved wife as 'stiff twin compasses' – which famously merges erotic, spiritual, and sexual registers to describe the heterosexual couple's union and constancy – becomes a way of ascribing many of the meanings that Donne attributed to his heterosexual union to Orinda's (Philips's) homoerotic union with Lucasia (Anne Owen): from the spiritual perfection of their love envisioned through the perfect circle the compass inscribes to the erotic and sexual longing of the lovers' bodies in their mutual erection when they are rejoined. While Donne's image of the legs of the compass has almost always been interpreted as referring exclusively to male erection, Philips's use suggests the female lovers' mutual clitoral erection.[4] However, while the sexual aspects of the erotic and affective relationship between the speaker and the young man are licensed by many patriarchal assumptions and institutions (including, for example, the sexual explicitness permitted by the poet's gender, as well as the social capital the male poet accrues precisely through the witty, sexual transgressiveness of his verse[5]), the sexual aspects of the erotic and affective relationship between Orinda and Lucasia struggle into being in the context of the very challenge they pose to these assumptions and institutions.

Licensing Same-Sex Erotic Desires, Love, and Sexual Acts: Homosocial Institutions in Early Modern England, 1550–1735

Alan Bray has shown that early modern English society's homosocial discourses and institutions underpinned and managed the formation of passionately committed same-sex relationships. His ground-breaking *Homosexuality in Renaissance England* (1982; rev. edn 1995) outlines the many early modern institutions that both suppressed and enabled male (and, I would add, female) same-sex erotic relationships. Of the enablers, the early modern household and the educational institution are perhaps the most important. All such households, except for the very poorest, included the related members of a family and its servants and/or apprentices. Unrelated and unmarried people of the same sex living together in close quarters – commonly sleeping two to a bed, looking for an outlet for libidinal energy in a culture where pre-marital heterosexual intercourse could mean pregnancy, social shame, and prosecution for bastardy – might well turn to same-sex acts

[4] A.B. Chambers, 'Glorified Bodies and the "Valediction: Forbidding Mourning".' *John Donne Journal* 1 (1982): 1–20. Recent histories of the body show that the clitoral erection was part of the 'intellectual baggage' of Donne and his contemporaries. For the Renaissance 'rediscovery of the clitoris' and its functioning in sexual arousal, see Traub, *Renaissance*, pp. 188–228. For an edition that unapologetically describes this 'erection' as female clitoral erection, see *John Donne: Selected Poems*, ed. Ilona Bell (London, 2006), p. 216, n32.

[5] See A.F. Marotti, *John Donne, Coterie Poet* (Madison, 1986), pp. 44–66.

and relationships. Moreover, masters' power over servants and apprentices, and teachers' power over students fostered both heterosexual and same-sex relations, but the latter usually enter the public record only when coercion or socially prominent individuals were involved. Otherwise such relationships apparently went unnoticed (Bray 42–51). Homoerotic relationships and acts between female servants and between a mistress and her maid were perhaps even more invisible than those between male household members. Margaret Hunt suggests that such relationships were apparently perceived either as 'harmless and beneath [...] notice' or as part of the 'physical endearments' conventional in women's friendships. A personal maid's intimate work – bathing, dressing, massaging, beautifying, and perhaps sharing a bed with the mistress – might well shade into erotic service and love (281). As Traub points out, and as texts as wildly diverse as Jacob's *Tractatus de Hermaphroditis* (see **2.1**), Mary Stuart's correspondence with Frances Apsley (see **5.3**), and the anonymously authored *Sappho-An* (see **7.9**) demonstrate, early modern cultural anxiety typically focused on women's same-sex erotic relationships only when these relationships became exclusive (thus interfering with their reproductive functions in marriage), expressed themselves in sexual acts that mimicked heterosexual intercourse (challenging male sexual prerogatives), and/or when these relationships potentially disrupted not just marriage's heterosexual economy but gender conventions as well as hierarchical and dynastic considerations (*Renaissance* 181; 188–97).

Grammar schools, universities, and the Inns of Court were exclusively male institutions, and encouraged male bonding between students, as well as the schoolmaster's authority over male pupils, all of which apparently fostered homoerotic attachments and created the circumstances within which same-sex acts might occur. The latter came to the attention of authorities, again, usually only when coercion or socially prominent individuals were involved (Bray, *Homosexuality* 51–3; Pittenger; Smith 81–5; and Stewart 84–121).[6] Latin was the linguistic and cultural milieu of these institutions, functioning in practical terms as the early modern period's diplomatic, economic, and intellectual *lingua franca*, and in symbolic terms as its marker of class, status, and power. Latin language and literature were thus the centre of the elite male's education, bonding him to his contemporaries and granting him access to a great deal of homophilic material. Studying classical writers and ancient as well as modern Latin texts on philosophy and natural science not only gave young men a sexual education largely unavailable to their female counterparts, but also reinforced young men's homoerotically charged educational environments and personal relationships (Smith 83–4;

[6] See the discussions of the Tudor humanist schoolmaster and playwright Nicholas Udall's relationships with his male students in Bray, Pittenger, Smith, and Stewart.

86–115). In this context, it is hardly surprising that some of the most erotic and emotionally moving verse that represents male same-sex relationships is written by young men for their school friends: Charles Goodall's published verse for his male friends, written during or inspired by their time together at Eton College and Oxford University (Merton College) (see **8.26** and **8.27**); Nicholas Oldisworth's manuscript poems for his dear Westminster School friend, Richard Bacon (see **8.17**); and William Lathum's pastoral elegy for his fellow Cambridge student and close friend, Nathaniel Weld (*Online Companion*).[7]

Lacking institutions like men's grammar schools and universities, women's education initially lacked a comparably intensive and wide-ranging same-sex bonding experience. By the 1650s, however, most larger towns and cities had some kind of female educational institution, and boarding schools, in particular, were on the increase throughout the period. Hunt notes that Mrs Salmon's school, one of two prominent gentlewomen's boarding schools in seventeenth-century London, claimed the poet Katherine Philips as a pupil. There she met at least one of the women who feature in her erotically charged poetry of female friendship: Mary Aubrey (see **9.14**). Young women's school curricula were perhaps less obviously integrated than young men's into a complex of same-sex desires and attitudes. With a curriculum that excluded Latin and Greek, and focused variously on English reading (and increasingly writing), religious instruction, household accountancy and management, modern languages (usually French), cooking, needlework, dancing, singing, and music, elite women were largely prepared to be wives and mothers. Lacking exposure to the classical Latin texts that reinforced male homoerotic relationships and desires, women still found ways of subverting the largely conservative motives of their education. An important subject in women's education, needleworking, particularly of biblical scenes portraying strong women such as Esther and Judith, challenged the silence and passivity that the activity aimed at cultivating (Frye 167). Needlework's all-female circles, comprised of mistress and maids, as well as of female friends and relations, suggest that women's educational curricula did indeed inform and foster homoerotic relationships. In *Midsummer Night's Dream*, Shakespeare certainly plays upon an apparently common connection between women's communal needle-working and the erotics of devoted female friendship in the figures of Hermia and Helena (see **9.4**).

The nature of women's school friendships, and their friendships within kinship, authorial, and affective circles generally, demands further attention.

[7] Men's homoerotic 'school' poetry has surprisingly received little sustained critical attention. For analyses of Goodall and Oldisworth, see Hammond, *Figuring*, pp. 32–8; 52–61. On Oldisworth, see Gouws, esp. pp. xv–xl.

Until recently, critics pointed to the lack of early modern prose treatises describing or referring to female same-sex friendship, in comparison to the large number on male same-sex friendship, and the generally dismissive way in which women's capacity for friendship is represented in this larger textual group. Early modern female friendship, unlike its male counterpart, apparently did not 'function as effectively as did men's to create and maintain legal, economic, and familial advantages', and thus 'in this context women's friendships were unmarked, naturalized, and as little subject to scrutiny as to celebration' (Traub, *Renaissance* 299).[8] However, as both Traub and Andreadis have argued, relying on Bray's insights concerning voluntary kinship and the way a broad range of men's social and familial relationships shaped and were shaped by men's passionate same-sex friendships, Katherine Philips's 'Society of Friendship' 'functioned as an alternative form of voluntary kinship' (Traub, *Renaissance* 300–1). This 'Society' formalized the way Philips and her female friends formed passionate erotic attachments as a counterbalance to marital relationships largely grounded in a woman's duty to family, class, religion, and politics. For Andreadis, Philips's use of the conventional image of idealized classical *amicitia* as the 'union' (or 'marriage') of two souls actually serves two purposes: it 'affirm[s] her passion for her female friends in her poems' and it 'create[s] a sociofamilial network of intimate relations [that] exemplifies female appropriation of masculine – and masculinist – ideology' ('Re-Configuring' 524–5).

The Sodomite and the 'Dear Friend': Literary Expressions of Male Same-Sex Desires, Relationships, Love and Sexual Acts, 1550–1735

Both what we might call provisionally the homophobic and the homophilic representations of male and female same-sex relationships, desires, and sexual acts are indeed very much shaped and affected by the language, imagery, and rhetoric of sodomy/tribadism and that constellation of images and discourses associated with the discourse of *amicitia*. Throughout this anthology's almost two-hundred-year time span, these discourses shift and develop. However, these representations and their interpenetration are also shaped by the changing conventions, forms of address, imagined audiences, and technologies of dissemination that attend on early modern literary

[8] For a full account of male same-sex friendship and voluntary kinship, see Bray, *Friend*, pp. 110–13, 213–19.

genres and modes. A focus on how particular literary genres and modes shaped and were shaped by the figure of the sodomite, the tribade, and the passionately devoted same-sex friend allows the modern reader to chart changes in the representation and import of these figures, as well as the ways in which these apparently opposed figures merge and interpenetrate. In turn, the modern reader can observe how the legal and religious definitions of the despised sodomite and tribade and the broader cultural definitions of the celebrated same-sex friend are, in turn, appropriated, deployed, and in many cases intermingled and contested through the resources provided by different literary genres and modes. Surprisingly, perhaps, we find that fissures and contradictions open up both in those imaginative works that condemn sodomy and the sodomite, and tribadism and the tribade, and those that celebrate same-sex friendship and the same-sex friend. Modern readers might sensibly assume that homophilic representations of passionate and erotic love between men and between women would be the monopoly of lyrical genres and utterances, while sexual activity between men and between women would find expression only in satiric genres and modes. However, ostensibly satiric literary works sometimes undermine their frequently xeno-homophobic agenda, and ostensibly celebratory works sometimes intermingle the figure of the faithful friend with that of the despised sodomite or tribade.

Satiric genres, discourses, and modes refer to the sodomite and sodomy in a variety of contexts.[9] In the sixteenth century, classical satire modelled on Juvenal and Horace depicted the sodomite either as the licentious gentleman/courtier with his ingle or catamite on one arm and his female punk or whore on the other; or as the physically abusive schoolmaster, whose corporal punishment of his students, his abuse of 'boyes buttockes', had been long acknowledged as erotically charged (Stewart 84–121; Bushnell 28–31). Both of these popular satiric types present sodomitical desires and activities as simply one aspect of the sexual and erotic pleasures available to those with power and wealth in the period, with the speaker's prostitute boy in John Donne's 'Satire 1' and John Marston's 'Satire 3' (see **8.9.1**) signifying the licentious courtier/gentleman's class status and power as a privileged consumer in London's urban economy. Inscribed within the misuse of class status and power, as well as the rejection of the ethical and cultural standards of ideal masculinity, then, Donne's and Marston's, as well as Ben Jonson's,[10]

[9] As a mode, satire functions 'to mark and defend boundaries' (3), and to indicate when such boundaries have been or are in danger of being violated. See Brian A. Connery and Kirk Combe, 'Theorizing Satire: A Retrospective Introduction', in *Theorizing Satire: Essays in Literary Criticism*, ed. B.A. Connery and K. Combe (London, 1995).

[10] The figure of the licentious gentleman who has sex with his page while courting his

satiric representations of sodomitical activity produce the curious effect of simultaneous condemnation and legitimization: the individual courtier/gentleman's sodomy represents, on the one hand, his moral, ethical, and gender corruption, and, on the other, his power and rank.[11] Likewise, the figure of the schoolmaster, sexually corrupting his students (as in Marston's 'Satire 3') or enjoying the satisfaction of his erotic desires through the sexual sublimation of corporal punishment, shows the extent to which these representations of sodomitical desires and acts were bound up with power and rank: this homoerotic relationship between the powerful scholar-teacher and his dependent youth-student was often inscribed within the uncomfortable and contradictory nexus of status and power that typified the humanist educational milieu. The schoolmaster's or tutor's rank was often far inferior to that of his pupils, but his power over them and their careers was widely acknowledged.

Into the seventeenth century, developments in satire as a mode of trenchant political as opposed to more general moral and ethical critique[12] meant that the satiric figure of the sodomite began to appear in works that had particular political axes to grind. Satiric and more generally critical or condemnatory representations of sexual relationships between older, elite males and younger, subordinate or dependent men, youths, or boys[13] take on varied political and nationalistic overtones. For example, Barnabe Barnes's tragedy *The Devil's Charter* (1607: see **8.11**) offers the ugly but conventional xeno-homophobic presentation of Pope Alexander VI as the sodomitical anti-Christ in the specific context of hysteria over possible Catholic insurgency in the wake of the Gunpowder Plot (1605). In Lady Mary Wroth's prose romance *Urania* (1621: see **8.12**), the contradictory figure of James I as 'the sodomite king' provokes a veiled examination of the

mistress appears in Jonson's *Every Man Out of His Humour* (1599) and *Epicoene* (1609), and is a familiar stage 'type'. See DiGangi, pp. 64–99.

[11] Rochester's libertine verse sometimes depicts the sexual relationship between the aristocratic speaker and his male objects of desire, usually the dependent page boy or lower-class youth; this relationship is as much about power as it is about desire (if not moreso). See Haggerty, *Men in Love*, pp. 6–9.

[12] See McRae, pp. 1–19.

[13] The use of 'boy' in various early modern homoerotic contexts owes at least as much to the influence of classical models, such as the Greek philosophers' consideration of the erotic relationship between tutor and student or between *eromenos* (the beloved boy) and *erastes* (the lover), or ancient lyrical poets' celebration of the beauty of youths and boys, as it does to early modern social reality. On the nature of the 'boy' as an erotic object in this period, see (for example) P. Stallybrass, 'Transvestism and the Body Beneath: Speculating on the Boy Actor', in *Erotic Politics*, ed. S. Zimmerman (New York, 1992), pp. 65–83; and L. Jardine, *Still Harping on Daughters* (Brighton, 1983).

relationship between sodomitical desire and statecraft. In the anonymous satirical poem *The Life and Death of John Atherton* (1641: see **3.2**), the sexual relationship between John Atherton, Bishop of Waterford and Lismore, and his appropriately named proctor John Child, emblematizes the established Church's and Archbishop Laud's emphasis on religious conformity and investment in 'papist' ceremony as threatening to destroy the Protestant nation, Church, and king. In John Wilmot, Earl of Rochester's closet drama *Sodom and Gomorrah* (1684: see **8.25**), King Bolloxinian's legalization of sodomy constructs a damning critique of Charles II and his government, particularly Charles's circumvention of Parliament, his French Catholic sympathies, and the concomitant disintegration of traditional structures of patronage and allegiance: King Bolloxinian's anal penetration of his grovelling courtiers showcases the degeneration of the bonds of mutual obligation and service between king and courtier into a crude sexual servicing of the king by his 'men'.

These satiric, condemnatory, and denigrating configurations of the sodomite and sodomy are in themselves interesting for what they tell a modern reader about the wide variety of ways this figure and discourse could be employed. However, even more interesting, perhaps, are the ambivalent or contradictory meanings produced by some of these texts. Hammond notes that Barnes's *The Devil's Charter* combines a highly typical representation of sodomy as a xeno-homophobic trope for England's religious, sexual, and national contamination by the 'other' (here, Catholic and Italian) with a highly contradictory erotic charge arising from the sensual pleasures provided to the audience by the Pope's lyrical wooing of the youthful Astor, Astor's anguished temptation to homoerotic desire and same-sex sexual acts, and the displaying of the young male actors' lovely bodies (Hammond 38–44). Likewise, Wroth's *Urania* does indeed, as Ellis Hanson has noted, respond to James I's homoerotic relationships with his various, younger male favourites,[14] through the numerous parallels between the unfolding of the eight-year relationship between James and Robert Carr, later Earl of Somerset, and that of Wroth's fictional duke and his unnamed favourite. While James's combination in his own person of king and sodomite was an unbearable contradiction, which Wroth 'solves' by dividing James into two fictional shadows – 'one a harmless but ineffectual sodomite, "bewitch'd" by a young man, the other a manly king who disregards the duke's affections and punishes the evil favourite' – this division has unexpected consequences.

[14] *Urania* appeared in a decade which saw, according to McRae, an outpouring of political satire in the form of clandestine verse and cheap pamphlets. James's same-sex erotic and sexual relationships with various favourites appear in a number of these. See *Early Stuart Libels: An Edition of Poetry from Manuscript Sources*, ed. A. Bellany and A. McRae, *Early Modern Literary Studies*, Text Series I (2005) http://purl.oclc.emls/texts/libelsl.

It helps resolve James's disruption of 'erotic [...] and patriarchal order' (139), but also produces a portrait of the duke as that most contradictory figure: the loving sodomite – here, a man of rank whose relationship with his younger, dependent, and less socially elevated favourite spans the fatherly, the affective, and the erotic, in much the same way as James's relationships with his favourites did, especially Buckingham (see Introduction to **5.1**). In comparison, the contradictory meanings attributed to sodomy in the *Atherton* pamphlet revolve around the author's decision to combine homoerotic with heteroerotic and autoerotic sexual acts as part of a thoroughgoing satire of the established Church leadership's spiritual and liturgical corruption. While meant as the *coup de grâce* of sexual depravity, the horror of Atherton's sodomitical relationship with Child, following hard on the heels of two bawdy, comic accounts of Atherton's sexual deception of his parishioners (which would not be out of place in a collection of fabliaux), is defused and undermined by the work's overall tonal instability. Even *Sodom and Gomorrah* inflects the obviously satiric and condemnatory presentation of sodomy as a synecdoche for political corruption with a tone of rampant libertinism, endowing King Bolloxinian, in particular, with a libidinous energy that makes him, if not admirable, at least never boring. Even the figure of the pederastic pedagogue finds ambivalent treatment in the period, since the sodomitical register that often accompanied the representation of teacher–student relationships does not exhaust these relationships' erotic possibilities or meanings. While the positive valences of the homoerotic love between humanist-schoolmaster and his young male student appear in a number of influential texts, most significantly Ascham's *The Schoolmaster* (1570) (*Online Companion*),[15] perhaps the most unusual example of pedagogical homoeroticism occurs in Marlowe's tragedy *Dido, Queen of Carthage* (1594) (*Online Companion*), where the erotic relationship between Jupiter and his beautiful cupbearer Ganymede comments on the play's heteronormative relationships by being the only erotic relationship to survive the genre's death drive (Orvis 101–3; 110–11).

The Restoration and early eighteenth century see a reconfiguration of satiric representations of sodomy and the sodomite, a hardening of attitudes towards this figure, and increasingly pervasive attempts to police the permeable and interpenetrating discourses of sodomy and male same-sex love. The late seventeenth and early eighteenth centuries, in particular,

[15] In *The Schoolmaster*, Ascham records a scene of shared reading between himself and his friend and pupil John Whitney, where this shared reading of the period's most influential Latin text on friendship, Cicero's *De Amicitia*, occurs in the context of their sharing the intimate physical space of a bed at Sir Anthony Denny's house in 1584. On this scene and the homoerotics of humanist reading and pedagogy, see Goldberg, *Sodometries*, p. 79; Smith, p. 84; and Stewart, pp. 122–60.

saw the simultaneous development of different images of the sodomite and different ends to which these images were employed: the sodomite became increasingly marked by a predominant and even exclusive interest in boys, youths, or men;[16] by both effeminacy and misogyny, expressed by taking on the gendered behaviours, speech patterns, and attributes of women, while holding women themselves in contempt as sexual partners; and by becoming a favoured juncture for anxieties about the increasingly complex relationship that was forming between sodomy, class, gender, masculinity, and national identity. Although critics continue to argue about the reliability of satiric and condemnatory texts as guides to the social reality of early eighteenth-century men's homoerotic relationships (see Chapter 6, Introduction), such texts undoubtedly signal a shift in how they were *imagined*. Represented as embedded in communities of like-minded individuals, the turn-of-the-century sodomite is identified by various markers absent from his sixteenth- and early to mid-seventeenth-century avatars: particular urban, architectural, and geographical spaces; transvestism; misogyny; effeminacy; and special forms of speech and comportment.

This shift in stereotypes, and in particular the connection between the so-called 'molly' and his defining social milieu of the molly house was a London phenomenon: the turn-of-the-century stage comedy Thomas Baker's *Tunbridge-Walks* (1703: see **8.29**) features a character, Mr Maiden, who owes much to details found in texts such as Ward's *Second Part of the London Clubs* (1709: see **6.5**) and in the oral narratives that were apparently circulating about this figure and his community, as well as to the characteristics of the earlier Restoration stage fop, particularly his 'refusal to fight, extreme complaisance, sexual passivity, avoidance of drunkenness, fondness for the company of women, concern with fashion, interest in singing and dancing, and delicacy of all kinds' (Staves 421).[17] Although Trumbach contrasts Maiden – the 'innocuous and gentle fop of the later years of the seventeenth century', a different version of which the reader can encounter in Dilke's comedy *Lover's Luck* (1696: see **8.28**) – with the mid-eighteenth century's 'sexually marked figure of contempt' (ctd in Haggerty, *Men in Love* 69), Maiden's lack of erotic interest in the play's women, his simultaneous mimicry of their femininity, and his lowly class status link him inextricably to the sensational and always contemptuously represented figure of the molly.

Although many late seventeenth- and early eighteenth-century satiric texts, then, are increasingly invested in the sodomite as a figure that helps manage the growing imbrication of ideal English masculinity, rigid class

16 See R. Trumbach, 'Heterosexual Male', pp. 99–127.

17 For the complex relationship between the Restoration and eighteenth-century fop and the sodomite, see Haggerty, *Men in Love*, pp. 44–53; Staves, pp. 414–15.

divisions, and heterosexual desire, some still produce an ambivalence towards the very 'sodomitical' types they set out both to create and denigrate. Thomas Gordon's *Love Letters* (1723: see **8.31**) is an excellent example of the way an obviously satiric, and indeed even libellous, text partly eludes the early eighteenth century's increasingly rigid divide between male same-sex sexual acts and male same-sex love and friendship. The representation of the relationship between the young ex-army captain Edward Wilson (d. 1694) and Charles Spencer, Third Earl of Sunderland (1675–1722), later First Lord of the Treasury (appointed 1717/18), aims at blackening the latter's character and denigrating his policies,[18] partly by representing the relationship between Wilson and Sunderland in terms familiar to a reader of the period's homophobic polemics: where both male partners are (to a certain extent) marked as effeminate and misogynist, and where both have thus irrationally surrendered their ideal English masculinity while despising the very gender they emulate: woman. At the same time, the paratextual materials and the affective nature of Wilson and Sunderland's relationship destabilize the text's homophobia and undermine its larger satiric purpose: to use the relationship to represent and comment on the economic chaos of the 1720s (McFarlane 97). Not only does Gordon's commentary (which comprises much more than half this brief text's length, and offers a narrative framework for the correspondence) suggest that the letters require 'massaging' in order to ensure that they are read only in the satirically libellous way that Gordon intends, but it also evinces an awareness of the threat that homoerotic affect poses to the text's satiric and denigrating programme. Oddly, instead of offering the standard, indeed ancient, justification for the satiric presentation of 'the scandal of the vice here described' – that this presentation will help the reader recognize and eschew this vice, of which as an Englishman he will be largely ignorant – Gordon invites the reader to mentally heterosexualize and thus beautify and render inoffensive the correspondence. Given that such advice would tend to undermine the satiric import of the text, Gordon clearly only recommends this strategy sardonically, meaning for the reader to feel *more* not *less* disgust with a male–male relationship expressed in terms appropriate to a male–female erotic and sexual liaison. At the same time, however, this advice opens up for the reader questions about the affective nature of Wilson's and Sunderland's relationship; clearly, the letters focus not simply on male same-sex sexual desire and acts but upon the emotions of love and jealousy. 'Greedy kisses' (4, 16) and 'melting ecstasy' (26) are part of the nobleman's love for Wilson, his 'dearest blessing' and his 'joy' (9, 6).

[18] See R. Norton, 'Introduction', *Love Letters* in *Eighteenth-Century British Erotica II*, 5.121–4.

Between 1550 and 1735, homophilic representations of male same-sex love, desire, and affective relationships shape and are shaped by an equally dizzying array of motivations, genres and modes, the latter including the sonnet, pastoral, lyric, epyllion, verse epistle, familiar letter, drama, translations and imitations of ancient Greek and Roman prose and poetry, as well as devotional verse, epic, and treatises on male friendship. However, these representations, particularly in the sixteenth and seventeenth centuries, do tend to pool in genres that rely directly on classical precedent, including the translation of classical homoerotic and homophilic works, ranging from Anacreon to Horace to Homer, as well as the imitation of classical homoerotic genres and modes, including the pastoral eclogue, love lyric, and romance, as well as those genres influenced more directly by the European and Petrarchan love lyric traditions. Perhaps equally important were classical works that allowed for the dialogic expression of both homophobic and homophilic points of view – as is the case with translations of classical dialogues, such as Plutarch's 'Of Love' (see **7.28.1**) and Lucian's *Dialogues* (see **7.29.1**; **7.30**; and *Online Companion*). The positive representations of passionate male same-sex love and attachment in classical martial relationships, for example, ranging from Homer's Achilles and Patroclus, to Virgil's Nisus and Euryalus, to Plutarch's 'Sacred Band' of warrior-lovers, were always erotically and sometimes sexually inflected in early modern readers' minds, indicated at least partly by the way these famous martial couples, in particular, appear in lists of classical male lovers, along with Zeus and Ganymede, and Hercules and Hylas. Early modern examples of male friendships based on this homoerotic martial ethos are ubiquitous. They range from the friendship of the princes Pyrocles and Musidorus in Sidney's *Arcadia* (see **8.3**) to the male couples in Book IV of Spenser's *Faerie Queene* (see **8.2**) to Coriolanus and Aufidius in Shakespeare's Roman tragedy *Coriolanus* (*Online Companion*) to the male homoerotic relationships in the heroic drama of the Restoration and the early eighteenth century, such as Dryden's *All for Love* and Nathaniel Lee's *The Rival Queens* (both 1677).

However, the apparent licensing of representations of male same-sex erotic love through appealing to the precedent of the ancients became increasingly problematic throughout the sixteenth, seventeenth and into the early eighteenth century, as the imbrication of these two categories and discourses (male friendship and sodomy) came to affect increasingly the translations and imitations of classical homophilic genres. Appealing to the precedent of classical practice was a compromised strategy as early as Richard Barnfield's imitation of Virgil's homoerotic 'Eclogue 2' in *The Affectionate Shepherd* (1594: see **8.4.1**; *Online Companion*). Ancient Greek verse, however, did offer a precedent for the combination of the erotic, the sexual and the affective in men's same-sex relationships,[19] and its emphasis on the elegiac mode, particularly in pastoral, was attractive to early modern writers: this mode allowed for the expression of homoerotic relationships involving love, sexual desire, and sexual acts, but marked these relationships, in Traub's words, as 'always already lost' or 'betrayed' by rejection, separation, or death, distancing them in a golden, lost world (*Renaissance* 174–5). The elegiac mode, particularly in early modern homoerotic pastoral and lyric, defuses or at least contains the potentially threatening aspects of male same-sex erotic love, at the same time that the mode allows it representation: in addition to Barnfield's *Affectionate Shepherd* and *Cythnia with Certain Sonnets* (see **8.5**), see Spenser's 'January' and 'April' eclogues from *Shepheardes Calender* (see **8.1.1** and **8.1.2**), the anonymous 'Pastoral Dialogue Concerning Friendship and Love' (*Online Companion*), the mid- to late seventeenth-century poets Goodall's, Oldisworth's, and Lathum's pastoral and lyric verse for their dear male friends, as well as Lewis Machin's verse narrative retelling of the love of Apollo and Hyacinthus (see **7.21**).

Unlike the seemingly similar adoption of elegiac pastoral as the preferred mode to express sixteenth- and early seventeenth-century female same-sex erotic relationships, pastoral and elegy do not manage male homoerotic relationships and desire by making them marginal to patriarchal orthodoxies. In sixteenth-century homoerotic pastoral, elegy and lyric, as well as in Donne's and Marston's satires, the relationship between the older man and the desired boy mirrors the way many relationships between men are figured in the period: as interconnecting hierarchies, where a man could expect to play (throughout his life) the role of superior and/or subordinate. Unlike in satire, however, where this relationship is reduced to the crude economics of power, in sixteenth-century homophilic genres and modes the relationship between the older male lover and his younger male beloved is full of the affective language adopted and adapted from the heterosexual love lyric, as well as the classical homoerotic eclogue and lyric.

Such positive representations, however, extend beyond those genres that had direct classical precedents to include devotional poetry, biblical epic, and the drama. Examples in each of these genres suggest that the homoerotic sexual desires of the male body are not always effaced from representations of men's passionately devoted love for each other. Sedgwick and Rambuss, for example, have both discussed the complex homoerotics of the devotional poetry of Herbert, Crashaw, Traherne, and (to a lesser extent) Donne (see **8.14**, **8.18**, **8.19** and **8.15**). In this verse, Christ's early modern body anticipates its 'unique position in modern culture as [a particular] image of the unclothed [...] male body, often *in extremis* and / or ecstasy', one meant

19 See, for example, Anacreon (**7.10–7.11**), Horace (**7.12**), and Catullus (**7.13–7.15**).

to be 'prescriptively [...] gazed at and adored'; like its modern counterparts, Christ's early modern representations cannot escape their compromising homoerotic reality even within a traditional Christian homophobia (Sedgwick 140). In Abraham Cowley's biblical epic *Davideis* (1656: see **8.20**), David's love for Jonathan is fashioned through the discourses of *amicitia* and a Christianized Neoplatonism; however, this relationship is also infused with a deep homoeroticism and a passionate appreciation of male beauty – mirroring Michael Drayton's focus in his earlier verse narrative, *David and Goliath* (1630: see **8.13**) – and a devotion to the male beloved that goes beyond the regards of family and rank; however, the fashioning of the relationship between David and Jonathan as a Christian 'answer' to the exemplar of classical *amicitia*, expressed through couples such as Achilles and Patroclus or Theseus and Pirithous, clearly sits uneasily within some early modern redactions: Thomas Elwood's epic on David (*Davideis* (1708–12), *Online Companion*) studiously eschews lyrical descriptions of the young men's love and any detailed account of David's beauty.

In the various genres of sixteenth- and early seventeenth-century drama, male homoerotic friendships abound. In romantic comedy, male homoerotic relationships give way before the pressures of compulsory heterosexuality: the heroine displaces her young male beloved's older male friend in works such as *Twelfth Night* and *The Merchant of Venice* in the genre's journey towards the renewal of the social contract in marriage and heterosexual fertility. In tragedy, such relationships and the passionate sexual desires that often accompany them tend to be sublimated within the rhetoric and structures of martial devotion, as in Shakespeare's Roman tragedies and histories, but there are instances where what is at issue is precisely the relationship between sodomy and male same-sex love, most famously in Christopher Marlowe's *Edward II* (1594: see **8.6**). Mortimer Jr and the play's other elite characters arguably deploy in an ideological and self-interested way the figure of the sodomite and the discourse of sodomy as weapons of political character assassination. Marlowe's emphasis on the way the discourse of sodomy is used to destroy Edward and Gaveston annihilates its claim to support the period's naturally and divinely ordained moral and ethical order, particularly given the fact that those characters who employ this discourse most obviously, such as Mortimer Jr, also represent the period's single most despised political stance: Machiavellianism. Even with Marlowe's complex charting of their very human and flawed relationship, Edward and Gaveston give the audience the only example of redeeming erotic love in the entire play. Sodomy and loving male same-sex sexual acts are, the play finally suggests, completely different.

The Tribade and the 'Dear Friend': Literary Expressions of Female Same-Sex Desires, Relationships, Love and Sexual Acts, 1550–1735

Looking for pre-1660 satiric representations of the tribade and tribadism, the reader finds none in the literary genres discussed above. For reasons that Traub has discussed at length,[20] there are no tribades on the Renaissance stage, in Renaissance romance, or indeed in Renaissance classical verse satire, although this figure does appear in the context of anti-Catholic and anti-monastic polemic. Unlike the figure of the sodomitical monk, priest, or bishop, the figure of the tribadic nun functions much more narrowly and, at least for Bale ('Votaries', *Online Companion*) and Erasmus (see **9.1**), much less representatively. If the monastic sodomite is *the* image of the utter spiritual, natural, and social chaos produced by Catholic doctrines and institutions, then the monastic tribade is a supplementary figure, and one whose same-sex sexual crimes are, like those of the monastic sodomite, simply the *coup de grâce* of a life of sexual and spiritual depravity; there are, in short, no female figures like Donne's or Jonson's gentleman sodomite or Marston's sodomitical schoolmaster. Given that these satirical representations are embedded in conventions of power and patriarchal prerogative, exact female equivalents unsurprisingly do not exist.[21] Satiric references to tribadism and the satiric figure of the tribade, in short, are rare in sixteenth- and early seventeenth-century literary texts. The three known references occur in Ben Jonson's lyric '10 ("And must I sing?")' (see **9.7.1**) and his satiric 'Epigram 49: Epigram on the Court Pucelle' (see **9.8.1**), and in Thomas Woodward's erotic verse epistle addressed to John Donne, 'To Master J.D.' (see **8.15.2**) Even these uses, however, differ wildly in tone and import. As David Robinson has noted, 'in a cultural milieu in which Poet and Muse were traditionally imagined as romantic, even sexual partners, female writing itself, regardless of context or content, sometimes gave rise to lesbian associations', as is the case specifically with Jonson's attack on the poet Cecilia Bulstrode in 'Epigram on the Court Pucelle' (19–20). Here, Bulstrode's female poetic productivity is represented as a perversion of woman's 'natural'

[20] See *Renaissance*, pp. 163–87.

[21] On the stage representation of the early seventeenth-century 'governess', see Jean Lambert, 'Early Modern Educational Culture: *The Wit of a Woman*', in *Performing Pedagogy in Early Modern England*, ed. K.M. Moncrief and K.R. MacPherson (Burlington, VT, 2011), pp. 131–45. The governess Balia in this 1604 anonymous stage comedy performs the role of encouraging the kind of same-sex attachments between her female students that we see in Shakespeare's *Midsummer Night's Dream*.

reproductive abilities, and the seizing of the male prerogative to dominate a partner in sexual intercourse: 'with tribade lust', she rapes the muse.[22] Jonson's '10 ("And must I sing")' likewise denigrates female homoeroticism, imagining Venus's 'new sports' as involving female same-sex intercourse with and among her traditional attendants, the three Graces, described as 'her tribade trine'. However, while Thomas Woodward's reference to the tribadic relationship between his muse and that of his friend Donne differs in tone from Jonson's verse, it still imagines 'the erotic exchange between the muses [as] provid[ing] the male poet with a novel means of appropriating female reproduction for his own creativity' (Traub, *Renaissance* 25). As Klawitter has so wisely noted, however, the tone of the poem is 'impishly sexual' and implies something of the 'bawdy talk teenage boys bandy about among themselves' (8, 10). An exception to this absence of satirical tribadic figures appears in allusions to Sappho's same-sex erotic relationships (see Introduction to **7.2–7.9**); however, even here the classical precedents for the representation of this figure, but also of the chastely loving female friend and the loving female couple, are much more severely limited[23] than is the case with the sodomite and the loving male couple.

Modern critics, however, have long looked to the many examples of cross-dressed heroines in early modern drama as a privileged point of access to women's same-sex erotic desires and the culture's fantasies and fears about them. Yet, as Goldberg and Traub have pointed out, focusing on *As You Like It*'s 'bawdy banter' between the cross-dressed Rosalind and love-sick Phebe, for example, runs the danger of ignoring other 'means of access into female erotic intimacy' and underestimating the effect of the required 'unmasking' of the cross-dressed heroine, her resumption of her place in a heterosexual economy, and this action's support of social and erotic orthodoxy (Traub, *Renaissance* 170). Instead, focusing on the love between women who are 'conventionally and symmetrically "feminine" in their outward demeanour' (i.e., not cross-dressed literally or figuratively) allows for a consideration of the terms within which female homoerotic love appears in the sixteenth and early seventeenth centuries. As the relationship between *Midsummer Night's Dream*'s Hermia and Helena demonstrates (see **9.4**), such homoerotic love is represented as a love that must give way before its culture's 'economic [and] political imperative: as each woman is re-secured in the patriarchal, reproductive order, her desires

[22] D.M. Robinson, *Closeted Writing and Gay and Lesbian Literature* (Aldershot, 2006). On this poem, see Traub, *Renaissance*, pp. 25–6; Andreadis, *Sappho*, pp. 45–6; and Wahl, pp. 49–51.

[23] For selections from the classical tradition's representation of tribades and loving female couples, see *Homosexuality in Greece and Rome: A Sourcebook of Basic Documents*, ed. Thomas K. Hubbard (Berkeley, 2003). For the authoritative account of male same-sex erotic, loving, and sexual relationships in Ancient Greece, see Davidson.

are made to conform to her "place"' (174). Written within the conventions not simply of stage comedy and romance (with its irresistible movement towards the heroine's marriage), but of elegy and the pastoral, such female lovers are situated in a world where their love is 'always already lost' and 'always about to be betrayed', as well as in 'a [...] golden age', safely distanced 'spatially and temporally' from the world of the reader (174, 175). Even the often-lauded representation of female same-sex erotic love in John Donne's 'Sappho to Philaenis' (see **7.7.1**) situates such love firmly in this elegiac tradition, and offers the added complication of fashioning this relationship through narcissism (through the emphasis on the rhetoric of bodily similitude between Sappho and her absent lover, Philaenis), not to mention through the male poet's ventriloquizing of the female poet-lover's experience.[24]

Although later seventeenth-century plays move away from this 'elegiac pastoralism' to represent 'female–female desire in the present tense', these plays also tend to focus less on 'loving female couple[s]' than on 'homoerotic pleasures [...] within a community of women' (Traub, *Renaissance* 175). This focus results in various displays of female–female desire, but finally functions to represent this desire 'as a distinct, if temporary and physically bounded, possibility' displaced by 'the force of a seemingly "natural", ultimately more powerful attraction to men' (177). Margaret Cavendish's *Convent of Pleasure* (1668: see **9.13**) 'explores the attractions of homoeroticism among women' while finally 'reaffirm[ing] the necessity of marital alliance as the price of a harmonious dramatic conclusion' (177), but this play also enacts and contains the anxiety that women's same-sex erotic relationships may become exclusive. As a 'temporary stage of female affectivity', women's same-sex erotic relationships could be represented simply as 'a "rehearsal" to the "natural" conclusion of marriage' and easily understood 'within the protocols of chastity' (186–7). Yet, the depiction of female homoerotic communities, such as Cavendish's secular convent of pleasure, with its affecting representation of men's predations and marriage's oppression, emphasizes the dangerous threat posed by these erotic relationships rather than the compensating fantasy of their 'insignificance'. In comparison with Marvell's 'Upon Appleton House' (see **9.11**), which treats the convent as a site of religious, sexual, and social perversion triumphantly eradicated by masculine martial valour, Cavendish's *Convent of Pleasure* treats the convent as a site of orderly female pleasure and beauty, called into being and defined against the endemic violence and abuse of power that characterizes the world ruled by men, the world outside the convent walls. While Cavendish's play, however, finally sees the victory of heterosexual marriage over female same-sex erotic unions, such a conclusion is very much conditioned, as

[24] See E.D. Harvey, *Ventriloquized Voices* (London, 1992), pp. 116–39.

Traub points out, by stage comedy's traditional narrative trajectory towards marriage. In contrast, Aemilia Lanyer's long religious poem *Salve Deus Rex Judaeorum* (1611: see **9.5**) represents the love between women both in the poem's many dedicatory poems addressed by Lanyer to her female patrons, and also in the representation of the ecstatic relationship between the speaker and the feminized Christ. Lanyer's community of women 'presents homoerotic affection as a way for women to overcome the ravages of men's proprietary claims and as a positive ground for real-world communities' (Holmes 167). Even here, however, the projection of erotic female community into eternity is qualified by the elegiac tone of the volume's final poem 'The Description of Cookham' (see **9.5.8**), where Lanyer bids goodbye to her community and her beloved patron, Margaret, countess of Cumberland, and the work's overall apocalyptic mood.[25]

Mapped on top of this larger movement in the representation of female same-sex erotic relationships is the ancient theme of the '*amor impossibilis*', the impossible love between women, impossible because forbidden by Nature, but also by society (Traub, *Renaissance* 281). Charting the many ways in which different literary genres have shaped the presentation of the *amor impossibilis*, Traub concentrates initially on works that offer sex transformation as 'the imaginative means to elude impossibility' (288), especially in the many translations and redactions of the Ovidian sex transformation myth of Iphis and Ianthe, such as in Golding's and Sandys's translations of the *Metamorphoses* (1567 and 1632: see **7.17** and **7.18**) and the anonymous romance *Huon of Bourdeaux* (1600; *Online Companion*). The young cross-dressed maid, Iphis, in love with and engaged to her female beloved, Ianthe, despairs, lamenting that Nature, fate and the gods have all rendered their marital happiness impossible. Isis (Venus) solves this problem by transforming Iphis into a boy. As Traub indicates, this solution of the lamenting female lover's sex change appears in a wide variety of texts, although sometimes this sex change is literal and at other times metaphorical, as is the case with the introduction of the identical twin brother who stands in for the lamenting female lover's female object of desire in Shakespeare's *Twelfth Night* and Ariosto's *Orlando Furioso* (*Online Companion*). Moreover, although many other works, including Sidney's romance *Arcadia* (see **9.3**) and Wroth's romance *Urania* (see **9.6**), as well as Lyly's court comedy *Gallathea* (see **7.20**) and the Maitland Manuscript's 'Poem XLIX' (see **9.2**), employ the trope of the *amor impossibilis*, they treat very differently the whole 'solution' of a literal or metaphorical sex change for one member of the couple: the lament of

25 On the volume's apocalyptic qualities, see M. Loughlin, '"Fast ti'd unto them in a golden Chaine": Typology, Apocalypse, and Genealogy in Aemilia Lanyer's *Salve Deus Rex Judaeorum*', *Renaissance Quarterly* 53.1 (2000), pp. 133–79.

Sidney's heroine Philoclea focuses more 'on the subjective experience of desire' and implies a distaste for the solution of sex transformation; while Lyly's apparently straightforward appropriation of the sex transformation as the solution for his love-crossed, cross-dressed heroines, Phyllida and Gallathea, suggests that 'the reign of Nature is judged to be inadequate', since 'Love, at least when personified by a powerful goddess, can conquer Nature'; and 'Poem XLIX' takes advantage of the lyric mode and its removal from the narrative teleology of Ovidian myth, romance and stage play, to employ the appeal to sex transformation at the same time that it refuses to see the speaker's same-sex erotic desire and love for her beloved as either unnatural or impossible (Traub, *Renaissance* 287–90).

Both Traub and Andreadis describe a gradual disintegration of the separation between the chaste female friend and the tribade in the period. Andreadis says that by 1714 it becomes difficult to distinguish the signs of female friendship from those of tribadism; likewise, Traub suggests there was 'a collapse, over the course of the seventeenth century, of what previously seemed to be two mutually exclusive modes of embodiment, the tribade and the friend', where those signs and behaviours that had earlier 'been indices of feminine virtue' (e.g., kisses and embraces between female friends) gradually became subject to the same demonization that had accompanied the tribade (*Renaissance* 231). Both critics also see Katherine Philips and the mid- to late seventeenth-century poetry of female friendship as representing a significant juncture in this conflation between female friend and tribade. For Traub, Katherine Philips's homoerotic verse emphasizes 'the opposed claims of friendship and marriage' (*Renaissance* 295), and reformulates the terms of the female homoerotic elegy, with the speaker mourning no longer the bars of Nature for the impossibility of her erotic love for another women, but the 'physical absence of the beloved' and the obstacles created by the social world (296). Philips's lyrics, because they are not trapped within the teleology of narrative or drama, replace the traditional 'solution' to the *amor impossibilis* (a sex change for one member of the female couple) with one that validates and legitimizes this relationship by fashioning the couple in terms of an 'idealizing similitude' and innocence (Traub, *Renaissance* 297). Moreover, older discourses that had marked female same-sex erotic desire and relationships as unthreatening to patriarchal order began not simply to come under pressure but to be dismantled; as friendship became an aspect of companionate heterosexual marriage, passionate female friendship became increasingly viewed as unnecessary, and as looking suspiciously and threateningly like a substitute for companionate marriage (*Renaissance* 258–67).

Thus, late seventeenth and early eighteenth-century satires that feature the tribade and the exclusive female same-sex couple come to make more sense; the former figure was more available to people in print, and these satires became a method of managing the anxiety traditionally provoked both by this monstrous figure and also by the increasingly contaminated figure of the hitherto virtuous female same-sex friend. Satiric attacks were also aimed not just at the tribade and the contaminated female friend but at female same-sex coupling as an alternative to marriage. The increasing vociferousness and virulence of the satire directed at the tribade is intimately connected to the fear clearly expressed in Edmund Waller's 'On the Friendship betwixt Sacharissa and Amorett' (1645: see **9.9.1**) and John Hoadly's 'On the Friendship of Two Young Ladies' (1730: see **9.32**) that female same-sex erotic friendship was a challenge to heteronormativity, marriage, and more generally male sexual privilege. As in Edward Howard's poem 'Fricatrices: Or, A She upon a She' (1674: **9.15**), or the ballad 'Venus's Reply' (1699: see **6.2.2**), this challenge can be addressed in satiric terms that are witty, comic and bawdy. Even Aphra Behn's homoerotic verse, such as 'To the Fair Clarinda' and 'Verses Designed by Mistress A. Behn, to Be Sent to a Fair Lady' (see **9.18.1** and **9.19.1**), can be viewed as embedded in this anxiety-ridden context, with Clarinda described in terms that unite the 'sexualized vocabulary' of the hermaphrodite with the language, rhetoric, and attitudes of erotic female friendship (Traub, *Renaissance* 319). However, the disintegration of the boundaries between the tribade and chaste female friend and the challenge posed by the increased public visibility of this increasingly conflated, conflicted figure provokes satiric representations that are also increasingly sexually explicit, such as *An Epistle from Signora F———a to a Lady* (1727: see **9.31**); William King's *The Toast* (1732; 1736: see **9.33**); Jean Barrin's *Venus in the Cloister, or the Nun in her Smock* (first Engl. trans., 1683: see **9.16**); and the anonymous *Sappho-An* (c. 1735?/1749?: see **7.9**).

Terminology

Although some modern critics do employ the terms 'homosexual' and 'lesbian',[26] I have decided to use more neutral descriptors, such as 'homoerotic', 'same-sex erotic relationships', and 'same-sex erotic love'. Although these phrases are sometimes awkward, this drawback is outweighed by their usefulness in constantly reminding the reader of the historical and cultural specificity of such relationships, acts, and desires. However, I also use the

[26] See Traub, *Renaissance*, where the term *lesbian* appears italicized to indicate its problematic and provisional nature. For an early account of the controversy, see C.J. Summers, 'Homosexuality and Renaissance Literature: Or, The Anxieties of Anachronism', *South Central Review* 9 (1992), pp. 2–23.

terms 'sodomy/sodomite' and 'tribadism/tribade' when discussing aspects of these particular same-sex discourses, and the terms 'homosexual'/'lesbian' when I am marking a particular text or set of texts as having become crucial in charting the development of modern gay and lesbian identities (see Chapter 6, Introduction). For men, the most frequently used terms during the time span of this anthology include *sodomy* and its cognates (sodomite, sodometry, sodometries, sodomitical), *buggery* and its cognates (buggerer, bugger), *catamitus* (catamite), *cinaedus*, *ingle*, and *ganymede*; for women, *tribade*, *hermaphrodite*, and *fricatrice*. However, especially for women, circumlocutions for same-sex relationships and sexual acts abound: see Donoghue, *Passions* 1–8.

CHAPTER 1

Religious and Moral Writings

Introduction

The condemnation of male and female same-sex sexual acts is embedded in the earliest Christian theology regarding sexuality, heterosexual marriage, and reproduction: human genitalia were created for reproduction, mirroring the creative act of God. Thus, using the genitals for anything other than reproduction was a violation of God's intentions for the sexual and reproductive organs, of his command to Adam and Eve to 'be fruitful and multiply' (Gen. 1.28), and of his larger plan to increase the Christian faithful. The early Church confined legitimate sexual activity to heterosexual partners in Christian marriage within strictly defined limits, barring as sinful all non-reproductive sexual acts – including same-sex intercourse and other same-sex sexual acts, autoeroticism, *coitus interruptus*, heterosexual oral and anal sex, and even unusual sexual positions in heterosexual intercourse; even legitimate and authorized heterosexual intercourse within marriage could become an occasion for sin if the partners engaged in it solely for purposes of pleasure rather than reproduction (Borris, *Same-Sex* 24, 26). Given Christianity's conflicted representation of even marital, heterosexual intercourse and eroticism and its simultaneous valorization of virginity and sexual abstinence in texts such as Revelation 14.3–4 and 1 Corinthians 7.1, same-sex intercourse (sodomy and tribadism) was as a matter of course stringently condemned as one of those special 'crying sins'[1] so heinous that it brings upon its practitioners the immediate wrath of God. In short, same-sex intercourse, especially in its particular characterization as sodomy, was in a different category of sin from forbidden heterosexual acts (Borris, *Same-Sex* 28). In his discussion of Romans 1.24–31, Calvin calls sodomy the 'overthrowing of the whole order of nature'. In contrast, forbidden heterosexual acts within and outside of marriage were (according

[1] Along with murder, oppression of the poor, and the defrauding of the labourer.

to Thomas Aquinas, at least) less serious: they were violations of God's will, but not also violations of nature.

In terms of Scriptural prohibitions, the story of Sodom and Gomorrah (Genesis 19) was by far the most frequently discussed biblical condemnation of same-sex intercourse, and male same-sex anal congress was the most frequently alluded to same-sex act. Calvin suggests that the seriousness of the sin of the men of Sodom was demonstrated by the wholesale destruction of men, women, and children that God meted out as punishment, a conflagration signalling God's special hatred of this vice (*Online Companion*). This sin destroys two communities, taints the blood of the Sodomites' children, and leads to their destruction along with their parents'; this story makes sodomy the sin Christians should fear even to name, much less commit. Although female same-sex intercourse was sometimes treated in reference to Romans 1.26, many theologians understood this passage as referring to women's engagement in forbidden heterosexual acts; there is simply no well-developed body of theological commentary in England on the biblical basis for the condemnation of tribadism.

Attempting to undermine the spiritual and political authority of the Roman Catholic Church, English Protestant reformists often seized on sodomy as a highly charged and emotive anti-papal discourse, with female homoerotic sexual acts sometimes appearing as well. Perhaps the most famous of these reformists, the playwright, bishop and controversialist John Bale, attacked Catholicism's mandatory ecclesiastical celibacy as a trigger and veil for all kinds of sexual excesses; he claimed, as many reformists did, that Catholic celibacy for priests and other religious was unnatural, and encouraged men and women, their natural desires for the opposite sex frustrated, to seek out the more readily available members of their own sex; monasteries and nunneries became in such works the sites of wild homoerotic and heteroerotic intercourse. In *Acts of the English Votaries* (1564, 1551; *Online Companion*), he accuses the entire Roman Catholic hierarchy from the lowliest nun to the pope himself of adultery, pandering, sexual activity (heterosexual, homosexual, and autoerotic), infanticide, witchcraft, bastardy, murder, treason, blasphemy, and idolatry. These Catholic ecclesiastics have 'burnt in their own lusts one to another, that man with man, that is to say, monk with monk, nun with nun, friar with friar, priest with priest, wrought filthiness'. Bale's works are some of the earliest in a long English tradition conflating same-sex erotic acts and intercourse with a wide range of social, political, moral, and religious 'ills', although his focus is always on spiritual and ecclesiastical corruption, as in his drama uncompromisingly titled *A New Comedy* [...] *Concerning Three Laws of Nature, Moses, and Christ Corrupted by the Sodomites, Pharisees and Papists* (1548, 1562; *Online Companion*). Thomas Beard's *The Theatre of God's Judgements* (1597) a popular collection of anecdotes about divine wrath visited upon sinners of all types – prostitutes, adulterers, blasphemers, etc. – goes further than Bale, linking sodomy with Roman Catholic corruption, bestiality, atheism, cross-dressing, effeminacy, the general violation of gender boundaries, and both physical and spiritual monstrosity, as part of a wider project of constructing the godly nation. In a different context, the Puritan polemicist William Prynne's *Histrio-mastix* (1633) specifically condemns England's cross-dressed stage (where boys played the women's parts) as sodomitical, as does the popular pamphleteer Philip Stubbes' *Anatomy of Abuses* (1583; *Online Companion*); they, like Bale and Beard, see sodomy as dissolving natural and social boundaries. Biblical prohibitions play a large role in Prynne's text, but he argues finally that the cross-dressed stage effeminizes male actors and spectators both psychologically and (more strikingly) physically, threatening to make women out of men, and consequently making a man take on a woman's sexual desire for men: for Prynne, dress is constitutive of desire, and cross-dressing leads inexorably to sodomy.

Online Companion
Interested readers can find additional selections from the following religious and moral writers: John Calvin, John Bale, Philip Stubbes, John Rainolds, George Lesly, and Richard Baxter.

The Bible

1.1

From *Bible* (Authorized Version (1611))

1.1.1 Genesis 19.1–25 [The Story of Sodom and Gomorrah]

[God sends two angels to rescue Lot and his family from Sodom and Gomorrah's impending destruction. Lot offers them lodging, not knowing they are angels.]

19 […] [4] But before they lay down, the men of the city, even the men of Sodom, compassed the house round, both old and young, all the people from every quarter. [5] And they called unto Lot, and said unto him, 'Where are the men which came in to thee this night? Bring them out unto us, that we may know[1] them.' [6] And Lot went out at the door unto them, and shut the

[1] *know* have sex with.

door after him, [7] And said, 'I pray you, brethren, do not so wickedly. [8] Behold now, I have two daughters which have not known man; let me, I pray you, bring them out unto you, and do ye to them as is good in your eyes: only unto these men do nothing; for therefore came they under the shadow of my roof.' [9] And they said, 'Stand back.' And they said again, 'This one fellow came in to sojourn,[2] and he will needs be a judge. Now will we deal worse with thee than with them.' And they pressed sore[3] upon the man, even Lot, and came near to break the door. [10] But the men[4] put forth their hand, and pulled Lot into the house to them, and shut to the door. [11] And they smote the men that were at the door of the house with blindness, both small and great, so that they wearied themselves to find the door. [...] [17] And it came to pass, when they[5] had brought them[6] forth abroad, that he[7] said, 'Escape for thy life; look not behind thee, neither stay thou in all the plain; escape to the mountain, lest thou be consumed.' [...] [24] Then the Lord rained upon Sodom and upon Gomorrah brimstone and fire from the Lord out of heaven. [25] And he overthrew those cities, and all the plain, and all the inhabitants of the cities, and that which grew upon the ground. [...] [28] [...] and, lo, the smoke of the country went up as the smoke of a furnace.

1.1.2 Leviticus 18 and 20
[Laws Concerning Sexual Relations]

18 [...] [22] Thou shalt not lie with mankind, as with womankind: it is abomination. [23] Neither shalt thou lie with any beast to defile thyself therewith: neither shall any woman stand before a beast to lie down thereto: it is confusion. [24] Defile not you yourselves in any of these things, for in all these the nations are defiled which I cast out before you: [25] And the land is defiled: therefore I do visit the iniquity thereof upon it, and the land itself vomiteth out her inhabitants. [26] Ye shall therefore keep my statutes and my judgements, and shall not commit any of these abominations; neither any of your own nation, nor any stranger that sojourneth among you: [27] (for all these abominations have the men of the land done, which were before you,[8] and the land is defiled;) [28] That the land spew not you out also, when ye defile it, as it spewed out the nations that were before you. [29] For whosoever shall commit any of these abominations, even the souls that commit them,

[2] *sojourn* stay temporarily.
[3] *sore* violently.
[4] *men* angels (Lot's guests).
[5] *they* angels.
[6] *them* Lot, his wife, and daughters.
[7] *he* RSV has 'they' (angels).
[8] *men … you* Canaanites (previous inhabitants of the Promised Land).

shall be cut off from among their people. [30] Therefore shall ye keep my ordinance, that ye commit not any one of these abominable customs, which were committed before you, and that ye defile not yourselves therein [...]

[Penalties for Forbidden Sexual Relations]

20 [...] [12] And if a man lie with his daughter-in-law, both of them shall surely be put to death: they have wrought confusion;[9] their blood shall be upon them. [13] If a man also lie with mankind, as he lieth with a woman, both of them have committed an abomination: they shall surely be put to death; their blood shall be upon them. [14] And if a man take a wife and her mother, it is wickedness: they shall be burnt with fire, both he and they, that there be no wickedness among you. [15] And if a man lie with a beast, he shall surely be put to death, and ye shall slay the beast. [16] And if a woman approach unto any beast, and lie down thereto, thou shalt kill the woman, and the beast: they shall surely be put to death; their blood shall be upon them.

1.1.3 1 Samuel 16, 17, 18 and 20 [David's Anointing as the Next King of Israel by the Prophet Samuel]

16 And the Lord said unto Samuel, 'How long wilt thou mourn for Saul, seeing I have rejected him from reigning over Israel? Fill thy horn with oil, and go. I will send thee to Jesse the Bethlehemite: for I have provided me a king among his sons.' [...] [6] And it came to pass, when they[10] were come, that he[11] looked on Eliab, and said, 'Surely the Lord's anointed is before him.' [7] But the Lord said unto Samuel, 'Look not on his countenance, or on the height of his stature; because I have refused him: for the Lord seeth not as man seeth: for man looketh on the outward appearance, but the Lord looketh on the heart.' [...] [11] And Samuel said unto Jesse, 'Are here all thy children?' And he said, 'There remaineth yet the youngest, and, behold, he keepeth the sheep.' And Samuel said unto Jesse, 'Send and fetch him, for we will not sit down till he come hither.' [12] And he sent, and brought him in. Now he was ruddy, and withal of a beautiful countenance, and goodly to look to. And the Lord said, 'Arise, anoint him, for this is he.' [13] Then Samuel took the horn of oil, and anointed him in the midst of his brethren, and the Spirit of the Lord came upon David from that day forward.

9 *wrought confusion* committed incest (RSV).
10 *they* Jesse's sons.
11 *he* Samuel.

[David's Defeat of Goliath, the Giant Champion of Israel's Enemy, the Philistines]

17 [...] [32] And David said to Saul, 'Let no man's heart fail because of him; thy servant will go and fight with this Philistine.'[12] [33] And Saul said to David, 'Thou art not able to go against this Philistine to fight with him: for thou art but a youth, and he a man of war from his youth.' [34] And David said unto Saul [...] [36] '[...] this uncircumcised Philistine shall be as one of them,[13] seeing he hath defied the armies of the living God.' [...] [38] And Saul armed David with his armour, and he put a helmet of brass upon his head; also he armed him with a coat of mail. [39] And David girded his sword upon his armour, and he assayed[14] to go, for he had not proved[15] it. And David said unto Saul, 'I cannot go with these, for I have not proved them.' And David put them off him. [...][16] [42] And when the Philistine looked about and saw David, he disdained him, for he was but a youth, and ruddy, and of a fair countenance. [43] And the Philistine said unto David, 'Am I a dog, that thou comest to me with staves?'[17] And the Philistine cursed David by his gods. [44] And the Philistine said to David, 'Come to me, and I will give thy flesh unto the fowls of the air, and to the beasts of the field.' [45] Then said David to the Philistine, 'Thou comest to me with a sword, and with a spear, and with a shield; but I come to thee in the name of the Lord of hosts, the God of the armies of Israel, whom thou hast defied. [46] This day will the Lord deliver thee into my hand; and I will smite thee, and take thy head from thee; and I will give the carcasses of the host of the Philistines this day unto the fowls of the air, and to the wild beasts of the earth; that all the earth may know that there is a God in Israel. [47] And all this assembly shall know that the Lord saveth not with sword and spear, for the battle is the Lord's, and he will give you into our hands.'

[Using his sling, David kills Goliath, thereby winning the love of Jonathan, Saul's son and heir.]

18 And it came to pass, when he [i.e., David] had made an end of speaking unto Saul, that the soul of Jonathan was knit with the soul of David, and Jonathan loved him as his own soul. [2] And Saul took him that day and would let him go no more home to his father's house. [3] Then Jonathan

12 Terrified, no Israelite can be found to accept Goliath's challenge to single combat.

13 *them* David earlier kills a lion and bear for threatening his flock.

14 *assayed* attempted.

15 *proved* tested.

16 Carrying his staff, sling, and five smooth stones, David approaches Goliath.

17 *staves* staffs.

and David made a covenant, because he loved him as his own soul. [4] And Jonathan stripped himself of the robe that was upon him, and gave it to David, and his garments, even to his sword, and to his bow, and to his girdle.

[David becomes Saul's captain, and later marries Saul's daughter, Michal. Saul hates David's popularity; David reveals this to Jonathan.]

20 [...] [3] And David swore moreover, and said, 'Thy father certainly knoweth that I have found grace in thine eyes; and he sayeth, "Let not Jonathan know this, lest he be grieved." But truly as the Lord liveth, and as thy soul liveth, there is but a step between me and death.' [4] Then said Jonathan unto David, 'Whatsoever thy soul desireth, I will even do it for thee. [...]' [8] [David said] '[...] if there be in me iniquity, slay me thyself; for why shouldest thou bring me to thy father?' [9] And Jonathan said, 'Far be it from thee; for if I knew certainly that evil were determined by my father to come upon thee, then would not I tell it thee?' [10] Then said David to Jonathan, 'Who shall tell me? or what if thy father answer thee roughly?' [11] And Jonathan said unto David, 'Come, and let us go out into the field.' And they went out both of them into the field. [12] And Jonathan said unto David, 'O Lord God of Israel, when I have sounded my father about tomorrow any time, or the third day, and, behold, if there be good toward David, and I then send not unto thee, and show it thee; [13] the Lord do so and much more to Jonathan. But if it please my father to do thee evil, then I will show it thee, and send thee away, that thou mayest go in peace; and the Lord be with thee, as he hath been with my father. [14] And thou shalt not only while yet I live show me the kindness of the Lord, that I die not; [15] But also thou shalt not cut off thy kindness from my house forever: no, not when the Lord hath cut off the enemies of David every one from the face of the earth.' [16] So Jonathan made a covenant with the house of David, saying, 'Let the Lord even require it at the hand of David's enemies.' [17] And Jonathan caused David to swear again, because he loved him; for he loved him as he loved his own soul.

[At a feast, Jonathan tells Saul that he has given David permission to be absent on family business; Saul throws a spear at Jonathan in rage, and Jonathan then confirms to David Saul's murderous intentions.]

[41] [...] David arose out of a place toward the south, and fell on his face to the ground, and bowed himself three times: and they kissed one another, and wept one with another, until David exceeded.[18] [42] And Jonathan said to

[18] *exceeded* 'recovered himself' (RSV).

David, 'Go in peace, forasmuch as we have sworn both of us in the name of the Lord, saying, "The Lord be between me and thee and between my seed and thy seed forever".' And he arose and departed: and Jonathan went into the city.

1.1.4 2 Samuel 1.19–28
[David's Lament for the Deaths of Saul and Jonathan]

[...]

[19] The beauty of Israel is slain upon thy high places.
How are the mighty fallen!
[20] Tell it not in Gath, publish it not in the streets of Askelon,[19]
lest the daughters of the Philistines rejoice,
lest the daughters of the uncircumcised triumph.
[21] Ye mountains of Gilboa, let there be no dew,[20]
neither let there be rain upon you, nor fields of offerings:
for there the shield of the mighty is vilely cast away,
the shield of Saul, as though he had not been anointed with oil.
[22] From the blood of the slain, from the fat of the mighty,
the bow of Jonathan turned not back,
and the sword of Saul returned not empty.
[23] Saul and Jonathan were lovely and pleasant in their lives,
and in their death they were not divided.
They were swifter than eagles, they were stronger than lions.
[24] Ye daughters of Israel, weep over Saul,
who clothed you in scarlet, with other delights,[21]
who put on ornaments of gold upon your apparel.
[25] How are the mighty fallen in the midst of the battle!
O Jonathan, thou wast slain in thy high places.
[26] I am distressed for thee, my brother Jonathan.
Very pleasant hast thou been unto me;
thy love to me was wonderful, passing the love of women.
[27] How are the mighty fallen,
and the weapons of war perished!

[19] *Gath* and *Askelon* Philistine cities.

[20] *Gilboa* a mountain near the eastern pass into the valley of Jezreel; on its western slopes Saul and Jonathan were killed.

[21] *scarlet* precious dye; clothes so dyed were symbolic of wealth and honour.

1.1.5 Ruth [Ruth's Love for Naomi]

[The Israelite Naomi has lost her husband and two sons while living in the land of Moab. Naomi now intends to go home, leaving behind her non-Israelite daughters-in-law.]

1 [...] [8] And Naomi said unto her two daughters-in-law, 'Go return each to her mother's house: the Lord deal kindly with you, as ye have dealt with the dead, and with me. [9] The Lord grant you that you may find rest, each of you in the house of her husband.' Then she kissed them; and they lifted up their voice, and wept. [10] And they said unto her, 'Surely we will return with thee unto thy people.' [11] And Naomi said, 'Turn again, my daughters: why will you go with me? Are there yet any more sons in my womb, that they may be your husbands?[22] [12] Turn again, my daughters, go your way; for I am too old to have a husband. If I should say, I have hope, if I should have a husband also tonight, and should also bear sons; [13] would ye tarry for them till they were grown? Would ye stay for them from having husbands? Nay, my daughters, for it grieveth me much for your sakes that the hand of the Lord is gone out against me.' [14] And they lifted up their voice, and wept again: and Orpah kissed her mother-in-law, but Ruth cleaved[23] unto her. [15] And she said, 'Behold, thy sister-in-law is gone back unto her people, and unto her gods: return thou after thy sister-in-law.' [16] And Ruth said, 'Entreat me not to leave thee, or to return from following after thee: for whither thou goest, I will go; and where thou lodgest, I will lodge: thy people shall be my people, and thy God my God: [17] Where thou diest, will I die, and there will I be buried: the Lord do so to me, and more also, if aught but death part thee and me.' [...]

1.1.6 Romans 1 [Pagan Practices]

1 [24] Wherefore God also gave them[24] up to uncleanness[25] through the lusts of their own hearts, to dishonour their own bodies between themselves: [25] who changed the truth of God into a lie, and worshipped and served the creature more than the Creator, who is blessed forever. Amen. [26] For this cause God gave them up unto vile affections: for even their women did

[22] *Are ... husbands?* Levirate law demanded that a widow marry the brother of her dead husband and have children by him to continue the deceased's name (Deut. 25.5–10).

[23] *cleaved* clung; remained devoted [to her]. Cf. Gen. 2.24: 'Therefore shall a man leave his father and mother, and shall cleave unto his wife, and they shall be one flesh.'

[24] *them* idolatrous pagans.

[25] *uncleanness* moral and physical impurity.

change the natural use into that which is against nature: [27] and likewise also the men, leaving the natural use of the woman, burnt in their lust one towards another; men with men working that which is unseemly,[26] and receiving in themselves that recompense of their error which was meet.[27] [28] And even as they did not like to retain God in their knowledge, God gave them over to a reprobate mind, to do those things which are not convenient.[28] [...]

Thomas Beard (c. 1568–1632), polemicist and clergyman

Educated at Cambridge, Beard wrote Latin plays and highly apocalyptic, anti-Catholic pamphlets, but his most successful work was *The Theatre of God's Judgements* (1597), a compendium of vivid tales of divine retribution against unrepentant sinners that draws on a wide variety of classical, medieval, and contemporary writers, particularly the French Reformist minister Jean de Chassanion (1531–98). Immensely popular, *Theatre* expanded with each new edition (1612, 1631, and 1648).

1.2

From *The Theatre of God's Judgements* (1597)

1.2.1 Book 1, Chapter 32: Of Effeminate Persons, Sodomites, and Other Suchlike Monsters

Sardanapalus, King of Assyria, was so lascivious and effeminate that to the end to set forth his beauty, he shamed not to paint his face with ointments and to attire his body with the habits and ornaments of women, and on that manner to sit and lie continually amongst whores, and with them to commit all manner of filthiness and villainy. Wherefore, being thought unworthy to bear rule over men, first Arbaces his lieutenant rebelled, then the Medes and Babylonians revolted and jointly made war upon him till they vanquished and put him to flight. And in his flight he returned to a tower in his palace, which (moved with grief and despair) he set on fire and was consumed therein.

Suchlike was the impudent lasciviousness of two unworthy emperors,

[26] *men ... unseemly* 'men committing shameless acts with men' (RSV).

[27] *meet* fitting.

[28] *convenient* moral.

Commodus[1] and Heliogabalus, who laying aside all imperial gravity, showed themselves oftentimes publicly in woman's attire: an act as in nature monstrous, so very dishonest and ignominious. But like as these cursed monsters ran too much out of frame in their unbridled lusts and affections, so there wanted not many that hastened and emboldened themselves to conspire their destruction, as unworthy in their judgements to enjoy the benefit of this light.[2] Wherefore to one of them poison was ministered, and when that would take no effect, strangling came in the room[3] thereof, and brought him to his end; the other was slain in a jakes[4] where he hid himself, and his body (drawn like carrion through the streets) found no better sepulchre but the dunghill.

Touching those abominable wretches of Sodom and Gomorrah,[5] which gave themselves over with all violence, and without all shame and measure, to their infamous lusts, polluting their bodies with unnatural sins, God sent upon them an unnatural rain, not of water, but of fire and brimstone, to burn and consume them that were so hot and fervent in their cursed vices. So that they were quite rooted and raked out of the earth, and their cities and habitations destroyed; yea, and the very soil that bore them made desolate and fruitless, and all this by fire whose smoke ascended like the smoke of a furnace. Yea, and in sign of a further curse for to be a witness and a mark of this terrible judgement, the earth and face of that country continueth still parched and withered; and as Josephus[6] sayeth, whereas before it was a most plentiful and fertile soil, and as it were an earthly paradise bedecked with five gallant cities, now it lieth desert, inhabitable,[7] and barren, yielding fruit in show, but such as being touched turneth to cinders. In a word, the wrath of God is so notoriously and fearfully manifested therein, that when the Holy Ghost would strike a terror into the most wicked, he threateneth them with this like punishment, saying, "The Lord will rain upon each wicked one / Fire, snares, and brimstone, for his portion."[8]

Howbeit this maketh not[9] but that still there are too many such monsters in the world, so mightily is it corrupted and depraved. Neither is it any

1 *Commodus* Roman emperor (reigned 180–92 CE); reportedly engaged in cross-dressing, cunnilingus, and fellatio; had male slaves named after the male and female genitalia.

2 *light* sun.

3 *room* place.

4 *jakes* outhouse.

5 *Sodom and Gomorrah* See **1.1.1**.

6 *Josephus* first century CE Jewish historian.

7 *inhabitable* uninhabitable.

8 Ps. 11.6.

9 i.e., 'Even so these [terrible examples] have little effect.'

marvel, seeing that divers bishops of Rome,[10] that take upon them to be Christ's vicars and Peter's successors,[11] are infected with this filthy contagion. As namely Pope Julius III,[12] whose custom was to promote none to ecclesiastical livings save only his buggerers: amongst whom was one Innocent,[13] whom this holy father (contrary to the suffrages of the whole College[14]) would needs make cardinal.[15] Nay, the insatiable and monstrous lust of this beastly and stinking goat was so extraordinary that he could not abstain from[16] many cardinals themselves. John de la Casa,[17] a Florentine by birth, and by office archbishop of Benevento, and dean of his apostatical chamber,[18] was his legate and intelligencer in all the Venetian signories:[19] a man equal or rather worse than himself, and such a one as whose memory ought to be accursed of all posterity, for that detestable book which he composed in commendation and praise of sodomy,[20] and was so shameless, nay rather possessed with some devilish and unclean spirit, as to divulgate[21] it to the view of the world. Here you may see (poor souls) the holiness of those whom you so much reverence, and upon whom you build your belief and religion.

[...]

It is not for nothing that the law of God forbiddeth to lie with a beast and denounceth death against them that commit this foul sin.[22] For there have been such monsters in the world at some times, as we read in Caelius and Volterranus[23] of one Crathes a shepherd, that accompanied carnally with a she-goat. But the buck, finding him sleeping, offended and provoked with

[10] *divers* several, various (implies multiplicity without committing the writer to 'many' or 'few'); *bishops of Rome*: popes.

[11] *Christ's … successors* Mt. 16.18–19.

[12] *Julius III* (reigned 1550–55).

[13] *Innocent* Innocenzo Del Monte, Julius's young lover.

[14] *suffrages … College* i.e., the opinions of the College of Cardinals, the body that advised the pope on candidates for cardinal (the second highest rank in the Catholic Church); they opposed Innocent's elevation.

[15] *make cardinal* Innocent was appointed to this position in 1550.

[16] *abstain from* resist having sexual relations with.

[17] Archbishop Giovanni *della Casa* (1503–56), poet and papal chamberlain.

[18] *apostatical chamber* apostate or heretical chamber (sarcastic glance at 'apostolic').

[19] *legate* and *intelligencer* pope's ambassador and spy; *signories*: city-states.

[20] *detestable book … sodomy De laudibus sodomiae* ('In praise of sodomy'), a work libellously attributed to della Casa, which in fact never existed.

[21] *divulgate* make commonly known.

[22] Lev. 20.15–16.

[23] *Caelius* unidentified; *Volterranus*: Raffaelo Volterranus (Maffei) (1451–1522), Italian historian and humanist.

this strange action, ran at him so furiously with his horns that he left him dead upon the ground. [...]

William Prynne (1600–69), lawyer and writer

Puritan polemicist with more than two hundred works to his credit, Prynne targeted the cross-dressed English stage in *Histrio-mastix* (1633), but it was its condemnation of female actors, perceived as targeting Queen Henrietta Maria, lover of and performer in court masques, that led directly to Prynne's conviction and brutal punishment for sedition. Although an effective parliamentary propagandist, he opposed the execution of Charles I, and Charles II later appointed him keeper of the records. He published moral tracts and religious polemics until his death.

1.3

From *Histrio-mastix*[1] (1633)

1.3.1 Act 5, scene 6

[...] Lastly, this putting on of woman's array (especially to act a lascivious, amorous, whorish, lovesick play upon the stage), must needs be sinful, yea abominable, because it not only excites many adulterous filthy lusts, both in the actors and spectators, and draws them on both to contemplative and actual lewdness [...] which is evil, but likewise instigates them to self-pollution[2] [...] and to that unnatural, sodomitical sin of uncleanness to which the reprobate Gentiles were given over[3] (a sin not once to be named, much less than practised among Christians), which is worse. This the detestable examples of Heliogabalus, Sardanapalus, Nero and Sporus, the male-priests of Venus,[4] with the passive beastly sodomites in Florida, Gayra,[5]

1 *Histrio-mastix* As the work's subtitle suggests, 'Histrio-mastix' means 'The Players' Scourge, or Actors' Tragedy'.

2 *self-pollution* masturbation.

3 *to ... over* See **1.1.6**.

4 *male-priests of Venus* Orgies and male prostitution were believed part of Venus's worship.

5 *Gayra* on the South American coast. Gayran sodomites cross-dressed; their women who swore perpetual virginity became hunters and warriors. For Prynne's sources, see S. Purchas, *Purchas His Pilgrims*, 1.8.c7; 1.9.c1–c2.

and Peru, evidence:[6] who went clad in woman's apparel, the better to eliciate,[7] countenance, act, and colour their unnatural, execrable uncleanness, which I abhor to think of. This the usual practice of other ancient *incubi*,[8] who clothed their *galli*, *succubi*, *ganymedes*, and *cynaedi*[9] in woman's attire, whose virilities they did oft-times dissect,[10] to make them more effeminate, transforming them as near as might be into women, both in apparel, gesture, speech, [and] behaviour. And more especially in long, unshorn, womanish, frizzled,[11] lust-provoking hair and love-locks, grown now too much in fashion with comely pages, youths, and lewd, effeminate, ruffianly persons; as they were with these unnatural pagans, I dare not write, to amorous beastly purposes, to which they are strong allectives,[12] of which they were ancient symptoms, as sundry profane and Christian writers testify; [...] the more to extenuate this their unnatural wickedness, or rather the more freely to embolden, to allure and provoke them to the undaunted, unlamented practice of it, by reducing it as near to natural lewdness as they could devise; since few of them were so prodigiously impudent, so unnaturally outrageous at the first, as desperately to rush upon this unnatural filthiness in its superlative native vileness without some extenuating varnishes cast into it, to charm[13] their consciences and inflame their lusts. Yea, this the execrable precedents of ancient, of modern play-poets and players witness, who have been deeply plunged in this abominable wickedness, which my ink is not black enough to decipher. Witness the example of Sophocles, that famous Greek tragedian, whom [many ancient writers] have stigmatized for this sin. Witness St Cyprian[14] who writes thus of the womanish pantomimes and players in his time [...] Yea witness [...] with M[aster] Stubbes, his *Anatomy of Abuses*, where he affirms 'that players and play-haunters in their secret conclaves play the sodomites':[15] together with some modern examples of such, who have been desperately enamoured with players' boys thus clad in woman's apparel, so far as to solicit them by words, by letters, even actually to abuse them. All which [...] should make this very putting on of woman's apparel on boys, to act a

6 *evidence* demonstrate.

7 *eliciate* draw out.

8 *incubi* demons in male form who have sex with sleeping women.

9 *galli* priests of Cybele; they had an early modern reputation as sodomites; *succubi*: demons in female form who have sex with sleeping men; *ganymedes* and *cynaedi*: specifically, boys kept to satisfy the sexual desires of their masters; generally, sodomites.

10 *whose ... dissect* they often castrated them. See Cybele (Glossary).

11 *frizzled* curled.

12 *allectives* allurements.

13 *charm* allay the pangs [of]; put to sleep.

14 *St Cyprian* (d. 258), Bishop of Carthage and early Christian theologian.

15 For Stubbes, see *Online Companion*.

play, forever execrable to all chaste Christian hearts. Hence it is that sundry divines annex this text of Deuteronomy to the Seventh Commandment,[16] as a moral precept founded upon the very law of nature; because men's putting on of woman's raiment[17] is a temptation, an inducement not only to adultery but to the beastly sin of Sodom, which (sayeth Lactantius)[18] is most properly called adultery, because it is unnatural. [...] Yea, hence [...] those women who put on men's and men who put on women's apparel are said [...] not only to be abominable, but even to be an abomination to the Lord their God, because it is an occasion of, a violent provocation to that monstrous unparalleled sin of Sodom. [...] [I]t is abundantly evident by all these premises and (I suppose) by many players' and play-haunters' particular experience [...] that men's putting on of woman's apparel (especially to act a whore's, a bawd's, or sweetheart's womanish wanton part upon the stage, where all the solicitations and inescating[19] allectives to uncleanness do accompany it) is a preparative, an incendiary, not only to sundry noisome[20] lusts, to speculative, to practical adultery, whoredom, and the like: but even to the most abominable, unnatural sin of Sodom, to which men's inbred corruption, (as good authors testify) is over-prone; as the detestable examples of the flagitious[21] Sodomites, Canaanites, Jews, Gentiles, Corinthians, Italians, Turks, Persians, Grecians, Tartars, Chinois,[22] Celtae,[23] Peguans,[24] Floridians,[25] ancient Romans, Moors in Barbary, Gayrians, Peruvians, Jupiter and his Ganymedes, [...] and many others, yea the frequent sodomitical wickednesses of sundry unholy popes, cardinals, popish bishops, abbots, priests, friars, monks, (such are the unchaste fruits of their vowed and much-admired chastity) together with the frequent inhibitions, laws, and edicts against this prodigious villainy in Scriptures, councils, heathen states, and in our English statutes (which have made it capital,[26] as a late example of a memorable act of justice on an English peer[27] can witness) do more than testify; it cannot but be inexcusably sinful, both in the eyes of God, who literally prohibits it; and in the sight of natural, much

16 *the Seventh Commandment* 'Thou shalt not commit adultery.'

17 *raiment* clothing, attire.

18 *Lactantius* (c. 240–c. 320), early Christian apologist.

19 *inescating* enticing.

20 *noisome* noxious.

21 *flagitious* guilty of atrocious crimes.

22 *Chinois* Chinese.

23 *Celtae* Celts (Scots or Irish).

24 *Peguans* inhabitants of the city or district of Pegu (southern Burma).

25 *Floridians* natives of Florida.

26 *capital* punishable by death.

27 *English peer* Mervin, Lord Audley, executed for sodomy in 1631. See **3.3**.

more of Christian, men, who cannot but detest it. And so by consequence the plays themselves which are acted in such apparel (as all our masques and stage-plays for the most part are) must questionless be sinful, yea abominable, as men's putting on of woman's apparel is. [...]

CHAPTER 2

Pseudo-Medical Writings

Introduction

According to Kenneth Borris's extensive research, original early modern medical, pseudo-medical, and anatomical texts in Latin are surprisingly reticent about the physiological and anatomical aspects of homoerotic sexuality and desire.[1] This reticence is surprising in the academic Latin tradition. 'Modestly' veiled in Latin, the language of the intellectual and social elites of Europe, such texts were available only to the exclusive and relatively limited audience of professional physicians, anatomists, scientists, and educated gentleman who produced and consumed them. Moreover, as Borris goes on to point out, although early modern physicians, anatomists, and scientists were very well aware of classical and medieval Arabic texts' extensive discussions of homoerotic sexuality and desire – in works by figures such as Caelius Aurelianus, pseudo-Aristotle, and Avicenna (Ibn Sina) – and although these texts were highly respected (like most in the ancient tradition), these discussions did not make their way into original, learned anatomies and other scientific texts: 'Renaissance medical discourse on same-sex desires and practices appears to have been typically constituted by a paradox of unspeakable knowledge, whereby much of what highly valued ancient sources state on the subject (which would, according to conventional practice in the discipline, be cited often) could not even be restated, let alone further developed, in an independent original work in this field' (*Same-Sex* 116). Classical and Arabic investigations into homoerotic sexuality and desire entered the learned tradition only through the genre of the commentary (116), a learned disquisition on the content of a particular text, sometimes published alone and sometimes as an accompaniment to an edition of the text itself.

[1] For a full discussion, with excerpts from both English medical texts and translations from those available in Latin, see Borris, *Same-Sex*, pp. 115–56.

Kenneth Borris argues convincingly that this reticence springs from a profound disagreement between the ancients' naturalistic and Christianity's theological explanations for the causes of homoerotic sexual desire: the ancients' focus on the *causes* of homoeroticism as lying in the conditions the foetus experienced in the womb (what Borris calls 'congenital homoeroticism') made homoerotic desires and acts the result of a natural and 'innate predisposition', contradicting Christian theological assertions that such desires and acts were sins, wilfully practiced, and defined by God and man as *against* the laws of nature. The contradiction between the ancients' definition of same-sex acts and desires as natural and congenital,[2] and Christian definitions of them as unnatural and immoral tended to be resolved through silence; no original early modern Latin treatises 'acknowledge the theories of congenital homoeroticism, even to reject them' (116). Unsurprisingly, English texts, with their wider audiences, are even more thoroughly characterized by silences, elisions, and circumlocutions when dealing with the physiological and anatomical aspects of human sexuality, and thus discussion of the relationship between anatomy and the humoural complexion of the body in relation to same-sex desire and activity is even more thoroughly censored. For example, in *Anatomy of Melancholy* (1621), Robert Burton's encyclopaedic treatment of this mental illness, same-sex desires and sexual acts are discussed at length as particular symptoms of erotomania or love-sickness, but only because these acts and desires are discreetly veiled in Latin.[3]

The texts excerpted below and in the *Online Companion* dramatically demonstrate Borris's contention that there was a double standard in medical texts when it came to a description of male versus female same-sex erotic acts and desires. Although descriptions of both remain very rare in English texts in particular, women's same-sex desires and acts are at least acknowledged, although the natural 'causes' of these desires and acts are scrupulously avoided, and in fact these desires and acts are firmly inscribed in an essentializing discourse of clitoral abnormality and an erotic discourse of male voyeurism. The great medical maverick and popularizer Helkiah Crooke, for example, in his discussion of the anatomical composition and physiology of the female clitoris gives some space to a consideration of clitoral abnormalities in the context of female same-sex desires and acts: he notes that the hypertrophied clitoris, a clitoris that exceeds its usual

[2] Borris also points out that, although mainstream works by Galen and the Hippocratic tradition attempt to account for 'feminine males' and 'masculine females' by examining aspects of foetology, these works do not explicitly connect this lack of conformity to gender and sex roles with homoerotic desire and sexual acts (*Same-Sex*, pp. 115–16).

[3] For the way aspects of academic medicine and Latin classical treatises seeped down to the level of popular medicine and clinical practice, see Borris, *Same-Sex*, p. 115.

size to such an extent that it can and does function like a male penis, 'groweth to such a length that it hangeth without the cleft like a man's member, especially when it is fretted with the touch of the clothes, and so strutteth and groweth to a rigidity as doth the yard [i.e., penis] of a man. And this part it is which those wicked women do abuse called *tribades* (often mentioned by many authors, and in some states worthily punished) to their mutual and unnatural lusts' (*Microcosmographia* (1615), 238; *Online Companion*). In contrast, like all of his academic fellows and fellow popularizers, Crooke says absolutely nothing about male same-sex desires and acts in the course of his discussion of the male generative organs (Borris, *Same-Sex* 117). While this double standard is certainly, as Borris points out, connected to the relative insignificance of female same-sex acts and desires in comparison to those of men, it also reflects an anxious response to the way the clitoris came to be defined in the mid-sixteenth century as homologous to the penis, a homology that came to imply that all women had the potential to be hermaphrodites (117–19).

Both Giles Jacob's self-described 'airy entertainment' the *Tractatus de Hermaphroditis* (1718) and the anonymously authored, anti-masturbation tract *Supplement to the Onania* (1725?) exist at the very end of the period we are interested in. Here, at the beginning of the eighteenth century we see both continuity between and divergence from sixteenth- and early seventeenth-century contexts for the discussion of the causes of male and female homoerotic acts and desires: the development of the discourses of erotic voyeurism and of the discourses of nature, the natural, and the unnatural in relation to female homoerotic practices in particular. These combine together, in often very confused ways, to signal the development of the nascent connections between medical discourses generally and 'lesbian' identity (Borris, *Same-Sex* 116). Voyeuristic eroticism is most obvious in Jacob's text, although it is not entirely absent from the *Supplement to the Onania* even given that author's strenuous and largely convincing claims that the work has a serious moral and social purpose. *Tractatus*' most original sections – the three narratives depicting female homoerotic sexual acts and adventuring – dwell delightedly on the details of these sexual acts, engaging in some of the oldest markers of erotic and pornographic literature: a servant observing these acts through a peephole he has had drilled into the wall of his female employer's bedchamber; a cross-dressed male lover watching and even participating in the sexual intercourse between two women, finally convincing his desired object that a real penis is better than its dildo substitute; and the violent punishment of the female, hermaphroditic sexual adventurer, her genitals exposed to the gaze of men, and then forcibly excised by them (see below, and *Online Companion*).

While couched within a sincere and detailed Christian framework,

Supplement to the Onania's letter from the young woman who has been engaging for some years in sexual activity with her mother's maid cannot avoid the possibility of being read salaciously; the *Supplement*'s author recognizes as much in his preface, where he dismisses those who suggest that he has 'actually taught this practice [i.e., masturbation] to many, who without seeing [his] book would never have been guilty of it' (v); he becomes most angry, however, with the charge that he has written 'obscenely' and 'forward[ed] the corruption of manners' (vi), even though he acknowledges the enormous influence of the *Onania*'s and its *Supplement*'s autobiographical letters concerning the individual writers' habitual masturbation: 'I have known half a sentence of a silly letter rouse the conscience of a young man, whom the grave reasoning and solid arguments of the same book made no impression upon' (2). He is, of course, unwilling to entertain the notion that such letters might have a correspondingly powerful erotic effect on the reader.

Although Thomas Laqueur has acknowledged that any real account of the relationship between the discourses of masturbation and homosexuality needs to account 'for the novel, and sometimes paradigmatic, focus on girls and women masturbating and on knowledgeable female servants teaching them' (*Solitary* 260), not much critical work has yet been done on these common, early eighteenth-century tropes. Both *Tractatus* and *Supplement* focus partly on the role of clitoral hypertrophy in tribadic activity and hermaphroditic anatomy, but both are also concerned (in different ways) with the relationships between same-sex erotic partners. *Tractatus* suggests that a hermaphroditic woman's hypertrophied clitoris produces her sexual desire for members of her own sex, and allows her to satisfy it; her anatomy, then, makes her a tribade (cf. Schleiner; Traub, *Renaissance* 188–228; Donoghue, *Passions* 33–53, 206–12). In contrast, *Supplement* expresses a far more confused anatomical essentialism, with the author largely maintaining that a woman's prolonged indulgence in autoerotic practices and same-sex mutual masturbation enlarges the clitoris, subsequently allowing a woman to engage in penetrative sex with a female partner. At the same time, *Supplement* states that some clitoral hypertrophy arises naturally, and is not the result of a woman's diseased will, but that such naturally occurring clitoral hypertrophy can lead to tribadic sex, if the 'afflicted' woman surrenders to lust. *Supplement* suggests, then, that biology (an enlarged clitoris) precedes and creates same-sex desire; however, E.N.'s letter implies the opposite, that same-sex desire precedes and leads to same-sexual intercourse, producing in turn an enlarged clitoris. At the same time, both *Tractatus* and *Supplement* anxiously focus on the nature of the specific relationship which informs female same-sex sexual acts. E.N.'s relationship with her mother's maid primarily suggests the *Supplement*'s anxiety over the violation of class boundaries, while the various sexually intimate female relationships in *Tractatus* represent a more wide-ranging uneasiness over the challenge they pose to men's sexual and patriarchal prerogatives (*Online Companion*).

Online Companion
Interested readers can find additional selections from the following medical and pseudo-medical writers: Helkiah Crooke, Thomas Bartholin, Thomas Gibson, and Giles Jacob.

Giles Jacob (1686–1744), legal professional and writer

Jacob's writings range from legal textbooks and reference works to dramatic farces, satires, and verse. Reproducing conventional ancient and Renaissance medical knowledge about gender, sex, and hermaphroditism, the pseudo-medical text *Tractatus* also sets about titillating readers: its publication by the notorious Edmund Curll, responsible for the scandalous *Venus in the Cloister* (1724); its provocative Latin title, with its sexually charged word 'hermaphrodite'; and the voyeuristic observation of tribadic sex in the narrative of Margureta and Barbarissa, a common trope in early modern pornography, all provoke readers' sexual curiosity (Schleiner 246). For Jacob's pseudo-clinical discussion of hermaphroditism and his tale of Margureta and Barbarissa, see **2.1.2–2.1.4**, but for the lengthier tribadic adventures of Theodora and Amaryllis, and Diana and Isabella, consult the *Online Companion*.

2.1

From *Tractatus de Hermaphroditis: Or, A Treatise of Hermaphrodites* (1718)[1]

2.1.1 Preface

[...] I shall make no apology for my subject, notwithstanding an impudent libeller has endeavoured to load authors and publishers of works of this nature with the utmost infamy; and herein I admire at the front[2] of the fellow, to pretend to chastise others for writing only, when he practises a great deal more iniquity than any book extant can prompt him to every day that comes over his head.

My design in the following sheets is merely as an innocent entertainment

[1] Appended to an anonymous translation of Meibomius's *A Treatise of the Use of Flogging in Venereal Affairs*.

[2] *front* effrontery, impudence.

for all curious persons, without any views of inciting masculine-females to amorous trials with their own sex; and I am persuaded there will not be one single hermaphrodite the more in the world on account of the publishing this treatise.

It may be expected by some faithless persons that I should produce an hermaphrodite to public view as an incontestable justification of there being human creatures of this kind; but as I have no authority to take up the petticoats of any female without her consent, I hope to be excused from making such demonstrable proofs; and if I had such a power, the sight might endanger the welfare of some pregnant female, whose curiosity would spur her to a particular examination.[3]

The intrigues of my hermaphrodites are indeed very amazing, and as monstrous as their natures; but that many lascivious females divert themselves one with another at this time in this city is not to be doubted; and if any persons shall presume to censure my accounts, grounded on a probability of truth, I shall be sufficiently revenged in proclaiming them, what my hermaphrodites are found to be in the conclusion – old women.[4]

I confess, all histories of extraordinary conceptions from these intrigues,[5] or by women without actual copulation, are equally fabulous[6] with those of the engendering of men. It would be as surprising to find a man with a teeming belly,[7] as to see a woman increase there[in] merely by her own applications.[8]

I doubt not but this small treatise may put some persons upon previous examination of robust females, that they may be at a certainty with respect to mutual enjoyment; but I would not have them rashly conclude from large appurtenances only that they are unnatural, but, on the contrary, agreeable companions. To conclude, I fear not the censure of hermaphrodites, nor of those that would be such to satisfy their vicious inclinations; neither am I under any apprehensions from the censure of our reforming zealots.

[3] *the sight … examination* referring to the popular beliefs that pregnant women had unaccountable cravings, often for toxic or vile substances; and that the sight of horrific things might trigger miscarriage or the malformation of the foetus.

[4] *what … old women* The last female same-sex couple described in Jacob's text finally have their male genitalia violently excised, ending their sexual adventures; they decline into old age. See *Online Companion.*

[5] *intrigues* intercourse between hermaphrodites, or between hermaphrodites and anatomically 'normative' men or women.

[6] *fabulous* fictional, untrue (of the nature of fables).

[7] *teeming belly* i.e., pregnant.

[8] *by her own applications* i.e., perhaps, by bringing herself to orgasm through masturbation (female orgasm was long thought necessary for conception to occur). Jacob discusses 'monstrous conceptions' in the last section of the *Tractatus.*

2.1.2 A Treatise of Hermaphrodites

[The treatise begins with the assertion that hermaphrodites are an actual anatomical reality: 'Histories are full of confirmations that many persons in the world have had the privy parts of both sexes' (3). Noting that in the past hermaphrodites have tended not to marry anatomically 'normative' men or women for fear of exposure and execution, Jacob goes on to discuss the present treatment of people with both sets of generative organs.]

But the civil law does not regard hermaphrodites as monsters; it permits them to make a choice of either of the two sexes for the business of copulation, either in the capacity of men or women; but if the hermaphrodite does not perform his part agreeable to nature, the same law inflicts the punishment due to sodomy, because he has abused one part contrary to Nature's laws. This must be determined by the predominancy of the parts, for there are some hermaphrodites so very vigorous as to embrace women, and others whose parts are so disposed as to receive with pleasure the caresses of men; and where there is nothing to hinder the amorous action, but that they are capable of enjoying mutual pleasure, it would be a piece of injustice to prohibit their nuptials. [...]

[A detailed taxonomy of hermaphroditism follows, where 'five kinds of hermaphrodites' (6) are described. Jacob calls the first three types 'male hermaphrodite[s]' (9), and they are essentially men, capable of ejaculation in intercourse and begetting children, but have some anatomical peculiarities reminiscent of the vagina; the fourth type consists of female hermaphrodites, and they are essentially women, capable of conceiving and bearing children and menstruating, except they 'have the clitoris bigger and longer than others, and thereby impose upon the vulgar, who know but little of the parts they are composed of, and of these kinds of hermaphrodites, Columbus [i.e., the sixteenth-century anatomist Realdo Colombo] says he examined all the parts and found no essential difference from other women' (8). Fifthly, there are 'perfect hermaphrodites' (10), to whom a dominant sex category cannot be assigned, since they 'have neither the use of the one nor the other sex, and have their privy parts confused [...] but these sorts of persons are rather a kind of eunuchs than hermaphrodites, their penis being good for nothing, and their terms [i.e., menstrual periods] never flowing' (8–9). Jacob then proceeds to describe the external signs by which a person may perceive a hermaphrodite.]

Women having beards, and being of a large masculine size, have been sometimes, by the ignorant, accounted men, though they were true women; and it cannot be said that one sex is changed into another, for we never heard of men that became women, and that their privy parts were abolished, or turned within, in order to form the genital parts of a woman.[9] The hermaphrodites of Licetus,[10] which conceived and brought forth children, were real women taken for men, by reason of the length and bigness of their clitoris: and the fisherman's wife mentioned by Antonius de Palma[11] was only a male, called the third sort of hermaphrodites, undiscovered, which was afterwards manifested in the coming out of the parts of a man, when she had been fourteen years married. [...]

For the discovery of the male and female hermaphrodite, these observations will be serviceable: a person that is bold and sprightly, having a strong voice, much hair on the body, particularly on the chin and privy parts, with the rest of such signs as discover manhood, are certain demonstrations that the hermaphrodite has the privy parts of a man in a more predominant manner than those of the other sex; and contrariwise, if an hermaphrodite has good breasts, skin smooth and soft; if the terms appear at their due intervals; if there be a sparkling and agreeableness in the eyes, and if other signs are observed that commonly distinguish a woman from a man, these are arguments that the hermaphrodite has the privities of the female sex of a good conformation; and if the vagina is not too defective, such an hermaphrodite ought to pass for a woman.

I doubt not but there are many persons in the world of both species,[12] particularly of the female sex, who would willingly assume to themselves the parts belonging to hermaphrodites, if they could have a vigorous use of the members of both sexes, upon any lustful inclination. A lascivious female would be transported at the thoughts of acting the part of a man in the amorous adventure, and a lecherous male would propose equal pleasure in receiving the embraces he use[d] to bestow. But though most persons agree that women have the greatest sense of enjoyment in the act of copulation (as without all question they must by the situation and disposition of the parts), yet they would be more forward in satisfying this brutal[13] curiosity than those of the opposite sex. Men are more easy to be limited in the pleasures

9 *and it cannot be said … woman* a notion derived from the ancients, that women's reproductive organs were inverted versions of men's; women were believed physiologically 'colder' than men, lacking the 'heat' necessary to allow their vaginas to emerge from their bodies as penises.

10 *the … Licetus* as described in the Italian natural philosopher Fortunio Liceti's 1616 treatise *De Monstrorum Caussis, Natura, et Differentii* ('Concerning the Causes, Nature, and Differences of Monsters').

11 *Antonius de Palma* unidentified.

12 *species* sexes; kinds.

13 *brutal* i.e., after the manner of brute beasts; bestial.

of Venus than women; as they are endued with more reason,[14] so they are generally easily satisfied in those enjoyments which were chiefly designed for the propagating of their species.

[...]

The clitoris in women suffers erection and falling in the same manner as the penis in men; and the vagina likewise swells to make the passage straight and easy for the reception of the penis in the time of enjoyment. Sometimes the clitoris will grow out of the body two or three inches, but that happens not but upon extraordinary occasions, upon violent inclinations to copulation, overmuch heat of the privities,[15] etc., and by this means a man will be hindered from knowing[16] his wife; but the larger it is, so as no way to prevent their mutual embraces, the greater is the pleasure, especially to the female; and without this part the fair sex would neither desire the embraces of the males, nor have any pleasure in them, or conceive by them.[17]

Women well-furnished in these parts may divert themselves with their companions, to whom for the most part they can give as much pleasure as men do, but cannot receive in any proportion the pleasure themselves, for want of ejaculation, the crisis of enjoyment to the male in the intrigues of Venus.[18] I am informed that diversions of this nature are frequently practised by robust and lustful females, who cannot with any prospect of safety to their reputations venture upon the embraces of a man, though they are never so strongly inclined. The unnatural pleasures of this kind are finely illustrated in the following song, written by Mr Rowe,[19] which I take it will not be improperly inserted in this place.

[14] *endued with more reason* men were generally thought more able to restrain their emotions and physical desires than women, because men were believed to have a greater ability to reason.

[15] *privities* genitals.

[16] *knowing* having sex with.

[17] *and ... them* referring to the clitoris's essential role in female orgasm, and the consequent release of female semen (seed) leading to conception.

[18] *intrigues of Venus* sexual activity.

[19] *Mr Rowe* Nicholas Rowe (1674–1718), poet, playwright, and poet laureate (1715–18).

2.1.3 Song

While Sappho with harmonious airs,
  Her dear Philenis charms,[20]
With equal joy the nymph appears,
  Dissolving in her arms.[21]

Thus to themselves alone they are,
  What all mankind can give;
Alternately the happy pair
  All grant, and all receive.

Like the twin-stars, so famed for friends,[22]
  Who set by turns, and rise;
When one to Thetis' lap descends,[23]
  His brother mounts the skies.

With happier fate, and kinder care
  These nymphs by turns do reign,
While still the falling does prepare
  The rising to sustain.[24]

The joys of either sex in love,
  In each of them we read,
Successive each, to each does prove,
  Fierce youth and yielding maid.

2.1.4 Intrigues of Hermaphrodites and Masculine Females

The hotter the climate, the stronger are the inclinations to venery. When I was formerly in Italy, there happened a notable adventure in the neighbourhood of Rome between a certain lady called Margureta,[25] one of a noble family in the papal dominions,[26] and a lady of France, whose name was Barbarissa.[27]

[20] Cf. 'Sappho to Philaenis', **7.7.1**.
[21] *dissolving* experiencing sexual pleasure or orgasm.
[22] *twin-stars* the Gemini (Glossary).
[23] *Thetis* sea (daughter of the sea god, Nereus).
[24] *While … sustain* referring to the rising and falling of the tribadic clitoris as penis.
[25] *Margureta* meaning, 'pearl'.
[26] *papal dominions* states governed politically and spiritually by the pope.
[27] *Barbarissa* a variant on 'Barbara' ('foreign woman'), with an obvious play on 'barbarous' and 'barbarian'.

These two females were in their statures very near equal to the largest sized male; they had full and rough faces, large shoulders, hands, and feet, and but slender hips, and small breasts. In short, they resembled men in all respects but their dresses, their gaits, and voices, and indeed they were suspected to be hermaphrodites. These ladies, I am informed, paid frequent visits to each other, and 'twas always observed that nobody was admitted to their splendid entertainments, which heightened the curiosity of a servant in the family of Margureta to attempt a discovery of their intrigues, they always locking themselves in the moment they had dispatched[28] their suppers. In order to this, on a time, this servant, called Nicolini, with a piercing instrument of iron, and the assistance of an artificer,[29] ingeniously made a communication for the sight into the next room, by working a small hole through the wainscot, opposite to the bed, in the chamber wherein the two masculine ladies accustomed to solace themselves.

At the next meeting, Nicolini, to his no small surprise, had a prospect of the two females embracing each other, with a succession of kisses of no short duration. After this they both drew up their petticoats, and exposing their thighs to view, they mutually employed their hands with each other in the same manner, and with the same force of inclination, as a juvenile[30] gallant would make his approaches to what he most admires in a beautiful Belinda, at the same time continuing the closest salutations; at last one of the females threw herself down upon the bed, and displaying herself commodiously, the other immediately begun the amorous adventure, covering her companion so effectually that Nicolini could not possibly discover any farther particulars. They had not continued their sportings long before Margureta, which officiated now instead of the man, arose from Barbarissa, and turning towards the window with her clothes up in her arms, Nicolini immediately discovered something hang[ing] down from her body of a reddish colour, and which was very unusual. They both panting and almost breathless, retired from the bed to a table, where they sat down and refreshed themselves with sufficient quantities of generous wine. About an hour after this, they began to renew their frolics, and it being Barbarissa's turn to caress, who was not so masculine as Margureta, to incite the falling down and erection of her female member, she turned over a large book amply stored with obscene portraitures, wherein the amorous combat was curiously[31] described in the utmost variety of postures which were ever practiced or the head of a youthful and ingenious painter could invent; but this not having the effect expected, Margureta stripped herself naked, as

[28] *dispatched* finished.

[29] *artificer* handyman.

[30] *juvenile* youthful.

[31] *curiously* skilfully, minutely.

did likewise Barbarissa, and both dancing about the room, they gave each other repeated strokes with their hands on their white posteriors; and this likewise failing to move Barbarissa, Margureta opened a cabinet, and taking from thence a large birchen rod, she flogged Barbarissa lustily, her buttocks seeming to yield to that amorous discipline;[32] upon this, something appeared from the privities of Barbarissa, like unto what Nicolini had observed of Margureta, and they instantly put on their loose gowns, and ran to the bed, where Barbarissa embracing her companion, did her work effectually. After their sportings were over, that each had returned the favours received, they decently dressed themselves, and sat them down again to the table, where, after drinking a bottle or two of the richest Italian wines, they kissed each other in the most loving manner, and Margureta rang the bell for Nicolini to light Barbarissa downstairs, who immediately taking leave of Margureta, was carried in a chair to her place of residence.

This story sufficiently shows the unnatural intrigues of some masculine females where by the falling down and largeness of the clitoris they have been taken for men, as mentioned in my description of hermaphrodites, and are capable of every action belonging to a man, but that of ejaculation. I next insert an intrigue between two females more extraordinary than the former, by reason[33] in this, art was only employed, and in the other there was something of nature in it, though viciously applied. [...][34]

A Supplement to the Onania, Or the Heinous Sin of Self-Pollution (1725?)

A sequel to the enormously popular *Onania; Or, the Heinous Sin of Self-Pollution, and All Its Frightful Consequences, in both Sexes, Considered* (1716?; at least 19 editions by 1800), *Supplement* largely consists of letters purportedly from *Onania*'s readers to its anonymous author, outlining the medical problems springing from their habitual masturbation, followed by the author's commentary. The following, the only letter dealing with female homoerotic intercourse, introduces a lengthy section on hermaphroditism and tribadism.

Editions

Onania, or, The Heinous Sin of Self-Pollution [with] A Supplement to the Onania. Facsimile edition. New York: Garland, 1986.

32 *large ... discipline* Flagellation often features in sexual encounters between women in early modern texts (cf. **9.16.1**).

33 *by reason* since.

34 For the complete narratives of Theodora and Amaryllis, and of Diana and Isabella, see the *Online Companion*.

2.2

From *A Supplement to the Onania* (1725?)

2.2.1 To the Commendable Author of the *Onania*.

Oct. 16, 1725.

Sir,

This letter comes from a young female creature, but an old transgressor in the practice of that filthy pleasure which you have so justly exploded and condemned in your ingenious book of *Onania*, which I happily met with about ten days ago. But in all the cases therein enumerated there is not one that is parallel to mine, which as my welfare requires it, I must be obliged to relate, and is what I question, sir, whether you have ever once met with; nor could I tell it, though at the same time I bless the opportunity, but that I am sure you no more know the writer of it, nor ever will, than I know the author of *Onania*, or desire it.

I began, sir, the folly at eleven years of age, was taught it by my mother's chambermaid, who lay with me from that time all along till now, which is full seven years, and so intimate were we in the sin, that we took all opportunities of committing it, and invented all the ways we were capable of to heighten the titillation, and gratify our sinful lusts the more. We, in short, pleasured one another, as well as each ourselves, but whether by the hard usage of my parts by her, or myself, or both, or whether from anything in nature more in my make[1] than is customary to the sex, I don't know, but for above half a year past I have had a swelling that thrusts out from my body, as big, and almost as hard, and as long or longer than my thumb, which inclines me to excessive lustful desires, and from it there issues a moisture or slipperiness to that degree that I am almost continually wet, and sometimes have such a forcing, as if something of a large substance was coming from me, which greatly frightens both me and my maid. She went to a midwife about it, but did not, she says, tell her of our practice; the midwife said it was a bearing down of the womb, by weakness,[2] and told her what I should do, which I did, but to no purpose. Ever since I have been so, I have not had the

[1] *make* physical constitution.

[2] *bearing … weakness* Some early modern physicians held that the uterus might 'fall down' (become prolapsed) through overindulgence in heterosexual intercourse, but also through a natural constitutional weakness. A prolapsed uterus caused by autoerotic or female same-sex practices is not attested in the sources I have consulted, although diseases resulting from retention of female seed might be treated by masturbation and the attendant release of the seed through orgasm. *Onania* refutes and rejects this always controversial treatment.

course of nature,[3] have a great pain in my back, and my belly is swelled, am not near so strong as I was, my countenance much paler, and appetite less. It has almost distracted[4] me, and unfits me for my learning, and am afraid I am so hurt that it cannot be remedied. Oh! that I should be so wicked, I, who have had a much nobler education (and should know better) than is common to most of my sex; that am versed in the classics, and am designed by my friends, who are very rich, for something above the common station of my sex; I say, that I should so filthily debase myself, wrong my body, and, which is worse, my soul, is surprising even to myself! Had I read more the Bible, and less in Martial, Juvenal, Ovid,[5] etc., it had been better for me, but those books, Rochester,[6] and plays, at first debauched my silly fancy.[7] But I hope, as now both myself and maid have, on consulting your curious[8] discourse of self-pollution, abandoned the practice and resolved (through God's grace) to commit it no more, we shall find pardon, and my infirm body, from your hands, good sir, relief. She ails nothing, is a strong wench of twenty-seven; myself of a tender make and naturally inclined to be weakly, and but just turned of eighteen. I have with this sent you a guinea[9] fee, and desire your cordial advice what I had best to do, and your opinion of my case sealed up safe, directed for Mrs E.N. And I will send for it tomorrow morning at the bookseller's where this is left; and, sir, I must needs desire you to send this letter back that I may have the satisfaction of committing it to the flames myself. According to your answer, you shall hear further from,

Sir,
Your ever obliged, and
most obedient humble servant,
E. N.

Not, sir, but you may copy my letter first, and if you think worthwhile, to print it also in your next edition, as a caution to others; but would not that my hand be seen by any besides yourself, the circumstance of the relation, so as not to be known 'tis me, I have taken care of and guarded against.

[3] *course of nature* menstruation.

[4] *distracted* driven [me] mad.

[5] *Martial, Juvenal, Ovid* classical writers; referring specifically to Martial's satiric, erotic epigrams (including the homoerotic: see **7.23–7.26**); Juvenal's satires (which also focus on sexual licence and excess, including the homoerotic: see **7.27**); and Ovid's various erotic works, *Metamorphoses* (see **7.17–7.18**), *Ars Amatoria*, and *Heroides* (see **7.19**).

[6] *Rochester* See **8.21–8.25**.

[7] *debauched … fancy* corrupted my innocent imagination.

[8] *curious* minutely detailed.

[9] *guinea* an English gold coin worth £1 1s (£1.05) (a considerable sum in 1725).

[The author attributes E.N.'s condition to 'a relaxation of the clitoris', where the clitoris 'extends itself, and is enlarged when inflated to the exact likeness and size of a human penis erect, except that it has no perforation [...] nor is [it] altogether so long, but yet it erects and falls as that does, in proportion to the venereal [i.e., sexual] desire or inclination of the woman'. The author says that this condition is common among those women 'who are vigorous and lustful, and have given up themselves to the practice of self-pollution for any time' (154), although it can sometimes happen naturally as well with no moral imputation to the woman involved. He notes that he has only encountered one or two other female patients who have suffered from this condition, but that he has cured them completely and returned their organs to their natural size and condition by recommending chastity, some 'astringent foments' (cloths soaked in a medicinal substance that will contract soft organ tissues, like those of the clitoris) and 'a few internals' (a medicine taken internally; here, probably, a ring-shaped pessary, a device inserted in the vagina to support a prolapsed uterus). He further notes that this condition sometimes leads to the mistaken assumption that the sufferer has experienced a sex change, offering as refutation of this view Carr's sixteenth epistle on the apparent sex change of two nuns at Rome. (155)]

It is certain that in some women, especially those who are very salacious, the clitoris is so vastly extended that by hanging out of the passage it is mistaken for a penis; such have been called *fricatrices*:[10] by Caelius Aurelianus, *tribades*;[11] by Plautus, *subigatrices*,[12] and accounted hermaphrodites, because, as said before, they have been able to perform the actions of men with other women. Amatus relates of two Turkish women of Thessalonica;[13] and de Castro[14] says, he has also seen some women at Lisbon, punished for the like most filthy wickedness. In Creophagi, in Arabia, they circumcise the women that are so, by cutting away a certain apophysis[15] of musculous skin, that

[10] *fricatrices* from Latin, 'frico', to masturbate; women who have sex with other women.

[11] *Caelius Aurelianus*'s trans. of the Greek physician Soranos's *On Acute and Chronic Diseases* has an extended discussion of *tribades* and *pathics* (men who assume the receptive role in anal intercourse); unavailable in English between 1550 and 1735.

[12] *subigatrices* from Latin, 'subigo', [women who] fondle, handle [each other]. Plautus's Latin comedy *Truculentus* (late third century BCE) briefly mentions sex between a woman and her female slave.

[13] *Amatus* Amatus Lusitanus, Portuguese Jewish physician, (1511–68); perhaps in his multi-volume *Centuriae* (1549–61), containing case studies.

[14] *de Castro* Portuguese Jewish physician Rodrigo de Castro (1550–1627); perhaps in his work on women's disorders (1603).

[15] *apophysis* expanding or projected [part].

descends away from the superior part of the matrix,[16] which suffers erection in coition.[17] Lusitanus[18] tells us, Obs. 82, that a most renowned and honest virgin, having naturally a propended clitoris, which so provoked her to venery by only its unavoidable rubbing against her linen as she moved, that it gave much trouble and affliction to her soul, insomuch that with the consent of her parents, this physician was applied to, to cut it off, which he says, with the help of two skilful surgeons was done, and she cured and well ever after.

[...]

The following history, says an author, made a mighty noise both at Paris and Toulouse. A certain young woman at Toulouse had a relaxation of the vagina, resembling a man's penis, and some pretended that she abused it that way, it being six inches in length, and four in circumference in the middle, where it was very hard. It gradually increased from her childhood. She was searched[19] by the physicians there, who gave their opinion, it was a real penis; upon which the magistrates of the town ordered her to go in man's habit. In this equipage she came to Paris, where she got money by showing herself, till upon other assurances that she was a woman, and a promise of being cured, she was brought into the Hôtel Dieu,[20] where the descent was soon reduced, and she forced to resume her female dress, to her great regret.

Caliphanes[21] reports that beyond the Nasamones and about Matchlies there are ordinarily found hermaphrodites, which so much resemble both sexes that they have carnal knowledge one of another by turns; and this, by an expression in the young lady's letter aforegoing, and which introduced all this discourse about the clitoris, seems to be part of the practice between her and her bedfellow, the chambermaid.

[16] *matrix* womb.

[17] *In ... coition* Strabo, *Geography*, 3.196.

[18] *Lusitanus* Portuguese Jewish physician Zacuto Lusitanus? (1575–1642); perhaps in his case studies of rare conditions (1642).

[19] *searched* examined.

[20] *Hôtel Dieu* Paris hospital.

[21] *Caliphanes* unidentified, but this reference also appears in Sandys's commentary to Book 4 of his translation of Ovid's *Metamorphoses*.

CHAPTER 3

Criminal Pamphlets and the Law

Introduction

Although Western European cultures have always stigmatized and penalized same-sex intercourse between men (in particular), the penalties and the legal bodies responsible for trying and punishing offenders, as well as the legal definition and recognition of the seriousness of this act, fluctuated over the centuries. Canon law had long condemned male same-sex sexual acts, at least from the late fourth century CE, but the later Church courts were inconsistent in their treatment of offenders. Between 1470 and 1516, the London Church courts prosecuted only one sodomy case; the accused's 'non-appearance' before the court resulted in his excommunication, but not apparently in corporal punishment or heavy fines (Crompton, *Homosexuality* 362). The late Middle Age's revival of Roman law coupled with Scripture's emphasis on homoerotic acts and desires as inherently sinful gradually transformed these acts – in particular anal intercourse between men (sodomy) – from sins (governed by ecclesiastical law through the Church courts and the sacrament of confession) to crimes (governed by state law) (Borris, *Same-Sex* 76).

In England, same-sex sexual acts between men (called 'sodomy' and 'buggery' in English legal discourses) began to be regulated and punished by the state only with the 1533–34 statute against buggery (25 Henry VIII, Ch. 6; *Online Companion*). Although it could be interpreted as equally forbidding heterosexual and male same-sex anal intercourse, the 1533–34 statute not only ignored female same-sex intercourse altogether, but in practice the statute was applied fairly narrowly. As Borris demonstrates, although on the Continent such legislation could indeed apply to female same-sex intercourse (tribadism) and heterosexual anal intercourse, in practice it applied largely to anal penetrative sex between men. Prosecutions for tribadism were vanishingly rare on the Continent and simply non-existent in England; while for heterosexual anal intercourse they were "relatively rare" (*Same-Sex* 76). More importantly, however, even though this statute and those which followed it (with the exception of 1 Mary, Ch 1. [1553], *Online Companion*) made sodomy a felony or capital crime (punishable by hanging), they posed prosecutorial problems: in English case law, commentary and jurisprudence, sodomy was narrowly defined as anal sex between men with penetration and emission of semen; as a result, other sexual acts between men were effectively exempt from prosecution as capital crimes. However, as the Castlehaven trial suggests, legal prosecution and execution for sodomy could occur without proving anal penetration and emission (see **3.3** and **p. 84**). Even so, in practice, the narrowness of the legal definition of male same-sex sexual acts and (as Kenneth Borris has so insightfully shown) the peculiarities of English common law made successful prosecutions for sodomy highly unusual: to prove penetration and emission was difficult, since generally the only persons present were the two men having sex; given that both would be hanged if convicted (unless minors were involved, with one of the participants under the age of fourteen), it was rare for one partner to incriminate the other (but see Introduction to **3.2**). Unlike on the Continent (where convictions and executions for sodomy were fairly common), in England judicial torture could not be used to investigate such charges and compel a man charged with sodomy to confess and implicate his partner; thus, vanishingly few Englishmen were even prosecuted, much less convicted and executed for sodomy up to the beginning of the eighteenth century (*Same-Sex* 75–86). As Borris goes on to argue, such prosecutions and convictions before this point were largely confined to men who engaged in the anal rape of a minor, or men who were unfortunate enough to be observed in consensual anal sex by a third party. Thus, between 1558 and 1625, 'only six men are recorded as having been indicted for sodomy in the Home County assizes, with only one conviction' (Smith 48). Towards the end of the seventeenth century, the Societies for the Reformation of Manners (see Chapter 6, Introduction) managed to increase arrests for sodomy, partly because of the introduction of the new crime of attempted sodomy, which was much easier to prove in court (Borris, *Same-Sex* 85). More than 150 men were arrested between 1702 and 1726, and, although the vast majority were released for lack of evidence, four were convicted and hanged at the Maidstone Assizes, and another three at Tyburn, London (Goldsmith 8–9). The ballad 'The Women-Hater's Lamentation' (see **6.3**) states that three more committed suicide in the Southwark (London) prison, while awaiting trial. There were, however, many more convictions for the non-capital crime of attempted sodomy in this period, as in the case of the trial of Captain Edward Rigby (see **6.1**), and most of the persecutory and entrapping activity of the Societies resulted in this lesser charge (Norton, *Mother* 49ff). Conviction for attempted sodomy nevertheless led to serious penalties, including hefty fines, lengthy imprisonment, stocking, and brutal corporal punishment.

In England, the legal status and definition of sexual acts between women were even more complex. As Borris notes, Roman law lacked legal recognition of female same-sex sexual acts, but some Italian legal experts interpreted a late imperial statute as covering them (*Same-Sex* 75). Generally, such acts were overlooked under English law, since the language employed in the sodomy statutes 'was not interpreted as criminalizing relations between women' (Crompton, 'Myth' 11), even though (as religious writing suggests) biblical texts were sometimes interpreted as condemning both male *and* female same-sex intercourse. The English legal emphasis on sodomy as 'insertive', as anal penetrative sex between men involving the emission of semen, occluded female same-sex sexual acts. Edward Coke's influential commentaries on the statutes and jurisprudence relating to sodomy or buggery define this 'crime' as penetrative, anal sex between men with emission of semen, or penetrative sex between a man and an animal; however, for Coke, a woman can only be guilty of sodomy when she engages in bestiality; sexual relations between women are not an aspect of his discussion (*Online Companion*). As both Traub and Borris have pointed out, then, English legal commentaries were grounded in a phallocentric economy that made classifying sexual acts between women as sodomy 'strictly inconceivable' (*Renaissance* 165; *Same-Sex* 79). This 'overlooking' of sexual acts between women, however, was peculiar to England and Venice (Borris, *Same-Sex* 78). On the Continent, 'notably in such countries as France, Spain, Italy, Germany and Switzerland, lesbian acts were regarded as legally equivalent to acts of male sodomy and were, like them, punishable by death'; in fact, 'on occasion executions of women were carried out' in these other European nations ('Myth' 11). Although these were far rarer than executions of men, Crompton counts some twelve women executed for same-sex sexual acts in Europe prior to 1700, with another four women charged but acquitted for lack of evidence, although as he himself points out a wider and more systematic investigation of historical sources might well reveal further cases.

Online Companion
Interested readers can find additional selections from the following legal writings: England's 'Sodomy Statutes' and the works of Edward Coke.

The Arraignment, Judgement, Confession, and Execution of Humphrey Stafford, Gentleman (1607)

Unlike the sensational crime pamphlets of the period, and unlike the satiric and sexually explicit 'Atherton pamphlet' (see **3.2**), *Humphrey Stafford* focuses on defining Stafford as a good gentleman who sinned, making him much less a monstrous stereotype of vice than is the case either with Atherton or with Renaissance crime pamphlets' convicted murderers. Bearing out Bray's contention that sodomy was understood in the Renaissance as a sin that any man might commit, rather than a sign of a particular sexual orientation (*Homosexuality* 74–80), the pamphlet presents Stafford as the sodomite 'everyman', as the reader's neighbour, brother, friend, master, and fellow-Christian. The pamphlet emphasizes this representation by its constant 'generalizing' of Stafford's crime, suggesting that Stafford is executed as much for his sins of indolence, gluttony, and swearing as for sodomy. Stafford's eloquent remorse for his sinful life makes him a sympathetic and idealized figure of Christian repentance, a figure much emphasized in the text's preface (*Online Companion*).

Editions

Borris, Kenneth, ed., 'The Stafford Scandal, 1607.' *Same-Sex Desire in the English Renaissance*, 99–101 (excerpts only).

3.1

From *The Arraignment, Judgement, Confession, and Execution of Humphrey Stafford, Gentleman*

On the eleventh of May, 1607, was indicted at the King's Bench bar[1] at Westminster, before the reverend judges there, Humphrey Stafford,[2] gentleman, etc., for that he had upon the third of May, in the year of our Lord 1606, unnaturally and feloniously, contrary to the laws of God and the king, used unlawful company with two boys and had them carnally known, the one of them named Richard Robinson, the other Nicholas Cross, the one about the age of seventeen years, the other of thirteen or fourteen years. The place of the fact[3] committed was at the said Humphrey Stafford's lodging, then in the parish of St Andrews in Holborn.[4] To which fact he pleaded not guilty. [...]

Being come unto the bar, his indictment was again read, whereunto he had before pleaded not guilty, whereupon was presently impanelled a jury of gentlemen for his trial. Then were called into the court his accusers: to wit,

[1] *King's Bench* the court of record; supreme court of common law; *bar*: the railing where prisoners stood for legal proceedings.

[2] *Humphrey Stafford* unidentified. His crime is not named on the title page, another indication of the work's eschewing of sensationalism.

[3] *fact* act; crime.

[4] *St Andrews in Holborn* central London.

the two boys, Robinson and Cross, and one of their father and mother. [...] [A]n oath was administered unto those four aforenamed that they should speak the truth and nothing but truth. The two boys upon their oaths did directly charge him with the fact, and the particulars thereof: as the time when, the place where, the manner how, the circumstances both precedent and consequent (which here for modesty sake I overpass). The man and the woman testified only some matters ensuing upon the fact, for confirmation of the truth of the boys' allegations, showing that the boys had received hurt thereby, and that they were forced to use the help of a surgeon for their cure. Master Stafford still denied the fact, affirming and protesting that he was guiltless therein, excusing himself that if he had offended it was in wine.[5] But the jury after a little deliberation returned him guilty, whereupon one of the judges made an exhortation unto him, withal demanding what he could say for himself, wherefore judgement should not be pronounced against him? Whereupon Master Stafford desired three or four days' respite before sentence were pronounced: 'For,' said he, 'I have something to speak, which for some causes unto myself known I cannot now utter.' But the honourable bench being not satisfied with that dilatory answer, judgement was presently pronounced: that he should be conveyed from thence to the place of execution, there to be hanged till he were quite dead. The sentence pronounced, the prisoner was returned back to the place from whence he came, where he remained until the tenth of the same month of June, being Wednesday following, in which time he disposed himself to godward,[6] having made his will, and bequeathed his body to be buried in the church of St George in Southwark.

During the time of his being in prison, the knowledge of his fact and the report of the sentence pronounced against him coming unto some recusants[7] in the King's Bench prison, they studied much how they might separate him from the body of our Church,[8] being a gentleman of good descent, unto which end they wrote a certain letter unto him in Latin, which was closely[9] conveyed unto him, therein persuading him that there was no salvation in our Church, and that he should not admit of any of our ministers to confer with him, but that he should be confessed by some seminary priest,[10] which letter Master Stafford having received, showed it unto some of his friends

5 *in wine* i.e., that he was drunk at the time of the offence.

6 *disposed ... godward* prepared himself to meet God.

7 *recusants* Roman Catholics.

8 *our Church* Protestant church (Church of England).

9 *closely* secretly.

10 *confessed ... priest* receive the sacrament of Confession, where he would confess and be absolved of his sins, by a Catholic priest. English Protestantism had rejected Confession, seeing it as a perverse Catholic invention with no Scriptural basis.

and being himself in conscience persuaded of the truth of our religion, he acknowledged a detestation of the Romish faith and religion, subscribed with his own hand, which was also witnessed by the presence of some others, present at the same time, some of them being men of reverend esteem, who with their own mouths reported it unto me, which makes me presume of the truth thereof, they being men of known good report, and such as I verily think, make conscience of[11] speaking the least untruth wittingly. Which thing I the rather mention, because the world may see how the papists seek by all means possible, both in prison and out of prison, to withdraw his Majesty's subjects from the truth of religion, unto the acknowledgement of the false doctrine of the whore of Babylon,[12] and that they more especially labour with and aim at men of great birth and calling, rather than mean personages, whereby may be gathered that they do it more of policy than for conscience sake.

[...]

The day of his death being come, he prepared himself thereunto cheerfully, and at his setting forwards, he called for a clean band,[13] and other things, and being asked the reason why he regarded those things: 'Oh,' said he, 'I am now going to a more joyful marriage.'

He obtained (by request) of Master Arundel (the under-marshal of the King's Bench prison) that he might go on foot to his death,[14] who himself with Master Cartwright, minister of St George's Church (who had laboured much with him for his soul's health) did also bear him company, having on the one side his brother, and on the other side his kinsman, Master William Stafford. And amongst others who accompanied him to his death, was lame Master Paget[15] (a reverend preacher of God's word) who also administered him greatest comfort at his death. [...]

[...]

[A]nd then immediately he began to make a general acknowledgement of his sins.[16] Then said Master Paget, 'I pray you that you will satisfy the world for this fact, for which you are now to die. I desire not the particulars of it.'

Master Stafford replied with a loud voice, 'I acknowledge that I have

11 *make conscience of* scruple at.

12 *whore of Babylon* destroyer of the righteous (Rev. 17.3–6); common Protestant image for the Catholic Church.

13 *band* a collar or ruff worn around the neck.

14 *that … death* instead of being placed upon a hurdle and dragged.

15 *Master Paget* Eusebius Pagit (1546/7–1617) nonconformist London clergyman and powerful preacher.

16 *And … sins* Stafford has arrived at the place of execution.

deserved death, but yet I could not perform mine intention' – whereat he bowed towards a preacher and other his friends – adding with a very low voice, 'for I could not put it in execution for drunkenness.'

Then Master Paget willed him to testify unto the world, whether he were not one of those atheists of the world, who denied that there was a God?

'No,' said he, 'although my former life misspent might justly occasion this question to be moved, yet I utterly disclaim it, hoping to be saved by the alone[17] merits of Christ Jesus, and not by any merits of mine own; and although it may be justly said that Humphrey Stafford lived a most wretched life, yet bear me witness, I beseech you, that now I die a most repentant sinner.'

Then Master Paget, in this his agony and conflict for his sins, comforted him with the examples of many repentant sinners, who upon their true repentance were received into grace and pardoned, as namely that of Jonah, of Manasseh, the Prodigal Child, the Thief upon the Cross,[18] at which words, Master Stafford like the true penitent publican beat his breast, lifting up his hands and eyes towards heaven.[19]

Then said Master Paget, 'Be of good comfort, and pray that thou mayest be that "brand taken out of the fire".'[20]

He replied that he hoped he was, and that his spark of joy was turned into a flame.

'Seeing,' said Master Paget, 'he is so penitent, let us not cast him down further with the burden of his sins than happily in this so small a space I shall be able to raise him again.'

'Now,' said Master Paget, 'shall we sing a psalm unto the praise of God?'

'I will,' said he, 'bear you company.' Whereupon was sung the twenty-fifth psalm, beginning thus: 'I lift up my heart to thee', etc.

The psalm being ended: 'Now,' said Master Paget, 'I hope you are able to pray yourself.'

'I will follow you,' said he, 'if you please to begin.' Whereupon Master Paget made a brief but effectual prayer, which Master Stafford prayed after him, that the Lord would mollify and soften his hard heart, which till

[17] *alone* sole.

[18] *of Jonah … Cross* all types of the repentant and forgiven sinner: God forgives *Jonah*'s attempt to flee his prophetic calling, rescuing him from the belly of a whale; God forgives the repentant Israelite king *Manasseh* for idolatry, blasphemy, and murder (2 Kings 21; 2 Chron. 33.12–20); the *Prodigal Child* (more commonly, 'son') sins against his father, repents, and is lovingly forgiven (Lk. 15.11–32); crucified with Jesus, the *Thief upon the Cross* repents his crime, professes belief in Jesus, and is promised a place in Paradise (Lk. 23.39–43).

[19] *penitent … heaven* Lk. 18.10–14.

[20] *brand … fire* Zechariah 3.2.

then had been so obdurate, and pardon and forgive his manifold sins and wickedness, which so long he had wallowed in. After which he devoutly repeated the mother of all prayers, the prayer of Christ in the Gospel,[21] that fountainhead of all petitions, through which the springs of God's mercies are opened unto us, as on the contrary, unthankfulness is *ventus urens*,[22] 'a parching wind', that dries up all the passages and choketh the fountains of God's free mercies and bounties unto us.

All this while Master Stafford stood upon the lower-most step of the ladder, and being ready to ascend the executioner threw down an ash-coloured silk garter to fasten his hands, whereat, said he: 'It shall not be needful, for I am resolved to die.'

'Nay, but,' said Master Paget, 'you know not what extremity of pain may force you unto, whereby you may wrong yourself.'

'Then,' said Master Stafford, 'let it be so.'

Then he fastened his own bands before him, (and his soul doubtless fastened unto everlasting peace in Christ the Redeemer), but yet so as if he had but strove to unloose them, it might easily have been performed.

Ascending higher upon the ladder with a loud and audible voice, he out of true and perfect contrition, acknowledged again that he had been a grievous offender many and diverse ways, and lifting up his voice to the people, prayed that his death might be a warning to all others, to beware how they gave up themselves to wine, swearing, and company-keeping with such as he termed 'good fellows', which from his youth he had greatly delighted in; but especially he wished that all men would have a care never to delight in making of men drunk, which, as it should seem, was the sin his soul then chiefly stood guilty of. Furthermore, also thanking the Lord for one especial comfort, which his soul now at the hour of his death rejoiced in: to wit, that he was guiltless of the blood of any man, which might well be a great joy and invaluable comfort unto a soul untimely departing.

'I forgive,' said he, 'all the world, and him that sought my blood, even as I would that the world should forgive me, for they were not mine enemies that brought me to mine end and this my death, but God of his mercy called me, that I might be saved from eternal death.' Then said he again with a loud voice, 'I beseech you, let me hear you speak cheerfully that you freely forgive me.' Whereat there was an exceeding great noise with the people's praying and condescending:[23] for this, his true and unexpected contrition in his end, made amends for all his former sins of his life, though never so loathsome and unnatural.

[21] *prayer … Gospel* The Lord's Prayer (Mt. 6.9–13; Lk. 11.2–4).

[22] *ventus urens* Jeremiah 18.17 (Latin Vulgate).

[23] *condescending* agreeing.

As he was thus preparing for death, having before unbraced his bosom, and looking upon his own breast: 'I think,' said he, 'I shall be long in dying, because I am whole-chested.' Whereupon Master Paget out of a Christian love wished the hangman to show him as much favour as he could in his death, and not to put him to any more torment than needs he must.

Whereunto Master Stafford replied that if he were two whole years in dying, he would willingly undergo it, for his sins had deserved it; yet that his joys in Christ's mercies were exceeding, and that he hoped assuredly that all his sins were pardoned, withal confessing that he had consumed much in riotousness, and abhorred living, which might have relieved many a poor creature and done many thousands good, but to his exceeding present sorrow he had spent all most vainly and wickedly. The executioner being some ways moved, swore a great oath, which Master Stafford hearing, reproved him for it, telling him that such courses had brought him to this end.

He took his last farewell of his brother, withal importuning him not to be unmindful of some private business wherewith he had formerly acquainted him, who much grieving for his brother, and not able to endure to see him die, departed a little before his turning off.

'Go now, brother,' said he. 'Farewell till we meet in heaven.'

And perceiving that his brother took his death so heavily: 'I hope,' said he, 'Master Paget will comfort you.' Who answered that he would do what God would enable him unto, if he pleased to resort unto him. Then took he his leave of divers, and amongst the rest, he spoke very heartily unto Master Arundel, under-marshal of the King's Bench, thanking him for his extraordinary favours and kindness showed unto him in the time of his imprisonment.

The halter being put about his neck: 'Come,' said he, 'this halter is more welcome unto me than ever was ruff or falling band.'[24] Whereupon his friends looking heavily, he desired them not to be discomforted, for they should see him die like a Christian, and in that they should have joy and comfort of him. For whereas by reason of the wild affections and unbridled follies of his youth, they had had but small comfort of him in his former life, he strove now to make amends by putting the more into his death, which indeed (not without great cause) gave them all much cause of rejoicing. For a notorious general sinner dying all the time of his riotous life, to godwards, as soon as he heartily repents him of his sins, then he begins his life with God, when he proves a dead man unto the world, and utterly mortifies all his filthy affections: so he never truly lived till death touched him, and a true feeling of all his former offences. The sense and apprehension of death makes men

[24] *ruff or falling band* fashionable accoutrements for the neck. See **n13**.

wise, and those that have spent most follies in their youth, reap most wisdom at such an hour.

A little before his turning off the ladder: 'I had thought,' said he, 'to have leaped off, which yet I will not do, lest I should be thought to die desperately,[25] and yet the world shall see I will not die fearfully.'

His countenance could not be perceived to alter much at any time, because he was a man of high colour (for he was of a very sanguine complexion), yet now death seemed a little to take possession in his eye, for his look began to be heavy (for who amongst a million is so hardy-valiant at the door of whose heart death arrives not fearful) knowing we must all give account to God the Auditor at the dreadful Day of Judgement, that Auditor whom man's shallow wit cannot describe: incomprehensible, just, respecting no person. The king is his bailey,[26] to give him account, as well as the beggar; 'tis not thy person, not thy state, not thy power, not thy authority and place in this world which God respects: that Auditor will not be with bribes corrupted; not riches, and the unspeakable numberless treasures of the world, but pure hearts and consciences, washed in the blood of that immaculate lamb,[27] prevail with his mercies.

The physicians are of opinion that a bone being broken in the leg or elsewhere if it be skilfully set is faster[28] ever after than any of the rest, so the true repentant sinner, having a broken and contrite heart in this world for his offences past, may have a surer affiance and trust in that rock Christ Jesus, for 'through tribulation and hearty sorrow we enter into peace and everlasting glory',[29] and 'there is more joy in heaven for one sinner that repenteth, than for many that need no repentance'.[30]

Now being upon the point of turning off, he strove much with himself to express the heartiness of his repentance unto the world, for as his own words gave him out: 'I am,' said he, 'the most penitent man in the world.' Withal adding that 'if his sins were in number as many as the sands upon the seashore, or the drops of water that are therein, yet were God's mercies above them all.'[31] 'Yea,' said he, 'his mercies are far more than the sins of all this company, and yet here (looking about him) are a great many'; and so praying earnestly to God to receive his soul into his kingdom, he willed the executioner to do his office, but his face being yet not well-covered, the

25 *die desperately* commit suicide.

26 *bailey* bailiff.

27 *washed … lamb* Rev. 7.14.

28 *faster* stronger.

29 *through … glory* partly based on Isaiah 57.1–2.

30 Lk. 15.7. Jesus's statement prefaces a series of parables (including 'the Prodigal Son') about repentance and forgiveness.

31 *if … all* based on Prayer of Manasseh vers. 9; Ps. 139.18.

executioner staying a little, he again added, 'Thou hast redeemed me, O Lord God of my salvation; into thy hands I commend my spirit.[32] Now, executioner, I pray thee, do thy office.'

And then immediately he was turned off the ladder, not without great lamentation of the multitude and general praying for the happiness of his soul.

After that his body had fully satisfied the law, it had on the morrow Christian burial in St George's Church in Southwark.

Mors illis lucrum.[33]

John Atherton (1598–1640), bishop

Atherton's early life as a married man and parish minister was marred by rumours that he had fathered his sister-in-law Susan's illegitimate child (born 1623), perhaps prompting his departure for Ireland. As Bishop of Waterford and Lismore (appt. 1636) Atherton successfully wrested back Church lands illegally expropriated by powerful Anglo-Irish noblemen. Dogged by rumours of serious sin – incest with his niece and complicity in the murder of their infant daughter – Atherton was finally brought down by his proctor John Child's 1640 accusations of sodomy (with Child himself), fornication, and adultery. Child's motivations remain a mystery: his revelations resulted in his own execution (March 1641). Atherton confessed to heterosexual fornication, but denied the capital charge of sodomy. Whether or not Atherton was guilty of the sodomy for which he died remains unclear. Nicholas Barnard, the minister who counselled Atherton, maintained his innocence. Today, some scholars speculate that Atherton may have been 'framed' by powerful enemies seeking revenge for their newly lost lands.

A particularly extreme salvo in the Revolutionary period's invective-laden 'debate' on religion and episcopacy, *John Atherton* focuses on Atherton's sexual crimes and spiritual depravity as symbols of the established Church's pervasively corrupt leadership. Like the sodomy rampant among the Church's bishops, the speaker suggests, Archbishop William Laud's (1573–1645) 'innovations' in church ritual, his emphasis on conformity, and his investment in 'papist' ceremony threaten to destroy the Protestant nation and its king. However, the pamphlet's satiric aims, particularly its attempts to degrade in the reader's eyes Atherton and by extension Laud and all Church

[32] *into … spirit* Jesus's last words on the cross (Lk. 23.46). See also Psalm 31.5 (Geneva Bible).

[33] Latin, 'Death is gain to [men such as these]'.

officials, are fatally compromised by the very sin that is the narrative's *coup de grâce*: sodomy. Atherton's heterosexual excesses are presented as bawdy, titillating, and comic: the two most detailed descriptions of Atherton's antics are essentially fabliaux, focusing on the bishop's clever cuckolding of two parishioners. However, sodomy is not amenable to such an approach. Unlike Atherton's heterosexual acts and desires, sodomy is defined as demonic, destructive not just of the nation but of creation itself.

3.2

The Life and Death of John Atherton, Lord Bishop of Waterford and Lismore[1] (1641)

Confusion, give my thoughts once leave to be
Exempted from thy lawless tyranny:
If for the space of but one poor half hour,
Oh, give me leave to sit in quiet's bower,
That I with patience may delineate,
In lines of life this prelate's sordid state,[2]
Who first in England did his life receive,
His education Oxford did him give,
Thence to a benefice preferred he was,[3]
In which he viciously his time did pass,
And although married to a handsome wife,
Blest with sweet children, th'only joy of life,
Yet so far baseness did in him prevail,
That unto lust he himself set to sail,[4]
Deflowered virgins, marriage beds defiled,
With many other vicious crimes too viled
To be conceived; beyond all measure proud,
Impudence and ambition did him shroud.
Amongst his flock he sowed seditious strife,
Set friend 'gainst friend, husband against wife.
So that 'mongst many he did live alone,
And loving none, beloved was of none.

[1] The sensational aims of the pamphlet are clear on the title page, which features prominently Atherton's crimes: 'incest, buggery, and many other enormous crimes'.

[2] *prelate* high Church official.

[3] *benefice* parish position including an income to support himself; *preferred*: advanced.

[4] *set to sail* gave free rein to.

Lastly through pride, high fare, and lustful life,[5]
Incest committed with the sister of his wife,
For which he sued his pardon, and then fled
To Ireland, where a worser life he led.
There through insinuation did obtain,
The parsonage of St John, became chaplain
Unto that honoured lord and worthy peer,
Lord Chancellor there, Lord Viscount Loftus here,[6]
By whose assistance he did eke require,[7]
To be sub-dean of Christ-church, one step higher,
Whose goodness for to guerdon he did prove[8]
A Judas, and betrayed him for his love,[9]
Brought him into disgrace with that great sir,
Who brooked no rival nor competitor,
Strafford's stern earl, a man of eminent height,[10]
Knowledge, and wit had it been governed right.
Courage and resolution to those high
Employments he had given him, but why
Should he his merits banish and so die,
Imping his wings with false felicity?[11]
Winning on him, by him he was preferred[12]
Unto the bishopric of Waterford,
And of Lismore, where he did five years lord it[13]
In such sort, as all good men much abhorred it.
But in the interim, mark what did befall,[14]
If so he had had any grace at all,
At which he aimed, but not the grace of God,
But at such grace as had our graceless Laud,

[5] *high fare* rich food (with implications of luxury and excess). Gluttony was believed a spur to and a sign of sexual over-indulgence.

[6] Adam Loftus, First Viscount Loftus of Ely (1568–1643), Lord Chancellor of Ireland. Notoriously quarrelsome, his stormy professional relationship with Wentworth (later Earl of Strafford) led to Loftus's demotion and imprisonment at Wentworth's order (1638).

[7] *eke require* also request.

[8] *guerdon* repay.

[9] *Judas* betrayer of Christ.

[10] *height* great promise.

[11] *imping* engrafting.

[12] *winning on him* playing on his good nature.

[13] *lord it* behave arrogantly.

[14] *mark* take particular note of.

He surely warnèd was to mend his life,
By his own sister Master Leakey's wife,
Which Master Leakey's mother being dead,
And in her lifetime conscious how he led
His lustful life, her ghost in ghastful wise[15]
Did oft appear before her sister's eyes,
But she fear-stricken durst not speak unto it,[16]
Till oft appearing forced her to do it:
Then thus she spoke: 'Mother-in-law, what cause
You from your rest, to my unrest thus draws?'
Who answered, 'Daughter, 'tis the wicked life
Your brother leads: warn him to mend his life;
If not, then plainly tell him 'tis decreed,
He shall be hanged; bid him repent with speed,
Then shall my restless spirit be at rest,
And not till then.' Thus vanished. She addressed
Herself for travail, into Ireland went[17]
With this sad message unto him was sent:
Which how he took to heart may plain appear
By the slight answer he returnèd her:
'What must be, shall be. If I must, I must die;
Marriage and hanging come by destiny.'[18]
Thus scoffed her counsel, sent her back, and when
She was returned, he grew far viler then[19]
He was before, if viler man may be,
For one bad act before, committed three.
Here, lord-like prelates, two things I propound,
Or leave your seas, or in them your vice drowned.[20]
If ye will bishops be, be such as was
That godly Timothy: make him your glass.[21]
Shun avarice, shun extortion, shun vain pride,
Shun hate, dissimulation; let your guide
Be godliness. Shun lust, shun buggery,

15 *ghastful wise* frightful way.

16 *durst* dared.

17 *travail* 'travel'; also, 'labour'.

18 Proverbial, 'Wedding is destiny, and hanging likewise' (J. Heywood, *Proverbs* (1546) 1.3.88).

19 *then* i.e., than.

20 *seas* i.e., sees (with the obvious pun); a 'see' is a bishop's jurisdiction.

21 *Timothy* St Paul's trusted companion and fellow evangelist, among the first Christian bishops; *glass*: mirror.

Shun incest, rape, and shun adultery.
Be practisers of every honest thing.
Be meek like Christ, your bishop, lord and king,
So may you live beloved, and die to life,[22]
Not by the axe or by the hangman's knife,[23]
A halter as this bishop here hath done,[24]
When being hanged yourselves do scarce bemoan.
And proctors be ye warned by John Child's fall,
Lest that his fate betide unto you all.[25]
Lust, avarice, extortion of fees
Caused him at London Bridge his life to leese.[26]
Y'are alike guilty: let not the same thing
Draw you like him to Heaven in a string.[27]
Now to the bishop, we return again,
With whose loathed crimes I loathe to foul my pen.
A strict list being taken of each whore
He was known to use amounts to sixty-four.
Nor was it out of frailty he did sin
In this vile sort, that might excused have bin.[28]
For when that nature failed all these to please,
To provoke lust he used cantharides,[29]
Nor did this bravo, as some lechers use[30]
When they have acted sin, seek to excuse
The same by mincing or a flat denial;[31]
He scorned such baseness. Let him make a trial[32]
Of any neighbour's wife, as oft he did,

[22] *die to life* reject this life in favour of eternal life (Col. 2.20 and 3.1–17).

[23] *hangman's knife* with which the hangman would dole out aspects of capital punishment (disembowelling, cutting out the heart, castration, etc.) and non-capital punishment (cutting off an offender's ears; slitting his nose, etc.).

[24] *halter* noose of the gallows.

[25] *betide* happen.

[26] *leese* lose; *London Bridge*: error for 'Bandon Bridge', borough and market town (County Cork, Ireland).

[27] *string* rope of the gallows.

[28] *bin* been. Atherton cannot claim that he acted unthinkingly, because overwhelmed by passion.

[29] *For ... cantharides* When unable to get an erection through natural means, he used artificial ones. *Cantharides* is an aphrodisiac.

[30] *bravo* reckless desperado.

[31] *mincing* extenuating.

[32] *make a trial* tempt to illicit sex (literally, 'he made an attempt on or tested [their sexual virtue]').

He would not have his dealing to be hid.
He'd rather justify the act for good,
As thus, "twas done to purify the blood',[33]
Or if a barren womb he chanced to prove,
'Twas cause 'he did not the stone-colic love.'[34]
Some women he did do in charity[35]
And some because they used good cookery,
Knew how to please his palate as his bed,
So that at once his corpse and lust he fed.
Thus many salves he had for many sores
But still the cure was wrought by the art of his whores.
If not, t'advance his lust this lustful elf[36]
Had tricks enough whereby to help himself.[37]
A man well known in Waterford had need
To borrow a hundred pounds; in hope to speed[38]
Unto this reverend lord he did address
Himself, and his suit, which thus he did express:[39]
'My lord, I oft have tasted of your favour
And promises to do me good, which rather
Induceth me unto this bold request:
Your lordship will be pleased to make me blest
With the loan of 100 pound which I'll repay
Within a month or else on any day
Your lordship shall appoint.' This courteous lord
Answered, 'Sir, you shall have it on your word[40]
And more to do you good, but let your wife
Be present, lest there should be any strife,

33 *'twas … blood* It was believed that semen was a super-refined blood product, and that ejaculation purged the body of this substance.

34 *stone-colic* disorder attributed to kidney stones. *Kidneys* had long been believed a centre of sexual desire. Atherton argues that his excessive sexual activity is a preventative against kidney-stones.

35 *do in charity* i.e., have sex with as a favour [to them] (with blasphemous irony: 'charity' (or love) is that gift bishops should cultivate above all others in their Christian communities). Cf. **n54**.

36 *elf* demon.

37 *Had … himself* referring to the two incidents (below) where Atherton seduces wives in his congregation; but also referring to Atherton's skill in autoerotic practices.

38 *speed* be successful.

39 *suit* request.

40 *on your word* 'simply because you've asked', but also 'without having to sign a promissory note'.

If you should fail for to repay the same,
Or I for breach of payment should make claim.'
He grants, and goes, she comes, the money's ready,
So is my lord, and the poor cuckold's needy.
'Sir,' say'th my lord, 'though't be an entire sum,[41]
It is odd money that to me is come.[42]
Amongst it all there's but one piece of gold
That with the rest not easy to be told,[43]
Go draw it out within my study door.
I'll trust you there, but will not many more.
But 'cause your credit's cracked, I'll keep the key,[44]
The door being locked meanwhile your wife shall stay
And talk with me.' 'Tis granted, in his seat[45]
The bishop mounts, and does the well-known feat.[46]
Another when his lordship's watch digressed,[47]
As he himself did always, to a feast[48]
He invites himself: which ended, he requests
The goodman of the house (there being no guests[49]
To spoil his sport) that he would set his watch
At his sundial, at which he doth catch,[50]
Proud of such favour, goes without denial,
Meanwhile another's set by his wife's noon dial.[51]
These are but tricks of youth; now arm your ears
With patience for to hear of pallid fears.
Suppose a devil from th'infernal pit,
More monster-like than e'er was devil yet,
Contrary to course, taking a male fiend[52]

[41] *though't … sum* although the entire [agreed upon] sum is here.

[42] *odd* different denominations, kinds, etc.

[43] *told* counted; but, perhaps, also 'found'.

[44] *'cause* because; *cracked*: damaged.

[45] *seat* female genitalia (usually, when it 'belongs' to a man through the bond of marriage: Atherton occupies the husband's rightful 'place').

[46] *mounts* sexually 'climbs up on'; usually said of animals.

[47] *watch digressed* when his watch (timepiece) was not keeping proper time.

[48] *he … always* Atherton, like his watch, 'digressed' (pun on 'digressed', meaning 'to go wrong, to deviate').

[49] *goodman* title of respect for a man under the rank of gentleman.

[50] *at which … catch* he responds eagerly to this request.

[51] *noon-dial* female genitalia; at noon the hands of the clock both point upwards, an image of erection.

[52] *course* to the course of nature.

To sodomize with him: such was the mind
Of this lord bishop; he did take a Child
By name, not years, acting a sin so viled,
As is forenamed; this Child a proctor too,[53]
Nor him alone, but his parrator he must do;[54]
These and a thousand like, these he hath done,
Besides endeavouring to eclipse the sun
Of this our sky, by making Charles' Wain draw
Sublunary, by subverting the law[55]
Fundamental, and putting in the place,[56]
Commission high, pope's canons, great Laud's grace.[57]
For the subverting of such devilish plots,
From staining of our kingdom with such blots,
For th'happy reign of our most sacred king,
And those that from the royal stock do spring,
For parliament, and health of martial men,[58]
All loyal subjects cry with me, 'Amen.'

[53] *viled* degraded; *proctor*: an agent for the collection of tithes and other church fees.

[54] *parrator* A *paritor* summons offenders to appear in ecclesiastical court to answer (usually) sexual offences; *do*: see **n35**.

[55] *by … Sublunary* Here, sodomy strikes at the order of the natural world. 'Charles's Wain' is another term for the constellation known as 'the Plough' or 'the Great Bear'; thus, sodomy draws this constellation down below the level of the moon, upsetting the celestial hierarchy. King Charles I (reigned 1625–49), mentioned below, is elsewhere described as the 'royal waggoner' and the English nation as his 'wain' (waggon) (J. Davies, 'Charles His Waine', *Poems*, ed. A.B. Grosart, 2.237). Sodomy also, then, threatens the relationship between king and nation.

[56] *law fundamental* basic law of the state and nature; pun on 'fundament' ('anus' or 'buttocks'); thus, 'law pertaining to the anus'.

[57] The writer connects the subversion of natural and state law with Archbishop Laud's promotion of what many English Protestants saw as a return to Roman Catholic ritual and theology. The *High Commission*, the highest ecclesiastical court in England, had been established under Elizabeth I to try cases involving opposition to the Church of England and the monarch's supreme authority over it. Used extensively by Laud, the court was widely perceived as an 'un-English' violation of common law principles in favour of procedures smacking of the Catholic Inquisition, particularly the rejection of the right not to incriminate oneself during a trial. The High Commission was abolished in 1641; *pope's canons*: ecclesiastical laws laid down by papal decree.

[58] *martial* warlike, 'manly'.

Mervin Touchet, Lord Audley, Second Earl of Castlehaven (1593–1631), nobleman

Castlehaven's early life included a financially advantageous marriage and inheritance of his family estates. His conversion to Catholicism, however, in the 1620s lent credibility to the charges of sodomy later brought against him, although he had apparently returned to Protestantism before his second marriage to Lady Anne Brydges (née Stanley), Lady Chandos (1580–1647). She and her eldest daughter Elizabeth went to live with Castlehaven at his estate, Fonthill Gifford. Married unhappily to Castlehaven's son and heir, James, Elizabeth became sexually involved with one of her father-in-law's 'favourites', Henry Skipwith, a man of low rank and Castlehaven's trusted confidante. Upset by his father's gifting of vast sums to Skipwith and by the underling's appropriation of Elizabeth, James complained to the king. An investigation resulted in two felony charges against Castlehaven: accessory to the rape of his wife, along with the principal actor, his servant Giles Broadway, and sodomy, with his manservant Florence Fitzpatrick. Castlehaven denied all the charges, insisting that his family were conspiring against him for financial gain. While 26 of the 27 jurors convicted Castlehaven of being an accessory to the rape of his wife, their verdict to convict on sodomy was hotly contested, with only 15 in favour and 12 dissenting (Herrup 87). Refusing to admit his guilt, and denied a royal pardon, Castlehaven was executed, as were Broadway and Fitzpatrick.

Editions

Borris, Kenneth, ed., 'The Castlehaven Scandal, 1630–31' (excerpts from the 1631 State Papers account, including the execution of Broadway and Fitzpatrick). *Same-Sex Desire in the English Renaissance*, pp. 101–13.

Norton, Rictor, ed., 'The Trial of Mervyn Touchet, Earl of Castlehaven (1631)', 'The Trial and Execution of Broadway and Fitzpatrick (1631)', and 'Verses Following the Trial of the Earl of Castlehaven (1631).' *Homosexuality in Eighteenth-Century England.*

3.3

From *The Arraignment and Conviction of Mervin Lord Audley, Earl of Castlehaven* (1642/3)[1]

[The Lord High Steward (Thomas, Lord Coventry) opens the case for the prosecution, announces the indictments, and charges the jury to be fair and impartial.]

[1] The arrest of a group of men for sodomy in 1699 seems to have spurred a new edition of the following text in that year, capitalizing on the sensational event (see 'Preface', A3).

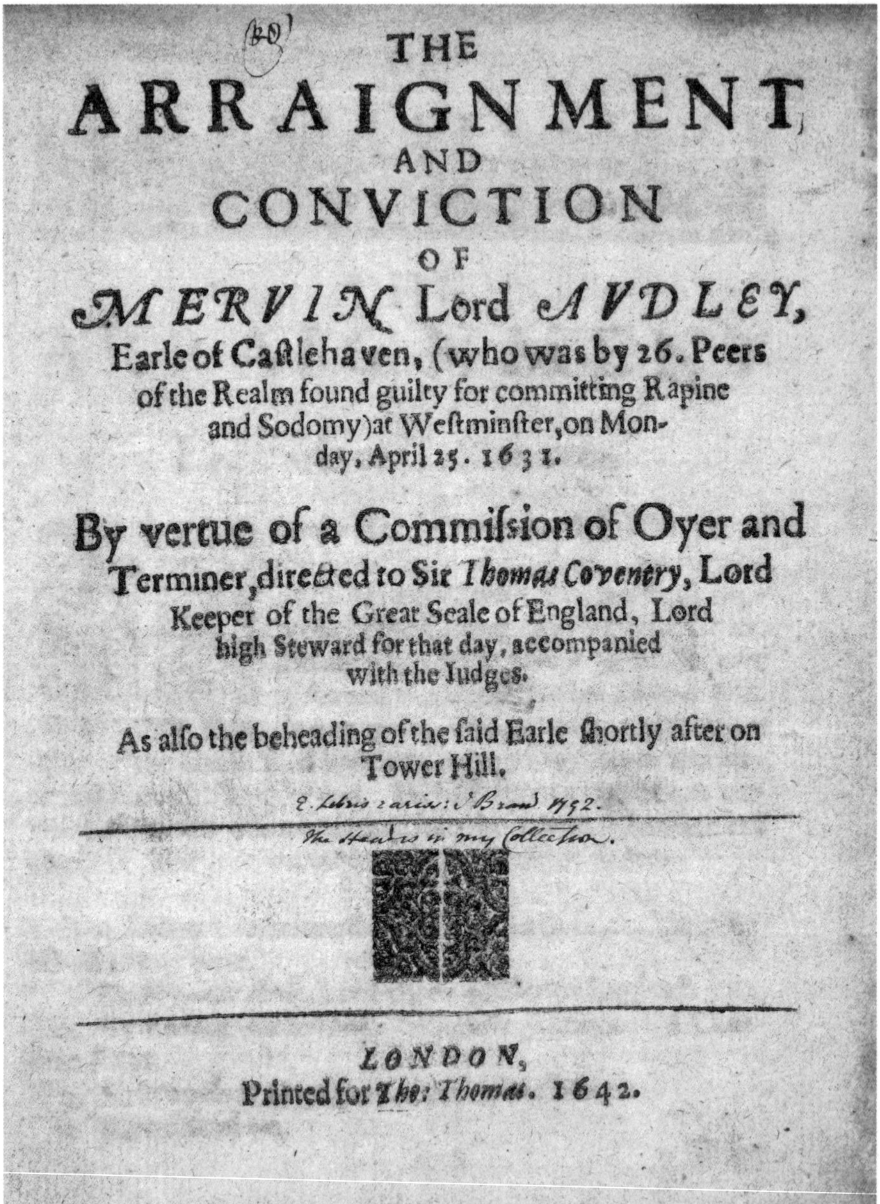

THE
ARRAIGNMENT
AND
CONVICTION
OF
MERVIN Lord AVDLEY,
Earle of Castlehaven, (who was by 26. Peers of the Realm found guilty for committing Rapine and Sodomy) at Westminster, on Monday, April 25. 1631.

By vertue of a Commission of Oyer and Terminer, directed to Sir Thomas Coventry, Lord Keeper of the Great Seale of England, Lord high Steward for that day, accompanied with the Judges.

As also the beheading of the said Earle shortly after on Tower Hill.

LONDON,
Printed for Tho: Thomas. 1642.

1 Title page from *The Arraignment and Conviction of Mervin Lord Audley, Earl of Castlehaven* (1642).

2 Portrait from *The Arraignment and Conviction of Mervin Lord Audley, Earl of Castlehaven* (1642).

[…]

Master Attorney said, 'My Lord High Steward, and it please your Grace, there are two indictments against Mervin Lord Audley, the first for rape, the second for sodomy; the prisoner is honourable, the crimes dishonourable of which he is indicted. If it falls out to be true, which is to be left to trial, I dare be bold to say, never poet invented nor historiographer writ of any so foul, though Suetonius hath curiously set out the vices of some of the emperors which had absolute power,[2] and that might make them fearless of any manner of punishment, and besides were heathens and knew not God; yet none of them came near this lord's crime. This is a crime of that rarity in our nation that we seldom know of the like, and the other that we scarce hear of it, but they are of that pestilential nature that, if they be not punished, they will draw from Heaven heavy judgements upon this kingdom. I can speak with comfort that all my time, both in his Majesty's royal father's life, and since he came to his crown,[3] I never had occasion to speak in this place against any peer of the realm before now, and God knows I do it now with sorrow, and I hope I shall not have occasion to do so much again; but his Majesty who is the pattern of virtue, not only as king, but in his person also, in whom it is hard to judge whether he excel most in justice or mercy, but I rather think in mercy, for he would have my Lord Audley, the prisoner at bar, heard with as much favour as such a crime as this can be; when he first heard it, he gave strict accompt[4] that the trial should be searched,[5] that his throne and people should be cleared from so grievous sins, and therefore he was indicted in his own country,[6] according to the law, by gentlemen of worth. The bill is found,[7] and now he is brought to this bar to be tried by his honourable peers, such as of whose wisdom and sincerity there can be no question, but to have an honourable hearing.'

[Master Attorney describes the laws pertaining to rape before proceeding to those pertaining to sodomy.]

[…] [F]or the *crimen sodomiticum*, our law had no knowledge of it till the 15 Henry VIII, by which statute it was made felony; and in this there is no

[2] *Suetonius … power* in the ancient Roman historian's *History of the Twelve Caesars*; *curiously*: exactly.

[3] *both … crown* i.e., in the reigns of James I (1603–25) and Charles I (1625–49).

[4] *accompt* instructions.

[5] *searched* examined closely.

[6] *in … country* i.e., county (to ensure the appearance of fairness).

[7] *found* ascertained to be valid.

more question, but only whether it be *crimen sodomiticum sine penetratione*.[8] And the law the 5 of Elizabeth sets it down in general words, and where the law doth not distinguish neither must we. I know you will be curious[9] how you give the least mitigation of so abominable a sin which brought such plagues after it, as we may see in Genesis 18, Judges 14, Romans 1.

But, my lords, it seemed to me strange at the first, how a nobleman of his quality should lust to such abominable sins, but when I found he had given himself over to lust, and find that *nemo repente sit pessimus*,[10] and that if men once habit themselves in ill, it is no marvel if they fall into any sin; and that he was constant in no religion, but in the morning would be a papist, in the afternoon a protestant. I shall be bold to give your Grace a reason why he became so ill: he believed not God. Then what may not a man run into? But I find things beyond imagination, for I find his intentions bent to have his wife naught,[11] which the wickedest man that ever I heard of before would have virtuous and godly, how bad soever himself be, and him lewd to his own wife. If she love him, she must love Henry Skipwith, whom he loves above all, and not in any honest love, but in a dishonest. He gives his reason by Scripture: she was now subject to him,[12] and therefore if she did ill at his command, it was not her fault but his, and he would answer it. He lets this Skipwith, whom he calls his favourite, spend of his purse £500 per annum, and if his wife or daughter would have anything, though necessary, they must lie with Skipwith and have it from him, and not otherwise; also telling Skipwith and his daughter that he had rather have a child by him than by anybody else. But this thing I had rather should come out of the mouths of the witnesses than from me.

3.3.1 The Several Examinations and Depositions Before the Lords

Walter Biggs's examination[13]

Anktill[14] was a page to Sir Henry Smith, and had no means[15] when he came to my Lord Audley. He entertained him[16] for a page eight years, and then let him

[8] Latin, 'a crime of sodomy without [with no] penetration'.

[9] *curious* careful.

[10] Latin, 'No one becomes wicked overnight'.

[11] *naught* promiscuous.

[12] Gen. 3.16.

[13] *Walter Biggs* Castlehaven servant.

[14] *John Anktill* younger son of a gentry family; Castlehaven's page, estate manager, advocate for the family's interests as an MP (1621); and Castlehaven's son-law, marrying Lucy, a daughter from the earl's first marriage (Herrup 19).

[15] *means* estate; money.

[16] *entertained* had [him] in service.

keep horses in his ground, by which I think he enriched himself £2000, but he never sat at the table with him until he had married his daughter, then gave him to the value of £7000. Henry Skipwith[17] was sent from Ireland by my lord to be a page to my lady (his father and mother were very mean[18] folks); there he spent out of my lord's means £500 per annum, and he gave him at one time £1000 and hath made divers deeds of lands to him. My lord was at first a Protestant; after the buying of Fontaine, [he] turned his religion.[19]

Lord Audley, his examination[20]
He sayeth Henry Skipwith had no means when he came to him [i.e., Castlehaven], and that he had given him £1000 and that Skipwith did lie with him when he was straightened in room;[21] and that he gave a farm of £100 to Anktill that married his daughter, and at other times to the value of £7000, and that there was one Blandina[22] in his house fourteen days and bestowed an ill disease there, and therefore he sent her away.

[The Lord High Stewart interjects, urging Castlehaven 'not to deny those things which are clearly proved' (7).]

The Countess's examination[23]
The first or second night after we were married, Anktill came to his bedside whilst we were in bed, and the lord spoke lasciviously to her, and told her, her body was his, and that if she loved him, she must love Anktill, and if she lay with any man with his consent, it was not her fault, but his.

He would make Skipwith come naked into her chamber and bed, and delighted in calling up his servants, making them show their privities,[24] and her look on, and commended those that had the largest.

Broadway[25] lay with her whilst she made resistance, and my lord held her hands, and one of her feet, and she would have killed herself afterwards with a knife, but that he took it from her: and before that act of Broadway she had

[17] *Henry Skipwith* Never charged with any crime in the scandal, and considerably enriched, he vanishes from the public record after 1632 (Herrup 114).

[18] *mean* low-ranking.

[19] *Fontaine* Fonthill Gifford; *turned his religion*: converted to Catholicism.

[20] *Lord Audley* James (b. 1612), Castlehaven's son, by his first wife.

[21] *straightened in room* i.e., when beds were lacking.

[22] *Blandina* later called a prostitute.

[23] *the Countess* After Castlehaven's execution, Anne retired to her mother's country estate, and at her mother's petition Charles I granted her a pardon. Resuming her former title, and never remarrying, she died in 1647 (Herrup 111–13).

[24] *privities* genitals.

[25] Giles *Broadway* man of low rank, another Castlehaven servant; tried, convicted, and executed for the rape of the countess, July 1631 (Herrup 19; 94–6).

never done it.[26] He delighted to see the act done, and made Anktill come into the bed with them, and lie with her whilst he might see it, and that she cried out.

[...]

Henry Skipwith's examination
He spent £500 per annum of the lord's purse. He lay for the most part in bed with the earl; he [Castlehaven] gave him his house in Salisbury, and a manor of £160 per annum; and that he usually lay with the young lady,[27] and there was love before and afterwards.[28] And that my lord said he would rather have a boy of his getting than of any other; and that she was but thirteen years old when he lay with her, and that he could not enter her body without art; and that my lord gave her things to open her. That Blandina lived half a year in my lord's house, and was a common whore.

Fitzpatrick's examination[29]
The lord made him lie with him at Fonthill and Salisbury, and once in the bed, *et semen consumpsit*,[30] but did not penetrate his body; and that he heard he did so with others. That Skipwith lay with the young lady often, and that the lord would have a boy by him; that Blandina lived half a year in the lord's house and was a common whore.

[...]

The young Lady Audley's examination[31]
That she was married to her husband by a Romish[32] priest in the morning, and at night by a prebend[33] of Kilkenny; that she was first tempted to lie with Skipwith by the Earl of Castlehaven, and that she had no means[34] but that

26 *she ... it* she would never have done [this act] if Broadway [and Castlehaven] had not forced her.

27 *lady* Elizabeth Brydges, Lady Audley, James's wife.

28 *before and afterwards* Probably Skipwith means that he did not force Elizabeth, that she loved him both before they had intercourse and afterwards.

29 Florence (or Lawrence) *Fitzpatrick* another Castlehaven servant; tried, convicted, and executed for sodomy with Castlehaven, July 1631 (Herrup 95–6).

30 Latin, 'and spent his seed' (i.e., emitted semen).

31 See **n27**. After Castlehaven's execution, she and James were briefly reconciled, but soon separated again, with James finally abandoning her altogether for a mistress and a life on the Continent. Elizabeth was dogged by the scandal and financial troubles, as well as family and social isolation for the rest of her life. She never remarried, dying in 1679 (Herrup 17–18; 109–11).

32 *Romish* Roman Catholic.

33 *prebend* minister; they had both Protestant and Catholic weddings.

34 *means* money; income.

which Skipwith gave her. But she would not lie with Pawlet; he [Castlehaven] solicited [her] also to lie with Greene;[35] that he [Castlehaven] saw Skipwith and she lie together divers[36] times, and nine of the servants in the house had likewise seen it.

When he [Castlehaven] solicited her[37] he said her husband loved her not, and that he would turn her out of doors if she did not, and if she would not he would tell her husband she did. That he [Skipwith] used a wyld[38] to enter her body first: that he usually lay with her, and it was with the earl's privity.[39]

Broadway's examination

He lay at the bed's feet,[40] and in the night he [Castlehaven] called for tobacco, and as he brought it, caught him, and bid him come to bed to him and his wife, and held one of his wife's legs, and both her hands, and at last he [Broadway] lay with her, notwithstanding her resistance.

Then he [Castlehaven] used his [Broadway's] body like a woman, *sed nunquam penetravit, quamvis inter femine, semen suum consumpsit.*[41]

[…]

The Earl's examination

He desired to be pardoned in those things of which he must accuse himself, and that condemnation should not come out of his own mouth.[42]

Master Attorney General said, 'You have seen the clearness of the cause proved, and I know your wisdoms to be such as you well know in so dark a business a clearer cannot be; for let a man be never so wicked, he will not call witnesses to see it.'

Lord High Steward asked, 'whether may a wife be witness against her husband?'

[35] *Pawlet* and *Greene* unidentified; probably Castlehaven servants.

[36] *divers* a word implying multiplicity but without committing the writer to 'many' or 'several'.

[37] *solicited her* i.e., to have sex with Skipwith.

[38] *wyld* uncertain, but perhaps another reference to the instrument used to widen her vagina to allow for sexual intercourse (see **p. 83**).

[39] *privity* private knowledge.

[40] *bed's feet* perhaps at the bed's foot, or in a cot that could be pushed under the master's bed during the daytime.

[41] Latin, 'but he (Castlehaven) never penetrated him (Broadway) after the manner of a man with a woman, even though he (Castlehaven) expelled his seed'.

[42] *He … mouth* claiming the right to non-self-incrimination. The State Papers 1641 account contains Castlehaven's lengthy defence, absent in this published account (Herrup 126–9).

Judges' answer: 'In civil causes she cannot; in criminal she may, especially where she is the party grieved.'

Lord High Steward asked, 'whether buggery was within the statute, without penetration?'

Judges' answer: 'It may, the use of the body to spend seed doth it.'

[...]

Then the lords went away to consider, and after their return the Lord Steward asked one by one, first of the indictment of rape, to which they all answered, 'Guilty'; then to the other, and fifteen found him guilty, and the rest not.

Lord Audley spoke for himself, that 'his wife had been naught, and had a child which he concealed to save her honour', and that 'his son now became twenty-one years of age, and he old, that the one would have lands, the other a younger husband, and therefore they plotted his death'.

Then the lieutenant was called to bring out the prisoner, who when he was come to the bar, the Lord High Steward spoke to him in this manner:

'Mervin, Lord Audley, you have been indicted, and have pleaded not guilty, and put yourself on God and your peers, who have found you guilty of both, and therefore my heart grieveth that [which] my tongue must utter, but justice is the way to cut off wickedness. Oh, think upon your offences, which a Christian ought scarce to name, and which the depraved nature of man, which carries us to all vice, yet hates this unnatural sin! And you have not only offended against the nature, but the rage of a man, jealousy. And though you die not for it, yet you have abused your daughter, and having honour and fortune to leave behind, you would have had the spurious seed of a varlet to inherit both.

'But, my lord, it grieves me to see you stand against a truth apparent and concluded upon. How God might have taken you away in your sins! And therefore I hope he hath reserved you as a subject of mercy; when you were blinded in your sins, he sends you to see this day of shame to turn you to him; and seeing he doth in a manner draw you, spend the rest of your time in tears and repentance, and this day's work is a correction for many crimes' corruption.'

[The Lord High Stewart formally condemns Castlehaven to death.]

CHAPTER 4

Travel Writings

Introduction

English travel narratives that deal with the sexual customs of other cultures, particularly those of the New World and the East, often present sexual licentiousness as endemic, sometimes touching specifically on sodomy and tribadism. However, by far the most detailed presentations of same-sex erotic relationships in non-European cultures are those relating to Turkey and the Turkish seraglio, where both sodomy and tribadism are represented as springing from a rigidly observed and religiously mandated separation of the sexes. Early modern European travel writers usually reflect the assumption that Eastern households generally and the seraglio or harem specifically were places of 'barbarous cruelties and extravagant sensualities' (Chew qtd in Vitkus 13), with 'the Ottoman sultan's palace a proverbial site for sexual excess, sadistic entertainment, and private, pornographic spectacle'. Islamic men of the East and North Africa were stereotyped as aggressively and excessively promiscuous; Islamic women as cauldrons of lust under a veil of 'virtue and chastity' (Vitkus 13–14).

Of the following presentations of tribadism in Africa and the East, Africanus's is unsurprisingly the most measured. In a telling rejection of superstition, Africanus asserts that tribadic relationships do not spring from demonic possession, as he asserts is the popular conception in Africa and the Middle East, but are instead part of a 'confidence' subculture, where women desiring other women manipulate husbands into colluding in their own cuckoldry. By presenting Islamic culture as condemning tribadism, Africanus suggests the moral and ethical equivalency between Islamic Fez and Christian Europe, but the picture he presents probably could not have avoided feeding his European readers' assumption that Islam and the East were once again sites of 'aberrant' sexuality. In contrast, de Nicolay presents tribadism as endemic to Turkish culture, perversely encouraged by the Turkish husband's stereotypical jealous possessiveness and his wielding of tyrannical domestic power. His domestic despotism makes his wife (or wives) seek sexual freedom at the all-female public baths. Playing on English fears about what women get up to when there is no male surveillance, de Nicolay represents these baths as 'hotbeds' of female homoerotic acts and desires. Tavernier's account of the Ottoman Sultan's seraglio likewise suggests that the tyrannical authority of men over women and of officers of both sexes over their male and female subordinates results in widespread same-sex desires, intercourse, and erotic acts generally: heterosexual men and women of the seraglio turn to members of their own sex because of their enforced celibacy, the most intimate expression of their total domination by the Sultan and his officials.

Mary Wortley Montagu's eye-witness accounts of the women's baths and the seraglio contest in particular de Nicolay's and Tavernier's second-hand information and their popular stereotypes of Eastern women as abject, enslaved, deceitful, and voraciously licentious. At the same time, Montagu's representation of her encounters with Turkish women at the baths and in the aristocratic household does not avoid the erotic aspects of women's relationships, although her imagining of the invisible presence of the male painter at the women's baths has led to some discussion of the voyeuristic male gaze. Many critics, such as Grundy, Heffernan, Still, Weitzman and Wunder, have also debated the extent to which these letters in particular both participate in and critique the emerging discourse of Orientalism, as well as the extent to which these representations are imbricated in a critique of women's legal, sexual, and social oppression in early eighteenth-century English society.

Online Companion
Interested readers can find additional selections from the following travel writers: Richard Hakulyt and Richard Head.

Leo Africanus [al-Hassan bin Muhammed al-Wazzan al-Fasi] (1486/88–c. 1554), writer and traveller

Native of Granada but raised in Fez (Morocco), Africanus travelled extensively, at least partly in the service of his sultan, Muhammad II al-Burtuqali. He was apparently engaged, however, on personal business when in 1518 he was captured by Spanish pirates and presented as a gift to Pope Leo X. Freed upon converting to Christianity, Africanus lived first in Rome, where he wrote *The Description of Africa* (completed, 1526), and later in Bologna, where he wrote an Arabic–Hebrew–Latin medical dictionary and an Arabic grammar. Translated into many European languages and frequently plagiarized, *The Description of Africa* was seen as unequalled in its accuracy and comprehensiveness, although it focuses largely on those regions that Africanus knew well: the Gold Coast, Benin, the Congo, the Sudan, and of course Morocco.

Editions

Africanus, Leo, *History and Description of Africa* (1600), trans. J. Pory, ed. R. Brown. London: Hakluyt Society, 1896.

4.1

From *A Geographical History of Africa* (2nd edn, 1600)[1]

4.1.1 The Fortune-Tellers and Some Other Artisans in Fez[2]

[…]

[…] The third kind of diviners[3] are women-witches, which are affirmed to have familiarity with devils. Some devils they call red, some white, and some black devils; and when they will tell any man's fortune, they perfume themselves with certain odours, saying that then they possess themselves with that devil which they called for. Afterward changing their voice, they feign the devil to speak within them; then they which come to inquire aught, with great fear and trembling ask these vile and abominable witches such questions as they mean to propound; and lastly, offering some fee unto the devil, they depart. But the wiser and honester sort of people call these women *sahacat*, which in Latin signifieth *fricatrices*,[4] because they have a damnable custom to commit unlawful venery[5] among themselves, which I cannot express in any modester terms. If fair women come unto them at any time, these abominable witches will burn in lust towards them no otherwise than lusty younkers[6] do towards young maids, and will in the devil's behalf demand for a reward that they may lie with them; and so by this means it often falleth out, that thinking thereby to fulfil the devil's command they lie

[1] Translated by John Pory (1572–?1636), Cambridge graduate and colonial administrator.

[2] From Bk 3. This section appears verbatim in *Purchas His Pilgrims* (1625 edn), Bk VI, chpt. 1–3, p. 796.

[3] *diviners* fortune-tellers.

[4] *fricatrices* women who have sex with other women. See **2.2.1 n10**.

[5] *venery* sexual practices.

[6] *younker* fashionable young man.

with the witches. Yea, some there are, which being allured with the delight of this abominable vice, will desire the company of these witches, and feigning themselves to be sick, will either call one of the witches home to them, or will send their husbands for the same purpose; and so the witches, perceiving how the matter stands, will say that the woman is possessed with a devil, and that she can no way be cured, unless she be admitted into their society. With these words her silly husband being persuaded doth not only permit her so to do, but makes also a sumptuous banquet unto the damned crew of witches, which being done, they use to dance very strangely at the noise of drums, and so the poor man commits his false wife to their filthy disposition. Howbeit, some there are that will soon conjure the devil with a good cudgel out of their wives; others feigning themselves to be possessed with a devil will deceive the said witches, as their wives have been deceived by them.

Nicolas de Nicolay (1517–c. 1583), French cartographer

Resulting largely from first-hand observations during a French diplomatic embassy to the Ottoman Empire, de Nicolay's *Les Navigations, Peregrinations et Voyages Faits en la Turquie* (1568) was quickly translated into several European languages, including English. His highly regarded maps and sea charts and a translation of Pedro de Medina's *The Art of Navigation* complete his major works.

4.2

From *The Navigations, Peregrinations, and Voyages Made into Turkey* (1585)

4.2.1 Chap. 22. Of the women of Turkey going unto the baths, and of their apparel and manner of cleanness

The Turks' wives [...] do delight at all times to haunt the baths, as well for the continuance of their health as beautifying of their persons, which is not to be reputed as spoken of the women of base estate or condition, but likewise of the great and notable dames, which ordinarily do frequent the baths two or three times in the week, not the public but their private baths, which for the most part they have very fair within their houses or *sarails*,[1] but such as are of the meaner degree go unto them at the least once in the week, if by

[1] *sarails* seraglios.

other[s] they will be esteemed not infamed or scarce honest.[2] And notwithstanding they will not gladly fail to go thither for two several[3] occasions: the one being for the observation of their Mahumetical[4] law, which as before I have said forbiddeth them not to make their prayers within the mosques except first their bodies be washed and purified, notwithstanding that few women do enter into the same mosques but such as are dames of great reputation and authority; the other and principalest reason is, to have good occasion and honest excuse to go abroad out of their houses, within the which they are continually closed up for the great jealousy of their husbands, or rather for the observing of the ancient custom of their ancestors, which after that sort kept their wives and daughters closed up in the backsides of their houses, which they call *ginaises*; so as the Turkey women being shut up without permission to go abroad [...] except it be going to the baths, whereto they nevertheless go with their faces covered to bring their jealous husbands out of suspicion, which continually so keep them under subjection and closed in, [...] oftentimes under colour of going to baths, they resort to other places where they think good to accomplish their pleasures, and come home again in good time without the knowledge or perceiving of their husbands, wherein they fear nothing at all, for that to those baths no men do frequent, so long as the women are there. [...] [S]ometimes they do go ten or twelve of them together, and sometimes more in a company, as well Turks as Grecians, and do familiarly wash one another, whereby it cometh to pass that amongst the women of Levant,[5] there is very great amity proceeding only through the frequentation and resort to these baths. Yea, and sometimes [they] become so fervently in love the one of the other as if it were with men, in such sort that perceiving some maiden or woman of excellent beauty, they will not cease until they have found means to bathe with them, and to handle and grope[6] them everywhere at their pleasures, so full they are of luxuriousness and feminine wantonness. Even as in times past were the *tribades*, of the number whereof was Sappho the Lesbian which transferred the love wherewith she pursued a hundred women or maidens upon her only friend Phaon.[7] And therefore considering the reasons aforesaid – to wit: the cleansing of their bodies, health, superstition, liberty to go abroad, and lascivious voluptuousness – it is not to be marvelled at that these baths are so accustomably frequented of the Turks, and that likewise the women of estate[8]

[2] *infamed* of poor or scandalous reputation; *honest*: chaste, virtuous.

[3] *several* separate.

[4] *Mahumetical* Islamic.

[5] *Levant* eastern Mediterranean.

[6] *grope* clutch; but, also, 'embrace tightly'.

[7] *Sappho* and *Phaon* See Introduction to **7.2–7.9**; see also **7.19**.

[8] *estate* high rank.

do so gladly go thither in the morning betimes for to remain there until dinnertime. [...]

Jean-Baptiste Tavernier (1605–89), baron of Aubonne, French courtier, merchant, and traveller

Tavernier's extensive travels included journeys to England, Eastern Europe, Turkey, Persia, and Palestine. Suffering personal and financial reversals, as well as persecution for his Protestantism, Tavernier briefly came under the patronage of the elector of Brandenburg. He died on his way through Russia to Asia. *Les Six Voyages de Jean-Baptiste Tavernier* was first translated into English in 1677.

4.3

From *Collections of Travels Through Turkey into Persia and the East Indies* (2nd edn, 1684): A New Relation of the Inner-Part of the Grand Seignior's Seraglio[1]

4.3.1 Chapter 2: Of the First Court of the Seraglio, and particularly, of the Infirmary

[The infirmary clearly functioned as a space where the rigid rules of the seraglio could be temporarily circumvented: wine, relaxation, and a partner for homoerotic intercourse could all be procured.]

Nor is the drinking of wine the main inducement which makes those counterfeit sick persons to seek out pretences to go and pass away some days in the infirmary; insomuch that some have the lewd artifice to put themselves into a slight fever which is presently removed. A detestable passion, and which is in a manner natural to them though it be against nature, makes them study all the imaginable ways to satisfy it. This proves a hard matter for the *ichoglans*[2] to do while they are in their chambers observed and

[1] *Grand Seignior* sultan or supreme ruler of the Ottoman Empire; *seraglio*: the sultan's private apartments and those of his servants. The women's apartments (for his wives, concubines, and female slaves) were the most inaccessible.

[2] *ichoglans* boys from conquered Christian communities; beautiful, intelligent, and well-born, they were educated and severely disciplined under their supervisors, the white eunuchs (see **n9**); a boy-*ichoglan* would be page to the sultan, his family, and officers, and could rise to be an officer (*bassa* or *bashaw*).

watched night and day by severe overseers, who never pardon them the least misdemeanour.

For though the Grand Seignior be himself subject to the same passion, the very name whereof causes a horror, yet he orders cruel punishments to be inflicted on those who shall presume to imitate him. He does what he can to prevent the mischief, which he would not have countenanced by his example, and imposes the prevention of it as a task upon the eunuchs, a vigilant sort of animals, whose eyes are always open. But in the infirmary, all these precautions prove fruitless; the eunuchs belonging to that place being corrupted partly by presents, partly by treats, or being made drunk with wine, or some other liquors, they bring in thither some young lads, of whom there is great store in the city of Constantinople. The better to over-reach the eunuchs, they put those young lads into the habits of the *halvagis*,[3] and so the cheat succeeds, in regard they are the attendants on the officers of the seraglio, and all the errands they have to do in the city.

Of these *halvagis*, there is ordinarily to the number of six hundred, and they have only their clothing and sustenance allowed them, without any wages, till such time as they have served thirteen or fourteen years. [...] [T]heir most considerable gain proceeds from the infamous commerce of those young lads whom they bring in to their masters, and whom they cunningly slip into the infirmary, after they had put them into habits like their own. [...]

The *hasteler-agasi*, or chief overseer of [the] infirmary, is indeed continually at the gate with five or six other eunuchs, and carefully observes whatever goes in or comes out. But all that vigilance will not do the work; nay, though he had a hundred eyes, yet were it impossible for him to discern those young lads amidst the great number of those *halvagis* [...] But if it should happen that the said superintendent eunuch should have any secret information of what's designed, and seems as if he would make some noise about it, he is presently appeased with a silk vest or some other present, and 'tis thence that he derives his greatest advantages. In fine,[4] that brutish passion is so ordinary amongst the Turks and generally over all the Eastern parts, that notwithstanding all the endeavours that has been used to prevent the effects of it, they will hardly ever be able to do it. There happened a memorable example of this in my time. Two pages of the chamber, who could not have the convenience of executing their wicked design in the seraglio, would needs aggravate their crime by going into the mosque to satiate their brutality.[5] After prayers were ended, they suffered all the people to go out, and, having

[3] *halvagis* servants of *grandees* (eminent seraglio-officers); *halvagis* could leave and enter the seraglio at will.

[4] *fine* conclusion.

[5] *brutality* bestial desires; after the manner of brute beasts.

so well hid themselves that he who shut the doors could not perceive them, they fell to the doing of an action whereof the very idea causes horror.

[...]

4.3.2 Chapter 13: Of the Cup-bearers' Quarters, and of Divers Other Apartments.

[...]

But it were to be wished that they would not so much concern themselves in keeping those places[6] so clean provided they could forbear polluting them with those detestable impurities, which I should gladly have left unmentioned, did I not fear the reproach might be made to me of my having been defective in point of exactness. [...] It is a subject which is to be slightly passed over, that so there may be but imperfect ideas left of it. It is therefore in those places that the pages make their nocturnal assignations, in order to the committing of the worst of all crimes, which yet they find it very difficult to put in execution, because they are so narrowly watched; and if they are taken in the very act, they are punished with so great severity that sometimes they are even drubbed[7] to death. [...] In like manner, to prevent the committing of that infamous act in the places where they take their repose there are two torches lighted, which last all the night, and three eunuchs are ever and anon going their rounds, by which means the pages are deprived of the opportunities, which otherwise they might have, to offend.

But we need not go far to find out the source of this evil: the strictness of the restraint they are in and their being deprived of the sight of women induce those young men to practise such defilements, and hurry the Turks into a gulf to which they, by an execrable passion, are naturally but too much inclinable. The *ichoglans*, who are brought very young into the seraglio, know not what a woman is but by the instinct of nature; and there are some of them who for one day's sight and enjoyment of a woman would be content to die the next. All those nations generally have so great a bent to lubricity,[8] that it seems impossible they should quit it but with their lives. What they cannot do one way, they endeavour to do another; and they of the seraglio do all they can to elude the inspection of their overseers. The reader may call to mind the action of the two pages [...] and that single example is

6 *those places* lavatories.
7 *drubbed* flogged.
8 *lubricity* lasciviousness.

enough to show how they seek out all the ways imaginable to satisfy their brutish passion.

[…]

4.3.3 Chapter 17: Of the Women's Apartment

I make a chapter by itself of the apartment of the women only to entertain the reader with the impossibility there is of having a perfect knowledge of it, or getting any exact account either what the accommodations of it are, or how the persons who are confined therein behave themselves. There is not in all Christendom any monastery of religious virgins, how regular and austere soever it may be, the entrance whereof is more strictly forbidden to men than is that of this apartment of the women: insomuch that my white eunuch,[9] who has supplied me with so particular a description of the inner part of the seraglio, could give me no certain information of this quarter of it, where the women are lodged. […] [B]esides the Grand Seignior himself, and sometimes the physician in case of great necessity, there never enters any man into it, nor no woman besides those who live in it and they are never permitted to go out of it, unless it be in order to their confinement in the Old Seraglio.[10]

[…]

[…] It may also be conjectured that there is in this quarter an observance of the same regulations as there are in the chambers of *ichoglans*: that some of the more ancient maids are mistresses over the younger ones, and are, night and day, employed in observing their actions; and that their involuntary restraint forces them to the same unseemly actions amongst themselves as the brutish passions of those young men engages them in, whenever they can find the opportunities to commit them. And this presumption has no doubt given occasion to the fabulous[11] story which is related of their being served up with cucumbers cut into pieces, and not entire, out of a ridiculous fear lest they should put them to indecent uses, they who have forged the story not knowing that it is the custom in the Levant to cut the fruit across into great thick slices, as I shall make it appear in the chapter where I treat of gardens. But it is not only in the seraglio that that abominable vice reigns, but it is

[9] *white eunuchs* partially castrated (testicles removed); supervised *ichoglans* and other servants. The black eunuchs were completely castrated (all external genitalia removed), and they alone guarded the women's quarters.

[10] *unless … confinement* i.e., during labour and childbirth. The seraglio women's maids and ladies-in-waiting are the other exceptions.

[11] *fabulous* fictitious.

predominant also in the city [of] Constantinople and in all the provinces of the empire; and the wicked example of the men, who slighting the natural use of womankind are mutually inflamed with a detestable love for one another, unfortunately inclines the women to imitate them.

Of this there was a strange instance in the time of Solyman the Magnificent.[12] An old woman was guilty of such an excess of extravagance, as to put on man's clothes, and to give out that she had bought a *chiaoux*'s[13] place, the better to compass her design of obtaining the only daughter of a tradesman of Constantinople, with whom she was desperately fallen in love, having made fruitless attempts, by other ways, to satisfy her infamous inclinations. The father not suspecting anything of her wicked intentions, and being withal poor, grants her his daughter, the marriage is solemnized [...] and the imposture having been discovered the very wedding night, the old woman was condemned the next day to be thrown into the sea, there to quench the Gomorrhean[14] inflammations of her lewd desires. This story is to this day related in Constantinople, and I have had it from several good hands.

These insatiable salaciousness[es] amongst the women are the effects and consequences of the same inclinations in the men; and the Turks are so much the more execrable and abominable as to this particular[15] the more they are permitted a plurality of wives. But whether it happens through a just punishment from Heaven, or proceed from their sorceries, which are common and allowed in Turkey, and ordinarily practised by the women in opposition to one another to appropriate the affections of their husbands, it has always been observed that the Turks who keep many women are not so well-stored with children as they who observe conjugal chastity and confine themselves to one.

[...]

Lady Mary Wortley Montagu (1689–1762), writer, traveler, and inoculation pioneer

Daughter of an aristocratic family, wife to the diplomat Edward Wortley Montagu (1678–1761), and writer of poems, essays, and fiction, Montagu is best known for her letters written during the seventeen months she spent in Turkey, accompanying her husband on a diplomatic embassy. Indicating her familiarity with Turkish culture and literature, *Letters* was published

12 Suleiman I (c. 1494–1566), sultan of the Ottoman Empire (1520–66).

13 *chiaoux* Sultan's messenger.

14 *Gomorrhean* i.e., in the manner of the sodomites of Gomorrah (see **1.1.1**).

15 *particular* specific [vice].

only posthumously, although Montagu's revisions suggest that she meant it to appear in print. Her most significant extra-literary accomplishment was in introducing and promoting smallpox inoculation in England. Falling ill-fatedly in love with a Venetian count, Francesco Algarotti, Montagu left for the Continent in 1739, spending time in Avignon, Brescia, Venice and Padua, dying finally of breast cancer.

The following selections are from the first published edition, but major variations from Montagu's manuscripts are noted, following Isobel Grundy's 1997 edition, *Selected Letters.*

Editions

Montagu, Lady Mary Wortley, *Selected Letters*, ed. I. Grundy. London: Penguin, 1997.

—. *Complete Letters of Lady Mary Wortley Montagu*, ed. R. Halsband. Oxford: Clarendon, 1965–67.

—. *Turkish Embassy Letters*, ed. M. Jack. Athens: University of Georgia Press, 1993.

4.4

From 'The Turkish Embassy Letters'
(comp., 1716–18; publ., 1763)

4.4.1 Letter XXVI. To the Lady ———.

Adrianople, April 1. O.S.,[1] 1717.

I am now got into a new world where everything I see appears to me a change of scene [...] I won't trouble you with a relation of our tedious journey, but I must not omit what I saw remarkable at Sophia,[2] one of the most beautiful towns in the Turkish Empire and famous for its hot baths that are resorted to both for diversion and health. I stopped [t]here one day on purpose to see them [...] I went to the *bagnio*[3] about 10 o'clock. It was already full of women. [...] I was in my travelling habit, which is a riding dress,[4] and certainly appeared very extraordinary to them, yet there was not one of them that showed the least surprise or impertinent curiosity, but received

[1] *O.S.* 'Old Style', referring to the dating of the letters according to the English Julian calendar, as opposed to the Continental Gregorian calendar; Julian calendar dates are 11 days earlier than Gregorian.

[2] *Sophia* in Bulgaria.

[3] *bagnio* public bath.

[4] *riding dress* female riding habit.

me with all the obliging civility possible. I know no European court where the ladies would have behaved themselves in so polite a manner to such a stranger. I believe, upon the whole, there were 200 women, and yet none of those disdainful smiles and satiric whispers that never fail in our assemblies when anybody appears that is not dressed exactly in the fashion. They repeated over and over to me, 'Uzelle, pek uzelle', which is nothing but, 'Charming, very charming'. The first sofas were covered with cushions and rich carpets, on which sat the ladies, and on the second their slaves behind them, but without any distinction of rank by their dress, all being in the state of nature, that is, in plain English, stark naked, without any beauty or defect concealed. Yet there was not the least wanton smile or immodest gesture amongst them. They walked and moved with the same majestic grace which Milton describes our general mother with.[5] There were many amongst them as exactly proportioned as ever any goddess was drawn by the pencil of a Guido or Titian,[6] and most of their skins shiningly white, only adorned by their beautiful hair divided into many tresses hanging on their shoulders, braided either with pearl or ribbon, perfectly representing the figures of the Graces.

I was here convinced of the truth of a reflection that I have often made, that 'if it were the fashion to go naked, the face would be hardly observed'. I perceived that the ladies of the most delicate skins and finest shapes[7] had the greatest share of my admiration, though their faces were sometimes less beautiful than those of their companions. To tell you the truth, I had wickedness enough to wish secretly that Mr Gervase[8] could have been there invisible. I fancy it would have very much improved his art to see so many fine women naked in different postures, some in conversation, some working,[9] others drinking coffee or sherbet, and many negligently lying on their cushions while their slaves (generally pretty girls of seventeen or eighteen) were employed in braiding their hair in several pretty fancies.[10] In short, 'tis the women's coffee house,[11] where all the news of the town is told, scandal invented, etc. They generally take this diversion once a week, and stay there at least four or five hours, without getting cold by immediate coming out of the hot bath into the cool room, which was very surprising to

[5] *general mother* Eve (*Paradise Lost*, 4.287–324; 9.386–96).

[6] *Guido* Reni (1575–1642) and *Titian* (c. 1480/5–1576), Italian painters, partly famed for their sensuous female nudes.

[7] *of … shapes* 'with the finest skins and most delicate shapes' (Grundy 149).

[8] *Gervase* Charles Jervas (Jarvis) (1675–1739), fashionable portrait painter.

[9] *working* embroidering or sewing.

[10] *fancies* 'manners' (Grundy 149).

[11] *coffee house* in England, an exclusively male space for socializing, discussing current affairs, and drinking coffee.

me. The lady that seemed the most considerable[12] amongst them entreated me to sit by her and would fain[13] have undressed me for the bath. I excused myself with some difficulty. They being, however, all so earnest in persuading me, I was at last forced to open my skirt[14] and show them my stays,[15] which satisfied them very well, for I saw they believed I was so locked up in that machine, and that it was not in my own power to open it, which contrivance they attributed to my husband. I was charmed with their civility and beauty and should have been very glad to pass more time with them, but Mr Wortley resolving to pursue his journey the next morning early, I was in haste to see the ruins of Justinian's church,[16] which did not afford me so agreeable a prospect as I had left, being little more than a heap of stones.

Adieu, madam. I am sure I have now entertained you with an account of such a sight as you never saw in your life and what no book of travels could inform you of, as 'tis no less than death for a man to be found in one of these places.

4.4.2 Letter XXXIII. To the Countess of ——[17]

Adrianople, April 18, O.S. [1717]

[...]

[...] so much her[18] beauty effaced everything I have seen, nay, all that has been called lovely either in England or Germany. I must own that I never saw anything so gloriously beautiful, nor can I recollect a face that would have been taken notice of near hers. She stood up to receive me, saluting me after their fashion, putting her hand to her heart with a sweetness full of majesty that no court breeding could ever give. She ordered cushions to be given me and took care to place me in the corner, which is the place of honour. I confess [...] I was so struck with admiration that I could not for some time speak to her, being wholly taken up in gazing. That surprising harmony of features! that charming result of the whole! that exact proportion of body! that lovely bloom of complexion unsullied by art![19] the unutterable

12 *most considerable* of the highest rank.

13 *fain* willingly.

14 *skirt* The copy text (1763) has 'shirt', but Grundy emends to 'skirt'.

15 *stays* early corset.

16 *Justinian's church* St Sophia (Hagia Sophia) in Sofia, Bulgaria.

17 The addressee has been identified as Montagu's sister, Frances Erskine, countess of Mar (1690–1761).

18 *her* i.e., Fatima (wife of the Kahya, an important official); she has invited Montagu to dine at her house.

19 *art* cosmetics.

enchantment of her smile! But her eyes! large and black, with all the soft languishment of the blue! every turn of her face discovering some new grace![20] After my first surprise was over, I endeavoured by nicely[21] examining her face to find out some imperfection, without any fruit of my search but my being clearly convinced of the error of that vulgar notion, that a face exactly proportioned,[22] and perfectly beautiful[23] would not be agreeable, Nature having done for her with more success what Apelles[24] is said to have essayed, by a collection of the most exact features to form a perfect face; add to all this, a behaviour so full of grace and sweetness, such easy motions, with an air so majestic yet free from stiffness or affectation that I am persuaded, could she be suddenly transported upon the most polite throne of Europe, nobody would think her other than born and bred to be a queen, though educated in a country we call barbarous. To say all in a word, our most celebrated English beauties would vanish near her.

[…]

[…] I am afraid you will accuse me of extravagance in this description. I think I have read somewhere that women always speak in rapture when they speak of beauty, but I cannot imagine why they should not be allowed to do so. I rather think it virtue to be able to admire without any mixture of desire or envy. The gravest writers have spoke with great warmth of some celebrated pictures and statues. The workmanship of Heaven certainly excels all our weak imitations, and I think has a much better claim to our praise. For me, I am not ashamed to own I took more pleasure in looking on the beauteous Fatima than the finest piece of sculpture could have given me. […]

[…]

Her fair maids were ranged below the sofa to the number of twenty, and put me in mind of the pictures of the ancient nymphs. I did not think all Nature could have furnished such a scene of beauty. […] This dance was very different from what I had seen before.[25] Nothing could be more artful or more proper to raise *certain ideas*. The tunes so soft! the motions so languishing! Accompanied with pauses and dying eyes! half falling back and then recovering themselves in so artful a manner that I am very positive the coldest and most rigid prude upon Earth could not have looked upon

[20] *grace* 'charm' (Grundy 163).

[21] *nicely* closely.

[22] *exactly proportioned* 'perfectly regular' (Grundy 163).

[23] *perfectly beautiful* phrase absent from Grundy's edition.

[24] *Apelles* (fourth century BCE), reputedly the finest ancient Greek artist, famed for his Aphrodite (i.e., Venus) Anadyomene at Kos.

[25] Fatima has ordered her servants to play and dance for Montagu.

them without thinking *of something not to be spoke of.* I suppose you may have read that the Turks have no music but what is shocking to the ears, but this account is from those who never heard any but what is played in the streets, and is just as reasonable as if a foreigner should take his ideas of English music from the bladder and string, or the marrow bones and cleavers.[26] I can assure you that the music is extremely pathetic.[27] [...]

When the dance was over, four fair slaves came into the room with silver censers[28] in their hands and perfumed the air with amber, aloes-wood, and other scents.[29] After this they served me coffee upon their knees in the finest Japan china with *soûcoupes*[30] of silver gilt. The lovely Fatima entertained me all this while in the most polite agreeable manner, calling me often 'Uzelle Sultanam', or 'the beautiful Sultana', and desiring my friendship with the best grace in the world, lamenting that she could not entertain me in my own language. When I took my leave two maids brought in a fine silver basket of embroidered handkerchiefs. She begged that I would wear the richest for her sake, and gave the others to my woman and interpretess. I retired [...] and could not help thinking I had been some time in Mahomet's Paradise,[31] so much I was charmed with what I had seen. [...]

[26] *bladder ... cleavers* makeshift, street instruments.

[27] *pathetic* moving.

[28] *censers* vessels for the burning of incense.

[29] *scents* 'rich scents' (Grundy 165).

[30] *soûcoupes* French, 'saucers'.

[31] *thinking* 'fancying' (Grundy 165); *Mahomet's Paradise*: the place of rest for the faithful Islamic dead. Western societies usually caricatured this paradise as a place of sybaritic luxury and sexual licence, populated by sexually willing *houris* or lovely women.

CHAPTER 5

Letters

Introduction

An ubiquitous early modern genre, the letter was something that most literate people would have produced, its popularity prompting the publication of a number of letter-writing manuals in the sixteenth and seventeenth centuries. These celebrate and idealize, in particular, the familiar letter not just as a necessary bridge between separated friends but in the words of Angel Day as a capturing and conveying of 'the familiar speech of the absent' (*English Secretary* (1586), 1), and as an essential aspect of building and maintaining friendships: 'Love is the life of friendship, letters are / The life of love' and 'Speech is the index, Letters ideas are / Of the informing soul' (J. Howell, 'To the Reader', *Epistolae Ho-Elianae* (1645),15; Henderson 331–3). Not only do familiar letters reveal the inner mind of the writer, they often imply an intimacy and a capacity for conveying desire, which perhaps increase in intensity of expression precisely because they are predicated on the absence of the beloved. In the words of John Donne's famous verse epistle 'To Sir Henry Wotton': 'Sir, more than kisses, letters mingle souls: / For thus friends absent speak' (see **8.15.7**). At the same time, even though familiar letters were defined as an intimate sharing of the correspondents' inner lives, thoughts, and secrets, they could be and often were affected in their diction, forms of address, and rhetorical strategies by their generic conventions; their social, familial, and political contexts; and their possible persuasive intents. As David Bergeron has noted in his wonderful edition of the correspondence between James I and VI and his male favourites, familiar letters were also often dangerous because they could and did reveal personal, familial, and perhaps even state secrets; such letters could also be radically transgressive in their emphasis on fostering love and desire, particularly between correspondents of different social ranks, resulting in a disintegration of social boundaries; and particularly when the desires they expressed reveal and construct a love that deviated from the heteronormative (9).

King James I and VI (1566–1625), King of Scotland (1567–1625) and England (1603–25)

Although an ineffective financial manager, James set the groundwork for the union of England and Scotland; largely avoided the persecution of religious minorities; and did not expect all his bishops to hold his own Calvinist views. Sponsor of the finest translation of the Bible in English, the Authorized Version (1611), James was (for all his vaunted love of hunting) an intellectual, a scholar with a sincere love of learning, a patron of literature, and an accomplished writer; his works include the political treatises *The True Law of Free Monarchies* (1598) and *Basilikon Doron* (1599), as well as verse in Scots and a treatise on Scottish poetry. James married Anne, daughter of King Frederick II of Denmark, in 1589; the couple had three children: Henry, Elizabeth, and Charles (Charles I (1600–49)).

George Villiers, First Duke of Buckingham (1592–1628), courtier

Confidante and adviser to two kings, George Villiers initially impressed James with his beauty, poise, and conversation. Supplanting James's previous favourite, Robert Carr, Earl of Somerset, Villiers rose swiftly from Viscount (1616), to Earl (1617), to Marquis (1618), and finally to Duke of Buckingham (1623). Buckingham's talents and commitment to James's service were demonstrated in his reorganization and revitalization of the navy. His relationship with James's eldest son, Charles, was cemented into a lasting and deep friendship during their joint incognito visit to Spain in 1623, in an unsuccessful attempt to win the Spanish Infanta as Charles's wife. Under Charles, Buckingham encouraged England's wars with Spain and France, their disastrous outcomes leading to his parliamentary impeachment. With no evidence for charges ranging from nepotism to bribery to the murder of James I, the impeachment crumbled, Charles refusing to surrender his most trusted adviser. Buckingham, however, was assassinated in 1628 by a former soldier, John Felton, who had been convinced by Parliament's remonstrance of that year that killing Buckingham would be a service to the nation.

James I and Royal 'Homosexuality' Among the Critics

James's homoerotic preferences were well known among his contemporaries, with the diarist Sir John Oglander (1585–1655) noting that '[James] loved young men, his favourites, better than women, loving them beyond the love of men to women. I never saw any fond husband make so much or so great dalliance over his beautiful spouse as I have seen King James over his favourites, especially the Duke of Buckingham' (qtd in Bergeron 196).[1] Certainly James's generosity to Buckingham exceeded what he had shown to his earlier favourites, and Buckingham amassed a vast fortune, which he spent largely in the service of his royal masters.

Reactions to James's and Buckingham's relationship are of a piece with reactions to the couple's intimate correspondence. Seventeenth- and eighteenth-century commentators portray the relationship as distasteful and morally repugnant (Ashton 105–39),[2] while twentieth-century critics tend to see James's love for Buckingham as 'unfairly' suggesting that same-sex erotic desire, love, and sexual acts were a component of their relationship, sometimes translating this love into the register of filial affection, sometimes pointing to the fact that James's encouragement to his favourites, including Buckingham, to marry precludes any homoerotic feelings for these men (Bergeron 107–09; Young). Even James's twenty-first century *DNB* biographer Jenny Wormald dismisses the issue by suggesting that only literary critics, and not historians, are interested in the question of the sexual aspects of the king's relationship with his favourites.[3] According to Bergeron, the James–Buckingham correspondence constitutes a record of the longest, most loving, and most mutual of James's relationships with his favourites. Bergeron describes their body of letters appreciatively as 'an artful text of love', a record of a love both 'multi-faceted' and 'full of tension and complexity', a correspondence that contains both 'quotidian details' and 'soaring expressions of love and gratitude' (126–7). He places these comments in the context of the more common response to the letters' language, imagery, and content, which are described by some eighteenth-century historians as 'fulsomely familiar' and 'indecent', as well as 'nauseous'; by some twentieth-century writers as 'repulsive' and 'revolting', as well as full of 'maudlin sentimentality' (126–7); and by Wormald as having a 'sugary sentimentality' that modern readers will find distasteful. Readers will arguably be struck more by the letters' passion and their fusing of the language of marital, fatherly, and erotic devotion.

Editions

Bergeron, David M., *King James and Letters of Homoerotic Desire*. Iowa City: University of Iowa Press, 1999.

[1] In a 1713 translation of Xenophon's *Hiero*, the Emperor Hiero describes his love for the beautiful youth Dailochus; the translator's long footnote compares this same-sex relationship with that of James and his two favourites, presumably Carr and Buckingham.

[2] For early Stuart clandestine satire focused on James and his male favourites, see McRae, esp. pp. 44–50 and pp. 75–82.

[3] For a cogent examination of the political valences of these relationships, see McRae, pp. 118–27.

5.1

From 'Letters'

5.1.1 To George Villiers, Marquess of Buckingham[4] [December 1622?]

My only sweet and dear child,

I am now so miserable a coward, as I do nothing but weep and mourn: for I protest to God I rode this afternoon a great way in the park without speaking to anybody and the tears trickling down my cheeks, as now they do that I can scarcely see to write. But alas, what shall I do at our parting? The only small comfort I can have will be to pry in thy defects with the eye of an enemy, and of every mote[5] to make a mountain, and so harden my heart against thy absence. But this little malice is like jealousy, proceeding from a sweet root; but in one point it overcometh it, for as it proceeds from love so it cannot but end in love. Sweetheart, be earnest with Kate[6] to come and meet thee at Newhall[7] within eight or ten days after this. Cast[8] thee to be here tomorrow, as near about two in the afternoon as thou can, and come galloping hither. Remember thy picture[9] and suffer none of the Council[10] to come here. For God's sake write not a word again and let no creature see this letter. The Lord of heaven and earth to bless thee, and my sweet daughter, and my sweet little grandchild, and all thy blessed family, and send thee a happy return, both now and thou knows when, to thy dear dad and Christian gossip.[11]

JAMES R.

[4] The following letters are from Bergeron's edition; reprinted by permission of University of Iowa Press.

[5] *mote* speck (of dust).

[6] *Kate* affectionate diminutive for Lady Katherine Manners (?1603–49), Buckingham's wife.

[7] *Newhall* Buckingham's Essex mansion, just outside Chelmsford.

[8] *cast* plan.

[9] *thy picture* miniature portrait; exchanging them was a sign of intimacy and friendship. See James's letter to Buckingham (28 Feb 1623): 'I have no more to say but that I wear Steenie's picture in a blue ribbon under my waistcoat next my heart' (153). Buckingham says James wears 'my unworthy picture [...] next the worthiest heart living' (Madrid, 24 March 1623; p. 188). Cf. **8.6.3 n26**.

[10] *Council* Privy Council, comprised of ministers of state.

[11] *gossip* godparent; also, 'intimate friend'.

5.1.2 To George Villiers, Duke of Buckingham [December 1623?]

My only sweet and dear child,

Notwithstanding of your desiring me not to write yesterday, yet had I written in the evening if, at my coming out of the park, such a drowsiness had not come upon me as I was forced to sit and sleep in my chair half an hour. And yet I cannot content myself without sending you this present, praying God that I may have a joyful and comfortable meeting with you and that we may make at this Christmas a new marriage ever to be kept hereafter; for, God so love me, as I desire only to live in this world for your sake, and that I had rather live banished in any part of the earth with you than live a sorrowful widow's life without you. And so God bless you, my sweet child and wife, and grant that ye may ever be a comfort to your dear dad and husband.

JAMES R.

5.1.3 Buckingham to King James [Undated]

Dear Dad and Gossip,

Your last command was I should write merrily and short. How may you expect of performance of this from me, having filled my heart so full of thoughts? For my reception yesterday when I came, my entertainment being there, and my leave-taking was such, nay I say such, sir, that all the way hither I entertained myself your unworthy servant with this dispute, whether you loved me now (my ever dear master, here give me leave to say, a full heart must either vent itself or break, and that oftentimes the senses are better expressed in absence and by letter than otherwise: you know full thoughts cause long parentheses) better than at the time which I shall never forget at Farnham,[12] where the bed's head could not be found between the master and his dog. Sir, if you mark not well the parenthesis, it does break the sense that was my desire, and if therein I did deceive, it was with my goodwill.

To conclude, these thoughts are never likely to break your faithful servant's heart, which whensoever it shall be truly and thoroughly searched, shall be found full of love, faith, and obedience to you – in one thing excepted, that I will not be so hastily rich as you would make me, though covetously I will

[12] *Farnham* Farnham Castle (Surrey), where, during a 1615 royal progress, James and Villiers apparently had their first sexual encounter. A few months earlier, James had made Villiers a knight and gentleman of the bedchamber.

make myself so in this, eternally to deserve your blessing, which I humbly crave as

Your Majesty's most humble slave and dog,

Steenie.[13]

I pray you, sir, tell your sweet Baby Charles[14] that I will wait of you both before many hours pass, and by the grace of God be at the death of a stag with you.

5.1.4 Buckingham to King James[15] [Madrid, undated, May? 1623]

Dear Dad and Gossip,

It cannot but have been an infinite trouble to have written so long a letter and so soon, especially at this painful time of your arms; yet wish I not a word omitted, though the reading forced blushes, deserving them no better, neither is it fit I should ever dissemble with my master. Wherefore I confess truly I am not a jot sorry for the pains you have taken;[16] this might argue I love myself better than my Maker,[17] but my disobedience in this, with my humble obedience in all my future actions, shall witness the contrary; and I can boldly say it is not in the power of your large bountiful hand and heart ever hereafter either to increase my duty and love to you, or to overvalue myself as you do, by thinking it fit I should be set so far beyond my fellows. There is this difference betwixt that noble hand and heart, one may surfeit[18] by the one, but not by the other, and sooner by yours than his own; therefore give me leave to stop, with mine, that hand which hath been but too ready to execute the motions and affections of that kind obliging heart to me. As for that argument that this can be no leadening case to others, give me leave to say, it's true only in one (but that's a great and the main) point; for I grant that I am more than confident, you will never love none of your servants (I will be saucy here) better than Steenie; thus it will be no leadening case.[19] But

[13] *Steenie* Scottish contraction of 'Stephen'. The Christian martyr Stephen had 'the face of an angel' (Acts 6.15).

[14] *Baby Charles* affectionate nickname used by Buckingham and James.

[15] Buckingham's letter thanks James for Buckingham's recent elevation to the dukedom, the highest rank in the English peerage. Buckingham accompanied Charles to Madrid on 18 Feb. 1623, remaining there for six months.

[16] *pains ... taken* trouble you have spent.

[17] *Maker* James.

[18] *surfeit* point at which a person is 'full'.

[19] *As for that argument ... no leadening case* the sense seems to be: 'You, O King, have argued that your generosity to me will not discourage others [i.e., will not be a *leadening*

you cannot deny but it may be a precedent of emulation hereafter, to those that shall succeed you, to express as much love as you have done to me; and I am sure they may easily find many fitter subjects.

So if it be unfit in respect of the number, this way it will be increased; but I maintain it is unfit in respect there is not here, as in other places, a distinction betwixt dukes' and kings' children; and before I make a gap or a step to that parity between them and other subjects, I'll disobey you, which is the most I can say or do. I have not so much unthankfulness to deny what your Majesty sayeth, that my former excuse of the disproportion of my estate is taken away;[20] for you have filled a consuming purse, given me fair houses, more land than I am worthy of, to maintain both me and them, filled my coffers so full with patents of honour,[21] that my shoulders cannot bear more; this I say is still a good argument for me to refuse, but you have not been contented to rest here, when I thought you had done more than enough, and as much as you could but hath found out a way, which to my heart's satisfaction, [is] far beyond all; for with this letter, you have furnished and enriched my cabinet with so precious a witness of your valuation of me, as in future times it cannot be said, that I rise as most courtiers do, through importunity. For which character of me, and incomparable favour from you, I will sign, with as contented, nay as proud a heart,

Your poor Steenie,
as Duke of Buckingham

Constance Fowler [née Aston] (d. 1664), poet and letter writer

Sister of the poets Herbert Aston (1614–88/9), and Gertrude Thimelby (1617–88), Constance Fowler was part of a literary Roman Catholic family, well acquainted with the writers Drayton, Crashaw, Caryl, and Fanshawe. Constance wrote eight letters to Herbert, while he accompanied their father, Sir Walter Aston, on a Spanish diplomatic embassy. Promoting the marriage of Herbert and Katherine Thimelby (1617/18–58) – the daughter of a Lincolnshire Catholic family, and Constance's dear friend – these letters

case]; they will not assume that there is no largesse or favour left for them. I agree with this argument, except in one and the most important respect: they cannot hope to compete with me for a space in your heart. There is no more such love to give others: I have indeed monopolized your love, if not your favour and largesse.'

20 *my ... away* James has given Buckingham the resources necessary to support his new position as duke.

21 *patents of honour* i.e., James's bestowing of offices, titles, lands, and privileges upon Buckingham.

accomplished their end: Herbert and Katherine married (1638), and had ten children before her death in 1658. In Herbert's poetry, Katherine is 'Seraphina', whom he describes in his grief as 'suit[ing] Paradise before the fall, / Blest copy of the lost original' (Clifford 1.203).

Constance Fowler's letters to her brother concerning their mutual love for Katherine Thimelby have long struck modern readers as containing language usually reserved to express heterosexual desire. As the letters in this section suggest, however, Constance's language is by no means unprecedented. Traub has noted that at least one collection of model letters, Markham's *Hobson's Horse-load of Letters* (1617), contains an epistolary exchange between two gentlewomen with distinctly erotic language and imagery (*Renaissance* 184–5). While for Mendelson and Crawford, Constance's letters about her love for Katherine indicate the difficulty of describing seventeenth-century women's passionate attachments in terms of a modern sexual sensibility (244–5), for Traub these letters are another example of the way female same-sex erotic desire is made to vanish, to not 'signify' in this period, to be coded as a temporary site of passion on the way to a woman's 'true' emotional fulfillment in marriage. Absorbed within codes of female emotional sensitivity and chastity, Constance's letters reveal the extent to which the language of female same-sex passion could be licensed when in the service of a heterosexual economy (Mendelson and Crawford 246).

Editions

Clifford, Arthur, ed., *Tixall Letters*, 2 vols. London: Longmans, 1815.

5.2

From Constance Fowler to Herbert Aston[1]

My dearest brother,

[...] I believe I am blest with the most perfectest and constant lover as ever wom[a]n was blest with. Oh, if you would know the story of our affection, you must come hither and read volumes of it, afore you can be able to understand half the dearness of our love. I keep them a-purpose for your sight, and no creature breathing but myself ever saw them or knows of them else. You will say, I am certain, when you peruse them, that there was never any more passionate affectionate lovers than she and I, and that you

[1] *Tixall Letters*, vol. 1, no. 23, pp. 107–27. Clifford remarks: 'The following letter is one of the greatest curiosities in the epistolary style that I have ever met with' (p. 107, n.).

never knew two creatures more truly and deadly[2] in love with one another than we are. And I will now let you see as many passages[3] how we came to be such lovers as I have time to declare. First, then, you must know, to obey you, and being indeed truly taken with the praises you writ of her, I presently [...] sought by all the ways I could possible devise to be better known to her than yet I was. [...] For after I had made known to her by letters how infinitely I honoured her, and how I had done so since I first saw her here, she writ me the sweetest answers, that from that very hour I confess I have been most deadly in love with her as ever lover was; and so much she did increase my admiration of her by many of these letters, that I could never since think anyone worth the honouring but she. [...] Believe it, she is so far above my expression that you cannot conceive half her worth by it. Therefore, do not think the passionateness of my affection makes me speak more of her than truth; [...] it was my happy fortune to meet her by chance with Sir John and my Lady Thimelby at Tixall[4] [...] and such was our misery that we could not have that time to converse more than by silent expressions, for none but ourselves knew all or anything of that which have passed betwixt us, and therefore she durst not take notice of me but as one she honoured being her choice's[5] sister. [...] But as she [Katherine] thus discoursed to her[6] as she sat between us, she would sometimes give a look to me as if by chance her eye had so wandered, and then she would steal the prettiest words to me, that you would have been taken extremely if you had seen and heard her: 'Oh,' she would softly say, 'that I might speak my thoughts to you', and then again 'Oh, what worlds would I give I might possess you but one half hour to myself! How unfortunate am I to meet you here with your sister; if I have any private conference with you, she will take it ill, and perhaps think I am inconstant, and that I honour you more than she, and it may be she believes she has as much obliged me.' – 'She will not leave us.' – 'Oh, what shall I do? My soul is full, and I would fain[7] have you know some of my miseries; I shall not be blest with such an opportunity again this great while, and yet I know not how to make use of it, I am full of so many fears.' – 'Oh, that I had my thoughts writ now that I might have stole them to you', and many such dark speeches as these did she by bits steal to me if my sister did but look away, or any of her brothers hold her the least in discourse. [...]

2 *deadly* extremely.

3 *passages* incidents.

4 *Sir John and my Lady Thimelby* parents of Katherine; visiting the Aston family estate at Tixall, Staffordshire.

5 *her choice's* Herbert's.

6 *her* Constance's sister, Gertrude Aston; she later married Katherine's brother.

7 *fain* eagerly.

[...]

[...] do what you can to compass that happiness for yourself which I so thirst after, that my dearest friend and you being united in one, your hearts may likewise become one, and so I may keep them with more ease in my breast than now I can, they being divided. [...] Never creature loved two with more equal affection than I dote on you both. [...] For I speak it to you with my eyes drowned in tears; I think, nay, I am certain the grief of it[8] would kill me [...] and I command you to do so,[9] and to make her happy in your affection, if it be possible, as you tender the life and happiness of her who has ever been most constant in being

Your dear affectionate lover,

Constance F.

I am so mad with love, that if I have writ any nonsense here, you must forgive it, for I know nothing I do. [...]

Mary Stuart, later Mary II (1662–94)

Elder daughter of James, Duke of York, later James II (1633–1701), wife of William of Orange (1650–1702), and sister of Anne (later Queen Anne (1665–1714)), Mary became joint ruler of England with her husband William in the crisis of 1688. Although characterized by James II's supporters as a hard-hearted, undutiful daughter, Mary was much loved by her supporters, proved an able queen, and was celebrated for her moral virtue and piety. At fifteen, she entered her arranged and childless marriage with William, which initially caused her much unhappiness, as he was physically unprepossessing, emotionally reserved, and largely indifferent to her. Her letters show that she later came to love him. William's grief when she died of smallpox shows that he had come in turn to appreciate her during their seventeen-year marriage.

Frances Apsley, later Lady Bathurst (d. 1727)

Daughter of Sir Allen Apsley, an important official in the households of Charles II and James II, Frances Apsley married Sir Benjamin Bathurst (d. 1704) in 1682; he was a significant figure in finance and government. Frances gave birth to twin boys in 1683, but neither survived. In 1686 she gave birth again, but this child also died (Hamilton 126–7; 161).

8 *it* Herbert and Katherine's separation.

9 *to do so* i.e., attempt by all means to marry Katherine.

Interpreting the Terms of Endearment in the Stuart–Apsley Letters

Although its dating is notoriously difficult, the correspondence between Princess Mary and Frances Apsley apparently began around 1675 when Mary was about thirteen, and Frances probably between the ages of seventeen and eighteen; it continued until after Mary's marriage to William in 1677 (McClain 510; cf. Bathurst 30–1). As 'Mary Clorine', Mary assumed the role of wife in relationship to her epistolary husband, 'Aurelia', the penname adopted by Frances. Twentieth-century critics have generally viewed Mary's more than eighty letters to Frances as grotesquely inflated expressions of devotion (Beaven ctd in Bathurst 16); excused them as reflecting the passionate language of 'a romantic young lady to a girl friend' (Bathurst 13); psychologized them as expressions of 'adolescent romanticism and subconscious sexuality' (Gregg 21), or as the sublimation of Mary's desire for maternal love (Gordon and Lawton 80); dismissed them as expressing a 'mock affection' for Frances that Mary later translated into 'real devotion' to William (Speck, *DNB*); or scorned them as 'nonsense' (Green 33). Only rarely have these letters received any serious treatment: Gregg suggests that the passionate language might be traced to the girls' reading of French romantic fiction, while McClain examines how the letters are shaped by the literary conventions of the period's poetry, drama, and novels, and by Mary's adoption of the terms of libertine address popular between Charles II and his courtiers and mistresses. Her letters to Frances may represent an early attempt to create her own relationships outside the influence of the extended family of Charles II's deceased favourite, George Villiers, Duke of Buckingham (506).

Editions

Bathurst, Benjamin, ed., *Letters of Two Queens*. London: Robert Holden, 1925.

5.3

From 'Letters'

5.3.1 Letter 17[1]

Two letters already you have had today, dear Aurelia,[2] from me: I hope you will read the third. Though you, I suppose, are tired with them now, I hope

[1] Letters are reproduced from Bathurst's edition, above. 'Letter 17', pp. 60–1.

[2] *Aurelia* character in Massinger's tragicomedy *The Maid of Honour* (1621).

my pardon is sealed by you, dear, dear, dear, dear, dear, dear Aurelia. I may, if I can, tell you how much I love you, but I hope that is not doubted; I have given you proofs enough. If not, I will die to satisfy you. Dear, dear husband, if all my hairs were lives, I would lose them all twenty times over to serve or satisfy you in any doubt of my love. Think but if you were married to Mr Sute[3] who is, as I guess, the man in the world you love best: how much you would expect he should love you or how much you would love him – so, nay a thousand times more, longer, better should I, nay I do, love you.

I love you with a heart entire; I am for you all one desire;
I love you with a flame more lasting than the vestals' fire;[4]
Thou art my life, my soul, my all that heav'n can give;
Death's life with you; without you death to live.

What can I say more to persuade you that

I love you with more zeal than any lover can,
I love you with a love that ne'er was known by man.

I have for you excess of friendship, more of love than any woman can for woman, and more love than ever the constantest lover had for his mistress. You are loved more than can be expressed by your ever obedient wife, very affectionate friend, humble servant; to kiss the ground where on[c]e you go, to be your dog in a string,[5] your fish in a net, your bird in a cage, your humble trout.[6]

Mary Clorine[7]

Saturday, three o'clock in the afternoon.

5.3.2 Letter 20[8]

Though you are not at leisure to write to your poor wife, yet you may in your spare minutes read what I send you; it is but to confirm you of what I have so often told you: how much I love you, which though you want faith to believe, is as true as an oracle. Indeed I am poor in everything but love, poor but content – for what greater riches can I desire than love of you? And I hope it is repaid by you, for if you did but love me as I do you, I could live

3 *Mr Sute* unidentified.

4 *vestals' fire* The vestals were virgin-priestesses of Vesta, goddess of the hearth; they maintained her temple's sacred fire.

5 *in a string* on a leash.

6 *trout* slang, 'trusted friend'.

7 *Clorine* common name in pastoral works, such as John Fletcher's *The Faithful Shepherdess* (1608).

8 Bathurst, pp. 65–6.

and be content with a cottage in the country, and cow, a stuff petticoat and waistcoat in summer, and cloth in winter,[9] a little garden – to live upon the fruit and herbs it yields – or if I could not have you so to myself, I would go a-begging, be poor but content. What greater happiness is there in the world than to have the company of them one loves? To make your happiness complete, though mine would wish you alone – be so: I wish her[10] with us; I am sure then you would be pleased. When I have made you happy, so I will die, I hope you'll shed some tears for my death and wish me as happy in heaven as I have made you on earth, though but in thought.

5.3.3 Letter 31[11]

I had not patience, my dear husband, till tomorrow, but I must needs have an answer by this messenger, for Mrs Rose[12] told me yesterday you were not well, but Mrs Depuei[13] told me you were well, but had not slept well for the noise of clocks. Hearing all this, I did not know which to believe, but my fear of your being ill make[s] me send this to inquire and to satisfy myself. You went away so much sooner than I expected that I did not see my dear to take my leave of her, though I know you did not design to take it publicly. Yet I hoped you would have had some discourse better than we had that night before, for I was then so sleepy I did not know what I did or said. I hope you will keep your word with me and not forget your poor Clorine that loves you better than can be expressed. If you should not believe your one, true wife – which I hope you do – she has no way to show it but by writing to you, so that if you will not believe her she must die condemned, which God forbid she should ever give you cause; I'm very sure she never will, and I hope you never will be so much mistaken as to think of any such thing. But of all things, pray be not in the fashion to keep mistresses to break your poor wife's heart. Indeed I am impatient till I hear from you. Pray, do not delay but answer my letter by this same messenger, and believe me your true wife, humble servant, and most affectionate and loving friend,

Mary Clorine

Pray, remember me to my lady,[14] and send me word how she does.

[9] *stuff petticoat and waistcoat* undergarments of plain, light fabric; *cloth*: wool.

[10] *her* unidentified.

[11] Bathurst, pp. 80–1; occasioned by Mary's marriage to William, and her subsequent departure for Holland.

[12] *Mrs Rose* unidentified.

[13] *Mrs Depuei* unidentified.

[14] *my lady* lack of dating makes identification difficult: perhaps Frances's older sister (see **n19**).

5.3.4 [Copy of a letter from Frances to Mary][15]

Since it was my hard fate to lose the greatest blessing I ever had in this world, which was the dear presence of my most beloved wife, I have some comfort that she is taken from me by so worthy and so great a prince, for so he is in the opinion of all good men. Your Highness has put a hard task upon me to treat you with the same familiarity as becomes a fond husband to a beloved wife he dotes upon, whom I ought to reverence and adore as the greatest princess now alive. When I flatter myself with the blessing God and yourself have given me in so dear a wife, I think what the Scripture says, 'that man and wife are but one body',[16] and then your heart is mine; I am sure mine is yours. But if I behave myself to you as I am bound in duty to your Highness, I must ask your pardon for my presumption; yet since my life depends upon it – for I can live no longer than your favour shines upon me – it will be a great charity in your Highness to continue your love and bounty to a husband that admires you and dotes upon you, and an obedient servant that will always serve and adore you.

5.3.5 Letter 32[17]

The Hague, December 17th, [1677]

I am very much ashamed that my dearest husband should write to me first, for though there could not be a greater pleasure in the world to me, yet it was my duty as wife to have writ first; and I hope you will be so kind to me to believe it was for want of time, for you may imagine that not being well settled and having a great deal of company perpetually so take up my time that I was fain[18] to rise this morning before day to write some few letters of which yours was the first that was writ. I have but one thing to trouble you with: to remember me to your sister Apsley and let my lady Wentworth[19] know I would have writ to her myself to have thanked her for her news-book[20] but that I have not time, so desire you to do it for me. I am willing to write a little to as many of my friends as I can; therefore, you will excuse me if I do not say much to you whom I love like my own life, and do not think my love

15 Bathurst, pp. 82–3.

16 Gen. 2.24 (Adam's description of his union with Eve).

17 Bathurst, pp. 83–4; he describes this letter as Mary's answer to the above.

18 *fain* obliged.

19 *Wentworth* Frances's older sister, Isabella (b. 1649), who married Sir William Wentworth in 1667 (Bathurst, p. 25).

20 *news-book* early bound newspaper.

is so weak that crossing the sea will put it out. Be just to me and love me with all your heart, and I shall ever be your kind, loving wife

Mary Clorine

You see though I have another husband I keep the name of my first.

5.3.6 Letter 35[21]

Honslerdyck, August 9th, [1678]

I have a hundred thousand pardons to beg of my dear, dear husband, who if I did not know to be very good and hope she loves me a little still I could not so much as hope to be forgiven. But those considerations make me, though very criminal for not having writ since I was well again, begin to believe that so charitable a body as yourself can't know how sorry I am for the fault and continue long angry. But if anything in the world can make amend for such a fault, I hope trusting you with a secret will, which though in itself 'tis not enough, yet I tell you 'tis one yet I would hardly give myself leave to think on it, nor nobody leave to speak of it, not so much as to myself; and that I have not yet writ the duchess[22] word, who has always charged me to do it in all her letters. It is what I am ashamed to say, but seeing it is to my husband I may, though I have reason to fear because the sea parts us you may believe it is a bastard; but yet I think upon a time of need I may make you own[23] it, since 'tis not out of the four seas; in the meantime, if you have any care of your own reputation, consequently you must have of your wife's too: you ought to keep this a secret, since if it should be known, you might get a pair of horns[24] and nothing else by the bargain. But, dearest Aurelia, you may be very well assured, though I have played the whore a little, I love you of all things in the world. Though I have spoke as you may think in jest all this while, yet for God's sake if you love me, don't tell it, because I would not have it known yet for all the world, since it cannot be above six or seven weeks at most, and whenever you do hear of it by other people never say that I said anything of it to you. In the meantime, I beg of you to say nothing as you hope ever to be trusted another time.

[21] Bathurst, pp. 91–2. The letter refers to Mary's first pregnancy, which (like all her pregnancies) did not come full term.

[22] *duchess* Mary of Modena, James, Duke of York's second wife, and thus Mary's stepmother.

[23] *own* accept responsibility for the paternity of.

[24] *horns* traditional sign of the cuckold, a man sexually deceived by his wife.

CHAPTER 6

The New 'Homosexual' Subculture, 1700–30

Introduction

In 1691, the Societies for the Reformation of Manners were formed to cleanse England of sin and degeneracy. Although the Societies had many targets, including prostitution, swearing, Sabbath-breaking, and general lewdness, they focused on sexual sin, and particularly on male same-sex erotic relationships, practices, and early communities, engineering the entrapment and subsequent prosecution of 'homosexuals', especially those who were apparently beginning to meet in groups regularly in London. The English naval commander Edward Rigby was only the Societies' earliest and most famous victim. In 1707 and 1726, the Societies instigated mass arrests of 'homosexuals', taken in raids on meeting places throughout London, including the so-called 'molly houses', as well as public parks and the Royal Exchange. Most of those arrested were later released, since most early eighteenth-century arrests for sodomy did not result in trials and convictions, much less executions, although trials and convictions for attempted sodomy, a non-felony, increased throughout the eighteenth century (Chapter 3, Introduction).

Samuel Stevens, probably an agent of the Societies, reported witnessing the activities at a molly house on 14 November 1725:

> I found between 40 and 50 men making love to one another, as they called it. Sometimes they would sit on one another's laps, kissing in a lewd manner, and using their hands indecently. Then they would get up, dance and make curtsies, and mimic the voices of women. O, fie, Sir! – Pray, sir. – Dear sir. Lord, how can you serve me so? – I swear I'll cry out. – You're a wicked devil. – And you're a bold face. – Eh ye little dear toad! Come, buss [i.e., kiss]! – Then they'd hug, and

> play, and toy, and go out by couples into another room on the same floor, to be married, as they called it. (qtd in Norton, *Mother* 55)

Trial transcripts and published polemics describing and condemning the new 'homosexual' subculture have, however, proved highly controversial sources, particularly when they have been used to date the shift from Renaissance to modern models of 'homosexual' identity. A comparison of the most influential writers on this topic – Alan Bray, Randolph Trumbach, Rictor Norton, and more recently Cameron McFarlane – suggest the complexity of the textual evidence, and the difficulty of interpreting it, as well as connecting it with actual relationships between men during this period, not to mention with nascent notions of modern 'homosexual' identity. Rictor Norton and Alan Bray essentially agree in seeing the molly houses and the new kind of 'homosexual' culture they supported and expressed as indicating the rise of new forms of 'homosexuality', involving markers of transvestism and effeminacy, and indicating 'a radical extension of the meaning of homosexuality' (Bray, *Homosexuality* 88–9); the largely 'socially diffused homosexuality' of the Renaissance and seventeenth century changed profoundly, becoming a 'continuing culture', with new material markers, such as 'clothes, gestures, language, particular buildings and public places' that came to connote 'homosexuality' for the subculture's participants and for its observers in the larger society (92). Richard Trumbach argues, in fact, that late-seventeenth and early eighteenth-century London saw the replacement of an earlier image of the rake or debauched man who had sex with both women and boys (see **8.9.1**) with the image of the male, effeminate 'homosexual', whose relations were strictly with other effeminate males, signalling 'a profound shift [...] in the conceptualization and practice of male homosexual behaviour' ('Sodomitical' 118).

There are problems, however, in treating intensely homophobic texts such as the ones selected below as correlating closely to actual social practices. For example, as McFarlane points out, Ward's *Second Part of the London Clubs* (1709) is excessively 'over-the-top' and short on crucial details: the molly house's location, how Ward discovered it, whether or not he actually observed the activities that took place there, and, if he did not, how he came upon his knowledge of its inner workings all remain unclear (McFarlane 63–5). The single most provocative aspect of Ward's account, however, is the mollies' staging of a mock birth and christening. Although modern critics continue to debate how closely, if at all, his description reflects an actual same-sex community practice,[1] clearly it is an integral part of the text's deliberately

[1] For some positions in this debate, see Norton, *Mother*, pp. 97–102 and McFarlane, pp. 60–8. It seems fairly clear that this description has socio-cultural precedent: Norton

excessive representation of the molly clubs as threats to England's natural, social, and reproductive order, a threat neatly eradicated by the Societies, the text's symbol of social conservatism (McFarlane 65–7). Ward's description, in fact, complicates our perception that the new 'homosexual' is characterized largely at the turn of the century by an increasingly strong link between sodomy and effeminacy. As McFarlane has demonstrated, Ward is able to present the mollies misogynistically as having degenerated into effeminacy, and he is able to present them as basing their new identity on an excessive, unsanctioned misogyny, a hatred of women that would eradicate the very continuation of the human species and the 'natural' order (66–8).

Like their sixteenth-century predecessors Bale (*Online Companion*), Beard (see **1.2.1**) and Prynne (see **1.3.1**), the following writers engage in virulent xeno-homophobia, painting 'homosexuality' as a foreign vice bent on the destruction of the English nation. However, they also begin to treat more systematically and at greater length the relationship between 'homosexuality,' masculinity, class identity, and the English national character. *Plain Reasons*, *Hell upon Earth*, Dunton's 'He-Strumpets', and Ward's *London Clubs* are all invested in a conservative gender and class hierarchy, where each text presents the sodomite's sexual and gender degeneracy as connected with his redefinition as a man whose erotic interests completely preclude women, but whose behaviours, roles, and attire are stereotypically feminine (Trumbach, 'Heterosexual Male' 114–15). *Plain Reasons* links the degeneration of the ideal English gentleman with sodomy, showing how much being a man, or more specifically a gentleman, in the eighteenth century was coming to be predicated on a 'normalization of homophobia' (Edelman 119). Moreover, in *Plain Reasons* and 'He-Strumpets', the writer's masculinity is predicated on his power over the effeminized male 'other' that the work depicts. In *Plain Reasons* men's kissing of each other, an increasingly common trope in early eighteenth-century descriptions of sodomy, encapsulates the image of the sodomite's body as penetrable and abject in contrast to that of the writer: masculine, impenetrable, self-controlled (McFarlane 46–9; Edelman 122–3).

'Lesbianism' receives only passing mention in *Plain Reasons* and appears in none of these other moral polemics. Like Dryden in his introduction to his translation of Juvenal's 'lesbian' orgy in 'Satire 6' (see **7.27.1**), *Plain Reasons* depicts female same-sex eroticism very conventionally as a foreign vice unknown to Englishwomen; the author dismisses it as the product of 'overly-refined' societies (Donoghue, *Passions* 258, 261). When the author considers women in the context of same-sex kissing, moreover, he betrays his unwillingness to attribute to women the same 'sodomitical' urges as men, largely

offers a number of sources that cite the practice of the mock birth. Cf. a community's performance of this ritual to shame a local sodomite in Rollinson, pp. 70–97.

because his solution to the problem of sodomy depends on women's active support of conventional gender and sexual roles.

Edward Rigby (*fl.* 1693–1711), English naval commander

The Societies for the Reformation of Manners' first victim in their systematic entrapment of 'homosexuals', Rigby was earlier acquitted of sodomy by a naval court. Although charged with and convicted of attempted sodomy with one William Minton, Rigby did not serve the year-long prison sentence, fleeing instead to the Continent, where he became a French naval captain. Although his ship, the French man-of-war the *Toulouse*, was captured by the English in 1711, Rigby escaped and continued his distinguished career. Rigby's arrest may be one of the first signs of London's new 'homosexual' subculture, with the preface to a 1699 edition of Castlehaven's trial for sodomy linking arrests in that year with 'the infamous example of that monster Ri[g]by, and other notorious sodomites' (A3). The ballads 'The Women's Complaint to Venus' and 'Venus's Reply' (below) respond to Rigby's conviction.

Editions

Norton, Rictor, ed., 'The Trial of Capt. Edward Rigby' (1698) (with transcriptions of relevant news-book accounts) and 'The Women's Complaint to Venus.' *Homosexuality in Eighteenth-Century England.*

6.1

From *An Account of the Proceedings Against Captain Edward Rigby*[1] (1698)

An indictment was found[2] against Captain Rigby, for that he, the seventh day of November last, did solicit, incite, and, as well by words as other ways, endeavour to persuade one William Minton (of about the age of nineteen years) to suffer him, the said Rigby, to commit the crime of sodomy with him, the said Minton. [...]

Captain Rigby being sensible of his guilt, and unwilling the same

[1] The title continues: 'at the sessions of Gaol-Delivery, held at Justice-Hall in the Old Bailey, on the Wednesday the seventh day of December, 1698, for intending to commit the abominable sin of sodomy, on the body of one William Minton'; *sessions of Gaol-Delivery*: a court held in order to try prisoners after an en masse clearing of their prison (*gaol*); *Old Bailey*: London's central criminal court.

[2] *found* ascertained to be valid.

should be disclosed to the world, would not therefore plead 'not guilty' to his indictment; neither would he confess the same, but demurred[3] to the indictment, in hopes, as his council alleged, that they might find some fault therein; but upon arguing the demurrer, the court were of [the] opinion the indictment was good, and therefore judgement was given against Rigby, which was the same as if he had pleaded guilty. And on the last day of the sessions,[4] the Council for the King demanded judgement against him, which could not be adequate to his crime; and for the information of the court, in order to give a just and exemplary judgement, prayed, that several affidavits[5] which were produced might be read, which accordingly were read; whereby it appeared, that on Saturday the fifth of November last, Minton standing in St James's Park to see the fireworks,[6] Rigby stood by him and took him by the hand, and squeezed it; put his privy member erected into Minton's hand; kissed him, and put his tongue into Minton's mouth, who being much astonished at these actions went from him; but Rigby pursued him, and accosted him again; and after much discourse prevailed with Minton to tell him where he lodged, and to meet him the Monday following about five o'clock at the George Tavern in the Pall Mall,[7] and to inquire for Number 4. Minton the next day acquainted Charles Coates, Esquire[8] (with whom he lived) with what had happened to him the night before, and desired his advice and direction therein; who with a worthy divine then present (being willing to detect and punish the villainy designed by Rigby) directed Minton to apply himself to Thomas Railton, Esquire, a justice of the peace for Middlesex; who being informed of what passed between Rigby and Minton, appointed his clerk with a constable and two other persons, to go with Minton to the George Tavern, who were to stay in some room adjoining to

3 *demurred* A defendant who 'demurs' admits that the facts of the crime alleged by the Crown (the plaintiffs and prosecution) are true, but that they are not sufficient to entitle the plaintiffs to prevail in their action. Rigby's demurrer probably declared that errors in law in the indictment meant the invalidation of the prosecution. When no errors were found, Rigby found himself convicted on his own agreement to the facts of the crime.

4 *sessions* court held four times a year.

5 *affidavits* written statements used in a trial as judicial proof.

6 *St James's Park* notorious place for sexual assignations and prostitution in Restoration London; popular 'homosexual cruising ground', a place where men could find other men for the purposes of sex (Norton, *Mother*, pp. 66, 71, 90–1); *fireworks*: for Guy Fawkes' Day.

7 *George Tavern … Mall* Cf. the molly house at the Royal Oak alehouse, in the same London area (Norton, *Mother*, p. 58).

8 *Esquire* title for young men who were members of the highest ranks of the English gentry. Coates was Minton's employer and Thomas Bray's associate (Norton, *Mother*, p. 44).

the room whereinto Minton should go: and if any violence should be offered to him, upon crying out 'Westminster', the constable and his assistants should immediately enter the room.

That on Monday the seventh of November last, about four o'clock in the afternoon, Rigby came to the George Tavern, and left Number 4 at the bar, with directions, that if any inquired for that number to send them to him; after Rigby had been about an hour at the Tavern (Minton not coming), Rigby called up one of the drawers,[9] and in a passionate manner, bid him go to Minton's lodgings and inquire for a young gentleman; and if he were within, to tell him a gentleman stayed for him at the George Tavern. The drawer accordingly went, but Minton not being within, the drawer returned that answer to Rigby.

That about six o'clock Minton came to the George Tavern, inquired for Number 4, and was showed into the room where Rigby was, and the constable and his assistants were placed in a room adjoining. Rigby seemed much pleased upon Minton's coming, and drank to him in a glass of wine and kissed him, took him by the hand, put his tongue into Minton's mouth, and thrust Minton's hand into his (Rigby's) breeches, saying, 'He had raised his lust to the highest degree.' Minton thereupon asked, 'How can it be? A woman was only fit for that.' Rigby answered, 'Damn 'em, they are all poxed.[10] I'll have nothing to do with them.' Then Rigby sitting on Minton's lap kissed him several times, putting his tongue into his mouth, asked him, 'if he should f— him;' 'how can that be,' asked Minton. 'I'll show you,' answered Rigby, 'for it's no more than was done in our forefathers' time.' And then to incite Minton thereto, further spoke most blasphemous words, and said, 'That the French king[11] did it and the Czar of Muscovy made Alexander, a carpenter, a prince for that purpose,' and affirmed, 'he had seen the Czar of Muscovy through a hole at sea lie with Prince Alexander.'[12] Then Rigby kissed Minton several times, putting his tongue in his mouth, and taking Minton in his arms, 'wished he might lie with him all night, and his lust was provoked to that degree, he had ——[13] in his breeches, but notwithstanding he could f—[14] him.' Minton thereupon said, 'Sure you cannot do it here.' 'Yes,' answered

[9] *drawers* bartenders.

[10] *poxed* infected with sexually transmitted disease.

[11] *French king* Louis XIV (1638–1715) had many heterosexual affairs, but the reference is probably to Louis's brother Philippe, Duc d'Orléans (1640–1701), perhaps the most famous 'homosexual' in French history (after Henri III).

[12] *Czar of Muscovy* and *Prince Alexander* Peter the Great (1672–1725) and his young lover Alexander Danilovich Menshikov; they visited England in 1698 (Norton, *Mother*, p. 45).

[13] —— ejaculated.

[14] *f—* fuck.

Rigby, 'I can,' and took Minton to a corner of the room, and put his hand into Minton's breeches, desiring him to pull them down, who answered, 'he would not, but he (Rigby) might do what he pleased;' thereupon Rigby pulled down Minton's breeches, turned away his shirt, put his finger to Minton's fundament,[15] and applied his body close to Minton's, who feeling something warm touch his skin, put his hand behind him, and took hold of Rigby's privy member, and said to Rigby, 'I have now discovered your base inclinations, I will expose you to the world, to put a stop to these crimes;' and thereupon Minton went towards the door. Rigby stopped him and drew his sword, upon which Minton gave a stamp with his foot, and cried out 'Westminster'; then the constable and his assistants came into the room, and seized Rigby, who offered the constable a gratuity[16] to let him go, which he refusing, carried Rigby before Sir Henry Dutton Colt,[17] before whom Minton charged Rigby (who was present) with the fact[18] to the effect before related; who being asked by Sir Henry Colt, whether the fact Minton had charged him with were true, Rigby denied not that the charge against him was true, only objected against some inconsiderable circumstances, which no ways tended to the lessening of the charge.

That after all the informations were read, Rigby was asked by the court, 'what he had to say for himself': he desired that a gentleman's affidavit, who was present when this matter was transacted might be read; the court told him that 'that gentleman stood indicted in the same indictment with him, for being aiding, advising, and assisting to him in committing his crime, and therefore could not be an evidence for him.'[19] Rigby was asked by the court 'what further he had to say': he insisted on his innocency, that he was misadvised by his council in demurring the indictment, which if he had known had been confessing of the fact in case the court had been of [the] opinion that the indictment was sufficient, he would not have done it;[20] but seeing the law was so he must submit to it; he said he was drunk, and might kiss Minton several times. To which it was answered by the King's Council, that 'his (Rigby's) council had well advised him, and he knew his guilt to be such, that it would be proved by

15 *fundament* anus.

16 *gratuity* bribe.

17 *Sir Henry Dutton Colt* (d. 1731), First Baronet Colt, Lord Chief Justice; in Kent, he condemned four sodomites to death.

18 *fact* crime.

19 *gentleman … him* probably, Edward FitzGerald: he accused the minister William Tipping of pressuring him to falsely accuse Rigby of sodomy. Rejecting the accusation, the court recommended perjury charges against FitzGerald and a co-accuser (Norton, *Mother*, pp. 47–8).

20 *which … it* i.e., if Rigby had understood the consequences of demurring, he would not have done so (see **n3**).

three or four witnesses beyond all contradiction, and therefore Rigby demurred to the indictment in hopes thereby his crime would not be disclosed, as it must have been if he had pleaded not guilty to his indictment, and submitted to a trial; but as the fact had now been made public in court; and it also appearing that he was not drunk when he committed it.'

It was therefore prayed by the King's Council that the court would give an exemplary judgement against him, for that crime of which, by his own confession, he stood convicted, and was not in its nature to be aggravated.[21]

And the judgement which was pronounced by the court against Rigby was, viz.

That he stand three several[22] days in the pillory for the space of two hours, from eleven o'clock to one, in each of those days.

The first day over against the George Tavern in the Pall Mall; the second day at Charing Cross;[23] and the third day at Temple Bar.[24]

That he pay a fine of £1,000 to the king.

That he lie in prison for a year, after he shall have paid his fine.

And that before he be discharged out of prison, he shall find sufficient sureties for his good behaviour for seven years.

6.2

From *A Collection of the Most Choice and Private Poems*[1] (1699)

6.2.1 The Women's Complaint to Venus (1698)

How happy were good English faces
  Till monsieur from France[2]

[21] *aggravated* Certain crimes could be made more serious by their surrounding circumstances (*aggravated*); the Crown argues that Rigby's crime is not subject to this kind of gradation, presumably because if Rigby had indeed penetrated Minton, the crime would be sodomy, instead of attempted sodomy. In other words, Rigby's crime of attempted sodomy cannot be *aggravated* because what he has done is as 'bad' as it gets.

[22] *several* separate.

[23] *Charing Cross* on the main road between Westminster and London; a site of public executions and corporal punishment.

[24] *Temple Bar* south-west boundary between the cities of London and Westminster.

[1] MS. Collection. Reprinted by permission of Brotherton Collection, Leeds University Library.

[2] *monsieur from France* reflecting the English stereotype of sodomy and sexual sin generally as foreign vices.

Taught pego a dance[3]
To the tune of 'Old Sodom's Embraces'.[4]

But now we are quite out of fashion:
Poor whores may be nuns
Since men turn their guns[5]
And vent on each other their passion.

In the reign of good Charles the Second,
Full many a jade[6]
A lady was made,
And the issue right noble was reckoned.[7]

But now we find to our sorrow,
We are overrun
By sparks of the bum[8]
And peers of the realm of Gomorrah.[9]

The beaus too, whom most we relied on,[10]
At night make a punk[11]
Of him that's first drunk,
Though unfit for the sport as John Dryden.[12]

The soldiers, whom next we put trust in,
No widow can tame
Or virgin reclaim,
But at the wrong place will be thrusting.

[3] *pego* penis.

[4] *Old Sodom's Embraces* referring to the formula that followed printed ballad titles: 'To the tune of [...]'.

[5] *gun* penis.

[6] *jade* whore.

[7] *In ... reckoned* Charles II raised to the peerage many of his mistresses and the children he had with them.

[8] *sparks ... bum* sodomites; *spark*: effeminate young man.

[9] *Gomorrah* See **1.1.1**.

[10] *beau* licentious, dandyish young man. Cf. **6.4.1 n3**; **6.6 n2**; and **6.7.1 n6**.

[11] *punk* prostitute; whore.

[12] *as John Dryden* referring to Dryden's austere life; his only sexual 'scandal' was his mistress, Anne Reeves.

Fair Venus, thou goddess of beauty,
   Receive our complaint,
   Make Rigby recant,
And the soldiers henceforth do their duty.

6.2.2 Venus's Reply (1699)

Why nymphs these pitiful stories,
   But you are to blame,
   And have got a new game
Called flats with a swinging clitoris.[13]

Besides I have heard of wax tapers
   With which you get up
   And each other tup[14]
To cure the green sickness and vapours.[15]

I am told by a delicate seignior[16]
   Some matrons do ease
   Their lust and so please
They've not been lain with these ten years.

Your Frogmore frolics discover[17]
   Some reasons of art
   So play the man's part:
You are for no masculine lover.

[13] *flats* female same-sex intercourse; *swinging*: i.e., 'swiving' (copulating with).

[14] *Besides ... tup* referring to wax candles as makeshift dildos. Cf. *The Sappho-An* (1735?/49?): 'The chandler's art oft feeds a double flame, / First lights to bed and then her lust doth tame, / Warmed by the prurient, hot, corroding place, / The frequent motion working on apace; / Soon as the coming joy with her is felt, / The giving candle condescends to melt' (Canto 2); *tup*: mount sexually (originally, 'of a ram mounting an ewe').

[15] *green sickness* chlorosis (severe anaemia); believed caused by the virginal body's frustrated desire for sexual intercourse; orgasm could cure this condition by releasing long-retained and corrupted female 'seed' (semen); *vapours*: psycho-somatic hysteria, caused by a build-up of exhalations (gasses) in the uterus, which could be released by sexual activity.

[16] *by ... seignior* BL MS. Harley 7315 has 'with a delicate seignior', perhaps 'a dildo'.

[17] *Frogmore* Marginalia: 'L[ord] Fitzharding's seat near Windsor', referring to female same-sex sexual activity (*frolics*) at this peer's house.

At all which I am so offended,
   My son at men's hearts[18]
   Will throw no more darts
Till your lust and your lives are amended.

Forsake but these odd ways of sinning,
   And I'll undertake
   The arrantest rake[19]
Shall swinge you as at the beginning.[20]

6.3

The Women-Hater's Lamentation[1] (1707)

Editions

Norton, Rictor, ed., 'The Women-Hater's Lamentation (1707).' *Eighteenth-Century British Erotica II*, 5.83–6.

—, 'The Women-Hater's Lamentation (1707).' *Homosexuality in Eighteenth-Century England.*

To the tune of 'Ye Pretty Sailors All'.

Ye injured females see
Justice without the laws,[2]
Seeing the injury[3]
Has thus revenged your cause.

For those that are so blind
Your beauties to despise,

[18] *son* Cupid.
[19] *arrantest* most thoroughgoing; *rake*: man addicted to sensual and sexual pleasure.
[20] *swinge* See **n13**.

[1] Reprinted by permission of Guildhall Library, City of London. The title continues: 'Or, A New copy of verses on the fatal end of Mr. Grant, a woollen draper, and two others that cut their throats or hanged themselves in the Counter; with the discovery of near hundred more that are accused for unnatural despising the fair sex, and intriguing with one another'; *woollen draper*: dealer in woollen cloth; *Counter*: prison in Southwark (London). For reproductions of the ballad's accompanying woodcuts, see Norton (above), and Bray, *Homosexuality*, pp. 83, 94–5.
[2] *justice … laws* i.e., the accused men killed themselves before trial.
[3] *injury* in-custody suicides.

And slight your charms, will find
Such fate will always rise.

Of all the crimes that men
Through wicked minds do act,
There is not one of them
Equals this brutal fact.[4]

Nature they lay aside
To gratify their lust;
Women they hate beside,
Therefore their fate was just.

Ye women-haters, say
What does your breasts inspire,
That in a brutal way,
You your own sex admire?

Woman you disapprove,
(The chief of earthly joys),
You that are deaf to love,
And all the sex despise.

But see the fatal end
That does such crimes pursue:
Unnat'ral death attend
Unnat'ral lusts in you.

A crime by men abhorred,
Nor heaven can abide,
Of which when Sodom shared,[5]
She justly was destroyed.

But now, the sum to tell,
(Though they plead innocence),
These by their own hands fell,
Accused for this offence.

[4] *brutal fact* animalistic or bestial crime.
[5] *Sodom* See **1.1.1**.

A hundred more we hear
Did to this club belong,[6]
But now they scattered are,
For this has broke the gang.

Shop-keepers some there were,
And men of good repute,
Each vowed a bachelor,
Unnat'ral lust pursued.

Ye women-haters, then,
Take warning by their shame,
Your brutal lusts restrain,
And own a nobler flame.

Woman the chiefest bliss
That heaven e'er bestowed:
Oh, be ashamed of this,
You're by base lust subdued.

This piece of justice then
Has well revenged their cause,
And shows unnat'ral lust
Is cursed without the laws.

John Dunton (1659–1732), bookseller and writer

A periodical writer and successful Whig propagandist, Dunton claimed to have published some six hundred works, including devotional and political tracts, miscellanies and chapbooks.

Editions

Norton, Rictor, ed., 'The He-Strumpets (1707; 1710).' *Eighteenth-Century British Erotica II*, 5.87–96.

—, ed., 'The He-Strumpets (1707; 1710).' *Homosexuality in Eighteenth-Century England.*

6 *hundred … belong* For the numbers arrested (1701–20), see Norton, *Mother*, pp. 51–2.

6.4

From *Athenianism* (1710)[1]

6.4.1 Project IV. The He-Strumpets: A Satire on the Sodomite-Club

[...]
Lewd cracks repent, for 'tis the news,[2]
Your tails have burnt so many beaus,[3]
That now he-whores are come in use.[4]
Yes jilts! 'tis proved and must be said,[5]
Your tails are grown so lewd and bad,
That now men's tails have all the trade,[6]
Yet cracks are saints compared with them,
Who leave the whores to pick up men,
All cracks are found so full of ails,[7]
A new society prevails,
Called s—d—ites: men worse than goats,[8]
Who dress themselves in petticoats,
To whore as O—born did with O—tes.[9]
Modesty scarce can give a name
To such a catamitish flame;[10]
This lust as far as Sodom came;[11]
In Sodom men were so unclean,
That when the angels dressed like men,
They'd ask to fornicate with them.

[1] From the revised, enlarged fourth edn.

[2] *cracks* female prostitutes.

[3] *tail* vulva; specifically, 'the opening of the vagina'; *burnt*: given syphilis [to]; *beau*: elsewhere, the 'beau' is an effeminate 'homosexual' (see **6.7.1 n6**), but here, general licentiousness is emphasized. Cf. **6.2.1 n10**; and **6.6 n2**.

[4] *he-whores* male prostitutes.

[5] *jilts* whores.

[6] *tails* here, 'arses'.

[7] *ails* infections.

[8] *s—d—ites* sodomites.

[9] *O—born* and *O—tes* William *Osborne* (n.d.) was among a group of men who brought a charge of sodomy against the infamous informant Titus *Oates* (1648–1705). See Oates's *Narrative of the Horrid Conspiracy* (1680).

[10] *catamitish* sodomitical (referring to the receptive role in anal intercourse).

[11] *Sodom* See **1.1.1**.

Then sodomy is the abuse
Of either sex against the use
Of Nature, that should the babe produce.
[…]
The men who thus their lust confine
Do dote upon he-concubine,
Do ply (that's whore) near the Exchange:[12]
Here men turn cracks – 'tis wondrous strange:
Yet very true, for these exclude
All women from their interlude,[13]
Yet act what's carnal, vile, and rude.
The very 'Change can scarce escape
This loathsome, nasty Sodom rape.
But what's your number, brutes? Be free:
'Tis said your gang is forty-three
That whore (as 'twere) in sodomy.
He-whore! The word's a paradox:
But there's a club hard by the Stocks,[14]
Where men give unto men the pox.[15]
Such whoring (for I'll call it so)
Is against God and Nature too,
And makes man's tail a sort of stew.[16]
Such rob the women of their rights
(Their tails could keep the peace a' nights)
But for this club of sodomites.
These dote on men, and some on boys,
And quite abandon female joys,
To act a vice so full of shame,
That brutes would fly, and blush to name.
For even goats are grown so poor
That he with he does never whore.

[Dunton here contrasts the sodomite and exclusively heterosexual animals.]

Sukey (for so 'tis said you greet[17]
The men you pick up in the street)

[12] *Exchange* See **6.6 n21**.
[13] *interlude* entertainment.
[14] Dunton's footnote: 'Stocks-Market' (i.e., London meat and fish market).
[15] *pox* syphilis.
[16] *stew* brothel; whore.
[17] *Sukey* male 'homosexual' (familiar form of 'Susan' or 'Susanna').

En't you a monster thus to quench,[18]
And make men's tails a sort of wench?
In short (and worse cannot be said)
You are he-strumpets in the bed.
Oh fie! Remember Sodom's miss:[19]
Unnat'ral tails was all their vice;
Your flame is worse, that thus rebel,
For sodomy's the flame of hell.
O J—nes! O sodomitish wretch![20]
Should you be damned you could not grutch;[21]
You make your very country blush.
He-lust! It looks so vile in print,
There's none will stand a trial in't.
They J—nes no sooner did accuse,
And two in'th' Compter full as loose,[22]
But they straight fly to hempen noose,
Jermain a clerk that lived in'th' East,[23]
Ber—den, a he-whoring beast,[24]
And forty s—d—ites at least,[25]
No sooner did their lewdness flame,
But cut their very throats for shame.
Thus of all tails men's are the worst,
Not but the females' vie in lust;
For women's tails so wanton grow
They breed unnat'ral vices too.
They change the nat'ral use and feature
Into a crime which ruins nature:
Yea, sodomy they will permit,
(A vice they never can commit)
Though kissing each other's something lik't.
There's b—ry, a beastly sin,[26]

18 *thus to quench* to satisfy your desire [with same-sex sexual acts].

19 *miss* sin.

20 *J—nes* Jones (Norton, 'He-Strumpets', *Homosexuality in Eighteenth-Century England*).

21 *grutch* complain.

22 *Compter* Counter (see **6.3 n1**).

23 Dunton's footnote: '*Jermain*, late clerk of St Dunstan's in the East, who being charged with s—d—y, cut his throat with a razor.'

24 *Ber—den* unidentified.

25 *s—d—ites* sodomites.

26 *b—ry* buggery (here, sex with an animal; also frequently used of hetero- or 'homosexual' anal intercourse).

Is not a vice too lewd for them:
For 'tis not forty years ago,
A crack was hanged [f]or whoring so;
Her sparks were but a dog or two.[27]

[Dunston accuses the common female prostitute of being syphilitic as well as willing to engage in anal sex and bestiality. He then satirizes women who are sexually free but protest that they are not whores because they accept no money for their favours.]

Thus tails have been unnatural,
In men, in wives, in cracks, in all:
But still (as I observed before)
The sodomite does highest soar;
For men with very men will whore;
With men! They'll whore with incubus;[28]
If he's they care not what's the curse:
Their tail's so hot, they can't be worse.
Nor man nor turkey can escape;[29]
Scarce Jack himself avoid a rape:[30]
All must go padlocked, if the rogue
Should bring this he-vice into vogue.
If men invent new l—ry,[31]
Suspect thy stable's chastity:[32]
Or, which is yet a lewder flight,
Believe thyself a sodomite.
Thus tail of man (add women to't)
When Sodom's vice has burnt it out,
It is no tail, but perfect brute.[33]
Brute! Oh no! It tempts to evil;
It is no brute, but perfect devil.

[27] *sparks* lovers. Cf. **6.2.1 n8**.

[28] *incubus* demon who takes on male form to have sex with sleeping women.

[29] *turkey* believed a licentious, syphilis-ridden bird (object of King Bolloxinian's anal lust in *Sodom*: see **8.25.4 n59**).

[30] Dunton's footnote: 'The author of this satire.'

[31] *l—ry* lechery.

[32] *thy stable's chastity* i.e., because bestiality may become popular.

[33] Literally, 'It is no *tail* (human arse) but a *perfect brute* (a completely animalistic part)'; punningly, 'It is no *tale* (fiction, invention), but a *perfect* (true) *bruit* (rumour, report)'.

Edward (Ned) Ward (1667–1731), satirist and journalist

Writer of more than a hundred works, Ward specialized in satire focused on London social types and professions, as well as London 'low-life'. Tory supporter and high-church Anglican, Ward's political satires netted him one conviction for seditious libel (1706).

Editions

Norton, Rictor, ed., 'The Second Part, of the London Clubs (1709).' *Eighteenth-Century British Erotica II*, 5.111–20.

—, ed., 'The Mollies Clubs (1709–1710).' *Homosexuality in Eighteenth-Century England.*

6.5

From *The Second Part of the London Clubs* (1709)[1]

6.5.1 The Sodomites, Or Mollies Club

There are a particular gang of sodomitical wretches in town,[2] who call themselves mollies,[3] and are so far degenerated from all masculine deportment or manly exercises that they rather fancy themselves women, imitating all the little vanities that custom has reconciled to the female sex, affecting to speak, walk, tattle, curtsey, cry, scold, and mimic all manner of effeminacy. At a certain tavern in the city, whose sign I shall not mention because I am unwilling to fix an odium[4] on the house, they have a settled and constant meeting.[5] When they are met together, their usual practice is to mimic a female gossiping,[6] and fall into all the impertinent tittle-tattle that a merry society of good wives can be subject to. Not long since they had cushioned up the belly of one of their sodomitical brethren, or rather sisters, according to female dialect,[7] disguising him in a woman's nightgown, sarsenet-hood, and

[1] The other clubs are 'The No-Nose Club'; 'The Beaus Club'; 'The Farting Club'; and 'The Quacks Club'.

[2] *town* London.

[3] *mollies* sodomites; male 'homosexuals'. Cf. **6.6 n7**.

[4] *odium* shame.

[5] *settled … meeting* i.e., regular, rule-governed meeting.

[6] *gossiping* originally, a celebration for a child's birth or christening; later, a meeting of idly talking women.

[7] *female dialect* slang of the burgeoning 'molly' subculture of eighteenth-century London (Norton, *Mother*, pp. 92–6).

night-rail,[8] who when the company were met, was to mimic the wry faces of the groaning woman, to be delivered of a jointed-baby[9] they had provided, and to undergo all the formalities of a lying-in.[10] The wooden offspring to be afterwards christened, whilst one in a high-crowned hat, [and an] old beldam's pinner,[11] representing a country-midwife, and another dizened up[12] in a housewife's coif for a nurse, and all the rest of an impertinent decorum of a christening.[13]

And for the further promotion of their unbecoming mirth, everyone was to talk of their husbands and children, one extolling the virtues of her husband, another the genius and wit of their children; whilst a third would express himself sorrowfully under the character of a widow.

Thus everyone in his turn makes scoff of the little effeminacy and weaknesses which women are subject to when gossiping o'er their cups, on purpose to extinguish that natural affection which is due to the fair sex, and to turn their juvenile desires towards preternatural polotions.[14] No sooner have they ended their feasts and run through all the ceremonies of [a] theatrical way of gossiping, than they begin to enter upon their beastly obscenities, that no man who is not sunk into a state of devilism[15] can think on without blushing: which practice they continued till they were happily routed by the conduct of some of the under-agent to the Reforming Society;[16] so that several of them were brought to open punishment, which happily put a period to[17] their scandalous revels.

Hell upon Earth

After recounting London's vices and crimes, *Hell* describes the fop's vanity in his appearance, to which he will sacrifice the satisfaction of his other vicious desires; stupid, imitative, and 'composed of pride, ignorance, conceit,

8 *sarsenet* soft silk; *night-rail*: dressing-gown.

9 *jointed-baby* doll with jointed limbs.

10 *lying-in* all-female gathering of a pregnant woman's friends and relations at her labour and delivery.

11 [*and an*] Norton's emendation of 'I am' (from 1710 edn) (*Eighteenth-Century British Erotica* II, 5.388n); *beldam's pinner*: old woman's cap.

12 *dizened up* decked out.

13 *the … christening* Cf. similar mock births, one using a jointed doll, one a Cheshire cheese (Norton, *Mother*, p. 98). See Chapter 6, Introduction.

14 *preternatural polotions* unnatural pollutions (usually, ejaculation from masturbation).

15 *devilism* devilish behaviour.

16 *under-agent to the Reforming Society* investigator for the Societies for the Reformation of Manners.

17 *put … to* brought to an end.

vainglory and imagination', the fop 'knows no other end of his being than to swagger in the streets, and resort to public places to be gazed at' (35). *Hell* does not directly connect the fop with 'homosexual' desire, but does include the following anecdote.

6.6

From *Hell upon Earth* (1729)

Last summer I happened to be at Bristol, and coming up in the stagecoach I was agreeably diverted with a narrative that is well worth notice. There was in company a grave merchant, an ancient gentlewoman, a young Irishman,[1] two young ladies and myself. The merchant said little, the old gentlewoman heard little, the beau[2] and the two ladies had all the discourse, and I sat as judge to determine the controversy. The theme was love, which was argued and defended with a great deal of judgement on both sides. The first night on the road he took me aside and told me, he believed them to be good-natured ladies, for that they had granted him an appointment, and that he doubted not but ere morning to gain the ascendant over them; and accordingly next day affirmed to me, he had been happy in their embraces. This he confirmed with such circumstantial probabilities, that I readily believed it matter of fact. But how was he struck with shame and confusion, when he found the two young ladies metamorphosed into two young gentlemen, that for their diversion, and to pass the time away, had purposely put on the disguise to conceal their sex, and had assumed an air suitable to their appearance, to mortify some fond, conceited, passionate, whining *enamorado*.[3]

[After describing how people waste their time (gossiping, gaming, visiting, etc.), *Hell* finally discusses sodomy (on page 41 of a 62-page treatise), the first time it has been mentioned since the title page.]

The late proceedings in our courts of law have furnished us with ample proofs that this town abounds too plentifully with a sect of brutish creatures called sodomites; a sect that ought to be excluded from all civil society and human conversation.[4] They exceed the worst beasts of the field in the

[1] *Irishman* 'homosexuality' was conventionally represented as a foreign (especially, Catholic) vice in early modern England.

[2] *beau* foppish, licentious young man. Cf. **6.2.1 n10**; **6.4.1 n3**; and **6.7.1 n6**.

[3] *enamorado* lover.

[4] *conversation* social interaction.

filthiness of their abominations. The birds of the air couple male and female to propagate generation, and every animal moves by a natural instinct; but man, exclusive of all others, forms ideas destructive to himself, and grows fond of new inventions which are repugnant to divine institution and the fundamental laws of nature; he is grown hardened in iniquity, having abandoned himself to all manner of vice, and is not ashamed to act crimes which expose him to the severity of the laws and the contempt of the world. I have heard that one Tolson, who lately kept a brandy-shop at Charing Cross,[5] and was transported for felony, whose constitution was so depraved and ruined that he could contain nothing within him, and who was not ashamed to confess that he received that debility by human conversation and the vile practice of buggery;[6] and that once having caught a foot-soldier in bed with his wife, he insisted upon no other satisfaction than to commit the detestable sin of sodomy with him, which the other complied with, and so the affair was made easy. It is a melancholy sight to see men in full strength and vigour go to public executions unpitied and unlamented, loaded with the highest guilt, that can neither hope or expect any mercy in this, and may justly dread the punishments in the world to come. The greatest criminal has some people that may drop some pitying expressions for his unhappy and untimely fate and condole his dismal circumstances; while those persons who fall by the laws for sodomy can expect neither pity [n]or compassion.

It would be a pretty scene to behold them in their clubs and cabals, how they assume the air and affect the name of 'Madam' or 'Miss', 'Betty' or 'Molly',[7] with a chuck[8] under the chin, and 'Oh, you bold pullet, I'll break your eggs,'[9] and then frisk[10] and walk away to make room for another, who thus accosts the affected lady with, 'Where have you been, you saucy queen?[11] If I catch you strolling and caterwauling,[12] I'll beat the milk out of your breasts, I will so'; with a great many other expressions of buffoonery and ridiculous affectation. If they can procure a young smug-faced[13] fellow,

[5] *Charing Cross* See **6.1 n23**.

[6] *human conversation* i.e., 'natural', heterosexual intercourse; *buggery*: bestiality or anal intercourse (either heterosexual or 'homosexual'). Cf. **6.4.1 n26**.

[7] *Betty* sodomite (cf. the older meaning: 'man who does woman's work'); *Molly*: sodomite (cf. the older meanings: 'lower-class woman'; 'prostitute').

[8] *chuck* playful or amorous tap.

[9] *pullet* young, inexperienced person (usually said of women). Cf. **8.29.3 n56**; *eggs*: testicles.

[10] *frisk* have a lively sexual encounter [with].

[11] *queen* originally, 'whore or hussy' (possible, but not necessarily, a prostitute). *OED* says the meaning 'ostentatiously effeminate, male homosexual' dates to 1893.

[12] *strolling* sexually soliciting; *caterwauling*: behaving lecherously.

[13] *smug-faced* sleek-faced.

they never grudge any expense, and it is remarkable these effeminate villains are much fonder of a new convert than a bully[14] would be of a new mistress.[15]

They have also their walks[16] and appointments,[17] to meet and pick up[18] one another, and their particular houses of resort[19] to go to, because they dare not trust themselves in an open tavern.[20] About twenty of these sort of houses have been discovered, besides the nocturnal assemblies of great numbers of the like vile persons, what they call the markets, which are the Royal Exchange, Lincoln's Inn Bog-Houses, the South-side of St James's Park, the piazzas of Covent Garden, St Clement's churchyard, etc.[21]

[The tract concludes with portraits of cynics contemptuous of religion, social snobs, worldly men, thieves and housebreakers, blasphemers and cursers, and finally hack writers.]

Plain Reasons for the Growth of Sodomy in England (1728?; 1730?)

Later plagiarized in its entirety in *Satan's Harvest Home* (1749), *Plain Reasons* begins with a nostalgic description of the ideal English gentleman's upbringing: educated for scholarship and war, the boy became a man dedicated to serving 'his king, his country, and his family' (5), reproducing his virtues and physical integrity in his children, being himself free 'from debauch'. This traditional upbringing has been superseded, however, by a pampering of young gentlemen, effeminating them so that they are unfit for friendship with a man or marriage to a woman: 'What can be expected from such an enervated effeminate animal? [...] Should [his wife] at last bring him a child, what can we hope from so crazy a constitution? But a

14 *bully* whore's protector.

15 *mistress* whore.

16 *walks* places of habitual resort.

17 *appointments* assignations.

18 *pick up* approach someone (especially, a stranger) in a public place for sexual purposes.

19 *houses of resort* brothels; more specifically, 'molly houses'.

20 *tavern* Although generally more respectable than the alehouse, the *tavern* was still a well known centre of illicit sexual activity.

21 *the markets ... etc.* *Royal Exchange*: fashionable London shopping district; *Lincoln's Inn*: one of the four Inns of Court, where young men were trained in law; *bog-house*: public toilet; *St James's Park*: See **6.1 n6**; *Covent Garden*: notorious for prostitution and brothels; *piazza*: infamous meeting place for heterosexual and 'homosexual' assignations. See Norton, *Mother*, pp. 70–91; *St Clement's churchyard*: parish burial ground at this Eastcheap (London) church.

feeble, unhealthy infant, scarce worth the rearing; whilst the father, instead of being the head of the family, makes it seem as if it were governed by two women' (9).

Editions

Norton, Rictor, ed., 'Plain Reasons (1730?).' *Eighteenth-Century British Erotica II*, 5.189–218.

6.7

From *Plain Reasons for the Growth of Sodomy in England*

6.7.1 Chapter II. The Effeminacy of Our Men's Dress and Manners, Particularly Their Kissing Each Other

I am confident no age can produce anything so preposterous as the present dress of those gentlemen who call themselves 'pretty fellows': their head-dress, especially, wants nothing but a suit of pinners[1] to make 'em downright women. But this may be easily accounted for, as they would appear as soft as possible to each other, anything of manliness being diametrically opposite to such unnatural practices, so they cannot too much invade the dress of the sex they would represent. And yet with all this, the present garb of our young gentlemen is most mean[2] and unbecoming. 'Tis difficult to know a gentleman from a footman by their present habits. The low-heeled pump is an emblem of their low spirits; the great harness buckle is the height of affectation; the silk waistcoat all be-laced, with a scurvy blue coat like a livery frock[3] has something so poorly preposterous it quite enrages me; I blush to see 'em aping the running footmen,[4] and poising a great oaken plant, fitter for a bailiff's follower[5] than a gentleman. But what renders all more intolerable is the hair stroked over before and cocked

[1] *pinner* close-fitting women's cap (usually worn by women of high status).

[2] *mean* debased; lower-class.

[3] *scurvy* contemptible, worthless; *livery frock*: clothing marking a person as the servant of a particular family.

[4] *running footman* servant who ran before his master's carriage.

[5] *poising … follower* holding a stout staff ready to use on people apprehended by the bailiff; this traditional 'peasant' weapon is set up implicitly against the gentleman's traditional weapon: the sword.

up behind, with a comb sticking in it, as if it were just ready to receive a head-dress. Nay, I am told some of our tip-top beaus[6] dress their heads on quilted hair caps,[7] to make 'em look more womanish; so that Master Molly[8] has nothing to do but slip on his head-cloths[9] and he is an errant[10] woman, his rueful face excepted; but even that can be amended with paint,[11] which is as much in vogue among our gentlemen as with the ladies in France. [...] But to see 'em dressed for a ball or assembly in a parti-coloured silk coat is the height of my aversion. They had better have a mantua and petticoat[12] at once, than to mince the matter thus, or do things by halves.

But of all the customs effeminacy has produced, none more hateful, predominant and pernicious than that of men's kissing each other. This fashion was brought over from Italy (the mother and nurse of sodomy),[13] where the master is oftener intriguing with his page[14] than a fair lady. And not only in that country but in France, which copy from them, the contagion is diversified, and the ladies (in the nunneries) are criminally amorous of each other,[15] in a method too gross for expression. I must be so partial to my own countrywomen to affirm, or at least hope, they claim no share of this charge; but must confess, when I see two ladies kissing and slopping[16] each other in a lascivious manner, and frequently repeating it, I am shocked to the last degree; but not so much as when I see two fulsome fellows slavering every time they meet, squeezing each other's hand, and other like indecent symptoms. And though many gentlemen of worth are oftentimes, out of pure good manners, obliged to give into it, yet the land will never be purged of its abominations till this unmanly, unnatural usage be totally abolished, for it is the first inlet to the detestable sin of sodomy.

Under this pretext, vile catamites[17] make their preposterous addresses, even in the very streets; nor can anything be more shocking than to see a couple of creatures, who wear the shape of men, kiss and slaver each other

[6] *beau* fop; effeminate 'homosexual'. Cf. **6.2.1 n10**; **6.4.1 n3**; **6.6 n2**; and **8.29.2 n34**.

[7] *dress* 'do up' one's hair; *caps*: forms on which wigs (here, 'heads') were prepared for wearing.

[8] *Molly* See **6.5.1 n3** and **6.6 n7**.

[9] *head-cloths* parts of an ornamental attire for the female head.

[10] *errant* thorough.

[11] *paint* cosmetics.

[12] *manuta* loose woman's gown; *petticoat*: decorative underskirt.

[13] *Italy ... sodomy* widely believed since at least the English Reformation.

[14] *page* boy or youth employed as a personal attendant.

[15] *ladies ... other* another commonplace assumption (see **9.1.1** and **9.16**).

[16] *slopping* slobbering over.

[17] *catamites* sodomites (usually referring to the receptive role in anal intercourse).

to that degree as is daily practised even in our most public places, and, generally speaking, without reproof, because they plead in excuse, that 'it is the fashion'. Damned fashion! Imported from Italy amidst a train of other unnatural vices! Have we not sins enough of our own, but we must eke 'em out with those of foreign nations, to fill up the cup of our abominations, and make us yet more ripe for divine vengeance?[18]

Till of late years,[19] sodomy was a sin in a manner unheard of in these nations; and indeed, one would think where there are such angelic women, so foul a sin should never enter into imagination. On the contrary, our Sessions-Papers are constantly stained with the crimes of these beastly wretches;[20] and though many have been made examples of, yet we have but too much reason to fear that there are numbers yet undiscovered, and that this abominable practice gets ground every day.

Instead of the pillory, I would have the stake[21] be the punishment of those who in contradiction to the laws of God and man, to the order and course of nature, and to the most simple principles of reason preposterously burn for each other, and leave the fair, the charming sex neglected. [...]

[...]

If such a resolution[22] was more universal, the sons of Sodom would lose many proselytes, in being baffled out of one of their principal advances; for under pretence of extraordinary friendship, they entice unwary youth from this first step to more detestable practices, taking many times the advantage of their necessities[23] to decoy them to their ruin. [...] I hope the manly and generous Britons who yet survive will take what I say into consideration, and show themselves friends to the fair sex by opposing all inlets to the sin of sodomy, of which man-kissing is the very first.

With this all other effeminacies should be abolished, and each sex should maintain its peculiar[24] character. I hope the ladies will not stand in need of any advice from me, yet I could wish that some among them would seem less amorous of one another; for though woman kissing woman is more suitable

18 *cup ... vengeance* Rev. 17.4.

19 *of late years* recently.

20 *Sessions-Papers ... wretches* Twenty such accounts were published (1726–28) (Norton, *Eighteenth-Century British Erotica II*, 5.390n).

21 *pillory* contraption to publicly restrain an offender for humiliation, physical abuse, etc., from passers-by; *stake*: where persons would be bound for execution by burning. On the Continent, convicted sodomites were often burned at the stake; in England, they were hanged.

22 *such a resolution* i.e., replacing kissing with shaking hands.

23 *necessities* poverty.

24 *peculiar* distinctive.

to their natural softness, and indeed more excusable than the like practice in the contrary sex; yet it ought to be done (if at all) with modesty and moderation, lest suggestions, which I hope are false, and which to me seem improbable, should bring such ladies under censure, who give themselves too great liberties with each other. For as the age increases in wickedness, new vices may arise; and since they themselves see how fulsome it is in gentlemen, I hope they will abstain from all appearance of evil, and contribute to the intended reformation, not only by scorning and deriding such wretches of men who shall openly affront them by kissing each other in their presence, but that they will set the gentlemen a pattern, and shame them out of it by using a kiss, if it must be used, in so decent a manner and with so great restraint that the most envious shall find no cause of censure.

[...]

6.7.2 The Petit Maitre,[25]
An Odd sort of An Unpoetical Poem, In the Trolly-lolly Style[26]

By a gentleman commoner.[27]

Tell me, gentle hob'dehoy![28]
Art thou girl, or art thou boy?
Art thou man, or art thou ape;
For thy gesture and thy shape,
And thy features and thy dress,
Such contraries do express:
I stand amazed, and at a loss to know,
To what new species thou thy form dost owe?

By thy hair combed up behind,
Thou should'st be of womankind,
But that damned, forbidding face
Does the charming sex disgrace;
Man or woman, thou art neither,
But a blot, a shame to either;
Nor dare to brutehood even to make pretence,[29]
For brutes themselves show greater sign of sense.

25 *Petit Maitre* French, meaning literally, 'little master'; fop.
26 *trolly-lolly style* after a refrain in comic songs; thus, reflecting careless gaiety.
27 *gentleman commoner* one of the privileged class of university undergraduates.
28 *hob'dehoy* hobbledehoy: awkward youth.
29 *brutehood* the status or nature of animals.

By thy jaws all lank and thin,
By that forced unmeaning grin,
Thou appear'st to human eyes,
Like some ape of monst'rous size.
Yet an ape thou can'st not be;
Apes are more adroit than thee.
Thy oddities so much my mind perplex,
I neither can define thy kind or sex.[30]

Art thou substance, art thou shade?
That thus monst'rously arrayed,
Walking forth in open day,
Dost our senses quite dismay?
Unghastly, yet thou only can'st provoke,[31]
Our rage, our detestation, and our joke.

If thou art a man, forbear
Thus, this motley garb to wear;[32]
Do not reason thus displace;
Do not manhood thus disgrace;
But thy sex by dress impart,
And appear like what thou art:
Like what thou art, said I, pray pardon me;
I mean appear like what thou ought'st to be.

[30] *kind* species.

[31] *unghastly* unghostly (also, 'unghastly', meaning 'not able to cause terror').

[32] *motley* extravagant (clothes); glancing at the older meaning: costume of a jester.

CHAPTER 7

The Classical Tradition in Translation

Introduction

The humanist recovery of Latin and Greek texts revealed to early modern readers the homoerotic relationships of celebrated Greek and Roman men, such as Plato, Socrates, Alcibiades, Alexander the Great, and Virgil. Moreover, classical texts often presented such relationships positively or at least neutrally. Plutarch's influential biographies of famous Greeks and Romans, for example, comment censoriously only on men whose homoerotic desires and acts were part of a general sensual excess, such as the Macedonian general Demetrius (*Online Companion*); far more numerous are the biographies that present approvingly the often martially based love relationships of his subjects: many of Plutarch's twenty-three biographies of famous Greek men depict positively men's erotic relationships with their *eromenoi* (young male beloveds; beloved boys), often youths in training for martial and civic manhood. Both Plutarch's biography 'The Life of Pelopidas' (*Online Companion*) and his dialogic treatise 'Of Love' (see **7.28.1**) describe the 'Sacred Band', a Theban group of 150 pairs of martial male lovers whose victories in battle are traced back to the mutual erotic devotion of the older *erastes* (lover) for his younger *eromenos*. Plato's *Symposium*, likewise, offers a series of speeches in praise of homoerotic love between men, where such love is celebrated as heroic (a true lover will die for his male beloved); as a higher form of love (intellectual and spiritual) versus a lower (carnal) form reserved for boys and women; and as the oldest and most 'natural' type of love. Although in *Symposium* Socrates argues that a man should finally transcend his love of a beautiful boy, and this love's most virtuous end is to lead a man to the love of beauty itself, in Plato's *Phaedrus* the love between the *erastes* and *eromenos* is exalted, although the type of same-sex acts a male couple may legitimately engage in is largely limited to touching, kissing, and embracing.

Certainly, however, there is a general, though by no means absolute, divide between Greek and Latin literature's treatment of the *erastes–eromenos* relationship, since the former tends to treat male homoerotic relationships more favourably than does the latter. Plutarch's works, for example, may be one of our only sources for information about the Sacred Band, but his 'Of Love' is a debate concerning the relative merits of homoerotic relationships versus heterosexual marriage, where the latter is the clear victor. In short, early modern Latin and Greek literate readers would encounter both works celebrating the erotic love between, for example, the male poet and the young male beloved, and poems that satirized same-sex acts and desires for a variety of reasons (e.g., to attack enemies or political opponents or critique indolence and sensual abandonment). More generally, Greek and Latin texts celebrating and idealizing male friendship, particularly Cicero's *Laelius: On Friendship* (*Online Companion*), could be read, and indeed apparently were, in early modern England as sanctioning the most intense emotional bonds between men, and as licensing their passionate expressions of love. However, Cicero's discourse on heterosexual and male same-sex erotic love in *Tusculan Disputations* (*Online Companion*) is quite typical of Latin literature, in describing both forms of love as equally dangerous and to be avoided, while Suetonius's *History of the Twelve Caesars* goes further, deeming male same-sex relationships, desires, and acts as demeaning and unmanly, associating both with political degeneracy and the abuse of power.

While *Symposium* and *Phaedrus* were kept from the Greek and Latin illiterate public until the later eighteenth century,[1] a surprising amount of material depicting and discussing male same-sex erotic relationships, desires, and sexual acts was translated into English before 1750. Such translations were not subject to uniform censorship and it is misleading to group them all under the label 'crudely bowdlerized' (Smith 289–90 n9). Different classical genres and early modern perceptions of their purposes made for different levels of explicitness in translation. Broadly, the classical love lyric and particularly the satiric epigram tend to be fairly explicit about male same-sex erotic relationships, desires, and sexual acts, and thus tend to be more expurgated and 'tamed' in translation than is the case with such relationships, desires and acts in classical biography or epic where these are usually aspects of martial bonding and heroic love. Similarly, in late seventeenth-century translations of Juvenal's complete satires sexually obscene and scatologically explicit material is more often retained and (relatively) clearly translated than is the case with comparably 'obscene' material in Horace's, Catullus's and Martial's epigrams and lyrics. Early modern writers and readers perceived Juvenal's satiric work as having a more general set of social targets

[1] *Symposium* was translated into English in bowdlerized form only in 1767, deleting entirely Alcibiades' discussion of his erotic love for Socrates; *Phaedrus* was not translated into English until 1792, although this translation maintains the original's focus on male–male love.

than Martial's, Horace's, or Catullus's, even though all three were perceived as aiming at revealing, shaming, and (hopefully) correcting human vice and folly. As result, Juvenal's putative 'obscenities' were more often retained in translation than similarly perceived passages in these other major classical poets. Moreover, when material dealing with male and female homoerotic relationship, desires, and acts is missing from a volume of early modern translations, this absence is often but not always a result of the translator's or editor's homophobia; sometimes an early modern translation worked from faulty Latin or Greek manuscripts. Lucian's famous 'Dialogue 5' from *Dialogues of the Courtesans* (see **7.31.1**), depicting female same-sex desires and acts, and his 'Dialogue of Jupiter and Ganymede' (see **7.29.1–7.29.2**), depicting the establishment of the erotic and sexual relationship between the god and the beautiful youth, are both missing from Erasmus's most widely printed Latin edition, perhaps accounting partly for the former's lack of translations in particular. On the other hand, although Martial does not receive an English translation of his complete epigrams in this period, his early Latin manuscripts (including Venice, 1482; and London, 1615) are complete, although the 1670 London Latin edition deletes most of the poet's famous epigrams satirizing men who engage in same-sex sexual acts.

Early modern translators managed their originals' various homoerotic and homosatiric materials in several ways.

1. *Deletion, Expurgation, Vagueness, and 'Mistranslation'.* The most extreme method of dealing with a classical poet's homoerotic lyrics and satires of same-sex erotic desires and acts was silent deletion, and early modern England saw many more volumes of *selections* from particular classical poets than translations of their complete works (e.g., Anacreon, Horace, Martial, Theocritus, and Tibullus). This approach allowed the translator to quietly ignore 'inappropriate' material. For example, Hawkins prefaces his 1625 translations from Horace with a comment typical of volumes of this poet's selected works: he rejects Horace's 'wanton and looser poems' to focus on his 'moral and serious odes'. Horace's most famous homoerotic lyrics (4.1 and 4.10; 7.12) are simply deleted from Ashmore (1621) and Holyday (1652), while Harington (1684) deletes 4.10. Interestingly, Harington is the only translator in the period to draw such decided attention to his deletions, replacing each dropped or truncated poem with the assertion that he has done so 'on good grounds'. Likewise, selections from Martial's epigrams almost always delete his most sexually obscene and homoerotically explicit poems (such as 1.91's satire of the tribade Bassa (see **7.23.1**), and 4.42's celebration of boyish beauty and pederastic sex). Translators also resort to the closely allied technique of expurgation. Stanley's 1651 translation of Anacreon's odes, for instance, consistently drops 'unseemly' homoerotic passages, including all those referring to Anacreon's love for the beautiful boy,

Bathyllus; Abraham Cowley's contributions to Willis's multi-authored volume of selected translations from Anacreon (1683) expurgates the one reference to Bathyllus in his translation of the *Anacreontea*'s 'Ode 10. The Swallow'. Likewise, Harington deletes the last section of Horace's 4.1 (the address to the beloved boy, Ligurinus), saying it has been 'on good grounds omitted'.

As Juvenal's 1644 translator Stapylton states, a translator's diction and usage can also help 'purge' a writer of 'inappropriate' material (A3v). While both Stapylton and Holyday (1673) are fairly clear that something sexual is going on between the women in Juvenal's 'Satire 6', only Dryden indicates unequivocally that a same-sex sex orgy is under way (see **7.27.1**). Vagueness, however, is a popular strategy that most often takes the form of obscuring the gender of the male love object – as Pope does in his translation of Horace's 4.1 (composed 1730s), where the boy beloved is addressed simply as 'too dear' and 'too cruel'. Other translators simply erase the homoerotic love of the speaker, as Coxwell does when he recasts the relationship between the speaker and Ligurinus in Horace's 4.10: the speaker warns Ligurinus that if the boy continues to scorn those who love him, eventually no 'tender virgin [i.e., woman]' will want him. Giving the original's 'beloved boy' a sex change is, also, a relatively frequent strategy, with (for example) Horace's Ligurinus becoming the scornful mistress Lisetta in Manning's 1730 translation of 4.10. Similarly, Killigrew's 1695 translation of Martial's epigrams, apart from deleting many poems, recasts many more, making both the beloved boy Diadumenus and an unnamed serving boy 'maids' (3.65; 9.26), and transforming the praise of boyish beauty into the praise of girlish beauty (4.42).

2. *Contextualization.* Sometimes translators defuse the putative 'obscenity' of the classical homoerotic lyric by contextualizing it in a larger verse miscellany, slipping it in without further comment, as is the case with Thomas Ball's translation of the *Anacreontea*'s 'Ode 10. The Swallow' (see **7.11.1**) and Lovelace's translations of Catullus (see **7.13.1**). Translators' prefaces sometimes also place a classical writer's homoerotic works in a historical and/or biographical context: Dryden's relatively explicit translation of the female same-sex orgy in Juvenal's 'Satire 6' was perhaps partly enabled by his prefatory statement firmly situating such sexual acts and desires in the ancient past (*Online Companion*); likewise, Brown's straightforward presentation of female same-sex intercourse in Lucian's 'Dialogue 5' may result partly from the editor Dryden's conviction that same-sex relationships in Lucian's works reflect the ancient writer's 'secret inclination to it' ('Life of Lucian', *Works of Lucian* (1710–11), 29–30). Most fascinating is the case of the first English translations of Catullus's homosatiric and homoerotic lyrics, which posed more problems for early modern translators than perhaps any other classical poems of this type. Putting aside Lovelace's unique translation of one of the Juventius lyrics (see **7.13.1**), Catullus's verse concerned with male

same-sex love relationships, desires, and sexual acts first appears via an English translation of a French novel concerning the poet's life and loves, Jean de La Chapelle's *Les Amours de Catulle* (1680). *The Adventures of Catullus* (1707: see **7.14**) puts Catullus's homoerotic and homosatiric poems for and about the beautiful youth Juventius in a heterosexual context, laboriously explaining that 'Juventius' is simply a 'pen-name' for Catullus's beloved mistress, Crastinia. This heterosexualizing of Catullus's love for Juventius, however, subsequently disappeared when the translations from *Adventures* were reprinted without their narrative context at the end of a 1713 translation of Petronius's *Satyricon* (*Online Companion*), where the explicitly presented love affair between Petronius's central character Encolpius and his male slave-lover Giton ends up reinforcing the homoerotic and homosatiric nature of Catullus's lyrics.

3. *Reception History, Allegorization, and Didacticism.* The allegorizing and Christianizing of classical writers also helped license the translation of homoerotic material into English. Often called 'the Roman Homer', Virgil was one of the first pagan poets to be reinterpreted for Christian audiences and sensibilities. As a result, Virgil's homoerotic pastoral poem 'Eclogue 2' was frequently allegorized through prefaces and marginal commentary, with the Italian humanist Vives typically asserting that the love of the shepherd Corydon for the scornful but beautiful shepherd-boy Alexis is an allegory of Virgil's platonic love of the poet and statesman Cornelius Gallus, and Virgil's desire for his patronage, a transformation of homoerotic desire into the more acceptable register of patronage plea that occurs also in other translations (*Online Companion*). Dryden (1697) in contrast acknowledges the long tradition of Virgil's love for his young male slaves Alexander and Cebes (traced back to Aelius Donatus's 'Life of Virgil' (c. 350 CE)), but strenuously asserts its platonic nature (see **7.16.1**). Ovid's epic mythological poem *Metamorphoses* was also subject to Christian reinterpretation early in its post-classical reception, and its Latin editions and vernacular translations were typically couched in moralizing commentary and allegorical explication, as is the case with Ovid's most famous early modern translations (those of Golding and Sandys: see **7.17** and **7.18**). Sandys, for example, says that Iphis' transformation into a boy so she can wed her beloved Ianthe shows that the ancients believed 'that men should despair of nothing; since all things were in the power of the gods to give; and give they would what was justly implored' (Commentary on Book 9), offering as well a number of precedents in the past and present for such sex changes. Golding's Christianizing and allegorizing strain in his translation of Ovid's *Metamorphoses* leads him to describe the poem as a model text for the reader's moral, ethical, and spiritual instruction, a 'sea of goods and jewels' ('To the Reader', l. 183).

As the above discussion suggests, classical representations of female same-sex erotic love, desire, and sexual acts are rare, and early modern translations are even rarer. It is only in the case of the Greek poet Sappho, increasingly acknowledged in the early modern period as a lover of both men and women, that classical material dealing with female homoerotic relationships comes within the ken of the general reader. For a discussion of the ways translation strategies interact with changing conceptions of female authorship and gender to fashion the representation of Sappho and her representations of female same-sex love and desire, see Introduction to **7.2–7.9**.

Online Companion
Interested readers can find additional selections from the following classical writers in translation: Aelian; Anacreon; Aristaenetus; Quintus Lutatius Catulus; Catullus; Cicero; Diogenes Laertius; Horace; Juvenal; Lucian; Martial; Ovid (*Metamorphoses*' 'Afterlife'); Petronius; Plutarch; Sappho (Sappho's 'Afterlife'); Achilles Tatius; Theocritus; Tibullus; Virgil; and Xenophon.

Homer (*fl.* eighth century BCE), Greek epic poet, author of the *Iliad* and the *Odyssey*

Probably a native of Ionia, Homer and his works were viewed by the ancients as repositories of wisdom and examples of poetic excellence. Imitated by numerous classical writers, including Virgil and Lucretius, they were first translated into Latin by Livius Andronicus (284–204 BCE).

George Chapman (1559/60–1634), poet and dramatist

Writer of some fifteen plays, as well as narrative poetry, Chapman is still best known for his translations of Homer. His complete translation of the *Iliad* was published in 1611, and was followed three years later by a translation of the *Odyssey*.

7.1

From *The Iliad*

7.1.1 Book 18

[The great Greek warrior Achilles has just learned of his male beloved Patroclus's death at the hands of the Trojan hero Hector, although the book opens with Achilles' terrible premonition of Patroclus's fate.]

[...]

This said, grief darkened all his pow'rs. With both his hands he rent[1]
The black mould from the forcèd earth and poured it on his head,
Smeared all his lovely face, his weeds (divinely fashionèd)[2]
All 'filed and mangled, and himself he threw upon the shore,[3]
Lay as laid out for funeral, then tumbled round, and tore
His gracious curls. His ecstasy he did so far extend[4]
That all the ladies won by him and his now-slaughtered friend
(Afflicted strangely for his plight) came shrieking from the tents
And fell about him, beat their breasts, their tender lineaments
Dissolved with sorrow. And with them wept Nestor's warlike son,[5]
Fell by him, holding his fair hands in fear he would have done
His person violence; his heart (extremely straight'ned) burned,[6]
Beat, swelled and sighed, as it would burst. So terribly he mourned
That Thetis, sitting in the deeps of her old father's seas,
Heard and lamented. [...]

7.1.2 Book 23

[After killing Hector in battle, Achilles falls asleep; Patroclus's ghost appears, reproaching Achilles for not having given him speedy and honourable burial.]

[...]

'Dost thou sleep, Aeacides, am I[7]
Forgotten of thee? Being alive, I found thy memory
Ever respectful, but now, dead, thy dying love abates.
Inter me quickly; enter me in Pluto's iron gates;[8]
For now the souls (the shades) of men fled from this being beat
My spirit from rest and stay my much desired receipt
Amongst souls placed beyond the flood. Now every way I err[9]

[1] *This said* the report of Patroclus's death; *his*: Achilles'.

[2] *weeds* clothing.

[3] *'filed* defiled.

[4] *ecstasy* frenzy.

[5] *Nestor's warlike son* Antilochus, eldest son of King Nestor of Pylus, one of the Greek generals.

[6] *straight'ned* torturously stretched.

[7] *Aeacides* Achilles.

[8] *iron gates* entrance to the classical Underworld.

[9] *err* wander, stray.

About this broad-doored house of Dis. Oh, help then to prefer
My soul yet further; here I mourn, but had the funeral fire
Consumed my body, never more my spirit should retire
From hell's low region: from thence souls never are retrieved
To talk with friends here, nor shall I. […]

[…]

Oh, then, I charge thee now take care
That our bones part not, but, as life combined in equal fare[10]
Our loving beings, so let death. When from Opunta's tow'rs
My father brought me to your roofs (since ('gainst my will) my pow'rs,
Incensed and indiscreet at dice, slew fair Amphidamas),
Then Peleus entertained me well; then in thy charge I was
By his injunction and thy love: and therein let me still
Receive protection. Both our bones provide, in thy last will,
That one urn may contain, and make that vessel all of gold
That Thetis gave thee – that rich urn.' This said, sleep ceased to hold
Achilles' temples, and the shade thus he received: 'O friend,
What needed these commands? My care, before, meant to commend
My bones to thine, and in that urn. Be sure thy will is done.
A little stay yet, let's delight, with some full passion
Of woe enough, either's affects; embrace we.' Opening thus
His greedy arms, he felt no friend: like matter vaporous
The spirit vanished under earth and murmured in his stoop.

[Achilles gives Patroclus a lavish funeral procession and pyre.]

In midst of all was borne
Patroclus' person by his peers; on him were all heads shorn,
E'en till they covered him with curls. Next to him marched his friend
Embracing his cold neck, all sad since now he was to send[11]
His dearest to his endless home. Arrived all where the wood
Was heaped for funeral, they set down. Apart Achilles stood,
And, when enough wood was heaped on, he cut his golden hair. […]

[…]

[…] all night swift-foot Achilles threw
Wine from a golden bowl on earth, and steeped the soil in wine,[12]

10 *fare* condition.

11 Cf. Andromache, who cradles her dead husband Hector's head in Bk 14.

12 *steeped … wine* libation, a common Greek funerary practice.

Still calling on Patroclus' soul. No father could incline
More to a son most dear, nor more mourn at his burnèd bones,
Than did the great prince to his friend at his combustions –
Still creeping near and near the heap, still sighing, weeping still.

[...]

7.1.3 Book 24

The games performed, the soldiers wholly dispersed to fleet,[13]
Supper and sleep their only care. Constant Achilles yet
Wept for his friend; nor sleep itself, that all things doth subdue,
Could touch at him. This way and that he turned, and did renew
His friend's dear memory – his grace in managing his strength,
And his strength's greatness – how life racked into their utmost length
Griefs, battles, and the wraths of seas in their joint sufferance.
Each thought of which turned to a tear. Sometimes he would advance
(In tumbling on the shore) his side, sometimes his face, then turn
Flat on his bosom, start upright. Although he saw the morn
Show sea and shore his ecstasy he left not, till at last
Rage varied his distraction. Horse, chariot, in hast[14]
He called for, and (those joined) the corse was to his chariot tied,[15]
And thrice about the sepulchre he made his fury ride,
Dragging the person. [...]

[...]

[16]'Achilles, that withstands
All help to others, you can help – one that hath neither heart
Nor soul within him that will move or yield to any part
That fits a man; but lion-like, uplandish and mere wild,[17]
Slave to his pride, and, all his nerves being naturally compiled
Of eminent strength, stalks out and preys upon a silly sheep –
And so fares this man. That fit ruth that now should draw so deep[18]
In all the world being lost in him, and shame (a quality

[13] *games* athletic contests in Patroclus's honour: chariot-racing, wrestling, sword fighting, etc.

[14] *hast* haste.

[15] *corse* Hector's body: Achilles refuses it decent burial, and actively degrades it.

[16] The god Apollo, enraged over Achilles' mistreatment of Hector's body, speaks here to the other gods.

[17] *uplandish* barbaric.

[18] *fit ruth* decent sorrow.

Of so much weight that both it helps and hurts excessively
Men in their manners) is not known, nor hath the pow'r to be
In this man's being. Other men a greater loss than he
Have undergone – a son, suppose, or brother of one womb;
Yet, after dues of woes and tears, they bury in his tomb
All their deplorings. Fates have given to all that are true men
True manly patience, but this man so soothes his bloody vein
That no blood serves it; he must have divine-souled Hector bound
To his proud chariot, and danced in a most barbarous round
About his loved friend's sepulchre, when he is slain. 'Tis vile,
And draws no profit after it. […]'

[Jove sends Thetis to Achilles with a command to surrender Hector's body to the Trojans.]

[…] His reverend mother then
Came near, took kindly his fair hand, and asked him: 'Dear son, when
Will sorrow leave thee? How long time wilt thou thus eat thy heart,
Fed with no other food, nor rest? 'Twere good thou wouldst divert
Thy friend's love to some lady; cheer thy spirits with such kind parts
As she can quit thy grace withal. The joy of thy deserts[19]
I shall not long have; death is near and thy all-conquering fate,
Whose haste thou must not haste with grief, but understand the state
Of things belonging to thy life, which quickly order. […]'

[Priam visits Achilles to plead for his son's body, but Achilles has already determined that he will obey Jove's command.]

[…] the corse Achilles' own hand laid
Upon a bed, and, with his friends, to chariot it conveyed.
For which forced grace (abhorring so from his free mind) he wept,
Cried out for anger, and thus prayed: 'O friend, do not except
Against this favour to our foe (if in the deep thou hear)
And that I give him to his sire; he gave fair ransom; dear
In my observance is Jove's will, and whatsoever part
Of all these gifts by any mean I fitly may convert
To thy renown here and will there, it shall be poured upon
Thy honoured sepulchre.' […]

[…]

[19] *quit* repay.

Sappho (b. c. 630 BCE), Greek lyric poet

Born on the island of Lesbos, Sappho was probably married, and had a daughter (probably named Cleis), and a brother. Highly celebrated by the ancients – originating the metre that came to bear her name (the Sapphic), and earning the title 'the Tenth Muse' – Sappho has seen most of her verse lost, except one complete poem and fragments of others. Many of her poems apparently deal with the love between women and girls, often elegiac in tone, but she also composed religious and wedding songs. Ovid's 'Sappho to Phaon' (*Heroides*) depicts Sappho's love for the male ferryman Phaon, her abandonment by him, and her despairing suicide by leaping off a cliff on the island of Leucas (Leucadia) into the sea, but, although highly influential in fashioning her representation throughout the medieval and early modern periods, the story has no support from other ancient sources.

Sappho's After-Life: Imitation, Inspiration, Denigration. In early modern England, Sappho was the most famous classical woman whose primary emotional and sexual relationships were with other women, although explicit discussion of this aspect of her sexuality was generally confined to Latin texts until the seventeenth century. Much more widely known, however, was the Ovidian legend about her love for Phaon; Ovid's 'Sappho to Phaon', one of his *Heroides*, letters from women to their often faithless lovers, recasts her as a lover both of women and of men, although the poem essentially charts Sappho's possession by the heterosexual desire for Phaon as that which usurps her love and desire for her female beloveds. Early modern English translations recast Sappho as a heterosexual mistress, suppressing to a greater or lesser extent her same-sex desires and relationships, a tradition that John Lyly takes advantage of in his play *Sappho and Phao* (1592: see **7.6**), and which receives its most decided expression in Henry Glapthorne's pastoral, romance tragedy *Argalus and Parthenia* (1639; *Online Companion*). In fact, Turbervile's translation of Ovid's 'Sappho to Phaon' (see **7.19.1**) was the first and last in the sixteenth-century period to be so explicit about the primary and erotic nature of Sappho's same-sex relationships. *Heroides*' three mid-seventeenth-century translators generally either elide Sappho's relationships with her female lovers or transform them into instances of her general sexual lasciviousness. In Thomas Heywood's 1624 translation, for instance, Sappho's enormous sexual appetite encompasses both women and men; he presents her hedonism and 'unnatural' desires as finally punished by her ultimately unrequited passion for Phaon, by her being forced to watch as Phaon enjoys the favours of her previous female companions, and by her being stripped of her poetic abilities and audience through lust, jealousy, and despair (Andreadis 28–37). Sappho is also the early modern exemplar of female poetic excellence, but her celebration by ancient writers like Horace and Catullus was felt so incompatible with her sexual relationships that two Sapphos early emerged: one, the poet praised for her skill; the other, the sexually voracious whore. Calling an early modern woman writer another 'Sappho' became initially a conventional method of praising her poetic talent. As Sappho's same-sex erotic relationships became more widely known in the seventeenth and early eighteenth centuries, however, such praise was increasingly qualified and accompanied by an emphasis on the particular woman writer's chastity (see Wharton, *Online Companion*).

Although increasingly condemnatory discussions of tribadism appear in both Latin and vernacular medical texts from the sixteenth century onwards, Sappho's erotic reputation only becomes linked with tribadism in these non-literary discourses around the mid-seventeenth century (Andreadis 39). Many early and influential medical writers, such as Fallopius (1562) and Laurentius (1595), name the reality of female same-sex sexual intercourse in their relatively clinical studies of clitoral anatomy and physiology, as do their later but much more censorious English counterparts, such as Helkiah Crooke (*Microcosmographia*, 1615; *Online Companion*) and Thomas Gibson (*Anatomy*, 1682; *Online Companion*). As Andreadis notes, however, Sappho first appears as the exemplar and early classical practitioner of tribadism in English language medical discourse in Thomas Bartholin's *Bartholinus Anatomy* (1653, 1663; *Online Companion*). This identification seems to have quickly proliferated in other genres, such as William Walsh's 1691 mock defense of women (see **7.8**), where Sappho does not simply practice tribadism, but has been 'promoted' to its inventor. By the beginning of the eighteenth century, Sappho had become an increasingly 'contaminated' figure, subject to the disapproving insistence of scholars on her same-sex erotic and sexual relationships, and to the bawdy contempt of popular satirists: the anonymous *The Sappho-An* (see **7.9**) makes Sappho not just the inventor of tribadism, but also of the dildo, further cementing the representation of tribadism as modelled on penetrative heterosexual intercourse; even the *Heroides*' moving presentation of Sappho's heteroerotic love, betrayal, and loss is degraded in Stevenson's and Radcliffe's early eighteenth-century burlesques (*Online Companion*), where Sappho the dignified and honoured classical poet becomes a vulgar, predatory, syphilitic whore.

Sir Philip Sidney (1554–86), courtier, soldier, and poet

Educated at Oxford, Sidney spent his life in service of queen and country, dying on the Continent in the cause of international Protestantism; he was later elegized as the pattern of the English gentleman. His works include the sonnet sequence *Astrophil and Stella* (1591); his influential defence of imaginative writing *Apology for Poetry* (1595); translations of *Psalms* (with his sister Mary, *comp.* mid–1580s/early 1590s); and his never-out-of-print prose romance *Arcadia* ('The New Arcadia') (1590, 1593).

7.2

From 'The Old Arcadia' (comp. 1577–80)

7.2.1 My Muse, What Ails This Ardour? (Fragment 31)[1]

My musc what ails this ardour
To blaze my only secrets?
Alas, it is no glory
To sing my own decayed state.
Alas, it is no comfort
To speak without an answer.
Alas, it is no wisdom
To show the wound without cure.

My muse what ails this ardour?
My eyes be dim, my limbs shake,
My voice is hoarse, my throat scorched,
My tongue to this my roof cleaves,
My fancy amazed, my thoughts dulled,
My heart doth ache, my life faints,
My soul begins to take leave.
So great a passion all feel,
To think a sore so deadly
I should so rashly rip up.

My muse what ails this ardour?
If that to sing thou art bent,
Go sing the fall of old Thebes,
The wars of ugly centaurs
The life, the death of Hector,
So may thy song be famous;
Or if to love thou art bent,
Recount the rape of Europe,[2]

[1] Only the second stanza adapts lines from Sappho's 'Fragment 31' (preserved in Longinus's *On the Sublime* (c. first century CE)). Cf. *Greek Lyric* 1.31.78–81.

[2] *Europe* Europa (Glossary).

Adonis' end, Venus' net,
The sleepy kiss the moon stole;
So may thy song be pleasant.[3]

My muse what ails this ardour
To blaze my only secrets?
Wherein do only flourish
The sorry fruits of anguish,
The song thereof a last will,
The tunes be cries, the words plaints,
The singer is the song's theme
Wherein no ear can have joy,
Nor eye receives due object,
Ne pleasure here, ne fame got.[4]

My muse what ails this ardour?
'Alas,' she say'th, 'I am thine,
So are thy pains my pains too.
Thy heated heart my seat is,
Wherein I burn, thy breath is
My voice, too hot to keep in.
Besides, lo here the author
Of all thy harms; lo here she
That only can redress thee,
Of her I will demand help.'

My muse, I yield, my muse sing,
But all thy song herein knit:
The life we lead is all love,
The love we hold is all death,
Nor aught I crave to feed life,
Nor aught I seek to shun death,
But only that my goddess
My life, my death, do count hers.

[3] *Or … pleasant* all are appropriate subjects for love poetry; *Venus' net*: 'Venus and Mars' (Glossary); *moon*: Diana. See also Endymion (Glossary).

[4] *Ne … ne* neither … nor.

Pierre Bayle (1647–1706), Huguenot classical scholar and professor of philosophy

Famed French classicist whose academic career was often stymied by his Protestantism and commitment to religious tolerance, Bayle focused on writing after losing his teaching position in 1693. His influential *Dictionnaire historique et critique* (1697; rev. edn, 4 vols, 1702) is widely viewed as a monument to Enlightenment intellectual ideals. Selections from Bayle's extensive footnotes (lettered) appear at the end of this extract.

7.3

From *An Historical and Critical Dictionary* (1710)

7.3.1 Sappho

Sappho was one of the most renowned women of all antiquity for her verses and her amours. [...] She composed a great number of odes, epigrams, elegies, epithalamiums, etc. All her verses run upon love, and had such natural and moving charms that 'tis no wonder if she was called the Tenth Muse. Strabo looks on her as a wonder, and says that never any woman could come near her in poetry.[5] There remains nothing[c] of so many poems she made but some small fragments which the ancient scholiasts[6] have cited, and a hymn to Venus, and an ode to one of her mistresses:[7] For you must know that her amorous passion extended even to the persons of her own sex,[d] and this is that for which she was most cried down. Suidas[8] has preserved the names of three of her mistresses, who spoiled her reputation and defamed themselves by a strange singularity which was imputed to their commerce. He has also preserved the names of three of her female scholars[9] whom she did, without doubt, initiate in her mysteries. Since Lucian does not observe that the women of the isle of Lesbos, who he says were very subject to this

[5] *Strabo ... poetry* (64 BCE–c. 24 CE), traveller and geographer; see his *Geography* 13.424.

[6] *fragments* See **7.5.4**; *scholiasts*: ancient commentators upon a classical writer.

[7] *a ... mistresses* See 'Hymn to Venus' (Fragment 1) (**7.5.2**) and 'An Ode' (Fragment 31) (**7.5.3**).

[8] *Suidas* author of the tenth century CE encyclopaedia, the *Suda*.

[9] *three ... mistresses ... scholars* her mistresses were Atthis, Telesippa, and Megara; her scholars, Anagora of Miletus, Gongyla of Kolophon, and Euneika of Salamis (*Suda* Online, sigma 107).

passion, learned it of Sappho,[10] 'tis better to imagine that she found it already established in her country than to make her the inventor of it. Be it as it will, Sappho always passed for a famous *tribas*,[11] and some think that it was for this reason, that some surnamed her *mascula Sappho*.[e] If her design was to pass by and neglect the other half of mankind, she was frustrated of her expectation; for she fell desperately in love with Phaon, and did in vain all that she could to make him love her. But he despised her and forced her by his coldness to throw herself from a high rock to extinguish her devouring flame. Oh! What a cruelty! […]

[…]

It's said that the Mytileans[12] did her the honour after her death to stamp their money with her image. Some authors make mention of another Sappho.[k]

7.3.2 Bayle's Footnotes

[c] *There remains etc.*} […] The piece[13] which he[14] cites out of his 'Notes on *Anacreon*' shows us that he was persuaded that Sappho writ this ode for a woman she was in love with. We shall see in the following remark that his daughter was not of this opinion; yet 'tis a very probable one.

[d] *Extended even to the persons of her own sex*} I cannot blame the charity of Mrs Le Fèvre,[15] who has endeavoured for the honour of Sappho to render the fact uncertain; but I think her too reasonable to be vexed at us for believing our own eyes. The ode which Longinus has mentioned is not in the style of a friend writing to a friend: it savours of love all over, and not of friendship; otherwise, Longinus, who was so good a judge, would not have brought it as a model of the art with which great masters represent things. He would not, I say, have given us as an example of that art, the manner wherewith the symptoms of an amorous fury are collected in that ode […]; and Plutarch would not have cited this same ode to prove that love is a divine fury, which causes more violent enthusiasms than those of the priestess of Delphi, of the

10 *Since … Sappho* See **7.31.1**.

11 *tribas* tribade, a woman who has sex with other women.

12 *Mytileans* citizens of the island of Lesbos's most important city, Mytilene.

13 *the piece* 'An Ode' (Fragment 31) (see **7.5.3**).

14 *he* Famed French classicist Tanneguy Le Fèvre (1615–72) produced editions of Sappho, Anacreon, Virgil, Horace, and others.

15 *Mrs Le Fèvre* Anne Le Fèvre (later Dacier, c. 1651–1720), daughter of Tanneguy Le Fèvre. Her 1681 prose translation of Sappho includes a heterosexualized life of the poet, whose poetic excellence, Anne claimed, prompted her 'slanderous' characterization as a tribade; Anne later translated Homer (1699 and 1708).

Bacchants,[16] and of the priests of Cybele. [...] People were so persuaded in Ovid's time that Sappho loved women as men do, that he makes no difficulty of introducing her making a sacrifice to Phaon of the female companions of her debauchery:

The girls of Pyrrha and Methyme do not delight me,
And I am not delighted by any other crowd of girls from Lesbos.
Vile to me is Anactorie, vile is the fair Cydno;
Not pleasing to mine eyes, as she used to be, is Atthis,
And a hundred others whom I have loved not without crime:
Base man, one alone possesses what belonged to a multitude.

Lesbians, beloved ones, who made me infamous,
Stop coming in an eager group to hear my lyre song.[17]

Horace is another evidence against her in the complaints he supposes she made of the maids of Lesbos: 'Et Aeoliis fidibus querentem, Sappho puellis de popularibus';[18] for if she had complained that the ladies of her country envied her merit, she would not have chosen the young ones for the subject of her complaint. But because she had spoke to them of love, and the greatest part of 'em were either too simple, or, to speak better, too crafty to be catched, and those who had complied had made her infamous; for this reason she complained of the young maids. This verse of Ovid, 'Stop coming in an eager group to hear my lyre song', shows that the women of Lesbos had done justice to her fine verses. To conclude, I leave it to a new Father Sánchez[19] to decide whether a married woman who had complied with the passion of Sappho would have committed adultery and made her husband a cuckold. I do not know whether this question has escaped the inexhaustible curiosity of the casuists about matrimonial causes.

16 *Bacchants* Bacchus (Glossary).

17 *The girls of Pyrrha ... song* Ovid, 'Epistle 15: Sappho to Phaon', *Heroides*, ll. 15–20; 201–2. I have substituted here my own translation for the original Latin that appears at this point. Thanks to Michael Treschow (UBC-O) for his generous and invaluable assistance. For an early modern translation, see **7.19.1 n72** ('Pyrino is forgot ... from them to thee hast wyrd') and **7.19.1 n114** ('Ye Lesbian lasses ... I charge you come no more').

18 Ode 2.13.24–5: 'and Sappho complaining on her Aeolian strings about the girls of her city'.

19 Thomas *Sánchez* (1550–1610), Spanish Jesuit and casuist, published a lengthy work on marriage's moral and doctrinal aspects (1602); casuistry was popularly viewed as a type moral philosophy that encouraged the self-serving perversion of absolute principles.

Let us confirm this by the testimony of a great wit,[20] who did not believe that his complaisance for Mrs Le Fèvre should go so far as to approve the pains she has taken in favour of Sappho. After the death of her husband, says he, 'Sappho, though young, renounced marriage, but not the pleasure of loving. She had a soul too passionate to be without it; which may be easily judged by the tenderness all over her poems, which has put her above all the poets as to that point. So finding herself too weak to vanquish so violent an inclination as that, she wholly gave herself up to it, and loved all manner of ways, far beyond the bounds which modesty naturally prescribes to her sex. 'Tis in vain to justify her on that head; it cannot be done but at the expense of truth; and neither her aversion for the shameful love of Charaxus,[21] nor all the honours she received from the Lesbians,[22] can wash off a stain which all those who have spoke of her could not disguise, notwithstanding the elogies[23] they have given her, and which her own works evidence more clearly still. Many beautiful women are put in the number of her mistresses.'

[e] *the surname of* mascula Sappho} It's not so easy as it's thought to know truly what Horace means by *mascula Sappho* [*Epistles* 1.19.28]; but if he pretended to reproach her with her love against nature, it's easy to know he took the wrong time. The epithet would be very faint and too far-fetched without necessity. There are, notwithstanding, learned men who understand it so. Chabot[24] places among them the interpreter of Juvenal, and Porphyrion,[25] an ancient scholiast upon Horace [...] however it be with the ancient commentators, 'tis certain that the moderns do commonly mention three opinions about the sense of *mascula Sappho*: 1. That this word means that she was a *tribas*; 2. That it denotes the inclination she had for the sciences, instead of handling the spindle and distaff; 3. The courage she had to precipitate herself at Leucate[26] [...] 'Horace and Ausonius,' says he,[27] 'when

20 *great wit* Longe-Pierre in 'The Life of Sappho', prefacing a translation of Sappho's poems into French (Bayle 5.46).

21 *Charaxus* her brother, who loved the courtesan Rhodope.

22 *Lesbians* inhabitants of Lesbos.

23 *elogies* eulogies, expressions of praise.

24 *Chabot* Pierre Gaultier-Chabot (1516–97) wrote an influential commentary on Horace.

25 Pomponius *Porphyrio*, early third century CE scholar.

26 *precipitate ... Leucate* i.e., Leucas. See Introduction to **7.2–7.9** (Sappho's biographical headnote).

27 *he* André Thevet's 1584 *Les Vrais Portraits et Vies des Hommes Illustres* accepts the fiction of 'the two Sapphos' in order to sanitize her biography of any homoerotic inclinations. Even Sappho's heterosexual passion for Phaon is transferred to this 'other'

they called this Lesbian woman the *mascula*, meant nothing else but that she did what was proper for men, in composing so excellent verses, or that she had undertaken to get into those beautiful places of Leucate, near which the men durst not come.' […] 'This therefore,' continues he, 'is to wrong our Sappho and to calumniate her without reason, since the divine philosopher Plato admired her for her dexterity and vivacity of wit, and for her profound wisdom, which set her, not only above the rest of her sex, but also above the most able men.'

[Bayle concludes by agreeing with opinion 1 above.]

[k] *Of another Sappho*} Mr Moréri says there are some who mention a second maid of this name of Erythrae, who made verses, and that 'tis the opinion of Athenaeus, lib. 13.[28] Athenaeus does not say that this other Sappho was a poet, or that she was born at Erythrae. He says that she was of Eressus, and by profession a courtesan, and that she fell in love with Phaon. According to this opinion the great Sappho, the Sappho of Mytilene, who made such excellent poems, might, without much trouble, be reinstated into a good reputation; there would be nothing else to do but to transport her bad fame upon the other Sappho. The mischief is, that a lame passage of Athenaeus, seconded as much as you please by Aelian,[29] is not to serve us for a guide preferably to a thousand authorities that are against it. […]

Ambrose Philips (1674–1749), writer and translator

Cambridge fellow, tutor, and MP (Irish House of Commons), Philips was also a writer of well-received pastoral eclogues, plays, journalism, and political satire. His translations of Sappho (1713) appeared again in the 1748 edition of his poems that he saw through the press just before his death.

Sappho. Neither Sappho, Thevet insists, could ever have committed the 'crime' of loving other women.

[28] Louis *Moréri* (1643–80), scholar and author of *Le Grand Dictionnaire Historique* (1674); *Athenaeus* (*fl.* c. 200 CE), Greek writer of *Deipnosophistae* ('The Learned Banqueters').

[29] *Aelian* in his first- to second-century CE *Historical Miscellanies.* This fiction also appears in Suidas (*Suda* Online, sigma 108).

7.4

From *The Odes of Sappho* (1713)[30]

The Life of Sappho

This admired lady, who has so long enjoyed the glorious title of the Tenth Muse, has yet the common misfortune of suffering by a confused story. For the critics pretend that there were two of this name, both of the same country, both near the same times, and both inclined to the same studies. Perhaps indeed this may have been an original mistake in Athenaeus (Lib. 13, p. 596), on whose authority the remark is generally built. However, since it's impossible so much as to distinguish the persons, the characters must lie blended as they have hitherto done, and the surviving nymph must own the faults as well as the virtues of her forgotten namesake.

[...]

Of her own sex, her three intimate friends and companions were Atthis, Telesilla, and Megara (Suidas),[31] on account of whom her character suffered so much from the charge of dishonest and unnatural pleasure, it being a constant tradition that her amorous humour was not satisfied with the addresses of men, but that she was willing to have her mistresses too, as well as her gallants. Indeed the incomparable French lady, who has lately adorned her relics,[32] is very ingeniously singular in defending her from this unhappy imputation. But however she may defy the rest of the world, yet since Mr Dacier[33] has declared for the common opinion, she will certainly submit to the superior judgement of her husband.

[...]

Her lyrics, of which she wrote nine books, besides her compositions in other strains (Suidas), have gained the prize for sweetness and force with all the grave judges of antiquity, and such as cannot be suspected of gallantry and compliment. The only two pieces which remain entire have been both preserved by the masters of eloquence, while they allege them for the best instances and patterns of some extraordinary graces. One is a hymn to

30 Contained in the multi-authored volume, *Works of Anacreon and Sappho*.

31 *Suidas* See **n8**.

32 *the incomparable French lady … relics* Anne Dacier (née Le Fèvre). See **n15**.

33 *Mr Dacier* André Dacier (1651–1722), French classicist and husband of Anne. His edition of Horace's works (1681–89) includes a commentary on Ode 2.13 agreeing with Philips's representation of Sappho's same-sex loves.

Venus, which we find in Dionysius Halicarnassus;[34] the other, an amorous ode addressed to one of the young maids that she admired; and this we meet with in Longinus.[35] The last of the two is the most esteemed, and is still acknowledged (as Longinus first produced it) for the inimitable example of the most artificial[36] union, or rather combat, of all the passions, and of all the moving circumstances that can enliven a piece.

[...]

John Addison (*fl.* 1735–36), translator

All that is known about Addison is that he translated Sappho's and Anacreon's verse (1735), and Petronius's *Satyricon* (1736). He probably had a university education, since his works show his knowledge of Greek.

7.5

From *The Works of Anacreon [...] To which are added the Odes, Fragments, and Epigrams of Sappho* (1735)

7.5.1 The Life of Sappho

[...] but he[37] leaving her a widow very young, she would never accept of any second match; not enduring to confine that passion to one person, which, as the ancients tell us, was too violent in her to be restrained even to one sex. Her censures of Charaxus,[38] we may presume, were before her own conduct lay so open to reproof.

A little fragment of hers acquaints us, that two of her female favourites were called Atthis and Andromeda:[39] the names of the others, as delivered to us by antiquity, are Telesilla, Megara, Cydno, Mnaïs, and Cyrene.

But no one seems to have been the object of her admiration so much as the lovely Phaon. At first he was a kind of ferryman, as is reported, and thence fabled to have carried Venus over the stream, and to have received

[34] Dionysius of *Halicarnassus*'s *On Literary Composition* (c. 30 BCE) (Fragment 1).

[35] *Longinus* See **n1**.

[36] *artificial* consummately artistic.

[37] *he* Cercolas of Andros, Sappho's husband, by whom she had a daughter, Cleis (Addison 251).

[38] *Charaxus* See **n21**.

[39] *A ... Andromeda* See **7.5.4**.

3 ‘Portrait of Sappho’, from John Addison, trans., *The Works of Anacreon … to which are added the Odes, Fragments and Epigrams of Sappho* (1735).

from her as a reward, the favour of growing the most beautiful man in the world.[40]

This inconstant lover having withdrawn himself into Sicily to avoid her, she took a voyage in pursuit of him, and there and upon that occasion, it's imagined she composed her 'Hymn to Venus'.

[...]

It's certain her soul seemed formed of love and poetry; she felt the passion in all its warmth, and described it in all its symptoms. Horace calls her *mascula Sappho*, which Porphyrion explains of the energy of her poetry; and Plutarch[41] compares her to Cacus, the son of Vulcan, who breathed out nothing but flame.

7.5.2 A Hymn to Venus (Fragment 1)

Many-sceptred Queen of Love,
Guile-enamoured child of Jove,
Ever-honoured! cease my smart,
Nor oppress thy vot'ry's heart.[42]

But, propitious, Oh descend!
And my tuneful vows attend.
From thy father's gold-roofed court,
Once they charmed thy kind resort.

Thee thy wanton sparrows drew,
Swift on sable wings they flew;
As they through the raptured air,
Lightly-quiv'ring bore thy car.[43]

They returned. You, goddess, smiled,
And with looks divinely mild,

[40] See Introduction to **7.2–7.9** (Sappho's biographical headnote).

[41] Plutarch, *Moralia*, 'Of Love': 'to make mention of Sappho among the Muses. The Romans write in their history, that Cacus, the son of Vulcan, breathed and flashed flames of fire from his mouth. And in truth the words that Sappho uttereth be mixed with fire, and by her verses testifieth the ardent and flaming heat of her heart' (1147). Plutarch then translates Fragment 1.

[42] *vot'ry's* votary's.

[43] *Thee ... car* Sparrows, doves, or swans drew Venus's chariot (*car*); *sparrows*: emblem of licentiousness.

Asked, 'what griefs my peace betrayed,
Why I called you to my aid.

'Whence my mind's soft frenzy grew?
What coy youth I would subdue?[44]
Whom engage in artful toils?[45]
Who my Sappho's heart beguiles?

'Though thy gifts and thee he slight,
He shall soon with gifts invite;
Though he freeze, he soon shall burn,
Thy fond victim in his turn.'

Once again, Oh hear my prayer!
Loose the bands of am'rous care.
Present bless the suppliant's fires,
Grant me all my heart desires.

7.5.3 An Ode (Fragment 31)[46]
On a Young Maid whom She Loved

Happy as a god is he,
That fond youth, who placed by thee,
Hears and sees thee sweetly gay,
Talk and smile his soul away.

That it was alarmed my breast,
And deprived my heart of rest.
For in speechless raptures tossed,
Whilst I gazed, my voice was lost.

The soft fire with flowing rein,
Glided swift through ev'ry vein;
Darkness o'er my eyelids hung;
In my ears faint murmurs rung.

[44] In the original, the beloved object is a girl or woman, not a youth. Addison implicitly acknowledges that he changes the sex of the speaker's beloved from female to male on the basis of the line's emendment by Tanneguy Le Fèvre. See **n14**.

[45] *artful* crafty; *toils*: bonds.

[46] Translations from Catullus onwards often transform the speaker into a man.

Chilling damps my limbs bedewed;
Gentle tremors thrilled my blood;
Life from my pale cheeks retired;
Breathless, I almost expired.

7.5.4 Dire Love, Sweet-bitter Bird of Prey [Based on Fragments 130 and 131][47]

Dire love, sweet-bitter bird of prey!
  Whom nothing can control,
Ah me! Dissolves my life away,
  And melts my inmost soul.

The charming Atthis, who so late
  To Sappho vowed her care;
Now makes Andromeda her fate,
  And leaves me to despair.[48]

Sappho's After-Life: Imitation, Inspiration, Denigration

John Lyly (1554–1606), writer

Graduate of Oxford (MA, 1575) and author of the spectacularly successful prose fictions *Euphues, the Anatomy of Wit* (1578) and its sequel *Euphues and His England* (1580), Lyly was also a successful popular and court dramatist, although he never received the preferment he expected. His plays include *Campaspe*, *Sappho and Phao*, and *Gallathea* (perf. 1588), and other plays for the Children of St. Paul's acting company. *Sappho and Phao* was presented to Elizabeth I on the evening of Shrove Tuesday, 1584.

[47] Addison's footnote: 'This ode was written by Sappho upon two favourite maids, of whom she was jealous.' Cf. *Greek Lyric* 1.130.146–7; 131.148–9.

[48] *Atthis* and *Andromeda* two of Sappho's female beloveds. See **7.3.1** and **7.3.2, note d**.

7.6

From *Sappho and Phao* (1592)

[Annoyed with Sappho's resistance to love, Venus orders her son Cupid to make Sappho and the beautiful ferryman Phao passionately in love with each other. Seeing their mistress sick, Sappho's gentlewomen send for Phao, reputedly skilled in the making of sleeping draughts. Alone, Sappho admits her love.]

7.6.1 Act 3, scene 3

[…]

SAPPHO. Ah! Impatient disease of love, and goddess of love thrice unpitiful! The eagle is never stricken with thunder, nor the olive with lightning; and may great ladies be plagued with love? O Venus, have I not strewed thine altars with sweet roses? Kept thy swans in clear rivers? Fed thy sparrows with ripe corn, and harboured thy doves in fair houses? […] Didst thou nurse me in my swaddling clouts[49] with wholesome herbs that I might perish in my flowering years by fancy?[50] I perceive, but too late I perceive, and yet not too late. […] Resist it[51] Sappho, whilst it is yet tender […] but alas it fareth with me as with wasps who feeding on serpents, make their stings more venomous: for glutting myself on the face of Phao, I have made my desire more desperate. Into the nest of a halcyon, no bird can enter but a halcyon, and into the heart of so great a lady can any creep but a great lord? […] my desires the more they swerve from reason, the more reasonable seem they. When Phao cometh, what then? Wilt thou open[52] thy love? Yea. No, Sappho, but staring in his face 'till thine eyes dazzle, and thy spirits faint, die before his face. Then this shall be written on thy tomb: that though thy love were greater than wisdom could endure, yet thine honour was such as love could not violate. […]

[…]

[Song]

49 *swaddling clouts* cloths in which new-borns were wrapped.
50 *fancy* love.
51 *it* love.
52 *open* reveal.

SAPPHO. O cruel love! On thee I lay
My curse which shall strike blind the day:
Never may sleep with velvet hand
Charm thine eyes with sacred wand;
Thy jailors shall be hopes and fears;
The prison-mates – groans, sighs, and tears;
Thy play to wear out weary times,
Fantastic passions, vows and rhymes;
Thy bread be frowns, thy drink be gall,[53]
Such as when you Phao call.
The bed thou liest on be despair;
Thy sleep, fond dreams; thy dreams, long care.[54]
Hope (like thy fool) at thy bed's head,
Mock thee, till madness strike thee dead;
As Phao, thou dost me with thy proud eyes
In thee poor Sappho lives; for thee she dies.

[Phao leaves without Sappho revealing her love for him. Venus, now herself mad with love for Phao, gets Cupid to relieve Sappho of her love for the ferryman.]

7.6.2 Act 5, scene 2

[A room in Sappho's palace. Enter Sappho, Cupid, Mileta,[55] Venus.]

[. . .]

CUPID. My mother is in love with Phao. She willed me to strike you with disdain of him and him with desire of her.

SAPPHO. Oh, spiteful Venus! Mileta, give him some of that.[56] What else, Cupid?

CUPID. I could be even with my mother, and so I will if I shall call you 'mother.'

SAPPHO. Yea, Cupid, call me anything so I may be even with her.

CUPID. I have an arrow with which if I strike Phao, it will cause him to loathe only Venus.

SAPPHO. Sweet Cupid, strike Phao with it. Thou shalt sit in my lap: I will rock thee asleep and feed thee with all these fine knacks.

[53] *gall* the type of an intensely bitter substance.

[54] *fond* infatuated; foolish.

[55] *Mileta* Sappho's maidservant.

[56] *that* i.e., they are feeding Cupid delicacies.

CUPID. I will about it. [*Exit* CUPID.

SAPPHO. But come quickly again. Ah, unkind Venus, is this thy promise to Sappho? But if I get Cupid from thee, I myself will be the Queen of Love.[57] I will direct these arrows with better aim and conquer mine own affections with greater modesty. Venus' heart shall flame and her love be as common as her craft. [...]

[Venus, finding Cupid sitting in Sappho's lap and claiming her as mother, threatens them both with terrible punishments.]

SAPPHO. Venus, be not choleric. Cupid is mine. He hath given me his arrows, and I will give him a new bow to shoot in. You are not worthy to be the lady of love, that yield so often to the impressions of love. Immodest Venus, that to satisfy the unbridled thoughts of thy heart, transgressest so far from the stay of thine honour. How sayest thou, Cupid: wilt thou be with me?

CUPID. Yes.

SAPPHO. Shall not I be on earth the goddess of affections?

CUPID. Yes.

SAPPHO. Shall not I rule the fancies of men and lead Venus in chains like a captive?

CUPID. Yes.

SAPPHO. It is a good boy!

[...]

VENUS. Well, I will be even with you both, and that shortly. [*Exit.*

SAPPHO. Cupid, fear not. I will direct thine arrows better. Every rude ass shall not say he is in love. It is a toy made for ladies, and I will keep it only for ladies.

CUPID. But what will you do for Phao?

SAPPHO. I will wish him fortunate. This will I do for Phao because I once loved Phao; for never shall it be said that Sappho loved to hate, or that out of love she could not be as courteous as she was in love passionate. Come, Mileta, shut the door.

[*Exeunt.*

[In the last scene of the play, it is Phao who continues in his hopeless passion for Sappho, determining to return to work as a ferryman.]

57 *Queen of Love* one of Venus's most common epithets.

John Donne (1572–1631)

Educated at Oxford, Cambridge and the Inns of Court, Donne's early life was shaped by his family's Roman Catholicism, by the hostility this religion faced in Protestant England, and by his unsanctioned marriage (1600) with Anne More, the niece of his powerful employer, Sir Thomas Egerton. Briefly imprisoned and socially ostracized for this marriage, Donne's hopes for a public, secular career were destroyed, but after years of soul-searching, his conversion to Protestantism and his ordination (1615) led to his appointment as dean of St Paul's Cathedral (1621). Unlike his religious prose, most of his secular poetry, including his verse epistles and erotic elegies, was published only posthumously.

7.7

From *Poems* (1633)

7.7.1 Sappho to Philaenis[58]

Where is that holy fire which verse is said
   To have? Is that enchanting force decayed?
Verse that draws Nature's works from Nature's law,
   Thee, her best work, to her work cannot draw.
Have my tears quenched my old poetic fire;
   Why quenched they not, as well, that of desire?
Thoughts, my mind's creatures, often are with thee,
   But I, their maker, want their liberty.
Only thine image in my heart doth sit,
   But that is wax and fires environ it.
My fires have driven, thine have drawn it hence;
   And I am robbed of picture, heart, and sense.
Dwells with me still mine irksome memory,
   Which both to keep and lose grieves equally.
That tells me how fair thou art: Thou art so fair,
   As gods, when gods to thee I do compare,
Are graced thereby; and to make blind men see
   What things gods are, I say they're like to thee.
For if we justly call each silly man[59]

58 *Philaenis* Greek, 'female friend'.
59 *silly* pitiable.

A little world, what shall we call thee than?[60]
Thou art not soft, and clear, and straight, and fair,
As down, as stars, cedars, and lilies are,
But thy right hand, and cheek, and eye, only
Are like thy other hand, and cheek, and eye.
Such was my Phao awhile, but shall be never,
As thou wast, art, and, oh, may'st be ever.
Here lovers swear in their idolatry
That I am such; but grief discolours me.
And yet I grieve the less, lest grief remove
My beauty, and make me unworthy of thy love.
Plays some soft boy with thee, oh there wants yet
A mutual feeling which should sweeten it.
His chin, a thorny hairy unevenness
Doth threaten, and some daily change possess.
Thy body is a natural paradise,
In whose self, unmanured, all pleasure lies,
Nor needs perfection; why shouldst thou than[61]
Admit the tillage of a harsh rough man?[62]
Men leave behind them that which their sin shows,
And are as thieves traced, which rob when it snows.[63]
But of our dalliance no more signs there are
Than fishes leave in streams, or birds in air.
And between us all sweetness may be had;
All, all that nature yields, or art can add.
My two lips, eyes, thighs, differ from thy two,
But so, as thine from one another do;
And, oh, no more; the likeness being such,
Why should they not alike in all parts touch?
Hand to strange hand, lip to lip none denies;
Why should they breast to breast, or thighs to thighs?
Likeness begets such strange self flattery,
That touching myself, all seems done to thee.
Myself I embrace, and mine own hands I kiss,
And amorously thank myself for this.
Me, in my glass, I call thee; But alas,

[60] *little world* commonplace Renaissance comparison between the individual and the cosmos, where a person was thought to comprise a miniature version of created nature; *than*: then.

[61] *than* then.

[62] *tillage* common agricultural metaphor for sexual intercourse.

[63] *traced* tracked.

When I would kiss, tears dim mine eyes and glass.
Oh, cure this loving madness, and restore
Me to me; thee, my half, my all, my more,
So may thy cheeks' red outwear scarlet dye,
And their white, whiteness of the galaxy,
So may thy mighty amazing beauty move
Envy in all women, and in all men love,
And so be change, and sickness, far from thee,
As thou by coming near, keep'st them from me.

William Walsh (1662–1708), MP and writer

A member of Dryden's literary circle, Walsh wrote in a variety of genres, from love lyrics and epigrams to fictional love letters in prose. Addressed to Eugenia, the Countess of Kingston, probably Walsh's mistress, *Dialogue Concerning Women, Being a Defence of the Sex* presents the opinions of the woman-hating Misogynes and the woman-loving Philogynes. Although Misogynes repeats conventional stereotypes about women, he focuses on their propensity to lust. Misogynes' subsequent list of sexually voracious women is equally conventional, except it includes possibly the earliest identification of Sappho as the inventor of tribadism. Philogynes' equally standard list of virtuous women concludes with an attempt to silence Misogynes' charges against Sappho, not because he is morally outraged, but because he does not want to give women the opportunity to reproach men for their much longer history of same-sex erotic relationships.

7.8

From *A Dialogue Concerning Women* (1691)

[...]

[MISOGYNES] [...] Sappho, as she was one of the wittiest[64] women that ever the world bred, so she thought with reason it would be expected she should make some additions to a science[65] in which all womankind had been so successful. What does she do then? Not content with our sex, she begins amours with her own, and teaches us a new

[64] *wittiest* most ingenious, clever, or skilful.
[65] *science* here, a body of knowledge concerning sexual lust.

sort of sin, that was followed not only in Lucian's time,[66] but is practised frequently in Turkey at this day.[67] You cannot but be sensible, sir, that there is no necessity of going so far for instances of their lewdness, and were it civil to quote the lampoons,[68] or write the amours of our own time, we might be furnished with examples enow[69] nearer home.

[70]*Here, madam, I could not forbear telling my friend, that his disputant grew scurrilous. He told me, considering him as a woman-hater, he thought 'twas no more than his character required; and that if I compared his discourse with what others had said against 'em,[71] I should think him a very well-bred man.*

[...]

[PHILOGYNES]. [...] We might tell you further, sir, that this modesty too often hinders 'em from making their virtues known; that they are not of those eternal scribblers who are continually plaguing the world with their works; and that it is not the vanity of getting a name, which several of the greatest men of the world have owned to be the cause of their writing, that is the cause of the women's. Had not Sappho been so much in love, 'tis possible we had never heard any mention of one of the greatest wits that ever was born; had not Cicero and Quintillian given us accounts of Cornelia [...] and Hortensi[a],[72] they had never done it themselves; had not Jane Grey[73]

66 Walsh's marginal note: 'See his Dialogue between Cleonarium and Leaena.' See **7.31.1**.

67 Walsh's marginal note: 'See Tavernier's Travels.' See **4.3.3**.

68 *lampoon* vicious satire on an individual.

69 *enow* enough.

70 The speaker here is the work's narrator, presumably to be identified with Walsh.

71 *'em* women.

72 *Cornelia* (d. by 100 BCE) was the second daughter of Publius Cornelius Scipio Africanus. Her marriage to Tiberius Sempronius Gracchus produced twelve children although only three survived to adulthood (Tiberius and Gaius became famed tribunes). After her husband's death she remained a widow, refusing all offers of marriage – even reportedly one from Ptolemy VIII – and dedicated herself exclusively to the education of her children. *Hortensia* was the daughter of the famous Roman orator Quintus Hortensius Hortalus (d. 49 BCE), Cicero's most serious legal and oratorical rival. Reportedly, when the triumvirs ordered 14,000 women to make a list of their possessions so that they might be taxed by the state, Hortensia pleaded the women's case so successfully that she won an exemption for 1,000 of them. She and her orations (which do not survive) are celebrated by Quintilian (c. 35–100 CE), Latin writer and rhetorician, who notes that this particular oration 'is still read and not merely as a compliment to her sex' (*Institutio Oratoria*, trans. H.E. Butler, 1.1.6).

73 *Jane Grey* (1537–54), daughter of an aristocratic family, she was executed by order

been put to death, her virtues had never been so much taken notice of; had not the Portuguese nun been deserted by her gallant, we had missed some of the most passionate letters that these latter ages have produced;[74] and had not Anna Maria Schurman's[75] works been published by a friend, without her consent, we had not the benefit of 'em. We may tell you too that 'tis not only in respect of their own sex that they are admired, but even of ours; that of those two odes we have yet of Sappho, we owe one to Dionysius Halicarnassus, the other to Longin[us],[76] the two best critics of Greece, who chose 'em out for examples to their rules, before any of the men's; that 'The Epistle of Sappho to Phaon', which is esteemed the most delicate of Ovid's is supposed to be taken out of her writings; that Corinna was five times victorious over Pindar, the best lyric poet of our sex.[77]

[...]

[PHILOGYNES] [...] whatever Sappho's life and conversation were, there is nothing in her writings but what represents the most tender and delicate passion in the world. [...] For the Queen of Sheba, there is no mention in Scripture of her travelling for anything but to be satisfied with the wisdom of Solomon; however, if you will believe she went to him for the same reason that Thalestris did to Alexander the Great,[78] it was no such great matter in countries where it was thought no sin, if the one had a mind to have a child by the wisest man in the world, and the other by the bravest. [...] But not a word more, I beseech you, of Sappho nor her new crime. Let Lucian be forgotten for putting us in mind of it, and let it be cloistered up

of Mary I for her unwilling involvement in an attempt to place Jane on the throne of England; famous for her staunch Protestantism and learning.

[74] *Portuguese nun ... produced* a reference to *Letters of a Portuguese Nun* (*Les Lettres Portugaises*), an epistolary fiction which was believed at the time the genuine letters of a Portuguese nun to her lover Noel Bouton, Marquis de Chamilly (1635–1715).

[75] *Anna Maria Schurman* (1607–78), Dutch artist, writer, and scholar, whose *De ingenii muliebris* [...] (1641) was highly influential. Translated in 1659 as *The Learned Maid, or Whether a Maid May Be a Scholar.*

[76] See **n34** and **n1**.

[77] *Corinna* (*fl.* third century BCE?), Greek poet to whom some fifty books of epigrams and odes were attributed of which only a handful of verses remain; *Pindar*: celebrated Greek poet to whom seventeen books of verse were attributed; only his victory odes and some fragments survive.

[78] *Thalestris*, Queen of the Amazons, sought out *Alexander the Great* so that she could have a child by him; she spent thirteen days having sex with him and then departed for home, believing she had conceived.

> within the walls of a Turkish seraglio.[79] I speak not this in behalf of the female sex, but of our own; for if they should once hear of this argument and fall upon us with Socrates,[80] Plato,[81] and all those heroes of antiquity, whom Plutarch and Lucian produce in defence of a like sin in our sex; should they mention Anacreon, Tibullus, Martial, and all those poets who have eternized their infamy in their writings; and after that show you what progresses this crime has made not only in the Turk's dominion but even in Spain and Italy: I am sure, sir, you would wish you had said nothing of a point that may be so severely made use of against ourselves.

[...]

The Sappho-An

Probably the nadir in Sappho's early modern representations, this mock-heroic poem offers the licentious, sexually voracious, and heterosexual Sappho so familiar from the eighteenth to the early twentieth centuries. Alexander Pope's thoroughly heterosexualized version of Sappho in his translation of Ovid's 'Sappho to Phaon' and his vituperative attacks on his erstwhile friend Lady Mary Wortley Montagu, whom he partly presents in the guise of Sappho as promiscuous, syphilitic, and repulsive, may to a certain extent have licensed *The Sappho-An*'s degraded representation of the ancient poet (Reynolds 123–5). However, Stevenson's and Radcliffe's late seventeenth-century burlesques of Ovid's 'Sappho to Phaon' are even earlier precedents for Sappho's representation as the vulgar, diseased prostitute (*Online Companion*). Modern critical assessments vary: Traub suggests that *The Sappho-An* implies the increasingly blurred division between female friendship and tribadism (*Renaissance* 316), while Donoghue sees its title as an indication of how widely known the link had become between Sappho and female same-sex erotic and sexual relationships (*Passions* 261). Wahl sees the poem as containing an early example of a popular later stereotype: the ageing lesbian in pursuit of younger women (86, 321 n31), but believes the poem represents lesbians less harshly than their contemporary male homosexual counterparts, the mollies, since, unlike the mollies, the goddesses do not seek to transform their gender.

The author of *The Sappho-An* remains unidentified. The suffix 'an' refers

79 *seraglio* harem.

80 Walsh's marginal note: 'Socrates was in love with Alcibiades.' See Plutarch, 'Life of Alcibiades', *Online Companion.*

81 Walsh's marginal note: 'Plato writes verses to Aster, a boy with whom he was in love' (*Greek Anthology* 7.669–70).

to membership or association (as in Anglican or Roman (Catholic)), and points to the way the homoerotic and autoerotic sexual acts in the work are constituted as marking an early Sapphic affiliation between various female characters (from goddesses to contemporary Englishwomen). The work lacks a print publication date, but the University of Kansas copy bears the title page inscription 'Toms Coffee House, April 10 1749'. Critics have assigned it dates as early as c. 1735 and as late as that year.

7.9

From *The Sappho-An*[82] (c. 1735?/1749?)

7.9.1 Canto 1

Swains of Britannia's happy, gladsome isle,[83]
Who wait submissive on the fair one's smile;
And all the soothing arts of lovers try
In hope to make the cruel nymph comply;
Know, whilst you idle thus away your time,
Women in secret joys consume their prime;[84]
Some fav'rite, or handy young coquette,[85]
Steals the rich prize you vainly strive to get;
Of them be cautious, but the artful prude
Watch most, for she will thoughtless girls delude.
At break of day when you have often mourned
Your tender billet-doux, unread, unreturned,[86]
And thought some happier rival in the place
Where you expected the long-wished embrace:

[82] The title page continues: 'An Heroic Poem, of Three Cantos. In the Ovidian Style, Describing the Pleasures which the Fair Sex Enjoy with Each Other. According to the Modern and Most Polite Taste. Found amongst the Papers of a Lady of Quality, a great Promoter of Jaconitism'; *Jaconitism*: probably an error for Jacobitism, the label given to supporters of the exiled James III and opponents of the reigning monarch, George II (1727–60). The Whigs generally portrayed the Tories as secret Jacobites. The title page epigram is from Ovid's 'Sappho to Phaon', where Sappho rejects all her female lovers in favour of Phaon (ll. 15–19; see Introduction to **7.2–7.9** and **7.3.2 n17**).

[83] *swain* lover (especially in pastoral poetry).

[84] *prime* early adulthood.

[85] *handy* 'conveniently available', but also 'sexually skilful with her hand'; *coquette*: flirtatious, wanton woman.

[86] *billet-doux* love letter.

Your lovely nymph, in private, quenched her flame
With some experienced, well known crafty dame,
Who knew the softest way to reach her heart,
And proudly vied with nature in her art.

[Apologizing to modest young women readers, the author distinguishes between the natural love of a young woman 'who clasp[s] the vig'rous youth' and the unnatural love of women who 'Amazonian warfare vainly wage, [...] Inverting nature in a horrid way' (11). Claiming he will reveal women's secrets, he calls upon the Roman chastity goddess Bona Dea as his muse; however, this invocation is intentionally ironic, given that Bona Dea's exclusive worship by women is the pretext for the well known female same-sex orgy in Juvenal's 'Satire 6' (see **7.27.1**).]

Do thou with gentle beams inspire my verse,
The progress of thy vot'ries to rehearse,[87]
When in soft dalliance they waste the night,
To form some new invention of delight:
Oh, paint the blissful scene, the soft distress,
Which only gentle murmurs can express!
Think, on the couch you see the lovely maid
Extended, and her limbs for pleasure spread;
To her own sex a treasure she resigns,
A treasure richer than Peruvian mines.

[The author claims heterosexual love was first corrupted by lust, the destruction of Sodom being an 'emblem of false love' and of those 'who from the dictates of true nature swerve' (13).]

Fearful of shame, they tried a curious art,[88]
And saw the doves their cooing joys impart;[89]
From thence they learned, that even suction eased,
And by partition both were highly pleased.[90]
In ancient Greece the ladies knew full well
Who best in these Olympics could excel;
There, as from dews the bees their honey sip,

[87] *vot'ries* votaries.

[88] *shame* i.e., attendant on illicit heterosexual intercourse (exposure or pregnancy); *they*: women.

[89] *doves* one of Venus's emblematic birds.

[90] *partition* unclear: perhaps, a 'portion or part' (of sexual intercourse) referring to the women's pleasuring of each other without a penis or dildo.

The dames would dwell upon the ruby lip;
Till, by their joys excited, they rise high'r,
And dart the tongue to raise the glowing fire;
Nor stopped they there, but full fruition sought,
The finger was an useful, charming thought.[91]

[Fearing the shame of bastardy, ancient women used pre-pubescent boys for sexual pleasure, and the boys most desired were feminine in appearance. The author describes how Venus used her own son, Cupid, as a sexual toy, when she endured a forced abstinence from her lover, Mars. Mentioning the bisexual loves of some gods, the author details Juno's rage at Jove's many infidelities, and the gods' general enjoyment of boys becomes the justification for the goddess's exploration of female same-sex acts.]

[92]'Nor mine alone is this disgrace; look round
Th' Olympian court, no god is honest found:
For not the female bed alone they court,
But ruddy boys afford them filthy sport.
There sticks the rancour, venom there corrodes,
That poisons even the divine abodes.
If their sex thus can find their own delight,
Sure we *some way* each other may invite!
Here then my fury rests, I'll straight convene[93]
The jealous goddesses t'attend their queen.'

7.9.2 Canto 2

[Hermes tries to warn his fellow gods about the danger the goddesses's meeting poses to their sovereignty, but he is simply laughed at. The author then gives portraits of the main players at Juno's gathering: Cytherea [i.e., Venus], Minerva, Diana, Vesta, Ceres and her daughter Proserpine, Cybele, Hebe, the Naiads (sea nymphs), and finally Sappho.]

Juno herself, with features stern and strong,
High nose, thin lips, and chin acute and long,
Whilst spread about some bristly hairs appear,
Such as when yonkers their first off'rings shear;[94]

91 *And dart … thought* referring to cunnilingus, although here finger succeeds tongue as an instrument of arousal.

92 The speaker is Juno.

93 *straight* immediately.

94 *yonker* fashionable young man; *first off'rings shear*: i.e., shave their first chin hairs.

Her dress was female, but her manly step
Seemed as she'd wrestle, throw the bar, or leap;
From C—rt—r these she borrowed, lusty maid,[95]
Who makes the H—ckn—y husbands all afraid;[96]
For neither science comes to her amiss,[97]
The spouse she'll bully, and the wife she'll kiss.

[...]

From sylvan scenes of hawthorn glens and trees,
The huntress nymph appears bare to the knees,[98]
Her manlike sinews, hardened by the chase,
Strain, stretch, and crack at thoughts of the embrace;
Yet man she scorns, and whilst she inward burns,
Nature's strong current on itself returns.
Diana thus bold Philony appears,[99]
Whose loud-toned pack the Hampshire forests fears.
From them retreating to the inmost shade
Where no bold eyes their privacy invade;
She with her nymphs their lovely limbs unbind
To be all o'er kissed by the bawdy wind.
Or, laving in the stream, to water give
Th' embraces man most gladly would receive;
In vain they beat the wave, the wave supplies
Fresh warmth, from whence more wanton they arise;
Then stretched on verdant banks in pairs they lie
And to posteriors friendly birch apply;[100]
The gentle titillation swells the veins
Till oozing ichor leaves some faintish stains:[101]
Imperfect bliss! mere miniature of joy!
Formed to raise longings and high lust destroy.

In antiquity, a young man's first beard shavings were often ceremoniously offered to the gods as a token of his entrance into manhood.

[95] *C—rt—r* There are a number of indications, like this one, that contemporary Englishwomen are being covertly referred to, but they all remain unidentified. See **n99** and **n128**. Cf. **n134** (two male contemporaries).

[96] *H—ckn—y* Hackney (area of London notorious for its prostitutes).

[97] *science* practice requiring trained skills.

[98] *huntress nymph* Diana (Glossary).

[99] *Philony* unidentified. See **n95**.

[100] *birch* Bundles of birch twigs served as whips. For flagellation as a technique of sexual arousal, see **2.1.4 n32** and **9.16.1 n39**.

[101] *ichor* fluid supposed to flow like blood in the veins of the classical deities.

[...]

Mark yon fell dame who, tott'ring in her gait,[102]
Steps solemn on, fond to preserve her state,[103]
Cybele hight, the mother of the gods[104]
Who long has revelled in her dark abodes.
A matron's image shrouds her shrivelled skin,
With furrowed brows and features lank and thin;
Yet still her palsied hand would grasp the chief[105]
That floods her veins and renovates her life;
But long debarred from that to art she flies,
And the kind bosom of a virgin tries;
Whose rising sap with genial juices crowned[106]
Make her faint spirits from their dotage bound;
Her arid limbs entwined, close suction ply,
And drain the melting porous nymph quite dry;
Who yields her vigour to relieve the crone,
And whilst she gives her vigour taints her own;
So tea and spices though they're closely pent[107]
Receive the neighb'ring filth's obnoxious scent.
   Behind her Hebe comes in bloom of youth
Formed for congenial love, soft joys, and truth;
Blushing and radiant as the rosy morn,
When heav'nly smiles doth Nature's face adorn,
Arrayed in ev'ry grace to charm mankind,
To clasp the youth in am'rous folds inclin'd.
But, ah! too soon those beauties all will fade,
And lust perfidious sully the bright maid.
No jocund bridegroom leaps into her arms,
But the old dotard rifles all her charms,
Till like a dying flow'r she pines and droops,
And in mid-age with impotence she stoops;
From her sunk cheeks declines the lively dye,
And faintly rolls the heavy, languid eye.

[...]

102 *fell* terrible.
103 *fond* eager.
104 *hight* called.
105 *palsied* shaking; *chief*: penis.
106 *juices* sexual lubrication.
107 *closely pent* securely confined.

To close the scene, quite ripe for am'rous sport
The Lesbian, though no goddess, fills the court:[108]
Man's solid bliss she to the full had tried,
Nor to the other sex her aid denied;
Awful she rushes in and claims a part[109]
To add new vigour to the blunted dart;[110]
Amazed the conclave sat, her threat'ning front[111]
Carried dismay and insolence upon't.
For Phaon still she sighed, a tender boy,
Who spurned her hostile love and warrior joy;
For Nature in exuberance of lust,
Her parts had formed adapt to either gust:
The wide receiver (most capacious space!)[112]
With ease the largest chieftain could embrace,[113]
And when the trembling damsel lay supine
To seeming virile force she could incline:
Nature benevolent thrust forth elate
The part that forms to bliss, or goads to hate.[114]
Hence, ev'ry Hero on her bosom fell
And how she tickled girls they best can tell.[115]
'Forgive this rude intrusion,' now she cries.
'Ripe to redress our sex's wrongs I rise!
A nobler way remains in Nature's womb
To fix our joys eternally to come.'

[Before Sappho is allowed to make her suggestion, the author interrupts to offer a list of all the ways that woman has found to pleasure herself sexually without a man, principally through bestiality: some have been pleasured by their lapdogs, others have achieved orgasms through riding hard their horses.]

108 *Lesbian* Sappho.
109 *awful* either 'awe-inspiring' (meant sarcastically) or simply 'appalling'.
110 *blunted dart* flaccid or worn-out penis.
111 *front* face.
112 *receiver* vagina.
113 *chieftain* penis.
114 *For Nature in exuberance … hate* referring either to Sappho's tribadic anatomy, where her enlarged clitoris can function penetratively like a penis, or to her hermaphroditism, where Nature has endowed her with both male and female sexual organs. The description of her 'seeming virile force' may suggest the former, but 'Nature in exuberance of lust, / Her parts had formed adapt to either gust' the latter.
115 *tickled* copulated with; here, 'masturbated'.

'My poor endeavours shall support the claim,
Love is my life, and love is all my aim;
Man's rough, ingrateful sex henceforth I scorn,
May all, like me, their cold embraces spurn;
Woman to woman's breast can best supply
The stream of love, when once the pulse beats high.
Come then, ye virgins of the tender make,[116]
Of unfelt joys and circling bliss partake.'
Thus Sappho spoke, and at the grateful close,
A pleasing murmur through th'assembly rose.
Mild as when o'er the rill, or through the trees,
In whispers gently swells the vernal breeze.
They smiled assent, and from her starry throne,
Great Juno thus her sentiments made known:
'Celestial sisters! Arbiters of fate!
Know from my soul sincerely man I hate;
No more the scrubbing of a rustic kiss
Shall rough my face, rude antidote to bliss.
Freedom to all is given; your schemes propose;
At liberty your secret thoughts disclose.
Say, who the noblest science can improve,
With arts unknown to dull, mechanic love;
[...]
Be't yours to bound, to leap, your limbs to spread,
And wanton lewdly on the genial bed;
Satiate with man, all nature's stock explore,
And pluck assistance from her endless store.
Begin: who first our infant hopes can rear,
Shall in a full assembly transport share.'

[Ceres suggests using carrots or parsnips as penis substitutes, an idea rejected by Juno as undignified for goddesses. Juno suggests eunuchs instead: they can't make one pregnant. However, Hebe reveals that she herself has had sex with Ganymede and he has confessed that Jove 'in another mode hath love expressed', clearly referring to anal intercourse. Hebe warns that ganymedes are unlikely to keep ladies' secrets, and implies they may attempt anal intercourse with their female partners, a sexual act that the group deplores as 'Italian mimicry' (36).]

[116] *tender make* delicate constitution.

7.9.3 Canto 3

[Canto 3's central preoccupation is the dildo. Sappho recommends it, and demonstrates its effectiveness on the test maiden.]

When Hebe ceased, alert, with manly air,
Sappho rose from off her iv'ry chair,
Beneath her robe the sacred prize she held,
Whose large protub'rance was but ill concealed.
'Cease, cease,' she cries, 'your needless search suspend!
Well-versed in love, let me the conflict end;
A curious artist that through nature pried,
Has ev'ry wish our hearts could form supplied;
He gives us man without the plague of males,
Which will untired remain when nature fails;
The conscious blush must rise whene'er I think
What arts we use when drooping standards sink;[117]
In vain the lily hand with genial fire
Strives with fresh heat the mortals to inspire;
When round their limbs robust we gently twine,
And fondly hope to make the centres join;
Repugnant to our joys, the ruler, dead,[118]
Hangs like a fading flow'r its livid head;
Nor can our heaving breasts new strength excite,
The darting tongue no longer can invite;
When we to rushing joy go boldly on,
Supine and indolent they tumble down;
Baulked in our bliss, we to reproaches fly,
And noise and tumult for kind sighs supply;
No more we clasp him in our tender arms,
No more his colder breast our bosom warms;
Who then such frail felicity would trust,
Or value those imperfect efforts most,
When solid joys are always at command,[119]
And court the pressure of your eager hand?
For this the burnished iv'ry rears its head,
Waiting for coral of a lovely red;
Or if too rude the polished engine seems,

[117] *standards* penises.
[118] *ruler* penis.
[119] *solid* physically solid; reliable.

The velvet cov'ring keeps it from extremes;
In shape complete, nor can ye aught despise,
For to your choice they shall adapt the size.'
  She said, and with a more majestic mien
Produced at once the wonderful machine.[120]
Not more the Greeks rejoiced when Ilium's fate,
Which on its stol'n Palladium did await,[121]
The sly Ulysses cautiously drew out
And charmed the wond'ring chiefs and vulgar rout.
With rapture all beheld it, and applause
In Iös loud, the silent image draws.[122]
Immediate trial is the next demand,
The trial claims a gently trembling hand;
Kind Sappho soon administers her aid,
And drives the dart into the yielding maid.

[The goddesses' joint decision to improve the use of the dildo leads to Diana's testing of it, and Minerva's improvement on it: she places a small tube in the middle of it which (at the touch of a finger) emits warm liquid, mimicking penile ejaculation. In a brief survey of the dildo's history, the author says it was first used in China, and then came via trade to Spain, Italy and France, before finally landing in Britain.]

Returning Charles this blessing brought and more,[123]
To fill the magazine of lech'ry's store.[124]
These all the ladies of his court enjoyed,
Though for disguise a hogshead were destroyed;
Of this facetious Butler loudly sings,
Best poet to the bawdiest of k—ngs.[125]
  Oh! could I trace the dear succession down,

[120] *machine* dildo. See 'engine', above.

[121] *Palladium* statue of Pallas Athena, the goddess of wisdom, believed to safeguard Troy (*Ilium*); the Greek warriors Diomedes and Ulysses steal the statue in order to ensure Troy's fall.

[122] *Iös* 'Io, Io Paean': ancient Greek ritual cry of celebration and acclamation.

[123] *Charles* II returned to the throne 1660, with the restoration of the monarchy; notoriously licentious king, with many mistresses and illegitimate children.

[124] *magazine* munitions storehouse.

[125] *These … k—ngs* The poet Samuel Butler's *Dildoides. A Burlesque Poem* (1706) recounts 'the Burning [of] a Hogshead [i.e., a large cask] of dildoes in 1672', as part of Parliament's 'prohibiting of French Goods'. Butler notes the dildos varied in size depending on whether experienced court ladies or virgins were their intended users.

How it the country raised, and spread the town,
As outside nervous should my verses prove,
Yet softer than the milk-distilling love.[126]
   Like sects opposed the stronger root it took,
And soon the chief of women men forsook;[127]
They change their habits, alter ev'ry air,
And see in Joseph's puny miss appear;[128]
The bold virago mankind seems to ape,[129]
And for that purpose varies ev'ry shape;
The yielding girl to gentler postures turns,
And gives to woman what to man she scorns.
   The diff'rent symptoms take: the female rake,[130]
The cock of hat and furzy wig bespeak;[131]
She rides her trotting nag aside 'tis true;[132]
But ye pale-looking nymphs how rides she you?[133]
Full flushed, and of the Amazonian kind,
She dreads no storms, nor fears the rougher wind;
All morn most briskly she pursues the chase,
Then on your couch imprints the lewd embrace.
   With languid eyes, and feeble trembling pulse,
That baffles all the skill of Sl—ne or H—se[134]
Forever lazy, and forever dull
Craving eternally, yet never full;
Stretched on a couch, or lolling in a chair,
The indigent receiver doth appear.[135]
The sport a-while may sick'ning life sustain.
But soon 'tis o'er, and endless is the pain.
   Would ye, young girls, who glow with health and love,

Charles II reportedly loved Butler's *Hudibras*, a mock chivalric epic that skewered the monarchy's opponents.

[126] *milk-distilling love* a woman's stroking of the penis, producing milk (semen).

[127] *chief of women* i.e., most women, but with a glance at 'the most masculine of women'. Cf. **n105**; **n113**.

[128] *Joseph* unidentified. See **n95**.

[129] *virago* mannish woman; also, 'male sexual athlete'.

[130] *rake* promiscuous man.

[131] *cock of hat* hat worn with a rakish tilt; *furzy*: fuzzy.

[132] *aside* side-saddle, as was proper for a woman.

[133] *rides* copulates with.

[134] *Sl—ne* Sir Hans Sloane, prominent court physician to Queen Anne, George I, and George II; *H—se*: Sir Edward Hulse, important London physician.

[135] *receiver* whore. But cf. **n112**.

The blissful minutes of your lives improve,
Ne'er throw the balm of luscious love away,[136]
And voluntary dwindle to decay;
Nor bathe a stupid tool, when the same joys,[137]
May bring ye pretty girls and chatt'ring boys;
Rather avow your love, confess your flame,
And nature boldly own, devoid of shame.
Let the mean herd, the shaggy, pallid crew,
Their forced, their made-up bliss at home pursue;
Woman was made for man, so nature meant,
And ev'ry fibre answers the intent;
Who sins against it thc creation wrongs,
Must rank with beasts, nor to mankind belongs.

[The poem concludes with the fictional speaker saying that she is dying because of her indulgence in non-reproductive sex, and she begs young female readers to avoid her fate.]

Anacreon (c. 575–c. 490 BCE), Greek poet

Court poet in Samos and Athens, reportedly Anacreon was the lover of the aristocrat Critias (c. 460–403 BCE); lived to age eighty-five; died choking on a grape; and vied with Polycrates, King of Samos, for the love of the beautiful boy Smerdies. The hedonistic tenor of the following translations from the *Anacreontea*, poems in imitation of Anacreon, helped produce Anacreon's early modern reputation as the sweetest of lyricists and the most impious of drunkards. His love for the youth Bathyllus was well known: the couple regularly appear in conventional lists of famous classical same-sex lovers; Horace comments on 'soft Anachreon' who 'for Bathyllus burn'd, / And oft his Love he sadly mourned' ('Epode 14', trans. Thomas Creech (1684), 176).

Francis Willis (n.d.), Abraham Cowley (1618–67), John Oldham (1653–83), Thomas Wood (n.d.), and S.B

We know nothing about Willis and his collaborators, with the exception of Cowley (see Introduction to **8.20**) and Oldham, Oxford graduate, libertine poet, satirist, and translator.

[136] *balm* male semen.
[137] *stupid tool* dildo.

7.10

From *Anacreon done into English out of the original Greek* (1683)[1]

7.10.1 XXVI. Bathyllus[2]

If painter thou true life can'st draw,
Now, now, my fair Bathyllus show.
On's hair a charming blackness lies,
And even thence a light does rise.
Make wand'ring little curls to dance
In a well-ordered negligence.
His high forehead bright as the morn[3]
Black, narrow eyebrows do adorn.
Through which, as from a bow that's bent
Sharp arrows from his eyes are sent.[4]
To my heart let them a passage bore,
And make me love him more.
Make fierce, black eyes, that thousands slew,
Yet make 'em kind and courteous too.
This angry part by Mars was sent,
This mildness here by Venus lent.
That down th'admirer drives,
And this the criminal forgives.
His cheeks with youth and blushes dressed,
By fairest apples are expressed.[5]
Let modesty o'er all command,
Else the piece will blush to mend your hand.[6]
His red, plump lips and little mouth
Will puzzle and torment us both.
Pretty, delicious, – oh, they've outgone
All art and all description.
But let sweet smiles around 'em play,
And there becoming moistures lay;

[1] For S.B.'s preface, see *Online Companion.*

[2] Anonymous translator. Cf. 'Anacreontea', *Greek Lyric* 2.17.184–7.

[3] *high forehead* conventional mark of beauty.

[4] *Through … sent* The Petrarchan mistress's eyes often shoot darts of love into her lover's.

[5] *By … expressed* Cf. **7.25.5**.

[6] *your hand* i.e., [the work] of the painter's hand.

To them let eloquence be joined,
As if for rhetoric designed.[7]
They must at least a motion make,
And even silence seem to speak:
Like that of the spheres let it be,
A sweet but unheard harmony.[8]
And in this charming face, let all
Be stately and majestical.
O'er's slender, ivory neck I'll pass,[9]
And with more joy do downwards hast.[10]
His breast is full in every part,
For it contains Anacreon's heart.
Smooth are his hands, both long and white,
Which kisses must from all invite.
Here through blue veins pure blood does glide;
Here on it oft the soul does ride.
To this fair place o'erjoyed it runs,
Long stays it makes, and quick returns.
His large, big belly all approve;
'Tis in drunk'ness graceful and in love.
His thighs to marble I'd compare,
But that they soft and tender are;
Loose quivering flesh in whiteness lies,
And stiff cold age with fire supplies.
Let there be now a thin slight shade,
Or anything or nothing made.
An inward tickling only draw,
And love's first pleasant itchings show;[11]
Even now let flowing Nature try
To pass the bounds of chastity.
But see your art is too unkind:
It does not show the charms behind,
Charms that seem now lovelier far,
Because they hidden are.
On him I will not feet bestow,
For lovers never look so low.

[7] *rhetoric* persuasiveness.

[8] *Like … harmony* Spheres (Glossary).

[9] *O'er's* Over his

[10] *hast* haste.

[11] *Let … show* Cf. 'Anacreontea', *Greek Lyric* 2.17.187, which refers to Bathyllus's 'simple member that already desires the Paphian [Venus]'.

I only this of you shall claim,
That you'd the piece 'Apollo' name.[12]
And if you e'er Apollo see,
Call't Bathyllus in effigy:
For both are gods, both loved by me.

Thomas Ball (1669/70–1723), translator and Cambridge graduate

Two Books of Elegies contains translations of selections from Ovid's *De Tristibus*, original poems, seven of Anacreon's other odes (including the homoerotic 'Ode 3' (33)), and translations from Horace, Moschus, and Bion.

7.11

From *Two Books of Elegies* (1697)

7.11.1 Ode 12: The Swallow[13]

Say, thou damned disturber of my rest,
Thou prattling swallow, worst of all thy nest,
How shall I punish thee? for I'll no more
Endure thy early noise as heretofore;
What if I clipped thy wings? or cut thy tongue?
As Tereus, Philomela served when young?
For when Bathyllus moves with softest charms,
And I all melting lie within his arms,[14]
The boy I loose, by your confounded note,[15]
So often echoed through your squeaking throat.

[12] *piece* painting.

[13] Cf. 'Anacreontea', *Greek Lyric* 2.10.172–5.

[14] *melting* often used in early modern love poetry to mean 'experiencing orgasm' or 'extreme erotic pleasure'.

[15] *loose* 'release', or perhaps 'lose' (since dawn means the end of their embraces, as they rise to meet the day).

Horace (65–8 BCE), Latin poet

Son of an Italian freedman and client of the literary patrons Maecenas and the Emperor Augustus, Horace produced six major works: *Satires*, *Epodes*, *Odes*, *Carmen Saeculare*, *Epistles*, and *Ars Poetica*. Bisexuality and a general indifference to the gender of the beloved mark much of Horace's love poetry; he speaks of his own 'thousand passions for girls, thousand passions for boys' (*Satires* 2.3.325). In *Odes*, the speaker sexually desires and longs for a specific boy (Ligurinus) (4.1; 4.10); symbolizes the sensual pleasures of life in the beautiful boy generally (1.4, 1.32, 1.38); and voyeuristically describes the boy's beauty and the erotic desire he awakens in girls (3.19). As in most ancient homoerotic Latin verse, the male love object in Horace's odes is a beautiful pubescent or adolescent slave.

Henry Rider (*fl.* 1623–38), translator

We know almost nothing about Henry Rider, except that he was a Cambridge graduate (BA, 1626–27; MA, 1630) and the first translator of Horace's complete odes and epodes into English.

7.12

From *All the Odes and Epodes of Horace*
(1638; 2nd edn, 1644)

7.12.1 Ode 4.1:[1] A complaint that Venus hath made him a lover again. He dotes upon Ligurinus, and desires Venus to forsake him, and go to the house of Paulus Maximus[2]

O Venus, intermitted many a day,[3]
Dost thou again wage wars? Spare, spare, I pray.
I am not now as I before did stand
Under my lovely Cynarae's command.[4]

[1] For this poem's history of deletion in selected translations, see '1. Deletion, Expurgation, Vagueness, and Mistranslation' (Chapter 7, Introduction). Translations by Smith (1649), Brome (1660), Creech (1684), and Coxwell (1718) clearly depict the speaker's homoerotic desire.

[2] *Paulus* Fabius *Maximus*, Roman nobleman and consul, friend of Ovid and Augustus.

[3] *intermitted* i.e., you who have suspended or left off.

[4] *Cynarae* Cynara, a female beloved in Horace's verse.

Spare, cruel mother of all-pleasing love,
A man 'bout fifty years of age to move,
Now hardened to thy soft commandments: go
Where young men's pleasing prayers do thee woo;
In Paulus Maximus his palace you,
Being winged with cygnets of a purple hue,[5]
More opportunely may together feast,
If you delight to fire a fitting breast:
For he, being both noble and complete,
And for poor souls condemned ne'er silent yet,[6]
And a youth of a hundred tricks beside,[7]
Shall spread the ensigns of thy war full wide.[8]
And when he shall triumph, being of more power
Than the late gifts of his competitor,
Near to the Albane springs he'll set up thee[9]
All marble underneath a citron tree.
There with thy nose thou shalt draw much sweet smell,
And there thou shalt be pleasèd very well
With intermixèd music of the lute,
And Berecynthian pipe, and with the flute.[10]
There youths with tender virgins twice a day,
While that they do thy deity display,[11]
According as is now the Salian guise,[12]
With their clean feet thrice on the ground shall rise.
Me neither woman now nor boy doth move,
Nor a too credulous hope of mutual love;
Nor doth it please me to contend with wine,
Nor with fresh flowers my temples round to twine.
But why, O Ligurinus, why alas
Do my rare seen tears o'er my cheeks thus pass?
Wherefore in silence, no way fit at all,
Amidst my words does my smooth tongue thus fall?
Now close-clinged in my nightly dreams I woo thee,

[5] *cygnets* Swans drew Venus's chariot.

[6] *And ... yet* i.e., Paulus was an eloquent advocate for apprehensive defendants.

[7] *tricks* accomplishments.

[8] *ensigns* flags.

[9] *Albane springs* Alban Lake, about 15 miles from Rome.

[10] *Berecynthian pipe* double pipe, one of which sounds bass notes.

[11] *display* acknowledge; worship.

[12] *guise* style; *Salian*: pertaining to the ancient Roman Salii or priests of Mars, god of war.

Now through the grass of Mars his field pursue thee,
So swift of foot, and cruel-hearted thee
Among the streams that every-moving be.

7.12.2 Ode 4.10: The poet tells Ligurinus that when the flower of his youth is past, he shall grieve to think he had not that understanding then which now he hath

O thou, yet cruel, and imperious grown
By Venus' gifts, when the unhopèd down[13]
Shall steal upon thy pride, and thy hairs shed
Which now fly o'er thy shoulders, and thy red
That's choicer than the damask rose's grace,
Being changed shall turn unto a wrinkled face:
Thee, Ligurinus, thou wilt cry (alas)[14]
(When thou shalt see thee, not thee, in thy glass):
'When I was young why had I not this mind?
Or to these thoughts why not sound cheeks assigned?'

Catullus (c. 84–54 BCE), Latin poet

Catullus's love poems on his relationship with the married 'Lesbia', probably Clodia, wife of the consul Quintus Metellus Celer, in their movement from happiness to bitter despair over her infidelity, influenced many early modern writers. Catullus also wrote a cycle of poems for and about the beloved boy, the aristocratic youth Juventius, of which only 'Carmen 48' – where Catullus desires almost limitless kisses from Juventius – and 'Carmen 99' – where Catullus steals a kiss from the youth – appeared in English before 1735 without any qualification of or explanation for their homoerotic content.

Of the other poems in this cycle, 'Carmen 15?' and 'Carmen 21?' deal generally with rivals who pose a sexual threat to the beloved youth, while 24 and 81, focus on the speaker's reproaches for Juventius' sexual relationships with other men; of these, only 15? and 21? appear in English before 1735. *Carmina* 24 and 81, as well as Catullus's many homosatiric assaults on enemies and rivals (e.g., 16, 74, and 80), had to wait until well into the twentieth century for frank translations.

[13] *unhopèd down* undesired, first growth of the beard. Maturing from boy to man made Ligurinus an unsuitable object of male erotic desire in the classical world.

[14] In the original, 'alas' is part of Ligurinus's own lament, and Rider's punctuation suggests that it can be read that way, but also as a parenthetical expression of grief by the speaker.

Richard Lovelace (1617–57), poet, royalist army officer, and Oxford graduate

Wounded and imprisoned in Charles I's service, Lovelace published his only volume of verse *Lucasta* (1649) a year after his incarceration in 1648, with the 1659 expanded edition published posthumously. While the volume's poems for the mistress Lucasta are justly famous, Lovelace's translations from Latin and Greek poets have received little attention.

7.13

From *Lucasta: Posthume Poems* (1659)

7.13.1 To Juvencius

Juvencius, thy fair sweet eyes,
If to my fill that I may kiss,
Three hundred thousand times I'd kiss,
Nor future age should cloy this bliss;
No, not if thicker than ripe ears
The harvest of our kisses bears.

Jean de La Chapelle (1651–1723), French dramatist, prose writer, and member of the Académie Française

Author of many highly regarded works, such as *Cléopâtre* (1681), *Marie d'Anjou, Reine de Majorque* (1682), and *Les Amours de Tibulle* (1722), de La Chappelle's *Les Amours de Catulle* (1680) was translated anonymously into English in 1707. On the following Catullus and Petronius texts, see '2. Contextualization' (Chapter 7, Introduction).

7.14

From *The Adventures of Catullus* (1707)

[The name of the beautiful and much-admired Roman youth Juventius becomes the name Catullus gives the lovely aristocrat Crastinia in the verse he writes for and about her. After courting and winning her favour, Catullus voyages to Bythinia, and asks his friend Aurelius to look after his 'boy' while he is gone.]

7.14.1 (Carmen 15)

Aurelius, I entreat your care[1]
Of me, and of my love's affair;
Modest's the favour I request:
If ever what is good or chaste
Was entertained within your breast,
Chastely preserve my boy from harm,
Not from the mob in streets that swarm,
That busied travel here and there,
From them there is no cause of fear;
But from yourself, a man in pow'r,[2]
Who good and bad alike deflow'r,[3]
E'en take your swing of lust abroad,[4]
By no such thing as conscience awed;
Caress what other youth you please,
But not in him disturb my ease.
For rest assured, if your base mind
Drive you to act a treason of this kind,
You may with justice surely dread
My vengeance shall o'ertake your head.
So wretched then shall be thy fate,
So despicably mean thy state,
As to receive in public view
What is to lewd adulterers due.[5]

[Acting as Caesar's 'go-between', Aurelius turns Juventius (Crastinia) against Catullus.]

7.14.2 (Carmen 21)

Aurelius, you the chief and head
Of those who niggard tables spread,

[1] *Aurelius* possibly Marcus Aurelius Cotta, praetor (54 BCE).
[2] In the original, Catullus also specifically fears Aurelius's *pene* (penis).
[3] *deflow'r* rob of virginity.
[4] *take your swing of* allow yourself to freely indulge in.
[5] *What … due* In the original, Aurelius is threatened with radishes and mullets (a spiny fish) up the anus (a traditional Roman humiliation for adulterers).

And are with next to nothing fed,
Not only those who breathe this air,
But all that are to come and were:
You'd fain debauch my pretty boy,[6]
That is his master's love and joy.
Nor do you hide your base design,
But with him in discourses join;
All ways and means in public tried,
As you stick closely to his side.
But all attempts in vain shall be,
The snares you lay for him and me,
Thou villain, shall entangle thee.[7]
Not but I'd see't, and hold my tongue
Did you make love, well-fed and strong.
Now for him I with grief could burst,
Lest he from you should learn to thirst;
Lest he, poor boy, should know the way
Of feeding upon air all day.[8]
Wherefore I counsel you decline,
While you well are, this lewd design.
But you'll ne'er cease to seize the youth,
Till I have drenched your nasty mouth.[9]

[As the narrative continues, Catullus writes the following poem attacking Caesar's sexual licentiousness, partly in retaliation for Caesar's seduction of Juventius (Crastinia).]

7.14.3 (Carmen 57)

No two male harlots e'er agreed
More perfectly in thought and deed
Than Caesar and Mamurra, who[10]

[6] *fain* eagerly.

[7] *The snares … entangle* In the original, these lines refer to fellatio from the point of view of the man being fellated. For a modern translation, which more plainly reflects the speaker's threat to humiliate and subordinate Aurelius by forcing him to perform this sexual act on the speaker, see Peter Green, trans. *Poems of Catullus* (Berkeley, 2005), p. 67.

[8] *feeding … day* living on empty promises. In the original, Catullus fears Juventius's corruption will involve the boy's experiencing excessive desire like Aurelius's.

[9] *drenched … mouth* Cf. **n7**.

[10] *Caesar* Gaius Julius Caesar (100–44 BCE), Roman general. Caesar's 'bisexuality' was well known. For Caesar's purported same-sex relationship with King Nicomedes,

The same ill courses both pursue.
No wonder, both alike inclined
Have the same vices of the mind,
Which on it still impressed shall stay,
Hopeless of being washed away.
One bed has always both contained,
Both have a little learning gained.
Nor is one's lust more hot than t'other's,
The two he-whores and mere twin-brothers.[11]
Joint rivals of the ladies grown,[12]
And to their sex prefer their own.
No two male harlots e'er agreed
So perfectly in thought and deed.

7.15

From *The Works of Petronius Arbiter* (1713)

7.15.1 (Carmen 48)

Juventius, might I kiss those eyes,
  That such becoming sweetness dart,
The numbers might to thousands rise,
  Yet be too few to satisfy my heart.
A heart no surfeit would allow,[13]
  Ev'n though the harvest of our kisses were,
More thick than what succeeds the plough,
  And speaks the blessings of a fruitful year.

7.15.2 (Carmen 99)

Lovely Juventius, while you toyed I stole
A kiss, that got th' ascendant of my soul,

see Suetonius's *History of the Twelve Caesars. Mamurra*, an army officer and engineer, accompanied Caesar to Britain (55 BCE) and earlier to Gaul, where he accumulated vast wealth. Catullus elsewhere calls him sneeringly 'Mentula' ('prick' or cock').

11 *he-whores* male prostitutes.

12 i.e., they are rivals with women for the attentions of men.

13 *surfeit* condition of being over-full.

Sweeter than is ambrosia to the taste,[14]
But not unpunished for my thievish haste;
For to this gain succeeds a greater loss,
I seem as if whole hours upon a cross.
Yet not excuses you, nor tears allow,
But cruelty sits frowning on your brow;
For I no sooner my excuses make,
But wish to be more faulty for your sake:
As my moist lips run over at your sight,
And melt with an impatience of delight.
Besides, what gives increase to this my pain,
No sense of what I suffer you retain,
But make me like a slave to drag the chain.
Fresh torments with fresh beauties you create,
And in exchange my love's returned with hate.
So grievous are my suff'rings, and so sore,
Th' ambrosian kiss is worse than hellebore.[15]
Since I for kissing this return receive,
Believe't, I'll kiss no more without your leave.

Virgil (70–19 BCE), Latin poet

Educated in Cremona, Rome, and Milan, Virgil returned to his family farm to study and write. His supporters included the noble literary patron, Maecenas, and the Emperor Augustus. His *Eclogues* (*Pastorals* or *Bucolics*, ten pastoral poems), *Georgics* (four agricultural poems), and the *Aeneid* (an epic on the establishment of Rome) are all founding texts in the Western literary tradition.

John Dryden (1631–1700), writer

Educated at Cambridge, and producer of plays, verse, literary criticism, and translations, Dryden began writing professionally in the late 1650s. Of his classical translations, his Virgil was particularly celebrated. Charles II made him poet laureate a year after the publication of *Annus Mirabilis* (1667), and Dryden satirized Charles's enemies with devastating effectiveness in *Absalom and Achitophel* (1681–2). After 1688, his conversion to Roman Catholicism and support of James II lost him political favour and the poet laureateship.

[14] *ambrosia* food of the gods.
[15] *hellebore* plant used to make a bitter, purgative medicine.

7.16

From *The Works of Virgil* (1697)[1]

7.16.1 The Life of Publius Virgilius Maro

[...] he[2] was certainly of a very amorous disposition, and has described all that is most delicate in the passion of love; but he conquered his natural inclinations by the help of philosophy; and refined it into friendship, to which he was extremely sensible.[3] [...]

[...]

But however he stood affected to the ladies, there is a dreadful accusation brought against him for the most unnatural of all vices, which by the malignity of human nature has found more credit in latter times than it did near his own. This took not its rise so much from the Alexis,[4] in which pastoral there is not one immodest word, as from a sort of ill-nature that will not let anyone be without the imputation of some vice; and principally because he was so strict a follower of Socrates and Plato. In order therefore to his vindication, I shall take the matter a little higher.

The Cretans were anciently much addicted to navigation, insomuch that it became a Greek proverb (though omitted, I think, by the industrious Erasmus): 'A Cretan that does not know the sea.'[5] Their neighbourhood gave them occasion of frequent commerce with the Phoenicians,[6] that accursed people, who infected the Western world with endless superstitions and gross immoralities. From them it is probable that the Cretans learned this infamous passion, to which they were so much addicted that Cicero remarks (in his book *De Republica*) that it was a disgrace for a young gentleman to be without lovers.[7] Socrates, who was a great admirer of the Cretan Constitutions, set his excellent wit to find out some good cause and use of this evil inclination, and therefore gives an account wherefore beauty is to

[1] Includes Virgil's *Pastorals* (i.e., Eclogues), *Georgics*, and *Aeneid.*

[2] *he* Virgil.

[3] *sensible* sensitive.

[4] *the Alexis* See **7.16.2**.

[5] Erasmus, *Adages*, I.ii.31: 'The Cretan [is ignorant or frightened of] the sea' (i.e., men who pretend to be ignorant of something they understand intimately).

[6] *Phoenicians* Phoenician ship captains offered boys for sale to wealthy buyers (*Odyssey* 14.297, 15.449).

[7] *Cicero ... lovers* Among the Spartans 'it [is] disgraceful for adolescent boys not to have lovers' (4.3–4).

be loved in the following passage (for I will not trouble the reader, weary perhaps already, with a long Greek quotation):

> There is but one eternal, immutable, uniform beauty, in contemplation of which our sovereign happiness does consist. And therefore a true lover considers beauty and proportion as so many steps and degrees, by which he may ascend from the particular to the general, from all that is lovely of feature, or regular in proportion, or charming in sound, to the general fountain of all beauty and perfection. And if you are so much transported with the sight of beautiful persons, as to wish neither to eat or drink, but pass your whole life in looking on them, to what ecstasy would it raise you to behold the original Beauty, not filled up with flesh and blood, or varnished with a fading mixture of colours, and the rest of mortal trifles and fooleries, but separate, unmixed, uniform, and divine, etc.[8]

Thus far Socrates, in a strain, much beyond the *Socrate Chrétien* of Mr Balsac;[9] and thus that admirable man loved his Phaedo, his Charmides, and Theatetus;[10] and thus Virgil loved his Alexander, and Cebes, under the feigned name of Alexis. He received them illiterate, but returned them to their masters, the one a good poet and the other an excellent grammarian. And to prevent all possible misinterpretations, he warily inserted into the liveliest episode in the whole *Aeneid*, these words, *Nisus amore pio pueri*.[11] And in the sixth, *quique pii vates*.[12] He seems fond of the words, *castus*, *pius*, *virgo*,[13] and the compounds of it; and sometimes stretches the use of that word further than one would think he reasonably should have done, as when he attributes it to Pasiphae herself.

[...]

[8] Plato's *Symposium*, 211–12.

[9] *Le Socrate Chrétien* ('The Christian Socrates') (1652) by Jean-Louis Guez de Balzac (1597–1654), French historiographer.

[10] *Phaedo*, *Charmides*, and *Theatetus* young male participants with Socrates in the Platonic dialogues that bear their names.

[11] *Nisus ... pueri* The older warrior Nisus's relationship with his beloved boy Euryalus was platonic: 'Euryalus was famed for beauty and flower of youth, Nisus for dutiful love of the boy' (*Aeneid* 5.296). See *Online Companion*.

[12] *Aeneid* 6.662 praises men who in their lifetime were 'priests and pure'.

[13] Latin, 'chaste, sacred, maiden/virgin'.

7.16.2 Virgil's Eclogues
[Eclogue 2] The Second Pastoral, or, Alexis[14]

The argument

The commentators can by no means agree on the person of Alexis, but are all of opinion that some beautiful youth is meant by him, to whom Virgil here makes love in Corydon's language and simplicity. His way of courtship is wholly pastoral: he complains of the boy's coyness; recommends himself for his beauty and skill in piping; invites the youth into the country, where he promises him the diversions of the place, with a suitable present of nuts and apples. But when he finds nothing will prevail, he resolves to quit his troublesome amour, and betake himself again to his former business.

Young Corydon, th' unhappy shepherd swain,
The fair Alexis loved, but loved in vain:
And underneath the beechen shade, alone,
Thus to the woods and mountains made his moan:
'Is this, unkind Alexis, my reward,
And must I die unpitied, and unheard?
Now the green lizard in the grove is laid,
The sheep enjoy the coolness of the shade;
And Thestilis wild thyme and garlic beats[15]
For harvest hinds, o'erspent with toil and heats:[16]
While in the scorching sun I trace in vain
Thy flying footsteps o'er the burning plain.
The creaking locusts with my voice conspire,
They fried with heat, and I with fierce desire.
How much more easy was it to sustain
Proud Amaryllis, and her haughty reign,
The scorns of young Menalcas, once my care,
Though he was black, and thou art heav'nly fair.[17]
Trust not too much to that enchanting face;
Beauty's a charm, but soon the charm will pass:
White lilies lie neglected on the plain,
While dusky hyacinths for use remain.
My passion is thy scorn; nor wilt thou know
What wealth I have, what gifts I can bestow,

[14] For early modern imitations of this eclogue, see **8.1.1** and **8.4.1**.

[15] *Thestilis* countrywoman (appears in Theocritus).

[16] *hinds* country labourers.

[17] *black* black-haired.

What stores my dairies and my folds contain:
A thousand lambs that wander on the plain,
New milk that all the winter never fails,
And all the summer overflows the pails.
Amphion sung not sweeter to his herd,
When summoned stones the Theban turrets reared.[18]
Nor am I so deformed; for late I stood
Upon the margin of the briny flood:[19]
The winds were still, and if the glass be true,
With Daphnis I may vie, though judged by you.
Oh, leave the noisy town! Oh, come and see
Our country cots, and live content with me![20]
To wound the flying deer, and from their cotes[21]
With me to drive a-field the browsing goats:
To pipe and sing, and in our country strain
To copy, or perhaps contend with Pan.
Pan taught to join with wax unequal reeds,
Pan loves the shepherds, and their flocks he feeds,
Nor scorns the pipe; Amyntas, to be taught,
With all his kisses would my skill have bought.
Of seven smooth joints a mellow pipe I have,
Which with his dying breath Damaetas gave:
And said, "This, Corydon, I leave to thee;
For only thou deserv'st it after me."
His eyes Amyntas durst not upward lift,
For much he grudged the praise, but more the gift.
Besides two kids that in the valley strayed,
I found by chance, and to my fold conveyed:
They drain two bagging udders every day;
And these shall be companions of thy play.
Both flecked with white, the true Arcadian strain,[22]
Which Thestilis had often begged in vain:
And she shall have them, if again she sues,
Since you the giver and the gift refuse.

[18] *Amphion … reared* Jove's son, Amphion, inventor of music, raised the walls of Thebes by playing his lyre.

[19] *briny flood* sea.

[20] *cots* cottages.

[21] *cotes* shelters.

[22] *Arcadian* pertaining to Arcadia, a country in the middle of the Peloponnesus; highly celebrated by ancient poets for its mountains, forests, and fertile plains, Arcadia was traditionally the home of shepherds and herdsmen, skilled in war and music.

Come to my longing arms, my lovely care,[23]
And take the presents which the nymphs prepare.
White lilies in full canisters they bring,
With all the glories of the purple spring;
The daughters of the flood have searched the mead[24]
For violets pale, and cropped the poppy's head,
The short narcissus and fair daffodil,
Pansies to please the sight, and cassia sweet to smell:[25]
And set soft hyacinths with iron blue,
To shade marsh marigolds of shining hue.
Some bound in order, others loosely strowed,
To dress thy bow'r, and trim thy new abode.
Myself will search our planted grounds at home,
For downy peaches and the glossy plum:
And thrash the ches'nuts in the neighb'ring grove,
Such as my Amaryllis used to love.
The laurel and the myrtle sweets agree;
And both in nosegays shall be bound for thee.
Ah, Corydon, ah poor unhappy swain,
Alexis will thy homely gifts disdain;
Nor, should'st thou offer all thy little store,
Will rich Iolas yield, but offer more.[26]
What have I done, to name that wealthy swain,
So powerful are his presents, mine so mean!
The boar amidst my crystal streams I bring,
And southern winds to blast my flow'ry spring.
Ah, cruel creature, whom dost thou despise?
The gods to live in woods have left the skies.
And godlike Paris in th' Idean grove,
To Priam's wealth preferred Oenone's love.
In cities which she built, let Pallas reign;
Tow'rs are for gods, but forests for the swain.
The greedy lioness the wolf pursues,
The wolf the kid, the wanton kid the browse:[27]
Alexis, thou art chased by Corydon;
All follow sev'ral games, and each his own.

[23] *care* that which causes anxiety or grief.

[24] *mead* meadow.

[25] *cassia* a type of cinnamon.

[26] *Iolas* as the poem makes clear, a wealthy shepherd, and Corydon's rival for Alexis' love.

[27] *browse* tender shoots.

See from afar the fields no longer smoke;
The sweating steers unharnessed from the yoke,
Bring, as in triumph, back the crooked plough;
The shadows lengthen as the sun goes low.
Cool breezes now the raging heats remove;
Ah, cruel Heaven! that made no cure for love!
I wish for balmy sleep, but wish in vain;
Love has no bounds in pleasure or in pain.
What frenzy, shepherd, has thy soul possessed?
Thy vineyard lies half pruned, and half undressed.[28]
Quench, Corydon, thy long unanswered fire;
Mind what the common wants of life require.
On willow twigs employ thy weaving care;
And find an easier love, though not so fair.'

Ovid (43 BCE–17/18 CE), Latin poet

Educated in Rome for a public career, Ovid became a poet instead. His works include *Amores* (a collection of love elegies); *Heroides* (imagined letters from women to their often faithless lovers); *Metamorphoses* (a series of mythological poems, each dealing, as the title suggests, with supernatural transformations); and *Ars Amatoria* (*Art of Love*, a satiric poem on adultery and courtship). According to Ovid's own account, Augustus banished him from Rome on account of the sexual explicitness of *Ars Amatoria*, and his indiscretion concerning some scandal involving Augustus's family. Ovid died in exile.

Arthur Golding (1535/6–1606), writer and translator

Educated at Cambridge, Golding's works include the first complete English translation of Caesar's *Gallic Wars* and Ovid's *Metamorphoses* (1567). While constituting Golding's most important work, *Metamorphoses* is not typical of his output, comprised largely of translations of religious works and other nonfiction prose; even his two original works aim at inculcating Protestant doctrines.

[28] *undressed* untended.

7.17

From Ovid's *Metamorphoses* (1567)

7.17.1 Book 2 (The Story of Callisto)

[...]

Now as he often went and came it was his chance to light[1]
Upon a nymph of Nonacris, whose form and beauty bright[2]
Did set his heart on flaming fire. She usèd not to spin[3]
Nor yet to curl her frizzled hair with bodkin or with pin.[4]
A garment with a buckled belt fast girded did she wear
And in a white and slender caul slight trussèd was her hair.[5]
Sometime a dart, sometime a bow she usèd for to bear.[6]
She was a knight of Phoebe's troop. There came not at the mount
Of Menalus of whom Diana made so great account.[7]
But favour never lasteth long. The sun had gone that day
A good way past the point of noon: when weary of her way
She drew to shadow in a wood that never had been cut.
Here off her shoulder by and by her quiver did she put.
And hung her bow unbent aside, and couched her on the ground,
Her quiver underneath her head, whom when that Jove had found
Alone and weary: 'Sure,' he said, 'my wife shall never know[8]
Of this escape, and if she do, I know the worst I trow.[9]
She can but chide; shall fear of chiding make me to forslow?'[10]
He counterfeiteth Phoebe straight in count'nance and array,[11]
And says, 'O virgin of my troop, where didst thou hunt today?'
The damsel started from the ground and said, 'Hail, goddess dear,
Of greater worth than Jove (I think) though Jove himself did hear.'

1 *he* Jove (Glossary).

2 *nymph of Nonacris* Callisto (Glossary).

3 *spin* emblematic work symbolizing the ideal early modern woman and wife.

4 *frizzled* synonym for 'curl'; *bodkin*: synonym for '[hair] pin'.

5 *caul* netted cap.

6 *dart* spear.

7 *There … account* i.e., there was not another virgin of her company whom Diana held in such great esteem. *The mount / Of Menalus* is a mountain in Arcadia. See **7.16.2 n22**.

8 *wife* Juno (Glossary).

9 *escape* minor sexual transgression; *trow*: suppose.

10 *forslow* delay.

11 *counterfeiteth* impersonates; *straight*: immediately; *array*: clothing.

Jove heard her well and smiled thereat, it made his heart rejoice
To hear the nymph prefer him thus before himself in choice.
He fell to kissing: which was such as out of square might seem,[12]
And in such sort as that a maid could nothing less beseem.[13]
And as she would have told what woods she rangèd had for game,
He took her fast between his arms, and not without his shame,
Bewrayèd plainly what he was and wherefore that he came.[14]
The wench against him strove as much as any woman could;[15]
I would that Juno had it seen, for then I know thou would
Not take the deed so heinously: with all her might she strove.
But what poor wench or who alive could vanquish mighty Jove?
Jove having sped flew straight to heav'n. She hateth in her heart[16]
The guiltless fields and wood where Jove had played that naughty
  part,[17]
Away she goes in such a grief as that she had well nigh
Forgot her quiver with her shafts and bow that hangèd by.
Dictina guarded with her train and proud of killing deer,
In ranging over Menalus espying called her near.
The damsel hearing Phoebe call did run away amain,[18]
She fearèd lest in Phoebe's shape that Jove had come again,
But when she saw the troop of nymphs that guarded her about,
She thought there was no more deceit, and came among the rout.[19]
Oh Lord, how hard a matter is't for guilty hearts to shift[20]
And keep their count'nance: from the ground her eyes scarce durst she
  lift.
She pranks not by her mistress' side, she presses not to be[21]
The foremost of the company, as when she erst was free.[22]
She standeth muët: and by changing of her colour ay[23]

[12] *out of square* unusual, atypical.

[13] *And … beseem* And in a way that nothing could be less seemly for a *maid* (virgin).

[14] *bewrayèd* revealed. 'And not without his shame' perhaps suggests he exposes his genitals, but more likely his erection is obvious beneath his clothes.

[15] *wench* young woman.

[16] *sped* succeeded.

[17] *naughty* immoral.

[18] *amain* with all her might.

[19] *rout* troop.

[20] *shift* change.

[21] *pranks* proudly displays herself.

[22] *erst* not long ago.

[23] *muët* mute; *ay*: continually.

The treading of her shoe awry she plainly doth bewray,[24]
Diana might have found the fault but that she was a may.[25]
A thousand tokens did appear apparent to the eye,
By which the nymphs themselves (they say) her fault did well espy.

[...]

[Diana later dismisses the pregnant, dishonoured Callisto from her train. After Callisto gives birth to a boy (Arcas), Juno transforms her into a bear. As a young man, Arcas is out hunting, and is on the verge of killing his own mother. Taking pity on mother and son, Jove prevents the murder and transforms each into a constellation.]

7.17.2 Book 10 (The Story of Ganymede; The Story of Hyacinthus and Apollo)

[...]

[...] [26] 'I erst in graver verse
The Giants slain in Phlaegra fields with thunder, did rehearse,
But now I need a meelder style to tell of pretty boys[27]
That were the darlings of the gods; and of unlawful joys
That burnèd in the breasts of girls, who for their wicked lust
According as they did deserve, receivèd penance just.
The king of gods did burn erewhile in love of Ganymed
The Phrygian, and the thing was found which Jupiter that sted[28]
Had rather be than that he was. Yet could he not beteem[29]
The shape of any other bird than eagle for to seem,
And so he, soaring in the air with borrowed wings, trussed up
The Trojan boy, who still in heav'n e'en yet doth bear his cup,
And brings him nectar, though against Dame Juno's will it be.
And thou Amyclae's son (had not thy heavy destiny[30]
Abridgèd thee before thy time) hadst also placèd been
By Phoebus in the firmament. How be it (as is seen)
Thou art eternal so far forth as may be. For as oft

[24] *The ... awry* proverbial, meaning 'to fall from virtue'.

[25] *may* maid.

[26] The speaker is Orpheus (Glossary).

[27] *meelder* milder.

[28] *sted* instead.

[29] *beteem* think proper.

[30] *Amyclae's son* Hyacinthus (Glossary); *Amyclae*: the town founded by Hyacinthus's father, Amyclas.

As wat'ry Pisces giveth place to Aries that the soft[31]
And gentle springtide doth succeed the winter sharp and stowre:[32]
So often thou renew'st thyself, and on the fair green clowre[33]
Dost shoot out flow'rs. My father bore a special love to thee[34]
Above all others. So that while the god went oft to see
Eurotas and unwallèd Spart, he left his noble town[35]
Of Delphos (which amid the world is situate in renown)[36]
Without a sovereign. Neither harp nor bow regarded were.
Unmindful of his godhead he refusèd not to bear
The nets, nor for to hold the hounds, nor as a painful mate[37]
To travel over craggèd hills, through which continual gait
His flames augmented more and more. And now the sun did stand
Well near midway between the nights last past and next at hand.
They stripped themselves and 'nointed them with oil of olive fat.
And fell to throwing of a sledge that was right huge and flat.[38]
First Phoebus, peising it, did throw it from him with such strength[39]
As that the weight drove down the clouds in flying. And at length
It fell upon substantial ground, where plainly it did show
As well the cunning as the force of him that did it throw.[40]
Immediately upon desire himself the sport to try,
The Spartan lad made haste to take up unadvisedly
The sledge before it still did lie. But as he was in hand
To catch it, it, rebounding up against the hardened land,
Did hit him full upon the face. The god himself did look
As pale as did the lad, and up his swounding body took.[41]
Now culls he him, now wipes he from the wound the blood away,[42]
Another while his fading life he strives with herbs to stay.
Naught booted leechcraft. Helpless was the wound. And like as one[43]

31 *Pisces* zodiacal sign of late winter; *Aries*: zodiacal sign of early spring.
32 *stowre* stour: fierce.
33 *clowre* grassy ground.
34 *my father* Apollo.
35 *Eurotas* river near Sparta.
36 *Delphos* i.e., Delphi, location of Apollo's most famous temple, and dwelling place of his renowned oracle.
37 *painful mate* painstaking companion.
38 *sledge* large hammer, used for throwing in athletic contests.
39 *peising* estimating weight by lifting.
40 *cunning* skill.
41 *swounding* fainting.
42 *culls* hugs.
43 *Naught booted leechcraft* medical treatment was useless.

Bruised violet stalks or poppy stalks or lilies growing on
Brown spindles, straight they withering droop with heavy heads and are
Not able for to hold them up, but with their tops do stare
Upon the ground: So Hyacinth, in yielding of his breath,
Chopped down his head. His neck, bereft of strength by means of death,
Was even a burden to itself, and down did loosely writhe
On both his shoulders, now at one and now at other lithe.[44]
'Thou fad'st away, my Hyacinth, defrauded of the prime
Of youth,' quoth Phoebus, 'and I see thy wound my heinous crime.
Thou art my sorrow and my fault: this hand of mine hath wrought
Thy death: I like a murderer have to thy grave thee brought.
But what have I offended though, unless that to have played,[45]
Or if that to have lovéd, an offence it may be sayed.[46]
Would God I render might my life with and instead of thee.
To which sith fatal destiny denieth to agree,[47]
Both in my mind and in my mouth thou evermore shalt be.
My viol striken with my hand, my songs shall sound of thee,
And in a new-made flow'r thou shalt with letters represent
Our sighings. And the time shall come ere many years be spent,
That in thy flow'r a valiant prince shall join himself with thee,
And leave his name upon the leaves for men to read and see.'[48]
While Phoebus thus did prophesy, behold, the blood of him
Which dyed the grass, ceased blood to be, and up there sprang a trim
And goodly flow'r, more orient than the purple cloth ingrain,[49]
In shape a lily, were it not that lilies do remain
Of silver colour, whereas these of purple hue are seen.
Although that Phoebus had the cause of this great honour been,
Yet thought he not the same enough. And therefore did he write
His sighs upon the leaves thereof: and so in colour bright
The flow'r hath *AI AI* writ thereon, which letters are of grief.[50]

[44] *now … lithe* now on the one and now on the other [shoulder] bent.

[45] *played* engaged in fun and games; also, 'engaged in amorous play, had sexual intercourse with'.

[46] *sayed* said.

[47] *sith* since.

[48] *That in thy flow'r … see* Enraged when denied the dead Achilles' armour, the Greek warrior Ajax (the *valiant prince*) killed an entire flock of sheep, and then stabbed himself. His blood was transformed into the hyacinths that bear his name.

[49] *orient* radiant, shining; *ingrain*: dye thoroughly.

[50] *AI* *Greek*, 'alas'.

George Sandys (1578–1644), writer and translator

Educated at Oxford, Sandys travelled extensively, later writing an influential account of the Middle East. *Metamorphoses* was published in 1626, and again in 1632 in a sumptuous edition dedicated to Charles I and his queen. Its first five books were written in England; two more en route to Virginia and Sandys's new role as colony treasurer; and the remaining eight during his time in the colony (1621–25). Sandys later translated Virgil's *Aeneid* (Book 1, 1632), the Psalms, and the Song of Solomon (1641).

7.18

From *Metamorphoses* (1632)

7.18.1 Book 9 (The Story of Iphis and Ianthe)

[The goddess Isis appears in a dream to the expectant mother Telethusa, deeply grieved over her husband's command that her newborn, if it is a girl, be killed. Telethusa obeys Isis' command to pretend that it is a boy.]

Increasing throes at length a girl disclosed.[51]
Both by the father and the world supposed
To be a boy; so closely hid and known
But to the mother, and the nurse alone.
He pays his vows, and of his father's name[52]
It Iphis calls, which much rejoiced the dame –
To each sex common, nor deceives thereby –[53]
Who still with pious fraud conceals her lie.
A boy in show, whose looks should you assign
To boy or girl, love would in either shine.
At thirteen years her father her affied[54]
To yellow-tressed Ianthe: she the pride
Of Phaestian virgins for unequalled fair,
Telestes' daughter, and his only heir,
Like young, like beautiful, together bred,
Informed alike, alike accomplishèd:

[51] *throes* labour pains.
[52] The baby is named after her grandfather.
[53] *common* i.e., Iphis is a unisex name.
[54] *affied* betrothed.

Like darts at once their simple bosoms strike,
Alike their wounds; their hopes, Oh, far unlike!
The day they expect. Ianthe thought time ran[55]
Too slow, and takes her Iphis for a man.
Poor Iphis loves, despairs; despair ejects
Far fiercer flames: a maid, a maid affects.
'What will become of me,' she weeping said,
'Whom new, unknown, prodigious loves invade!
If pitiful, the gods should have destroyed
Or else have given what might have been enjoyed.
No cow a cow, no mare a mare pursues:
But harts their gentle hinds, and rams their ewes.
So birds together pair. Of all that move,
No female suffers for a female love.
Oh, would I had no being! Yet, that all
Abhorred by Nature should in Crete befall,
Sol's lust-incensèd daughter loved a bull:[56]
They male and female. Mine – Oh, far more full
Of uncouth fury! for she pleased her blood,[57]
And stood his error in a cow of wood;[58]
She, for her craft, had an adulterer.
Should all the world their daring wits confer,
Should Daedalus his waxen wings renew
And hither fly: what could his cunning do?
Can art convert a virgin to a boy?
Or fit Ianthe for a maiden's joy?
No, fix thy mind; compose thy vast desires;
Oh, quench these ill-advised and foolish fires!
Think of thy sex, or even thyself abuse:[59]
What may be, seek, and love as females use.[60]
Hope wings desire; hope Cupid's flight sustains;
In thee thy sex this deads. No watch restrains[61]
Our dear embrace, nor husband's jealousies,
Nor rigorous sires, nor she herself denies:
Yet not to be enjoyed. Nor canst thou be

55 *The day* their marriage day.
56 *daughter* Pasiphae (Glossary).
57 *pleased her blood* satisfied her sexual desire.
58 *stood his error* endured his fury or extravagant passion.
59 *abuse* masturbate.
60 *use* are accustomed to.
61 *this* hope; *deads*: destroys.

Happy in her, though men and gods agree!
Now also all to my desires accord:
What they can give, the easy gods afford;
What me, my father, hers, herself, would please
Displeaseth Nature, stronger than all these.
She, she forbids. That day begins to shine,
Long wished, wherein Ianthe must be mine!
And yet not mine. Of mortals most accurst!
I starve at feasts and in the river thirst!
Juno, ô Hymen, wherefore are you come?[62]
We both are brides, but where is the bridegroom?'
Here ended. Nor less burns the other maid,
Who, Hymen, for thy swift appearance prayed.
Yet Telethusa fears what she affects;
Protracting time, oft want of health objects;[63]
Ill-boding dreams, and auguries oft feigns,
But now no colour for excuse remains.[64]
Their nuptial rites, put off with such delay,
Were to be solemnized the following day:
When she unbinds hers and her daughter's hair,
And holding by the altar formed this pray'r:
'Isis – who Paraetonium, Pharos' Isle,
Smooth Mareotis, and seven-channelled Nile,[65]
Cheer'st with thy presence – thy poor suppliants hear!
Oh, help in these extremes, and cure our fear!
Thee, goddess, thee of old, these ensigns I[66]
Have seen and know: thy lamps, attendancy,
And sounding timbrels, and have thee obeyed.
To me, impunity; life, to this maid,
Thy saving counsel gave. To both renew
Thy timely pity.' Tears her words pursue.
The goddess shakes her altar; when the gate
Shook on the hinges, horns that imitate
The waxing moons through all the temple flung
A sacred splendour; noise-full timbrels rung.

62 *Juno, ô Hymen* Greek wedding song refrain, invoking the marriage deities.

63 *want* lack.

64 *colour* pretext.

65 *Isis* Egyptian fertility goddess; ecstatic music/dance characterized her rites. *Paraetonium* (a city), *Pharos' Isle* (off the coast of Alexandria), *Mareotis* (a lake), and the *Nile* are all in Egypt.

66 *ensigns* signs (the lamps, attendancy, and timbrels (tambourines), below).

The mother, glad of this successful sign,
Though not secure, returns from Isis' shrine.
Whom Iphis follows with a larger pace
Than usual; nor had so white a face.
Her strength augments; her look more bold appears;
Her short'ning curls scarce hang beneath her ears;
By far more full of courage, rapt with joy:
For thou, of late a wench, art now a boy.
Gifts to the temple bear, and *Iö* sing!
Sing joy! Their gifts they to the temple bring;
And add a title, in one verse displayed:
What Iphis vowed a wench, a boy he paid.
The morning night dismasks with welcome flame:
When Juno, Venus, and free Hymen came,
To grace their marriage; who, with gifts divine,
Iphis the boy, to his Ianthe join.

George Turbervile [Turberville] (1543/4–c. 1597), poet and translator

Educated at Oxford, Turbervile published five significant works, including his translation of Ovid's *Heroides* and a collection of original verse, *Epitaphs, Epigrams, Songs and Sonnets* (1567). Family tragedy marred his literary success: the murder of his brother, Nicholas, and Turbervile's own killing of a man in self-defence. He married in 1574, after which he seems to have stopped writing.

7.19

From *Heroical Epistles* (1567)

7.19.1 The Seventeenth Epistle: Sappho to Phaon[67]

[…]

As straw doth kindle soon,
  when Eurus 'gins to drive
The flash into the fertile fields:

[67] In modern editions, numbered the fifteenth epistle.

even so I fry alive.[68]
To Aetna Phaon now[69]
hath ta'en his way in haste:
And me poor wench as great a fire
as Aetna's flame doth waste.
I cannot frame my frets,[70]
my stubborn strings do jar:
For why indeed of quiet minds[71]
such verses tokens are.
Pyrino is forgot,
ne dryads do delight[72]
My fancy: Lesbian lasses eke[73]
are now forgotten quite.
Not Amython I force,[74]
nor Cydno passing fine:[75]
Nor Atthis, as she did of yore,[76]
allures these eyes of mine.
Ne yet a hundred moe[77]
whom (shame ylaid aside)
I fancied erst: thou all that love[78]
from them to thee hast wryd.[79]
In thee doth feature flow,
thy years for dalliance apt:
Thy face, O face, 'tis thou that hast
my shaken senses rapt.[80]

68 *Eurus* god of the east wind; *flash*: sudden burst of lightning.

69 *Aetna* Etna, volcanic mountain (in Sicily).

70 *frame my frets* arrange the frets [on my instrument], with the obvious pun on 'frets' as 'anxieties' or 'cares'.

71 *for why* because.

72 *Pyrino … delight* 'Pyrino' seems to be Turbervile's mistranslation of Ovid's reference to 'Pyrriades puellae' (the girls of Pyrrha). See **7.3.2, note d**. A *dryad* is a wood nymph, a semi-divine entity in the form of a lovely woman, attached to some particular woodland haunt or tree.

73 *eke* also.

74 *force* rape.

75 *passing fine* surpassingly beautiful.

76 *Pyrino … Atthis* Sappho's female lovers.

77 *moe* more.

78 *erst* first.

79 *wryd* turned.

80 *rapt* enraptured.

A quiver and a lute[81]
  take thou in hand, and thee
Apollo men will deem: don horns
  and Bacchus thou shalt be:[82]
And Phoebus Daphne loved,
  King Minos' darling dear[83]
God Bacchus liked, yet neither of both
  a cytheron's string could steare.[84]
But me Pegasian nymphs[85]
  have learned on the lute,
And throughout all the world is borne
  of Sappho's songs the brute.[86]

[...]

I sang, I mind it well,
  (for lovers fix in breast
Forepassed toys), and thou the whilst
  to kissing thee addressed.
Those busses liked thee eke,[87]
  for every point I was
Befancied well: but most when we
  to Venus' pranks did pass.[88]
Then did my wanton tricks
  and lofty mounting, more[89]
With sugared words delight thy mind
  (my Phaon) than of yore.
And that when both our joys
  confounded were, I lay
With weary limbs, and languor lame
  and had no word to say.

81 *quiver* and *lute* symbols of Apollo.

82 *don … be* Bacchus, sometimes depicted with horns; he and Apollo were famously beautiful.

83 *King Minos' darling dear* Ariadne (Glossary).

84 *cytheron* cithern (guitar-like instrument); *steare*: stir.

85 *Pegasian nymphs* Muses (Glossary).

86 *brute* report.

87 *busses* kisses; *eke*: also.

88 *Venus' pranks* erotic play.

89 *mounting* the 'rising' of her songs (with play on 'copulating [with]'; usually said of animals).

Now are Sicilian trulls[90]
  thy novel prey, I see:
In Lesbos what make I? a wench
  of Sicill I will be.
O Nysian matrons, O
  Sicilian dames, I say,
This loit'ring guest of ours expel
  your country bounds I pray.
Ne let his glosing tongue[91]
  your list'ning ears beguile:
For why to us he hath ere this
  yused that self-same style.
And Lady Venus thou
  that knowen art to dwell,
Rue on thy poet's piteous plight
  among the Sicans fell.[92]

[...]

What wonder, if with such
  a beardless youth I were
Attached, whose tender childish years
  allowed his chin no hair?
I dread, Aurora, least[93]
  for Cephalus thou would
Ychosen him: save that thy for-
  mer rape doth thee withhold.[94]
If Phoebe view him once,
  that all surveys with eye,[95]
My Phaon shall be quickly forced
  in slumber long to lie.[96]
In ivory wagon would
  Dame Venus to the stars

90 *trulls* whores; licentious women.

91 *glosing* lying.

92 *Sicans fell* dangerous Sicilians.

93 *least* lest.

94 *for* in place of. *Cephalus* was happily married to Procris. Aurora, goddess of the dawn, fell in love with him and carried him away. When he rejected Aurora, she returned him to his wife; *rape*: kidnapping (of Cephalus).

95 *eye* i.e., the moon, over which the goddess Phoebe (Diana) held sway (Glossary).

96 *If ... lie* Phaon's fate would be that of the beautiful shepherd boy, Endymion (Glossary).

Borne him: but that she feared he would
  have coyed the god of wars.[97]
O thou that neither art
  a boy, nor man in sight
But aptest age: of all thy race
  the most excellent wight,
Come hither, come, and to
  my bosom make retowre:[98]
No love I crave in faith of thee
  but thee to love the powre.

[...]

By love, that never far
  may from thy breast astart,
And sacred sisters nine (my saints)[99]
  whom I embrace with heart,
I swear: when one exclaimed
  (I wrote ne'er who) to me
And said, 'Now, Sappho, jogs thy joy,
  thy Phaon now doth flee,'
I had no tears to shed,
  my lips did language lack,
Mine eyes did want their gushing tears
  my fault'ring tongue it stack[100]
Unto the roof, and icy cold
  my fearful breast did rack.
When grief was somewhat swagged,[101]
  and sorrow 'gan to slake:[102]
I howl'd with toren locks, and with[103]
  my fist my body strake:[104]

[...]

Then I to Phoebus will
  my pleasant lute bequeath:

97 *coyed* seduced; *the god of wars*: Mars (Venus's lover).
98 *retowre* return.
99 *sacred sisters nine* the Muses (Glossary).
100 *stack* stuck.
101 *swagged* assuaged.
102 *'gan* began.
103 *toren* torn.
104 *strake* struck.

LIB I. 163

The Argument of the one and twentieth Epiſtle.

PHaon *being ſometimes a Boatman*, Venus *came unto him, and deſired to be carried over the water gratis, which he did, not knowing her to be a Goddeſs, whereupon ſhe gave him a Box of Oyntment, wherewith anoynting himſelf, he became ſo beautiful, that all the Women in the Iſle* Lesbos *were in love with him, eſpecially* Sappho *did impatiently affect him. But when*Phaon *went to* Sicily, Sappho *out of the heat of her love, and fear of his diſdain, deſperately*

M 2 *reſolved*

4 and **5** ‘Sappho Leaps into the Sea from the Leucadian Rock’, from Wye Salstonstall, trans., ‘Sappho to Phaon’, *Ovid’s Heroical Epistles Englished by W.S.* (1686).

reſolved to throw herſelf into the Sea, from Leucas *a* Promontory *of* Spire. *But yet unconſtant to her firſt reſolve, ſhe endeavours by this Epiſtle to recal him back, and gain his love, of which ſhe formerly deſpaired, and to win him to diſlike of his preſent eſtate and manner of life. Laſtly, ſhe uſeth all* Arguments *that might move him to pity. And in this Epiſtle* Ovid *hath moſt lively expreſt the ſoft and amorous affection of love.*

SAPPHO *to* PHAON.

SOon as thou doſt behold my ſtudious hand,
Whence the Letter comes doſt thou underſtand?
Or unleſs in it thou *Sappho*'s name read,
Doſt thou not know from whence it doth proceed?
Thou may'ſt wonder why I in this verſe write,
Since I in *Lyrick* numbers do delight.
The Weeping Elegy will fitting prove
To ſuit unto our ſad and mournful love.
But in light *Lyrick* verſes there appears
No doleful harmony, that may ſuit tears.
For as a field of corn on fire, whoſe flame
The Eaſtern wind doth blow up, and maintain,
Doth burn apace, being fanned by the wind,
Even ſo the flame of love doth fire my mind.
Though *Phaon* live near *Ætna*, far from me,
My flames of love hotter than *Ætna* be.
So that verſes to my Harp I cannot ſet,
" A quiet mind doth verſes beſt beget.
The *Dryads* do not help me at this time,
Nor *Lesbian*, nor *Pierian* Muſes nine.
I hate *Amythone*, and *Cydnus* white,
And *Athis* is not pleaſant in my ſight.
And many others that were lov'd of me,
But now I have plac'd all my love on thee.

Thy

And bravely cause to be engraved
 this verse, or two beneath:
  O Phoebus this her lute
  Hath Sappho left to thee:
  For in that art she during life
  And thou did well agree.
Fie (Phaon) why dost thou[105]
 me to Actaeum drive:[106]
And thou thyself mayst make return
 and save thy love alive?
More healthful than the flood
 of Leucas thou mayst be:[107]
And by thy beauty's seemly shape
 Apollo unto me.
And canst thou (oh) more hard
 than rock, and ruthless wave,
If so I die, the title of
 my death endure to have?
Ah, how much better might
 my breast conjoin with thine,
Than thus be cast from craggy cliff
 to sea of surging brine?
That self-same breast which thou
 commended hast so oft:
And which with passing wisdom fraught
 thy self (friend Phaon) thought.
Now would I were facund,[108]
 but dolour hinders art:[109]
And all my wit is me bereft
 by long enduring smart.
My wonted vein in verse
 is overdry become:
My low'ring lute laments for woe,
 my harp with dool is dumb.[110]
Ye Lesbian lasses all

[105] *fie* exclamation of disgust.

[106] *Actaeum* in some writers, another name for the Leucadian cliff or rock from which Sappho in despair leapt to her death.

[107] *of Leucas* i.e., Leucadian (see **n106**).

[108] *facund* eloquent.

[109] *dolour* sorrow.

[110] *dool* grief.

6 'Sappho Writing with Winged Cupid', from Sir Carr Scrope, trans., 'Sappho to Phaon', *Ovid's Epistles* (1720).

7 'Portrait of Sappho' by Jean Le Blond (c. 1594–1666)

that border on the lake:
And ye that of the Aeolian town
your names are thought to take:[111]
Ye Lesbian lasses (that
for cause I loved you sore[112]
Breed my defame) unto my harp[113]
I charge you come no more.[114]
Look what did like you erst,[115]
of that is Phaon sped:[116]
Alas, poor wretch, 'my Phaon' I
had very near ysaid.[117]
Cause Phaon to retire
and then your poet will
Revert again: 'tis he that doth
both make and mar my skill.
What? Do my prayers prevail
or pierce his steely breast?
Or is he standing stiff at stay,
a retchless rigorous guest?[118]
Or do the puffing winds transport
my words into the west?
The gale that hence conveys
my voice, oh that it might
Reduce thy fleeing bark again[119]
and bring thy ship in sight.
O overling'ring lad,
in faith if thou were wise,
Thou wouldst attempt to make return
and follow mine advise.[120]
What? Wilt thou come? Or no?
we for thy ship prepare
Our vowèd gifts: why doth thy stay

111 *And … take* Lesbos is in Aeolia (Asia Minor).
112 *for cause* because; *sore*: deeply.
113 *defame* infamy.
114 *Ye Lesbian … come no more* Cf. **7.3.2, note d**.
115 *erst* previously.
116 *sped* possessed.
117 *ysaid* said.
118 *retchless* reckless.
119 *reduce* draw back; *bark*: small ship.
120 *advise* advice.

enforce our hearts to care?
Avail and loose thy bark,
take seas, for Venus, she
That came of seas, will calm the surge:
come off, the gale will be
As friendly to thy coming keel[121]
as thou wouldst wish to see.
At helm will Cupid sit,
and steer thy ship to land:
he both will hoise and hale the sails[122]
with skilful boatswain's hand.
Or if thy pleasure be
from Sappho far to trudge:
(Who never did deserve so ill
of thee, thyself be judge),
At least let cruel lines
will her, unhappy wench,
Unto Leucadian ford to flee[123]
and there her corpse to drench.

***Metamorphoses*' Afterlife: Imitations and Inspirations**

John Lyly (1554–1606)

For his biography, see Introduction to **7.6**.

7.20

From *Gallathea* (1592)

[Tityrus and Melebeus, the fathers (respectively) of the lovely maidens Gallathea and Phyllida, disguise their daughters as boys to protect them from Neptune's decree: their community's loveliest virgin must be sacrificed to a

[121] *keel* ship.
[122] *hoise* hoist; *hale*: set.
[123] *Leucadian ford* See **n106**.

sea-monster. The two maidens meet and fall in love, each thinking the other a boy, although each quickly coming to suspect that the other is actually a girl. Meanwhile, Cupid, rejected by one of Diana's nymphs, causes them all to fall in love. Diana captures Cupid, angering Venus. Their contention ends with Neptune's intervention: Cupid is freed, in exchange for cancelling the virgin sacrifice.]

7.20.1 Act 5, scene 3

Enter TITYRUS, MELEBEUS *at one door,* GALLATHEA *and* PHYLLIDA *at another*

NEPTUNE. But soft, what be these?[124]
TITYRUS. Those that have offended thee to save their daughters.
NEPTUNE. Why, had you a fair daughter?
TITYRUS. Ay, and Melebeus a fair daughter.
NEPTUNE. Where be they?
MELEBEUS. In yonder woods, and methinks I see them coming.
NEPTUNE. Well, your deserts have not gotten pardon, but these goddesses' jars.[125]
MELEBEUS. This is my daughter, my sweet Phyllida.
TITYRUS. And this is my fair Gallathea.
GALLATHEA. Unfortunate Gallathea, if this be Phyllida!
PHYLLIDA. Accursed Phyllida, if that be Gallathea!
GALLATHEA. And wast thou all this while enamoured of Phyllida, that sweet Phyllida?
PHYLLIDA. And couldst thou dote upon the face of a maiden, thyself being one, on the face of fair Gallathea?
NEPTUNE. Do you both, being maidens, love one another?
GALLATHEA. I had thought the habit agreeable[126] with the sex, and so burned in the fire of mine own fancies.
PHYLLIDA. I had thought that in the attire of a boy there could not have lodged the body of a virgin, and so was inflamed with a sweet desire which now I find a sour deceit.
DIANA. Now, things falling out as they do, you must leave these fond, fond[127] affections. Nature will have it so, necessity must.
GALLATHEA. I will never love any but Phyllida. Her love is engraven in my heart with her eyes.

[124] *soft* 'just a moment'.
[125] *jars* quarrellings.
[126] *habit agreeable* clothing matching [to].
[127] *fond* foolish.

PHYLLIDA. Nor I any but Gallathea, whose faith is imprinted in my thoughts by her words.

NEPTUNE. An idle[128] choice, strange and foolish, for one virgin to dote on another, and to imagine a constant faith where there can be no cause of affection. How like you this, Venus?

VENUS. I like well and allow it. They shall both be possessed of their wishes, for never shall it be said that Nature or Fortune shall overthrow Love and Faith. Is your love unspotted, begun with truth, continued with constancy, and not to be altered till death?

GALLATHEA. Die, Gallathea, if thy love be not so.

PHYLLIDA. Accursed be thou, Phyllida, if thy love be not so.

DIANA. Suppose all this, Venus, what then?

VENUS. Then shall it be seen that I can turn one of them to be a man, and that I will.

DIANA. Is it possible?

VENUS. What is to Love or the Mistress of Love[129] impossible? Was it not Venus that did the like to Iphis and Ianthe?[130] How say ye, are ye agreed, one to be a boy presently?

PHYLLIDA. I am content, so I may embrace Gallathea.

GALLATHEA. I wish it, so I may enjoy Phyllida.

MELEBEUS. Soft, daughter, you must know whether I will have you a son.

TITYRUS. Take me with you, Gallathea. I will keep you as I begat you: a daughter.

MELEBEUS. Tityrus, let yours be a boy, and if you will, mine shall not.

TITYRUS. Nay, mine shall not, for by that means my young son shall lose his inheritance.

MELEBEUS. Why, then get him to be made a maiden, and then there is nothing lost.

TITYRUS. If there be such changing, I would Venus could make my wife a man.

MELEBEUS. Why?

TITYRUS. Because she loves always to play with men.

VENUS. Well, you are both fond:[131] therefore, agree to this changing or suffer your daughters to endure hard chance.

MELEBEUS. How say you, Tityrus, shall we refer it to Venus?

TITYRUS. I am content, because she is a goddess.

VENUS. Neptune, you will not dislike it?

[128] *idle* senseless.

[129] *Mistress of Love* one of Venus's many epithets.

[130] *Venus … Ianthe* In *Metamorphoses*, Isis affects this transformation: the ancients saw Isis and Venus as versions of the same goddess.

[131] *fond* foolish.

NEPTUNE. Not I.
VENUS. Nor you, Diana?
DIANA. Not I.
VENUS. Cupid shall not.
CUPID. I will not.
VENUS. Then let us depart. Neither of them shall know whose lot it shall be till they come to the church door.[132] One shall be; doth it suffice?
PHYLLIDA. And satisfy us both. Doth it not, Gallathea?
GALLATHEA. Yes, Phyllida.

[...]

Lewis Machin (*fl.* 1607–13), poet and playwright

Machin was a writer for the boys' theatre company, the King's Revels, where he may have collaborated with *Mirrha*'s co-writer, William Barksted. *Mirrha, the Mother of Adonis, or Lust's Prodigies* (1607), a versification of Ovid's tale of Mirrha and her incestuous love for her father, concludes with Machin's eclogues: the last two recount the tragic love of the sun god, Phoebus Apollo, for the beautiful mortal youth, Hyacinthus.

7.21

From *Mirrha, the Mother of Adonis* (1607)

7.21.1 Apollo and Hyacinth

Apollo weary, let his courses breathe,[133]
Whilst he descended to this earth beneath.
Armed with his bow and shafts he walked the woods
To hear the muttering of the shallow floods.
The little birds did sing on every briar,
Making the green-boughed trees their music's quire,[134]
And with sweet notes these harmless singers strove
To chant an anthem to the gods above.

[132] *church door* where marriages were performed.
[133] *courses* coursers: large, powerful horses that pulled Phoebus Apollo's sun chariot across the sky.
[134] *quire* choir loft.

Phoebus was ravished, hearing of this noise,[135]
Vowing he would forsake his heavenly joys
To live on earth, if no more harm were found
Than did appear upon that pleasant ground.
But he did after find this false world's pleasure
Joy for a minute, trouble without measure.
Thus wand'ring up and down without this grove
He spied a boy that after game did rove.
His bow was in his hand, shafts by his side,
His curlèd hair did all his shoulders hide.
A well-shaped face he had, pleasing to view,
A fine straight body and a heart most true.
Apollo stayed and gazed upon his face,
Supposing him mortal of Jove's race,
And that blind archer, that doth wound all hearts,
Had now quite overcome the god of arts,
For he did dote upon this lovely youth,
Whose heart was all composed of melting ruth.[136]
And seeing Phoebus come, the boy did stay him,
He said, 'Youth, will you walk?' He'd not deny him
But went along together hand in hand,
And Zephyr with calm wind their faces fanned.
Then Phoebus said, Fair youth, what make you here,[137]
Kind courteous stranger for to kill the deer?
To hear the birds to sing, the waters glide:
Tumbling in curls along a green bankside.
More sweet content in harmless woods is found
Than in great cities; there doth sin abound.
But here hunt's quiet keeps us company,
Free from all cares, and bad society.
Here grows high grass: let's sit and make it flat,
And so beguile swift time with pleasing chat.
So hand in hand, they sat them on the ground,

135 *ravished* captivated.

136 *ruth* compassion.

137 Here I cease using direct quotations marks, since it is difficult to be sure where the question ends and the response begins. Given the traditional innocence of Hyacinthus, he probably responds to Apollo's question with 'Kind courteous … bankside' (in which case the question mark here is misplaced) and Apollo's response is 'More sweet content … chat.' However, Machin's Hyacinthus is unusual: the syntax suggests *he* approaches and speaks to Apollo *first*, so perhaps he is more worldly wise than is typical. I have inserted direct quotation marks later where the division of speech is unambiguous.

Where little birds did make harmonious sound,
But Phoebus' heart did pant and leap with joy,
When he beheld that sweet, delicious boy.
His eyes did sparkle love, his heart flamed fire:
To see this sweet boy smile is his desire.
Then with an ardent gripe his hand he crushed,[138]
And then he kissed him, and the boy then blushed,
That blushing colour so became his face
That Phoebus kissed again, and thought it grace
To touch his lips; such pleasure Phoebus felt
That in an amorous dew his heart did melt.
And thus he dallied with his amorous kisses,
Forgetting of the world that his light misses.
More joy he had, when this day did approach,
Than in his shining crown or burning coach.[139]
Wearied with toying they left off their play,[140]
And conquering night had now o'ercome the day,
Casting her sable curtains o'er the sky.
Then said the boy, 'I to my rest must hie.'[141]
'And I,' said Phoebus, 'must into the sea,
To sport with Thetis till the break of day.
Tomorrow when my chariot's in the west,
Then meet me here, for that's my times of rest.'
'I will,' quoth Hyacinth, 'till then, farewell,
The parting of true friends all pains excel.'
Phoebus turned coward and was quite dishearted;
At last he came and kissed him, and so parted.[142]

7.21.2 Apollo and Hyacinth (Part 2)

Grim night being past, the morning star appeared,
And bright Aurora had the welking cleared.[143]
Then Phoebus, drawn forth by his fiery team,
Gilded the hills, the fields, and wat'ry stream.[144]

[138] *gripe* grip; clasp.
[139] *burning coach* See **n133**.
[140] *toying* sporting amorously (sexual activity, usually falling short of intercourse); *play*: synonym for 'toying' (cf. **n45**).
[141] *hie* hasten.
[142] *he came* probably, Apollo approaches and kisses Hyacinthus, but see **n137**.
[143] *Aurora* goddess of the dawn; *welking*: i.e., 'welkin' or 'sky'.
[144] *gilded* i.e., with light.

So swiftly flew his steeds through scorching flames
As if he ran for the Olympic games.
But 'twas not so: Apollo made that haste,
Longing till he his Hyacinth embraced.
And Hyacinth, sweet youth, the time respected;[145]
Gods' love by mortals should not be neglected.
There sat he down by a clear running brook,
And like Narcissus doteth with each look
He casts upon himself. There had he died
But that bright Phoebus did his beauty hide:
In over-dark'ned clouds to stop his self-loved error,
No shape he saw in nature's wat'ry mirror.
And now Apollo waving towards the west,[146]
Unteamed his fiery steeds, and let them rest,
Whilst he descended on this ball of earth,
To sport with Hyacinth, strange unknown mirth[147]
For which the gods were angry and decreed
They would remove the cause: the boy must bleed.
Now Phoebus for to see his love did haste him;
Then Hyacinth came running and embraced him.
More joy had Phoebus in this Spartan lad
Than heaven-born love in Phrygian Ganymed.
His love to Daphne (that chaste beaut'ous nymph)
Was not so great as to his Hyacinth.
All female pleasures, which he did adore,
Are dull to those of his male paramour;[148]
And having passed some hours in delight,
They would go walk to Delphos ere that night[149]
Should dark the world, for they went to see
The sport there made by the land's peasantry.
And being come to a fair spacious plain,
There might they see each nymph had got a swain:
Some dancing after pipes, others were running
At barley break, and with their homely cunning[150]

145 *the time respected* he was punctual.

146 *waving* moving [to and fro with the wind].

147 *sport* engage in amorous behaviour or sexual intercourse. Cf. **n45** and **n140**.

148 *paramour* lover.

149 *Delphos* i.e., Delphi (see **n36**).

150 *barley break* game played by three male–female pairs: one couple would attempt to catch the others, who were allowed to break apart and take different partners to avoid capture.

Sought to delight themselves and those stood by;
Others for nimble footing there did try,
Who best deserved the worth; some threw at length[151]
The heavy sledge, and therein showed their strength,
Which pleased Apollo best; then he would prove
His strength in it, and threw it far above
The expectation of the standers-by,
For through the clouds the sledge did seem to fly;
And Hyacinth, being eager for to throw,
Ran to the place ere that it fell below
Upon the earth, and falling on firm ground
Against his face the heavy sledge rebounds,
And struck him to the earth; the god did sound,[152]
When he beheld that fatal deadly wound,
But being revived, he hollowed in his ear,[153]
To call back life, 'O, Hyacinth, my dear,
Leave me not thus! I will court Destiny
For to revoke th[y] doom. Thou shalt not die!'
Grief would not help; in gore there lay his brain,
And so Apollo's Hyacinth was slain.
But yet the god still wept upon his wound,
Till with his tears there sprung from out the ground
A flower where his bleeding corpse lay dead,
Shaped like a lily, but this flower was red.
The people wondered when they saw this done,
But then he showed himself bright like the sun,
Which filled them all with fear. They kneeling said,
'Tell us thy will, and it shall be obeyed.'
[154]'Then build a stately temple o'er this flow'r,
And dedicate it to his matchless power
That kept my heart in thrall, that lovely boy,
Beauty of mankind, and Apollo's joy,
And every year to make a solemn feast
In honour of my friend but now deceased.
And for my part, I'll walk in shadow groves,
Consort with virgins' ghosts, slain by false loves;
No more I'll touch my viol or my lute,
Nor speak to gods or men (true grief is mute).'

[151] *worth* prize.

[152] *sound* faint.

[153] *hollowed* cried out loud.

[154] Apollo responds.

So he departed, wringing of his hands,
And they to do those things that he commands.
The gods, for missing of their wonted light,
Sent Mercury to know of him if night
Should still possess the world. He made reply,
'Three days for Phaethon did I leave the sky,
But Hyacinth was dearer. For his wrack[155]
Six days the world shall mourn in solemn black.'
But Hermes used such cunning, he did force
Phoebus again to take his wonted course.[156]
And so to Heaven he went with Mercury,
Whose tongue had power to o'errule Destiny.
Yet since the earth had robbed him of his friend,
He vowed this curse until the world should end:
Half of the year, his beams should comfort shine
The rest to rain and frost he would resign,
And that because his sorrow here had birth,
Trouble and grief should still possess the earth.

Thomas Heywood (c. 1573–1641), poet, actor, dramatist, and prose writer

Collaborator on some two hundred plays, Heywood's most famous independent works include the domestic tragedy *A Woman Killed with Kindness* (1603) and a defence of the stage, *Apology for Actors* (1612). His ambitious five-play cycle – *The Golden Age*, *The Silver Age*, *The Brazen Age*, and *The Iron Age* (2 parts) (1611–13) – relates the pagan history of the world from the establishment of the reigns of Jupiter and Saturn to the fall of Troy. His other major works include translations of Sallust and Ovid, a history of women (*Gynaikeion* (1624)), and *Pleasant Dialogues and Dramas* (1637), which contains many classical translations (including fifteen of Lucian's dialogues; see **7.29.2**).

[155] *wrack* destruction.
[156] *wonted* customary.

7.22

From *The Golden Age* (1611)

[In exchange for his elder brother Titan's relinquishment of his claim to the throne of Crete, Saturn has agreed to kill all his new-born sons, ensuring the accession of Titan's children. Sybilla, Saturn's wife, secretly sends their new-born Jupiter away to the court of King Milliseus of Epire. Completing a peace treaty between Milliseus and King Lycaon, son of Titan, the adult Jupiter is betrayed by Lycaon, but defeats him, is elected king, and falls in love with Callisto, Lycaon's daughter. Callisto rejects him and joins Diana's virgin community. Unable to surrender her, Jupiter cross-dresses and goes to join her.]

7.22.1 Act 2, scene 1

[...]

DIANA. These sports, our fauns, our satyrs, and ourselves[157]
Make (fair Callisto) for your entertain.[158]
Pan, the great god of shepherds, and the nymphs
Of meads and fountains, that inhabit here,
All give you welcome with their rural sports,
Glad to behold a princess of your birth
A happy citizen of these meads and groves.
These satyrs are our neighbours, and live here,
With whom we have confirmed a friendly league
And dwell in peace. Here is no city-craft;
Here's no court-flattery: simpleness and sooth,[159]
The harmless chase and strict virginity[160]
Is all our practice. You have read our orders,
And you have sworn to keep them. Fair Callisto,
Speak: how esteem you them?
CALLISTO. With reverence.
Great queen, I am sequestered from the world,
Even in my soul hate man's society
And all their lusts, suggestions; all court-pleasures
And city-curiosities are vain,

[157] *sports* dancing, singing, rural games.
[158] *entertain* entertainment.
[159] *sooth* truth.
[160] *chase* hunt.

And with my finer temper ill agree,
That now have vowed sacred virginity.

[...]

DIANA. Where's Atlanta?
ATLANTA. Madam.
DIANA. Is there no princess in our train,[161]
As yet unmatched to be her cabin-fellow,
And sleep by her?
ATLANTA. Madam, we all are coupled[162]
And twined in love, and hardly is there any[163]
That will be won to change her bedfellow.
DIANA. You must be single till the next arrive,
She that is next admitted of our train,
Must be her bed-companion, so 'tis 'lotted.
Come fauns, and nymphs, and satyrs, girt us round
Whilst we ascend our state, and here proclaim[164]
A general hunting in Diana's name.

Enter JUPITER *like a nymph or a virago.*[165]

JUPITER. There I strid[166] too wide. That step was too large for one that professeth the strait order:[167] what a pitiful coil[168] shall I have to counterfeit this woman, to lisp (forsooth), to simper and set my face like a sweet gentlewoman's made out of ginger-bread! Shall I venture or no? My face I fear not: for my beard being in the nonage[169] durst never yet look a barber in the face. And for my complexion, I have known as brown lasses as myself have gone for current.[170] And for my stature, I am not yet of that giant size, but I may pass for [...] a virago or a good manly lass. If they should put me to spin, or to sew, or any such gentlewoman-like exercise, how should I excuse my

[161] *train* group.
[162] *coupled* 'paired'; also, 'joined in wedlock or sexual union'.
[163] *twined* intertwined; but, perhaps, 'twinned': intimately united.
[164] *state* throne.
[165] *virago* manly woman.
[166] *strid* strode.
[167] *strait order* austere way of life.
[168] *coil* fuss.
[169] *in the nonage* under-developed.
[170] *brown* without a woman's conventionally white complexion; *gone for current*: been accepted as genuine [females].

bringing up? Tush, the hazard is nothing, compared with the value of the gain. [...] But howsoever

Be my loss certain, and my profit none,
'Tis for Callisto's love, and I will on.

[...]

JUPITER. Hail, divinest queen.
I come to do thee service.
DIANA. A manly lass, a stout virago,
Were all our train proportioned to thy size,
We need not fear men's subtle treacheries.
Thy birth and fortunes?
JUPITER. Madam, I derive
My birth from noble and high parentage:
Respect of your rare beauty, with my love
And zeal I still bear to a virgin's life,
Have drawn me to your service.
DIANA. Welcome, lady. Her largeness pleaseth me. If she have courage proportioned with her limbs, she shall be champion to all our wronged ladies. You, Atlanta, present her oath.
[*Her oath is given on Diana's bow.*

[...]

ATLANTA. You shall vow chastity:
JUPITER. [*Aside*] That's more than I can promise. Well, proceed.
ATLANTA. You never shall with hated man atone,[171]
But lie with woman or else lie alone.
JUPITER. Make my oath strong, my protestation deep,
For this I vow by all the gods to keep.
ATLANTA. With ladies you shall only sport and play,[172]
And in their fellowship spend night and day.
JUPITER. I shall.
ATLANTA. Consort with them at board and bed,
And swear no man shall have your maidenhead.
JUPITER. By all the powers both earthly and divine,
If e'er I los't, a woman shall have mine.
DIANA. Now you're ours, you're welcome, kiss our hand!

[171] *atone* reconcile; perhaps, also, 'join together physically'.

[172] *sport* amuse oneself; also, 'engage in amorous behaviour or sexual intercourse'; *play*: See **n45**.

You promise well, we like you, and will grace you.
And if with our election yours agree,[173]
Callisto here your bed-fellow shall be.

[...]

[Jupiter and Calisto rest in an isolated bower, while the others go hunting.]

[...]

CALLISTO. Come, shall's lie down a little?
JUPITER. Sooth, I will.
[*Aside*] I thirst in seas and cannot quaff my fill
Behold before me a rich table spread
And yet poor I am forced to starve for bread:
We be alone, the ladies far in chase,
And may I die an eunuch by my vow,
If bright Callisto you escape me now.
[*To Callisto*] Sweet bed-fellow, your hand. What have I felt
Unless blanched snow, or substance not to melt?
CALLISTO. You gripe too hard.
JUPITER. Good sooth, I shall not rest
Until my head be pillowed on thy breast.
CALLISTO. Lean on me then.
JUPITER. So shall I wrong mine eyes
To have your face to look up the skies,
Oh, how I love thee! Come, let's kiss and play.[174]
CALLISTO. How?
JUPITER. So a woman with a woman may.
CALLISTO. I do not like this kissing.
JUPITER. Sweet, sit still.
Lend me thy lips that I may taste my fill.
CALLISTO. You kiss too wantonly.[175]
JUPITER. Thy bosom lend,
And by thy soft paps let my hand descend.[176]
CALLISTO. Nay, fie, what mean you?
JUPITER. Prithee, let me toy.[177]
I would the gods would shape thee to a boy,
Or me into a man.

[173] *election* choice.
[174] *play* See **n45**.
[175] *wantonly* lasciviously.
[176] *paps* nipples.
[177] *toy* dally.

8 'Jupiter and Callisto', from Ovid, *P. Ovidii Nasonis Metamorphoseon libri XV* (Venice, 1565).

CALLISTO. A man, how then?
JUPITER. My sweet, lie still, for we are far from men.
Lie down again. Your foot I oft have praised,
Aye, and your leg. Nay, let your skirt be raised:
I'll measure for the wager of a fall,[178]
Who hath the greatest great or smallest small.
CALLISTO. You are too wanton, and your hand too free.
JUPITER. You need not blush to let a woman see.
CALLISTO. My bareness I have hid from sight of skies,
Therefore may bar it any lady's eyes.
JUPITER. Methinks you should be fat; pray, let me feel.[179]
CALLISTO. Oh, God, you tickle me.[180]
JUPITER. Lend me your hand,

[178] *fall* the loser of the wager shall agree to a wrestling match (a *fall*); Jupiter hints at Callisto's imminent sexual fall.

[179] *fat* plump.

[180] *tickle* the modern meaning, but also 'to be pleasurably stirred or moved; to be sexually played with'.

And freely taste me: note how I will stand,[181]
I am not ticklish.
CALLISTO. Lord, how you woo!
JUPITER. We maids may wish much, but can nothing do.
CALLISTO. I am weary of this toying.
JUPITER. Oh, but I
In this Elysium could both live and die.
[*Aside*] I can forbear no longer, though my rape
Be punished with my head, she shall not 'scape.

[Jupiter reveals himself, carries off the resistant Callisto, rapes her (offstage), and impregnates her. Consequently, Diana banishes her. Refusing Jupiter's marriage proposal, Callisto gives birth to a boy, Archas. Later, the grown Archas, savage and bestial in keeping with his nurture in the wilderness, attempts to kill Callisto. Saved by Jupiter, Callisto delivers Archas to his care, refuses to be Jupiter's queen, and departs, vanishing from the action of the play.]

Martial (c. 40–104 CE), Latin poet

Member of the Roman literary elite, and friend of Seneca and Juvenal, Martial searched for imperial patronage, but was only moderately successful, returning to Spain around 98 CE. Martial's twelve-book *Epigrams* (comp. c. 86–101 CE) consists of brief poems, usually addressed to and/or about a particular individual or personality type, often satiric, and usually concerned with larger issues of social mores and values.

R. Fletcher (*fl.* 1650s)

Perhaps Robert Fletcher, Warwickshire gentleman. Perhaps a London law student and friend of the poets Carew and Suckling, Fletcher may have fought for the king during the Civil War, publishing his only work, *Ex Otio*, after these chaotic years. Absorbed into John Cleveland's *Poems* (1659), Fletcher's original verse became part of this more famous poet's oeuvre, contributing to the former's literary and biographical obscurity.

Editions

Woodward, D.H., ed., *Poems and Translations of Robert Fletcher*. Gainesville: State University of Florida Press, 1970.

181 *taste* 'touch', but also 'test'; *stand*: not recoil (playing on 'become sexually erect').

7.23

From *Ex Otio Negotium,*
Or, Martial His Epigrams Translated[1] (1656)

7.23.1 Epigram 1.91 (1.90): Ad Bassam tribadem[2]

'Cause amongst males thou ne'er was seen to be
Nor as unchaste no fable feignèd thee,[3]
But all thy offices dischargèd were[4]
By thy own sex, no man intruding there,
I grant thou seem'dst Lucretia to our eye,
But (Oh, mistake!) Bassa th' art out on't, fie.
Two twats commit the fact, and dare it can,[5]
Whiles a prodigious lust supplies the man.[6]
Th' hast made a riddle worth the Theban guile:[7]
Where no man is, adultery bred the while.

7.23.2 Epigram 9.26 (9.25): In Afrum[8]

As oft as we thy Hyllus do behold[9]
Filling thy wine, thy brows do seem to scold.
What crime is't, I would know to view thy boy?

[1] *Ex Otio Negotium* Latin, 'From leisure business' (i.e., from seeming inactivity one can fulfil public duty).

[2] Latin, 'To the Tribade, Bassa'; *tribade*: a woman who has sex with other women.

[3] *fable* rumour.

[4] *offices* business; services.

[5] *twat* vagina. However, *twat*'s use here and in other texts, especially lampoons and satires, also suggests its more general meaning: 'female genitalia'. But cf. **7.23.5** where *twat* refers to both vaginal and anal orifices; *fact*: crime, outrage.

[6] In the original, Bassa has an enlarged clitoris (*prodigiosa Venus*) that allows her to play the man's penetrative role in intercourse.

[7] *Theban guile* The monstrous Sphinx would accost travellers outside Thebes. If they were unable to answer a particular riddle, the Sphinx killed them. Only Oedipus solved it, and when he did the Sphinx killed herself.

[8] Latin, 'On Afer'. *Afer* is a pretentious boaster who appears in *Epigrams* 4.37, 78; 6.77; 9.6; 10.84. He marries a man, the 'bearded Callistratus', in 12.42.

[9] *Hyllus* This common slave name was also that of the hero Hercules' son. A 'Hyllus' appears in four other epigrams, but of these only 4.7 (where the speaker expresses continued sexual interest in Hyllus after he has become a man) seems unquestionably addressed to this same beloved youth. Cf. the homosatiric and heterosatiric content of 2.51 and 2.60, respectively. I could find no English translation of 4.7 before 1735.

We look upon the gods, the stars, the sky,
Shall I fling back as when a Gorgon lies[10]
Steeped in the cup? and hide my face and eyes?
Great Hercules was fierce in cruelty
Yet we might see his pretty Hylas free;
Nor would great Jove have aught in wrath to say
If Mercury with Ganymede did play.
Afer, if then we must not view thy loose
Soft ministers that serve thee in thy house,
Invite such men as Phineus to be
Thy guests or Oedipus that ne'er could see.[11]

7.23.3 Epigram 11.7 (11.6): Ad Romam[12]

In scythe-crowned Saturn's feasts, wherein[13]
The box of dice doth reign as king,
All-covered Rome, thou dost permit[14]
Me now to sport my fluent wit,
So I suppose, for thou did'st smile,
Thence we are not forbid the while.
Ye pallid cares, far hence begone!
I'll speak whate'er I think upon,
Sans any studièd delay;
So fill me out three cups, my boy,
Such as Pythagoras did give
To Nero when he here did live,
But, Dindymus, fill faster too,[15]
For sober I can nothing do.
When I am drunk up to the height
Full fifteen poets seize me straight.
Now give me kisses, such as were
Catullus his and if they are

[10] *Gorgon* horrific monster; looking upon it would turn one to stone.

[11] *Phineus* and *Oedipus* were legendary Greek kings who went blind.

[12] Latin, 'To Rome'.

[13] Saturnalia, feast of the god *Saturn*, inverted the social order and suspended the limits on sensual indulgence.

[14] *all-cover'd* In the original, *pilleata* (cap-wearing) refers to the traditional Saturnalian cap: symbol of licence.

[15] *Dindymus* This beautiful slave boy also appears in *Epigrams* 5.83 (as the object of the speaker's erotic pursuit) and 10.42 (on Dindymus's kisses); a eunuch named Dindymus who may (or may not) be the same person appears in 6.39, 11.81, and 12.75.

So numerous as his are said to be,[16]
I will Catullus' sparrow give to thee.[17]

7.23.4 Epigram 11.23 (11.22): In Paediconem masturbantem[18]

'Cause thou dost kiss thy boy's soft lips with thy
Rough chin, and with stripped Ganymede dost lie,
Who does deny thee this? 'tis well. At least
Frig not thyself with thy lascivious fist,[19]
This in light toys more than the prick offends,
Their fingers hasten and the man up sends.[20]
Hence, goatish rankness! sudden hairs, a beard[21]
Springs forth to wond'ring mothers much admired.
Nor do they please by day when in the bath
They wash their skins. Nature divided hath
The males: half to the girls born to be shown,
The other half to men: Use then thy own.[22]

7.23.5 Epigram 11.44 (11.43): In Uxorem[23]

Caught with my boys, at me my wife the froe[24]
Scolds, and cries out she hath an arse-hole too.
How oft hath Juno thus reproved loose Jove?
Yet he with Ganymede doth act his love.
Hercules bent his boy, laid by his bow,
Though Megara had haunches too we know.[25]

[16] *Now … be* Catullus asks his mistress Lesbia for thousands of kisses ('Carmen 5').

[17] *Catullus' … thee* i.e., I will give you my penis (satisfy you sexually). The Latin, 'passer' (sparrow) was slang for 'penis'. Cf. 'Carmen 3', where the poet memorializes Lesbia's dead sparrow, envied for its physical closeness to her.

[18] Latin, 'On a Masturbating Boy-Lover [sodomite]'.

[19] *frig* masturbate. In the original, the speaker is reproved for masturbating the boys, not himself.

[20] In the original, Martial states that masturbating boys is far worse than having anal intercourse with them; *man*: penis.

[21] *goatish* lustful.

[22] In the original, Martial says nature created a youth's anus for the pleasure of men, his penis for that of girls.

[23] Latin, 'On His Wife'.

[24] *froe* Dutch, 'wife'; here, sexually available woman.

[25] *haunches* buttocks.

Phoebus was tortured by the flying wench,[26]
Yet the Oebalian lad those flames did quench.[27]
Though much-denied Briseis from him lay
Achilles with Patroclus yet did play.
Give not male names then to such things as thine,
But think thou hast two twats, O wife of mine.[28]

Thomas May (c. 1596–1650), historian, translator, playwright, and poet

May's translations of Lucan (1627), Virgil (1628), and Martial (1629), and his original dramas on classical figures such as Cleopatra and Antigone obliquely address late Stuart political corruption, especially the power of Buckingham, and the limits of monarchical authority. May early cultivated royal and aristocratic patronage, although his principled objections to monarchy were public knowledge. Later, he became one of Parliament's most effective propagandists and historians.

7.24

From *Selected Epigrams of Martial* (1629)

7.24.1 Epigram 3.64 (3.65): To Diadumenus

What smell ripe apples bit by virgins fair,
Or what Cilician saffrons' fragrant air,[29]
What blooming vines with blossoms lately filled,
Or springing pastures cropped by sheep do yield;
What myrtles, chafèd amber, Eastern gums,[30]
Arabian incense rising in pale fumes;
What meadows lightly wet with summer show'rs,
Or nard in chaplets made of sweetest flow'rs:[31]
All this, fair boy, thy fragrant kisses be.
What would they, didst thou give them full and free?

26 *flying wench* Daphne (Glossary).
27 *Oebalian lad* Hyacinthus (Glossary).
28 *twat* Cf. **n5**.
29 *Cilician* from Cilicia, a country in Asia Minor, on the coast, north of Cyprus.
30 *chafèd* heated. A fossil resin, *amber* was burned as incense.
31 *nard* fragrant perfume; *chaplet*: wreath for the head.

7.24.2 Epigram 6.68: On the Death of the Boy, Eutychus[32]

Weep, nymphs, for your misdeeds all Lucrine lake;[33]
Let Thetis feel your sorrow and partake.
Drowned in the Baian waters, Eutychus
Is lost: thy dear companion, Castricus,
That knew thy thoughts, thy cares that gently eased,
The loved Alexis, which our poet pleased.[34]
Perchance the wanton nymph within the lake
Thee naked saw, and sent young Hylas back;
Or else the goddess movèd with delight
Of thy embrace neglects th'Hermaphrodite.[35]
Whatever caused thy sudden rape, to thee[36]
Let both the earth and water gentle be.

7.24.3 Epigram 9.57 (9.56)

To Libya goes Splendophorus to war.
Cupid, thy shafts for this fair boy prepare,
Those shafts, which youths and tender virgins wound;
Light let thy spear in his soft hand be found.
The breast-plate, helm, and shield I leave to thee;
To fight in safety, naked let him be.
No arrow, sword, nor dart could hurt in war
Parthenopaeus whilst his face was bare.[37]
He whom this youth shall wound will die of love,
And happy too so sweet a fate to prove.
Whilst yet thy chin is smooth, fair boy, come home;
Grow not a man in Affric, but at Rome.[38]

32 This epigram is one of five addressed to Martial's patron, friend, and fellow poet Castricus (6.43; 7.4, 37, and 42); the epigram mourns Castricus's loss of his beloved slave boy Eutychus (whose name, ironically, means 'the fortunate or lucky one').

33 *Lucrine lake* i.e., the Lucrine lagoon, in Campagnia, adjoining the gulf of Baiae. Castricus either had a villa or vacationed regularly on its shores (6.43).

34 *our poet* Virgil. See **7.16.2**.

35 *Or … th'Hermaphrodite* Hermaphroditus (Glossary).

36 *rape* forcible seizing upon.

37 *Parthenopaeus* boy-warrior, famously beautiful.

38 *Affric* i.e., Africa.

Sir John Heath (1614–91), lawyer, royalist, and attorney-general of the duchy of Lancaster

Of Heath's two manuscript copies of his translations from Martial's epigrams, MS Additional 27343 is the earlier, containing numerous alterations, deletions, and substitutions; MS Egerton 2982 is the later, relatively fair copy, reflecting these changes, but containing many other changes and additions, including poems such as 11.79 (78) which do not appear in Additional 27343. Egerton 2982 is, however, also missing sections that appear in Additional, and so a complete comparison of the two versions is impossible. Both are in Heath's own hand (BL Manuscripts Catalogue online).

7.25

From *Martial's Epigrams* (BL MS Egerton 2982 and MS Additional 27343)[39]

7.25.1 Epigram 6.34 (Egerton 2982, fol. 199r): To Diadumenus

Come, kiss me close. How often, wouldst thou know?
Thou bidst me number the salt waves that flow;
Or shells spread on th'Aegean shores to count;
Or swarming bees on the Cecropean mount;[40]
Or tell the hems and claps o' th' crowded rout,[41]
When to the theatre Caesar first comes out.
Not all those kisses Lesbia frankly gave
To sharp Catullus are what I would have:[42]
Those are too few which any numbers hold;
Give me the kisses that can ne'er be told.[43]

7.25.2 Epigram 8.46 (Egerton 2982, f. 218v): To Cestus: A Boy

With such rare form, what innocence thou hast,
Sweet boy! Than young Hippolytus more chast![44]

39 Reprinted by permission of the British Library.
40 *Cecropean* Attican or Athenian.
41 *tell* count; *hems and claps*: applause; *rout*: audience.
42 *frankly* unreservedly; *sharp*: witty.
43 *told* numbered, with a pun on 'related, described'.
44 *chast* chaste.

With thee Diana's self would swim; with thee
The Cybele, rather than her Phrygian, be.[45]
Thou, with thy modest kisses, Ganymede,
Juno herself consenting, mightst succeed.[46]
Happy that spouse, though ne'er so coy, that can
(Her virgin zone untied) first write thee man.

7.25.3 Epigram 9.12 (9.11) (Egerton 2982, f. 230r): Of Earinus: Domitian's Boy[47]

The name o' th' year's best (wished for) part, the spring,
Which violet and rose doth with it bring;
Of Hybla's, and of Attic, flow'rs doth smell;[48]
All odours which i' th' Phoenix' nest doth dwell:
(Earinus) in which con-centred meet
All that in nectar and ambrosia's sweet:[49]
A name, of which fair Atys would be proud;
Which Ganymede would beg to be allowed;
A name, which once pronounced i' th' Roman court
All loves, and beauties, thither would resort;
That name, so noble, soft, so delicate,
In verse, as smooth and soft, I would relate.
But there a syllable so rough I find
To verse's measure 'twill not be confined.[50]
Greek poets yet 'Earinus' would say:
Who rules of quantity do not obey;[51]
But the same word, all in a breath are found
Boldly sometimes, both short and long, to sound.
We Latins such quaint licence dare not use,[52]
Whose duty binds to a severer muse.

[45] *her Phrygian* 'Cybele and Attis' (Glossary).

[46] *Thou, ... succeed* Cf. Additional: 'Thou, with thy modest kisses might'st succeed, / Juno herself consenting, Ganymede.'

[47] *Earinus* eunuch cup-bearer of Emperor *Domitian* (51–96 CE); 'Earinus' means 'of the spring'.

[48] *Hybla* mountain famous for its flowers and honey; *Attic*: i.e., Attica, region in central Greece, famously fertile.

[49] *Nectar* and *ambrosia* drink and food of the gods.

[50] *That name ... confined* Earinus's name has four syllables, one too many for Martial's metre.

[51] *quantity* length of a syllable.

[52] *quaint licence* clever tricks.

7.25.4 Epigram 9.58 (9.57) (Egerton 2982, ff. 227v–228r): Of Hedyle

Nothing's more worn than Hedyle's cloak. No not
The handles of an antique brazen pot;
Or slave's thigh smoothèd with a ten years chain;
Or mule's neck galled, and then skinned o'er again;[53]
Or stones i' th' cart-routs of highways; or those
That shine like glass, where the sea overflows;
Or spades, with digging vineyards, polishèd;
Or threadbare gown, that covers beggars dead;
Or bruisèd wheels of the dull muleteers;
Or a wild ox's sides which his den wears;
Or whetted fangs of a fierce o'er-grown boar;
Yet there's one thing, (he'll not deny) 's worn more
Than Hedyle's cloak. His —— that is sore.[54]

7.25.5 Epigram 11.9 (11.8) (Additional 27343, pp. 140–1): Of His Boy's Kisses

Like balsams chaffed by some exotic fair,[55]
Or from a saffron field fresh gliding air;
In winter chests like apples ripening,
Or grounds o'erspread with budding trees in spring:
Like silken robes in royal presses, and[56]
Gums suppled by a virgin's soft white hand;[57]
As broken jars of Falerne wines do smell,[58]
Far off, or flow'ry gardens where bees dwell;
Perfumers' pots, burnt incense lost i' th' air,
Chaplets new-fall'n from rich perfumed hair:
What more? All's not enough: mix all t' express
My dear boy's morning kisses' sweetnesses.
You'ld know his name. I'll naught but 's kisses tell.[59]
I doubt, I swear, you'd know him fain too well.[60]

53 *galled* rubbed (usually by an instrument like a harness) until the skin beneath is raw.
54 —— arse.
55 *balsam* aromatic oil; *fair*: beloved woman.
56 *presses* storage chests.
57 *gums* resins, burned as incense.
58 *Falerne* highly prized wine.
59 *'s* his.
60 *fain* eagerly.

7.25.6 Epigram 11.79 (11.78) (Egerton 2982): To Victor[61]

Female embraces, Victor, now enjoy!
Let p— learn, at length, a new employ.[62]
The virgin's ready now with wedding stole:[63]
Your new bride, now, your page's locks will poll.[64]
For once she'll give you leave to use your boy,
Fearing your first encounters to enjoy:
After, your nurse and mother will't deny;
Saying, 'A wife, now, not a boy, you'll try.'
Alas, what heats must p—, what pains con wont[65]
Endure? If then a stranger to a c—[66]
Unto some suburb-whore put it to school.[67]
A maid won't teach you play the man, but fool.

Thomas Dilke (*fl.* 1678–98), writer

Educated at Oxford, Dilke was an army lieutenant under Lord Raby, later earl of Strafford. Of Dilke's three comedies, *The Lover's Luck* (1696) was quite successful, but *The City Lady, or Folly Reclaimed* (1697) and *The Pretenders, or Town Unmasked* (1700) were reportedly flops. In the 'Preface' to his brief collection of very free adaptations from Horace, Martial, Anacreon, and Petronius (1698), Dilke claims, 'I have [...] adapted my authors to our present circumstances of time and custom, so that their notions might be relished with as little expense of thought as possible' (2). The reader may compare the following adaptation with Thomas May's stricter translation in the *Online Companion* and **7.25.2**.

[61] In the original, Victor's inexperience with heterosexual intercourse must be remedied by visiting prostitutes. Victor's bride will allow her husband anal intercourse once, while she fears vaginal penetration, but soon her mother and nurse will forbid this, reminding Victor that 'she's your wife, not your boy'; all three finally forbid sex with the boy.

[62] *p—* prick (penis).

[63] *stole* long robe.

[64] *poll* cut.

[65] *con wont* perhaps, 'can want'. Heath may mean 'what pains can your penis's lack [of experience with women] endure'. Or perhaps 'what pains can your penis's [sexual] need [for your page or for your wife] endure'?

[66] *c—* cunt.

[67] *suburb-whore* prostitute.

7.26

From *XXV Select Allusions to Several Places of Horace, Martial, Anacreon, and Petron[ius]* (1698)

7.26.1 Epigram 8.46

Charming Alexis is so sweet a boy,[68]
To look on him is more than to enjoy.
No blushes yet did ever grace
A more bewitching, modest face.
Whene'er I see the lively red
His tender cheeks o'erspread,
Methinks they do invite me to a kiss:
Yet seem to say, that I must struggle for the bliss.
The youth that did the Mighty Thund'rer move[69]
Had never eyes more fraught with love.[70]
He that with lightning could the world destroy
Stooped to the flames of his dear lovely boy.
How then can wretched I,
Whom all the pangs of love do thus enrage
Forbear to try
Whether Alexis won't my panting pains assuage?

Juvenal (c. 50/65–after 130 CE), Latin satirist

Possibly born in Aquinum, Juvenal lived in Rome, was a friend of Martial, may have had independent means, and was perhaps a member of the imperial elite. He wrote sixteen satires (although the last is unfinished) sometime between 110 and 130 CE.

John Dryden (1631–1700)

For his biography, see Introduction to **7.16**. On 'Satire 6', see '1. Deletion, Expurgation, Vagueness, and Mistranslation' (Chapter 7, Introduction).

[68] In the original, the poem is addressed to the boy Cestus; the lovely slave boy Alexis appears in 8.63, and Virgil's beloved boy of the same name is alluded to in 5.16, 6.68, 7.29, 8.55, 73.

[69] *the youth* Ganymede; *the Mighty Thund'rer*: Jove. See 'Jove and Ganymede' (Glossary).

[70] *fraught* full.

7.27

From *The Satires of Decimus Junius Juvenalis*[1] (1693)

7.27.1 Satire 6

[...]

The secrets of the goddess named the Good,[2]
Are e'en by boys and barbers understood:
Where the rank matrons, dancing to the pipe,[3]
Gig with their bums, and are for action ripe;[4]
With music raised, they spread abroad their hair;
And toss their heads like an enamoured mare:
[Confess their itching in their ardent eyes
While tears of wine run trickling down their thighs.][5]
Laufella lays her garland by, and proves[6]
The mimic lechery of manly loves.[7]
[Provokes to flats some battered household whore
And heaving up the rubster does adore,][8]
Ranked with the lady, the cheap sinner lies,

[1] A multi-authored volume edited by John Dryden, who also translated 'Satire 6', below. The lines in square brackets were cancelled before the volume was published, because they were too explicit. See W.B. Carnochan, 'Some Suppressed Verses in Dryden's Translation of Juvenal VI', *TLS*, 21 January 1972: pp. 73–4.

[2] *the Good* Bona Dea, goddess of female chastity; her rites were restricted to women.

[3] *rank matrons* grossly licentious wives.

[4] *Gig* move to and fro; *action*: sexual activity.

[5] Cf. Stapylton (1660): 'Then how they long for't! when it comes, what cries, / What torrents of old wine flow down their thighs!' (167); Holyday (1673): 'Where these astonished Maenads n'er shame / To run with rowling hair. Oh, forward flame!' (99).

[6] *Laufella* in some mss, 'Saufeia'; if a real person, she has remained unidentified, although both names suggest her aristocratic origins; given to drunkenness, Laufella appears in 'Satire 9' as a priestess of Vesta, goddess of the hearth. Traditionally, Vesta's priestesses were virgins.

[7] *mimic ... loves* i.e., she imitates the man's role in sexual intercourse. Stapylton (1660): 'Laufella wenches at the nimble heave / Dares challenge, and the garland does receive' (168). Holyday (1673): 'The lewd Laufella makes a game of sin: / Rewards proposes and rewards does win' (100). Holyday excuses his translation from being more explicit about the exact nature of the sin and the reward (117 n35).

[8] *flats* female same-sex intercourse; *rubster*: here, the penetrative partner in tribadic intercourse.

For here not blood, but virtue gives the prize.[9]
Nothing is feigned in this venereal strife;
'Tis downright lust, and acted to the life.
So full, so fierce, so vigorous, and so strong;
That, looking on, would make old Nestor young.[10]
Impatient of delay, a general sound,
An universal groan of lust goes round;
For then, and only then, the sex sincere is found.
Now is the time of action; now begin,
They cry, and let the lusty lovers in.
The whoresons are asleep; then bring the slaves
And watermen, a race of strong-backed knaves.
[Bring any thing that's man: if none be nigh
Asses have better parts their places to supply.]
I wish, at least, our sacred rites were free
From those pollutions of obscenity:

[...]

I hear your cautious counsel, you would say,
Keep close your women, under lock and key.
But, who shall keep those keepers' women, nursed
In craft, begin with those, and bribe 'em first.
The sex is turned all whore; they love the game,
And mistresses and maids are both the same.
The poor Ogulnia on the poet's day[11]
Will borrow clothes, and chair, to see the play:
She, who before, had mortgaged her estate;
And pawned the last remaining piece of plate.[12]
Some are reduced their utmost shifts to try:
But women have no shame of poverty.
They live beyond their stint; as if their store[13]
The more exhausted, would increase the more:
Some men, instructed by the lab'ring ant,[14]
Provide against th' extremities of want;

[9] *blood* rank, status; *virtue*: i.e., 'physical strength'; also, 'unusual ability' [in sexual technique].

[10] *Nestor* King of Pylos; extraordinarily long-lived.

[11] *Ogulnia* if a real person, she remains unidentified; her name is that of an ancient patrician family or *gens*.

[12] *plate* dishes, cups, etc. (of precious metal).

[13] *stint* allowance; *store*: possessions; money.

[14] *lab'ring ant* by-word for hard work and prudence.

But womankind, that never knows a mean,[15]
Down to the dregs their sinking fortune drain:
Hourly they give, and spend, and waste, and wear;
And think no pleasure can be bought too dear.
There are who in soft eunuchs place their bliss,[16]
To shun the scrubbing of a bearded kiss,
And 'scape abortion; but their solid joy
Is when the page, already past a boy,
Is caponed late; and to the gelder shown,[17]
With his two pounders, to perfection grown.[18]
When all the navel-string could give, appears;[19]
All but the beard; and that's the barber's loss not theirs.
Seen from afar, and famous for his ware,
He struts into the bath among the fair:
Th' admiring crew to their devotions fall;
And, kneeling, on their new Priapus call.
Carved for his lady's use, with her he lies;
And let him drudge for her, if thou art wise;[20]
Rather than trust him with thy fav'rite boy;
He proffers death in proffering to enjoy.

Plutarch (c. 50–120 CE), Greek philosopher and historian

Born to a wealthy and respected family in the city of Chaeronea (in Boeotia, a region in central Greece), Plutarch was a prolific writer of moral philosophy, dialogues, commentaries, polemics, religious history, and biography. Sadly, of his reported 227 works we possess now only seventy-eight.

Philemon Holland (1552–1637), scholar and translator

Cambridge graduate, Coventry schoolmaster, and practising physician, Holland's monumental classical translations include Livy's *History of Rome* (1600); Pliny the Elder's *Natural History* (1601); Plutarch's *Moralia* (1603);

15 *a mean* moderation.
16 *There are who* i.e., There are those who.
17 *caponed* castrated; *gelder*: castrater.
18 *two pounders* testicles.
19 *navel-string* umbilical cord.
20 *drudge* labour sexually (connotations of 'wearisome toil').

Suetonius's *History of the Twelve Caesars* (1606); and Xenophon's *Cyropaedia* (1632).

7.28

From *Moralia* (1603)

7.28.1 Of Love

Summary

This dialogue is more dangerous to be read by young men than any other treatise of Plutarch, for that there be certain glances here and there against honest marriage to uphold indirectly and underhand the cursed and detestable filthiness covertly couched under the name of the love of young boys. But minds guarded and armed with true chastity and the fear of God may see evidently in this discourse the miserable estate of the world, in that there be found patrons and advocates of so detestable a cause: such I mean as in this book are brought in under the persons of Protogenes and Pisias. Meanwhile they may perceive likewise in the combat of matrimonial love against unnatural pederasty not to be named, that honesty hath always means sufficient to defend itself for being vanquished, yea and in the end to go away with the victory. [...]

[Protogenes notes that marriage is necessary for procreation, but says the bond has nothing to do with true (pederastic) love, which is a noble love of the youth's mind, not a sexual lust for his body. Daphnaeus mocks this stance, noting sensibly that philosophers always say this, but still choose beautiful boys for their beloveds. Plutarch's father finally intervenes, and much of the rest of the dialogue concerns his disquisition on love and marriage. Although he is firmly on the side of heterosexual marriage as exemplifying amity and virtue, he also speaks approvingly of the type of martial male–male love that was understood as typical of Spartan society, and which Plutarch also discusses in his description of the Sacred Band ('Life of Pelopidas', *Online Companion*). In the following extracts, the speaker is Plutarch's father.]

[...] 'There came to aid the Chalcidians, at what time as there was hot war in Thessaly against the Eretrians, this Cleomachus.[1] Now the Chalcidians

[1] *Cleomachus* of Pharsalus fought in the Lelantine War for the city of Chalcis or Chalkida, on the Greek island of Euboea (late eighth century BCE).

seemed to be strong enough in their footmen, but much ado they had, and thought it was a difficult piece of service, to break the cavalry of their enemies and to repel them. So they requested Cleomachus, their ally and confederate, a brave knight, and of great courage, to give the first charge, and to enter upon the said men of arms. With that, he asked the youth whom he loved most entirely, and who was there present, "whether he would behold this enterprise, and see the conflict." And when the young man answered, "Yea," and withal, kindly kissing and embracing him, set the helmet upon his head, Cleomachus much more hardy and fuller of spirit than before assembled about him a troop of the most valourous horsemen of all the Thessalians, advanced forward right gallantly, and with great resolution set upon the enemies, in such sort as at the very first encounter he broke the front, disarrayed the men of arms, and in the end put them to flight. Which discomfiture, when their infantry saw, they also fled; and so the Chalcidians won the field and achieved a noble victory. Howbeit, Cleomachus himself was there slain, and the Chalcidians show his sepulchre and monument in their marketplace, upon which there standeth, even at this day, a mighty pillar erected. And whereas the Chalcidians before time held this *pederasty* or love of young boys an infamous thing, they of all other Greeks ever after affected and honoured it most. [...] hereupon it cometh that the Chalcidians use to chant such a carol as this:

> Sweet boys, fair imps extract from noble race,[2]
> Endued besides with youth and beauty's grace,
> Envy not men of arms and bold courage,
> Fruition of your prime and flow'ring age,
> For here as well of love and kind affection,
> As of prowess, we all do make profession. [...]

[...]

And in our city of Thebes,[3] O Pemptides, did not one Ardetas give unto a youth, whom he loved, a complete armour the day that he was enrolled soldier, with the inscription of Ardetas his own name? And as for Pammenes,[4] an amorous man and one well-experienced in love matters, he changed and altered the ordinance in battle of our footmen heavily armed, reproving Homer as one that had no skill nor experience of love for ranging the Achaeans by their tribes and wards, and not putting in array the lover

[2] *imps* noble male children.

[3] *Thebes* the most important city in Boeotia, a region in central Greece.

[4] *Pammenes* early leader of the Theban fighting force, the Sacred Band, comprised of 150 pairs of lovers (c. 379/80–338 BCE); it won famous victories against the Spartans, but Philip II of Macedon had it massacred.

close unto him whom he loveth; for this indeed had been the right ordinance, which Homer describeth in these words:

> The Morians set so close, and shield to shield
> So jointly touched, that one the other held.[5]

And this is the only battalion and army invincible, for men otherwhiles[6] in danger abandon those of their tribe, their kindred also, and such as be allied unto them. Yea, and believe me, they forsake their own fathers and children, but never was there enemy seen that could pass through and make way of evasion between the lover and his darling, considering that such, many times, show their adventurous resolution in a bravery, and how little reckoning they make of life, unto them being in no distress nor requiring so much at their hands. [... One] chanced in fight to fall grovelling upon his face, and when his enemy lifted up his sword to give him a mortal wound, he requested him to stay his hand awhile until he could turn his body that his friend, whom he loved, might not see him wounded in his back part. And therefore we may see that not only the most martial and warlike nations are most given to love – to wit, the Boeotians, Lacedaemonians, and Candiots[7] – but also divers renowned princes and captains of old time: as, namely, Meleager, Achilles, Aristomenes, Cimon, Epaminondas.[8] [...] To come now unto Hercules: hard it were to reckon and number his loves (they were so many), but among others, men honour and worship to this day Iolaus, because they take him to have been Hercules his darling, in so much as upon his tomb the manner is of lovers to take a corporal oath and assurance of reciprocal love.

[...]

Yea, but there be many enormious[9] and furious parts, will some one say, that are played by such as are in love with women. And be there not more (I pray) by those that are enamoured upon boys? Do but mark him who uttereth these passionate words:

[5] *Achaeans* a general term for the Greeks; *Morians*: i.e., the Myrmidons, a legendary people of ancient Greek, famed as warriors, and in Homer's *Iliad* commanded by Achilles. For these scenes of male martial bonding, see *Iliad* 13.131ff.; 16.215ff.

[6] *otherwhiles* at other times.

[7] *Boeotians* See **n3**; *Lacedaemonians*: Spartans; *Candiots*: inhabitants of Candia (the isle of Crete).

[8] *Meleager* ancient hero, one of the Argonauts; *Aristomenes* (*fl.* c. 660 BCE), Messenian warrior hero, who received cult honours after his death; *Cimon* (c. 510–450 BCE), Athenian nobleman and general; he won many victories against the Persians; *Epaminondas* (d. 362 BCE), Theban general and statesman, whose dear friend was Pelopidas.

[9] *enormious* outrageous, monstrous.

So often as these eyes of mine behold
That beardless youth, that smooth and lovely boy
I faint and fall: then wish I him to hold
Within mine arms, and so to die with joy:
And that on tomb were set where I do lie,
An epigram, mine end to testify.

But as there is a furious passion in some men doting upon women, so there is as raging an affection in others toward boys, but neither the one nor the other is love.

[…]

But to the end that we may not range too far, nor use any superfluous and nugatory words, yourself do know that these *pederasties* are of all other[10] most uncertain […] Bion the Sophister[11] was more rough and odious in his words toward such, when he termed the first down or hairs appearing upon the face of beautiful youths "Harmodii" and "Aristogitones";[12] for that by them lovers were delivered out of the tyranny of such fair persons, when they begin once to bud and put forth. But these imputations are not justly charged upon true lovers. As for that which Euripides said, it was pretty, and carried some elegancy with it; for as he embraced and kissed fair Agathon,[13] even when his beard began to grow, he said that, "of fair persons, the very latter season of the autumn was lovely and beautiful." But I say more than so, namely, that the loveliness of honest women passeth not away with rivels,[14] wrinkles, and hoary hairs, but continue always even to their sepulchre and tombs of memorial. Again, there are but a few couples in that other sex, of true lovers; but of men and women joined in wedlock, an infinite number, who to the very last hour have kept most faithfully their loyalty and hearty love reciprocally one unto the other.' […]

[10] *other* i.e., other loves.

[11] *Bion* (c. 325–c. 255 BCE), Greek philosopher of the Sophist school.

[12] *Harmodii* and *Aristogitones* the plural forms of the names *Harmodius* and *Aristogeiton*, lovers and aristocratic assassins of the Athenian tyrant Hipparchus; executed, but later celebrated as fathers of democracy; ancient writers make Hipparchus's attempt to seduce Harmodius, the youth of the relationship, one of the prime motivations for the assassination.

[13] *Euripides* and *Agathon* Greek tragedians; the seventy-year-old Euripides fell in love with the forty-year-old Agathon.

[14] *rivels* furrows.

Lucian of Samosata (*fl.* second century CE), Greek writer

Abandoning his early life as a rhetorician and itinerant philosopher, Lucian wrote satiric dialogues, philosophic works, essays, and satiric prose fiction. Thirty-six of his dialogues survive, their favourite targets being philosophers, religious hypocrites, historians, rhetoricians, and the gods.

Thomas Heywood (c. 1573–1641)

For his biography, see Introduction to **7.22**.

7.29

From *Pleasant Dialogues and Dramas* (1637)

7.29.1 The Argument of the Dialogue entitled 'Jupiter and Ganymede'

Jove's masculine love this fable reprehends,
And wanton dotage on the Trojan boy.[1]
Shaped like an eagle, he from th'earth ascends,
And bears through th'air his new delight and joy.
In Ganymede's expressed a simple swain,[2]
Who would leave Heaven, to live on earth again.

7.29.2 The Dialogue

JUPITER. Now kiss me, lovely Ganymede, for see,
We are at length arrived where we would be:
I have no crooked beak, no talons keen
No wings or feathers are about me seen;
I am not such as I but late appeared.[3]
GANYMEDE. But were you not that eagle who late feared
And snatched me from my flock? Where is become

[1] *wanton dotage* licentious love; *Trojan boy*: Ganymede. See 'Jove and Ganymede' (Glossary).
[2] *swain* herdsman.
[3] *late* recently.

That shape? You speak now, who but late were dumb.
JUPITER. I am no man, fair youth, as I appear,
Nor eagle, to astonish thee with fear:
But king of all the gods, who for some reason
Have by my power transhaped me for a season.[4]
GANYMEDE. What's that you say? You are not Pan, I know:
Where's then your pipe? or where your horns, should grow
Upon your temples? where your hairy thighs?
JUPITER. Thinks Ganymede that godhood only lies in rural Pan?
GANYMEDE. Why not? I know him one:
We shepherds sacrifice to him alone.
A spotted goat into some cave we drive,
And then he seizeth on the beast alive.
Thou art but some child-stealer, that's thy best.[5]
JUPITER. Hast thou not heard of any man contest[6]
By Jove's great name? nor his rich altar viewed
In Gargarus, with plenteous show'rs bedewed?[7]
There seen his fire and thunder?
GANYMEDE. Do you then
Affirm yourself the same, who on us men
Of late poured hail-stones? he that dwells above us,
And there makes noise; yet some will say doth love us?
To whom my father did observance yield,
And sacrificed the best ram in the field.
Why then (if you of all the gods be chief)
Have you, by stealing me, thus played the thief,
When in my absence the poor sheep may stray,
Or the wild ravenous wolves snatch them away?
JUPITER. Yet hast thou care of lambs, of folds, of sheep,
That now art made immortal, and must keep
Society with us.
GANYMEDE. I no way can
Conceive you. Will you play the honest man,[8]
And bear me back to Ida?
JUPITER. So in vain
I shaped me like an eagle, if again
I should return thee back.

4 *for a season* for a while.
5 *best* best explanation possible.
6 *contest* swear.
7 *Gargarus* famously fertile Greek mountain.
8 *conceive* understand.

GANYMEDE. My father, he
By this hath made inquiry after me;
And if the least of all the flock be eaten,
I in his rage am most sure to be beaten.
JUPITER. Where shall he find thee?
GANYMEDE. That's the thing I fear,
He never can climb up to meet me here,
But if thou beest a good god, let me pass
Into the mount of Ida where I was:
And then I'll offer, in my thankful piety,
Another well fed goat unto thy deity,
(As price of my redemption) three years old,
And now the chief and prime in all the fold.
JUPITER. How simple is this innocent lad? a mere
Innocuous child. But Ganymede now hear:[9]
Bury the thoughts of all such terren dross,[10]
Think Ida and thy father's flocks no loss:
Thou now art heavenly, and much grace mayst do
Unto thy father and thy country too.
No more of cheese and milk from henceforth think,
Ambrosia thou shalt eat, and nectar drink,[11]
Which thy fair hands in flowing cups shalt fill
To me and others, but attend us still;
And (that which most should move thee) make thy abode
Where thou art now, thou shalt be made a god,
No more be mortal, and thy glorious star
Shine with refulgence, and be seen from far.[12]
Here thou art ever happy.
GANYMEDE. But I pray,
When I would sport me, who is here to play?[13]
For when in Ida I did call for any,
Both of my age and growth it yielded many.
JUPITER. Playfellows for thee I will likewise find,
Cupid, with divers others to thy mind,
And such as are of both thy years and size,
To sport with thee all what thou canst devise:

[9] *innocuous* harmless.

[10] *terren* earthly.

[11] *Ambrosia* and *nectar* food and drink of the gods. Consuming the former would confer immortality.

[12] *refulgence* radiance.

[13] *sport* recreate.

Only be bold and pleasant, and then know
Thou shalt have need of nothing that's below.
GANYMEDE. But here no service I can do indeed,
Unless in heaven you had some flocks to feed.
JUPITER. Yes, thou to me shalt fill celestial wine,
And wait upon me when in state I dine:
Then learn to serve in banquets.
GANYMEDE. That I can
Already, without help of any man:
For I use ever when we dine or sup,[14]
To pour out milk, and crown the pastoral cup.[15]
JUPITER. Fie, how thou still remember'st milk and beasts,
As if thou wert to serve at mortal feasts!
Know, this is heaven, be merry then and laugh;
When thou art thirsty thou shalt nectar quaff.
GANYMEDE. Is it so sweet as milk?
JUPITER. Prized far before,
Which tasted once, milk thou wilt ask no more.
GANYMEDE. Where shall I sleep a-nights? what, must I lie
With my companion Cupid?
JUPITER. So then I
In vain had raped thee: but I from thy sheep[16]
Of purpose stole thee by my side to sleep.
GANYMEDE. Can you not lie alone? but will your rest
Seem sweeter, if I nuzzle on your breast?
JUPITER. Yes, being a child so fair.
GANIYMEDE. How can you think
Of beauty, whilst you close your eyes and wink?
JUPITER. It is a sweet enticement, to increase
Contented rest, when our desire's at peace.
GANYMEDE. Aye, but my father every morn would chide,
And say, those nights he lodged me by his side
I much disturbed his rest; tumbling and tossing
Athwart the bed, my little legs still crossing
His: either kicking this way, that way sprawling,
Or if he but removed me, straightways yawling:[17]
Then grumbling in my dreams, (for so he said)
And oft times sent me to my mother's bed:

14 *use* am accustomed.
15 *crown the pastoral cup* fill until foam rises above the brim.
16 *raped* kidnapped.
17 *straightways yawling* immediately yelling.

And then would she complain upon me worse.
Then if for that you stole me, the best course
Is even to send me back again; for I
Am ever so unruly where I lie,
Wallowing and tumbling, and such coil I keep,[18]
That I shall but disturb you in your sleep.

JUPITER. In that the greater pleasure I shall take,
Because I love still to be kept awake.
I shall embrace and kiss thee then the ofter,
And by that means my bed seem much the softer.

GANYMEDE. But whilst you wake I'll sleep.

JUPITER. Mercury, see
This lad straight taste of immortality;
And making him of service capable,
Let him be brought to wait on us at table.

Ferrand Spence (*fl.* 1682–89), translator

Perhaps a graduate of Cambridge, Spence published a number of translations of French works, ranging from early novels to historical and geographical treatises. The first to translate Lucian's complete works into English (five volumes), Spence apparently did not work from the original Greek as his title page claims, but from Perrot d'Ablancourt's 1634 French version. For an account of Spence's work, see H. Craig, 'Dryden's Lucian', *Classical Philology* 16.2 (1921): pp. 141–63.

7.30

From *Lucian's Works* (1684–85)

7.30.1 The Loves: A Dialogue between Lycinus and Theomnestus

This dialogue consists principally of two harangues: In the one, the love of women is maintained; and in the other, that of boys; which is the honest or honourable love according to the doctrine of the Platonics. However, the author endeavours maliciously and slyly under that pretext to introduce the filthy and unnatural love; but the other opinion therein is so well defended that none can hereby be corrupted; and it serves rather to show that this

18 *wallowing* tossing about; *coil:* disturbance; *keep*: make.

vice has only passion for its plea, for all its reasons are chimerical and confound friendship with love, and vice with virtue.

[The woman-loving Charicles and the boy-loving Callicratides debate whether heterosexual or male same-sex erotic love is superior. Charicles argues that heterosexual love is natural and male same-sex erotic love unnatural, the latter resulting from humanity's fall from the innocent Golden Age into increasing corruption. The lack of male same-sex sexual acts among animals and the fact that the continuance of species relies on heterosexual intercourse demonstrate the naturalness of heterosexual love. Scorning philosophical claims that male same-sex love should be understood as an asexual love of the beloved's mind – pointing out the obvious sexual component of wise men's love for beautiful, young boys – Charicles argues that women enjoy as well as give sexual pleasure.]

[Charicles] [...] 'Now this is what cannot be said of the love of boys; for they are so far from receiving any contentment in that sport, that they undergo pain; which they sufficiently manifest by their tears, even after the pain is over, without speaking of the eternal regret which dwells upon their spirits; insomuch that the greatest affront that can be done them is to upbraid them with this crime. Now, if people may sift farther into matters which it's neither handsome to say nor do: if I became so mad as to deviate from the ordinary course of nature,[19] I should rather choose it might be with a woman than with a boy, because a woman's a more lovely object, and can endow me with either of those pleasures,[20] whereas a boy can only confer on me the least. Thus, if women can also please us in this point, let us at least retrench that other love, unless we would allow 'em to love one another, like the tribadians,[21] and so beget a monstrous and unimaginable animal; for how much more just is it, that women become men, than to see men become women, since each thing tends to its perfection?'[22]

[As patron of his discourse, Callicratides calls upon 'Celestial Love, the father of hidden mysteries and patron of friendship', Cupid in his guise as the 'wholly perfect' and 'first-born principle'.]

[19] i.e., by having anal rather than vaginal intercourse.

[20] *either ... pleasures* anal or vaginal intercourse.

[21] *tribadians* *tribades*, women who have sex with other women.

[22] *For ... perfection* a commonplace of classical and early modern medicine and natural philosophy.

[CALLICRATIDES] [...] 'As for marriage, it was introduced out of necessity, for the preservation of the species; but the love of boys is a work of reason. Now,[23] such things as have been invented for pleasure or for decency are much more noble and more perfect than those which are done out of present necessity; as the honest is preferable before the useful and the necessary. During the rudeness[24] of the first age, when art and experience had not yet found out the conveniences of life, people were contented with common things, as not having had the leisure or the wit to find out others. Thus men lived in the beginning on herbs, fruits, and roots; but after having found out the way of sowing and reaping corn, they left this primitive nourishment to beasts; and none were so enamoured of antiquity as to go about to reduce us to the acorns[25] of our forefathers. [...] Wherefore, let no man ask examples of the love of boys in the primitive ages, for that of women was then too necessary for the propagation of humankind; but it introduced itself by degrees into the world with philosophy,[26] as did also eloquence and politeness. So that the last inventions are not to be condemned as if they were the worst; nor ought we to prefer the one love before the other, because it is the more ancient; but keeping the old customs as necessary, commend the new as better.

I could not forbear laughing when I heard Charicles propose to us the example of beasts and Scythians,[27] as if he repented his being born a man or a Greek rather than a Barbarian. For it is not at all strange that beasts, that have not the use of reason, do not make use of these inventions; and that dull uncivilized nations have not the advantages of those which are refined and polite. Now if brute animals were capable of reason, they would not lead a savage and vagabond life, as they do, but would live together, and found cities and republics. Lions do not love lions. Why? Because they do not philosophize. Other beasts in like manner, because they are not capable of friendship; but reason and experience have made known to men, and particularly to those who are most civilized, that man is more worthy of being beloved than woman.

[23] Spence's marginal note: 'All sort[s] of extravagances may be defended in this way.'

[24] *rudeness* lack of sophistication, uncivilized nature.

[25] *acorns* foraged, not cultivated, food; symbol of savagery.

[26] *it ... philosophy* Pederastic love is a frequent topic in Greek philosophy. See Plato's *Phaedrus* and *Symposium*.

[27] *Scythians* inhabitants of Scythia, a region covering parts of northern Europe into Asia; by-word for utter barbarity for such practices as cannibalism and turning the skulls of travellers into drinking cups.

And therefore, Charicles, don't condemn what you don't know, or what is not at all your province, and do not prefer a fond, silly amour before a celestial love; but put off with age the passions of youth,[28] so to make way for the entertaining more noble habitudes.[29] Consider, if you have not yet done it, that there are two sorts of love: the one, childish, which cannot be governed by reason and is only the work of Nature; the other, celestial and divine, which only inspires holy desires, and is nowhere to be found but in great personages, who being full of the God, only approve of that pleasure which is mingled with virtue. For true it is, according to the tragedian,[30] that love inspires two diverse passions, or rather these are two different things expressed under one and the same name; as there are two sorts of bashfulness, the one good, and the other bad. Wherefore it is not to be thought strange that passion has usurped the name of virtue, and that the love of good will and that of concupiscence are called by the same appellation.'

[Callicratides then offers a conventional misogynist portrait of a woman's life: full of vanity, extravagance, gluttony, lust, and infidelity.]

[CALLICRATIDES] [...] 'But now let us set against this life, that of a young boy, for the better knowing the difference: as soon as he is up and dressed, without so much fluster and fiddle faddle,[31] he goes abroad under the conduct of his tutor, followed by some servants, who carry for him not combs and looking-glasses, and the other equipage of luxury, but notebooks and volumes, which contain the bravest actions of antiquity proposed for his imitation. Sometimes they'll carry yea[32] his harp, if he goes to a music meeting. After having spent part of the morning in the sciences,[33] he disciplines himself in arms, in riding or wrestling, and other exercises of the body, already meditating, while in peace, the laborious trade of war. Afterwards he bathes lightly and eats with sobriety, that he may be capable, after having dined, to settle to serious things; for he still devotes the rest of his time to study. And having thus spent the whole day in the

28 *but ... youth* Plutarch's 'Of Love' argues that erotic love of boys is a mark of immaturity; marital love of women, of maturity.

29 *habitudes* habits.

30 *the tragedian* Euripides.

31 *fiddle faddle* fuss [about trivial matters].

32 *yea* certainly.

33 *sciences* learning.

exercises of virtue, he sleeps all the night without disquiet, and void of trouble.

What man, unless one that is altogether insensible, but would love such a youth, since in a mortal body he exercises immortal virtues? May I live in peace with him the rest of my days, without abandoning him one moment, and enjoying all my life long his lovely conversation! If he falls sick, as human life is subject to a thousand accidents, I'll be sick with him. If he goes to sea, I'll follow him. If he's attacked, I'll be his defender. If he's taken, I'll renounce my freedom. If he dies, I'll accompany him to the grave, and we'll both be laid in the same tomb. Such were Orestes and Pylades, for I'll have none but heroes for my example, who lived together from their tenderest infancy; revenged both the death of a father; ran both the same fortune. If the one was sick, the other comforted him, and felt his sufferings more sensibly than his own. If one was accused, the other was his vindicator. Their friendship was not confined within the bounds of Greece; they carried it as far as Scythia; and when they arrived in Taurica Chersonesus,[34] the one being persecuted by the revengeful Furies of his mother, the other, though in a sad condition, rendered him the devoirs[35] not only of a friend but of a parent. And when 'twas decreed that the one should stay to be sacrificed to Diana, and that the other should go carry the news thereof to Mycenae, each of 'em strove and stickled[36] to die for his friend, as if he had lived in him, and was dead in himself. Thus, when this love, which is formed from the cradle, comes to be confirmed by age and reason, then he whom we had loved begins to render us the like; and friendship is reinforced in such a manner that it's difficult to know the lover from the beloved, the passion of the one being passed and inculcated into the soul of the other, as an image which reflects in a looking-glass.

Why, then, do you condemn, as a strange sensuality, a doctrine received from heaven, which has been transmitted from hand to hand down to us, and which we cultivate as being conformable to our nature, and confirmed by the example of heroes? This Socratical discipline is approved of by oracles, who have judged that personage the wisest of all men.[37] For among the other precepts he

[34] *Taurica Chersonesus* a large European peninsula, at the south-west of what is now the Crimea; an isthmus connected it to Scythia (see **n27**); its inhabitants, the Tauri, were widely considered savage.

[35] *devoirs* duties.

[36] *stickled* endeavoured.

[37] *This … men* The Delphic Oracle labelled Socrates the wisest of men.

has bequeathed us for the living well, he approves the love of boys as a thing useful to the Republic.[38] So that we ought to love 'em after his example, as he did Alcibiades, without consuming our love in fleeting joys and short-lived pleasures;[39] but extending it even to old age, in revering this sacred bond; for by these means, life will be sweet and pacific,[40] the conscience not being tormented with any remorse nor sullied with any crime; and the reputation of persons who shall have lived after this manner will still live after they are dead. Nay, and heaven, according to the doctrine of philosophers, will receive 'em at their departure from the earth.'

[...]

[The debate's moderator Lycinus decides in favour of the love of boys, and then asks his friend Theomnestus if he approves this judgement.]

THEOMNESTUS. D'ye doubt it? And d'ye think me incapable of seeing what is rational? I was so transported during your relation that I thought myself at Cnidos, and that this house was the goddess's temple.[41] But to tell you freely my opinion, and to conceal nothing from you in a festival day, and the festival too of Hercules, who was very gallant, much an amourist, and a sparkish sort of god,[42] I find Callicratides his harangue somewhat too grave and serious, and I fancy 'twould be a penance, loving a handsome youth, and lying with him, to remain like a Tantalus,[43] with water up to the very eyes without being able to quench one's thirst; for it is not sufficient to behold the person you love, or to sit by him listening to his pretty prattle; but as if there were a certain orderly progression in pleasure, the first degree of love is to see the object beloved, and then when seen to touch (or if we may talk naturally) to feel it: so that although we do but touch it with the tip of our fingers, at the same instant a sensible[44] delight runs swiftly circulating with the blood through the whole body. Now

38 *he … Republic* Socrates qualifiedly recommends the chaste love of boys in Plato's *Republic*, 403: 'a friend should use no other familiarity to his love than a father would use to his son, and then only for a noble purpose, and he must first have the other's consent'.

39 *as … pleasures* Alcibiades (Glossary).

40 *pacific* peaceful.

41 *Cnidos … Temple* At this temple the debaters and Lycinus see a statue of the goddess Venus; each values its physical assets in terms of his own sexual preferences: Charicles lauds the statue's breasts and womanly figure; Callicratides its beautiful bottom.

42 *sparkish* amorous.

43 Spence's marginal note: 'This is a raillery' (i.e., a satirical or ironic remark).

44 *sensible* acutely pleasurable.

after we are come thus far, without any difficulty, we make in the third place an essay[45] for a kiss. Not at the first onset, that curious eager one, but such as by gradually applying lips to lips, does almost give off before the very contact, having no manner (Heaven knows!) of slavering suspicion about it; and then my gentleman, being grown more brushingly[46] bold, and coming up close to the business in hand, falls a-melting more and more into more exquisite embraces, sometimes also stealing a lambent[47] kiss; nor does he suffer either of his hands to lie idle all this while. For the free and undenying hugs in things carnal are of the formal essence of pleasure. So with his right hand swimmingly slipping down the bosom, he presses the breasts, which according to nature do moderately stick out, and all around handles the delicate and rising belly, and so proceeds to the fine down of youth. So that love, having got so much power, and so many fortresses in his hand, meditates something more glorious, and is flushed on for greater and warmer enterprises. Then grounding his effort upon the thighs, he discharges all his artillery.[48] Now may I always love boys in this manner. But let them that trifle away their time about sublime and foolish speculations, and are only philosophers in their supercilious looks, feed the unlearned with a company of grave and senseless words, and continue to joy and bask themselves in their chimerical flame; but for our parts, let us imitate Socrates, who was not content with merely loving Alcibiades, but lay[49] with him; which is not to be wondered at all, since Achilles did the like with Patroclus, which may be easily conjectured from his extreme sorrow for his death, and from certain circumstances of his affliction, which speak his passion rather than his amity.[50] Now there are those perhaps will say, that this is somewhat too smutty and obscene to be spoken, but by Venus all is true.'

[…]

45 *essay* attempt.

46 *brushingly* perhaps an error for 'blushingly', but perhaps referring to the lover's rubbing up against his beloved.

47 *lambent* like a brightly shining flame that does not burn.

48 *discharges … artillery* ejaculates.

49 *lay* had sex.

50 *amity* friendship.

Thomas Brown (1663–1704), poet, dramatist, translator, and writer of non-fiction prose

Author of the first English translation of Lucian's 'Courtesans', Brown was a prolific professional writer and a first-class linguist and classicist. Although his posthumously published collected *Works* (1707–11, four vols) has many translations of classical and modern texts, including original dialogues in imitation of Lucian, 'Courtesans' is conspicuously absent, perhaps too salacious for a volume aimed at celebrating Brown and his works.

7.31

From *The Third Volume of the Works of Lucian* (1711)[51]

7.31.1 The Dialogues of the Courtesans[52] (Dialogue 5)

Cleonarium and Leaena

CLEONARIUM. We hear that rich Megilla courts thee as a man, and would enjoy thee; that you lie together acting I know not what. Prithee,[53] don't be a fool and blush, but plainly acquaint me with the secret.

LEAENA. Let my blushes inform you that there is something strange in it and not fitting for me to relate.

CLEONARIUM. By heavens, you shall acquaint me with the truth of the matter, and what satisfaction you receive when you enjoy one another in bed. Well, I perceive you don't love me, or else you would not conceal it from me.

LEAENA. I'll swear I love thee better than any of my own sex, and therefore can conceal nothing from thee. But really her inclinations are man-like, and her desire to caress the females as a man.

CLEONARIUM. I don't well apprehend what you mean, unless her fancy is changed, and she, like some women in the island of Lesbos,[54] takes the greatest delight and satisfaction in women.

LEAENA. You have hit it.

CLEONARIUM. Prithee, expound this matter: how she first solicited and won your compliance, and what followed.

[51] Multi-authored and edited by Dryden. See Introduction to **7.16**.

[52] Brown's note: He has avoided anything 'criminal in the original' in order to avoid offending even the most fastidious of readers ('Argument' 280).

[53] *prithee* please.

[54] *Lesbos* Sappho's homeland. See Introduction to **7.2–7.9**.

LEAENA. Why, she appointed a collation,[55] and invited Demonassa, the rich Corinthian and one well acquainted and exercised in the same mystery; they sent for me to sing and entertain them upon the harp, when it began to be late and the two ladies were well flustered with wine. They told me it was late, and they invited me to lodge between them. When we were in bed, they began to kiss me modestly; and afterwards, with that heat and passion as men inflamed with love, kissing close, and opening their mouths. Then they began to embrace me, and handled my breasts, and Demonassa would bite me in her kisses. All this while I was at a loss to guess what they meant, but when Megilla began to be warm in bed, she pulled off her tower or periwig,[56] and appeared like a robust champion, shaved close and ready to engage.[57]

I was frighted at the sight, but she said to me, 'Did you ever see a likelier young fellow? For you must know I am called Seignior Megillius, and have long since married this Demonassa my wife.'

I laughed at this, and said, 'Sir, we never took you for a man before, and little thought such an able Achilles should lurk among the virgins; and are you equipped in every point like an able warrior? And can you engage your wife at sharps[58] as men do?'

'I have that,' says he, 'that is sufficient to please a woman.'

'Then perhaps,' said I, 'you are an hermaphrodite, and able to give satisfaction at both weapons,[59] for as yet I don't understand your play.'

'Neither that,' said he, 'but I am in my inclinations a perfect man.'

'I have heard,' said I, 'that in Boeotia there was one Ismenadora was changed into a man, and was named Tiresias, and was a great prophet. Has any such matter happened to you?'

'Not at all. I am born with parts like you; but my mind, inclinations, and desires are man-like, and covet to enjoy that beautiful sex.'

'Then,' said I, 'you have lust more than sufficient.'

Then Megilla courted me to a compliance, and gave me a rich jewel. We embraced, and she seemed infinitely transported with pleasure.

CLEONARIUM. Come, come, you need not scruple to tell me all.

LEAENA. Forbear to ask any further. I have satisfied your curiosity as far as I may. Let my blushes make out the rest.

55 *collation* light meal.

56 *tower* high women's headdress; *periwig*: stylized wig, fashionable for men and women in the eighteenth century.

57 *shaved … engage* shaving one's head was a common practice among Greek athletes.

58 *at sharps* with a penis.

59 *both weapons* penis and clitoris.

CHAPTER 8

Literature: Representing Male Same-Sex Erotic Relationships and Desires

Edmund Spenser (?1552–99), poet

Educated at Cambridge, where he met his dear friend and mentor Gabriel Harvey, Spenser later became the Earl of Leicester's secretary, and gained the support and patronage of Sir Walter Ralegh and Sir Philip Sidney. Spenser's works include the immediately popular *Shepheardes Calender* (1579); the sonnet sequence *Amoretti* and marriage poem *Epithalamion* (both 1595); the mythopoetic allegory of Tudor court life *Colin Clouts Come Home Againe*; and the epic romance *The Faerie Queene*, which he wrote during his state employment in Ireland. *The Faerie Queene*'s six completed books were published in 1596, with the 'Mutabilitie Cantos' added in 1609. The work was popular and apparently netted Spenser a royal pension.

Like *Shepheardes Calender*'s dedicatory letter, the work's extensive commentary or gloss (attributed to the fictional friend E.K.) is probably the collaborative work of Spenser and Harvey. E.K. identifies Colin Clout, the work's central shepherd-poet, as Spenser, concealed under an assumed name 'as sometime did Virgil [in his *Eclogues*] under the name of Tityrus'; critics largely agree that Hobbinol, the older shepherd hopelessly in love with Colin, and Spenser's 'very special and most familiar friend, whom he entirely and extraordinarily beloved' is Harvey. E.K.'s notes, however, eagerly dispel the idea that the relationship between these pastoral characters 'savour[s] of disorderly love, which the learned call *paederastikē* [pederasty]'. E.K. objects that such an opinion 'is gathered beside his [i.e., Spenser's] meaning', linking the love of Hobbinol and Colin with Socrates' platonic love of Alcibiades and other youths. Citing Plato's dialogue *Alcibiades*, Xenophon's writings (*Symposium*, 8.6–43; and *The Memorable Things of Socrates*), and those of

Maximus Tyrius (*Dissertationes*, 21.8), E.K. asserts 'that such love is much to be allowed and liked of, specially so meant, as Socrates used it – who sayeth that indeed he loved Alcibiades extremely, yet not Alcibiades' person but his soul, which is Alcibiades' own self. And so is *paederastikē* much to be preferred before *gynerastikē* (that is, the love which enflameth men with lust toward womankind), but yet let no man think that herein I stand with Lucian [see **7.29–7.31**] or his devilish disciple Unico Aretino ["Aretino", Glossary] in defense of execrable and horrible sins of forbidden and unlawful fleshliness'.

A Note on the Texts

The anthology's texts of *The Shepheardes Calender* and *The Faerie Queene* are based on the first editions. Spenser's deliberate use of archaic words and phrases as part of his poetics means that his works are rarely modernized in terms of spelling, punctuation or orthography. Out of consideration for the general reader, however, I have followed the lead of D. Brooks-Davies, leaving dialect and archaic forms as they appear in the original, but otherwise normalizing capitalization and modernizing spelling as well as occasionally punctuation.

8.1

From *The Shepheardes Calender* (1579)[1]

8.1.1 January: Aegloga prima

Argument

In this first eglogue Colin Clout[2] a shepherd's boy complaineth him of his unfortunate love, being but newly (as seemeth) enamoured of a country lass called Rosalind:[3] with which strong affection being very sore travailed,[4] he compareth his care-full case[5] to the sad season of the year, to the frosty ground, to the frozen trees, and to his own winter-beaten flock. And lastly, finding himself robbed of all former pleasance and delights, he breaketh his pipe in pieces, and casteth himself to the ground.

1 Subtitle: 'Containing twelve eglogues proportionable to the twelve months'. Dedicated to Spenser's patron, Sir Philip Sidney.

2 *Colin Clout.* See Introduction to **8.1**.

3 *Rosalind* Rosalind is a 'feigned name' for the poet's 'love and mistress', a practice with precedent in the ancients and moderns (E.K.).

4 *sore travailed* severely tormented.

5 *care-full case* sorrowful situation, one 'full of cares or griefs'.

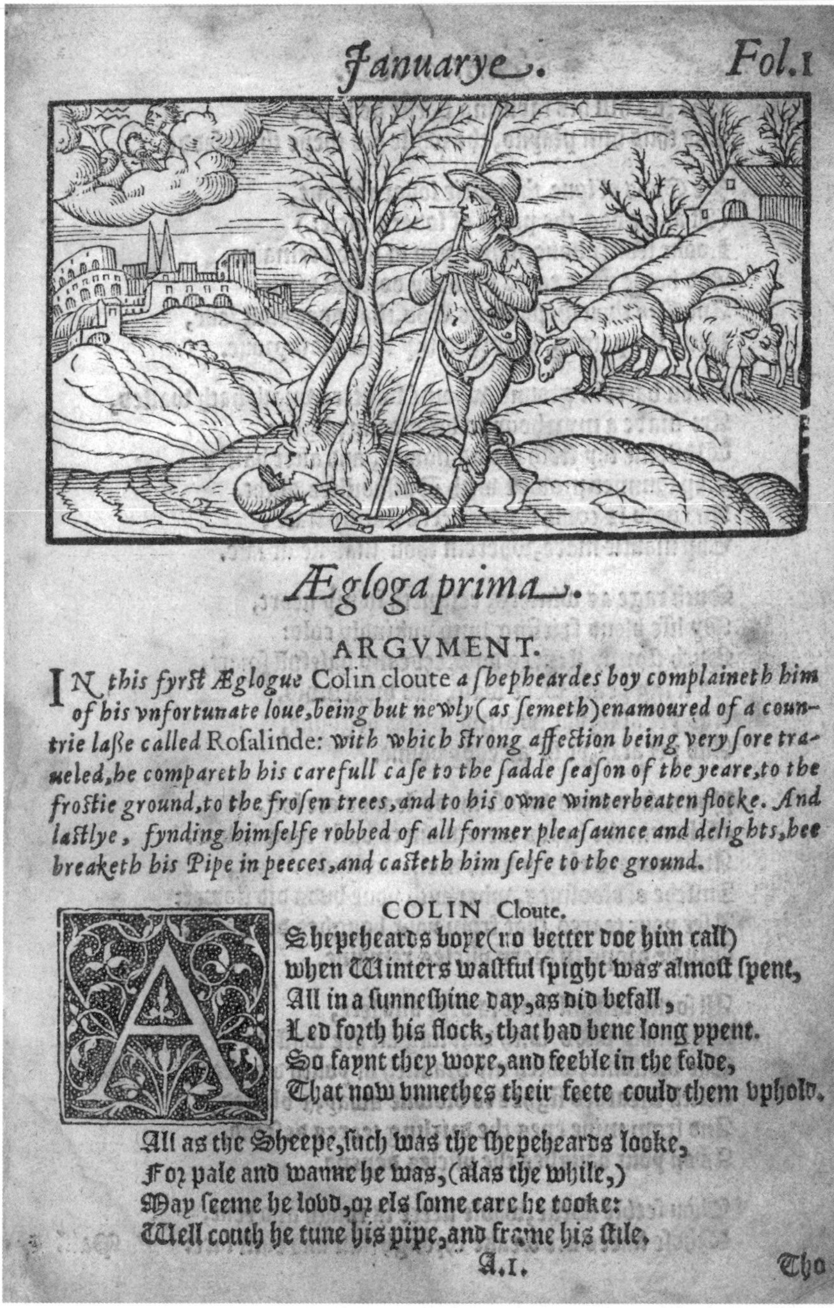

Januarye. Fol.1

Ægloga prima.

ARGVMENT.

IN this fyrst Æglogue Colin cloute a shepheardes boy complaineth him of his vnfortunate loue, being but newly (as semeth) enamoured of a countrie lasse called Rosalinde: with which strong affection being very sore traueled, he compareth his carefull case to the sadde season of the yeare, to the frostie ground, to the frosen trees, and to his owne winterbeaten flocke. And lastlye, fynding himselfe robbed of all former pleasaunce and delights, hee breaketh his Pipe in peeces, and casteth him selfe to the ground.

COLIN Cloute.

A Shepeheards boye (no better doe him call)
when Winters wastful spight was almost spent,
All in a sunneshine day, as did befall,
Led forth his flock, that had bene long ypent.
So faynt they woxe, and feeble in the folde,
That now vnnethes their feete could them vphold.

All as the Sheepe, such was the shepeheards looke,
For pale and wanne he was, (alas the while,)
May seeme he lovd, or els some care he tooke:
Well couth he tune his pipe, and frame his stile.

A.1. Tho

9 Illustration from Eclogue 1 (January),
from Edmund Spenser, *Shepheardes Calender* (1579)

Colin Clout

A shepherd's boy (no better do him call),
When Winter's waste-full spite was almost spent,
All in a sunshine day, as did befall,
Led forth his flock that had been long ypent.[6]
So faint they woxe, and feeble in the fold,[7]
That now uneaths their feet could them uphold. [8]

All as the sheep, such was the shepherd's look,
For pale and wan he was, (alas the while),
May seem he loved, or else some care he took;
Well couth he tune his pipe, and frame his style.[9]
Tho to a hill his fainting flock he led,[10]
And thus him plained, the while his sheep there fed:[11]

'Ye gods of love, that pity lovers' pain,
(If any gods the pain of lovers pity),
Look from above, where you in joys remain,
And bow your ears unto my doleful ditty;[12]
And Pan, thou shepherds' god, that once didst love,
Pity the pains that thou thyself didst prove.[13]

Thou barren ground, whom winter's wrath hath wasted,
Art made a mirror to behold my plight:
Whilom thy fresh spring flowered, and after hasted[14]
Thy summer proud with daffadillies dight.[15]
And now is come thy winter's stormy state,
Thy mantle marred, wherein thou masked'st late.

Such rage as winter's reigneth in my heart,
My life-blood freezing with unkindly cold:[16]

6 *ypent* pent up.
7 *woxe* grew.
8 *unearths* 'scarcely' (E.K.).
9 *couth* 'could' (E.K.).
10 *tho* then.
11 *plained* lamented.
12 *ditty* song.
13 *prove* undergo.
14 *whilom* previously.
15 *dight* adorned.
16 *unkindly* unnatural.

Such stormy stours do breed my baleful smart,
As if my year were waste and woxen old.[17]
And yet, alas, but now my spring begun,
And yet, alas, it is already done.

You naked trees, whose shady leaves are lost,
Wherein the birds were wont to build their bow'r,
And now are clothed with moss and hoary frost
Instead of blossoms, wherewith your buds did flow'r:
I see your tears, that from your boughs do rain,
Whose drops in dreary icicles remain.

All so my lustful leaf is dry and sere,[18]
My timely buds with wailing all are wasted:
The blossom, which my branch of youth did bear,
With breathèd sighs is blown away and blasted,
And from mine eyes the drizzling tears descend,
As on your boughs the icicles depend.[19]

Thou feeble flock, whose fleece is rough and rent,
Whose knees are weak through fast and evil fare,[20]
May'st witness well by thy ill government,
Thy master's mind is overcome with care.
Thou weak, I wan; thou lean, I quite forlorn:
With mourning pine I, thou with pining mourn.[21]

A thousand sithes I curse that care-full hour,[22]
Wherein I longed the neighbour town to see:[23]
And eke ten thousand sithes I bless the stour,
Wherein I saw so fair a sight as she.
Yet all for naught: such sight hath bred my bane.[24]
Ah God, that love should breed both joy and pain.

[17] *stours* 'fits' (E.K.); here, 'inner emotional storms'; *baleful smart*: painful suffering; *woxen*: become.

[18] *lustful* vigorous; *sere*: 'withered' (E.K.).

[19] *depend* hang.

[20] *evil fare* poor food.

[21] *pine* waste away [from grief].

[22] *sithes* 'times' (E.K.); *care-full*: See **n5**.

[23] *neighbour town* 'the next town' (E.K.); here, probably a farm or village.

[24] *bane* grief; destruction.

It is not Hobbinol wherefore I plain,[25]
Albe my love he seek with daily suit:[26]
His clownish gifts and court'sies I disdain, [27]
His kids, his cracknels, and his early fruit.[28]
Ah foolish Hobbinol, thy gifts bene vain:[29]
Colin them gives to Rosalind again.

I love thilk lass (alas, why do I love?),[30]
And am forlorn, (alas, why am I lorn?).
She deigns not my goodwill but doth reprove,[31]
And of my rural music holdeth scorn.
Shepherd's device she hateth as the snake,[32]
And laughs the songs that Colin Clout doth make.

Wherefore, my pipe, albe rude Pan thou please,
Yet for thou pleasest not where most I would;
And thou unlucky Muse, that wont'st to ease
My musing mind, yet canst not when thou should:
Both pipe and Muse shall sore the while aby.'[33]
So broke his oaten pipe, and down did lie.

By that, the welkèd Phoebus 'gan avail[34]
His weary wain, and now the frosty Night[35]
Her mantle black through heaven 'gan overhale.[36]
Which seen, the pensive boy half in despite
Arose, and homeward drove his sunnèd sheep,
Whose hanging heads did seem his care-full case to weep.

[25] *Hobbinol* See Introduction to **8.1**.

[26] *albe* although.

[27] *clownish* rustic; *court'sies*: courtesies.

[28] *His … fruit* 'an imitation of Virgil, *Eclogues* 2.56' (E.K.). *Kids*, *cracknels* (biscuits) and *early fruit* are all gifts from Virgil's Corydon to his scornful male beloved, Alexis (see **7.16.2**).

[29] *bene* are.

[30] *thilk* this.

[31] *deigns* accepts.

[32] *device* poetic invention; perhaps, also, 'conversation'.

[33] *sore … aby* meanwhile severely pay the penalty.

[34] *welkèd* diminishing in brightness; *Phoebus*: the sun; *avail*: 'bring down' (E.K.).

[35] *wain* waggon (i.e., the sun in setting).

[36] *overhale* 'draw over' (E.K.).

8.1.2 April: Aegloga quarta

Argument

This eglogue is purposely intended to the honour and praise of our most gracious sovereign, Queen Elizabeth. The speakers herein be Hobbinol and Thenot, two shepherds: the which Hobbinol being before mentioned, greatly to have loved Colin, is here set forth more largely, complaining him of that boy's great misadventure in love, whereby his mind was alienate and withdrawn not only from him who most loved him, but also from all former delights and studies, as well in pleasant piping as cunning rhyming and singing, and other his laudable exercises. Whereby he taketh occasion, for proof of his more excellency and skill in poetry, to record a song, which the said Colin sometime made in honour of her Majesty, whom abruptly he termeth Elisa.

Thenot *Hobbinol*

Thenot.

Tell me good Hobbinol, what gars thee greet?[37]
What? hath some wolf thy tender lambs ytorn?
Or is thy bagpipe broke, that sounds so sweet?[38]
Or art thou of thy lovèd lass forlorn?[39]
Or bene thine eyes attempered to the year,[40]
Quenching the gasping furrows' thirst with rain?
Like April show'r, so streams the trickling tears
Adown thy cheek to quench thy thristy pain.[41]

Hobbinol

Nor this, nor that, so much doth make me mourn,
But for the lad, whom long I loved so dear,[42]
Now loves a lass that all his love doth scorn:[43]
He plunged in pain, his tressèd locks doth tear.[44]

Shepherds' delights he doth them all forswear,
His pleasant pipe, which made us merriment,

[37] *gars thee greet* 'causeth thee weep and complain' (E.K.).
[38] *bagpipe* In the January woodcut, Colin's bagpipe lies broken at his feet.
[39] *forlorn* 'left and forsaken' (E.K.).
[40] *attempered to the year* 'agreeable to the season of the year' (E.K.).
[41] *thristy* thirsty.
[42] *lad* 'Colin Clout' (E.K.).
[43] *lass* 'Rosalind' (E.K.).
[44] *tressèd* 'wreathed and curled' (E.K.).

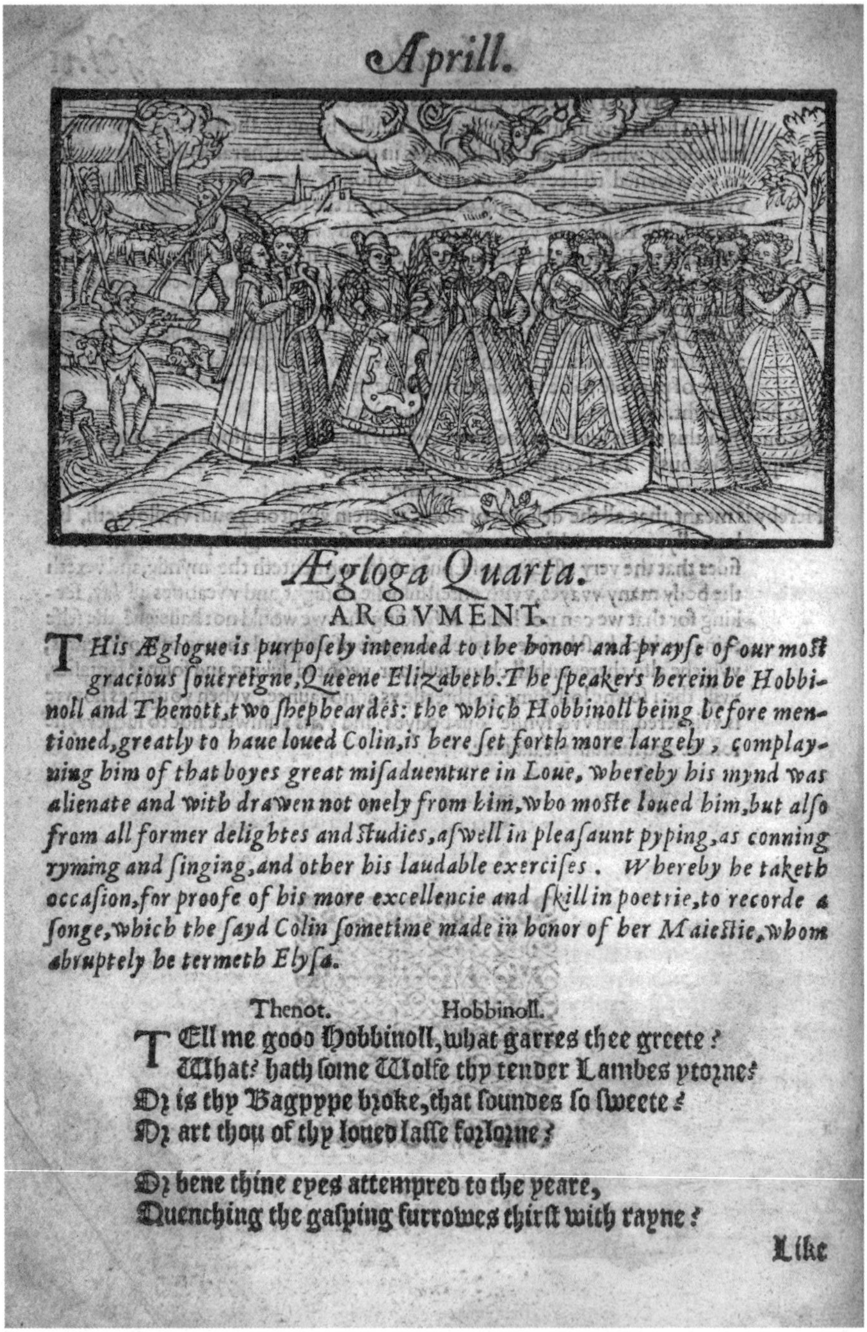

Aprill.

Ægloga Quarta.

ARGVMENT.

THis Æglogue is purposely intended to the honor and prayse of our most gracious souereigne, Queene Elizabeth. The speakers herein be Hobbinoll and Thenott, two shepheardes: the which Hobbinoll being before mentioned, greatly to haue loued Colin, is here set forth more largely, complayning him of that boyes great misaduenture in Loue, whereby his mynd was alienate and with drawen not onely from him, who moste loued him, but also from all former delightes and studies, aswell in pleasaunt pyping, as conning ryming and singing, and other his laudable exercises. Whereby he taketh occasion, for proofe of his more excellencie and skill in poetrie, to recorde a songe, which the sayd Colin sometime made in honor of her Maiestie, whom abruptely he termeth Elysa.

Thenot. Hobbinoll.

TEll me good Hobbinoll, what garres thee greete?
What? hath some Wolfe thy tender Lambes ytorne?
Or is thy Bagpype broke, that soundes so sweete?
Or art thou of thy loued lasse forlorne?

Or bene thine eyes attempred to the yeare,
Quenching the gasping furrowes thirst with rayne?

Like

10 Illustration from Eclogue 4 (April),
from Edmund Spenser, *Shepheardes Calender* (1579).

He wilfully hath broke, and doth forbear
His wonted songs, wherein he all outwent.[45]

Thenot
What is he for a lad, you so lament?[46]
Is love such pinching pain to them that prove?[47]
And hath he skill to make so excellent,[48]
Yet hath so little skill to bridle love?

Hobbinol
Colin thou kenn'st, the southern shepherd's boy:[49]
Him Love hath wounded with a deadly dart.
Whilom on him was all my care and joy,
Forcing with gifts to win his wanton heart.

But now from me his madding mind is start[50]
And woos the widow's daughter of the glen:[51]
So now fair Rosalind hath bred his smart,
So now his friend is changèd for a fren.[52]

[…]

8.2

From *The Faerie Queene* (1596)

8.2.1 The Fourth Book of the Faerie Queene:[53] Canto 10

[Earlier, we learn that Amoret is one of twin daughters born to the nymph Chrysogone, after she was impregnated by the sun: Amoret is raised by Venus; Belphoebe by Diana. The knight Scudamour lands on Venus's island,

45 *outwent* excelled.
46 *What … lad* '"What manner of lad is he?"' (E.K.).
47 *prove* experience [it].
48 *make* 'to rhyme and versify; […] this word […] comprehend[s] all the skill of poetry' (E.K.).
49 *kenn'st* knowest.
50 *madding* distraught; *start*: rushed away.
51 *widow's … glen* 'Rosalind' (E.K.).
52 *fren* 'stranger' (E.K.).
53 The title of Book 4 continues: 'Containing the Legend of Cambel and Telamond, Or, Of Friendship'.

defeating twenty knights to win the shield of love that will allow him to claim Amoret. Passing figures representing the delays and obstacles to love, Scudamour arrives at Venus's garden, at the centre of which lies her temple and his prize, Amoret.]

In such luxurious plenty of all pleasure,[54]
It seemed a second paradise to ghesse,[55]
So lavishly enriched with nature's threasure,
That if the happy souls, which do possess
Th'Elysian fields, and live in lasting bless,[56]
Should happen this with living eye to see,
They soon would loath their lesser happiness,
And wish to life returned again to be,
That in this joyous place they mote have joyance free.[57]

Fresh shadows, fit to shroud from sunny ray;
Fair launds, to take the sun in season dew;[58]
Sweet springs, in which a thousand nymphs did play;
Soft rumbling brooks, that gentle slumber drew;
High reared mounts, the lands about to view;
Low looking dales, disloign'd from common gaze;[59]
Delightful bow'rs, to solace lovers true;
False labyrinths, fond runners' eyes to daze;[60]
All which by nature made did nature' self amaze.

And all without were walks and alleys dight,[61]
With divers trees, enranged in even ranks;[62]
And here and there were pleasant arbours pight,[63]
And shady seats, and sundry flow'ring banks,
To sit and rest the walkers' weary shanks,
And therein thousand pairs of lovers walked,
Praising their god, and yielding him great thanks,

[54] Stanzas 23–8; *luxurious*: lavish.

[55] *to ghesse* one might assume.

[56] *Elysian fields* classical dwelling of the blessed dead.

[57] *mote* might.

[58] *launds* glades.

[59] *disloign'd* distant.

[60] *false labyrinths* hedge mazes that deceive the person entering about the right direction; *fond*: foolish; loving.

[61] *dight* adorned.

[62] *divers* various kinds [of].

[63] *pight* planted.

Ne ever aught but of their true loves talked,
Ne ever for rebuke or blame of any balked.[64]

All these together by themselves did sport
Their spotless pleasures, and sweet love's content.
But far away from these, another sort
Of lovers linked in true hearts' consent;
Which loved not as these, for like intent,
But on chaste virtue grounded their desire,
Far from all fraud, or feignèd blandishment;
Which in their spirits kindling zealous fire,
Brave thoughts and noble deeds did evermore aspire.

Such were great Hercules, and Hylas dear;
True Jonathan, and David trusty tried;
Stout Theseus, and Pirithous his feare;[65]
Pylades and Orestes by his side;
Mild Titus and Gesippus without pride;
Damon and Pythias whom death could not sever:
All these and all that ever had been tied
In bands of friendship, there did live forever,
Whose lives although decayed, yet loves decayed never.

Which when as I, that never tasted bliss[66]
Nor happy hour, beheld with gazefull eye,
I thought there was none other heaven than this;
And 'gan their endless happiness envie,
That being free from fear and jealousy,[67]
Might frankly there their love's desire possess;
Whilest I through pains and perlous jeopardy,[68]
Was forced to seek my life's dear patroness:
Much dearer be the things which come through hard distress.

[After passing allegorical figures representing love, hate, and concord, Scudamour enters the inner temple.]

64 *balked* stopped talking.

65 *feare* comrade, partner.

66 *I* Scudamour.

67 Later in the epic, Scudamour becomes *jealous* of Britomart, after being convinced that his wife's rescuer (whom he believes a man) has possessed her sexually. Amoret is *fearful* during her imprisonment by the enchanter Busirane in Book 3.

68 *perlous* perilous.

Right in the midst the goddess self did stand[69]
  Upon an altar of some costly mass,
  Whose substance was uneath to understand:[70]
  For neither precious stone, nor durefull brass,[71]
  Nor shining gold, nor mould'ring clay it was;
  But much more rare and precious to esteem,[72]
  Pure in aspect, and like to crystal glass,
  Yet glass was not, if one did rightly deem,
But being fair and brickle, likest glass did seem.[73]

But it in shape and beauty did excel
  All other idols, which the heathen adore,
  Far passing that, which by surpassing skill
  Phidias did make in Paphos Isle of yore,
  With which that wretched Greek, that life forlore,
  Did fall in love: yet this much fairer shined,[74]
  But covered with a slender veil afore;[75]
  And both her feet and legs together twined
Were with a snake, whose head and tail were fast combined.[76]

The cause why she was covered with a veil
  Was hard to know, for that her priests the same
  From people's knowledge laboured to conceal.
  But sooth it was not sure for womanish shame,[77]
  Nor any blemish, which the work mote blame;[78]
  But for, they say, she hath both kinds in one,[79]

69 Stanzas 39–42.

70 *uneath* difficult.

71 *durefull* enduring.

72 *to esteem* in value.

73 *brickle* brittle.

74 *Phidias … love* (*fl.* early fifth century BCE), Greek sculptor, whose statues of Athena and Zeus were widely celebrated; Spenser is perhaps thinking here of the equally famed Greek sculptor Praxiteles' Aphrodite (Venus) at Cnidus, with which a young man reportedly fell in love. He hid himself one night in the Temple and masturbated on the statute; he vanished and it was speculated he had thrown himself into the sea; *Paphos Isle*: island sacred to Venus, central to her ancient cult.

75 *slender* thin.

76 *snake … combined* ancient image of generation and the cycle of birth and death.

77 *sooth … for* truly, it surely was not because of.

78 *mote* might.

79 *kinds* As *Venus Hermaphroditus*, she combines both sexes.

Both male and female, both under one name:
She sire and mother is herself alone,
Begets and eke conceives, ne needeth other none.

And all about her neck and shoulders flew
A flock of little loves, and sports, and joys,[80]
With nimble wings of gold and purple hue;[81]
Whose shapes seem'd not like to terrestrial boys,
But like to angels playing heavenly toys;[82]
The whilest their eldest brother was away,
Cupid their eldest brother; he enjoys
The wide kingdom of love with lordly sway,
And to his law compels all creatures to obey.

[…]

'So all the world by thee at first was made,[83]
And daily yet thou doest the same repair:
Ne aught on earth that merry is and glad,
Ne aught on earth that lovely is and fair,
But thou the same for pleasure didst prepare.
Thou art the root of all that joyous is,
Great god of men and women, queen of th'air,
Mother of laughter, and wellspring of bliss,
O grant that of my love at last I may not miss.'

[…]

Thus sate they all a round in seemly rate:[84]
And in the midst of them a goodly maid,
Even in the lap of Womanhood there sate,
The which was all in lily white arrayed,
With silver streams amongst the linen strayed;
Like to the morn, when first her shining face
Hath to the gloomy world itself bewrayed,[85]
That same was fairest Amoret in place,
Shining with beauty's light, and heavenly virtue's grace.

80 *sports* amorous play.
81 *gold and purple* kingly colours.
82 *toys* games.
83 Stanza 47. Scudamour here addresses Venus; *thee*: Love/Venus; the love, sexual desire, and drive to reproduction she instils in all creatures.
84 Stanza 52; *a … rate*: fittingly, in a circle.
85 *bewrayed* revealed.

[…]

With that my shield I forth to her did show,[86]
Which all that while I closely had concealed;
On which when Cupid with his killing bow
And cruel shafts emblazoned she beheld,
At sight thereof she was with terror quelled,
And said no more: but I which all that while
The pledge of faith, her hand engagèd held,[87]
Like wary hind within the weedy soil,[88]
For no entreaty would forgo so glorious spoil.[89]

And evermore upon the goddess' face
Mine eye was fixed, for fear of her offence,
Whom when I saw with amiable grace
To laugh at me, and favour my pretence,[90]
I was embold'ned with more confidence,
And nought for niceness nor for envy sparing,
In presence of them all forth led her thence,
All looking on, and like astonished staring,
Yet to lay hand on her, not one of all them daring.

She often prayed, and often me besought,
Sometime with tender tears to let her go,
Sometime with witching smiles: but yet for naught,
That ever she to me could say or do,
Could she her wished freedom fro me woo;
But forth I led her through the Temple gate,
By which I hardly past with much ado:
But that same lady which me friended late[91]
In entrance, did me also friend in my retrate.[92]

[…]

[86] Stanzas 55–7; *her*: the matron who guards Amoret and her attendants.

[87] *her* Amoret's.

[88] *soil* pool used as a refuge by hunted animals. A *hind* is a female red deer.

[89] *spoil* plunder.

[90] *pretence* rightful claim.

[91] *but … lady* I would have passed only with difficulty if that lady had not; *lady*: Concord.

[92] *retrate* retreat.

Sir Philip Sidney (1554–86)

For his biography, see Introduction to **7.2**.

8.3

From *The Countess of Pembroke's Arcadia* ('The New Arcadia') (1593)

[After receiving several terrible prophecies involving himself, his wife, Gynecia, and their two beautiful daughters, Pamela and Philoclea, Basilius, King of Arcadia, has withdrawn to the country. The princes Musidorus and Pyrocles, however, fall in love with the princesses: Pyrocles with Philoclea, and Musidorus with Pamela. In order to get close to the women, the former disguises himself as the Amazon Zelmane, and the latter as the shepherd Dorus. Romantic complications ensue: Basilius falls in love with Zelmane thinking her the woman she appears to be; Gynecia falls in love with Zelmane strongly suspecting 'her' to be a man; Philoclea only gradually identifies her love for Zelmane as a passion that goes beyond sisterly love or same-sex friendship.]

8.3.1 Book 1, chapter 12

[Pyrocles is the first of the princes to fall to love; Musidorus takes this event badly.]

[...] he[1] saw a sight which persuaded and obtained of his eyes that they would abide yet a while open. It was the appearing of a lady who, because she walked with her side toward him, he could not perfectly see her face, but so much he might see of her that was a surety for the rest that all was excellent.

Well might he perceive the hanging of her hair in fairest quantity in locks, some curled and some as it were forgotten, with such a careless care and an art so hiding art that she seemed she would lay them for a pattern whether nature simply or nature helped by cunning[2] be the more excellent: the rest whereof was drawn into a coronet of gold richly set with pearl, and so joined all over with gold wires and covered with feathers of diverse colours that it was not unlike to a helmet, such a glittering show it bore, and so bravely it

1 *he* Musidorus.
2 *cunning* art, skill.

was held up from the head. Upon her body she wore a doublet[3] of sky-colour satin, covered with plates of gold and, as it were, nailed with precious stones that in it she might seem armed. The nether[4] part of her garment was so full of stuff[5] and cut after such a fashion, that though the length of it reached to the ankles, yet in her going one might sometimes discern the small of her leg,[6] which with the foot was dressed in a short pair of crimson velvet buskins,[7] in some places open,[8] as the ancient manner was, to show the fairness of the skin. Over all this she wore a certain mantle made in such manner, that coming under her right arm and covering most of that side, it had no fastening on the left side but only upon the top of her shoulder, where the two ends met and were closed together with a very rich jewel: the device[9] whereof, as he after saw, was this: a Hercules made in little form, but set with a distaff in his hand, as he once was by Omphale's commandment, with a word in Greek but thus to be interpreted, 'Never more valiant.' On the same side, on her thigh she wore a sword which, as it witnessed her to be an Amazon[10] or one following that profession, so it seemed but a needless weapon, since her other forces were without withstanding.

But this lady walked out-right[11] till he might see her enter into a fine close[12] arbour. It was of trees, whose branches so lovingly interlaced one the other that it could resist the strongest violence of eyesight; but she went into it by a door she opened, which moved him, as warily as he could, to follow her, and by and by[13] he might hear her sing this song with a voice no less beautiful to his ears than her goodliness was full of harmony to his eyes:

Transformed in show, but more transformed in mind,
  I cease to strive, with double conquest foiled:
For, woe is me, my powers all I find
  With outward force, and inward treason, spoiled.

For from without came to mine eyes the blow,
  Whereto mine inward thoughts did faintly yield:

3 *doublet* close-fitting men's garment.
4 *nether* lower.
5 *stuff* material.
6 *small of her leg* lower leg.
7 *buskins* boots.
8 *open* ornamentally slit.
9 *device* image and accompanying explanatory motto.
10 *Amazon* female warrior.
11 *out-right* directly onwards.
12 *close* concealed.
13 *by and by* soon.

Both these conspir'd poor reason's overthrow;
False in myself, thus have I lost the field.

Thus are my eyes still captive to one sight;
Thus all my thoughts are slaves to one thought still:
Thus reason to his servants yields his right;[14]
Thus is my power transformed to your will.
What marvel then I take a woman's hue,
Since what I see, think, know, is all but you?

This ditty gave him some suspicion, but the voice gave him almost assurance who the singer was; and therefore boldly thrusting open the door and entering into the arbour, he perceived indeed that it was Pyrocles thus disguised: wherewith not receiving so much joy to have found him as grief so to have found him, amazedly looking upon him (as Apollo is painted when he saw Daphne suddenly turned into a laurel) he was not able to bring forth a word; so that Pyrocles (who had as much shame as Musidorus had sorrow) rising to him, would have formed a substantial excuse, but his insinuation being of blushing and his division of sighs, his whole oration stood upon a short narration[15] what was the cause of this metamorphosis. But by that time Musidorus had gathered his spirits together, and yet casting a ghastful[16] countenance upon him as if he would conjure some strange spirit, he thus spoke unto him:

'And is it possible that this is Pyrocles, the only young prince in the world formed by nature and framed by education to the true exercise of virtue? Or is it indeed some Amazon that hath counterfeited the face of my friend in this sort to vex me? For likelier sure I would have thought it that any outward face might have been disguised than that the face of so excellent a mind could have been thus blemished. [...] See with yourself how fit it will be for you in this your tender youth, born so great a prince, and of so rare not only expectation but proof, desired of your old father, and wanted of your native country, now so near your home to divert your thoughts from the way of goodness to lose, nay, to abuse your time. Lastly to overthrow all the excellent things you have done, which have filled the world with your fame [...] Remember (for I know you know it) that if we will be men, the reasonable part of our soul is to have absolute commandment, against which, if any sensual weakness arise, we are to yield all our sound forces to the

14 *servants* the five senses.

15 *insinuation ... division ... narration* referring to the traditional parts of a formal oration: the introduction, the division of the material, and the statement of the central argument.

16 *ghastful* terrible.

overthrowing of so unnatural a rebellion; wherein how can we want courage, since we are to deal against so weak an adversary that in itself is nothing but weakness? Nay, we are to resolve that if reason direct it, we must do it; and if we must do it, we will do it; for, to say "I cannot," is childish, and "I will not," womanish.

'And see how extremely every way you can endanger your mind: for to take this womanish habit, without you frame your behaviour accordingly, is wholly vain; your behaviour can never come kindly[17] from you but as the mind is proportioned unto it: so that you must resolve, if you will play your part to any purpose, whatsoever peevish imperfections are in that sex, to soften your heart to receive them – the very first down-step to all wickedness. For do not deceive yourself, my dear cousin, there is no man suddenly either excellently good or extremely evil, but grows either as he holds himself up in virtue or lets himself slide to viciousness.

'And let us see what power is the author of all these troubles: forsooth love, love, a passion, and the basest and fruitlessest of all passions. Fear breedeth wit; anger is the cradle of courage; joy openeth and enableth the heart; sorrow, as it closeth, so it draweth it inward to look to the correcting of itself; and so all of them generally have power towards some good by the direction of reason. But this bastard love (for indeed the name of love is most unworthily applied to so hateful humour)[18] as it is engendered betwixt lust and idleness; as the matter it works upon is nothing but a certain base weakness which some gentle fools call a gentle heart; as his adjoined companions be unquietness, longings, fond[19] comforts, faint discomforts, hopes, jealousies, ungrounded rages, causeless yieldings; so is the highest end it aspires unto a little pleasure with much pain before and great repentance after. But that end, how endless it runs to infinite evils, were fit enough for the matter we speak of; but not for your ears, in whom, indeed, there is so much true disposition to virtue.

'Yet thus much of his worthy effects in yourself is to be seen, that (besides your breaking laws of hospitality with Kalander[20] and of friendship with me) it utterly subverts the course of nature in making reason give place to sense,[21] and man to woman. And truly I think hereupon it first got the name of love: for indeed the true love hath that excellent nature in it, that it doth transform the very essence of the lover into the thing loved, uniting and, as it were, incorporating it with a secret and inward working. And herein do these kinds

[17] *kindly* naturally.

[18] *humour* inclination.

[19] *fond* foolish.

[20] *Kalander* Arcadian nobleman, who welcomes Musidorus and Pyrocles into his home.

[21] *sense* sensuality.

of love imitate the excellent: for as the love of heaven makes one heavenly, the love of virtue, virtuous, so doth the love of the world make one become worldly: and this effeminate love of a woman doth so womanize a man that, if he yield to it, it will not only make him an Amazon, but a launder, a distaff-spinner[22] or whatsoever other vile occupation their idle heads can imagine and their weak hands perform. [...]

'I do now beseech you even for the love betwixt us (if this other love have left any in you towards me) and for the remembrance of your old careful father (if you can remember him that forget yourself) lastly, for Pyrocles' own sake (who is now upon the point of falling or rising) to purge yourself of this vile infection. Otherwise give me leave to leave off this name of friendship as an idle title of a thing which cannot be where virtue is abolished.'[23]

[...]

'Alas,' said he, 'Prince Musidorus, how cruelly you deal with me. If you seek the victory, take it, and, if you list,[24] the triumph. [...] But truly you deal with me like a physician that, seeing his patient in a pestilent fever, should chide him instead of ministering help, and bid him be sick no more; or rather like such a friend that, visiting his friend condemned to perpetual prison and laden with grievous fetters, should will him to shake off his fetters or he would leave him. I am sick, and sick to the death. I am prisoner, neither is there any redress but by her to whom I am a slave. Now, if you list, leave him that loves you in the highest degree: but remember ever to carry this with you, that you abandon your friend in his greatest extremity.'

And herewith the deep wound of his love, being rubbed afresh with this new unkindness, began, as it were, to bleed again in such sort that he was unable to bear it any longer; but gushing out abundance of tears, and crossing his arms over his woeful heart, as if his tears had been out-flowing blood, his arms an over-pressing burden, he sunk down to the ground. Which sudden trance went so to the heart of Musidorus that, falling down by him and kissing the weeping eyes of his friend, he besought him not to make account of his speech which, if it had been over-vehement, yet was it to be borne withal, because it came out of a love much more vehement: that he had not thought fancy could have received so deep a wound; but now finding in him the force of it, he would no further contrary it but employ all his service to medicine it in such sort as the nature of it required. But even this kindness made Pyrocles the more melt in the former unkindness, which his

22 *launder*: laundry-woman; *distaff-spinner*: spinner of thread for cloth; traditional lower-class women's occupations.

23 *a ... abolished* Friendship can only exist between virtuous men. See Cicero's *Laelius* (*Online Companion*).

24 *list* wish.

manlike tears well showed, with a silent look upon Musidorus, as who should say: 'And is it possible that Musidorus should threaten to leave me?'; and this struck Musidorus' mind and senses so dumb, too, that for grief being not able to say anything, they rested with their eyes placed one upon another, in such sort as might well paint out the true passion of unkindness to be never aright but betwixt them that most dearly love.

And thus remained they a time, till at length Musidorus, embracing him, said, 'And will you thus shake off your friend?'

'It is you that shake me off,' said Pyrocles, 'being for my unperfectness unworthy of your friendship.'

'But this,' said Musidorus, 'shows you more unperfect, to be cruel to him that submits himself unto you. But since you are unperfect,' said he, smiling, 'it is reason you be governed by us wise and perfect men. And that authority will I begin to take upon me with three absolute commandments: the first, that you increase not your evil with further griefs: the second, that you love her with all the powers of your mind: and the last commandment shall be, you command me to do what service I can towards the attaining of your desires.'

Pyrocles' heart was not so oppressed with the two mighty passions of love and unkindness but that it yielded to some mirth at this commandment of Musidorus that he should love; so that something clearing his face from his former shows of grief:

'Well,' said he, 'dear cousin, I see by the well choosing of your commandments that you are far fitter to be a prince than a counselor, and therefore I am resolved to employ all my endeavour to obey you, with this condition: that the commandments you command me to lay upon you shall only be, that you continue to love me, and look upon my imperfections with more affection than judgement.'

'Love you?' said he. 'Alas, how can my heart be separated from the true embracing of it without it burst by being too full of it?'

[...]

Richard Barnfield (1574–1620), writer

Educated at Oxford (BA, 1592) and possibly at Gray's Inn (London), Barnfield was a friend of the poet Francis Meres and associated with Sidney and Spenser. He wrote four works: *Greene's Funerals* (1594), *The Affectionate Shepherd* (1594), *Cynthia* (1595), and a collection of poems and verse pamphlets (1598).

Online Companion

From Barnfield's *The Affectionate Shepherd* and *Cynthia with Certain Sonnets*, and 'A

Pastoral Dialogue Concerning Friendship and Love' in Cicero's *Laelius: A Discourse of Friendship* (1691).

8.4

From *The Affectionate Shepherd* (1594)

8.4.1 The Tears of an Affectionate Shepherd Sick for Love, or The Complaint of Daphnis for the Love of Ganymede

Scarce had the morning star hid from the light[1]
Heaven's crimson canopy with stars bespangled,
But I began to rue th'unhappy sight[2]
Of that fair boy that had my heart entangled;
    Cursing the time, the place, the sense, the sin;
    I came, I saw, I viewed, I slippèd in.

If it be sin to love a sweet-faced boy,
(Whose amber locks trussed up in golden trammels[3]
Dangle adown his lovely cheeks with joy,
When pearl and flowers his fair hair enamels),
    If it be sin to love a lovely lad,
    Oh then sin I, for whom my soul is sad.

His ivory-white and alabaster skin
Is stained throughout with rare vermilion red,
Whose twinkling starry lights do never blin[4]
To shine on lovely Venus (beauty's bed),
    But as the lily and the blushing rose,[5]
    So white and red on him in order grows.

[…]

Oh, would she would forsake my Ganymede,[6]
Whose sugared love is full of sweet delight,

1 *morning star* Venus.
2 *rue* regret.
3 *trammels* tresses of hair (usually applied to women).
4 *blin* cease.
5 *lily* and *rose* conventional emblems of the Petrarchan mistress's perfect complexion.
6 *she* Guendolena (she and Ganymede are in love with each other).

Upon whose forehead you may plainly read
Love's pleasure 'graved in ivory tables bright;
    In whose fair eyeballs you may clearly see
    Base love still stained with foul indignity.

Oh, would to God he would but pity me,
That love him more than any mortal wight;[7]
Then he and I with love would soon agree,
That now cannot abide his suitor's sight.[8]
    Oh, would to God (so I might have my fee)[9]
    My lips were honey, and thy mouth a bee.

Then shouldst thou suck my sweet and my fair flower
That now is ripe, and full of honey-berries;
Then would I lead thee to my pleasant bower[10]
Filled full of grapes, of mulberries, and cherries;
    Then shouldst thou be my wasp or else my bee,
    I would thy hive, and thou my honey be.

I would put amber bracelets on thy wrists,
Crownets of pearl about thy naked arms;
And when thou sitt'st at swilling Bacchus' feasts,
My lips with charms should save thee from all harms;
    And when in sleep thou tookst thy chiefest pleasure,
    Mine eyes should gaze upon thine eyelids' treasure.

[…]

And when it pleaseth thee to walk abroad
(Abroad into the fields to take fresh air),
The meads with Flora's treasure should be strowed[11]
(The mantled meadows and the fields so fair).
    And by a silver well (with golden sands)
    I'll sit me down and wash thine ivory hands.

And in the sweltering heat of summer time,
I would make cabinets for thee, my love;[12]

7 *wight* creature.
8 *his suitor* i.e., Daphnis.
9 *fee* reward.
10 *bower* arbour.
11 *meads* meadows; *Flora*: goddess of flowers and the spring; *strowed*: strewn.
12 *cabinets* summer houses or garden bowers.

Sweet-smelling arbours made of eglantine
Should be thy shrine, and I would be thy dove.
    Cool cabinets of fresh green laurel boughs
    Should shadow us, o'er-set with thick-set yews.[13]

Or if thou list to bathe thy naked limbs[14]
Within the crystal of a pearl-bright brook,
Paved with dainty pibbles to the brims,[15]
Or clear, wherein thyself thy self mayst look,
    We'll go to Ladon, whose still trickling noise[16]
    Will lull thee fast asleep amids thy joys.

Or if thoult go unto the river side[17]
To angle for the sweet fresh-water fish,
Armed with thy implements that will abide
(Thy rod, hook, line) to take a dainty dish:
    Thy rods shall be of cane, thy lines of silk,
    Thy hooks of silver, and thy baits of milk.

[...]

Or if thou dar'st to climb the highest trees
For apples, cherries, medlars, pears, or plums,[18]
Nuts, walnuts, filbeards, chestnuts, cervices,[19]
The hoary peach, when snowy winter comes:
    I have fine orchards full of mellowed fruit,
    Which I will give thee to obtain my suit.

Not proud Alcynous himself can vaunt[20]
Of goodlier orchards or of braver trees
Than I have planted; yet thou wilt not graunt
My simple suit; but like the honey bees
    Thou suckst the flow'r till all the sweet be gone,
    And lov'st me for my coin till I have none.

[13] *yew* tree often planted in churchyards (symbolizing grief).
[14] *list* wish, desire.
[15] *pibbles* pebbles.
[16] *Ladon* Arcadian river. On its banks the nymphs Daphne and Syrinx were transformed (Glossary).
[17] *thoult* i.e., thou wilt.
[18] *medlar* fruit (like the *cervice*), edible only when over-ripe.
[19] *filbeards* filberts.
[20] *Alcynous* king of a famously fertile and beautiful island (*Odyssey*, Bk 6); *vaunt*: boast.

[...]

All these, and more, I'll give thee for thy love;
If these, and more, may 'tice thy love away:[21]
I have a pigeon-house, in it a dove,
Which I love more than mortal tongue can say;
  And last of all, I'll give thee a little lamb
  To play withal, new weanèd from her dam.

But if thou wilt not pity my complaint,
My tears, nor vows, nor oaths, made to thy beauty,
What shall I do? But languish, die, or faint,
Since thou dost scorn my tears and my soul's duty:
  And tears contemned, vows and oaths must fail,[22]
  For where tears cannot, nothing can prevail.

Compare the love of fair queen Guendolin
With mine, and thou shalt see how she doth love thee:
I love thee for thy qualities divine,
But she doth love another swain above thee;[23]
  I love thee for thy gifts, she for her pleasure,
  I for thy virtue, she for beauty's treasure.

And always (I am sure) it cannot last,
But sometime nature will deny those dimples;
In stead of beauty (when thy blossom's past)[24]
Thy face will be deformed, full of wrinkles:
  Then she that loved thee for thy beauty's sake,
  When age draws on, thy love will soon forsake.

But I that loved thee for thy gifts divine,
In the December of thy beauty's waning,
Will still admire (with joy) those lovely eine,[25]
That now behold me with their beauty's baning:[26]
  Though January will never come again,
  Yet April years will come in showers of rain.

21 *'tice* entice.
22 *contemned* disdained.
23 *swain* shepherd (in pastoral verse); wooer.
24 *in stead* in the place of.
25 *eine* eyes.
26 *baning* cursing.

When will my May come, that I may embrace thee?
When will the hour be of my soul's joying?
Why dost thou seek in mirth still to disgrace me?
Whose mirth's my health, whose grief's my heart's annoying.
  Thy bane my bale, thy bliss my blessedness,[27]
  Thy ill my hell, thy weal my welfare is.[28]

Thus do I honour thee that love thee so,
And love thee so, that so do honour thee,
Much more than any mortal man doth know,
Or can discern by love or jealousy.
  But if that thou disdain'st my loving ever,
  Oh, happy I if I had loved never.

[…]

8.5

From *Cynthia, with Certain Sonnets* (1595)[29]

8.5.1 Sonnet 1

Sporting at fancy, setting light by love,
There came a thief and stole away my heart,
  (And therefore robbed me of my chiefest part)
Yet cannot reason him a felon prove.
For why his beauty (my heart's thief) affirmeth,
  Piercing no skin (the body's 'fensive wall)
  And having leave, and free consent withal,
Himself not guilty, from love guilty tearmeth,
Conscience the judge, twelve reasons are the jury.
  They find mine eyes the beauty t'have let in,
  And on this verdict given, agreed they bin:[30]
'Wherefore, because his beauty did allure ye,
  Your doom is this: in tears still to be drowned,
  When his fair forehead with disdain is frowned.'

27 *bane* fatal mischance; *bale*: suffering; death.
28 *weal* and *welfare* synonyms for 'happiness'.
29 For the work's preface about the controversy apparently generated by *The Affectionate Shepherd* (see **8.4.1**), consult *Online Companion*.
30 *bin* been.

8.5.2 Sonnet 6

Sweet coral lips, where Nature's treasure lies,
The balm of bliss, the sovereign salve of sorrow,
  The secret touch of love's heart-burning arrow,
Come quench my thirst or else poor Daphnis dies.
One night I dreamed (alas 'twas but a dream)
  That I did feel the sweetness of the same,
  Wherewith inspired, I young again became,
And from my heart a spring of blood did stream;
But when I waked, I found it nothing so,
  Save that my limbs (methought) did wax more strong[31]
  And I more lusty far, and far more young.
This gift on him rich Nature did bestow.
  Then if in dreaming so, I so did speed,[32]
  What should I do, if I did so indeed?

8.5.3 Sonnet 7

Sweet Thames, I honour thee, not for thou art
  The chiefest river of the fairest isle,
  Nor for thou dost admirers' eyes beguile,
But for thou hold'st the keeper of my heart,
For on thy waves, (thy crystal-billowed waves),
  My fairest fair, my silver swan is swimming,
  Against the sun, his prunèd feathers trimming,
Whilst Neptune his fair feet with water laves.
Neptune, I fear not thee, not yet thine eye,
  And yet (alas) Apollo loved a boy,[33]
  And Cyparissus was Silvanus' joy.
No, no, I fear none but fair Thetis I,
  For if she spy my love, (alas) ay me,
  My mirth is turned to extreme misery.

8.5.4 Sonnet 8

Sometimes I wish that I his pillow were,
  So might I steal a kiss, and yet not seen,

[31] *wax* grow.
[32] *speed* attain [my] desire.
[33] *a boy* See 'Apollo and Hyacinthus' (Glossary).

So might I gaze upon his sleeping eyne,
Although I did it with a panting fear.
But when I well consider how vain my wish is,
Ah, foolish bees, (think I) that do not suck
His lips for honey, but poor flowers do pluck
Which have no sweet in them, when his sole kisses
Are able to revive a dying soul.
Kiss him, but sting him not, for if you do,
His angry voice your flying will pursue.
But when they hear his tongue, what can control
Their back-return? for then they plain may see
How honey-combs from his lips dropping be.[34]

8.5.5 Sonnet 11

Sighing and sadly sitting by my love,
He asked the cause of my heart's sorrowing,
Conjuring me by heaven's eternal king
To tell the cause which me so much did move.
'Compelled,' quoth I, 'to thee will I confess:
Love is the cause, and only love it is
That doth deprive me of my heavenly bliss.
Love is the pain that doth my heart oppress.'
'And what is she,' quoth he, 'whom thou dost love?'
'Look in this glass,' quoth I. 'There shalt thou see
The perfect form of my felicity.'
When, thinking that it would strange magic prove,
He opened it, and taking off the cover,
He straight perceived himself to be my lover.

8.5.6 Sonnet 12

Some talk of Ganymede th'Idalian boy,
And some of fair Adonis make their boast;
Some talk of him whom lovely Leda lost,[35]
And some of Echo's love that was so coy.[36]
They speak by hearsay, I of perfect truth;
They partially commend the persons named,

[34] Cf. the groom's description of the bride's lips (Song of Songs, 4.11).
[35] *him* Castor (Glossary).
[36] *Echo's love* Narcissus (Glossary).

And for them sweet encomiums have framed,[37]
I only t'him have sacrificed my youth.
As for those wonders of antiquity,
And those whom later ages have enjoyed,
(But, ah, what hath not cruel death destroyed?
Death, that envies this world's felicity),
They were (perhaps) less fair than poets write,
But he is fairer than I can indite.[38]

8.5.7 Sonnet 14

Here; hold this glove (this milk-white cheveril glove)[39]
Not quaintly over-wrought with curious knots,[40]
Not decked with golden spangs, nor silver spots,[41]
Yet wholesome for thy hand as thou shalt prove.
Ah no, sweet boy, place this glove near thy heart,
Wear it, and lodge it still within thy breast,
So shalt thou make me (most unhappy) blest.
So shalt thou rid my pain, and ease my smart:
'How can that be?' (perhaps) thou wilt reply,
'A glove is for the hand not for the heart,
Nor can it well be proved by common art
Nor reason's rule.' To this, thus answer I:
'If thou from glove dost take away the g,
Then glove is love: and so I send it thee.'

8.5.8 Sonnet 17

Cherry-lipped Adonis in his snowy shape
Might not compare with his pure ivory white,
On whose fair front a poet's pen may write,
Whose rosiate red excels the crimson grape.
His love-enticing delicate soft limbs
Are rarely framed t'intrap poor gazing eyes;
His cheeks the lily and carnation dyes[42]
With lovely tincture which Apollo's dims.

37 *encomium* panegyric.
38 *indite* express.
39 *cheveril* kid-skin.
40 *quaintly over-wrought* elaborately decorated; *curious*: overly intricate.
41 *spangs* spangles.
42 *His … dyes* See **n5**.

His lips ripe strawberries in nectar wet,
  His mouth a hive, his tongue a honey-comb,
  Where muses (like bees) make their mansion.
His teeth pure pearl in blushing coral set.
  Oh, how can such a body sin-procuring
  Be slow to love, and quick to hate, enduring?

Christopher Marlowe (1564–93), poet and playwright

Educated at Cambridge (MA, 1587), Marlowe wrote some of the most influential Elizabethan dramas, including *Tamburlaine*, Parts I and II (1590; 1593), *Doctor Faustus* (1604), and *Edward II* (1594), as well as narrative verse (*Hero and Leander* (1598)), and classical translations. Dogged by serious legal troubles, Marlowe found himself under investigation on suspicion of atheism (and perhaps sodomy). Marlowe's violent death may have been linked to his unorthodox religious views, or to his work as a government spy. A warrant had been issued for his arrest, and two of the men involved in the fight that led to Marlowe's stabbing were also government agents.

Online Companion
From Marlowe's *Dido, Queen of Carthage* (1594); from Michael Drayton's *Piers Gaveston, Earl of Cornwall* (1593).

8.6

From *Edward II* (1594)

8.6.1 Act 1, scene 1

Enter GAVESTON *reading on a letter that was brought him from the* KING.[1]

GAVESTON. 'My father is deceased; come, Gaveston,
And share the kingdom with thy dearest friend.'
Ah, words that make me surfeit with delight![2]

[1] Piers *Gaveston* (d. 1312), Earl of Cornwall (granted, 1307) and royal favourite; son of a knight, Gaveston was by birth a gentleman, and (initially, at least) a valued member of the households of both Edward I and Prince Edward (later Edward II); *the King*: Edward II (1284–1327; reigned, 1307–27).

[2] *surfeit* engorge.

What greater bliss can hap to Gaveston,[3]
Than live and be the favourite of a king?
Sweet prince, I come; these, these thy amorous lines
Might have enforced me to have swum from France,
And, like Leander, gasped upon the sand,
So thou wouldst smile and take me in thy arms.
The sight of London to my exiled eyes
Is as Elysium to a new-come soul;
Not that I love the city or the men,
But that it harbours him I hold so dear,
The king, upon whose bosom let me die,[4]
And with the world be still at enmity.
What need the arctic people love starlight,
To whom the sun shines both by day and night?
Farewell, base stooping to the lordly peers;
My knee shall bow to none but to the king.
As for the multitude, that are but sparks
Raked up in embers of their poverty,
Tanti! I'll fan first on the wind[5]
That glanceth at my lips and flieth away.

[Gaveston speaks to three poor men who approach him looking for favour and assistance; he promises much but intends to do nothing for them; they leave and his thoughts return to Edward.]

I must have wanton poets, pleasant wits,
Musicians, that with touching of a string
May draw the pliant king which way I please.
Music and poetry is his delight;
Therefore I'll have Italian masques by night,[6]
Sweet speeches, comedies, and pleasing shows;
And in the day when he shall walk abroad,
Like sylvan nymphs my pages shall be clad,[7]
My men like satyrs grazing on the lawns
Shall with their goat-feet dance an antic hay;[8]

[3] *hap* happen.

[4] *die* faint (with play on 'achieve orgasm').

[5] *Tanti* Italian, 'Enough!' (an expression of contemptuous dismissal).

[6] *masques* spectacular dramatic entertainments with elaborate costumes, singing, and dancing.

[7] *sylvan* woodland.

[8] *antic hay* wild country dance.

Sometime a lovely boy in Dian's shape,[9]
With hair that gilds the water as it glides,[10]
Crownets of pearl about his naked arms,
And in his sportful hands an olive tree
To hide those parts which men delight to see,
Shall bathe him in a spring; and there hard by,[11]
One like Actaeon peeping through the grove,
Shall by the angry goddess be transformed,
And running in the likeness of an hart,
By yelping hounds pulled down, and seem to die.
Such things as these best please his Majesty.

[Hearing the nobles condemn him to Edward and threaten uprisings, Gaveston reveals his presence.]

GAVESTON. I can no longer keep me from my lord. [*He moves forward.*]
EDWARD. What, Gaveston! Welcome! Kiss not my hand;
Embrace me, Gaveston, as I do thee!
Why shouldst thou kneel; knowest thou not who I am?
Thy friend, thy self, another Gaveston![12]
Not Hylas was more mourned of Hercules
Than thou hast been of me since thy exile.
GAVESTON. And since I went from hence, no soul in hell
Hath felt more torment than poor Gaveston.
EDWARD. I know it. [*to* KENT] Brother, welcome home my friend.
[*to* GAVESTON] Now let the treacherous Mortimers conspire,
And that high-minded earl of Lancaster.
I have my wish, in that I joy thy sight,
And sooner shall the sea o'erwhelm my land
Than bear the ship that shall transport thee hence.
I here create thee lord high chamberlain,
Chief secretary to the state and me,
Earl of Cornwall, king and lord of Man.[13]
GAVESTON. My lord, these titles far exceed my worth.

[9] *Dian* Diana (Glossary).

[10] *gilds* implying the boy's hair is golden.

[11] *hard* close.

[12] Cf. *alter ipse amicus* Latin proverb, 'A friend is a second self'.

[13] *lord high chamberlain* most important officer in the king's household; *chief secretary to the state and me*: here, manager of the king's and government's correspondence; *king and lord of Man*: Gaveston gains sovereign powers similar to Edward's, but only over Man (an island in the Irish Sea, equidistant from Ireland and England).

KENT. Brother, the least of these may well suffice
For one of greater birth than Gaveston.
EDWARD. Cease, brother, for I cannot brook these words.
[*to* GAVESTON] Thy worth, sweet friend, is far above my gifts,
Therefore to equal it, receive my heart.
If for these dignities thou be envied,
I'll give thee more, for but to honour thee
Is Edward pleased with kingly regiment.[14]
Fear'st thou thy person? Thou shalt have a guard.
Wants thou gold? Go to my treasury.
Wouldst thou be loved and feared? Receive my seal,
Save or condemn, and in our name command
What so thy mind affects or fancy likes.[15]
GAVESTON. It shall suffice me to enjoy your love,
Which whiles I have, I think myself as great
As Caesar riding in the Roman street,
With captive kings at his triumphant car.[16]

[...]

[Gaveston's social elevation and his assault on the Bishop of Coventry enrage the nobles. Gaveston's return also further alienates Edward from his wife, Queen Isabella.]

8.6.2 Act 1, scene 2

[...]

MORTIMER JUNIOR. Madam, whither walks your Majesty so fast?
ISABELLA. Unto the forest, gentle Mortimer,
To live in grief and baleful discontent;[17]
For now my lord the king regards me not,
But dotes upon the love of Gaveston.
He claps his cheeks and hangs about his neck,
Smiles in his face and whispers in his ears;
And when I come he frowns, as who should say,
'Go whither thou wilt, seeing I have Gaveston.'
MORTIMER SENIOR. Is it not strange that he is thus bewitched?

[14] *regiment* authority.
[15] *affects* desires; *fancy*: whim.
[16] *car* chariot.
[17] *baleful* miserable.

[...]

[Backed by the power of the pope, whose legate threatens to excommunicate Edward and absolve his nobles of their allegiance, the nobles force Edward to exile Gaveston.]

8.6.3 Act 1, scene 4

[...]

EDWARD. It boots me not to threat; I must speak fair,[18]
The legate of the pope will be obeyed.
My lord, you shall be chancellor of the realm;
Thou Lancaster, high admiral of our fleet.
Young Mortimer and his uncle shall be earls,
And you, Lord Warwick, president of the North,
[*to* PEMBROKE] And thou of Wales. If this content you not,
Make several kingdoms of this monarchy,
And share it equally amongst you all,
So I may have some nook or corner left
To frolic with my dearest Gaveston.
BISHOP OF CANTERBURY. Nothing shall alter us; we are resolved.
LANCASTER. Come, come, subscribe.
MORTIMER JUNIOR. Why should you love him whom the world hates so?
EDWARD. Because he loves me more than all the world.
Ah, none but rude and savage-minded men[19]
Would seek the ruin of my Gaveston;
You that be noble born should pity him.
WARWICK. You that are princely born should shake him off.
For shame subscribe, and let the lown depart.[20]
MORTIMER SENIOR. Urge him, my lord.
BISHOP OF CANTERBURY. Are you content to banish him the realm?
EDWARD. I see I must, and therefore am content;
Instead of ink, I'll write it with my tears.
[*He signs the order for* GAVESTON*'s banishment.*]
MORTIMER JUNIOR. The king is love-sick for his minion.[21]

[...]

18 *boots* avails.
19 *rude* uncivilized.
20 *lown* man of low birth.
21 *minion* lover (with negative connotations: 'one kept to supply sexual favours').

EDWARD. How fast they run to banish him I love;
They would not stir, were it to do me good.
Why should a king be subject to a priest?
Proud Rome, that hatchest such imperial grooms,[22]
For these thy superstitious taper-lights,[23]
Wherewith thy antichristian churches blaze,
I'll fire thy crazèd buildings and enforce[24]
The papal towers to kiss the lowly ground,
With slaughtered priests make Tiber's channel swell,[25]
And banks raised higher with their sepulchres.
As for the peers that back the clergy thus,
If I be king, not one of them shall live.

Enter GAVESTON.

GAVESTON. My lord, I hear it whispered everywhere
That I am banished and must fly the land.
EDWARD. 'Tis true, sweet Gaveston. Oh, were it false!
The legate of the pope will have it so,
And thou must hence, or I shall be deposed.
But I will reign to be revenged of them,
And therefore, sweet friend, take it patiently.
Live where thou wilt – I'll send thee gold enough.
And long thou shalt not stay, or if thou dost,
I'll come to thee; my love shall ne'er decline.
GAVESTON. Is all my hope turned to this hell of grief?
EDWARD. Rend not my heart with thy too-piercing words.
Thou from this land, I from my self am banished.
GAVESTON. To go from hence grieves not poor Gaveston,
But to forsake you, in whose gracious looks
The blessedness of Gaveston remains,
For nowhere else seeks he felicity.
EDWARD. And only this torments my wretched soul,
That whether I will or no, thou must depart.
Be governor of Ireland in my stead,
And there abide till fortune call thee home.
Here, take my picture, and let me wear thine.[26]

[22] *grooms* servants.
[23] *taper-lights* candles lit for the dead and for liturgical purposes.
[24] *crazèd* flawed.
[25] *Tiber* Tiber River (Rome).
[26] The *pictures* that Edward and Gaveston exchange here are 'miniatures', small

Oh, might I keep thee here, as I do this,
Happy were I, but now most miserable.
GAVESTON. 'Tis something to be pitied of a king.
EDWARD. Thou shalt not hence; I'll hide thee, Gaveston.
GAVESTON. I shall be found, and then 'twill grieve me more.
EDWARD. Kind words and mutual talk makes our grief greater.
Therefore, with dumb embracement, let us part –[27]
Stay, Gaveston, I cannot leave thee thus.
GAVESTON. For every look my lord drops down a tear;
Seeing I must go, do not renew my sorrow.
EDWARD. The time is little that thou hast to stay,
And therefore give me leave to look my fill.
But come, sweet friend, I'll bear thee on thy way.
GAVESTON. The peers will frown.
EDWARD. I pass not for their anger; come, let's go.[28]
Oh, that we might as well return as go.

Enter EDMUND [EDWARD*'s brother, and Earl of* KENT] *and* QUEEN ISABELLA.

ISABELLA. Whither goes my lord?
EDWARD. Fawn not on me, French strumpet; get thee gone.[29]
ISABELLA. On whom but on my husband should I fawn?
GAVESTON. On Mortimer, with whom, ungentle queen –
I say no more; judge you the rest, my lord.
ISABELLA. In saying this, thou wrongst me, Gaveston.
Is't not enough that thou corrupts my lord,
And art a bawd to his affections,[30]
But thou must call mine honour thus in question?
GAVESTON. I mean not so. Your Grace must pardon me.
EDWARD. Thou art too familiar with that Mortimer,
And by thy means is Gaveston exiled;
But I would wish thee reconcile the lords,
Or thou shalt ne'er be reconciled to me.
ISABELLA. Your Highness knows it lies not in my power.
EDWARD. Away then, touch me not; come, Gaveston.

personal portraits; to exchange miniatures was a sign of intimacy and friendship. Cf. **5.1.1 n9**.

[27] *dumb* silent.

[28] *pass* care.

[29] *strumpet* whore.

[30] *bawd* pander; *affections*: desires; also, (sexual) passions.

ISABELLA. Villain, 'tis thou that robb'st me of my lord.
GAVESTON. Madam, 'tis you that rob me of my lord.
EDWARD. Speak not unto her; let her droop and pine.
ISABELLA. Wherein, my lord, have I deserved these words?
Witness the tears that Isabella sheds,
Witness this heart, that sighing for thee breaks,
How dear my lord is to poor Isabel.
EDWARD. And witness heaven how dear thou art to me.
There weep; for till my Gaveston be repealed,[31]
Assure thyself thou com'st not in my sight.

Exeunt EDWARD *and* GAVESTON.

ISABELLA. O miserable and distressèd queen!
Would when I left sweet France and was embarked,
That charming Circe, walking on the waves,
Had changed my shape, or at the marriage-day
The cup of Hymen had been full of poison,
Or with those arms that twined about my neck
I had been stifled, and not lived to see
The king my lord thus to abandon me.
Like frantic Juno will I fill the earth
With ghastly murmur of my sighs and cries,
For never doted Jove on Ganymede
So much as he on cursèd Gaveston.
But that will more exasperate his wrath;
I must entreat him, I must speak him fair,
And be a means to call home Gaveston.
And yet he'll ever dote on Gaveston,
And so am I forever miserable.

[Isabella successfully gets the nobles to rescind Gaveston's banishment. They plan to assassinate Gaveston when he returns.]

Enter KING EDWARD *mourning.*

[...]

EDWARD. He's gone, and for his absence thus I mourn.
Did never sorrow go so near my heart
As doth the want of my sweet Gaveston;

[31] *repealed* recalled from exile.

And could my crown's revènue bring him back,
I would freely give it to his enemies
And think I gained, having bought so dear a friend.
ISABELLA. Hark how he harps upon his minion.
EDWARD. My heart is as an anvil unto sorrow,
Which beats upon it like the Cyclops' hammers,[32]
And with the noise turns up my giddy brain[33]
And makes me frantic for my Gaveston.
Ah, had some bloodless Fury rose from hell,
And with kingly sceptre struck me dead,
When I was forced to leave my Gaveston.
LANCASTER. *Diablo*! What passions call you these?[34]
ISABELLA. My gracious lord, I come to bring you news.
EDWARD. That you have parleyed with your Mortimer.
ISABELLA. That Gaveston, my lord, shall be repealed.
EDWARD. Repealed? The news is too sweet to be true.
ISABELLA. But will you love me if you find it so?
EDWARD. If it be so, what will not Edward do?
ISABELLA. For Gaveston, but not for Isabel.
EDWARD. For thee, fair queen, if thou lov'st Gaveston;
I'll hang a golden tongue about thy neck,[35]
Seeing thou hast pleaded with so good success.
ISABELLA. No other jewels hang about my neck
Than these, my lord; nor let me have more wealth[36]
Than I may fetch from this rich treasury.
Oh, how a kiss revives poor Isabel.
EDWARD. Once more receive my hand, and let this be
A second marriage 'twixt thyself and me.
ISABELLA. And may it prove more happy than the first.
My gentle lord, bespeak these nobles fair
That wait attendance for a gracious look,
And on their knees salute your Majesty.

[Edward rewards his nobles and they all go in together to feast, except the Mortimers.]

[32] *Cyclops* one-eyed monsters, workmen of Vulcan, and creators of Jupiter's thunderbolts.

[33] *up* topsy-turvy.

[34] *Diablo* Spanish, 'the Devil!'; *passions*: passionate expressions (and the love that inspires them).

[35] *golden tongue* pendant in this shape.

[36] *these* probably, Edward's arms (he has embraced her).

MORTIMER SENIOR. Nephew, I must to Scotland; thou stayest here.
Leave now to oppose thyself against the king;
Thou seest by nature he is mild and calm,
And seeing his mind so dotes on Gaveston,
Let him without controlment have his will.
The mightiest kings have had their minions:
Great Alexander loved Hephaestion;
The conquering Hercules for Hylas wept;
And for Patroclus stern Achilles drooped.
And not kings only, but the wisest men:
The Roman Tully loved Octavius,
Grave Socrates, wild Alcibiades.[37]
Then let his Grace, whose youth is flexible
And promiseth as much as we can wish,
Freely enjoy that vain light-headed earl,
For riper years will wean him from such toys.[38]
MORTIMER JUNIOR. Uncle, his wanton humour grieves not me,
But this I scorn, that one so basely born
Should by his sovereign's favour grow so pert,
And riot it with the treasure of the realm
While soldiers mutiny for want of pay.
He wears a lord's revènue on his back,
And Midas-like he jets it in the court[39]
With base outlandish cullions at his heels,[40]
Whose proud fantastic liveries make such show
As if that Proteus, god of shapes, appeared.[41]
I have not seen a dapper jack so brisk;[42]
He wears a short Italian hooded cloak,
Larded with pearl; and in his Tuscan cap[43]
A jewel of more value than the crown.

[37] *Tully* (Cicero) and *Octavius* Caesar (later, Emperor Augustus) are the only unusual pair here: they were not close friends; Octavius respected the orator Cicero, but colluded in Cicero's death.

[38] *toys* trivialities.

[39] *Midas-like* like Midas, King of Phrygia, who turned everything he touched into gold; *jets it*: struts about arrogantly.

[40] *outlandish cullions* foreign, base-born fellows.

[41] *Proteus* shape-shifting sea deity.

[42] *jack* ill-mannered, lower-class fellow.

[43] *Italian hooded cloak* and *Tuscan cap* emphasizing Gaveston's connection with Italy, the stereotypical birthplace of sodomy.

Whiles other[s] walk below, the king and he
From out a window laugh at such as we,
And flout our train and jest at our attire.
Uncle, 'tis this that makes me impatient.
MORTIMER SENIOR. But, nephew, now you see the king is changed.
MORTIMER JUNIOR. Then so am I, and live to do him service:
But whiles I have a sword, a hand, a heart,
I will not yield to any such upstart.
You know my mind. Come, uncle, let's away.

8.6.4 Act 2, scene 2

Enter KING EDWARD, [ISABELLA] *the* QUEEN, LANCASTER, MORTIMER [Junior], WARWICK, PEMBROKE, KENT, attendants.

EDWARD. The wind is good. I wonder why he stays.
I fear me he is wrecked upon the sea.
ISABELLA. Look, Lancaster, how passionate he is,
And still his mind runs on his minion.[44]
LANCASTER. My lord—
EDWARD. How now, what news? Is Gaveston arrived?
MORTIMER JUNIOR. Nothing but Gaveston! What means your Grace?
You have matters of more weight to think upon;
The king of France sets foot in Normandy.[45]
EDWARD. A trifle! We'll expel him when we please.

[...]

EDWARD. My Gaveston!
Welcome to Tynemouth, welcome to thy friend.[46]
My absence made me droop and pine away;
For as the lovers of fair Danae,
When she was locked up in a brazen tower,
Desired her more and waxed outrageous,
So did it sure with me; and now thy sight
Is sweeter far than was thy parting hence
Bitter and irksome to my sobbing heart.
GAVESTON. Sweet lord and king, your speech preventeth mine,
Yet have I words left to express my joy:

44 *runs on* is obsessed with; *minion*: See **n21**.
45 *Normandy* in France (until 1450 a part of England).
46 *Tynemouth* town in Northumberland.

The shepherd nipped with biting winter's rage
Frolics not more to see the painted spring
Than I do to behold your Majesty.

[Peace is impossible; the nobles and Edward raise troops for a civil war. When Edward refuses to ransom Mortimer Jr's uncle, Mortimer Sr, taken in battle against the Scots, the king is condemned by all.]

MORTIMER JUNIOR. The idle triumphs, masques, lascivious shows,
And prodigal gifts bestowed on Gaveston[47]
Have drawn thy treasure dry and made thee weak;[48]
The murmuring commons overstretchèd hath.[49]
LANCASTER. Look for rebellion, look to be deposed:
Thy garrisons are beaten out of France,
And, lame and poor, lie groaning at the gates;
The wild O'Neill, with swarms of Irish kerns,[50]
Lives uncontrolled within the English pale;[51]
Unto the walls of York the Scots made road[52]
And, unresisted, drove away rich spoils.[53]
MORTIMER JUNIOR. The haughty Dane commands the narrow seas,
While in the harbour ride thy ships unrigged.[54]
LANCASTER. What foreign prince sends thee ambassadors?
MORTIMER JUNIOR. Who loves thee but a sort of flatterers?
LANCASTER. Thy gentle queen, sole sister to Valois,[55]
Complains that thou hast left her all forlorn.
MORTIMER JUNIOR. Thy court is naked, being bereft of those
That makes a king seem glorious to the world –
I mean the peers whom thou shouldst dearly love.
Libels are cast again thee in the street,[56]
Ballads and rhymes made of thy overthrow.

[47] *prodigal* lavish.
[48] *treasure* treasury.
[49] *The … hath* i.e., the gifts to Gaveston have overstretched [the resources of] the disgruntled common people to pay for them [through taxes].
[50] *O'Neill* powerful Irish clan; *kerns*: foot soldiers.
[51] *English pale* that part of Ireland over which English jurisdiction was established.
[52] *made road* have invaded.
[53] *spoils* plunder.
[54] *ride* are anchored; *unrigged*: with rigging (sails, ropes, etc) removed.
[55] *Valois* King Philippe IV of France.
[56] *again* against.

LANCASTER. The northern borderers, seeing their houses burnt,
Their wives and children slain, run up and down
Cursing the name of thee and Gaveston.
MORTIMER JUNIOR. When wert thou in the field with banner spread?
But once! And then thy soldiers marched like players,[57]
With garish robes, not armour; and thyself,
Bedaubed with gold, rode laughing at the rest,
Nodding and shaking of thy spangled crest[58]
Where women's favours hung like labels down.[59]

[With Edward occupied by Gaveston and preparations for his favourite's marriage to Edward's niece, the nobles attack. Gaveston and Edward leave the palace separately; Gaveston is captured and beheaded. The nobles then send Edward terms for peace.]

8.6.5 Act 3, scene 3

[...]

HERALD. The barons up in arms, by me salute
Your Highness with long life and happiness,
And bid me say as plainer to your Grace,[60]
That if without effusion of blood
You will this grief have ease and remedy,
That from your princely person you remove
This Spencer, as a putrefying branch[61]
That deads the royal vine whose golden leaves
Impale your princely head, your diadem,[62]
Whose brightness such pernicious upstarts dim,
Say they; and lovingly advise your Grace
To cherish virtue and nobility,
And have old servitors in high esteem,[63]
And shake off smooth dissembling flatterers.

[57] *players* actors.
[58] *crest* helmet's plume (here, ornately decorated).
[59] *favours* e.g., handkerchiefs that ladies gave to knights to wear into battle or tournaments.
[60] *plainer* complainant.
[61] *Spencer* i.e., Spencer, Jr, Edward's new favourite; historically, Hugh Despenser, the younger (d. 1326).
[62] *impale* encircle; *diadem*: crown.
[63] *old servitors* those who have served [you] for a long time.

This granted, they, their honours and their lives
Are to your Highness vowed and consecrate.
SPENCER JR. Ah, traitors, will they still display their pride?
EDWARD. Away! Tarry no answer, but begone.[64]
Rebels! Will they appoint their sovereign[65]
His sports, his pleasures, and his company?
Yet ere thou go, see how I do divorce
Spencer from me. *Embraces* SPENCER [JUNIOR].
Now get thee to thy lords,
And tell them I will come to chastise them
For murdering Gaveston. [...]

[Edward wins and imprisons the nobles, but later his brother Kent and Mortimer Junior escape, raise an army, and defeat him. Imprisoned and stripped of his supporters, Edward survives terrible prison conditions, as Mortimer Junior aims at the throne with the active connivance of Isabella, now his lover. Finally, Mortimer Junior sends assassins against him.]

8.6.6 Act 5, scene 5

[...]

EDWARD. Something still buzzeth in mine ears
And tells me, if I sleep I never wake.
This fear is that which makes me tremble thus;
And therefore tell me, wherefore art thou come?
LIGHTBORNE. To rid thee of thy life. Maltravers, come!

[*Enter* MALTRAVERS.]

EDWARD. I am too weak and feeble to resist;
Assist me, sweet God, and receive my soul.
LIGHTBORNE. Run for the table. [*Exit* MALTRAVERS.]

[*Enter* MALTRAVERS *with* GOURNEY, *carrying a table and hot spit.*]

EDWARD. Oh, spare me, or dispatch me in a trice!
LIGHTBORNE. So, lay the table down and stamp on it;
But not too hard, lest that you bruise his body.

64 *tarry* wait for.
65 *appoint* decide upon, determine; command.

[*They seize* EDWARD *and hold him down, laying the table on him.*
LIGHTBORNE *murders him with the spit. He screams and dies.*][66]

MALTRAVERS. I fear me that this cry will raise the town,
And therefore let us take horse and away.
LIGHTBORNE. Tell me, sirs, was it not bravely done?[67]

[After killing Lightborne, Gourney gets Maltravers to help him deliver Edward's body to Mortimer Junior. Edward's son then unites the nobles against Mortimer Junior and Isabella. The former is beheaded; the latter sent to prison until further investigation can be made of the extent of her culpability in the death of her husband.]

8.7

From *Hero and Leander* (1598)

8.7.1 Book 1 [Celebration of Leander's Beauty]

[...]

Amorous Leander, beautiful and young,
(Whose tragedy divine Musaeus sung)[68]
Dwelt at Abidus; since him dwelt there none[69]
For whom succeeding times make greater moan.
His dangling tresses that were never shorn,
Had they been cut, and unto Colchos borne,
Would have allured the vent'rous youth of Greece

[66] The 1594 edition lacks stage directions here, and so I have adopted this one and the preceding three from M. Wiggins and R. Lindsey's 1997 New Mermaids edition. Apart from clarifying the murderers' entrances and exits, Wiggins and Lindsey reject the decorous silence of earlier editions concerning Edward's horrific death, which Marlowe clearly bases on Holinshed's explicit description: the spit is thrust up Edward's anus (*Chronicles*, 1587 (London, 1807): 2.587). The red-hot spit, table, and featherbed are all named as the instruments of Edward's murder earlier in the scene.

[67] *bravely* well.

[68] *Musaeus* fifth century CE Greek poet; wrote the earliest extant poem on Hero and Leander.

[69] *Abidus* city of Asia, opposite the city of Sestus in Europe, separated from each other by a narrow strait, the Hellespont (now called the Dardanelles).

To hazard more than for the Golden Fleece.[70]
Fair Cynthia wished his arms might be her sphere;[71]
Grief makes her pale, because she moves not there.
His body was as straight as Circe's wand;
Jove might have sipped out nectar from his hand.[72]
Even as delicious meat is to the tast,[73]
So was his neck in touching, and surpast[74]
The white of Pelops' shoulder: I could tell ye,
How smooth his breast was, and how white his belly,
And whose immortal fingers did imprint
That heavenly path with many a curious dint,
That runs along his back; but my rude pen
Can hardly blazon forth the loves of men,[75]
Much less of powerful gods: let it suffice
That my slack muse sings of Leander's eyes,
Those orient cheeks and lips, exceeding his
That leapt into the water for a kiss
Of his own shadow, and despising many,
Died ere he could enjoy the love of any.[76]
Had wild Hippolytus Leander seen,
Enamoured of his beauty had he been:
His presence made the rudest peasant melt,
That in the vast uplandish country dwelt;
The barbarous Thracian soldier, moved with naught,[77]
Was moved with him, and for his favour sought.
Some swore he was a maid in man's attire,
For in his looks were all that men desire,
A pleasant smiling cheek, a speaking eye,[78]
A brow for love to banquet royally;
And such as knew he was a man would say,
'Leander, thou art made for amorous play:

70 *And … Fleece* Jason (Glossary).

71 *Cynthia* Diana; Endymion (Glossary); *sphere*: i.e., in place of the circuit of the moon over which Diana has control as its goddess.

72 *Jove … hand* 'Jove and Ganymede' (Glossary). Ganymede served Jove nectar in a cup, but Lysander could serve it more intimately out of his cupped hand.

73 *tast* i.e., taste.

74 *surpast* surpassed.

75 *blazon* describe fitly.

76 *exceeding … any* Narcissus (Glossary).

77 *barbarous Thracian* ancient type of savagery: war-loving, drunken, and licentious.

78 *speaking* highly expressive.

Why art thou not in love, and loved of all?
Though thou be fair, yet be not thine own thrall.'[79]

[*Leander swims the Hellespont,*[80] *attracting Neptune's attention.*]

[…]

With that he stripped him to the ivory skin,
And crying, 'Love, I come,' leapt lively in.
Whereat the sapphire-visaged god grew proud,[81]
And made his cap'ring Triton sound aloud,[82]
Imagining that Ganymede, displeased,
Had left the heavens; therefore on him he seized.
Leander strived, the waves about him wound,
And pulled him to the bottom, where the ground
Was strewed with pearl, and in low coral groves
Sweet singing mermaids sported with their loves
On heaps of heavy gold, and took great pleasure
To spurn in careless sort the shipwreck treasure.
For here the stately azure palace stood,
Where kingly Neptune and his train abode.
The lusty god embraced him, called him 'love',
And swore he never should return to Jove.
But when he knew it was not Ganymed,
For underwater he was almost dead,
He heaved him up, and looking on his face
Beat down the bold waves with his triple mace,
Which mounted up, intending to have kissed him,
And fell in drops like tears because they missed him.
Leander being up, began to swim,
And looking back, saw Neptune follow him;
Whereat aghast, the poor soul 'gan to cry,
'Oh, let me visit Hero ere I die.'
The god put Helle's bracelet on his arm,[83]
And swore the sea should never do him harm.
He clapped his plump cheeks, with his tresses played,

[79] *thrall* slave.

[80] *Hellespont* See **n69** and **n83**.

[81] *sapphire-visaged god* Neptune, god of the sea.

[82] *Triton* son of Neptune, usually depicted blowing on a conch-shell.

[83] *Helle*, daughter of King Athamas of Thebes. Fleeing her stepmother's persecution, Helle fell into the sea from the back of her flying golden ram, and was drowned; the Hellespont was named after her.

And smiling wantonly, his love bewrayed.[84]
He watched his arms, and as they opened wide,
At every stroke, betwixt them would he slide,
And steal a kiss, and then run out and dance,
And as he turned, cast many a lustful glance,
And threw him gaudy toys to please his eye,
And dive into the water, and there pry
Upon his breast, his thighs, and every limb,
And up again, and close beside him swim,
And talk of love. Leander made reply,
'You are deceived, I am no woman, I'
Thereat smiled Neptune, and then told a tale,
How that a shepherd sitting in a vale
Played with a boy so fair and kind,
As for his love both earth and heaven pined;
That of the cooling river durst not drink,
Lest water-nymphs should pull him from the brink.[85]
And when he sported in the fragrant lawns,
Goat-footed satyrs and upstaring fauns
Would steal him thence. Ere half this tale was done,
'Aye me,' Leander cried, 'th' enamoured sun,
That now should shine on Thetis' glassy bower,
Descends upon my radiant Hero's tower:
Oh that these tardy arms of mine were wings!'
And as he spake, upon the waves he springs.
Neptune was angry that he gave no ear,
And in his heart revenging malice bare:
He flung at him his mace, but as it went,[86]
He called it in, for love made him repent.
The mace returning back his own hand hit,
As meaning to be 'venged for darting it.
When this fresh bleeding wound Leander viewed,
His colour went and came, as if he rued
The grief which Neptune felt. In gentle breasts
Relenting thoughts, remorse, and pity rests.
And who have hard hearts and obdurate minds
But vicious, hare-brained, and illit'rate hinds?[87]
The god seeing him with pity to be moved,

84 *bewrayed* revealed.
85 *tale … brink* 'Hercules and Hylas' (Glossary).
86 *mace* three-pronged trident.
87 *hind* peasant.

Thereon concluded that he was beloved.
(Love is too full of faith, too credulous,
With folly and false hope deluding us.)
Wherefore, Leander's fancy to surprise,
To the rich ocean for gifts he flies:
'Tis wisdom to give much, a gift prevails,
When deep persuading oratory fails.

[…]

8.8

From BL Harley MS 6848, ff. 185–6[88]

8.8.1 A Note Containing the Opinion of Christopher Marly[89] Concerning his Damnable Judgement of Religion, and Scorn of God's Word

[…]

That the first beginning of religion was only to keep men in awe.

[…]

That Christ was a bastard and his mother dishonest.

That he was the son of a carpenter, and that if the Jews among whom he was born did crucify him they best knew him and whence he came.

[…]

That if there be any god or any good religion, then it is in the papists, because the service of God is performed with more ceremonies, as elevation of the mass, organs, singing men, shaven crowns, etc.[90] That all Protestants are hypocritical asses.

That if he were put to write a new religion, he would undertake both a more excellent and admirable method and that all the New Testament is filthily written.

88 Reprinted by permission of the British Library.

89 *Marly* Marlowe.

90 *elevation of the mass* raising of the host at the consecration; *shaven crowns*: tonsure of monks and other religious.

That the woman of Samaria and her sister[91] were whores and that Christ knew them dishonestly.

That St John the Evangelist was bedfellow to Christ and leaned always in his bosom,[92] that he used him as the sinners of Sodom.

That all they that love not tobacco and boys were fools.

[...]

These things, with many other, shall by good and honest witness be approved to be his opinions and common speeches and that this Marlowe doth not only hold them himself, but almost into every company he cometh he persuades men to atheism, willing them not to be afeared of bugbears and hobgoblins,[93] and utterly scorning both God and his ministers, as I, Richard Baines, will justify and approve both by mine oath and the testimony of many honest men [...] all men in Christianity ought to endeavour that the mouth of so dangerous a member may be stopped. [...]

RICHARD BAINES

John Marston (1576–1634), writer

Educated at Oxford (BA, 1594) and the Middle Temple, Marston wrote an early volume of verse (1598) – including imitations of Ovid and Juvenal – that was publicly burned under the Bishops' Ban of 1599. Famous today for his Italianate revenge tragedies and the influential social satire *The Malcontent* (c. 1603), Marston stopped writing plays for the public theatre about a year after being imprisoned for his part in a stage satire of the Scots that had angered James I. Ordained a minister in 1609, Marston served his parish from 1616 to 1631, then retired to London.

91 Jesus encounters the *woman of Samaria* at a well, and she believes in him after he tells her 'all that [she] ever did' (Jn. 4.39).

92 *St John the Evangelist* writer of the fourth gospel, traditionally identified with that gospel's unnamed 'beloved disciple' who 'leaned on [Jesus's] breast' (Jn 13.25; 21.20).

93 *bugbears* and *hobgoblins* childish objects of needless dread.

8.9

From *The Scourge of Villainy* (1598)

8.9.1 Satire 3[1]

[...]

O grievous misery!
Luscus hath left his female luxury.[2]
Aye, it left him; No, his old Cynic Dad[3]
Hath forced him clean forsake his Pickhatch drab.[4]
Alack, alack, what piece of lustful flesh
Hath Luscus left, his Priape to redress?[5]
Grieve not, good soul, he hath his Ganymed,
His perfumed she-goat, smooth combed and high fed.
At Hogsdon now his monstrous lust he feasts,[6]
For there he keepes a bawdy-house of beasts.
Paphus, let Luscus have his courtesan,[7]
Or we shall have a monster of a man.
Tut, Paphus now detains him from that bower,
And clasps him close within his brick-built tower.[8]
Diogenes, th'art damned for thy lewd wit,
For Luscus now hath skill to practise it.
Faith, what cares he for fair Cynedian boys?[9]
Velvet capped goats, Dutch mares? tut, common toys.[10]
Detain them all, on this condition

[1] Lines 33–82. The satire focuses on miserly fathers and their spendthrift, sexually licentious heirs.

[2] *Luscus* Latin, 'with one eye closed'.

[3] *Cynic* Greek philosophical school, popularly known for both its asceticism and its founder Diogenes' indulgence in shameless (and sometimes public) masturbation.

[4] *Pickhatch* London district notorious for prostitution; *drab*: whore, prostitute.

[5] *Priape* erect penis.

[6] *Hogsdon* Hoxton, just outside the City of London: popular place for lovers' trysts (embedded pun = 'Hog's den').

[7] *Paphus* The Greek sculptor Pygmalion fell in love with a female statue of his own creation (Galatea); Venus brought her to life; they wed, and had a son, Paphos (named after one of Venus's epithets).

[8] *clasps … tower* Danae (Glossary).

[9] *Cynedian boys* cinaedi (here, boys kept to sexually pleasure their masters).

[10] *toys* diversions.

He may but use the Cynic friction.[11]
  O now ye male stews, I can give pretence[12]
For your luxurious incontinence.
Hence, hence, ye falsed, seeming patriots,
Return not with pretence of salving spots,
When here ye soil us with impurity
And monstrous filth of Doway seminary.[13]
What though Iberia yield you liberty,[14]
To snort in source of Sodom villainy?
What though the blooms of young nobility,
Committed to your Rodon's custody,
Ye Nero-like abuse? yet near approach,[15]
Your new St Homer's lewdness here to broach.[16]
Tainting our towns, and hopeful academes,
With your lust-bating most abhorrèd means.
  Valladolid, our Athens 'gins to taste
Of thy rank filth: camphire and lettuce chaste[17]
Are clean cashiered now Sophi ringoes eat;
Candied potatoes are Athenians' meat.[18]
Hence holy-thistle, come sweet marrow pie,[19]
Inflame our backs to itching luxury.
A crab's baked guts, a lobster's buttered thigh,

[11] *Diogenes ... friction* See **n3**.

[12] *stews* prostitutes; *give pretence*: offer rationalizations.

[13] *Doway seminary* Roman Catholic seminary in Douai, France. Englishmen trained there as priests, returning home to reconvert Protestants; *falsed* and *seeming patriots*, they aim to heal the stain of heresy (*salving the spots*), but are really hypocrites and sodomites; *seminary*: college for training Roman Catholic priests, but also a 'seed-plot' (buried pun on 'seed' as 'semen'?).

[14] *Iberia* Spain, Europe's most powerful Catholic nation; both Spain and Italy were thought hotbeds of sodomy.

[15] *What ... abuse?* Rhodon, traitorous tutor of Cleopatra's son, Caesarion, either murdered Caesarion, or gave him up to Octavius Caesar. Like Rhodon and Nero (with his favourites), young nobles' priestly tutors sodomize and betray their charges.

[16] *St Homer* Saint-Omer, Jesuit school for sons of English Catholics.

[17] i.e., *our Athens* is either Oxford or Cambridge, which imitates the perversions of Catholic seminaries such as the Continental Catholic college *Valladolid*, and religious orders; *camphire* (camphor) *and lettuce*: cold vegetables (anti-aphrodisiacs).

[18] *clean cashiered* completely rejected; *now*: i.e., now that; *Sophi*: Cambridge undergraduates; *ringoes* (eryngo, candied root of the sea holly) and *candied potato* (yam): aphrodisiacs.

[19] *holy-thistle* antidote for certain poisons; heart-strengthener; *marrow*: beef marrow (sexual restorative).

I hear them swear is blood for venery.[20]
Had I some snout-fair brats, they should endure[21]
The new found Castilian callenture,[22]
Before some pedant-tutor in his bed
Should use my fry like Phrygian Ganymed.[23]
Nay then chaste cells, when greasy Aretine
For his rank 'fico', is surnamed divine:[24]
Nay then come all ye venial scapes to me,[25]
I dare well warrant you'll absolvèd be.

[...]

William Shakespeare (1564–1616), playwright and poet

Apart from writing the most famous plays in English literature, Shakespeare produced the narrative poems *Venus and Adonis* (1593) and *The Rape of Lucrece* (1594), as well as *Sonnets*. Some of Shakespeare's individual sonnets were clearly circulating in manuscript by 1598, but *Sonnets* itself was not published until 1609. Of the sequence's 154 sonnets, the first 126 address a young man, the rest a woman. *Sonnets* has long been assumed autobiographical and its figures have been variously identified: the young man, for instance, as Shakespeare's known patrons, Henry Wriothesley, Third Earl of Southampton, and William Herbert, Third Earl of Pembroke (to the former Shakespeare dedicated *Lucrece* and *Venus and Adonis*); the woman, the so-called 'dark lady', as Mary Fitton, courtier and mistress of William Herbert, and Aemilia Lanyer, poet and mistress of Henry Carey, First Baron Hunsdon.

Online Companion
From Shakespeare's *Coriolanus* (c. 1608)

[20] *Crabs* and *lobsters* aphrodisiacs; *venery*: sexual lust or activity.
[21] *snout-fair* fair of face (always with contemptuous overtones).
[22] *Castilian* Spanish; *calenture*: tropical disease: delirious sufferers saw the ocean as a green field, into which they tried to leap.
[23] *fry* children.
[24] *greasy Aretine ... divine* Aretino (Glossary); *fico*: obscene gesture.
[25] *venial scapes* minor errors.

8.10

From *Sonnets* (1609)

8.10.1 Sonnet 20

A woman's face with Nature's own hand painted[1]
Hast thou, the master mistress of my passion;[2]
A woman's gentle heart, but not acquainted[3]
With shifting change, as is false women's fashion;[4]
An eye more bright than theirs, less false in rolling,[5]
Gilding the object whereupon it gazeth;[6]
A man in hue, all hues in his controlling,[7]
Which steals men's eyes and women's souls amazeth;
And for a woman wert thou first created,
Till Nature as she wrought thee fell a-doting,[8]
And by addition me of thee defeated,[9]
By adding one thing to my purpose nothing:[10]
  But since she pricked thee out for women's pleasure,[11]
  Mine be thy love, and thy love's use their treasure.[12]

[1] *painted* with connotations of falsity; 'painting' (applying cosmetics) disguises a woman's flaws and enhances her assets; referring to woman's natural 'two-facedness'.

[2] *master mistress* The young man is 'double gendered' throughout the sequence; often feminized, he is also a womanizer and thus the 'master' of many 'mistresses'. Cf. **n21–3** and **n56**.

[3] *acquainted* buried pun on *quaint* (cunt).

[4] *shifting change* (1) woman's changeability; (2) woman's changing of clothes and her vain fascination with fashion.

[5] A *rolling* eye was a sign of untrustworthiness.

[6] *gilding* covering base metal with a thin gold leaf; same connotations as 'painting' (cf. **n1**).

[7] *hue* external appearance; expression.

[8] *fell a-doting* became infatuated [with].

[9] *and .... defeated* The 'addition' is the young man's penis. by making him a man, Nature deprives the speaker of the ability to consummate his sexual desire.

[10] *By ... nothing* The 'one thing' is again the young man's penis. Since 'nothing' was also a common slang term for the female genitalia, the speaker suggests that the young man's penis is for his purposes actually very important: as the equivalent of the female genitalia (*nothing*), the young man's penis represents the possibility of sexual consummation between the two.

[11] *pricked* selected (playing on 'prick', as 'penis').

[12] *thy ... treasure* i.e., let women enjoy you sexually so as to produce children (*treasure*).

8.10.2 Sonnet 29

When in disgrace with Fortune and men's eyes
I all alone beweep my outcast state,
And trouble deaf heaven with my bootless cries,[13]
And look upon myself and curse my fate,
Wishing me like to one more rich in hope,
Featured like him, like him with friends possessed,
Desiring this man's art and that man's scope,[14]
With what I most enjoy contented least;
Yet in these thoughts myself almost despising,
Haply I think on thee, and then my state,[15]
Like to the lark at break of day arising
From sullen earth sings hymns at heaven's gate;
   For thy sweet love remembered such wealth brings,
   That then I scorn to change my state with kings.

8.10.3 Sonnet 40[16]

Take all my loves, my love, yea, take them all;[17]
What hast thou then more than thou hadst before?
No love, my love, that thou mayst true love call;
All mine was thine before thou hadst this more.
Then if for my love thou my love receivest,[18]
I cannot blame thee for my love thou usest;[19]
But yet be blamed, if thou this self deceivest[20]
By wilful taste of what thyself refusest.[21]
I do forgive thy robb'ry, gentle thief,
Although thou steal thee all my poverty;

[13] *bootless* useless.

[14] *art* skill; *scope*: mental powers.

[15] *haply* by chance; *state*: condition.

[16] The young man has betrayed the speaker by sleeping with the speaker's mistress.

[17] *take* the modern meaning, but probably also, 'seize sexual possession of'.

[18] *for my love* in return for or (perhaps) in place of my love.

[19] *usest* often employed in a sexual sense in *Sonnets* (cf. **8.10.1 line 14**), here 'my love thou usest' means both 'you are having sex with my love or mistress' and (consequently) 'you abuse my love for and devotion to you'.

[20] *this self* in some editions, 'thy self'.

[21] By indulging in illicit sex but refusing marital intercourse, the young man is acting selfishly and obstinately; but perhaps, also, the speaker reproaches the young man for refusing to have sex with him, but doing so eagerly with the speaker's mistress.

And yet love knows it is a greater grief
To bear love's wrong than hate's known injury.
   Lascivious grace, in whom all ill well shows,
   Kill me with spites; yet we must not be foes.

8.10.4 Sonnet 41

Those pretty wrongs that liberty commits[22]
When I am sometime absent from thy heart,
Thy beauty and thy years full well befits,
For still temptation follows where thou art.
Gentle thou art, and therefore to be won;[23]
Beauteous thou art, therefore to be assailed;[24]
And when a woman woos, what woman's son
Will sourly leave her till he have prevailed?[25]
Ay me, but yet thou mightst my seat forbear,[26]
And chide thy beauty and thy straying youth,
Who lead thee in their riot even there[27]
Where thou art forced to break a twofold truth:[28]
   Hers, by thy beauty tempting her to thee,
   Thine, by thy beauty being false to me.

8.10.5 Sonnet 42

That thou hast her it is not all my grief,[29]
And yet it may be said I loved her dearly;
That she hath thee is of my wailing chief,
A loss in love that touches me more nearly.[30]
Loving offenders, thus I will excuse ye:

[22] *pretty* childish, innocent (usually used of women and boys); *liberty*: condition of being unrestrained; with sexual connotations: 'lasciviousness'.

[23] *gentle* Cf. the young man's 'gentle heart' (see **8.10.1 line 3**). Proverbial, 'All women may be won' (Tilley, W681).

[24] *assailed* wooed on all sides.

[25] *prevailed* with sexual connotations: 'successfully have intercourse with'.

[26] *seat* female genitalia, particularly when it is the 'property' of a particular man; the youth has appropriated the speaker's sexual 'place'.

[27] *riot* debauchery; *even there*: the mistress's genitalia.

[28] *twofold truth* the young man's friendship and love to the speaker, and the mistress's constancy or promise of love to the speaker.

[29] *hast* sexually possesses.

[30] *touches ... nearly* affects me far more deeply.

Thou dost love her, because thou know'st I love her,
And for my sake even so doth she abuse me,
Suff'ring my friend for my sake to approve her.[31]
If I lose thee, my loss is my love's gain,
And losing her, my friend hath found that loss;
Both find each other, and I lose both twain,
And both for my sake lay on me this cross:[32]
  But here's the joy: my friend and I are one;
  Sweet flattery! Then she loves but me alone.

8.10.6 Sonnet 53

What is your substance, whereof are you made,
That millions of strange shadows on you tend?[33]
Since every one hath, every one, one shade,
And you, but one, can every shadow lend.[34]
Describe Adonis, and the counterfeit[35]
Is poorly imitated after you;
On Helen's cheek all art of beauty set,
And you in Grecian tires are painted new.[36]
Speak of the spring, and foison of the year;[37]
The one doth shadow of your beauty show,[38]
The other as your bounty doth appear,[39]
And you in every blessèd shape we know.
  In all external grace you have some part,
  But you like none, none you, for constant heart.

8.10.7 Sonnet 57

Being your slave, what should I do but tend[40]
Upon the hours and times of your desire?

[31] *suff'ring* allowing; *approve*: commend; also, 'experience [her] sexually'.
[32] *cross* extreme sorrow.
[33] *shadows* in Platonic terms, the external realities of the world emanating from their perfect ideas or forms (their 'substance').
[34] *lend* The young man gives each shadow its being and attributes.
[35] *counterfeit* imitation.
[36] *tires* garments.
[37] *foison* abundance.
[38] *one* spring; *shadow*: image.
[39] *other* autumn (the time of foison).
[40] *tend* wait.

I have no precious time at all to spend,
Nor services to do, till you require.
Nor dare I chide the world-without-end hour[41]
Whilst I, my sovereign, watch the clock for you,
Nor think the bitterness of absence sour[42]
When you have bid your servant once adieu.
Nor dare I question with my jealous thought[43]
Where you may be, or your affairs suppose,[44]
But, like a sad slave, stay and think of naught
Save where you are how happy you make those.
   So true a fool is love that in your will,[45]
   Though you do anything, he thinks no ill.

8.10.8 Sonnet 61[46]

Is it thy will thy image should keep open
My heavy eyelids to the weary night?
Dost thou desire my slumbers should be broken
While shadows like to thee do mock my sight?[47]
Is it thy spirit that thou send'st from thee
So far from home into my deeds to pry,[48]
To find out shames and idle hours in me,
The scope and tenor of thy jealousy?[49]
Oh no, thy love, though much, is not so great;
It is my love that keeps mine eye awake,
Mine own true love that doth my rest defeat,
To play the watchman ever for thy sake.
   For thee watch I, whilst thou dost wake elsewhere,
   From me far off, with others all too near.

[41] *world-without-end* seemingly endless (referring to the last line of the doxology).

[42] *nor think* I do not dare think.

[43] *question* dispute.

[44] *suppose* guess at.

[45] *will* desire (with the obvious pun on the poet's name, common throughout *Sonnets*).

[46] The lover's troubling dream of the beloved is a common Petrarchan and romance trope.

[47] *mock* tantalize.

[48] *home* body ('home' of the young man's spirit).

[49] *scope* and *tenor* defined limits and purpose or aim.

8.10.9 Sonnet 93

So shall I live, supposing thou art true,[50]
Like a deceivèd husband; so love's face
May still seem love to me, though altered new,
Thy looks with me, thy heart in other place.
For there can live no hatred in thine eye,
Therefore in that I cannot know thy change.
In many's looks, the false heart's history
Is writ in moods and frowns and wrinkles strange,
But heaven in thy creation did decree
That in thy face sweet love should ever dwell;
Whate'er thy thoughts or thy heart's workings be,
Thy looks should nothing thence but sweetness tell.
  How like Eve's apple doth thy beauty grow,[51]
  If thy sweet virtue answer not thy show.[52]

8.10.10 Sonnet 98

From you have I been absent in the spring,
When proud-pied April, dressed in all his trim,[53]
Hath put a spirit of youth in everything,
That heavy Saturn laughed and leaped with him.[54]
Yet nor the lays of birds nor the sweet smell[55]
Of different flowers in odour and in hue
Could make me any summer's story tell,
Or from their proud lap pluck them where they grew;
Nor did I wonder at the lily's white,
Nor praise the deep vermilion in the rose;[56]
They were but sweet, but figures of delight,

[50] *so* i.e., in the way defined in Sonnet 92, in a state of blessed (and perhaps self-willed) ignorance concerning the youth's faithlessness; *supposing*: believing.

[51] *Eve's apple* fruit that tempted Eve for its beauty and desirability (Gen. 3.6); plucking and eating it against God's command led to humanity's expulsion from Paradise, and its fall into sin and death.

[52] *show* outer beauty; physical beauty should reflect a person's character (a Neoplatonic commonplace).

[53] *pied* multi-coloured.

[54] *Saturn* god and planet associated with winter, ageing, and disaster.

[55] *lays* songs.

[56] *Nor … rose* The *lily* and the *rose* are conventional emblems of the ideal colours of the Petrarchan mistress's perfect complexion.

Drawn after you, you pattern of all those.
  Yet seemed it winter still, and, you away,
  As with your shadow I with these did play.[57]

8.10.11 Sonnet 104

To me, fair friend, you never can be old,
For as you were when first your eye I eyed,
Such seems your beauty still. Three winters cold
Have from the forests shook three summers' pride,
Three beauteous springs to yellow autumn turned
In process of the seasons have I seen;
Three April perfumes in three hot Junes burned,
Since first I saw you fresh, which yet art green.
Ah, yet doth beauty, like a dial hand,[58]
Steal from his figure, and no pace perceived;
So your sweet hue, which methinks still doth stand,
Hath motion, and mine eye may be deceived;
  For fear of which, hear this, thou age unbred:[59]
  Ere you were born was beauty's summer dead.

8.10.12 Sonnet 126[60]

O thou, my lovely boy, who in thy pow'r
Dost hold Time's fickle glass, his sickle hour,[61]
Who hast by waning grown, and therein show'st
Thy lover's withering as thy sweet self grow'st;
If Nature, sovereign mistress over wrack,[62]
As thou goest onwards still will pluck thee back,[63]
She keeps thee to this purpose: that her skill
May Time disgrace and wretched minutes kill.[64]

57 *play* frolic; hinting at 'sexual activity'.
58 *dial* clock.
59 *age unbred* the future.
60 The last poem in Shakespeare's *Sonnets* addressing the young man.
61 *Time's glass* is *fickle* because its sands are always moving and shifting; it has a *sickle hour*, since Time causes things to grow towards ripeness, only to then destroy them (as the harvest is mown down with the reaper's scythe or *sickle*).
62 *wrack* ruin, decay.
63 *goest onwards* ages; *pluck thee back*: maintain thee [in thy present beauty].
64 *Time disgrace* i.e., show him he is not supreme.

Yet fear her, O thou minion of her pleasure![65]
She may detain, but not still keep, her treasure.
Her audit, though delayed, answered must be,
And her quietus is to render thee.[66]
( )
( )[67]

Barnabe Barnes (1571–1609), writer

Educated at Oxford, connected with the Essex faction at court, and later charged with but not prosecuted for attempted murder, Barnes produced only four works: the sonnet sequence *Parthenophil and Parthenophe* (1593), a collection of religious lyrics (1595), a translation of Cicero's *Offices* ('On Duties') (1606), and the Italianate tragedy *The Devil's Charter* (1607).

8.11

From *The Devil's Charter* (1607)

[Having sold his soul to the Devil, Pope Alexander VI plots to conquer Europe, while his children Caesar and Lucrezia engage in fratricide, murder, and adultery. Meanwhile, Alexander sexually pursues the political hostage Astor Manfredi, keeping 'the pearl of Italy, / [...] that virtuous young prince, / In beastly lust, and filthy sodomy'. In order to seize his reluctant young lover's estates, Alexander murders Astor and Astor's brother, Phillippo. Soon after, in a mix-up of bottles engineered by the Devil, Alexander finds himself poisoned by the wine he has meant for others. After a lengthy death-scene, Alexander is dragged off to hell.]

65 *minion* absolute dependant (often with sexual overtones).

66 *quietus* payment of [her] debt [to Time].

67 These two empty lines bracketed by parentheses occur in the original edition. The sonnet is truncated, only twelve lines long instead of the usual fourteen. For a summary of the various interpretations of these parentheses related to the themes of death, debt and repayment (echoing the language of accountancy in the sonnet), see *Shakespeare's Sonnets*, ed. K. Duncan-Jones (New York, 1997), p. 126 n12.

8.11.1 Act 3, scene 1

Enter ASTOR MANFREDI *with* PHILLIPPO.

ASTOR. [...] my life within the court of Rome,
Is much more loathsome to my soul than death,
And liberty more grief than servitude.
PHILLIPPO. I rather choose within the river Tiber
To drown myself, or from Tarpeyan hill[1]
My vexèd body to precipitate,
Than to subject my body to the shame
Of such viled, brutish, and unkindly lust.[2]
ASTOR. He that with fire and brimstone did consume
Sodom and other cities round about,[3]
Deliver us from this soul-slaying sin,
To which our bodies are made prostitute.

[Pope Alexander's right-hand man, Barnardo, enters with a summons for Astor.]

ASTOR. I was now going to Our Lady's mass,[4]
In Saint John Lateran's, where my ghostly father[5]
Attendeth me for my confession.
But thank his Holiness on my behalf,
In all due reverence and humility.
Tell him I mean – so soon as I return, [*Pause.*
To come according to my bounden duty. [*Exit* BARNARDO.
My case is desperate; what shall I do?
Phillippo, was there ever any man
Hunted with such unsatisfied rage?
PHILLIPPO. What, hath he sent again to visit you?
ASTOR. To visit me, nay to dishonour me!
Behold this ruby sent from his own finger,
Which as a bawd inviteth me to shame.[6]

[...]

1 *Tarpeyan hill* Roman rock-face, from which traitors were thrown to their deaths.
2 *viled* vile; *unkindly*: the modern sense, and 'unnatural'.
3 *He ... about* See **1.1.1**.
4 *Our Lady's mass* Roman Catholic service devoted to the Virgin Mary.
5 *ghostly father* priest who serves as an individual's spiritual director.
6 *bawd* pimp.

8.11.2 Act 3, scene 2

ALEXANDER *out of a casement.*

ALEXANDER. Astor? what, Astor? my delight, my joy,
My star, my triumph, my sweet fantasy,[7]
My more than son, my love, my concubine,
Let me behold those bright stars, my joy's treasure;
Those glorious well-attempered tender cheeks;[8]
That specious forehead like a lane of lilies;[9]
That seemly nose, love's chariot triumphant,
Breathing Panchaian odours to my senses;[10]
That gracious mouth, betwixt whose crimosin pillou[11]
Venus and Cupid sleeping kiss together;
That chin, the ball vowed to the queen of beauty,[12]
Now budding, ready to bring forth love blossoms:[13]
Astor Manfredi, turn thee to my love.
Come hither, Astor, we must talk above.
ASTOR. Betrayed? A slave to sin? What shall I say?
Most Holy Father——
ALEXANDER. Do not me forget:
I am thy brother, and thy dearest friend,
And though in age I love, know that desire
In riper years is pure and permanent,
Grounded on judgement, flowing from pure love:
Whereas the love lightning from young desire,
Fickle and feeble, will not long hold fire;
It is so violent it will not last.
They're blest whose lovers love when youth is past.
ASTOR. To call you 'friend' were too familiar,
To call you 'brother' sorts not with our years:
To call you 'father' doth import some fear,
Due to that age your Holiness doth bear.
ALEXANDER. Tell me not of mine age and holiness;

7 *star* punning on the meaning of 'Astor' (derived from the Greek for 'star').

8 *well-attempered* well-blended (the traditional white and red of the Petrarchan mistress's perfect complexion).

9 *specious* beautiful.

10 *Panchaian* part of Arabia, famed for its perfumes.

11 *crimosin pillou* crimson pillows (Astor's red lips).

12 *the … beauty* Paris (Glossary).

13 *love blossoms* Astor's first beard growth.

Thy sight sufficeth me to make me young.
Neither upbraid me with my sanctimony,
Love is the purest essence from above,
And to thy soul I would affix my love.
Come hither then and rest with me tonight;
Give me fruition of those amorous pits,
Where blinded Cupid close in ambush sits,
Who with his arrow (when thou laughed at Venus)
Shot through thy smiling cheeks, and did enchain us.
Thy chamber with ambrosial odours breatheth,
New loves and true loves unto them that entreateth,
And furious Mars made mild his faulcheon sheatheth[14]
At thy delicious aspect. See thy chamber:
The walls are made of roses, roof of lilies;
Be not ashamed to mount and venture it.
Here Cupid's altar, and fair Venus' hill is.[15]
Thy bed is made with spice and calamus,
With sinamond and spicnard Arabic,
With opobalsam and rich gums of Egypt;[16]
Music angelical of strings and voices,
With sundry birds in sugared symphony,
Where whistling wood-nymphs, and the pleasant choice is
Of antique action mixed with harmony,
Attend thy joyous entrance to this chamber.

PHILLIPPPO. Is it possible that the Devil can be so sweet a dissembler?

ASTOR. Yes, and play the pleasant part of a conceited amoret,[17]
For he can take the shape of a bright angel.

ALEXANDER. Now my sweet friend the joys of love doth mutter.
Thy mind too bashful is: speak, tongue; loves utter.
Thy coral gums cud love's pure quintessence,[18]
And thou thyself, fair boy, love's purest essence.

ASTOR. O blessed heavens, let Satan tempt no longer!
His force is powerful, yet thy strength much stronger,
He that with guileful baits' gilded untruth
So seeks to blast the blossom of my youth.

[14] *faulcheon* sword.

[15] *Venus' hill* with the obvious play on *mons Veneris* (Latin, 'the female pubic mound').

[16] *Calamus, sinamond* [cinnamon], *spicnard Arabic, opobalsam* [opobalsamum] and *gums* fragrant substances used in perfumes and oils.

[17] *amoret* sweetheart; wanton girl.

[18] *cud love's pure quintessence* speak words? chews his lips? (*cud* is an unusual word in the context).

ALEXANDER. Delicious fruits, divine confections,
Of herbs, roots, flowers of sundry fashions,
Preservatives drawn from the rich elixir,
Of finest gold, pure pearl, and precious stones,
Provided for thy divine appetite,
Wines of more price (made by th'industrious art,
In sacred distillations) than that nectar
Which Hebe bore, when Jove did most affect her.
PHILLIPPO. Satan, false god of lies and flattery!
How palpable is this gross villainy?
ALEXANDER. What, wilt thou come Manfredi to my chamber,
And bless me with thy precious breath of amber?[19]
ASTOR. After Our Lady's mass I will return.
Dear God, what furies in his soul do burn?
After the celebration of the mass,
I come, my lord. [*Exeunt* ASTOR *and* PHILLIPPO.
ALEXANDER. Come then, and let that pass.
Holla Barnardo! [ALEXANDER *tinkleth a bell.*
All business for this night I will adjourn.
Give good attendance that at his return
Astor may come to me, for my sick heart,
Till Astor with his beautiful embrace
Do bless my body – wounded with his dart –,
Can find no rest; love hath it in hot chase.

8.11.3 Act 4, scene 5

[Alexander has had the youths drugged.]

[ALEXANDER] [...] Sleep both secure upon your fatal bed.
Now that the god of silence, Morpheus,[20]
Hath with his signet of black horn sealed up[21]
Your languid eyelids loaden with pale death,
Sleep until you draw your latest breath.[22]
Poor, harmless boys, strangers to sin and evil,
Oh, were my soul as innocent as yours!

[19] *amber* ambergris (sperm whale extract used in perfumes).

[20] *Morpheus* god of sleep.

[21] *signet* seal [of authority]; *horn*: Morpheus's horn and ivory box of dreams; the black horn symbolized bad dreams, the white ivory, good.

[22] *latest* last.

This office is of highest consequence:[23]
In friendship, for I consider it,
I send you from a million of sorrows,
Into the flow'ry fields of Paradise,
There to go 'habit in the groves of myrtle,[24]
To feed on manna and to drink pure nectar,[25]
A cup of everlasting happiness;
Where such sweet music unconceivable,
Shall entertain your senses in sweet comfort,
As the delight thereof shall never die.

[...]

[*He stirreth and moveth them, opening both their bosoms.*[26]

[...]

Come out here now, you Cleopatra's birds,[27]
[*He draweth out of his boxes aspics.*[28]
Fed fat and plump with proud Egyptian slime
Of seven-mouthed Nilus, but now turned lean.
Take your repast upon these princely paps.[29]
[*He putteth to either of their breasts an aspic.*
Now Ptolemy's wife is highly magnified,[30]
Ensigning these fair, princely twins their death,[31]
And you my lovely boys, competitors
With Cleopatra, share in death and fate.
Now Charon stays his boat upon the strond,
And with a rugged forehead full of wrath
He thrusts a million from the shore of Styx
To give you waftage to the Elysian fields.[32]
I see their colours change and death sits heavy

[23] *office* the action Alexander is about to commit (the murder).
[24] *'habit* inhabit; *myrtle*: a plant sacred to Venus and an emblem of love.
[25] *manna* bread from heaven that sustained the wandering Israelites (Ex. 16.14–18); *nectar*: drink of the gods, sometimes said to convey immortality.
[26] *opening ... bosoms* He opens their shirts, exposing their chests.
[27] *birds* perhaps meant affectionately ('dear ones').
[28] *aspic* asp (poisonous serpent). Alexander copies Queen Cleopatra: she killed herself by applying asps to her breasts.
[29] *paps* nipples or breasts.
[30] *Ptolomy's wife* Cleopatra.
[31] *ensigning* instructing.
[32] *waftage* conveyance by boat.

On their fair foreheads with his leaden mace.
My birds are glutted with this sacrifice.
What now, proud worms? How tastes you princes' blood?
The slaves be plump and round. Into your nests.
[He taketh off the aspics and putteth them up in his box.
Is there no token of the serpents' draught?
All clear and safe. Well, now, fair boys, goodnight.

[...]

Lady Mary Wroth (?1587–1651/53), writer

Member of the literary Sidney family, Wroth produced several works, including the verse play *Love's Victory*, the sonnet sequence *Pamphilia to Amphilanthus*, and the prose romance *The Countess of Montgomery's Urania* (1621). Perceived as a roman-à-clef, *Urania*'s first part, with *Pamphilia to Amphilanthus* appended, was controversial. Sir Edward Denny, Baron of Waltham, complained that he was represented as the abusive Sirelius, and launched a vicious personal attack on Wroth. Like *Love's Victory*, *Urania*'s second part remained unpublished until the twentieth century. After the death of her husband, Wroth became the mother of two children by her cousin, William Herbert, Third Earl of Pembroke.

8.12

From *Urania* (Part I, 1621)

8.12.1 Book 1

[The page Allimarlus is on a quest to find the King of Romania's lost daughter, kidnapped on her way to her wedding. He encounters an old hermit, actually the Duke of Morea, who tells him the following story.]

'But weary at last of either,[1] as a hound will be who never so well loving hunting will at last take rest, so did I lie down at mine own home, determining to end my days in quiet plenteousness, taking my own delight, to add unto which I brought with me a virtuous lady, and such a one as might for goodness equal any of her rank and truly not unbeautiful. Yet so

[1] *either* i.e., the court and foreign travel.

much was I besotted on a young man, whom I had unfortunately chosen for my companion, as at last all delights and pastimes were to me tedious and loathsome if not liking or begun by him. Nay, my wife's company in respect of his was unpleasing to me.

Long time this continued, which continuance made me issueless,[2] wherefore I made him my heir, giving him all the present honour I could in my own power or by the favour of the king (who ever graced me much) procure him. But he, the son of wickedness, though adopted to me, esteeming possession far better than reversion,[3] gave place so much to covetousness as murder crept into credit to attain the profit, wherefore he practised[4] to make me away. My friends and kindred had before left me, expecting nothing but my ruin, seeing me so bewitched with my undoing. The plot was laid, and I thus betrayed where most I trusted.

The time being come for the execution, the hired man (being mine more for justness than his for rewards) came unto me, and upon promise of secrecy, discovered the truth unto me, making me besides promise to be persuaded by him, which was for some time to retire myself till a party were made in the country strong enough to pull down his pride, who had gained such power as he was grown more powerful than myself. Then might I be myself, and rule in safety.

I consented to the concealing, but never could be won to think of harming him whose ingratitude I believed sufficiently would one day burden him. But how often did I entreat and beseech him to perform his part, and satisfy his master in killing me, whose falseness and wickedness more grieved me than ten deaths (could I have suffered so many). Yet his honest care overruled me, and I submitted to his counsel.

Then took he my clothes, apparelling me fit for the change of my fortune. He, poor man, returning to my castle (for so till then it was), credibly reporting that I, going to swim – as often I did in this sweet river which runs along this valley – I was drowned, we being then in that place, and indeed the sweetest in the world. This in some kind was true (said he) for drowned I was in sorrow and tears, which could they have made a stream for bigness answerable to their swift falling, had questionless made his framed report true.

This being told, the duke, as then by my imagined death imaginarily he was, did make show of insupportable grief, being so possessed as he seemed disposed[5] of senses, furiously and suddenly stabbing the good man who for my life lost his own. This was counted a passionate act, love transporting

2 *issueless* childless.

3 *reversion* the right to inherit property.

4 *practised* plotted.

5 *disposed* dispossessed.

him so much beyond himself as he was not able to resist his own fury, while his devilish cunning did both set a gloss upon his brutishness and keep his treason unrevealed, the poor soul falling dead at his feet while he said, 'Take this for thy detested news-bringing.' Then did he make a solemn funeral for my dead mind, though living body. He apparelled himself and his court in mourning, which gave much content to the people who loved me, while indeed their black was but the true picture of his inward foulness.

My wife did presently retire to a house herself had built. But when he had (as he thought) sufficiently played with the people, he began to exercise his authority, beginning with my wife, picking a quarrel to bereave her of her estate, which he in short time did, turning her to seek her fortune. Patiently she took it. Having yet some jewels left her, she bought a little house in a thick and desert wood, where she was not long before I came unto her, discovering myself to both our equal passions of joy and sorrow. Privately we there continued many years, God in our poverty giving us an unexpected blessing, which was a daughter, who grew up and served us for a servant our means would not allow us, though our estates[6] required it.

[Seventeen years later, two princes, Amphilanthus and Parselius, discover the duke's plight. Parselius, Prince of Morea and son of the duke's overlord, intervenes.]

He[7] [...] commanded me the next day with my wife and daughter to attend him to the court, which fain[8] I would have refused, foreseeing that which soon after followed: the destruction of my once most-loved friend, who, though he had changed gratefulness to the contrary, and love to hate, yet my affection could not so much alter itself as to hate where once so earnestly I affected, or seek revenge on him whose good I ever wished.

But we obeyed. Then the sweet young prince presented me to his father, who instantly called me to mind, remembering many adventures which in our youths we had passed together, pitying my fortune as much as he had in younger days affected[9] me. Yet glad in some kind to recompense my faithful service to him, instantly sent for the usurper, who by reason of a journey the king made to see his realm and show it to his son before his departure, who was to go thence with his excellent cousin in a search by them undertaken, was come near to the place of the tyrant's abode. He refused to come, but soon by force he was brought before the king, who with mild fashion and royal majesty examined the business – which he confessed, but rather with a

6 *estates* social rank.
7 *he* Parselius.
8 *fain* willingly.
9 *affected* loved.

proud scorn than repentant heart. Wherefore the king, with just judgement, degraded[10] him, committing him to a strong tower whereinto he was walled up, meat given him in at the window and there to end his days, which were not long, pride swelling him so with scorn of his fall as he burst and died.

The dukedom after this sentence was restored to me; but truly I was not able to recover my former loss, wherefore humbly thanking the king and his son, besought them to give me leave to bestow it on my daughter, which was granted me, my wife, thinking she had seen enough when I was myself again, departing this life with joy and content. Besides, I made one suit more, which was that since the prince had with so much favour begun to honour me, it would please him to proceed so far as to bestow one of his young lords in marriage on my daughter. The king and prince both took this motion most kindly, wherefore choosing a hopeful young lord, and him the prince most loved, gave him to her.

[...]

This ended,[11] I went away, kissing the king's and prince's hands, undertaking a pilgrimage, which performed, I returned to this place where like a hermit still I live, and will continue while life is in me.' [...]

Michael Drayton (1563–1631), writer

Native of Warwickshire, Drayton was a prolific writer of pastoral eclogues, sonnets, lyrics, historical verse narratives, and *de casibus* tragedies (i.e., tragedies that depict the sudden fall of great men or women from the heights of wealth and power into despair and death); he also wrote a lengthy, influential verse description of England's topography, customs, and histories. Between approximately 1597 and 1604, Drayton also wrote and collaborated on some twenty plays.

Online Companion
From Drayton's *Piers Gaveston, Earl of Cornwall* (1593); from Francis Bacon's 'Of Beauty' (1625).

10 *degraded* reduced from high rank.

11 *This ended* i.e., his daughter's marriage and its attendant celebrations.

8.13

From *The Muses' Elizium* (1630)

8.13.1 David and Goliath

[...]

His curlèd tresses on his shoulders hung,
To which the dews at morn and eve so clung,
To the beholders that they did appear
As nature threaded pearl with every hair.
The bees and wasps, in wildernesses wild,
Have with his beauties often been beguiled,
Roses and lilies thinking they had seen,
But finding there they have deceivèd been,
Play with his eyes, which them that comfort bring,
That those two suns would shortly get a spring;
His lips in their pure coral liveries mock[1]
A row of pales cut from a crystal rock,[2]
Which stood within them, all of equal height.
From top to toe each limb so clean and straight,
By every joint of his that one might try,[3]
Or give true laws to perfect symmetry;
The vermin (oft) his sheep that would surprise
Became so charmed with th' splendour of his eyes,
That they forgot their ravine, and have lain
Down by his flocks [...]

[...]

Before grave Samuel David soon is brought,
Upon the prophet which most strongly wrought
When he beheld him beautiful and tall,
Of goodly presence, and well shaped withal,
His cheek a mixture of such red and white,[4]
As well with wonder might attract the sight,
A sprightful aspect, and so clear an eye,[5]

1 *mock* imitate.
2 *pales* posts.
3 *try* test.
4 *red and white* the traditional colours of the Petrarchan mistress's perfect complexion.
5 *sprightful* lively.

As shot a lightning at the standers-by,
His every gesture seen in it to bring
The majesty that might befit a king;

[...]

They him no sooner to Saul's presence bring,
But David's beauty so extremely took
The doting king, that in each glance or look,
He thought he saw high valour mixed with truth,
And near his person takes the lovely youth,
And who but David then with mighty Saul
His only favourite is, his all in all?

[...]

He caused an armour for him to be brought,[6]
But first of all a garment richly wrought
He puts upon the brave youth and then bad[7]
That in those goodly arms he should be clad;
Which put upon him as to stir he strives,
He thinks himself in manacles and guives,[8]
Their ponderousness him to the earth doth press;
These arms do make his activeness far less,
For he before had not been used to these,
Nor him at all their bois'trousness can please.
His gorget galled his neck, his chin beneath,[9]
And most extremely hindered him to breathe.
His curats sit too close upon his side;[10]
He in no hand his helmet can abide,
It is so heavy, and his temples wrings.
His pouldrons pinch him, and be cumbrous things,[11]
His gauntlets clumsy, and do wring his wrists,[12]
And be so stiff he cannot clutch his fists;
His guises they so strong and stubborn be[13]
That for his life he cannot bend his knee.

6 *he* Saul; *him*: David.
7 *bad* ordered.
8 *guives* shackles.
9 *gorget* throat armour.
10 *curats* cuirass: breast-plate and back-plate.
11 *pouldron* shoulder-plate.
12 *gauntlets* armoured gloves.
13 *guises* cuisses (thigh armour).

He knew not how to bear his brazen shield;
Such weapons shepherds were not used to wield:
Their weight and their unwieldiness was such,
And they restrained his nimbleness so much,
That he prayed Saul of these he might be freed:
'It is not armour that must do the deed.
Let me alone,' say'th he, 'and I'll provide
Myself of arms, this quarrel to decide.'[14]

[...]

When soon they saw a goodly youth descend
Himself alone, none after to attend
That at his need with arms might him supply,
As merely careless of his enemy.
His head uncovered, and his locks of hair
As he came on being played with by the air,
Tossed to and fro, did with such pleasure move,
As they had been provocatives for love;
His sleeves stripped up above his elbows were,
And in his hand a stiff short staff did bear,
Which by the leather to it, and the string,
They easily might discern to be a sling;
Suiting to these he wore a shepherd's scrip,[15]
Which from his side hung down upon his hip.
Those for a champion that did him disdain,
Cast with themselves what such a thing should mean,[16]
Some seeing him so wonderously fair
(As in their eyes he stood beyond compare),
Their verdict gave that they had sent him sure
As a choice bait their champion to allure;
Others again, of judgement more precise,
Said they had sent him for a sacrifice.

[...]

Which when Goliath saw, 'Why, boy,' quoth he,
'Thou desperate youth, thou tak'st me sure to be
Some dog (I think) and under thy command,
That thus art come to beat me with a wand.

[14] David kills Goliath using a single stone as sling shot.

[15] *scrip* pouch, bag.

[16] *cast* considered, pondered.

The kites and ravens are not far away,
Nor beasts of ravin that shall make a prey
Of a poor corpse, which they from me shall have,
And their foul bowels shall be all thy grave.'
  'Uncircumcisèd slave,' quoth David then,
'That for thy shape the monster art of men,
Thou thus in brass com'st armed into the field,
And thy huge spear of brass, of brass thy shield;
I in the name of Israel's God alone,
That more than mighty, that eternal one,
Am come to meet thee, who bids not to fear,
Nor once respect the arms that thou dost bear.
Slave, mark the earth whereon thou now dost stand.
I'll make thy length to measure so much land,
As thou liest grovelling and within this hour
The birds and beasts thy carcass shall devour.'

[...]

George Herbert (1593–1633), poet

Educated at Cambridge, Herbert abandoned a promising civic career for life as a country parish priest. Deeply committed to his Wiltshire parish, he had only three years to work at this calling before his early death at the age of forty. He remains best known for his collection of sacred verse, *The Temple* (1633).

8.14

From *The Temple* (1633)

8.14.1 Dullness

Why do I languish thus, drooping and dull,
  As if I were all earth?
Oh give me quickness, that I may with mirth[1]
    Praise thee brim-full![2]

[1] *quickness* liveliness.
[2] *thee* i.e., God, Herbert's addressee throughout the poem.

The wanton lover in a curious strain
  Can praise his fairest fair;
And with quaint metaphors her curlèd hair
    Curl o'er again.

Thou art my loveliness, my life, my light,
  Beauty alone to me:
Thy bloody death and undeserved, makes thee
    Pure red and white.[3]

When all perfections as but one appear,
  That those thy form doth show,
The very dust, where thou dost tread and go,
    Makes beauties here;

Where are my lines then? my approaches? views?
  Where are my window-songs?[4]
Lovers are still pretending, and ev'n wrongs[5]
    Sharpen their muse:

But I am lost in flesh, whose sugared lies
  Still mock me, and grow bold.
Sure thou didst put a mind there, if I could
    Find where it lies.

Lord, clear thy gift, that with a constant wit
  I may but look towards thee:
Look only, for to love thee, who can be,
    What angel fit?

John Donne (1572–1631), clergyman and writer

For his biography, see Introduction to **7.7**.

[3] *red and white* traditional colours of the Petrarchan mistress's perfect complexion (cf. Song of Songs 5.10).

[4] *window-songs* serenades (love songs).

[5] *pretending* wooing.

8.15

From *Poems* (1633)

8.15.1 To Master T.W.[1]

All hail, sweet poet, more full of more strong fire
  Than hath or shall enkindle any spirit:
  I loved what nature gave thee, but this merit[2]
Of wit and art I love not but admire;[3]
Who have before or shall write after thee,
Their works, though toughly labourèd, will be
  Like infancy or age to man's firm stay,
  Or early and late twilights to midday.

Men say, and truly, that they better be
  Which be envied than pitied: therefore I,
  Because I wish thee best, do thee envy:
Oh, wouldst thou, by like reason, pity me!
But care not for me: I, that ever was[4]
In nature's and in fortune's gifts, (alas,
  Before thy grace got in the Muses' school)[5]
  A monster and a beggar, am now a fool.[6]

Oh, how I grieve, that late born modesty
  Hath got such root in easy waxen hearts,
  That men may not themselves their own good parts[7]
Extol without suspect of surquedrie,[8]
For, but thyself, no subject can be found
Worthy thy quill, nor any quill resound[9]

[1] Thomas Woodward (b. c. 1576); about eighteen years old when this verse exchange took place (Klawitter, 'Verse Letters' 86–7).

[2] *what* everything.

[3] *wit* natural poetic talent; *art*: poetic proficiency gained by study and practice; *admire*: am amazed [at].

[4] *care not* do not experience undue anxiety [over me].

[5] *Before thy grace* in comparison with your poetic talents and skills.

[6] *monster* and *fool* conventional labels for the pining lover (male and female).

[7] *good parts* excellent qualities, playing on 'bodily or sexual parts' (Klawitter, 'Verse Letters' 89).

[8] *suspect of surquedrie* suspicion of arrogance or pride.

[9] *For but thyself no subject … resound* perhaps, 'There is no subject worthy thy *quill*

Thy worth but thine: how good it were to see
A poem in thy praise, and writ by thee.

Now if this song be too'harsh for rhyme, yet, as
The painter's bad god made a good devil,
'Twill be good prose, although the verse be evil,
If thou forget the rhyme as thou dost pass.
Then write, that I may follow, and so be
Thy debtor, thy'echo, thy foil, thy zany.[10]
I shall be thought, if mine like thine I shape,
All the world's lion, though I be thy ape.[11]

[In the Westmoreland manuscript, Donne's first verse letter to T.W. is followed by T.W.'s answer. Although there was clearly an exchange of poems going on between the two, we have only this one reply by Woodward; either he did not answer Donne's next poems, or these responses have been lost. According to W. Milgate, 'To Master J.D.' was detached from Donne's poem and copied into various other manuscripts.]

8.15.2 To Master J.D. (by Thomas Woodward)[12]

Thou send'st me prose and rhymes: I send for those
Lines, which being neither, seem or verse or prose.[13]
They're lame and harsh, and have no heat at all[14]
But what thy liberal beams on them let fall.
The nimble fire which in thy brain doth dwell
Is it that fire of heaven or that of hell?
It doth beget and comfort like heaven's eye
And like hell's fire it burns eternally.
And those whom in thy fury and judgement[15]
Thy verse shall scourge, like hell it will torment.

[pen] except thyself' and 'There is no subject worth writing about except thy *quill* [penis]' (Klawitter, 'Verse Letters' 89).

10 *echo* Cf. Echo (Glossary); *zany*: awkward mimic.

11 *lion* king of beasts; *ape*: ludicrous imitator.

12 Reprinted by permission of the Berg Collection, New York Public Library.

13 *I send for those / Lines* i.e., 'I send [in return] for your lines, lines of my own'; *or* … *or*: either … or.

14 *heat* physiological characteristic that distinguished the male body (hot and perfect) from the female body (cold and imperfect); necessary state for sexual arousal and conception.

15 *fury* divinely inspired creative frenzy of the true poet.

Have mercy on me and my sinful muse,
Which rubbed and tickled with thine could not choose[16]
But spend some of her pith and yield to be[17]
One in that chaste and mystic tribadree.[18]
Bassae's adultery no fruit did leave,[19]
Nor theirs which their swollen thighs did nimbly weave,
And what new arms and mouths embrace and kiss
Though they had issue was not like to this.[20]
Thy Muse, oh strange and holy lechery,
Being a maid still, got this song on me.[21]

8.15.3 To Master T.W.[22]

Haste thee harsh verse, as fast as thy lame measure[23]
Will give thee leave, to him, my pain and pleasure.
I have given thee, and yet thou art too weak,
Feet and a reasoning soul and tongue to speak.[24]
Plead for me, and so by thine and my labour,
I am thy Creator, thou my Saviour.[25]
Tell him, all questions, which men have defended
Both of the place and pains of hell, are ended;
And 'tis decreed our hell is but privation
Of him, at least in this earth's habitation:[26]
And 'tis where I am, where in every street
Infections follow, overtake, and meet.[27]

16 *rubbed* and *tickled* sexual play; tribadic (same-sex) intercourse of the men's female muses.

17 *spend … pith* ejaculate her female semen (*pith*) in her sexual climax with Donne's muse.

18 *tribadree* tribadism.

19 *Bassae* ancient tribade (see **7.23.1**).

20 *Nor… this* referring to Aristophanes' account of humanity's original sexual tripartism – male, female, and androgyne; thus, the muses' coupling may also be between two men (Klawitter, 'Verse Letters' 93).

21 *got* begot (implying insemination and reproduction).

22 Donne's reply to T.W.'s previous letter.

23 *measure* metre.

24 *feet* metrical units comprising a verse line (with a play on the literal meaning).

25 Clearly thought blasphemous, this line is deleted from most of the poem's copies. See W. Milgate, ed., *Satires, Epigrams, and Verse Letters of John Donne* (Oxford, 1967), p. 213.

26 *privation / Of him* absence of God.

27 *Infections … meet* perhaps dating the poem's composition to summer 1592 when plague was ravaging London (Milgate 213).

Live I or die, by you my love is sent,
And you'are my pawns, or else my testament.[28]

8.15.4 To Master T.W.

Pregnant again with th'old twins, Hope and Fear,[29]
Oft have I asked for thee, both how and where
Thou wert, and what my hopes of letters were;

As in our streets sly beggars narrowly
Watch motions of the giver's hand and eye,
And evermore conceive some hope thereby.

And now thine alms is given, thy letter'is read,[30]
The body risen again, the which was dead,
And thy poor starveling bountifully fed.

After this banquet my soul doth say grace,
And praise thee for'it, and zealously embrace
Thy love; though I think thy love in this case
  To be as gluttons, which say 'midst their meat,
  They love that best of which they most do eat.

8.15.5 To Master T.W.[31]

At once, from hence, my lines and I depart,
I to my soft still walks, they to my heart;[32]
I to the nurse, they to the child of art;[33]

Yet as a firm house, though the carpenter
Perish, doth stand; as an ambassador
Lies safe, how e'er his king be in danger:

28 *pawns* pledges (of my love); *testament*: last will and testament.

29 *Hope* and *Fear* the yearning lover's typical emotions in ancient and Renaissance poetry.

30 *now … read* referring to a lost letter from Woodward, characterized as an act of charity (*alms*).

31 Donne's last extant verse letter to Woodward.

32 *heart* Woodward.

33 *the nurse* [*of art*] Donne's solitary retreat; *child of* art: Woodward, as the superior poet, a characterization that Donne emphasizes throughout their exchange.

So, though I languish, pressed with melancholy,
My verse, the strict map of my misery,
Shall live to see that for whose want I die.

Therefore I envy them, and do repent,
That from unhappy me, things happy'are sent;
Yet as a picture, or bare sacrament,[34]
  Accept these lines, and if in them there be
  Merit of love, bestow that love on me.

8.15.6 To Master B.B.[35]

Is not thy sacred hunger of science
Yet satisfied? Is not thy brain's rich hive
  Fulfilled with honey which thou dost derive
From the arts' spirits and their quintessence?[36]
Then wean thyself at last, and thee withdraw
  From Cambridge, thy old nurse, and, as the rest,[37]
  Here toughly chew, and sturdily digest
Th'immense vast volumes of our common law;[38]
And begin soon, lest my grief grieve thee too,
  Which is, that that which I should have begun
  In my youth's morning, now late must be done;
And I as giddy travellers must do,
  Which stray or sleep all day, and having lost
  Light and strength, dark and tired must then ride post.[39]

If thou unto thy muse be marrièd,
Embrace her ever, ever multiply,
  Be far from me that strange adultery
To tempt thee and procure her widowhead.[40]
My muse, (for I had one), because I'am cold,
  Divorced herself: the cause being in me,

[34] *picture* portrait; *sacrament*: promise (legal term).

[35] Probably Beaupré Bell (d. 1638); attended Lincoln's Inn at the same time as Donne (c. 1594); Cambridge graduate (BA (1591), MA (1594)).

[36] *quintessence* essential quality (a term from alchemical distillation).

[37] *rest* fellow Cambridge graduates.

[38] At the Inns of Court, young men often, but not always, studied law in preparation for becoming lawyers.

[39] *post* with excessive haste.

[40] *widowhead* widowhood.

That I can take no new in bigamy,
Not my will only but power doth withhold.[41]
Hence comes it, that these rhymes which never had
Mother, want matter, and they only have
A little form, the which their father gave;[42]
They are profane, imperfect, oh, too bad
To be counted children of poetry,[43]
Except confirmed and bishopèd by thee.[44]

8.15.7 To Sir Henry Wotton[45]

Sir, more than kisses, letters mingle souls;
For thus friends absent speak. This ease controls[46]
The tediousness of my life; but for these
I could ideate nothing which could please,[47]
But I should wither in one day, and pass
To'a bottle of hay, that am a lock of grass.[48]
Life is a voyage, and in our life's ways
Countries, courts, towns are rocks or remoras;[49]
They break or stop all ships, yet our state's such
That, though than pitch they stain worse, we must touch.
If in the furnace of the even line,[50]

41 *My muse … withhold* i.e., 'My muse has divorced me because I am *cold* (sexually frigid and poetically sterile); since the reason she *divorced* me lies in my own coldness, I am unwilling and unable to marry another [muse]; such a marriage would constitute *bigamy*.'

42 *Hence … gave* referring to the ancient notion that the woman contributed *matter* (raw material) and the man *form* to a foetus. Since Donne cannot have sex with his estranged muse (now his divorced wife), his verses have only the form which (as the man) he can contribute.

43 *profane … poetry* A foetus produced with no maternal 'matter' is a physiological impossibility; thus, it would be unnatural or *profane* (unclean; polluted).

44 *bishopèd* confirmed (as in the sacrament of confirmation).

45 *Sir Henry Wotton* (1568–1639), diplomat, poet, and friend of Donne from his Oxford years. In the late 1590s (when this poem was probably written) both Wotton and Donne sought civic employment. The debate over which was preferable – public engagement or country retirement – was an ancient one.

46 *this ease* relief (of composing poems like this).

47 *these* these verse letters; *ideate*: imagine, create mentally.

48 *bottle* stack.

49 *remora* sucking-fish, believed able to stop any ship to which it attached itself.

50 *even line* equator.

Or under th'adverse icy poles thou pine,[51]
Thou know'st two temperate regions girded in
Dwell there: But oh, what refuge can'st thou win
Parched in the court and in the country frozen?
Shall cities, built of both extremes, be chosen?
Can dung and garlic be'a perfume? Or can
A scorpion and torpedo cure a man?[52]
Cities are worst of all three; of all three
(O knotty riddle) each is worst equally.
Cities are sepulchres; they who dwell there
Are carcasses, as if no such there were.[53]
And courts are theatres, where some men play
Princes, some slaves, all to one end and of one clay.
The country is a desert, where no good,
Gained as habits, not born, is understood.
There men become beasts, and prone to more evils;
In cities, blocks, and in a lewd court, devils.[54]
As in the first Chaos confusedly
Each element's qualities were in th'other three;[55]
So pride, lust, covetize, being several
To these three places, yet all are in all,
And mingled thus, their issue'incestuous.
Falsehood is denizened. Virtue'is barbarous.[56]
Let no man say there, Virtue's flinty wall
Shall lock vice in me, I'll do none, but know'all.
Men are sponges, which to pour out, receive,
Who know false play, rather than lose, deceive.
For in best understandings, sin began;
Angels sinned first, then devils, and then man.
Only perchance beasts sin not; wretched we
Are beasts in all but white integrity.
I think if men, which in these places live
Durst look for themselves and themselves retrive,[57]

[51] *adverse* hostile; perhaps simply 'opposite to'.

[52] *torpedo* electric ray, able to paralyze a swimmer.

[53] *no such* no such people (behaving as though they are alive, they are really the walking dead).

[54] *blocks* blockheads.

[55] In Renaissance cosmology, the universe was created from earth, air, fire, and water. God separated out these elements, creating true matter and order.

[56] *denizened* made a citizen.

[57] *Durst … themselves* 'dared to look at the world around them with their own eyes';

They would like strangers greet themselves, seeing then
Utopian youth grown old Italian.[58]
  Be thou thine own home, and in thyself dwell;
Inn anywhere, continuance maketh hell.[59]
And seeing the snail, which everywhere doth roam,
Carrying his own house still, still is at home,
Follow (for he is easy paced) this snail,
Be thine own palace, or the world's thy gaol.
And in the world's sea, do not like cork sleep
Upon the water's face, nor in the deep
Sink like a lead without a line, but as
Fishes glide, leaving no print where they pass,
Nor making sound, so closely thy course go;
Let men dispute whether thou breathe or no.
Only'in this one thing, be no Galenist. To make[60]
Court's hot ambitions wholesome, do not take
A dram of country's dullness; do not add
Correctives, but as chymiques, purge the bad.[61]
  But, sir, I'advise not you, I rather do
Say o'er those lessons which I learned of you,
Whom, free from German schisms, and lightness
Of France, and fair Italy's faithlessness,
Having from these sucked all they had of worth,
And brought home that faith which you carried forth,[62]
I throughly love. But if myself I'have won
To know my rules, I have, and you have

DONNE.

'dared to look into their own natures'; *retrive*: retrieve.

[58] *utopian* perfect; *Italian*: stereotype of the Italian as the epitome of moral corruption.

[59] *inn* dwell; *continuance*: staying somewhere for a long time.

[60] *be no Galenist* i.e., don't be like the followers of Claudius Galenus (second century CE physician), believing that medicinal cures should contain elements opposite to those in flux in the body (e.g., an illness arising from too much heat in the body would be cured by 'cold' medicines).

[61] *chymiques* chemists.

[62] *faith* Protestantism.

8.15.8 Holy Sonnet 14

Batter my heart, three-personed God, for you[63]
As yet but knock, breathe, shine, and seek to mend;[64]
That I may rise and stand, o'erthrow me, and bend[65]
Your force to break, blow, burn, and make me new.
I, like an usurped town to another due,
Labour to admit you, but oh, to no end;
Reason, your viceroy in me, me should defend,[66]
But is captived, and proves weak or untrue.
Yet dearly I love you, and would be loved fain,[67]
But am betrothed unto your enemy;
Divorce me, untie or break that knot again,
Take me to you, imprison me, for I,
Except you enthral me, never shall be free,[68]
Nor ever chaste, except you ravish me.[69]

Edmund Waller (1606–87), poet

Educated at Cambridge and Lincoln's Inn (London), and deeply committed to the royalist cause, Waller published *Poems*, his most important work, in 1645. Although escaping execution for his role in a planned insurrection against Parliament, Waller was forced into exile on the Continent in 1644. Later, however, he became a commissioner of trade (1655) in Cromwell's government, but resumed writing royalist verse at the Restoration, while at the same time defending parliamentary prerogatives against monarchical encroachment. His last published work, *Divine Poems*, appeared two years before his death.

[63] *three personed* reffering to the doctrine of the Trinity: God the Father, God the Son, and God the Holy Spirit.

[64] The first three verbs in this line have Scriptural resonance: *knock* (Mt. 7.7–8), *breathe* (Jn. 20.22), and *shine* (Num. 6.25).

[65] *rise and stand* with the reference to sexual erection.

[66] *viceroy* official who acts for a king or ruler.

[67] *fain* eagerly.

[68] *enthral* enslave.

[69] *ravish* 'rape'; but also 'overwhelm with astonishment or ecstasy'.

8.16

From *Poems* (1645)

8.16.1 On His Majesty's Receiving the News of the Duke of Buckingham's Death[1]

So earnest with thy God, can no new care,[2]
No sense of danger interrupt thy prayer?
The sacred wrestler till a blessing given
Quits not his hold but halting conquers heaven:[3]
Nor was the stream of thy devotion stopped
When from the body such a limb was lopped,[4]
As to thy present state was no less maim,
Though thy wise choice has since repaired the same.[5]
Bold Homer durst not so great virtue feign[6]
In his best pattern of Patroclus slain,
With such amazement as weak mothers use,
And frantic gesture he receives the news:[7]
Yet fell his darling by th'impartial chance
Of war, imposed by royal Hector's lance.
Thine in full peace and by a vulgar hand[8]
Torn from thy bosom left his high command.
   The famous painter can allow no place
For private sorrow in a prince's face.
Yet that his price might not exceed belief,
He cast a veil upon supposèd grief.
'Twas want of such a precedent as this
Made the old heathen frame their god amiss.
Their Phoebus should not act a fonder part
For the fair boy, than he did from his heart;

[1] George Villiers, Duke of Buckingham, intimate favourite of James I, and later of his son and heir, Charles I. See Introduction to **5.1**.

[2] *thy* here and throughout the poem, Waller addresses Charles I.

[3] *The sacred … heaven* Jacob wrestles with an angel, refusing to release it until it blesses him (Gen. 32.24–9).

[4] *such a limb* Buckingham.

[5] *wise choice* unidentified: Charles appointed various noblemen to the dead Buckingham's many offices.

[6] *feign* represent.

[7] *he* Achilles.

[8] *by a vulgar hand* Buckingham was murdered by a common soldier.

Nor blame for Hyacinthus' fate his own
That kept from him wished death, hadst thou been known.
 Yet he that weighs with thine good David's deeds,
Shall find his passion, not his love exceeds.
He cursed the mountains where his brave friend died,
But let false Ziba with his heir divide:[9]
Where thy mortal love to thy blest friends,
Like that of heaven upon their seed descends.[10]
Such huge extremes inhabit thy great mind,
God-like unmoved, and yet like woman kind:
Which of thy ancient poets had not brought
Our Charles his pedigree from heaven, and taught
How some bright dame compressed by mighty Jove[11]
Produced this mixed divinity and love?

Nicholas Oldisworth (1611–45), clergyman and poet

Educated at Westminster School, Oldisworth met there the young man who became his closest friend, and to whom many of his most affecting poems are addressed: Richard Bacon. Their personal contact was apparently largely limited to this early time in their lives. After their shared time at Westminster, they attended different universities: Bacon went to Trinity College, Cambridge (1627–28), his Catholicism preventing him from taking his degree; Oldisworth went to Christ Church, Oxford (BA, 1632; MA, 1635). Oldisworth took up the ecclesiastical living of Bourton-on-the-Hill (in the gift of his grandfather), and the life of a pastor. His marriage to Mary Chamberlayne (1611–1684) produced three daughters, two of whom predeceased him. Attempting to escape the plague that was ravaging London and its environs in 1644–45, Oldisworth and his family moved temporarily to Willington, Warwickshire. There, he produced the fair copy of his unpublished poems, which include those reflecting his passionate love for Richard Bacon, and there he died of the plague on 25 March 1645.

Richard Bacon (d. 1636)

Son of a London medicine dealer, Bacon left Cambridge for France, entering the Catholic English College at Douai in the autumn of 1629. In 1632, his

[9] *But … divide* 2 Sam. 19.24–30.

[10] *seed* children, descendants.

[11] The 'bright dame compressed [embraced] by mighty Jove' could refer to any of the god's many sexual conquests.

brother Matthew joined him there. A talented scholar who taught rhetoric at the College, Bacon died in Flanders of the plague.

Editions

Nicholas Oldisworth's Manuscript (Bodleian MS. Don.c.24), ed. J. Gouws. Tempe, AZ: RETS, 2009.

8.17

From *A Recollection of Certain Scattered Poems* (Bodleian MS. Don.c.24) (completed, 1644–45)[1]

8.17.1 To His Dear Wife, Marie Oldisworth (fol. 7r–v).

Sweet Mall,

We two have now been married five years: and hitherto (praised be God) we have wanted[2] nothing but peace. For my part, I thank God for those good days which I have seen in my youth, wherein I had leisure to please my own fancy, and to write such toys[3] as here do follow. And I doubt not but thou also, in those very days, hadst and didst enjoy thy fair, virgin-like contentments, though I then was not so happy as to know either them or thee. Time was (Mall) when tabrets and pipes were more respected than drums and trumpets,[4] which drums and trumpets were seldom heard in England but at a masque[5] or at a play. Time was, when I could ride from Bourton to London, both without company and without danger, and carry my pockets full of money.[6] But now where is that money? My gold-scales (thou knowest) lie useless and unemployed; nor do I see my sovereign's face in silver at home much oftener than I see his face in flesh and blood at Oxford.[7] Yet have I spent as much, in contributions and free-quarters,[8] as would not only have

[1] Reprinted by permission of the Bodleian Library, University of Oxford, owner of MS. Don.c.24, a fair copy in Oldisworth's own hand.

[2] *wanted* lacked.

[3] *toys* trifling compositions.

[4] *tabrets* [small drums] and *pipes*; *drums* and *trumpets* respectively, conventional images of peace and war. Oldisworth's fair copy was made during the Civil War.

[5] *masque* spectacular form of courtly dramatic entertainment.

[6] *Time … money* referring to the assaults, thefts, and highway robberies encouraged by the increasing lawlessness of war-torn England.

[7] *Oxford* Charles I's base of operations (1642–49).

[8] *contributions* and *free-quarters* respectively, money and supplies, and free room and board required from citizens for both the king's and Parliament's forces.

set me out of debt, but have begun competent portions[9] for thy two little daughters. I pray God send us patience, for although we are likely to stand in need of many things, yet are we likely to stand most in need of patience. So, entreating thee to be of good cheer, and not to trouble or disquiet thy mind with the fear and expectation of those evils, which perchance may never come; I rest

Thy true friend

NICOLAS OLDISWORTH.

From Willington.
1644. February 17.

8.17.2 To his friend beyond sea (fol. 9r)[10]

Friend: think not time, or wind, or place,
Or sea can hinder our embrace.
Our purer spirits still do meet,
And through the air, each other greet.
    Time, place, sea, wind,
    Are all combined
To make our absent joys more sweet.

Time only knows how to improve,
Not to blot out, or spoil, our love;
We have no time but what doth run
Governed by thee, more than the sun.
    Unless it be
    In thoughts on thee,
We never think, the day is done.

Place doth not sunder or divide
Our hearts, but makes them stretch more wide.
Our passions, which before did lie
In prison, now abroad do fly:
    The breadth of place
    Gives fancy space,[11]
And sets our souls at liberty.

[9] *competent portions* adequate dowries.

[10] Oldisworth's marginal note: 'These verses were written [in] 1629 to Mr. Richard Bacon, a hopeful youth who was sometimes a scholar of Westminster school, where he was generally praised and beloved. At last he died in travail [i.e., pain].'

[11] *fancy* imagination; also, 'love'.

And all the wind 'twixt us and thee,
Is but a puffing agony
Of sighs and blasts which do expire
From the vast depth of our desire.
    And this is wind
    Of such a kind,
As only blows, not cools the fire.

Instead of seas, our land doth swim
In brinish tears up to the brim;
Tears, which nor rage, storm, nor complain
But wait thee in a calmer strain:
    That when thou please,
    Thou may'st with ease
Take water and come back again.

8.17.3 To his friend beyond sea (fol. 28v)

Bacon, thou hardly wilt believe that we
Which are so zealous in commending thee
Should scarce endure to hear thy public praise:
Yet so it is. When any stranger says
Thou hast the active body of thy father
And thy fair mother's face, we had far rather
That he would swear how thou wert ugly grown,
Or how thy teeth and hair were not thine own.
Why art thou handsome? Beauty is the pride
Not of a gentleman, but of a bride.
  Truly we hope that though thou wentst from hence
Sweet, pretty, and delightful to the sense,
Time will impair thee so that we may find
No gifts at thy return but in thy mind.
Not that we wish thee any kind of ill
(We for thy welfare pray, we bless thee still)
But that we have no other way to prove
The constancy and pureness of our love.
What thanks deserve we, if we dote on feature?
A thing which ravishes each silly creature.
We dive into thy soul, and there find out
Jewels and mines not dreamt of by the rout.[12]

[12] *rout* common crowd.

Do, do, continue fine. This shall be all
Thy recompense: that where we used to call
Thee our dear brother, now another while
Our comely sister thee we will enstyle.[13]

8.17.4 On the Picture of Beauty (fol. 51v)[14]

Here joined you see white snow and purple fire:[15]
The one doth move, the other quench desire;
Fear not or freezing, or excessive heat:
The worst that can fall out is but cold sweat.
Oh, who of such a mixture can complain,
Where still the cure is equal to the pain?

8.17.5 A Paradox: To One Whom He Both Extremely Loved, and Extremely Hated (fol. 57r)

Thou best of good things, thou of bad things worst,
Oh how thou blest art, oh how thou art curst!
Thou sweetest bitter, I can scarce debate
If I should love thee more, or more thee hate.
Thou neither, and thou both, I do not know
Whether to call thee friend, or call thee foe:
Thou art the author of my greatest joys:
Thou art the author of my chief annoys.
Whate'er haps to me well, it springs from thee:
From thee it springs, whate'er haps ill to me.
Were it not for thee, I myself would kill:
Were it not for thee, I would yet live still.
At high noon thou dost blind me like the night:
By thee, I see at midnight, as by light.
Without thee, pleasure is a pain to me:
Pain to me is a pleasure, without thee.
Thou art the sauce which relishes my meat:
Thou art the bane which poisons what I eat.[16]
Thy horrid Furies oft me waking keep:
Thy smiling Graces lull me oft asleep.

13 *enstyle* name.

14 In another copy (Folger MS. V.a.170), the title is: 'On the Picture of Young Mr. Bacon, as it is set up beyond the sea, and entitled The Picture of Beauty'.

15 *white snow* his perfect complexion; *purple fire*: his lips.

16 *bane* noxious substance.

When through thy ice I freeze, clothes warm me not:
When through thy flames I burn, clothes are too hot.
Wine is no wine, unless to thee I drink:
Wine is no wine, if I on thee do think.
In thoughts, words, deeds, thou mak'st me to mistake:
In thoughts, words, deeds, thou me exact dost make.
My young god thou art, thou art my young devil;
To good thou draw'st me, thou me draw'st to evil:
And when I ill do, and when I do well,
Thou art my paradise, thou art my hell.

8.17.6 For a Gentleman. On the Embracing of his Friend (fol. 72v)

Let us alone, ye mortals, and permit
Us two for ay to be thus sweetly knit;[17]
Let us alone: we bid you all adieu,
Trouble not us, until we trouble you.
In naught but in ourselves we place our quiet;
As for the world, we totally defy it.
Possess thy yellow heaps, thou man of gold,
And purchase livings more than can be told,[18]
Only give us our love: whilst thou art poor
Amidst thy plenty, we in want find store;[19]
No treasure is so boundless as a friend;
He ne'er can lack who hath a man to spend.[20]
Tumble thy gaudy wenches, thou spruce lad,[21]
Whose highest aim is never to be sad,
Drink, sleep, use games, make feasts, dance masques, see plays,
And when in pleasure thou hast passed thy days,
At last confess that we have hit the right:
Chastely to join souls is the chief delight.
Enjoy thy crown, Great Turk, and reign as far[22]

17 *for ay* forever.

18 *livings* estates, possessions; *told*: related; counted.

19 *want* lack (of worldly wealth); *store*: abundance.

20 *spend* unlike the monetary treasure of worldly success, the spiritual treasure of true friendship cannot ever be *spent* (i.e., depleted or exhausted); therefore, the friend can never *lack* (be in want or need). 'Spend' could also mean in the period 'to experience sexual climax'.

21 *tumble* copulate with.

22 *Great Turk* head of the Ottoman Empire.

As any empires worth the having are;
Stretch out thy sceptre over lands and seas,
Throw down, build up, destroy, save what thou please;
Yet do not envy us: and thou shalt see
It will be long ere we do envy thee.

8.17.7 For a Gentleman. To Young Mr Henry Gresley (fol. 73r–v)[23]

Were I in heav'n, Hall, or were I with thee[24]
  (Thy presence is a heav'n to me)
By visions, not by words, I would disclose
  Why thee, on earth, my friend I chose.
The saints would ravish'd be, to learn my story,[25]
  And think, it added to their glory;
The angels would admire a mortal's love,
  And wish that they had such above.
First, I would show thee how thy pleasing face
  Promised a heart enriched with grace;
Through thy fair eyes I could espy within
  Much virtue, and scarce any sin.
This made me look so oft, and gaze on thee,
  That I thy inward worth might see;
More of the priest I had, than of the lover,
  And did high mysteries discover.
I saw a wit divine, which did not follow
  But did out-go, the sage Apollo;
Thy oracle was blind in no man's case,
  Best-sighted in thine own it was;[26]
Ripe were thy brains: thou seemedst to most men
  A youth of three score years and ten.[27]
I saw a modesty which did invite

[23] *Henry Gresley* (Greisley) (1613–78), translator. Like Oldisworth, he attended Westminster School and Christ Church; two years younger than Oldisworth, he matriculated at Christ Church (1634), during the time between Oldisworth's taking of his BA and MA. He was perhaps eighteen or nineteen at the time of this poem's composition.

[24] *Hall* play on the common nickname for Henry (Hal) and the opposite of heaven (hell) (Hammond, *Figuring* 37).

[25] *ravish'd* transported with ecstasy.

[26] *But did out-go … was* Apollo had the gift of futurity; his Delphic oracle was reputedly the wisest in the ancient world. See Apollo (Glossary).

[27] *three … ten* 70.

And yet did hinder my delight;
Thou wert so holy, thou to sleep or drink
Wouldst blush, and it too carnal think:
Oh, how thy noble blood mounted and flamed,
When to thee first I friendship named!
Pure friendship 'twas, and 'tis, else I should sure
The hell of losing thee endure.
I saw a conscience, which did scorn to fear,
It was so upright, and so clear;
To men thou gav'st their dues, but to the Lord
Thou didst thy very self afford.
Hence sprung thy peace, thy mirth, thy jolly rest:
The whole year seems to thee one feast.
Nothing e'er vexed thy soul but proffered wealth,
New honour, or continual health;
That which made others proud, did humble thee.
Thou with this world couldst ne'er agree.
What saw I else? a rare internal beauty,
Which to keep secret is my duty;
Some superstitious fools would thee adore,
Should I lay open all thy store.
While I thus viewed thy inside, I began
To count thee something more than man:
In each part, as thy body, so thy mind
Straight, sweet, heroic, I did find.
Tell me, ye cherubins, who dwell in light,[28]
Have I done well? Is my choice right?
Have I on goodness my affections placed,
And by a proxy God embraced?
Have I my Jesus in my Harry loved?
Is friendship now devotion proved?
If yea, then Christ smiles on our mutual troth,[29]
And is a third friend to us both.
An unity here is, if no Trinity,
I, thou, and Christ: Christ, thou, and I.[30]

28 *cherubins* angels.

29 *troth* truth, faithfulness; also, 'covenant'.

30 *An unity … I* Oldisworth's friendship with Henry, with Christ as a third partner, is a secular version of the divine Trinity (God the Father, God the Son (Jesus), and God the Holy Spirit).

8.17.8 On the Death of his Dear Friend, Mr Richard Bacon (fol. 74v)[31]

Richard Crashaw (1612/13–48), poet

Son of a Puritan preacher and devotional writer, Crashaw was educated at Cambridge (BA, MA), where he became fluent in several ancient and modern languages, and began writing verse, publishing a volume of Latin sacred poetry in 1634. Ordained an Anglican minister soon after 1638, Crashaw fled Cambridge before the occupying parliamentarian forces in 1643. On the Continent, he converted to Catholicism, and later accepted ecclesiastical positions in Rome and Loretto. His volume of sacred verse *Steps to the Temple* appeared in 1646 (expanded edn, 1648).

8.18

From *Steps to the Temple* (1646)

8.18.1 Blessed Be the Paps which Thou Hast Sucked (Luke 11)[1]

Suppose he had been tabled at thy teats,[2]
Thy hunger feels not what he eats;
He'll have his teat ere long (a bloody one),[3]
The mother then must suck the son.

8.18.2 Our Lord in his Circumcision to his Father[4]

To thee these first fruits of my growing death
(For what else is my life?) lo I bequeath.
Taste this, and as thou lik'st this lesser flood

[31] Uniquely in the manuscript, this heading is followed by a blank page.

[1] Luke 11.27, an unnamed woman's exclamation to Christ; *paps*: lactating breasts.

[2] *tabled* fed. For the image of God's maternal breast, see Ps. 34.8 and 1 Pet. 2.1–3; *teats*: nipples, breasts.

[3] *bloody teat* the spear wound in Christ's side, inflicted during his crucifixion.

[4] Lk. 2.21. The Feast of the Circumcision falls on 1 January in the Anglican calendar; associated with new beginnings.

Expect a sea, my heart shall make it good.
Thy wrath that wades here now, ere long shall swim;
The flood-gate shall be set wide ope for him.
Then let him drink, and drink, and do his worst,
To drown the wantonness of his wild thirst.
Now's but the nonage of my pains, my fears[5]
Are yet but in their hopes, not come to years.
The day of my dark woes is yet but morn,
My tears but tender and my death new-born.
Yet may these unfledged griefs give fate some guess,
These cradle-torments have their towardness.
These purple buds of blooming death may be,
Erst the full stature of a fatal tree.[6]
And till my riper woes to age are come,
This knife may be the spear's *praeludium*.[7]

8.18.3 On Our Crucified Lord, Naked and Bloody

Th' have left thee naked, Lord, Oh that they had;
This garment too I would they had denied.
Thee with thyself they have too richly clad,
Opening the purple wardrobe of thy side.
  Oh, never could be found garments too good
  For thee to wear, but these, of thine own blood.

8.18.4 On the Wounds of Our Crucified Lord

Oh, these wakeful wounds of thine!
  Are they mouths? or are they eyes?
Be they mouths, or be they eyne,[8]
  Each bleeding part some one supplies.

Lo! a mouth, whose full-bloomed lips[9]
  At too dear a rate are roses.
Lo! a blood-shot eye that weeps
  And many a cruel tear discloses.

[5] *nonage* infancy.

[6] Christ's drops of blood at his circumcision are likened to *purple buds, blooming* into the tree of the cross, soaked in his dying blood.

[7] *spear* See **n3**; *praeludium*: prefiguration.

[8] *eyne* eyes.

[9] *lips* 'edges of a wound', but also 'lips of the mouth'.

O thou that on this foot hast laid
   Many a kiss, and many a tear!
Now thou shalt have all repaid,
   Whatsoe'er thy charges were.

This foot hath got a mouth and lips,
   To pay the sweet sum of thy kisses:
To pay thy tears, an eye that weeps
   Instead of tears such gems as this is.

The difference only this appears,
   (Nor can the change offend)
The debt is paid in ruby-tears,
   Which thou in pearls did'st lend.

Thomas Traherne (c. 1637–74), writer

Educated at Oxford (BA, MA, BD), Traherne was probably ordained in 1657 and remained the rector at his Herefordshire parish until his death, although he also served briefly as private chaplain to Orlando Bridgeman, formerly Charles II's Lord Keeper of the Seal. Virtually unknown as a devotional writer during his lifetime, except among his close acquaintance, Traherne is now regarded as among the most important of the seventeenth-century religious poets. His verse was all published long after his death.

8.19

Love (publ., 1903)

   O nectar! O delicious stream!
O ravishing and only pleasure! Where
      Shall such another theme
Inspire my tongue with joys, or please mine ear?
      Abridgement of delights![1]
         And queen of sights!
O mine of rarities! O kingdom wide!
O more! O cause of all! O glorious bride!

[1] *abridgement* summary.

O God! O bride of God! O King!
O soul and crown of ev'ry thing!

Did not I covet to behold
Some endless monarch, that did always live
In palaces of gold,
Willing all kingdoms, realms, and crowns to give
Unto my soul! Whose love
A spring might prove
Of endless glories, honours, friendships, pleasures,
Joys, praises, beauties, and celestial treasures!
Lo, now I see there's such a King,
The fountainhead of ev'ry thing!

Did my ambition ever dream
Of such a Lord, of such a love! Did I
Expect so sweet a stream
As this at any time! Could any eye
Believe it? Why, all power
Is used here
Joys down from heaven on my head to shower,
And Jove beyond the fiction doth appear
Once more in golden rain to come
To Danae's pleasing fruitful womb.

His Ganymede! His life! His joy!
Or he comes down to me, or takes me up
That I might be his boy,
And fill, and taste, and give, and drink the cup.[2]
But these (though great) are all
Too short and small,
Too weak and feeble pictures to express
The true mysterious depths of blessedness.
I am his image, and his friend.[3]
His son, bride, glory, temple, end.[4]

[2] *cup* the gods' cup that Ganymede fills; also, the cup that holds the Eucharistic wine.

[3] *image* Gen. 1.26–7, 9.6.

[4] *son* ubiquitous label for the Christian believer (e.g., Gal. 4.5); *bride*: the Church and Christian believer are often depicted as the bride to Christ's bridegroom (Rev. 21.2–9; 22.17); *temple*: 1. Cor. 3.16–17; *Glory* and *end*: cf. Eph. 3.21. The Christian is Christ's *glory* though his redemption of humanity; the Christian is Christ's *end* (or purpose) in his incarnation.

Abraham Cowley (1618–67), writer and translator

Committed royalist and early proponent of the Royal Society, Abraham Cowley wrote (among other works) a tract in support of the advancement of science (1661), lyric verse, and translations from the classics. Just after 1643, Cowley abandoned and never completed his first epic (on the Civil War), but later mined some of this material for his second, also unfinished, sacred epic, *Davideis.*

Online Companion
From Thomas Ellwood's *Davideis: The Life of David, King of Israel* (1712).

8.20

From *Davideis*[1] (1656)

8.20.1 Book 2

[Cowley contrasts Saul's hatred with Jonathan's love of David.]

But Jonathan, his son, and only good,[2]
Was gentle as fair Jordan's useful flood.
Whose innocent stream as it in silence goes,
Fresh honours, and a sudden spring bestows
On both his banks to every flower and tree;
The manner how lies hid, th'effect we see.
But more than all, more than himself he loved
The man whose worth his father's hatred moved.
For when the noble youth at Dammin stood[3]
Adorn'd with sweat, and painted gay with blood,
Jonathan pierced him through with greedy eye
And understood the future majesty[4]
Then destined in the glories of his look;
He saw, and straight was with amazement strook,[5]
To see the strength, the feature, and the grace

[1] See **1.1.3–1.1.4**.
[2] *his* Saul's
[3] *Dammin* where David killed Goliath.
[4] Marginal note: 1 Sam. 18.1.
[5] *straight* immediately; *strook*: struck.

Of his young limbs; he saw his comely face
Where love and rev'rence so well mingled were;
And head, already crown'd with golden hair.
He saw what mildness his bold spirit did tame,
Gentler than light, yet powerful as a flame.
He saw his valour by their safety proved;[6]
He saw all this, and as he saw, he loved.
What art thou, Love, thou great mysterious thing?
From what hid stock does thy strange nature spring?
'Tis thou that mov'st the world through every part
And holdst the vast frame close, that nothing start
From the due place and office first ordained.
By thee were all things made, and are sustained.[7]

[Cowley lists all the things that obey the mysterious laws of Nature, even though man does not understand why.]

But thy chief palace is man's heart alone,[8]
Here are thy triumphs, and full glories shown,
Handsome desires, and rest about thee flee,
Union, inhaerence, zeal, and ecstasy.[9]
Thousand with joys cluster around thine head,
O'er which a gall-less dove her wings does spread,[10]
A gentle lamb, purer and whiter far[11]
Than consciences of thine own martyrs are,
Lies at thy feet; and thy right hand does hold
The mystic sceptre of a cross of gold.
Thus do'est thou sit (like men ere sin had framed
A guilty blush) naked, but not ashamed.[12]

[...]

6 *their* the Israelites.

7 *What art thou, Love ... sustained* Cf. Marsilio Ficino's popular fifteenth-century Neoplatonic interpretation of love and beauty in Plato's *Symposium* (Cowley's 'Notes to Book 2').

8 *thy* Love's. These lines create an image of the Christian Trinity, with God as love (Cf. 1 Jn. 4.16).

9 *inhaerence* inherency (i.e., when a quality is permanently existing in an object).

10 *gall-less* free from bitterness or malice; *dove*: emblem of peace; symbol of the Holy Spirit, the third person in the Trinity.

11 *lamb* symbol of Christ (Jn. 1.29; Rev. 5.12), the second person in the Trinity.

12 *naked, but not ashamed* Gen. 2.25.

Thou art a bright, but not consuming flame;
Such in th'amazèd bush to Moses came;[13]
When that secure its new-crowned head did rear,
And chid the trembling branches' needless fear.
Thy darts of healthful gold, and downwards fall
Soft as the feathers that they're fletched withal.[14]
Such, and no other, were those secret darts,
Which sweetly touched this noblest pair of hearts.
Still to one end they both so justly drew,
As courteous doves together yoked would do.[15]
No weight of birth did on one side prevail,
Two twins less even lie in Nature's scale.
They mingled fates, and both in each did share,
They both were servants, they both princes were.
If any joy to one of them was sent,
It was most his, to whom it least was meant,
And fortune's malice betwixt both was crossed,
For striking one, it wounded th'other most.
Never did marriage such true union find,
Or men's desires with so glad violence bind;
For there is still some tincture left of sin,[16]
And still the sex will needs be stealing in.[17]
Those joys are full of dross, and thicker far,[18]
These, without matter, clear and liquid are.
Such sacred love does heaven's bright spirits fill,
Where love is but to understand and will,
With swift and unseen motions; such as we
Somewhat express in heightened charity.
O ye blest One! whose love on earth became
So pure that still in heaven 'tis but the same!
There now ye sit, and with mixed souls embrace,

[13] Marginal note: 'Exo. 3.' Moses climbed Mount Horeb, encountering God as a flaming *bush* that was never consumed (2–6).

[14] *fletched* said of arrows when feathers are attached to their base (in order to stabilize them in flight).

[15] *dove* one of Venus's emblematic birds, sometimes depicted drawing her heavenly chariot; turtle-doves mated for life and were a popular emblem of marital fidelity and love. Cf. **n10**.

[16] *tincture* tinge.

[17] *sex* women.

[18] *Those joys* i.e., those related to the love of and desire for women; *dross*: foreign matter.

Gazing upon great Love's mysterious face,
And pity this base world where friendship's made
A bait for sin, or else at best a trade.
Ah, wondrous prince! who a true friend could'st be,
When a crown flattered, and Saul threatened thee!
Who held'st him dear, whose stars thy birth did cross!
And bought'st him nobly at a kingdom's loss!
Isra'el's bright sceptre far less glory brings;
There have been fewer friends on earth than kings.
To this strange pitch their high affections flew;
Till Nature's self scarce looked on them as two.
Hither flies David for advice and aid,[19]
As swift as love and danger could persuade,
As safe in Jonathan's trust his thoughts remain
As when himself but dreams them o'er again.
'My dearest lord, farewell,' said he, 'farewell.
Heaven bless the king; may no misfortune tell
Th'injustice of his hate, when I am dead;
They'are coming now, perhaps; my guiltless head
Here in your sight, perhaps, must bleeding lie,
And scarce your own stand safe for being nigh.
Think me not scared with death, howe'er 't appear,
I know thou can'st not think so: 'tis a fear
From which thy love and Dammin speaks me free;
I have met him face to face, and ne'er could see[20]
One terror in his looks to make me fly
When virtue bids me stand; but I would die
So as becomes my life, so as may prove
Saul's malice, and at least excuse your love.'
He stopped, and spoke some passion with his eyes;
'Excellent friend,' the gallant prince replies,
'Thou hast so proved thy virtues, that they're known
To all good men, more than to each his own.
Who lives in Israel that can doubtful be
Of thy great actions? for he lives by thee.[21]
Such is thy valour, and thy vast success,
That all things but thy loyalty are less.
And should my father at thy ruin aim,

[19] Marginal note: '1 Sam. 20.1.'

[20] *him* death.

[21] *he* the nation of Israel.

'Twould wound as much his safety as his fame.
Think them not coming then to slay thee here,
But doubt mishaps, as little as you fear.
For by thy loving God, who e'er design
Against thy life must strike at it through mine.'

[As a test of Saul's intentions towards David, the friends decide that David will not appear at the feast of the New Moon. Jonathan tells Saul that he has given David permission to visit his family. Enraged, Saul throws a spear at Jonathan, who leaves the feast to seek out his friend.]

The prince his danger, and his duty knew;[22]
And low he bowed, and silently withdrew.
   To David straight, who in a forest nigh[23]
Waits his advice, the royal friend does fly.
The sole advice, now like the danger clear,
Was in some foreign land this storm t'outwear.
All marks of comely grief in both are seen;
And mournful kind discourses passed between.
Now generous tears their hasty tongues restrain,[24]
Now they begin, and talk all o'er again.
A reverent oath of constant love they take,
And God's high name their dreaded witness make;
Not that at all their faiths could doubtful prove;
But 'twas the tedious zeal of endless love.
Thus ere they part, they the short time bestow
In all the pomp friendship and grief could show.[25]

[David falls asleep and has a vision of the future, and of the actions of his ancestors right down to the birth of Christ.]

8.20.2 Book 3

[David flees from Saul into Nob, Gath, and finally Moab, where he is welcomed at the Moabite court. Joab, who has gone to join David, recounts David's birth, family, skill in music and poetry, his temporary curing of

22 Marginal note: [1 Sam. 20] 'Ver. 34.'
23 Marginal note: [1 Sam. 20] 'Ver. 35.'
24 Marginal note: [1 Sam. 20] 'Ver. 41.'
25 *pomp* ostentatious display.

Saul's madness, his victory over Goliath, and finally David's love match with Saul's daughter, Michol.]

[...]

His beauty, youth, courage and wondrous wit,
In all mankind but Saul did love begit.[26]
Not Saul's own house, not his own nearest blood,
The noble cause's sacred force withstood.
You'have met no doubt, and kindly used the fame,
Of god-like Jonathan's illustrious name;
A name which every wind to heav'n would bear,
Which men to speak, and angels joy to hear.
No angel e'er bore to his brother-mind
A kindness more exalted and refined
Than his to David, which looked nobly down,
And scorned the false alarums of a crown.
At Dammin field he stood; and from his place[27]
Leapt forth, the wondrous conqueror to embrace;[28]
On him his mantle, girdle, sword, and bow,[29]
On him his heart and soul he did bestow.
Not all that Saul could threaten or persuade,
In this close knot the smallest looseness made.
Oft his wise care did the king's rage suspend.
His own life's danger sheltered oft his friend,[30]
Which he exposed a sacrifice to fall
By th'undiscerning rage of furious Saul.
Nor was young David's active virtue grown
Strong and triumphant in one sex alone.[31]
Imperious beauty too it durst invade,
And deeper prints in the soft breast it made,[32]
For there t' esteem and friendship's graver name,
Passion was poured like oil into the flame.

[Cowley describes Saul's two daughters, Merab and Michol: both beautiful, but the former proud and pitiless; the latter, sweet and compassionate.]

26 Marginal note: '1 Sam. 18.16'; *begit*: i.e., begat; produced.
27 Marginal note: '1 Sam. 18'; *he*: Jonathan.
28 *conqueror* David.
29 1 Sam. 18.4.
30 Marginal note: '1 Sam. 20.33.'
31 *one sex* i.e., among men.
32 Marginal note: '1 Sam. 18. 20, 28.'

The griefs she caused gave gentle Michol grief,[33]
She wished her beauties less for their relief,[34]
Even to her captives civil; yet th'excess
Of naked virtue guarded her no less.
Business and power Merab's large thoughts did vex,
Her wit disdained the fetters of her sex.
Michol no less disdained affairs and noise,
Yet did it not from ignorance, but choice.
In brief, both copies were most sweetly drawn;
Merab of Saul, Michol of Jonathan.

[...]

She checked her forward joy, and blushed for shame,[35]
And did his boldness with forced anger blame.[36]
The senseless rules, which first false honour taught,
And into laws the tyrant custom brought,
Which women's pride and folly did invent,
Their lovers and themselves too to torment,
Made her next day a grave displeasure feign,[37]
And all her words, and all her looks constrain
Before the trembling youth; who when he saw
His vital light her wonted beams withdraw,
He cursed his voice, his fingers, and his lyre,
He cursed his too bold tongue, and bold desire.
In vain he cursed the last, for that still grew;
From all things good its strong complexion drew:
His joy and hope their cheerful motions ceased,
His life decayed, but still his love increased.
Whilst she whose heart approved not her disdain,
Saw and endured his pains with greater pain.
But Jonathan, to whom both hearts were known
With a concernment equal to their own,[38]
Joyful that heav'n with his sworn love complied
To draw that knot more fast which he had tied,
With well-timed zeal, and with an artful care,

33 *she* Michol.
34 *their* her suitors'.
35 *she* Michol.
36 *his* David's. Michol desires him, but feels she has been too forward.
37 *feign* pretend.
38 *concernment* solicitude.

Restored, and bettered soon the nice affair.[39]
With ease a brother's lawful power o'ercame
The formal decencies of virgin-shame.
She first with all her heart forgave the past,
Heard David tell his flames, and told her own at last.
Lo, here the happy point of prosperous love!
Which e'en enjoyment seldom can improve!
Themselves agreed, which scarce could fail alone,
All Israel's wish concurrent with their own.
A brother's powerful aid firm to the side,
By solemn vow the king and father tied:
All jealous fears, all nice disguises past,[40]
All that in less-ripe love offends the tast,[41]
In either's breast their souls both meet and wed,
Their heart the nuptial-temple and the bed.

[...]

John Wilmot, Earl of Rochester (1647–80), libertine poet and courtier

Son of a royalist cavalry officer, Rochester served with distinction in the navy. Made a gentleman of the bedchamber to Charles II in 1666, Rochester was part of a court circle of witty and sensually indulgent young men, including his dear friend Henry Savile. Married in 1667 to the heiress Elizabeth Malet, whom he had tried to abduct two years earlier, Rochester died of syphilis at the age of thirty-two, having reportedly re-embraced Christian principles on his deathbed. Circulating almost entirely in manuscript and anonymously during his lifetime, Rochester's oeuvre poses some serious problems of attribution.

8.21

Love to a Woman

Love a woman! Th'rt an ass:[1]
'Tis a most insipid passion

39 *nice affair* requiring tact in handling.
40 *nice* shy.
41 *tast* taste.

1 *Th'rt* Thou art.

To choose out for thy happiness
   The dullest part of God's creation.

Let the porter and the groom,[2]
   Things designed for dirty slaves,
Drudge in fair Aurelia's womb[3]
   To get supplies for age and graves.

Farewell woman – I intend
   Henceforth every night to sit
With my lewd well-natured friend
   Drinking to engender wit.

Then give me health, wealth, mirth, and wine,
   And if busy love entrenches
There's a sweet soft page of mine[4]
   Can do the trick worth forty wenches.[5]

8.22

Nestor[6]

Vulcan, contrive me such a cup
   As Nestor used of old:[7]
Show all thy skill to trim it up
   Damask it round with gold.[8]

Make it so large that filled with sack[9]
   Up to the swelling brim

[2] *porter* and *groom* menial servants.

[3] *drudge* labour sexually (implying 'irksome toiling'); *Aurelia*: woman's name (Latin, 'gold').

[4] *page* boy or youth employed as a personal attendant.

[5] *trick* sexual act (implying its triviality or frivolousness); *wenches*: wanton women.

[6] 'Nestor' imitates classical songs in praise of drinking (cf. 'Anacreontea', *Greek Lyric* 2.4–5).

[7] The Greek general, Nestor, had an enormous, four-handled, golden drinking cup.

[8] *damask* decorate with rich designs.

[9] *sack* dry white Spanish wine.

Vast toasts on the delicious lake
  Like ships at sea may swim.[10]

Engrave no battle on its cheek
  (With war I've nought to do):
I'm none of those that took Mastricht
  Nor Yarmouth Leaguer knew.[11]

Let it no name of planets tell,
  Fixed stars or constellations
For I am no Sir Sidrophel,[12]
  Nor none of his relations.

But carve thereon a spreading vine,
  Then add two lovely boys;[13]
Their limbs in amorous folds entwine,
  The type of future joys.[14]

Cupid and Bacchus my saints are:
  May drink and love still reign.
With wine I wash away my cares,
  And then to Phill: again.[15]

10 *Vast … swim* Pieces of spiced toast would be placed in ale and sack.

11 During the Anglo-Dutch Wars (1652–74), England and France attacked the city of *Mastricht* (Netherlands); *Yarmouth Leaguer*: A *leaguer* was a military encampment. In 1673, troops were gathered at Yarmouth for an invasion of the Netherlands that never took place.

12 *Sir Sidrophel* comic astrologer in Samuel Butler's satiric epic romance *Hudibras* (2.3.106–1190).

13 *two lovely boys* Cupid; Bacchus (Glossary).

14 *type … joys* i.e., Cupid and Bacchus's embrace prefigures the joys of the afterlife.

15 *Phill:* perhaps, an abbreviation of 'Phyllis' (with an obvious play on 'fill').

8.23

To the Post Boy[16]

Son of a whore, God damn you, can you tell,
A peerless peer the readiest way to hell?[17]
I've out-swilled Bacchus, sworn of my own make
Oaths would fright Furies and make Pluto quake.
I've swived more whores more ways than Sodom's walls[18]
E'er knew or the College of Rome's Cardinals.[19]
Witness heroic scars – look here – ne'er go:[20]
Sear cloths and ulcers from the top to toe.[21]
Frighted at my own mischiefs I have fled
And bravely left my life's defender dead;[22]
Broke houses to break chastity and dyed
That floor with murder which my lust denied.[23]
Pox on't, why do I speak of these poor things?[24]
I have blasphemed my God and libelled kings.
The readiest way to hell? Come quick, ne'er stir![25]
Boy. The readiest way, my lord, 's by Rochester.[26]

[16] *post boy* one who assisted a person 'riding post' (where fresh mounts were stationed at intervals along a lengthy route).

[17] *peer* nobleman.

[18] *swived* copulated with; *Sodom's walls:* See **1.1.1**.

[19] *College … Cardinals* conventional English linking of sodomy with the Catholic hierarchy (cf. **1.2.1**).

[20] *heroic scars* from a confrontation involving Rochester, his friend Downs, and a local constable, in which Rochester fled, leaving Downs to be killed; also, perhaps, scars left by syphilitic pustules.

[21] *sear cloth* cerecloth, a waxed cloth to cover a wound or surgical incision; *ulcers*: secreting sores, a symptom of syphilis.

[22] *life's defender* Downs.

[23] Rochester and his friends broke into the constable's house, believing it was a brothel.

[24] *Pox on't* i.e., 'A curse on it!' (*pox*: syphilis, a sexually transmitted disease).

[25] *ne'er stir* don't go.

[26] *Rochester* punning on the Kentish town, Rochester.

8.24

Song

I rise at eleven, I dine about two,
I get drunk before seven, and the next thing I do;
I send for my whore, when for fear of a clap,[27]
I spend in her hand, and I spew in her lap:[28]
There we quarrel, and scold, till I fall asleep,
When the bitch, growing bold, to my pocket does creep;
Then slyly she leaves me, and to revenge th'affront,
At once she bereaves me of money and cunt.
If by chance then I wake, hot-headed and drunk,
What a coil do I make for the loss of my punk?[29]
I storm, and I roar, and I fall in a rage,
And missing my whore, I bugger my page.
Then crop-sick, all morning, I rail at my men,[30]
And in bed I lie yawning, till eleven again.

[27] *clap* gonorrhoea (sexually transmitted disease).

[28] *spend* ejaculate; *spew*: common synonym for 'ejaculate' among libertine poets, Rochester in particular; the older meaning of the word ('vomit') suggests the speaker's revulsion.

[29] *coil* tumult; *punk*: whore.

[30] *crop-sick* indigestion attendant on gluttony; *men*: servants.

8.25

From *Sodom and Gomorrah* (publ., 1684)[31]

8.25.1 [Scene 1] Act 1, scene 1

The scene an antechamber hung with Aretine's postures.[32] *Enter* BOLLOXINIAN, BORASTUS, PINE, POCKENNELLO, TEWLY.[33]

BOLLOXINIAN. Thus in the zenith of my lust I reign:
I eat to swive and swive to eat again.[34]
Let other monarchs who their sceptres bear
To keep their subjects less in love than fear
Be slaves to crowns, my nation shall be free:
My pintle only shall my sceptre be.[35]
My laws shall act more pleasures than command
And with my prick I'll govern all the land.
POCKENNELLO. Your Grace at once has from the powers above
A princely wisdom and a princely love.
Whil'st you permit your nation to enjoy
That freedom which a tyrant would destroy,
By this your royal tarse will purchase more[36]
Than all the riches of the king of Zoare.[37]

[31] Reprinted by permission of Oxford University Press. Also known as *Sodom, or the Quintessence of Debauchery*, this play's authorship remains doubtful. The text is from H. Love's Oxford edition, itself based on the two earliest versions contained in a single Princeton University manuscript, which differ substantially. Although there was apparently a published edition in 1684 (with the probably false imprint 'Antwerp'), it has not survived. I have modernized spelling and punctuation throughout, but have left elided obscenities and those that are fully 'spelled out' as they appear in Love's edition. I have also reproduced Love's doubled act and scene designations, a result of the fact that the two versions do not neatly coincide.

[32] *Aretine's postures* Aretino (Glossary).

[33] *Bolloxinian* from 'bollocks' (i.e., testicles, balls); *Borastus*: from Latin, 'astus' ('cunning', with obvious play on 'ass' and 'arse'); *Pine*: perhaps, from 'pine' (to long after); *Pockennello*: from 'pock' (a sexually transmitted pustule or the scar left by it); *Tewly*: perhaps from 'tewly' (delicate or sickly), but more likely from the verb 'tew' (to copulate with).

[34] *swive* copulate.

[35] *pintle* penis (popular term in Restoration lampoons, particularly to describe Charles II's penis).

[36] *tarse* penis.

[37] *Zoare* city where Lot takes refuge from the destruction of Sodom and Gomorrah (Gen. 19.20–3).

BORASTUS. May your most gracious pr— and cods be still[38]
As boundless in their pleasure as your will.
May plentiful delight of c—t and arse[39]
Be never wanting to your royal tarse.
May lust your pr— with flaming zeal incite
Ever to f— with safety and delight.[40]
BOLLOXINIAN. My pr—, Borast, thy judgement and thy care
Requires in a nice juncture of affair.[41]
BORASTUS. My duty's still my service to prepare.
BOLLOXINIAN. You are my council all –
POCKENNELLO. The bliss we own –
BOLLOXINIAN. But this advice belongs to you alone.
Borastus, c—ts no longer I admire:
The drudgery has worn out my desire.[42]
BORASTUS. Your Grace may soon to human arse retire.
BOLLOXINIAN. My pleasure for new c—ts I will uphold
And the reserves of kindness for the old.
I grant in absence dildos may be used
With milk of goats wherein our seed's infused.[43]
My pr— to bald c—t shall no more resort:
Merkins rub off and often spoil the sport.[44]

[...]

BOLLOXINIAN. As for my queen, her c—t no more invites,
Clad with the filtre of her nasty whites.[45]
Borastus spends his time I know not how
That choice of buggery is wanting now.
BORASTUS. I would advise you, sir, to make a pass
Once more at Pockennello's loyal arse;
Besides, sir, Pine has so gentile a skin[46]
'Twould tempt a saint to thrust his pintle in.

38 *pr—* prick; *cods*: testicles.
39 *c—t* cunt.
40 *f—* fuck.
41 *nice* delicate; requiring tactful handling.
42 *drudgery* sexual labour (implied that vaginal intercourse is 'irksome toil').
43 *seed* semen. Compare Bolloxinian's dildo with the one in *The Sappho-An* (see **7.9.3**).
44 *merkin* pubic wig (to compensate for pubic baldness due to sexually transmitted disease).
45 *whites* chronic vaginal infection; often considered a sign of sexually transmitted disease.
46 *gentile* soft, smooth.

TEWLY. When last, great sir, your pleasure did vouchsafe
To let poor Tewly's hand your pintle chafe,
You gently moved it to my arse when, lo,
Arse did the deed which white hand could not do.
BOLLOXINIAN. True, I remember how my sperm did flow.
Tewly, I'm in arrear to thy rewards.[47]
But let's be active while the time affords,
And Pockennello for my mate I choose:
His arse shall for a minute be my spouse.
POCKENNELLO. That spouse shall, mighty sir, although it's blind,
Prove to my lord both dutiful and kind.
It's all I wish that Pockennello's arse
May still find favour from your royal tarse.
BOLLOXINIAN. And next with Tewly I will have a touch –
And Pine –
PINE. Oh, sir, you honour us too much.
It was enough when me you did entrust
As harbinger unto your sacred lust.
But, as from heaven, your will can make us blest
Though we're unworthy when we do our best,
Nor your affections dare we claim as right.
BOLLOXINIAN. Those who my pleasure serve I must requite.
Henceforth, Borastus, set the nation free:
Let conscience have its force of liberty.
I do proclaim that buggery may be used
O'er all the land so c—t be not abused.
That's the proviso; this shall be your trust.
BORASTUS. All things shall to your order be adjust.
BOLLOXINIAN. To Buggeranthes let the grant be given[48]
And let 'em bugger all things under heaven.
BORASTUS. Straight this indulgence shall be issued forth[49]
From east to west and through the south and north.

[47] *in arrear* in arrears (perhaps with a pun on 'rear' meaning 'buttocks', although the *OED* dates this usage from 1716).

[48] *Buggeranthes* Bolloxinian's general; his name means 'the flower [or blooming] of buggery'.

[49] *Henceforth … forth* The legal and religious language here and elsewhere suggests a parody of Charles II's controversial and quickly rescinded Royal Declaration of Indulgence (1672), that gave religious freedom to Roman Catholics and Protestant Dissenters. Bolloxinian's statement 'Let conscience have its force of liberty' echoes the Declaration's granting of 'liberty to tender consciences'; the words 'grant' and 'indulgence' also suggest the link to Charles's proclamation (Elias 432–3).

[...]

BOLLOXINIAN. [...] Come, Pockennello, now my pintle burns,
In and untruss: I'll bugger you by turns.

End of Act 1

8.25.2 [Scene 2] Act 2, scene 2

[The ladies of the court, including Bolloxinian's queen, Cuntigratia (meaning 'free or loose cunt'), and her ladies-in-waiting, Clitoris, Fuckadilla, and Cunticula angrily discuss Bolloxinian's edict legalizing sodomy, and his decision to practice anal intercourse exclusively, and also only with other men. The garden setting for this scene features 'statues of naked men and women in various postures', the fountain fashioned after a urinating woman.]

8.25.3 First continuation [Scene A2]

CLITORIS. I've long considered of your royal want
And grieved to see your gaping cunt,
Touched your large womb and urged my frigger still,[50]
Tired my weak arm the pleasure to fulfil;
But c—t's dull motion all my hopes did kill.
At last my tongue with royal c—t did play
Whilst tickling motion forced the soul away:
You heaved and shoved till roapy sperm came down,[51]
Filled longing mouth and did my labours crown.
CUNTIGRATIA. Your pains were mighty and my sperm came slow.
Thrice had I charged my confident dildo,[52]
Thrice put it in, moved it with grace and art,
Called you, Clitoris, bid you reach my heart;
But the dull thing of gaping c—t afraid[53]
Spent on my thighs and robbed me of your aid.
CLITORIS. Then was the time!
CUNTIGRATIA. It was your tongue, like prick
Of charming boy or bloody neck of chick,[54]

[50] *frigger* dildo (from 'frig', meaning 'to masturbate; fuck').

[51] *roapy* viscous. Like men, women were believed to produce *sperm* (seed) and ejaculate it at the moment of orgasm.

[52] *charged* filled (with liquid). See **n43**.

[53] *dull thing* i.e., the dildo.

[54] *bloody ... chick* Comparing a small penis to the 'neck of [a] chick' parodies that of

Moved in my c—t, did my dull soul inspire,
Brought down my terms and made me all desire.[55]

[…]

CLITORIS. His boundless pleasure buggers all he meets,[56]
As linkboys, fiddlers, frigs in open streets,[57]
Forgets your joys—one c—t alone doth cloy
A man who all should uncontrolled enjoy.
Like him run on with pleasure, build your throne,
F—k, frig, spend, riot and the world's your own.
CUNTIGRATIA. I like your counsel: range the world about,
Grope for huge tarses, find the fittest out,
Try how they spend, display your greatest charms,
Open at once your cunt, your breast, your arms;
Fuck him to heights and, when his sperm is risen,
Send him to me, to all, to fuck to heaven.
Cunt tired out he shall to arse repair,
Bugger the part but frig me with the hair.

[…]

[The scenes not included here recount Prince Pricket's first sexual encounters with his sister, the Princess Swivia, and the waiting gentlewoman Cunticula; and Cuntigratia's unsuccessful attempt to seduce General Buggeranthes.]

8.25.4 [Scene B5] Act ___, scene 5

Enter BOLLOXINIAN, BORASTUS *and* POCKENNELLO.

BOLLOXINIAN. Since I have buggered human arse, I find
Pintle to cunt is not so much inclined.
What though the lechery be dry, 'tis smart,[58]

a large penis and 'a goose's neck' that occurs in various anatomy treatises (J. Grantham Turner, *Schooling Sex* (Oxford, 2003), p. 300).

55 *terms* menstrual blood. Cuntigratia's sexual deprivation has resulted in the stoppage of menstruation, a disorder for which intercourse was often recommended, at least for married women.

56 *his* Bolloxinian's.

57 Employed to light passengers along streets, *linkboys* were reputedly promiscuous; *fiddlers*: the obvious meaning, but also a sexually charged noun meaning variously 'vagina', 'penis', 'whore', and simply 'sexual partner'.

58 *smart* sharp.

And turkey's arse I love with all my heart;[59]
The lust which in those animals I see
Does far exceed all human lechery.
Their cunts by use improve their influence,
While ours grow void of pleasure, bounds or sense.
By oft fomenting, c—t so big does swell[60]
That pintle works like clapper in a bell,
All vacuum, no grasping flesh does glide
Or hug the brawny muscles of his side,
Tickling the nerves, prepuce and glance,[61]
Which all mankind with such delights intrance.

BORASTUS. Nature to them but one poor rule does give;
But man delights in various ways to swive.

POCKENNELLO. How simple was the lechery of old,
How full of shame, how feeble and how cold,
Confined to a formality of law
When woman ne'er her husband's p—tle saw
But when tame lust or duty made him draw,
Then fucked with such indifferent delight
As if pr— stood against the will in spite;
First rubbed, then spent, then groaned and so good night.
We the kind dictates of our sense pursue:
We study pleasures still and find out new.

BORASTUS. May, as the gods, his name immortall be
That first received the gift of buggery.

BOLLOXINIAN. Faces may change but c— is but c— still,
And he that fucks is slave to woman's will.

POCKENNELLO. True, Bolloxinian, should we daily bring
One dish to feast the palate of a king
And strive with various sauces to incite
The grandeur of his critique appetite,
Yet still the meat's the same; the change does lie
But in the sauces' great variety.
So 'tis with cunts' repeated dull delights:
Sometime they've flowers for sauce, sometime they've whites,[62]
Or crab-lice, which like buttered shrimps appear,
And may be served for garnish all the year.

59 *turkey* popularly believed a lustful, syphilis-ridden bird.

60 *fomenting* stimulating.

61 *glance* glans.

62 *flowers* menstrual blood; *whites*: See **n45**.

Enter BUGGERANTHES.

BORASTUS. My Liege, the general.
BOLLOXINIAN. Brave man of war,
How fares the camp?
BUGGERANTHES. Great sir, the soldiers are
In double duty to your favour bound:
They own it all, they swear and tear the ground,
Protest they'll die in drinking of your health
And creep into the other world by stealth,
Intending there among the gods to vie
Their Sodom's king with immortality.
BOLLOXINIAN. How, are they pleased with what I did proclaim?
BUGGERANTHES. They practise it in honour of your name.
If lust prevail they want no woman's aid:
Each buggers with content his own comrade.
BOLLOXINIAN. They know 'tis chargeable with c— to play.
BUGGERANTHES. It saves them, sir, at least a fortnight's pay.
BOLLOXINIAN. And arse they fuck, and bugger one another –
BUGGERANTHES. And live like man and wife, sister and brother.
Dildos and dogs with women do prevail.
I caught one frigging with a cow's bob tail.
'My lord,' said she, 'I do it with remorse
For I had once a passion for a horse,
Who in a moment grieved and pleased my heart.
I saw him standing pensive in a cart
With padded eye and back with sores oppressed,
And heavy halter hanging on his crest.
I grieved for the poor beast, I stroked his mane,
Pitied his daily labour and his pain,
When on a sudden from his scabbard flew
The stateliest yard that ever mortal drew,
Which clinging to his belly stiff did stand.
I tooked and grasped it with my loving hand,
And in a passion moved it to my c—t;
But he, to womankind not being wont,
Drew back his engine though my c—t could spare
Perhaps as much room as his lady mare.
At last I found his constancy was such
That he would none but his dear mistress touch.
Urged by his scorn, I did his sight depart
And to despair surrendered up my heart.

Now wand'ring o'er this vile (cunt-starving) land
I am content with what comes next to hand.'

BOLLOXINIAN. Such women ought to live. Pray find her out.
She shall a pintle have both stiff and stout.
Pr— shall hourly by her c—t be sucked:
She shall be daily by all nations fucked.
Industrious c—ts shall never pintles want:
She shall be mistress to the elephant.

BUGGERANTHES. Your Honour's matchless.

BOLLOXINIAN. I'll do'it. Let her swive.
I will encourage virtue while I live.

[...]

Enter TEWLY *and stranger with forty striplings.*[63]

BUGGERANTHES. So beautiful a troop I have not seen.

BOLLOXINIAN. How fares my brother Tarsehole and his queen?[64]

STRANGER. All hail and health from them was sent by me:
From these and this, O king, vouchsafe to see.

[...]

BOLLOXINIAN. Stranger, 'tis well. Thanks, and go tell thy lord
That what the limits of my land afford
He may like me command. What c—t does live
Within my precincts that are fit to swive
We'll send by Tewly. We intend a score
Of modest virgins, if we can find no more,
We shall with careful expedition send.
Meanwhile, our love and honour recommend.
Tewly, divert the stranger while he stays
With wine and with our Sodomean plays.
Receive him kindly, my command fulfil
And let him fuck and bugger what he will.
Here are my valued gems: these are to me
More than the riches of my treasury.
What does my crown or jewels do me good?
Jewels and gold are clay to flesh and blood.
Grace e'ry chamber with a pretty boy;
But here's my pretty darling and my joy.

[63] A gift from the King of Gomorrah, Bolloxinian's brother; *striplings*: youths.

[64] *Tarsehole* from 'tarse', meaning 'penis' (with the obvious play on 'arsehole').

Go and prepare what to my pleasure's due!
The choice of their apartments left to you.
[*Exeunt with the rest.*
Come, my soft flesh, our Sodom's dear delight:
To honoured lust thou art betrayed this night.
Lust with thy beauty cannot brook delay.
Between thy pretty haunches I will play.
[*Exeunt omnes.*

8.25.5 [Scene B7] Act 4, scene 5

[The court physician proclaims that a plague of syphilis has infected the whole nation; Queen Cuntigratia is dead and Bolloxinian's heir, Prince Pricket, is infected. Cuntigratia's ghost appears to foretell Bolloxinian's impending death and descent into hell.]

BOLLOXINIAN. Let heavens descend and set the world on fire!
We to some darker cavern will retire;
There on thy buggered a—se I will expire.[65]
[*Leering on* POCKENNELLO.

Enter fire and brimstone. A cloud of smoke arises.
The curtain falls.

[…]

Charles Goodall (1671–89), poet

Student of Eton College and Merton College (Oxford University), Goodall published his verse in the multi-authored *Poetical Recreations* (1688) and the solely authored *Poems and Translations* (1689). The latter contains thirty-three poems dedicated or addressed to male members of his Eton and Merton circles; eleven to women, some of whom are related to the men; and thirteen to the poet's (probably imaginary) mistress 'Idera', to whom Goodall addresses Theocritus's homoerotic 'Idyll 23'. Like all Goodall's homoerotic lyrics in *Poetical Recreations* that were reprinted in *Poems and Translations*, 'Idyll 23' is recast in heteroerotic terms, transforming the poem's scornful young man into a merciless young woman ('Theocritus,' *Online Companion*).

[65] *a—se* arse.

8.26

From *Poetical Recreations* (1688)

8.26.1 To Duserastes[1]

O cruel, proud, and fair,
Cause of my love, and cause of my despair!
When first a little sprouting beard
Those lovely lips and cheeks shall guard,
Not soft as down, but rugged, long, and hard;
When lovely locks that on your shoulders play
Shall turn to the cold hoary grey,
Or wasting time shall eat 'em quite away;
As when too much of working spoils
The very heart of fruitful soils,
And makes 'em, without moisture, hard and dry,
All plants and herbs do wither, fall, and die;
And when that lovely red and white
That in your charming cheeks do meet,
That make the lily and the rose[2]
Their sweetness and their colour lose,
Shall turn to wrinkles wan and pale,
And all your other charms shall fail:
Then as you go to gaze
Upon your former angel's face,
In your too-much-frequented looking-glass;
Then your own presence will you strive to shun,
And thus complain in a forsaken lover's tone:
'Why was I ever young?
Why was not beauty long?
Why had I ever charms, or why are they so quickly gone?'

8.26.2 The Vow. To the Same

Why do you vex me with continual fears,
And force out needless tears?
Why do you tell me I shall surely die,

[1] Based on Horace's 'Ode 4.10' (see **7.12.2**).

[2] *red and white*; *lily* and *rose* colours and emblems (respectively) of the Petrarchan mistress's perfect complexion.

Since courteous heav'n, and I,
Both in one resolution do comply?
That whensoever you are fled, unkind,
I will not stay, I cannot stay behind.
If envious Fate must strike the heart,
My better part,
Why should this lifeless lump of clay
Delay
To mount the skies to follow thee away?
Propitious Fate has spun
Both threads of life in one;
I've made a vow, yea I have sworn,
Nor will I fail (by heav'n) to perform:
We'll travel both together to our long, long home.

In spite of hell, to heav'n we will glide,
And all the heavy world below deride,
Attended by Jove's messengers on either side.[3]
Not Charon's shabby barge,
Shall have so great, so glorious a charge;
Apollo's chariot shall us both transport,
With Mercury our guide,
Above moon, stars, and sun, we'll glide,
Till we arrive to Jove's eternal court.[4]
There in immortal state
Shall I on yours, and you on Jove's left hand be set.
Nay, further still our glories shall extend:
You shall be worshipped as the god of beauty,
To you shall mortals pay all sacred duty.
My name shall signify a faithful friend;
Here shall our love no quarrels know, our joys no end.

[3] *Jove's messengers* the eagle, and Iris, the goddess of the rainbow.
[4] *Jove's eternal court* Olympus; heaven.

8.27

From *Poems and Translations* (1689)

8.27.1 To Mr G.L.: An Ode[5]

Dear George, the better part
Of my united, now divided heart,
Accept of these rude lines this paper bears,
Conceived in sorrow, and brought forth in tears,
Sad as th' occasion, hasty as thy flight.
Nor wonder, if with so much pains
They wrought their passage through my brains;
No wonder, if so hardly I the dirge indite,
Which ev'n my pen, clogged with grief, cannot write;
No wonder, if my verses lag behind,
Since my muse with tears is blind,
I to this prison here confined;
For sure no better is that place to me,
Whilst thou are absent, wheresoe'er it be.

Seven days are past, since I beheld thy face,
In which divinity itself is writ,
And angel all in every line of it,
Picture of beauty, and the stamp of grace.
Seven! to what immense number does that word amount![6]
Seven days! 7000 years in love's account.
Every minute is a day,
Every hour a tedious year,
In which the sun does once appear,
And in a moment vanishes away,
And leaves the miserable cloudy hemisphere.
Seven days! before I could my silence break,
Thy name in accents interrupted speak.
For seven long days upon the rack,[7]

[5] Possibly George Litton or Lytton (b. c. 1675/6), whose two brothers (Alexander and William) also attended Eton. Little more is known of his life, beyond the place of his birth (Windsor) and the names of his parents (Robert Litton of Windsor and Penelope, daughter of Thomas Baker).

[6] *seven* sacred number of perfection (e.g., the seven days of Creation).

[7] *rack* instrument of torture.

And overwhelmed with the dreadful storm,
  Grief haunted me like th'evil spirit of Saul;[8]
    Then in my wavering mind I thought,
What if I should myself to David's harp apply?[9]
  And might not numbers be a remedy?[10]
  I tried and found it nonsense all;
I tried again, and at the second draught,
Like old Deucalion's stones, all came to better form.[11]

To say, my life is bound in thine,
  Indeed were a tautology;
  For that as necessarily must be,
As that thou hast a soul divine.[12]
But to express the grief and consternation,
  When soul and body part;
  For such it is does seize my heart
That, that only is above my passion.
  Each day, my sun, since you withdrew your light,
  Has been an everlasting night;
  And yet still banished, Thyrsis, from thy sight!

I feel the pangs and tortures of a dying soul;
  Nay, I myself am dead, though but in part,
  Whilst you are my vicegerent in my heart,[13]
    And must command the whole.
'Tis this alone that does support
  My sinking spirits from the grave,
That though the scorpion stings, her blood can save.[14]
  Greatness and fortune do your absence court;

[8] *th'evil … Saul* Afflicted by an evil spirit, Saul was tempted to kill David, destined to be his successor as king of Israel (1 Sam. 16.14; 18.10–11).

[9] *to David's harp* i.e., to poetry and song; *David*: traditional author of the Psalms; his harp-playing soothed King Saul's troubled mind (1 Sam. 16.15–23).

[10] *numbers* verse.

[11] *Deucalion's stones* After a great flood that destroyed mankind, the only survivors, Deucalion and his wife Pyrrha, repopulated the earth by throwing stones behind them: they became men and women.

[12] *as that* since.

[13] *vicegerent* someone appointed by a ruler to exercise authority.

[14] *scorpion … save* Scorpion's oil (not blood) would cure the deadly effects of its tail's sting.

Though Fate does her malicious nature show,
To make such bitter streams from a sweet fountain flow.

Methinks I Pylades and Orestes see,
  And must admire their constancy;
    But when again I do recount
  To what vast sum my debts amount,
How infinitely I am obliged to thee,
Their friendship in the balance laid,
    And equally and fairly weighed
  Against my spotless love,
  Lighter than vanity does prove,
    Tilts up (like vapours that the air invade),
  Whilst mine is solid and does downward to its centre move:
No more to be compared, than atoms to the sun,
  Or little drops unto the boundless ocean.

Pylades proffered his own life ('tis true),
And bore that punishment was justly due
  To such a friend; but hadst thou died[15]
Instead of him, thou hadst been styled the matricide,[16]
  His horrid crime transferred to you;
That murder soon have put an end
  To that proverbial name of 'friend'.
But as thy matchless innocence[17]
  Could only be a capital offence,
Thy virtues I would ransom by my death,
And bless the author with my dying breath.

This I with less reluctancy could bear,
  Than such damnation to despair,
Than absence from that glorious sun,
Who lends all creatures light, and yet himself wants none.[18]

15 Goodall's marginal note: 'The "friend" is "Orestes, who killed his mother" and the "thou" is Pylades.'

16 Goodall's marginal note: 'This, according to Tully's [Cicero's] maxim in his treatise *De Amicitia* [i.e., *Laelius*] proves, that these two could not be true friends; for, says he, "Amicitia nisi in bonis esse non potest. Quid igitur? an caedes, bonum?"' (Friendship cannot exist except between good men. What follows? Is a murderer good?) (5.18; 18.65).

17 Goodall's marginal note: 'An apostrophe to his friend' [i.e., G.L.]; *apostrophe*: exclamatory address.

18 *wants* lacks.

'Tis from his rays I steal Promethean fire,[19]
Kindle my fatal spices and expire;[20]
Whose worth and virtues when I think upon,
Tossed by two different motions of my mind,
But both to the same end inclined,
I cannot be withheld, I must be gone.
My soul is on the wing,
But being stopped by cross necessity,
She makes a post of every wind,[21]
Sends word she fears you grow unkind,
Commits to every blast a sigh,
Then melts away into a piece of poetry:
So when the nightingale has gored her breast,[22]
She tunes her pipes, and quavers out her best,
And though in the extremity of pain,
Has not forgot her usual strain,
But sets herself to sing.

8.27.2 Solitude. To his dear Brother, Mr Ash Windham[23]

O Corydon! How I hug myself to think!
When in this troubled sea, the world,
All thrust into the main,
Till by a hurricane,
Through the abyss with vengeance hurled,
With horrible 'adieus,' they parting sink.

Whilst I upon the silent shore, secure,
Fear neither stormy wind nor tide,

[19] *Promethean fire* fire of life and poetic inspiration.

[20] Goodall's marginal note: 'An allusion to the Phoenix' (Glossary).

[21] *post* messenger.

[22] The nightingale pressing its breast against a thorn is obscurely linked to the tragic myth of Philomela, Tereus, and Procne (Glossary).

[23] *Ash Windham* (c. 1671–1749), Goodall's fellow student at Eton (c. 1685–91). 'Brother' indicates the closeness of their friendship, not any blood tie. Windham outlived his friend and went on to attend King's College (Cambridge) in 1690/1, travel and study in Italy, marry, and participate in politics (MP for Norfolk, 1708). He died in 1749 at the age of seventy-eight. The title is followed by a Latin epigraph: 'With thee forever I in woods could rest, / Where never human foot the ground has pressed; / Thou from all shades the darkness canst exclude, / And from a desert banish solitude' (Tibullus, *Elegies*, 3.19 (trans. A. Cowley, 'Of Solitude')).

With elevated soul,
Can move from pole to pole,
And through the aery regions glide,
Need only pity what they must endure.

The world will take no notice of my name;
Well then I'll let th' impostor see
I have my passions broke,
Brought pride to wear a yoke,
I'm as indifferent as she;[24]
No – I will never stop her trump of fame.[25]

That cursèd word 'the world' blisters my tongue,
It breathes out all the plagues of hell;
'Tis nonsense intricate,
Unintelligible state,
That puzzles all my brains to spell:
If I guess right, man's dust, the world is dung.

I never could any contexture find.[26]
Confusion only is her course,
Her joys but pleasant fictions,
A mass of contradictions,
All guilt, all trouble and remorse;
This is the world, or she or I am blind.

She never yet was in true colours drawn:
All, disappointments, pains, and fears,
One scene of misery,
Constant inconstancy,
Tempestuous world, a vale of tears,
For our chief happiness chance the only pawn.

Passions, and discontents, and jealousies,
Public war, and domestic strife,
Perjury and deceit:
This gall confounds the sweet,

[24] *she* the world.
[25] *trump* trumpet (loud acclamation).
[26] *contexture* unifying principle.

And poisons all the joys of life,
And our vain hopes must end in penitential sighs.

Oh! I am sick, and my head giddy turns;
The thoughts of noise I cannot bear,
Impertinence strikes me through;[27]
Business – that kills me too,
Death is less terrible than care;
To get from this fool's paradise my heart burns.[28]

Who would not then with us, dear friend, retire?
Accept the happiness to shroud
Under a shady screen,
To walk along unseen,
Wrapped like Aeneas in a cloud,
And see the world, as he did Troy, on fire.[29]

'Tis more than time, my soul, that we were gone;
Delay, my Corydon, does us wrong.
The world will grow more bold,
Still loath to quit her hold,
For her temptations they are strong.
Come then and put blind Pluto's helmet on.[30]

What a fair prospect now have we!
Can undisturbed together stand,
Enjoy ourselves, and all
The world her goods can call,
And touch the globe but with our hand,
And all things past, present, and future see.

Here at Earth's puffed up bubbles we can smile,[31]
Her fucused vanities despise,[32]

[27] *impertinence* unmannerly intrusion [upon a person].

[28] *get from* escape.

[29] *Wrapped … fire* When Aeneas and the fleeing Trojans arrive on the shores of Libya, Venus appears to Aeneas and Achates, conceals them in a cloud, and sends them off to Carthage to meet Queen Dido (1.411–586). Aeneas has earlier seen Troy burning, destroyed by the Greeks.

[30] The Cyclops gave a *helmet* of invisibility to *Pluto*, god of the Underworld.

[31] *bubbles* empty displays.

[32] *fucused* painted (with connotations of vanity, deceptiveness).

Divert with pleasant chat,
Discourse of this or that,
Still aiming to be truly wise,
With books, or harmless sport, the time beguile.[33]

Full of ourselves, what can we wish for more?
We find us work enough to tend
The habit of our soul,
Our passions to control,
To do the duties of a friend.
'Tis the mistaken world, not we, are poor.

Here in an empty theatre we sit,
Retired to keep our holy-day;[34]
Our minds the scenes must be,
The critical spectators we
Of one another's life, the play,
The authors and the judges of our wit.

If we have acted well in heaven's sight,
What though we hear no echoing stage?
Or when our state we change,
What though our names seem strange,
Unknown to a succeeding age?
Without that witness happy Democrite![35]

Why should we fame, that treacherous idol, court?
That sets us up for envy's mark,
That burns us with the rays
Of undeservèd praise,
Only to blind us in the dark,
To throw us down again for fear or sport.

Fame's breath is short, when she must trumpet loud:
'Tis seldom that she comes alone;
She's an unconstant guest,
That loves to change her nest.

33 *beguile* spend pleasantly.

34 *holy-day* holiday.

35 *Democrite* Democritus (c. 460 BCE–c. 370 BCE), Greek philosopher (the 'Laughing Philosopher'), famed for his modesty, rural retirement, contempt for money and status, as well as his cheerful attitude.

True worth, true praise would not be known;
The sun looks brightest through a silver cloud.

On an embroidered bank here we can pick and choose
An unbought, savoury, wholesome dish;
On leaves serve up our fare,
Perfumed with the sweet air.
Then Corydon! to complete our wish,
Our recreation, friendship and a muse.

Sometimes we take a pride to stand and see
Bees bring their yellow harvest home,
Unload their swelling thighs,
And as their goddess wise,
Spin it into their honeycomb.
Happy spectators! happy rivals we!

Sometimes upon a downy couch of grass,
On flowery cushions stretched we lie,
To hear a dying swan,
More sensible than man,
Warble forth a sweet elegy,[36]
Or in soft tunes the purling rivers pass.

Or else dissolved in ease, lay down our heads
In slumbers as our natures kind,
Bound in each other's arms
By virtue's strictest charms,
Lulled asleep by the whistling wind,
On easy velvet, fragrant violet-beds.[37]

The name Diogenes justly none can give,[38]
Nor churlish call our innocence;
With solitude thus crowned,
What firebrand can be found?[39]
Unless our happiness give offence,
For in the world, as out of it, we live.

36 *To … elegy* Swans were believed to sing beautifully just before dying.

37 *violet* spring flower associated with Venus; traditional symbol of faithfulness in love.

38 *Diogenes* of Sinope Cynic philosopher and by-word for misanthropy and incivility.

39 *firebrand* kindler of conflict.

Sometimes hear Echo her misfortunes tell,
See how she'll watch the lovely boy
Narcissus, as he looks
Into the crystal brooks.
Her vocal repartees enjoy,[40]
Or the melodious notes of Philomel.[41]

Sometimes in shady groves together walk,
And satisfied with humble sights,
See art and nature both digest
In Milton, Waller, and the rest.[42]
Full and unparalleled delights!
Of love and solitude divinely talk.

Each dryad that is worthy of the wound,[43]
Each tree that's worthy of the mark,
Our mutual friendship know,
Under our auspice grow,
'Thyrsis and Corydon' on the bark,
'Thyrsis and Corydon' the woods resound.[44]

But above all, the ash aspiring shoots,
Thy badge of honour proud to wear;
The ash, a tree for Jove,[45]
The ash, itself a grove,
Proud thy name in hers to bear,[46]
She nods her trembling head, and struts her swelling roots.[47]

The nymphs here take their rounds, and dance, and play;
The hamadryads at us peep;[48]

[40] *repartees* lively replies.

[41] *Philomel* the nightingale. See Philomela (Glossary). Cf. **n22**.

[42] John *Milton* (1608–74), author of the pastoral elegy 'Lycidas' and the biblical epic *Paradise Lost*; Edmund *Waller* (1606–87), best-known for his love lyrics.

[43] *dryad* tree-dwelling spirit, here, a synonym for 'tree'; *wound*: cutting of the lovers' names into the bark.

[44] The speaker finally names himself: *Thyrsis* (Glossary); see *Corydon* (Glossary).

[45] *ash* for the ancients, a sacred tree; symbol of solidity.

[46] *thy name* Ash Windham.

[47] *struts* juts forth, stretches out.

[48] *hamadryads* wood-nymphs.

Crocus and hyacinth some bring,[49]
Daisies, the maidenhead of the spring:[50]
Others behind us softly creep,
And steal our songs and pastorals away.

When our light hearts are for a looser rein,
To banquets we ourselves invite,
Consorts of music and of love,
Ambrosia from above;[51]
Verses for second course recite,
And with alternate trifles entertain.[52]

Or we converse with garden mysteries,
See the emulous roses blast;[53]
The loving ivy twine;[54]
The wall cling to the vine;
And Flora taking her repast:[55]
Adam might envy in his paradise.

And thus withdrawn from business, noise, and strife,
We double our few fleeting days,
And when together fled,
Fate having cut our thread,[56]
Were we sent back into this maze,
We'd act but the same scene, our former life.[57]

[49] *crocus* flower of the spring; *hyacinth*: flower born out of the tragic end of the love between Apollo and the beautiful boy, Hyacinthus; symbolic of love, faithfulness, and mourning; some varieties bloom around Easter. See 'Apollo and Hyacinthus' (Glossary).

[50] *daisies* symbol of innocence, virtue, and youth; emblem of pledged love between a knight and his lady; symbol of the resurrection (it blooms close to Easter); *maidenhead*: virginity (the state of being new).

[51] *ambrosia* food of the gods; consuming it conveyed immortality.

[52] *trifles* jokes; perhaps, amusing stories.

[53] *roses* emblem of romantic love (or *primroses*, early spring flower; emblem of youth and young love); *blast*: wither (after blooming). They are *emulous* of (desirous of imitating) the friends' indestructible love.

[54] The *ivy* (sometimes, the vine) twining around the oak was an emblem of mutual support in marriage and love.

[55] *Flora* Roman goddess of flowers and the spring.

[56] *cut our thread* Fates (Glossary).

[57] The poem concludes with a Latin epigram from Virgil, *Georgics*, 2.486–9, 493–4: 'let my delight be the country, and the running streams amid the dells – may I love the

8.27.3 Parting with Mr Tho[mas] Bebington[58]

Down by a river's side together sat
Thyrsis and Hylas, (such was once the state[59]
Of our first parents, in a friendly strife,[60]
Thus innocence might learn to square her life)
Where singing waters lulled themselves asleep,
And clouded heaven did sympathizing weep:
When pensive Thyrsis thus did silence break,
And all in tears to his loved Hylas speak.

Thyrsis
And canst thou, Hylas, thou, be so unkind
Thus to leave me and life behind?
And canst thou think of me without regret?
On love's account for millions run in debt?

Hylas
No, Thyrsis! Hylas can't unconstant prove,
Nor have I yet been wavering in my love;
But emulous fate summons us both to part:
Hast thou not a sufficient pledge, my heart?

Thyrsis
Yet out of sight I shall be out of mind.
Ah! Hylas, should you prove unkind,
Officious fate would need no other knife
To cut in two my ravelled thread of life.[61]

waters and the woods, though fame be lost. Oh, for those plains, and Spercheus, and Taygetus, where Spartan girls hold Bacchic rites. Oh, for one to set me in the cool glens of Haemus, and shield me under the branches' mighty shade' and 'Happy too is he who knows the woodland gods, Pan and old Silvanus and the sister nymphs'.

58 Thomas Bebington (b. c. 1674) was at Eton (c. 1687–91), before attending Christ's College (Cambridge); the seventeen-year-old student matriculated there and entered Gray's Inn in 1691. Beyond the names of his parents (Michael Bebington of St Margaret's, Westminster, and a woman named Constance), nothing else is known about him, except what the poem below implies: that he left England for an apparently lengthy sojourn in Holland.

59 *Thyrsis* Goodall; *Hylas*: Bebington. For Thyrsis and Hylas, see Glossary.

60 *first parents* Adam and Eve.

61 *thread of life* Fates (Glossary).

Hylas
Nature herself shall first unhingèd be,
The whole creation lose its symmetry,
Iron th' attractive loadstone shall forsake,[62]
When I the sacred league of friendship break.

Thyrsis
Into a confused chaos shall be hurled
The shattered atoms of the world.
The needle too the northern point shall shun,
And with my promise rivers backwards run.

Hylas
To Hylas then be sure you never fail
Kisses to send by every gentle gale.
Let Hylas be your talk, Hylas your dreams,
Transport me sighs over the Belgic streams.[63]

Thyrsis
To Thyrsis, without intermission, pay
Your bounden duty night and day;
And nothing less to Thyrsis than to heaven,
For life and love by both alike are given.
Pray to the gods; but I can hardly say
Whether to them you first presume to pray:
No—your first and last thoughts must be my due.
Come, Hylas! then once more renew
Your everlasting vow, before your long adieu.

Hylas
I swear by all the thunderbolts of Jove,
By those revengeful darts of injured Love,
By life and death, and all the powers above,
To comprehend them all, I swear by you,
That I forever will be just and true.

Thyrsis
May all the plagues that vengeance has in store
For infidelity, these and more,

62 *loadstone* magnet-like substance.
63 *Belgic* Belgian.

With aggravations, light on perjured me,
If I be guilty of unconstancy;
Or if an action be against me brought,[64]
Of one suspicious deed, or doubtful thought.

This said, ravish'd into an ecstasy,[65]
They would in their perfection die;[66]
And struggling hardly to themselves can come,[67]
Like prophets with their inspiration dumb.
Cupid the heavenly mediator came,
And with two arrows dipped in honour's flame,
Their golden points piercing through both their hearts,
For trial of their faith and virtue, parts.
Hylas the seas to Holland troubled bore,
And left deserted Thyrsis sighing on the shore.

Thomas Dilke (*fl.* 1678–98), writer

For his biography, see the Introduction to **7.26**.

8.28

From *The Lover's Luck* (1696)

[Sir Nicholas Purflew and Alderman Whim are joint-guardians to their kinswoman, Mrs Purflew, a beautiful and witty heiress. Of her three suitors – the fortune-hunting lawyer Mr Breviat; the 'self-admiring fop' Goosandelo; and Colonel Bellair – only the last is in love with Purflew. Breviat wins Whim's support for his suit by humouring his obsession with trading ventures; Goosandelo Sir Nicholas's by humouring his obsession with heraldry; both are inept suitors. True love and poetic justice triumph: Breviat ends up married to Purflew's cousin and confidante, the penniless

[64] *an action … brought* i.e., if a lawsuit is initiated against me; earlier, *aggravations* (those circumstances that make a crime more serious) and *perjured* (to lie under judicial oath) also have legal connotations.

[65] *ravish'd … ecstasy* transported into a rapturous state beyond physical sensation; but also, 'being taken into a realm of intense bodily pleasure'.

[66] *die* the obvious meaning; also, 'achieve sexual orgasm'.

[67] *hardly* scarcely; *come*: i.e., come back to their bodies.

and potentially wanton Mrs Pliant; Goosandelo to Jocand, Colonel Bellair's witty page-boy; and Bellair to Purflew.]

8.28.1 Act 1 [scene 3]

[...]

GOOSANDELO. If I am left to the lady,[1] I need not say a word of the matter,[2] though you see I have a happy talent in polite oratory, were there occasion.

SIR NICHOLAS. But, good sir, will you make love without speaking?

GOOSANDELO. I'll undertake to thaw a woman's heart, that's as cold as ice, with my bare appearance; and insensibly wriggle into her affections with my pretty, taking[3] movements, as thus: so I come into a room, and erect myself at a distance, thus; observe my eyes now. Then I jut[4] a little on, twisting myself thus. Now look how I set my feet. Then I gracefully handle my snuff-box, thus; pray, mind my hand. Now she smiles, I spring forwards, open my arms, and she, poor soul, drops into my bosom like a shooting star, and there dissolves to jelly.

SIR NICHOLAS. On my word, a notable odd way of courtship. Come, sir, will you honour me with your company to dinner? Alderman Whim and I keep a joint house over our joint trust:[5] But not a syllable of it[6] to him.

GOOSANDELO. No, no, mum's the word.

8.28.2 Act 2 [scene 1]

[...]

PLIANT. Oh cousin, it's Mr Goosandelo; he was the topping spark[7] at the Wells[8] this year.

PURFLEW. Yes, yes, Mr Goosandelo is a topping spark wherever he comes.

PLIANT. Do you know him?

1 *left ... lady* allowed to court Purflew without interference.
2 *matter* love and courtship.
3 *taking* alluring.
4 *jut* thrust [oneself] forward.
5 *joint house* single household; *joint trust*: Mrs Purflew.
6 *it* Goosandelo's wooing of Purflew and Nicholas's support of it.
7 *topping spark* best fop (said ironically).
8 *Wells* Epsom or Tunbridge Wells, fashionable watering-places.

PURFLEW. I know enough of him. The last time I was at the play with my aunt, I saw him making antic[9] grimaces, and playing a thousand monkey-tricks in [the] fop-box.[10]

PLIANT. You must not expect a Mr Breviat[11] of him, on my word.

PURFLEW. I must expect what's worse: shallow conceits, windy noise, and insufferable self-applause. I find the air sweetens, the beau[12] is making his approaches.

[...]

PLIANT. O Heavens! How came we, couz, without our knotting?[13] What will this gentleman think to see us idle?

GOOSANDELO. On my soul, ladies, I am violently concerned that you are without your huswif'ry;[14] I shall want[15] a great part of my discourse. 'Tis generally the first topic we fall upon when we make our addresses to persons of quality.[16]

PURFLEW. I should think, sir, 'twere a dry, crabbed subject.

GOOSANDELO. Ah, ah, ah; because it's so full of knots; but nothing is uneasy to a man of parts.[17] As I could say thus: 'You have knotted so long upon the thread of my affections, that your la'ship[18] has now worked up a piece sufficient to fringe round a squob[19] of repose, for my long languishing amour.' And a thousand such pretty things. But since I am left here by Sir Nicholas to make love,[20] how do you think I'll begin? In what shape? Like what?

PURFLEW. Why, you need not take the pains the gods of yore used to do. You see you have easy access to me in your own shape,[21] and that's more monstrous than any you can think on.

[9] *antic* grotesque.

[10] *monkey-tricks* foolish tricks; *fop*-box: theatrical box where foppish young men gathered to see and be seen.

[11] *Mr Breviat* from 'breviate', a lawyer's brief; also, a compendium or summary.

[12] *beau* fop, dandy (cf. its use in **6.2.1 n10**; **6.4.1 n3**; **6.6 n2**; and **6.7.1 n6**).

[13] *couz* cousin; *knotting*: fancy needlework.

[14] *huswif'ry* needlework.

[15] *want* lack.

[16] *quality* rank.

[17] *parts* talents.

[18] *la'ship* ladyship.

[19] *squob* cushion.

[20] *make love* woo.

[21] *in … shape* unlike Jove, who transformed himself into different forms to seduce human women.

GOOSANDELO. Nay, now I swear you talk by contraries. Here's a lady will tell you what killing work my shape has made in the world.[22]

PLIANT. I know, sir, you were ever reputed a very pretty gentleman.

GOOSANDELO. Phoo – everybody knows that! And my life on't this lady shall know it before I have done. I am positive I shan't want shafts, for I design to make love to you in the nature of a porcupine. I'll rustle my habiliments,[23] dart forth a poignant quill,[24] and strike you dead, I'gad.[25] Don't you find yourself wounded? Hah, madam. *Stands taking snuff.*[26]

PURFLEW. I must confess your complicated perfumes, and your cashified[27] breath have a little discomposed me. Therefore, pray sir, make love at a farther distance.

GOOSANDELO. Now by the Universal Light, I have no occasion for them, were they not customary to all those that are the exact models of wit and breeding. And now I talk of wit, do you see this diamond ring? This diamond ring?

PURFLEW. What, are you going to show hocus-pocus tricks? Have you got any of the German Artist's Powder la Pimp a la Pimp?[28] You should first put on a little blue jacket, tie a chain about your middle, and skip up and down the balcony to gather spectators ere[29] you begin. About, pug.[30]

GOOSANDELO. I find you begin to love me, by that pretty endearing word. But as I was saying, this ring guided by this hand, which is a hand I am not at all ashamed on –

PLIANT. That I vow you need not.

GOOSANDELO. – has writ in ladies' windows such mysterious things that

22 *killing … world* i.e., 'how many women I have made desperately in love with me on account of my fine appearance'.

23 *habiliments* weapons (here, Goosandelo's fashionable clothes).

24 *poignant quill* piercing quill pen.

25 *I'gad* 'Egad' (in God's name).

26 *snuff* powdered tobacco, taken by inhaling through the nostrils.

27 *cashified* referring to Goosandelo's overuse of expensive perfume and mouth fresheners.

28 *German … Pimp* The German Artist is unidentified, although the reference seems to be to one of the many 'treatments' for sexually transmitted disease provided by London's medical charlatans; like the magician doing his hocus-pocus tricks and the animal trainer (in the next sentence), such charlatans and showmen would publicly display their products or services, appealing to gathered crowds to purchase them.

29 *ere* before.

30 *About, pug* i.e., 'Start dancing, pug'. Purflew imagines Goosandelo as a costumed performing dog, chained to prevent escape.

the severest critics allow 'em to be wit itself epitomized. The shashes[31] at Kensington are full of the proofs of my genius, which I daily see entered into the tablets[32] of travellers. If you'll show me your closet,[33] I'll write something in your window there.

PURFLEW. Gently, spark.[34] Sure we have not proceeded yet so far as to admit you into my closet.

GOOSANDELO. No? I find you are unacquainted with the assurance that is inseparable with men of wit. We often rush into the closets of ladies that we never saw before. I was sent for the other day by a lady of no small rank to teach her a song in her closet. [...]

[...]

8.28.3 Act 5 [scene 1]

[...]

Enter EAGER,[35] *talking with* GOOSANDELO.

EAGER. 'Tis no otherwise than I expected. 'Sblud,[36] sir, you look very charming; with this presence you have power to kill like lightning at a distance. 'Tis but clapping your hat before your face, and taking it away again of a sudden – Flash! If ere a woman in Christendom would not fall as flat as a flounder, I'd perish.

GOOSANDELO. Maybe so. I vow – *Ha bien ajusté*![37] Let me die, Eager, I think thou dost not flatter me. *Looking in his glass, and pruning*[38] *himself.*

EAGER. Flatter you! You can't be flattered. Your perfections are unspeakable.

GOOSANDELO. I have now put on most of my graces in order to the celebrating my nuptials.

EAGER. Why, the bride can't choose but think she has got a young god in her arms.

GOOSANDELO. Gad! I am a violent fool to make love to mortals,

[31] *shashes* window sashes.
[32] *tablets* notebooks.
[33] *closet* private room.
[34] *spark* elegant, foppish young man.
[35] EAGER pimp or swindler; he profits from being an advocate for both Goosandelo and Breviat to the uncles.
[36] *'Sblud* 'God's blood'.
[37] *Ha bien ajusté* i.e., 'It [the clothing] is well-fitted'.
[38] *pruning* preening.

paltry flesh and blood. I should reserve myself for nymphs and goddesses.

EAGER. No doubt they'll come in search of you, if you'll have but patience. Was you ne'er attacked with a succubus[39] yet?

GOOSANDELO. Succubus, succubus, who's she? Some foreign princess, is it not?

EAGER. No, sir, no. They are black-eyed ladies of the royal blood of Pluto. When they find a man that's cast in something more than human mould as you appear to be, they slip gently into his bed when he's fast asleep, clasp their airy limbs about him, and so enjoy him in a dream.

GOOSANDELO. Pox on 'em! If those are they, I have 'em ev'ry night. They harass me off my legs.

EAGER. They are very busy when they find out such a complete, sweet, youthful person as yourself, especially if he's a lover of provocatives, such as shellfish, cavere, eringo-roots, pistachio-paste, Spanish chocolate, etc.[40]

GOOSANDELO. There's the business then, for I violently love all such things. [...]

[Breviat enters, Goosandelo's equally foolish rival for Purflew.]

GOOSANDELO. What, do you intend to be sharp upon me? If you do, look to yourself, for I'll ferk[41] you with repartee, I'll promise you. Eager, this is the gentleman that's like to carry the great fortune, Mrs Purflew.

BREVIAT. 'Twill be impossible if you make pretensions, sir.

GOOSANDELO. Oh, sir, I protest every moment you make fresh discoveries of your sense and judgement. Let me perish, if I han't forgot to be put on my scented leather-shoes! Gentlemen, a matter of high concern requires my attending upon myself to my own apartment. *Exit.*

BREVIAT. Was there ever such a fop in nature? And yet they tell me that the ladies dote on such fools.

EAGER. That the ladies love fools is true enough, but they must be harmless, credulous, passive fools, not such a self-admiring fool as Mr Goosandelo is, that insists so much on the theme of his dear

39 *succubus* demon that assumes a female shape to have sex with men while they sleep.

40 *provocatives* aphrodisiacs, such as *shellfish, cavere* (caviare), *eringo-roots* (candied roots of the sea holly), *pistachio-paste, Spanish chocolate* (as a drink).

41 *ferk* trounce, soundly defeat.

self that he can't afford the fair sex their share of worship and flattery.

BREVIAT. That I believe is very true.

[...]

8.28.4 Act 5 [scene 2]

[...]

BREVIAT. [*Leading up* PLIANT *to the* ALDERMAN *and* SIR NICHOLAS] Gentlemen, I have the honour to be your nephew, and humbly beg you will approve the choice your niece has made.

ALDERMAN. Aye, niece, have you been too nimble for us? Come, brother, since 'tis so, Mr Breviat is an ingenious, worthy gentleman; let's wish 'em joy.

SIR NICHOLAS. Ounz![42] What's the meaning of this?

GOOSANDELO. [*Leading up* JOCAND] Ah, ah, ah! Faith, lawyer, you are a little beside the point. Gentlemen, your beautiful niece has delivered her fair person to me. Under therefore your benign aspect, we shall shine the two brightest glories of this your hemisphere.

ALDERMAN. What a pox[43] is the matter now?

SIR NICHOLAS. Aye, aye, brother! Mr Goosandelo is a person of honour and quality; I think we shall do well to congratulate the match.

BELLAIR. [*Leading up* MRS PURFLEW] Make room here! I lay claim to this lady, who lately bore the name of Purflew, and am ready to justify my title.

SIR NICHOLAS and ALDERMAN. Bless us, who's this?

PURFLEW. [*Discovering herself*] I hope, uncles, the different measures in each of your conducts will excuse my choice of this gentleman, whom I have made my husband.

ALDERMAN. Pray, will you all unmask that these riddles may be explained!

BELLAIR. [*Discovering himself*] My name is Bellair. It shall be my care to set a true value on the blessing I have obtained.

OMNES.[44] Colonel Bellair!

ALDERMAN. Who have you got, Mr Breviat? [PLIANT *discovering herself*] What, my cousin Pliant!

BREVIAT. O Lord, what will become of me when I go the circuit![45] Faith,

[42] *Ounz* 'God's wounds'.

[43] *a pox* a mild oath, 'by the pox!' (where 'pox' refers to syphilis, a sexually transmitted disease).

[44] *Omnes* Latin, 'all'.

[45] *go the circuit* journey through certain appointed areas to fulfil legal duties.

I may now go and take a gentle swing into the other world,[46] and so finish the law upon myself.

PLIANT. Don't despair, sir; now I am yours, I may be allowed to own my affections for you, and since custom deprives our sex of making court where we like; when I was assured of my couz Purflew's pre-engagement, I took this method, and shall, I hope, by my duty, procure your esteem.

GOOSANDELO. [JOCAND *discovering himself*] Oh ye powers above! I have married a boy here.

OMNES. Ha, ha, ha, ha.

GOOSANDELO. And ha, ha, ha, too: I 'gad, I'm glad on't! It's a very pretty boy, by my soul. Come to my arms, my dear little Ganymede.

ALDERMAN. Fine doings, i'dad.[47] Ah, brother, we are well enough served for being so distrustful of each other.

SIR NICHOLAS. Since my niece has disposed of herself, I am glad she has made choice of you, sir. I am not unacquainted with the family of the Bellairs, and you, colonel, have added fresh laurels to the deeds of your worthy ancestors, and have maintained an indisputable character of a man of honour. Come, let's have another dance, and so in to the collation.[48]

[...]

Thomas Baker (b. 1680/81), lawyer and writer

Founder of the gossip-mongering periodical *Female Tattler*, Baker had varying success with his plays: the popular *The Humour of the Age* (1701) led to the acting company's prosecution for public immorality; the sensational *Tunbridge-Walks* (1703) was frequently performed until mid-century; the risqué but successful *An Act at Oxford* (1704) was banned; and *The Fine Lady's Airs* (1708) was a flop. Contemporaries believed that Mr Maiden, the effeminate fop of *Tunbridge-Walks*, was the author's self-parody.

Editions

Tunbridge-Walks; or, The Yeoman of Kent: A Critical Edition, Supervising Editor. R.W. Cooley. Editorial Team. K. Hepp, D. Leiter, E. Morris, and N. Thomson. University of Saskatchewan. 27 July 2007 <http://drc.usask.ca/projects/walks/index.html>.

46 *take … swing* be hanged.

47 *i'dad* Indeed.

48 *collation* light meal of delicacies.

Norton, Rictor, ed., 'Tunbridge-Walks; or The Yeomen of Kent (1703).' *Eighteenth-Century British Erotica II*, 5.1–82.

8.29

From *Tunbridge-Walks: Or, the Yeoman of Kent* (1703)

[Loveworth pursues the beautiful but amoral Hillaria, sister of his impecunious friend, Reynard; Reynard pursues Belinda, Woodcock the Yeoman of Kent's beautiful heir, whom Woodcock wants to marry a solid country squire. Squib, a fortune-hunter and 'a fluttering fop-militia captain' and Maiden, an overly fastidious 'fellow that values himself upon all effeminacies', vie for the attention of the ladies. Hillaria, who has attached herself to the country-weary but innocent Belinda in order to live off her money, is joined by Mrs Goodfellow, an ageing drinker; Penelope, supposedly her niece, 'an heroic trapes' (a slovenly, rude, ill-bred woman; later revealed to be a prostitute); and Lucy, Hillaria's maid.]

8.29.1 Act 1, scene 1

[...]

Enter MAIDEN.

MAIDEN. Are you for the walks, gentlemen?

REYNARD. Aye, but, Mr Maiden, you are very late today. The ladies will be all there before you.

MAIDEN. Why really, sir, I used to be dressed sooner; but I have been mightily out of order this morning with the vapours and the colic,[1] and was forced to stay to eat a little chicken broth – Pray, gentlemen, what new company have we here? They say there's a world of quality[2] come down this week.

WOODCOCK. Quality! What then! They'll neither furnish the Wells with more wit nor more money.

MAIDEN. But the ladies, sir, always respect people of rank. They say, Mr Woodcock, you have a fine daughter to dispose of[3] here. I design to make her some overtures.

[1] *vapours* woman's disorder (depression, hypochondria, hysteria, etc.); *colic*: severe stomach disorder.

[2] *quality* high-ranking individuals.

[3] *dispose of* marry off.

WOODCOCK. You? Thou effeminate coxcomb, dost think she'll like one of her own sex? [*Aside*] D'slife,[4] all the fops in this place have got a notion of my daughter; I shall have 'em bait her, as a parcel of hounds do a young leveret.[5] I'll go find her out, make her pack up her auls,[6] and we'll be gone tomorrow morning. [*Exit.*

LOVEWORTH. Prithee,[7] Frank, let's to the coffee-house, and leave these fools together.

REYNARD. I'll step but to my chamber, and follow you instantly.

[*Exeunt differently.*

SQUIB. Well, friend, and what accomplishments d'you pretend to with the ladies?

MAIDEN. Why, I can sing, and dance, and play upon the guitar; make wax-work and filigree, and paint upon glass.[8] Besides, I can dress a lady up a head[9] upon occasion, for I was put prentice to a milliner[10] once, only a gentleman took a fancy to me and left me an estate; but that's no novelty, for abundance of people nowadays take a fancy to a handsome young fellow.

SQUIB. And would soothe the women with these fooleries? They hate a nice[11] fop that's so much an image of themselves; and love a robust masculine fellow that will kiss 'em, tumble 'em, and touse 'em about.[12]

MAIDEN. [*Aside*] Poor silly creature! Lard, does he think fine ladies will suffer themselves to be used like oyster women?[13] Sir, I hope I hav'n't studied the ladies so long, not to know how to address 'em; neither have I taken so much pains to polish myself to be rejected for you. Therefore, you may give yourself what rough airs you please, and yet not succeed half so well as those that have a little more modesty.

SQUIB. Modesty! Here's a fellow now! Prithee, what does modesty signify? Did it ever get a lover a maidenhead,[14] a lawyer a cause, or a

[4] *D'slife* 'God's life'.

[5] *leveret* hare.

[6] *pack … auls* pack quickly.

[7] *prithee* pray thee; please.

[8] *Wax-work* (modelling figures in wax), *filigree* (jewel-work), and *paint*[*ing*] *on glass* are all female decorative domestic arts.

[9] *dress … head* i.e., put a lady's hair up in an elaborate coiffure.

[10] *milliner* seller (sometimes maker) of women's apparel, especially hats.

[11] *nice* overly fastidious.

[12] *Tumble* and *touse* engage in rough, amorous play before and during sex.

[13] *Lard* Lord. *Oyster women* gathered, bred, and often sold oysters (an aphrodisiac), but *oyster woman/wife* could also mean 'whore'.

[14] *get … maidenhead* i.e., enable a man to deflower a virgin.

courtier a place?[15] But to pretend to modesty in this age! Why, the women have laid it aside now, and are resolved, *a-la-mode en France*, to appear bare-necked, gallop without stays,[16] drink their bottle, keep fellows, and be out of countenance[17] at nothing. Thank heaven, modesty's an infamy my family can ne'er be branded with; for all my relations from the beginning have been either pimps, poets, attorneys, projectors,[18] stock-jobbers,[19] or custom-house officers.[20] But you may e'en quit your modesty, your airs, and your graces, for I resolve to engross all the ladies to myself, and if you dare meddle with one –

MAIDEN. D'you think I won't talk to 'em, and give 'em sweetmeats?[21]

SQUIB. That I grant you, but if you offer love to anything that's under fifty, above the degree of a chambermaid, and has a nose on her face, I'll cut your throat – [*Aside*] I may hector this fellow without danger.

MAIDEN. As to that matter, captain, we shall never quarrel; for if I can raffle[22] with the ladies, dance with them, and walk with 'em in public, I never desire any private love-favours from 'em.

[...]

8.29.2 Act 2, [scene 1]

[After a courting scene featuring Hillaria, Loveworth, Reynard and Belinda, Reynard and Belinda slip into a gambling shop to avoid Belinda's father, while Hillaria and Loveworth sit down with Mrs Goodfellow and her niece Penelope to have coffee. Maiden at this point enters with musicians, who perform a song.]

Song

[*While the song's performing,* MAIDEN *uses a fan, a pocket looking-glass, etc.*

If moving softness can subdue,
See, nymphs, a swain more soft than you:[23]

[15] *place* office.
[16] *stays* corset.
[17] *keep fellows* i.e., maintain their lovers financially; *out of countenance*: abashed.
[18] *projectors* swindlers.
[19] *stock-jobbers* unscrupulous stockbrokers.
[20] *custom-house officers* widely known to take bribes.
[21] *sweetmeats* confections.
[22] *raffle* gamble.
[23] *nymphs* beautiful women; *swain*: amorous young man.

We patch, and we paint,[24]
We're sick, and we faint,
To the vapours, and spleen we pretend;[25]
We play with a fan,
We squeak, and we scream,
We're women, mere women i' th' end.

Your airs we defy
Your beauty deny,
Be as gay, and as fine as you can;
Ye nymphs, have a care,
Be more nice, and more fair,
Or your lovers in time we may gain.

GOODFELLOW. Mr Maiden is the most useful person in such a public place, and distinguishes himself so obligingly by promoting ev'ry diversion.

MAIDEN. Oh, madam, I am master of the ceremonies here; appoint all the dancing, summon the ladies, and manage the music; though really these fiddlers are such a parcel of idle, scoundrel fellows, one has more trouble in keeping 'em together than Mr Rich has in governing the Drury Lane players.[26]

HILLARIA. But pray, Mr Maiden, how d'you employ yourself for want of an office[27] in London?

MAIDEN. Why, madam, I never keep company with lewd rakes that go to the nasty taverns, talk smuttily, and get fuddled,[28] but visit the ladies, and drink tea and chocolate. They think me the best creature, for they consult me mightily about their dress. I tell 'em when the sleeve's rolled too high, and the gown pinned too flat; fancy their knots, and help 'em make their patchwork;[29] and they call me Mrs Betty.[30]

[24] *patch* adorn [the face] with decorative patches; *paint*: apply cosmetics.

[25] *vapours* See **n1**; *spleen*: melancholy.

[26] Christopher *Rich* (1647–1714), lawyer and manager of the *Drury Lane* Theatre in London and its acting company. Rich underpaid his actors and removed their long-standing privileges, resulting in his most experienced actors setting up their own company in Lincoln's Inn Fields. Rich consistently defrauded those who remained.

[27] *want* lack; *office*: civil service or government position; perhaps simply 'professional occupation'.

[28] *fuddled* tipsy with drink.

[29] *fancy … knots* design their embroidery [patterns]; *patchwork*: needlework.

[30] *Betty* contemptuous label for a man who does work typically associated with women; for its slightly later adoption as term for 'effeminate homosexual' and 'sodomite', see **6.6 n7**.

Then, I have chambers at the Temple,[31] and keep a levee,[32] and a visiting-day; for since the lawyers are all turned poets, and have taken the garrets[33] in Drury Lane, none but beaus[34] live at the Temple now, who have sold all their books, burnt all their writings, and furnished the rooms with looking-glass and china.[35]

LOVEWORTH. But if you neither read, study, nor converse with men, how d'you employ your superfluous hours?

MAIDEN. Why, sir, I can pickle and preserve, raise paste,[36] and make all my own linen. Then I love mightily to go abroad in women's clothes. I was dressed up last winter in my Lady Fussock's cherry-colour damask,[37] sat a whole play in the front-seat of the box, and was taken for a Dutchwoman of quality.

[…]

8.29.3 Act 3, [scene 1]

[…]

SQUIB. […] But Mr Loveworth, here comes Maiden. Prithee, let's tease him a little. What if we get him to the tavern and make him drunk?

LOVEWORTH. With all my heart.

Enter MAIDEN.

They say, Mr Maiden, you are in the lampoon[38] that came out this morning, for having an affair with Mrs Motion your landlady's chambermaid.

MAIDEN. That's an impudent report, Mr Loveworth, only to spoil one's reputation among the ladies, for 'tis well known I have more modesty and never lay with a woman in my life.

SQUIB. And will your virtue gain you any credit with the ladies, you silly

[31] *chambers … Temple* rooms hired at either the Middle or Inner Temple, where lawyers were trained.

[32] *levee* reception of visitors (on one's rising from bed).

[33] *garret* small, cramped apartment at the top of a house; traditional residence of impoverished writers.

[34] *beau* fop (cf. its use in **6.2.1 n10**; **6.4.1 n3**; **6.6 n2**; and **6.7.1 n6**).

[35] *china* luxury product in the early eighteenth century.

[36] *raise paste* mould pastry to form a piecrust.

[37] *damask* elaborately embossed silk.

[38] *lampoon* scurrilous satire on an individual.

toad? If you would settle an interest[39] there, you must swear you ha' worried[40] half the sex; but thou hast'nt wit enough to subdue anything above a sempstress.[41]

MAIDEN. Lard! What signifies wit? How particular a wit would look at court nowadays; your poor scoundrel wits are forced to cringe to us men of figure.[42] I'm to have a dedication next winter. Well, a dedication is the prettiest thing: to see one's own name in the front of a book – To the Honourable Francis Maiden, Esquire; then to have the world told of one's airs, and equipage,[43] and the valour of one's ancestors. You may talk what you will of your wit and sense, but you'd part with all your qualifications to have my complexion.

SQUIB. O Lord, complexion! Who the devil minds that? And hast thou the assurance to despise men of wit and value thyself upon thy white gloves, thy honey-water bottle, and thy painted face?

MAIDEN. Well, were it not for a little art, one should look like other people. But what then, 'tis only a wash[44] from the Dove in Salisbury-Court, which all the quality use, and though I say it, when my face is set out to the best advantage, it has given many a lady a palpitation at the heart. But you know, captain, we have agreed not to quarrel. I hate testy folks; when I was at school, I could never abide the boys; they were always wrangling and fighting, but I loved mightily to play with the girls, and dress babies, and all my acquaintance now never quarrelled in their lives.

LOVEWORTH. No! What sort of people are they? Good now?

MAIDEN. Oh, the best creatures in the world. We have such diversion when we meet together at my chambers. There's Beau Simper, Beau Rabbitsface, Beau Eithersex, Colonel Coachpole, and Count Drivel,[45] that sits with his mouth open, the prettiest company at a bowl of virgin-punch.[46] We never make it with rum nor brandy like

39 *settle an interest* fix securely [your] rights or claims.

40 *worried* harassed (with violent connotations; cf. **n5** and **n12**).

41 *sempstress* seamstress.

42 *cringe* bow obsequiously; *men of figure*: fashionable men of rank.

43 *airs* behaviours; *equipage*: public accoutrements of wealth and rank (horse, carriage, apparel, etc.).

44 *wash* liquid cosmetic for the complexion.

45 *Beau* See **n34**; *Simper*: from 'simper', a silly, smiling look; *Rabbitsface*: from 'rabbit' as a timid, ineffectual person; *Coachpole*: perhaps referring to his lower-class status as a coachman; *Count*: the obvious play on 'cunt' (female genitalia); *Drivel*: the obvious meaning; also, 'drab, whore'.

46 *virgin-punch* alcoholic mixture containing no 'hard liquor'.

your sea-captains, but two quarts of mead[47] to half a pint of white wine, lemon-juice, borage,[48] and a little perfume. Then we never read gazettes,[49] nor talk of Venlo and Vigo,[50] like your coffee-house[51] fellows; but play with fans, and mimic the women, scream, hold up your tails,[52] make curtsies, and call one another 'madam'. But Mr Loveworth, are you for the dancing at Southborough tonight? I'm going to be all new-dressed.

LOVEWORTH. Aye, but we are too soon yet. Let's take a flask first at the Rummer.

MAIDEN. O Lard, I never go to the tavern.

SQUIB. But faith you shall. Mr Loveworth, let's force him along.

MAIDEN. O Lard, I shall be ravished! Captain, you are the rudest man. As I hope to be saved, I'll call out. Well, don't tumble[53] a body then, and I will go, but I never drink anything but Rhenish[54] and sugar.

SQUIB. Damn rotgut Rhenish! We'll have Mrs Motion's health in a bumper[55] of Barcelona!

MAIDEN. Oh! She's a bold pullet![56]

[*Exeunt.*

[By the end of the play, Reynard has outwitted Woodcock and has managed to marry his daughter, Belinda, by pretending to be a plain country squire with a large fortune. Hillaria promises herself to Loveworth, and the fools of the play, Squib and Maiden, are exposed and publicly humiliated: Squib is really a tailor, not a gentleman, and he ends up married to Penelope, a woman whom he has assumed to come from a good family, but who is in reality the prostitute Jenny Trapes. Maiden, who has earlier said that he was once a milliner's apprentice, is revealed to have no estate.]

47 *mead* alcoholic drink of fermented honey and water.

48 *borage* plant used in the making of cordials (invigorating drinks).

49 *gazettes* news-sheets.

50 *Venlo* (Netherlands) and *Vigo* (Spain) were combat sites during the war against France (declared in 1702).

51 *coffee-house* where men met to drink coffee and discuss current affairs, politics, gossip, etc.

52 *tails* skirts (perhaps glancing at 'arse; pudendum'); 'your' might be an error for 'our', or Maiden may be offering a piece of direct speech here (i.e., [we] scream, 'Hold up your tails').

53 *tumble* dishevel by treating roughly (cf. **n12**).

54 *Rhenish* German wine.

55 *bumper* cup filled to the brim (for drinking of toasts).

56 *pullet* young, inexperienced person (most often said of women) (cf. **6.6 n9**).

8.29.4 Act 5, [scene 1]

[…]

REYNARD [*Aside.*] […] But here comes soft Mr Maiden, mortified to the last degree, for after all his music, painting, and other fine accomplishments, he's discovered to have no estate.

ALL. No estate, ha, ha, ha.

REYNARD. Some gentleman it seems, pleased with his vanity, buzzed a plausible story in his ears, and brought him down hither to make him ridiculous.

HILLARIA. Poor Mr Maiden! But 'tis many a beau's[57] case to build a mighty appearance on a very slender foundation. The greatest beaus we have about town now are milliners, mercers,[58] lawyers' clerks, and 'tis such upstart fellows that ruin so many poor tradesmen; for amongst 'em all you'll scarce find a periwig[59] that's paid for.

Enter Maiden.

MAIDEN. What a pox! Must I go to the Change[60] again, and sell gloves and ribbons?

SQUIB. No estate! O Lord, Maiden, what will become of your airs now?

BELINDA. What pity 'tis, the fine Mr Maiden who does everything so much like quality, should be forced to turn mechanic.[61]

WOODCOCK. What will your patchwork and your filigree signify now, friend, without an estate to keep your follies in countenance?

HILLARIA. Come, come, Mr Maiden, ne'er be concerned: riches are only to supply other defects; your graces may command a lady with an estate at any time.

MAIDEN. Nay, whenever I marry, I don't doubt of a good fortune yet. When I was at the Change before, people used to call me 'handsome Mr Maiden'. I have a brother too, so like me, nobody can distinguish us, and we used to cheat folks, and lay it upon one another.[62]

[…]

[57] *beau* See **n34**.

[58] *mercer* merchant dealing in luxury cloth.

[59] *periwig* highly stylized wig.

[60] *Change* New Exchange (London shopping gallery specializing in luxury goods; fashionable meeting place).

[61] *mechanic* someone who works with his hands.

[62] Squib is subsequently subjected to equal public mockery (which Maiden participates in) when it is revealed that Squib's new wife Penelope (Jenny Trapes) is a prostitute.

Lady Mary Chudleigh (1656–1710), poet and essayist

Chudleigh's literary circle came to include John Dryden, the philosopher Mary Astell ('Almystrea' in Chudleigh's verse) and the poet Elizabeth Thomas ('Corinna'). While Chudleigh is 'Marissa' in some of her letters, other female epistolary and poetic addressees remain unidentified, including Eugenia, Emilia, and Clorissa (see **9.26**). *The Ladies Defence* (1709) as well as a number of her poems view critically conventional assumptions about love and marriage, but *Essays upon Several Subjects* (1701) examines wider moral and ethical subjects, such as justice, knowledge, humility, friendship, and love. Four of her six children with her husband George predeceased her.

Online Companion

From Cicero's *Laelius: A Discourse of Friendship* (1691); From Richard Baxter's *A Christian Directory* (1673) and *Reliquae Baxterianae* (1696).

8.30

From *Essays upon Several Subjects* (1710)

8.30.1 Of Love

[...]

Now this divine flame[1] can exert itself nowhere but in subjects equally good, in souls governed by the same principles, acting by the same unchangeable rules; there must be a joint inclination to virtue, a like sense of honour, the same notion of justice, as great an ardour for truth, and an exact conformity of thoughts; 'twill not reside where there's the least disparity, where there's anything impure, or debasing, anything that can in the least abate its fervour.

But where shall we find such a passion, such a happy agreement? Where is that pair to be found, whose hearts are fastened by such a divine, such an indissoluble cement, so generous and sublime an affection? Such lovers fear no rivals, admit of no distrusts, are strangers to jealousy, inconstancy, and all the other perturbations of sense: their fire burns too bright, is too intense to be extinguished, is too ardent to admit of any coldnesses, any neglects. They are one, and can no more be unkind to each other than to themselves; are but one mind, one soul in different bodies, and can no more cease to love than to be.[2]

1 *divine flame* love.

2 *Now … be* The first two paragraphs are based on Cicero's *Laelius* (*Online Companion*).

Profane[3] histories pretend to give us some instances of perfect friendships; they boast of a Pylades and an Orestes, but we ought to look on this as a fiction, as a story, dressed up by the poets, and as little to be credited as that of Pollux, who, they tell us, was so kind as to give his brother an equal share of his immortality. The greatest example of this sort that I've met with in any of their records is that of Damon and Pythias, and next to them Scipio and Laelius, Epaminondas and Pelopidas, Blosius and Tiberius Gracchus[4] may claim a place; and, for the honour of my own sex, give me leave to mention Hipparchia and Crates, Portia and Brutus, Sulpicia and Lentulus, Arria and Paetus, Paulina and Seneca;[5] but these are infinitely outdone by two illustrious names, by a royal pair, whose unprecedented friendship has the honour to be recorded in the Sacred Writ: I mean Jonathan and David.

Where was there ever seen a nobler, firmer, a more sacred union! How admirable was it in its beginning, its progress, and its conclusion! Where shall we meet with one so generous, so humble, so condescending, so tenderly affectionate, so unalterably constant as Jonathan, and so reciprocally kind as David? Who without wonder can see the son of a king, the heir apparent of a crown, a prince bred up amidst the flatteries of a court, amidst a crowd of fawning sycophants, caressing a poor despicable shepherd, one hardly known in Israel, not only giving him those praises which were due to the defender of his country, the conqueror of the great Goliath, but bestowing on him his heart, himself – the noblest present he could give, or love could ask!

That which breeds envy in narrow grovelling minds begets respect in brave and generous tempers. When he[6] saw that youth,[7] who was too weak to wear the ponderous garb of war, who fearless went to meet gigantic force, armed with no other weapon but a sling, return triumphant, and bringing

[3] *profane* secular.

[4] *Blosius* of Cuma reportedly said he would unhesitatingly obey all Emperor *Tiberius*'s orders.

[5] *Hipparchia* of Thrace married the Cynic philosopher *Crates*, her love springing from hearing his philosophical discourses. *Portia*, wife of *Brutus*, one of Julius Caesar's assassins, was a popular emblem of wifely devotion for committing suicide when she heard of Brutus's death. *Sulpicia*, wife of Roman politician Lucius Cornelius *Lentulus* (*fl.* first century BCE), braved great dangers to join her husband in exile. *Arria* (*fl.* first century CE) was the wife of Cecinna *Paetus*, Roman senator; when her husband was condemned for treason, she was determined to die with him; she stabbed herself and he followed her example; *Paulina and Seneca*: Nero commanded the Pythagorean philosopher Seneca to commit suicide; he did, but when his wife Paulina tried to follow him, Nero stopped her; she spent her remaining years in mourning.

[6] *he* Jonathan.

[7] *youth* David.

in his hand the trophy of his victory, his[8] head, who had bid defiance to a mighty host, and with his looks had almost gained the day, he felt a secret pleasure in his mind, the beginning of a growing flame; he admired his courage, gazed with wonder on him, with fixed attention heard him speak; each word increased esteem, and fanned the kindling fire; he found himself urged sweetly on, drawn by a delightful violence to knit his soul to his; love firmly tied the knot, and made them one.[9] From that dear moment they had no separate interest, no reserves, nothing that they could call their own: David to Jonathan was dearer far than empire, than glory, nay than life; his only business was to serve him, his happiness his whole concern. When his merit, joined with the acclamations of the people, had made the king his enemy, he, with the intensest zeal, became his advocate, defended his innocency, and, though 'twere with the hazard of his life, spoke what became a friend; neither the threatenings of an angry father, the jealousy of power, nor yet the slights and disregards that constantly attend a man disgraced and out of favour with his sovereign, could make him hide his thoughts. [...] [W]ith the generous Jonathan these considerations had no force; his affection made them all invalid.[10] When full of grief he went to tell him his life was sought, and that he must by flight endeavour to preserve it, how joyful was their meeting! how loath were they to part! None but such as feel the agonies of death, those last dissolving pangs which separate the soul and body, those loved companions, can have a true idea of their sorrow. How tenderly did they express their passion, with what ardour, what sincerity, renew their vows! What protestations did they make of everlasting kindness! But when the fatal minute came, the dire disjoining moment, how difficult was it to leave each other! How many were the essays[11] they made! Sighs stopped their words, and they could only look their thoughts, and by embraces tell the inward struggles of their souls, the pain they felt in being rent asunder! And when 'twas done, how sad were both![12] [...] so indefatigably kind is love, so busy, so inquisitive; it fears no hazard, declines no toil, dares anything, is restless till it can oblige. By it inspired, he visited the much wronged David, the persecuted innocent; his friendship still was firm, his constancy unshaken; the poor, the hated, the forsaken fugitive was still as dear to him as if he had been a monarch, and filled the greatest throne on Earth. Oh, with what joy did he again behold him, with what transporting pleasure! How did he strive to alleviate his grief, and comfort him in his distress! His words, like balm, distilled themselves into those smarting wounds his envious fate had made.

8 *his* Goliath's.

9 *When he saw that youth … head* 1 Sam. 17; 1 Sam. 18.1–4.

10 *When his merit, joined … invalid* 1 Sam. 19.1–7; 1 Sam. 20.25–34.

11 *essays* attempts.

12 *When full of grief he went to tell him … both* 1 Sam. 20.41–2.

[…] The promised exaltation of his friend[13] did not abate his love; he could well-pleased descend to let him rise; and look on his advancement as his own. […] How full of hopes were they the time would come when they should live together, and undisturbed enjoy the sweets of conversation, the most delicious banquet of the mind, that entertainment which only such a love as theirs could give, a passion so refined.

[…] Alas! How sad had been the parting of Jonathan and David had they then known that they must meet no more! Sure heaven in kindness to them concealed the fatal truth; it knew they could not bear the killing news, and kept them still in hopes of being happy, in expectation of succeeding bliss, till the retrieveless blow was given, and Jonathan was snatched away by death. […] But when the dismal tidings reached the ears of David, what tongue can tell his grief? 'Twas great beyond expression. He had lost the whole he loved, the best of friends, one in whom he durst confide, to whom he safely could impart his thoughts, who with him always shared his joys, and bore an equal part in every trouble, or rather took the burden on himself, was still his kind adviser, still his director in every strait, in every cross emergency of fortune. Oh! in what pathetic language does he speak his grief, how elegantly tell his sorrow! […] full of the tenderest sentiments that grief could cause, or love inspire. […][14]

[…]

O Jonathan! thou noblest of thy kind,
Thy fate was equal to thy godlike mind!
Upon thy heights on slaughtered bodies laid,
Thou hast thy own immortal trophy made!
Oh, what convulsive pangs for thee I feel!
Love strikes much deeper than the sharpest steel.
My pleasure's gone, my joys are wholly fled,
All, all is lost, my very soul is dead;
I'm but the echo of myself, a voice of woe;
In thee I lived, now no existence know.
While thou wert mine, heav'n had not sure in store
One dear delight, one single blessing more
That I could wish, to heighten my content;
Fancy itself could nothing more invent.
The whole I could desire in thee I found;
My life was with continual raptures crowned,

[13] 1 Sam. 16.12–13; 1 Sam. 20.30–1.

[14] Following is part of Chudleigh's version of David's famously beautiful elegy for Jonathan and Saul (2 Sam. 1.19–27).

And all my hours but one soft blissful round;[15]
The thoughts that thou wert mine made all my sorrows cease,
Amidst my num'rous toils gave me a halcyon peace;[16]
Contemned was ev'ry danger, ev'ry pain;[17]
Love made me cheerfully the greatest ills sustain.
When thou wert absent, then my busy mind
Did in thy dear remembrance solace find,
Revolved thy words, on each kind accent stayed,
And thy loved image in my breast surveyed,
Fancied thy eyes each tender glance returned,
And with engaging sweetness for thy David mourned.
But when thou didst me with thy presence bless,
Oh, who th' ecstatic transports can express![18]
Words are too poor, and language wants a name
For such a pure, immortal, fervent flame!
Awhile I looked, awhile could only gaze,
My face, my eyes, my heart, betrayed my glad amaze;
My soul to thine would force her speedy way,
Panting she stood, and chid her hind'ring clay;[19]
Trembling with joy, I snatched thee to my heart,
Did, with tumultuous haste, my thronging thoughts impart.
Troubl'd, thou heard'st me my past toils relate;
My suff'rings did a kind concern create,
And made thee, sighing, blame the rigour of my fate.
Oh, with what pity, what a moving air,
Did'st thou then vow thou would'st my hazards share,
Promis'd eternal faith, eternal love,
And kind to me, as my own soul didst prove,
Nay, kinder far, no dangers didst decline,
Exposed thy life to add a longer date to mine!
Such an affection to the world is new;
None can such wondrous proofs of friendship shew![20]
Not the fair sex, whom softest passions move,
Can with such ardour, such intenseness love.
But thou art lost! forever lost to me!
And all I ever prized is lost with thee:

15 *round* succession.
16 *halcyon* undisturbed.
17 *contemned* despised.
18 *transports* raptures.
19 *clay* body.
20 *shew* show.

Honour, and fame, and beauty lose their charms;
I'm deaf to the harmonious sound of arms,
Deaf to the calls of glory and of praise;
I'll near thy tomb conclude my wretched days,
In mournful strains employ my voice and lyre,
And, full of grief, by thy loved corpse expire.

How soon, alas! the mighty are destroyed!
Who can the dreadful stroke of fate avoid?
How are they fallen! who but lately stood
Like well-fixed rocks, and dared the raging flood!
They who dispersed their missive terrors round,
From whom their foes a swift destruction found,
Now lie, like common men, neglected on the ground.

Thomas Gordon? (d. 1750), writer

Committed Whig supporter, Gordon wrote many satiric pamphlets on Church and government corruption, as well as translations of Tacitus, Sallust, and Cicero. As Rictor Norton has argued, *Love Letters* (1723) exploits public curiosity about the mysterious life and violent death of the ex-army captain Edward Wilson (d. 1694), in order to blacken the character and denigrate the policies of Charles Spencer, Third Earl of Sunderland (1674–1722), First Lord of the Treasury (appointed, 1717/18).[1] Proceeded by a preface that disclaims mercenary motives on the part of the 'editor' and asserts the genuineness of the correspondence, and followed by a lengthy 'afterword' that fills in a set of narrative 'gaps', *Love Letters* has at its centre twenty epistles purporting to be the homoerotic correspondence of Sunderland and Wilson, in which Wilson is presented as a 'kept man', supported in style by his aristocratic lover (Norton 121–3). In Gordon's earlier work *The Conspirators* (1721), the corrupt, sodomitical Roman politician Catiline is a thinly veiled representation of Sunderland (*Online Companion*).

Editions

Kimmel, M.S., ed., *Love Letters*. New York: Haworth, 1990.
Norton, Rictor, ed., 'Love Letters (1723).' *Eighteenth-Century British Erotica II*, 5.121–82.

21 *missive terrors* projectiles (spears, arrows, etc.).

[1] For the other proposed candidates and the convincing argument in favour of Sunderland, see R. Norton, ed., *Love Letters*, pp. xiv–xvi, and 121–3. While most critics assert that the correspondence is entirely fictional (see McFarlane, pp. 92–5), Norton also mounts an interesting argument for its authenticity.

Online Companion
From Thomas Gordon's *The Conspirators* (1721).

8.31

From *Love Letters Between a Certain Late Nobleman and the Famous Beau Wilson* (1723)[2]

8.31.1 Letter 3. To Mr Wilson

I had not above a hundred pieces by me when I received yours,[3] which made me send, swift as the minutes, to the bank to fetch this. I would have my Willy believe, I am never so delighted, as when I am doing that which may convince him, how very dear he is to his nown[4] love. Then come away, the bath is ready, that I may wrestle with it,[5] and pit it, and pat it and — it; and then for cooler sport, devour it with greedy kisses; for Venus and all the poet's wenches are but dirty dowdies[6] to thee.

Put on the Brussels head
and Indian atlas I sent
yesterday.[7]

8.31.2 Letter 9. To the Lord ——

My Lord,

After a long, long fruitless expectation of your command how to direct to you,[8] which your lordship may remember was not fixed on, though I often urged it, I have been so wretched to construct it as a mark of your declining favour: as the tortures of my soul are inexpressible under such

[2] Published anonymously; *beau*: dandy or fop. Cf. **6.2.1 n10**; **6.4.1 n3**; **6.6 n2;** and **6.7.1 n6**.

[3] *pieces* i.e., of money; *yours*: your letter.

[4] *nown* 'own' (expression of affection).

[5] *it* Wilson (the speaker uses this pronoun in other letters to refer to Wilson); but, also, Wilson's *penis*.

[6] *dowdies* ugly women, shabbily dressed. Cf. Sunderland's misogyny: seducing a virgin is taking 'her dirty maidenhead' to silence rumours about his 'indifference' to women (Letter 11, p. 16).

[7] *Brussels head* headdress of Brussels lace; *Indian atlas*: gown of smooth Indian silk.

[8] *direct to you* i.e., to what address to send my letters.

bitter affliction, so are my joys as full to find them causeless. Those soft complaining passionate expressions[9] transported me beyond my strength to bear, and then revived me with your kind rebukes; what followed raised an ecstasy too great. The past conflicts of my mind, under the imaginary[10] displeasure of my dearest lord, made me regardless of the disorders of my body, which since your lordship has enjoined[11] shall be more my care.[12] My fate is wholly in your power, and you have vouchsafed to bless me above all men. Command me to be well and live; but not (for Oh! I cannot) live without you. Recall me from this restless banishment, or honour me with your loved presence here; the beauties of the place have such enticements which, with other reasons, I am informed, have long detained some persons of distinction on odd intrigues, perhaps not unworthy of your lordship's notice.

I am,

My Lord, etc.

8.31.3 Letter 15. To Mr Wilson

Is this thy faith? Is this thy return to all my foolish, lavish fondness? It seems I have taught you a trade, and harlot-like you intend to be as common as those abject wretches. [*We must beg pardon of the reader for omitting here some lines which are in the original of this letter, being too obscene to be inserted*] May every disease incident to them infect and destroy thee. What, couldst thou find none but that old, nauseous dog to kiss and slobber thee? Don't pretend to deny it, for by — I saw him. Had not a little regard to myself prevented, I had stabbed thee that moment.

I suppose you intend to hide your detested head in some hole to escape my rage; but my revenge shall find thee, and punish thy black ingratitude, an ingratitude so vile that thou deservest to be a terrible example to all that base fry.[13] Did not I take thee from a wretched, necessitous life, perplexed with petty duns,[14] and have raised thee to be the nation's wonder? Have I denied thee anything? But have been so lavish to make thee (or thou

[9] *those … expressions* Letter 8: 'Forgive me, my dear Willy, if I wrong thee; lay all the blame on this unruly passion. A plague confound those lying dogs of poets, who to delude and torture all mankind, would palm it on us as a heaven of pleasure – Damned spite, – It's hell to love and dote to madness, as I do on thee' (pp. 10–11).

[10] *imaginary* that which I imagined.

[11] *enjoined* commanded.

[12] *disorders … care* Sunderland laments Wilson's illness (Cf. Letter 7, p. 9: 'Should envious death take thee, my dearest blessing, from me, I am undone').

[13] *that base fry* those despicable youths.

[14] *duns* creditors' relentless demands for payment.

pretendest) to blush at my excess of bounty. But now I will be as boundless in my hatred as I have been profuse in my extravagant love. May all — torture thee, as thy baseness does me.

8.31.4 Letter 16. To the Lord ——

May all the detestable curses your lordship has been pleased to pronounce, with ten thousand more, inflict —— if I know or can guess what you mean.

Is it to try the bent of my mind under the most calamitous of all circumstances – your lordship's dread displeasure? as you have before done the other way in raising me from that abject fortune to your high grace, dispensing favours beyond my own aspiring hopes or vainest desires; which when I cease most gratefully to acknowledge, as is my duty, or give just cause of offence, either by action or omission, may all the valuable world, nay, what is infinitely preferable to all, your lordship's self, continue to hate, despise, and brand me for the most villainous of all that black and loathsome herd you have already ranked me with.

Am I not the creature of your framing, to rise, to fall, to live or die, to mould and fashion as you please? And should I dare to repine at, or more basely endeavour to hide myself from the fate you have allotted me? It is thinking too poorly of the wretch [that] your lordship once vouchsafed to honour with your love and esteem, which, perhaps, you'll see was not wholly misplaced when I have an opportunity to throw myself at your feet; in the meantime, devise as many tortures to rack this hated body as at present my soul endures, and let both fall a willing sacrifice to gratify your pleasures.

I am,

My Lord,

Your Lordship's most
faithfully, most entirely
devoted slave,

W. Wilson

8.31.5 Letter 17. To Mr Wilson

Sure thou art false for these eyes saw you suffer G——n[15] to kiss and slobber you. You have disarmed my anger, would you could my doubts. Let me see you, but come with certain proofs of thy faith, that I may not be fatal to thee and myself. Swear never to see that hated dog, and I'll believe thee. You have

15 *G——n* perhaps Sidney Godolphin, First Earl of Godolphin (1654–1712), well known for his heterosexual affairs and gambling (Norton, *Eighteenth-Century British Erotica II*, 5.389n).

a powerful advocate within, that would fain[16] find thee true; the very hope is a joy, great as ever filled my breast; then what must the certainty be? Add that to the many raptures thou alone could'st give, and I will be thy humble slave forever; but take heed or you'll find my wrath terrible, exceeding even the malice of women.[17]

[...]

[16] *fain* willingly.

[17] The relationship continues tumultuous: 'Letter 20' sees Wilson again protesting his constancy in the face of charges of heinous but unspecified 'crimes' (27).

CHAPTER 9

Literature: Representing Female Same-Sex Erotic Relationships and Desires

Desiderius Erasmus (?1466–1536), humanist scholar

Erasmus's major works are *Adages* (a collection of *sententiae* or wise sayings or maxims (1500)), the *Enchiridion* (a manual of Christian living (1503)), *The Praise of Folly* (a satire of contemporary European social and religious attitudes (1511)) and *Colloquies* (Latin dialogues on various social, moral, and religious topics (1518/19)). His Scriptural commentaries and editions of classical writers and the Church fathers profoundly influenced Renaissance scholarship and literature.

Sir Roger L'Estrange (1616–1704), politician

Cambridge educated and a committed royalist, L'Estrange spent much of the Civil War in exile on the Continent. After Cromwell's death, he published a series of notably intemperate pro-Stuart pamphlets. Appointed press censor, responsible for finding and arresting anti-government printers and booksellers, he also licensed politically and morally suitable works. His translations include Cicero's *Offices* (1680), Erasmus's *Colloquies* (1680; rev. exp., 1689), *Aesop's Fables* (1691; 1699), and the works of Josephus (1709).

9.1

From *Colloquies* (1689)

9.1.1 The Marriage Hater (Colloquy 7)

A girl takes a fancy to a cloister; her parents violently against it; and she herself in great affliction for want of their consent. A friend dissuades her; and lays before her the snare and danger of that course of life (the cheats, artifices, and abuses of the monks), preaches obedience to her parents, and advises her rather to work out her salvation in her father's house than in a convent.

Eubulus, Catharina.

[...]

EUBULUS. What was it that gave the first rise to this fatal[1] resolution?

CATHARINA. When I was a little girl, they carried[2] me into one of these cloisters, and showed me the whole college. The chapels were so neat, and the gardens so clean, so delicate, and so well-ordered that I fell in love with 'em, and then they themselves were so pure and glorious they looked like angels, so that (in short) which way soever I turned my eye, there was comfort and pleasure; and then I had the prettiest discourses with the nuns! I found two there that had been my play-fellows when I was a child; but I have always had a strange passion for that kind of life.

EUBULUS. I have no quarrel to the rules and orders of cloisters, though the same thing can never agree with all persons. If I were to speak my opinion, I should think it more suitable to your genius and manners to take a convenient husband and set up a college in your own house, where he should be the father of it and you the mother.

CATHARINA. I'll rather die than quit my resolution of virginity.

EUBULUS. Nay, 'tis an admirable thing to be a pure maid. But cannot you keep yourself so, without running yourself into a prison, never to come out again? Cannot you keep your maidenhead, I say, at home with your parents, as well as in a cloister?

CATHARINA. Yes I may, but 'tis not so safe though.

EUBULUS. Much safer truly, in my judgement, than with these brawny,

[1] *fatal* ruinous.

[2] *carried* took.

swill-bellied[3] monks. They are no capons,[4] I'll assure ye, whatever you may think of 'em; but may very probably be called 'fathers', for they commonly make good their calling to the very letter.[5] In times past, maids lived nowhere honester than at home, when the only metaphorical father they had was the bishop. [...]

[After painting a bleak picture of monks' drunkenness, illiteracy, imprudence, and general folly, Eubulus responds to Catharina's fears concerning the sometimes 'loose' behaviour of her parent's guests (the 'women are so given to talk smutty', and the men sometimes take advantage of the custom of the greeting kiss).]

EUBULUS. You may withdraw then if you find the company grow troublesome; and while they are chaunting and trifling,[6] you may entertain yourself with (Christ) your spouse, praying, singing, and giving thanks. Your father's house will not defile ye, and your goodness, on the other hand, will turn it into a chapel.

CATHARINA. But 'tis easier yet to be in a cloister.

EUBULUS. I do not disallow of a modest society; but yet I would not have you delude yourself with false imaginations. When ye come once to be wonted[7] there, and see things nearer at hand, you'll tell me another story. There are more veils than virgins, believe me.

CATHARINA. Good words, I beseech thee.

EUBULUS. Those are good words that are true words; and I never read of any more virgins than one that was a mother.[8]

CATHARINA. I abhor the thought on't.

EUBULUS. Nay, and more than that – the maids you speak of (let me assure you) do more than maids' business.

CATHARINA. Why so? If you please.

EUBULUS. Because there are more Sapphos among 'em for their bodies than for their brains.[9]

3 *swill-bellied* drunken.

4 *capons* castrated cocks (male chickens) (i.e., the monks' sexual equipment is intact).

5 *'fathers' ... letter* i.e., because they have fathered many illegitimate children.

6 *chaunting and trifling* singing and spending time frivolously.

7 *wonted* accustomed to be.

8 *any ... mother* The Virgin Mary (believed to have conceived Jesus through the power of the Holy Spirit, and not through sexual intercourse) is the only virgin mother. The nuns are mothers (through intercourse with the monks), but are not the virgins they are expected and commonly thought to be.

9 *Sapphos ... brains* For Sappho's mixed reputation (representing poetic excellence *and* female licentiousness, including tribadism), see Introduction to **7.2–7.9**.

CATHARINA. I do not understand ye.
EUBULUS. And I talk in cipher, my dear Kitty, because I would not have thee understand me.

[Eubulus offers any number of reasons for Catharina's remaining virtuously at home, but he cannot change her mind.]

9.1.2 The Penitent Virgin (Colloquy 8)

A virgin seduced into a cloister finds her error, repents of it, and in twelve days gets off again.

Eubulus, Catharina.

[At Catharina's abrupt return from the convent, Eubulus quizzes her about her experience. She describes below her confinement, constant surveillance, and attendance by several nuns before her entrance into the convent.]

[…]

EUBULUS. And did not your mind misgive you yet?[10]
CATHARINA. No, not at all. And yet I had so horrid a fright that I had rather die ten times over than be in that condition again.
EUBULUS. What might that be?
CATHARINA. It is not to be uttered.
EUBULUS. Come, tell me frankly. I am your friend.
CATHARINA. Will ye keep counsel?
EUBULUS. Yes, yes, without conditions. And I hope you know me better than to doubt it.
CATHARINA. I had a most dreadful apparition.
EUBULUS. Your evil genius[11] (it may be) that pushed ye forward into disobedience.[12]
CATHARINA. Nay, I am fully persuaded that it was no other.
EUBULUS. In the shape I suppose that we use to paint it? With a crooked beak, long horns, harpy's claws, and a swinging tail?[13]

[10] *misgive* fill [you] with foreboding.
[11] *evil genius* one of a person's two mutually opposed spirits (good and evil).
[12] *disobedience* i.e., against her father and mother who strenuously opposed her entry into the convent.
[13] *harpy* monster with woman's face and body, but bird's wings and claws; minister of divine vengeance.

CATHARINA. You may laugh as you will, but I had rather sink into the earth than see the fellow on't.[14]

EUBULUS. And were your women-solicitresses[15] then with you?

CATHARINA. No. And I would not so much as open my mouth to 'em of it, though they sifted[16] me most particularly, for you must know they found me almost dead with the surprise.

EUBULUS. Shall I tell you now what it was?

CATHARINA. Do, if you can.

EUBULUS. These women had absolutely bewitched you, or rather conjured your brains out of your noodle.[17] But did you hold out for all this?

CATHARINA. Yes, yes, for they told me that many were thus troubled upon the first consecration of themselves to Christ; but that if they got the better of the Devil that bout, he'd let 'em alone forever after.

[Eubulus then asks Catharina about the reason for her flight from the convent.]

EUBULUS. But what was it that brought ye off again?

CATHARINA. It was something very considerable, but I must not tell ye what. When I had been there six days, I got my mother to me. I begged and besought her as she loved my life to help me out again, but she would not hear on't, and bad[18] me hold to my resolution. Upon this I sent to my father and he chid[19] me too. He told me that I had made him master his affection, and that he would now make me overcome mine. When I saw this would do no good, I told them both that I would submit to die to please 'em, which would certainly be my fate if I stayed there any longer; and hereupon they took me home.

EUBULUS. 'Twas well you bethought yourself before you were in for good and all. But still ye say nothing of what it was that brought ye about so on the sudden.

CATHARINA. I never told it any mortal yet, nor will I tell it you.

EUBULUS. What if I should guess?

CATHARINA. You'll never hit it, I'm sure. Or if ye should, y'are never the nearer, for I'll not own it ye.

[...]

[14] *on't* on it (i.e., of it).

[15] *solicitresses* simply, women who solicit requests; also, enticers to immorality.

[16] *sifted* questioned closely.

[17] *noodle* head.

[18] *bad* ordered.

[19] *chid* rebuked.

Mary Maitland? (d. 1596), writer and copyist

Copyist of the Maitland family manuscripts and daughter of Sir Richard Maitland (1496–1586), poet and Keeper of the Privy Seal, Mary Maitland is compared to famous female poets, including Sappho, in the Maitland quarto's dedicatory poems, suggesting she may perhaps be the author of the following homoerotic female lyric.

Editions

Craigie, W.A., ed., *The Maitland Quarto Manuscript.* Edinburgh: Blackwood, 1920.
Farnsworth, J., 'Appendix' to 'Voicing Female Desire in "Poem XLIX"', *SEL* 36.1 (1995): 5–72.

9.2

From The Maitland Quarto MS

Poem 49 (As Phoebus in his spheris' height) (c. 1586)[1]

As Phoebus in his spheris' height[2]
Precels the cape crepuscular,[3]
And Phoebe all the starris' light,[4]
Your splendour, so madam I ween,
Does only pass all feminine
In sapience superlative,
Indued with virtues so divine,
As learnèd Pallas redivive.[5]

And as by hid virtue unknown
The adamant draws iron yairtill,[6]
Your court'ous nature so has drawn
My heart, yours to continue still:

[1] Reprinted by permission of the Pepys Library, Magdalene College Library, Cambridge.

[2] *Phoebus* sun. See Apollo (Glossary); *spheris'*: sphere's. I have maintained as much as possible the poem's original Scots.

[3] *precels the cape crepuscular* surpasses the twilight sky (*cape*).

[4] *Phoebe* moon. See Diana (Glossary); *starris*: two syllables.

[5] *redivive* revived.

[6] *adamant* rock with strong magnetic properties; *yairtill*: unto it.

So great joy does my sprite fulfil
Contempl'ing your perfection.[7]
Ye wield me wholly at your will
And ravish my affection.

Your peerless virtue does provoke,
And loving kindness so does move,
My mind to friendship reciproc,
That truth shall try so far above
The auncient heroicis' love[8]
As shall be thought prodigious:
And plain experience shall prove
More holy and religious.

In amity, Perithous
To Theseus was not so traist,[9]
Nor to Achilles Patroclus,
Nor Pylades to true Orest,
Nor yet Achates' love so lest[10]
To good Aenea, nor such friendship
David to Jonathan professed,
Nor Titus true to kind Josip.

Nor yet Penelope, I wis,[11]
So loved Ulysses in her days,
Nor Ruth the kind Moabitess
Naomi, as the Scripture says:[12]
Nor Portia, whose worthy praise
In Roman histories we read,
Who did devour the fiery brays
To follow Brutus to the deid.[13]

Would mighty Jove give me the hap[14]

[7] *contempl'ing* contemplating; *perfection*: four syllables.
[8] *auncient heroicis* either ancient heroes' or ancient heroic.
[9] *traist* faithful.
[10] *lest* last ('lasting').
[11] *I wis* I think.
[12] *Ruth* famed for her love of her mother-in-law, the Israelite Naomi (see **1.1.5**).
[13] *deid* death. Hearing of her husband *Brutus*'s death, *Portia* followed him by eating red-hot coals (*brays*).
[14] *hap* fortune.

With you to have your Brutus' part[15]
And, metamorphosing our shape,
My sex intil his vaill convert:[16]
No Brutus then should cause us smart
As we do now, unhappy women;
Then should we both, with joyful heart,
Honour and bless the band of Hymen.

Yea certainly we should efface
Pollux and Castor's memory;
And if that they deservèd place
Among the stars for loyalty,
Then our more perfect amity
More worthy recompense should merit:
In heaven eternal deity
Among the gods till inherit.[17]

And as we are, though to our woe,
Nature and Fortune do conjure;[18]
And Hymen also be our foe,
Yet love of virtue does procure
Friendship and amity so sure,
With so great fervency and force,
So constantly which shall endure,
That naught but deid shall us divorce.

And though adversity us vex,
Yet by our friendship shall be seen
There is more constancy in our sex
Than ever among men has been –
No trouble, torment, grief, or tein[19]
Nor earthly thing shall us dissever;
Such constancy shall us maintain
In perfect amity forever.

15 *part* Scots, 'pairt', meaning 'role' or 'place'; but also, 'penis' (Farnsworth, p. 64).

16 *intil* into; *vaill*: Scots, 'veil' or 'will.' The speaker hopes to be converted into Brutus's male body (his *veil* or casing of flesh), or she hopes more simply he (Jove) will (*vaill*) convert her sex into Brutus's (Farnsworth, pp. 65; 69 n19).

17 *till* to.

18 *conjure* conspire.

19 *tein* suffering.

Sir Philip Sidney (1554–86)

For his biography, see Introduction to **7.2**. For a brief summary of the *Arcadia*, see **8.3**.

Online Companion
From Ariosto's *Orlando Furioso* (trans., 1591); from *Huon of Bourdeaux* (trans., 1600).

9.3

From *The Countess of Pembroke's Arcadia*
('The New Arcadia') (1593)

9.3.1 Book 2, chapter 4

[…]

For whether it were that her[1] wit in continuance did find that Zelmane's friendship was full of impatient desire having more than ordinary limits, and therefore was she content to second Zelmane though herself knew not the limits, or that in truth true love, well considered, have an infective power, at last she fell in acquaintance with love's harbinger: wishing. First, she would wish that they two might live all their lives together, like two of Diana's nymphs. But that wish she thought not sufficient, because she knew there would be more nymphs besides them who also would have their part in Zelmane. Then would she wish that she were her sister, that such a natural band might make her more special to her. But against that, she considered that, though being her sister, if she happened to be married she should be robbed of her. Then grown bolder, she would wish either herself or Zelmane a man, that there might succeed a blessed marriage betwixt them. But when that wish had once displayed his ensign in her mind, then followed whole squadrons of longings that so it might be, with a main battle of mislikings and repinings against their creation, that so it was not. Then dreams by night began to bring more unto her than she durst wish by day, whereout[2] waking did make her know herself the better by the image of those fancies; […] For now indeed love pulled off his mask and showed his face unto her, and told her plainly that she was his prisoner. Then needed she no more paint her face with passions, for passions shone through her face; then her

1 *her* Philoclea's.
2 *whereout* out of which.

rosy colour was often increased with extraordinary blushing, and so another time, perfect whiteness descended to a degree of paleness; now hot, then cold, desiring she knew not what, nor how, if she knew what.

[...]

[...] laying all her[3] fair length under one of the trees, for a while she did nothing but turn up and down, as if she had hoped to turn away the fancy[4] that mastered her, and hid her face, as if she could have hidden herself from her own fancies.

At length with a whispering note to herself, 'O me, unfortunate wretch,' said she, 'what poisonous heats be these which thus torment me? How hath the sight of this strange guest invaded my soul? Alas, what entrance found this desire, or what strength had it thus to conquer me?' Then a cloud passing between her sight and the moon, 'O Diana,' said she, 'I would either the cloud that now hides the light of my virtue would as easily pass away as you will quickly overcome this let,[5] or else that you were forever thus darkened to serve for an excuse of my outrageous folly.'

Then looking to the stars, which had perfectly as then beautified the clear sky, 'My parents,' said she, 'have told me that in these fair heavenly bodies there are great hidden deities which have their working in the ebbing and flowing of our estates. If it be so, then, O you stars, judge rightly of me; and if I have with wicked intent made myself a prey to fancy, or if by any idle lusts I framed my heart fit for such an impression, then let this plague daily increase in me till my name be made odious to womankind. But if extreme and unresistible violence have oppressed me, who will ever do any of you sacrifice, O you stars, if you do not succour me? No, no, you will not help me. No, no, you cannot help me; sin must be the mother and shame the daughter of my affection. And yet are these but childish objections, simple Philoclea. It is the impossibility that doth torment me; for unlawful desires are punished after the effect of enjoying, but impossible desires are punished in the desire itself. Oh, then, ten times unhappy that I am, since where in all other hope kindleth love, in me despair should be the bellows of my affection; and of all despairs the most miserable which is drawn from impossibility. [...]

And yet, alas, why do I thus condemn my fortune before I hear what she can say for herself? What do I, silly wench, know what love hath prepared for me? Do I not see my mother as well, at least as furiously as myself, love Zelmane, and should I be wiser than my mother? Either she sees a

3 *her* Philoclea's.
4 *fancy* love.
5 *let* obstacle.

possibility in that which I think impossible, or else impossible loves need not misbecome me. And do I not see Zelmane (who doth not think a thought which is not first weighed by wisdom and virtue) doth not she vouchsafe to love me with like ardour? I see it; her eyes depose it to be true. What then? And if she can love poor me, shall I think scorn to love a woman as Zelmane? Away then all vain examinations of why and how! Thou lovest me, excellent Zelmane, and I love thee.' And with that, embracing the very ground on which she lay, she said to herself (for even to herself she was ashamed to speak it out in words) 'O my Zelmane, govern and direct me, for I am wholly given over unto thee.'

9.3.2 Book 2, chapter 17

[...]

[...] she[6] saw Zelmane lying upon a bank [...] 'Fair streams,' said she,[7] 'that do vouchsafe in your clearness to represent unto me my blubbered face, let the tribute-offer of my tears unto you procure your stay a while with me, that I may begin yet at last to find something that pities me, and that all things of comfort and pleasure do not fly away from me. But if the violence of your spring command you to haste away to pay your duties to your great prince, the sea, yet carry with you these few words, and let the uttermost ends of the world know them: a love more clear than yourselves, dedicated to a love, I fear, more cold than yourselves, with the clearness lays a night of sorrow upon me, and with the coldness inflames a world of fire within me.'

[...]

Philoclea, whose delight of hearing and seeing was before a stay from interrupting her, gave herself to be seen unto her, with such a lightning of beauty upon Zelmane that neither she could look on, nor would look off. At last Philoclea, [...] began to say: 'My father, to whom I owe myself, and therefore –'[8] when Zelmane (making a womanish habit to be the armour of her boldness, giving up her life to the lips of Philoclea, and taking it again by the sweetness of those kisses) humbly besought her to keep her speech for awhile within the paradise of her mind, for well she knew her father's errand, who should soon receive a sufficient answer. But now she demanded leave not to lose this long-sought-for commodity of time, to ease her heart thus far: that if in her agonies her destiny was to be condemned by Philoclea's mouth,

6 *she* Philoclea.

7 *she* Zelmane.

8 Basilius has sent Philoclea to find Zelmane.

at least Philoclea might know whom she had condemned. Philoclea easily yielded to grant her own desire. [...]

[Zelmane finally reveals her true gender to Philoclea.]

'[...] O only princess, attend here a miserable miracle of affection! Behold here before your eyes, Pyrocles, prince of Macedon, whom you only have brought to this game of fortune and unused[9] metamorphosis; whom you only have made neglect his country, forget his father, and lastly forsake to be Pyrocles! [...] I desire that my desire may be weighed in the balances of honour, and let virtue hold them. For if the highest love in no base person may aspire to grace, then may I hope your beauty will not be without pity. If otherwise you be (alas, but let it never be so) resolved, yet shall not my death be comfortless, receiving it by your sentence.'

The joy which wrought into Pygmalion's mind while he found his beloved image was softer and warmer in his folded arms, till at length it accomplished his gladness with a perfect woman's shape, still beautified with the former perfections,[10] was even such as, by each degree of Zelmane's words, creepingly entered into Philoclea, till her pleasure was fully made up with the manifesting of his being, which was such as in hope did overcome hope. Yet doubt would fain[11] have played his part in her mind and called in question how she could be assured that Zelmane was Pyrocles. But love straight stood up and deposed a lie could not come from the mouth of Zelmane. Besides, a certain spark of honour which rose in her well-disposed mind made her fear to be alone with him with whom alone she desired to be, with all the other contradictions growing in those minds which neither absolutely climb the rock of virtue nor freely sink into the sea of vanity. But that spark soon gave place, or at least gave no more light in her mind than a candle doth in the sun's presence; but even sick with a surfeit[12] of joy, and fearful of she knew not what [...] with a shrugging kind of tremor through all her principal parts, she gave these affectionate words for answer:

'Alas, how painful a thing it is to a divided mind to make a well-joined answer! How hard it is to bring inward shame to outward confession! And what handsomeness, trow[13] you, can be observed in that speech which is made one knows not to whom? Shall I say, "O Zelmane"? Alas, your words

[9] *unused* unaccustomed.

[10] *The joy ... perfections* Venus took pity on the famed Greek sculptor Pygmalion by bringing to life his statue of a woman so beautiful that he had fallen hopelessly in love with it.

[11] *fain* willingly.

[12] *surfeit* engorgement.

[13] *trow* think.

be against it! Shall I say, "Prince Pyrocles"? Wretch that I am, your show is manifest against it. But this, this, I well may say: if I had continued as I ought, Philoclea, you had either never been, or ever been Zelmane; you had either never attempted this change, set on with hope, or never discovered it, stopped with despair. [...] I fear me, my affection, ill hid, hath given you this last assurance. I fear indeed the weakness of my government before made you think such a mask would be grateful unto me; and my weaker government since makes you to pull off the visor. What shall I do then? [...] Shall I labour to lay marble colours over my ruinous thoughts? Or rather, though the pureness of my virgin mind be stained, let me keep the true simplicity of my word. True it is, alas, too true it is, O Zelmane (for so I love to call thee, since in that name my love first began, and in the shade of that name my love shall best lie hidden), that even while so thou wert (what eye bewitched me I know not) my passions were fitter to desire than to be desired. Shall I say then I am sorry, or that my love must be turned to hate, since thou art turned to Pyrocles? How may that well be, since when thou wert Zelmane, the despair thou mightest not be thus did most torment me? Thou hast then the victory; use it with virtue. Thy virtue won me: with virtue preserve me. Dost thou love me? Keep me then still worthy to be beloved.'

William Shakespeare (1564–1616)

For his biography, see Introduction to **8.10**.

9.4

From *A Midsummer Night's Dream* (c. 1594–95)

[There are four young people: Hermia, Helena, Lysander and Demetrius. Previously in love with Helena, Demetrius has rejected her in favour of Hermia, although Helena still passionately loves him. Hermia, however, loves Lysander and is dearly loved by him. When Egeus, Hermia's father, demands that Hermia marry Demetrius, Lysander and Hermia run away, pursued by Demetrius, followed by the love-sick Helena. Fairy magic results in both Demetrius and Lysander falling in love with Helena, and simultaneously scorning Hermia. As Act 3, scene 2 opens both men profess love for Helena, but she believes their extravagant professions are a cruel game instigated by her former friend, Hermia.]

Act 3, scene 2

[...]

HELEN. Lo, she is one of this confederacy!
Now I perceive they have conjoined all three
To fashion this false sport, in spite of me.[1]
Injurious Hermia, most ungrateful maid!
Have you conspired, have you with these contrived[2]
To bait me with this foul derision?
Is all the counsel that we two have shared –[3]
The sisters' vows, the hours that we have spent
When we have chid the hasty-footed time
For parting us – Oh, is all quite forgot?
All schooldays' friendship, childhood innocence?
We, Hermia, like two artificial gods[4]
Have with our needles created both one flower,
Both on one sampler, sitting on one cushion,
Both warbling of one song, both in one key,
As if our hands, our sides, voices, and minds
Had been incorporate. So we grew together,
Like to a double cherry, seeming parted,
But yet an union in partition,
Two lovely berries molded on one stem;
So, with two seeming bodies but one heart,
Two of the first, like coats in heraldry,
Due but to one and crownèd with one crest.[5]
And will you rend our ancient love asunder,
To join with men in scorning your poor friend?
It is not friendly, 'tis not maidenly.
Our sex, as well as I, may chide you for it,
Though I alone do feel the injury.
HERMIA. I am amazèd at your passionate words.
I scorn you not. It seems that you scorn me.
HELENA. Have you not set Lysander, as in scorn,
To follow me and praise my eyes and face?

[1] *in spite of me* to hurt me.
[2] *contrived* plotted.
[3] *counsel* confidences.
[4] *artificial gods* perhaps, referring to their artistic creations (needlework), below.
[5] A gentleman's coat of arms was often painted twice on his shield, but it would be capped by only one ornamental *crest.*

And made your other love, Demetrius,
Who even but now did spurn me with his foot,
To call me goddess, nymph, divine, and rare,
Precious, celestial? Wherefore speaks he this
To her he hates? And wherefore doth Lysander
Deny your love, so rich within his soul,
And tender me, forsooth, affection,[6]
But by your setting on, by your consent?
What though I be not so in grace as you,[7]
So hung upon with love, so fortunate,
But miserable most, to love unloved?
This you should pity rather than despise.

[...]

Aemilia Lanyer (1569–1645), poet

Daughter of one of James I's court musicians, wife of another, and mistress to Henry Carey, First Baron Hunsdon, Lanyer apparently served and was presumably educated in the household of Susan, dowager Countess of Kent, one of the dedicatees of her only work, the religious poem *Salve Deus Rex Judaeorum* ('Hail God, King of the Jews'). Recounting the passion, death, and resurrection of Christ, *Salve* also includes addresses to Margaret, Countess of Cumberland, Lanyer's central patron and chief dedicatee; eleven dedicatory pieces creating and celebrating a community of virtuous women; a proto-feminist assertion of women's rights; a defence of biblical women, including Eve; and the first country-house poem in English.

6 *tender* offer; *forsooth*: interjection, 'truly' (here meant sarcastically).
7 *grace* favour (with the men).

9.5

From *Salve Deus Rex Judaeorum* (1611)

9.5.1 To the Lady Lucy, Countess of Bedford[1]

Methinks I see fair Virtue ready stand,
T'unlock the closet of your lovely breast,[2]
Holding the key of Knowledge in her hand,
Key of that cabin where yourself doth rest,[3]
To let him in, by whom her youth was blest.[4]
  The true-love of your soul, your heart's delight,
  Fairer than all the world in your clear sight.

He that descended from celestial glory,
To taste of our infirmities and sorrows,
Whose heavenly wisdom read the earthly story
Of frail humanity, which his godhead borrows;[5]
Lo, here he comes all stuck with pale death's arrows,[6]
  In whose most precious wounds your soul may read
  Salvation, while he (dying Lord) doth bleed.

You whose clear judgement far exceeds my skill,
Vouchsafe to entertain this dying lover,[7]
The ocean of true grace, whose streams do fill
All those with joy, that can his love recover;
About this blessed ark bright angels hover,[8]

[1] Lucy Russell (née Harington) (1581–1627), courtier and literary patron, a popular early modern dedicatee; unlike Margaret, Countess of Cumberland, Bedford does not seem to have had a personal relationship with Lanyer.

[2] *closet* private room.

[3] *cabin* a synonym for 'closet', but glancing at 'cell of an anchorite', 'a poor rural dwelling', and 'heart'.

[4] *him* Christ.

[5] *which … borrows* referring to Christ's incarnation.

[6] *stuck … arrows* Christ's death is compared to that of St Sebastian (d. c. 300 CE). Many paintings of his martyrdom have erotic overtones; typically, Sebastian is a nude, dying figure, pierced with numerous arrows.

[7] *entertain* receive.

[8] *ark* receptacle for a holy object, like the Ark of the Covenant, in which the ancient Jews kept the tablets of the Law; here, Bedford's heart.

Where your fair soul may sure and safely rest,
When he is sweetly seated in your breast.

There may your thought as servants to your heart,
Give true attendance on this lovely guest,
While he doth to that blessed bow'r impart
Flow'rs of fresh comforts, deck that bed of rest,
With such rich beauties as may make it blest;
And you in whom all rarity is found,[9]
May be with his eternal glory crowned.

[...]

9.5.2 [An Invective against Outward Beauty Unaccompanied by Virtue][10]

That outward beauty which the world commends
Is not the subject I will write upon,
Whose date expired, that tyrant Time soon ends;
Those gaudy colours soon are spent and gone,
But those fair virtues which on thee attends
Are always fresh, they never are but one.
They make thy beauty fairer to behold
Than was that queen's for whom proud Troy was sold.[11]

As for those matchless colours red and white,[12]
Or perfect features in a fading face,
Or due proportion pleasing to the sight,
All these do draw but dangers and disgrace.
A mind enriched with virtue shines more bright,
Adds everlasting beauty, gives true grace,
Frames an immortal goddess on the earth,
Who though she dies, yet fame gives her new birth.

That pride of nature which adorns the fair,
Like blazing comets to allure all eyes,
Is but the thread that weaves their web of care,

[9] *rarity* unusual excellence of character.

[10] One of a number of marginal notes that organize the *Salve*'s material. They are included within square brackets throughout this selection.

[11] *queen* Helen of Troy (Glossary).

[12] *red and white* traditional colours of the Petrarchan mistress's perfect complexion.

Who glories most, where most their danger lies;
For greatest perils do attend the fair,
When men do seek, attempt, plot and devise,
  How they may overthrow the chastest dame,
  Whose beauty is the white whereat they aim.[13]

'Twas beauty bred in Troy the ten years' strife,
And carried Helen from her lawful lord;
'Twas beauty made chaste Lucrece lose her life,
For which proud Tarquin's fact was so abhorred;
Beauty the cause Antonius wronged his wife,
Which could not be decided but by sword;
  Great Cleopatra's beauty and defects
  Did work Octavia's wrongs, and his neglects.[14]

What fruit did yield that fair forbidden tree,[15]
But blood, dishonour, infamy, and shame?
Poor blinded queen, could'st thou no better see,
But entertain disgrace instead of fame?
Do these designs with majesty agree?
To stain thy blood, and blot thy royal name.
  That heart that gave consent unto this ill,
  Did give consent that thou thyself should'st kill.[16]

[...]

9.5.3 [Christ's Death]

His harmless hands unto the cross they nailed,
And feet that never trode in sinner's trace,
Between two thieves, unpitied, unbewailed,[17]

[13] *white* target.

[14] *Beauty … neglects* Mark Antony's tenuous alliance with Octavius Caesar was destroyed when Antony abandoned his wife Octavia, Octavius's sister, in favour of the famously beautiful and fascinating Cleopatra, Queen of Egypt.

[15] *forbidden tree* i.e., Antony's sin of adultery (with the obvious reference to the Tree of the Knowledge of Good and Evil, one of the two trees from which Adam and Eve are forbidden to eat (Gen. 2.17)).

[16] When she and Antony were defeated at the battle of Actium, Antony killed himself, and Cleopatra followed suit, using poisonous asps.

[17] *between two thieves* Mt. 27.38; Mk. 15.27; Lk. 23.32–43; Jn. 19.18.

Save of some few possessors of his grace,[18]
With sharpest pangs and terrors thus appailed,[19]
Stern Death makes way, that Life might give him place:
  His eyes with tears, his body full of wounds,
  Death last of pains his sorrows all confounds.

His joints disjointed, and his legs hang down,
His alablaster breast, his bloody side,[20]
His members torn, and on his head a crown[21]
Of sharpest thorns, to satisfy for pride:[22]
Anguish and pain do all his senses drown,
While they his holy garments do divide:[23]
  His bowels dry, his heart full fraught with grief,
  Crying to him that yields him no relief.[24]

9.5.4 [To My Lady of Cumberland][25]

This with the eye of faith thou may'st behold,
Dear spouse of Christ, and more than I can write;
And here both grief and joy thou may'st unfold,
To view thy love in this most heavy plight,
Bowing his head, his bloodless body cold;
Those eyes wax dim that gave us all our light,[26]
  His count'nance pale, yet still continues sweet,
  His blessed blood wat'ring his piercèd feet.

18 *unpitied … grace* Christ is 'unpitied, unbewailed' except by those 'few possessors of his grace', the predominately female disciples who do not abandon him at the cross (Mt. 27.55–6; Mk. 15.40–1; Lk. 23.48–9; Jn. 19.25–7).

19 *appailed* terrified.

20 *alablaster* alabaster.

21 *members* limbs.

22 *crown … thorns* Mt. 27.29; Mk. 15.17; Jn. 19.2; *satisfy for pride*: pay the price for humanity's sin of pride.

23 *they* the Roman soldiers; *garments do divide*: Mt. 27.35; Mk. 15.24; Lk. 23.34; Jn. 19.23–4.

24 *Crying … relief* i.e., Christ's cry to God from the cross: 'My God, my God, why hast thou forsaken me?' (Mt. 27.46; Mk. 15.34).

25 Margaret becomes the soul represented as the bride of her spouse, Christ. Taken from the biblical Song of Songs, a highly erotic wedding song, the imagery was commonly used to represent the relationship between Christ and the individual believer, as well as Christ and the Church.

26 *wax* grow.

O glorious miracle without compare!
Last but not least which was by him effected;
Uniting death, life, misery, joy and care,
By his sharp passion in his dear elected;[27]
Who doth the badges of like liveries wear[28]
Shall find how dear they are of him respected.
  No joy, grief, pain, life, death, was like to his,
  Whose infinite dolours wrought eternal bliss.

[...]

9.5.5 [Christ's Resurrection]

For he is rize from death t'eternal life,
And now those precious ointments he desires[29]
Are brought unto him by his faithful wife,
The holy Church; who in those rich attires,
Of patience, love, long-suff'ring, void of strife,
Humbly presents those ointments he requires:
  The oils of mercy, charity, and faith,
  She only gives that which no other hath.

9.5.6 [A Brief Description of his Beauty upon the Canticles][30]

These precious balms do heal his grievous wounds,
And water of compunction washeth clean
The sores of sins, which in our souls abounds;
So fair it heals, no scar is ever seen;
Yet all the glory unto Christ redounds,[31]
His precious blood is that which must redeem;
  Those well may make us lovely in his sight,
  But cannot save without his pow'rful might.

[27] *passion* the crucifixion and its immediately preceding events; also, 'suffering'; *elected*: chosen ones.

[28] *badges … liveries* clothing and accoutrements marking a person as the servant of a particular master.

[29] *those precious ointments* oils used to anoint Christ's dead body are transformed into a gift from bride (the Church) to groom (Christ).

[30] *Canticles* also called the Song of Solomon and the Song of Songs. See **n25**.

[31] *redounds* returns.

This is that bridegroom that appears so fair,[32]
So sweet, so lovely in his spouse's sight,
That unto snow we may his face compare,
His cheeks like scarlet, and his eyes so bright
As purest doves that in the rivers are,
Washèd with milk, to give thee more delight;
  His head is likened to the finest gold,
  His curlèd locks so beauteous to behold;[33]

Black as a raven in her blackest hue;[34]
His lips like scarlet threads, yet much more sweet
Than is the sweetest honey-dropping dew,[35]
Or honeycombs, where all the bees do meet;
Yea, he is constant, and his words are true,
His cheeks are beds of spices, flowers sweet;[36]
  His lips like lilies, dropping down pure myrrh,
  Whose love, before all worlds we do prefer.[37]

9.5.7 [To My Lady of Cumberland]

Ah! give me leave (good lady) now to leave
This task of beauty which I took in hand;
I cannot wade so deep, I may deceive
Myself, before I can attain the land;
Therefore (good madam) in your heart I leave
His perfect picture, where it still shall stand,
  Deeply engraved in that holy shrine,
  Environed with love and thoughts divine.

There may you see him as a God in glory,
And as a man in miserable case;
There may you read his true and perfect story,
His bleeding body there you may embrace,

[32] Cf. the groom's similar description of the bride, Song 4.7

[33] Cf. the bride's similar description of the groom, Song 5.10–12.

[34] *black* black-haired. Cf. Song 1.4–5 (Geneva); 5–6 (AV); part of the description of the bride's beauty, and the groom's.

[35] The groom describes the bride's lips as 'like a thread of scarlet' (4.3), and 'drop[ping] as the honeycomb: honey and milk are under [her] tongue' (4.11).

[36] Cf. the bride's description of the groom, Song 5.13, 6.2–3.

[37] An 'enclosed [virginal] garden', the bride grows orchard trees and sweet-smelling herbs and spices (Song 4.12–14).

And kiss his dying cheeks with tears of sorrow,
With joyful grief, you may entreat for grace;
   And all your prayers and your alms-deeds[38]
   May bring to stop his cruel wounds that bleeds.

Oft times hath he made trial of your love,
And in your faith hath took no small delight,
By crosses and afflictions he doth prove,[39]
Yet still your heart remaineth firm and right;
Your love so strong, as nothing can remove,
Your thoughts being placed on him both day and night,
   Your constant soul doth lodge between her breasts,
   This sweet of sweets, in which all glory rests.

[…]

The pilgrim's travels and the shepherd's cares
He took upon him to enlarge our souls;[40]
What pride hath lost, humility repairs,
For by his glorious death he us enrols
In deep characters, writ with blood and tears,
Upon those blessed everlasting scrolls;[41]
   His hands, his feet, his body, and his face,
   Whence freely flowed the rivers of his grace.

Sweet holy rivers, pure celestial springs,
Proceeding from the fountain of our life;[42]
Swift sugared currents that salvation brings,
Clear crystal streams, purging all sin and strife,
Fair floods, where souls do bathe their snow-white wings,
Before they fly to true eternal life:
   Sweet nectar and ambrosia, food of saints,[43]
   Which, whoso tasteth, never after faints.

38 *alms-deeds* charity.
39 *prove* test.
40 *enlarge* free.
41 *everlasting scrolls* Book of Life wherein the names of the saved are inscribed (Rev. 20.15).
42 *sweet … life* Rev. 22.1.
43 *nectar* and *ambrosia* drink and food of the gods; consuming the latter conveyed immortality.

This honey-dropping dew of holy love,[44]
Sweet milk, wherewith we weaklings are restored,
Who drinks thereof, a world can never move,
All earthly pleasures are of them abhorred;
This love made martyrs many deaths to prove,[45]
To taste his sweetness, whom they so adored:
  Sweetness that makes our flesh a burden to us,
  Knowing it serves but only to undo us.

[...]

9.5.8 The Description of Cookham[46]

[...]

But your occasions called you so away,[47]
That nothing there had power to make you stay.
Yet did I see a noble grateful mind,
Requiting each according to their kind,[48]
Forgetting not to turn and take your leave
Of these sad creatures, pow'rless to receive[49]
Your favour, when with grief you did depart,
Placing their former pleasures in your heart;
Giving great charge to noble memory,
There to preserve their love continually;
But specially the love of that fair tree,
That first and last you did vouchsafe to see,
In which it pleased you oft to take the air,
With noble Dorset, then a virgin fair;[50]
Where many a learnèd book was read and scanned
To this fair tree, taking me by the hand,

[44] See **n35**.

[45] *prove* experience, suffer.

[46] *Cookham* crown estate in Berkshire, near Maidenhead, temporarily occupied by Margaret, Countess of Cumberland and her household (including Lanyer), during Margaret's long-drawn-out legal battle to claim her dead husband's lands for their daughter, Anne.

[47] *you* Margaret.

[48] *requiting* rewarding.

[49] *sad creatures* trees of Cookham, mourning the countess's departure.

[50] *Dorset ... fair* before Anne's 1609 marriage to Richard Sackville, Third Earl of Dorset.

You did repeat the pleasures which had passed,[51]
Seeming to grieve they could no longer last.
And with a chaste, yet loving kiss took leave,
Of which sweet kiss I did it soon bereave,[52]
Scorning a senseless creature should possess[53]
So rare a favour, so great happiness.
No other kiss it could receive from me,
For fear to give back what it took of thee;
So I ingrateful creature did deceive it,[54]
Of that which you vouchsafed in love to leave it.
And though it oft had giv'n me much content,
Yet this great wrong I never could repent;
But of the happiest made it most forlorn,
To show that nothing's free from fortune's scorn,
While all the rest with this most beauteous tree,
Made their sad consort sorrow's harmony.

[...]

Each arbour, bank, each seat, each stately tree
Looks bare and desolate now for want of thee;
Turning green tresses into frosty gray,
While in cold grief they wither all away.
The sun grew weak, his beams no comfort gave,
While all green things did make the earth their grave.
Each briar, each bramble, when you went away,
Caught fast your clothes, thinking to make you stay.
Delightful Echo, wonted to reply[55]
To our last words, did now for sorrow die.
The house cast off each garment that might grace it,
Putting on dust and cobwebs to deface it.
All desolation then there did appear,
When you were going whom they held so dear.
This last farewell to Cookham here I give;
When I am dead thy name in this may live,
Wherein I have performed her noble hest,[56]

[51] *you* Margaret.

[52] *bereave* deprive. Kissing the tree directly after the countess has done so, Lanyer steals the countess's kiss for herself.

[53] *senseless* without senses; incapable of reason.

[54] *deceive* deprive.

[55] *wonted* accustomed.

[56] *hest* command.

Whose virtues lodge in my unworthy breast,
And ever shall, so long as life remains,
Tying my heart to her by those rich chains.[57]

Lady Mary Wroth (?1587–1651/53)

For her biography, see Introduction to **8.12**.

9.6

From *Urania*, Part I (1621)

9.6.1 Book 3

[The young prince Leonius rescues the shepherdess Veralinda from a beast; they fall mutually in love, but neither is aware of the other's feelings. On the advice of a shepherd, Leonius disguises himself as the shepherdess Leonia to approach Veralinda.]

As she[1] went on sadly bemoaning her solitary thoughts, she heard as pitiful a voice utter these unperfect joined words:

'Leonia, poor nymph,' said it, 'where is thy vow? Must Venus make thee change? O Love, coward Love, to steal thus to my heart! Couldest thou not have come bravely and contended with me in the chase, or taken me in the time when I did revile thee and scorn thy power? But to set upon me when I was quiet and safe, as I thought, treacherously to lie in wait and betray me when I was unarmed, naked, and without power to resist, and more for my shame when I had sworn to Diana! What punishment will that chaste goddess lay upon me for this offence? But, fool, why talk I of these poor things which in comparison of my woe are but blossoms? I love, and must love. What then? I will love, and die in love; then shall that cruel[2] see written in my heart that murder thus committed unkind. Alas, my soul melts as these tears, and yet to thee my pains are no more weighed than bubbles. My heart weeps blood: pity me then; say you do pity and save me.'

'Pity,' said the shepherdess, 'is that I want. What new companion in my woe have I found here?'

With that she went towards the place from whence as she imagined that

[57] *her* Margaret.

[1] *she* Veralinda.

[2] *cruel* i.e., cruel beloved.

sad voice did proceed, whenas a little from the bank under the shade of myrtle trees, which made as it were a cabin of themselves, lay a forest nymph, her apparel of colour and fashion like Diana, buskins upon her legs of white, her hair tied up, only some of the shortest and about the temples curled, crowned with roses and hyacinths. She lay with her head toward her, who with a soft pace went on till she came just behind her, then viewing her earnestly, her eyes being so full of love, as all loving creatures found a power in them to draw them to her call, especially those eyes which were so much hers as they could not stir but to her will, commanding them so, as she could with her looking on them with loving force, bring them to her own; and so it now proved, for those eyes which full of tears were seeing themselves in the stream, showing their watery pictures to each other, her earnest viewing the nymph with a natural humbleness to hers, drew her looks to her; joy then appeared in the nymph's face, yet straight was that clouded with sorrow. She rose, and with a timorous (though she imagined bashful) countenance and fashion, saluted her:

'I did think, fair nymph,' said the loving shepherdess, 'that it had been impossible for me to find any so like myself unhappily wounded.'

'Why, are you hurt, fair shepherdess?' said she. 'Alas, I am sorry for you, and wish your remedy, for none knows the torment of despair like to myself, and therefore in charity would have none else afflicted with it, but it is very strange that such beauty should complain.'

'Alas,' said she, 'oft times perfection is turned to the contrary, and so is it in me, if in me be that you spoke of. But I pray, sweet nymph, let me take boldness to demand of you, of whence you are and what hath brought you hither.'

'Love,' said she, 'for this must be the first and last of my discourse, all other matters how great soever being but dependences of this. My name,' said she, 'is Leonia. My profession was what my habits tell me to be, but love hath altered me, no more must I abuse my mistress who I served, since I have left her and a new one now have gained, a poor change, (yet the fruit of change) when for liberty and pleasure I get beggary and slavery. Then shun this passion, rare shepherdess, for nothing but misery follows it.'

'Alas, it is too late,' said she, 'you give this counsel out of time, for I am in the prison too fast locked by any means but by love to be freed.'

'Are you in love then?' said Leonia.

'Oh, hapless me! Why,' said the shepherdess, 'doth that grieve you?'

'It grieves me that such sweetness should be vexed.'

'It grieves me more,' cried she, 'that I love in despair.'

'Thus both afflict me,' said Leonia, 'and on these do I plain,[3] and in them die.'

[3] *plain* lament.

'Let us sit down and tell our woes,' said she.

'Mine are all endless,' said the nymph, 'yet I will not refuse to do what you command, for you may help me if you will but pity me.'

'I pity you,' said she, 'and love you, for in you I see (O dear remembrance) many things which represent my love unto mine eyes.'

With that the nymph did blush, the shepherdess went on: 'Be not offended, sweetest nymph,' said she, 'for he was excellent whom I did love and do love, rare for true beauty and valour, and oh, too brave[4] for me.'

'None can be so,' sighed she, 'fair shepherdess, for the fairest, and bravest must sue to you for grace. But I did blush to hear that I should seem so favourably blessed in your all-conquering eyes as to be thought but to resemble him, that happy man, whom your great goodness loves. But to go on, I was by my own suit to my parents chosen a nymph, and accepted into the number and service of Diana's servants, being given to all those sports that goddess did affect, but especially to throwing my dart[5] at marks, and shooting in my bow at beasts, or anything, so cunning I was in that exercise, as I could hit a bird at great distance. Oft times I would take my greyhounds and course[6] the deer or hare, being so nimble as I could follow them where'er they went. These and many other harmless delights I lived in, till one day sacrificing to Diana, unhappily for me, there came a youth, who having killed a terrible beast offered it to the goddess, as the princess of the woods and deserts. This offering proved strange, making my heart the victim bleeding, and lying on the altar, dedicated to his love, thus doubly had he conquered. I fainted, fearing the chaste goddess, yet I was rescued by Venus, who promised her assistance, but not so well armed by her, as not afraid of Diana, I fled from those parts, and since have I roamed about, directed by mine own despair, for never since have I seen my love. The forgetful goddess having enough in winning, but scorning too much care, hath I fear forgotten me, contented with my yielding, but careless of my proceeding. I seek still, but I know not with what hope. I have wept and grieved, and so I fear still must, and thus lives and perpetually laments the poor, unblessed Leonia.'

The shepherdess catching her in her arms, 'Ah, my companion in my woes,' said she, 'let us still live together fittest for our fortunes. Let our tears be shed together, our sighs breathed together, and let us never part, but always keep together.'

This was what the nymph desired, being so glad of that embracement as she could have found in her heart to have forgot her habits, but danger of losing all if not governed with modesty, till apter time gain fitter opportunity

[4] *brave* excellent.

[5] *dart* spear.

[6] *course* hunt.

of discovery, she only with an affectionate kiss, and that she would not suffer herself to miss, being such a one as liked Veralinda (for so the shepherdess was called) better than any of her fellows' kisses, for this seemed more passionately kind, gave liberty to that, and then began her own discourse thus:

'My name is Veralinda, daughter I am to the king's shepherd, who dwells upon yonder hill; his place, estate in goods, and some kind of thing in me, which these people here call "beauty", hath made me to be sought by many, but I have still refused all, truly I must say with some neglectiveness; for which I am punished, and if I flatter not myself above my merit, the pain being more than the offence, for I am made to love in despair, to hope in loss, and affect one I know not, or can aspire to thought of ever seeing him again. Destiny prevailing in this, and I am left a poor example of the Fates' tyranny: for how can I hope that if I meet him he could fancy me? – he a knight, I a poor maid; he a prince it may be, and surely is, for princely virtues dwell in him, beauty unexpressable, and such as – but in you – I never saw any like him, and so like are you, as I love you for his sake so much as love can command love to the image of their dear. Valiant he is above expression, and mild, and courteous; but what doth grieve my soul most, is, he surely loves.'

'And surely would love you,' said the nymph, 'if he could be but happy with the knowledge. In the mean space, grace me with your favour, which I will strive like him to merit. Let me enjoy those sweet embracements you would yield to him and think I am your love, which I will do by you, and in that thought till we be blessed with perfecter enjoyings, we shall have some ease.'

She condescended, and so they kissed again. Wishing and loving, they remained, passing many such pleasant times, till at last the wonder of such affection 'twixt women was discovered, and it may be, had then been brought to light, had not the shepherdesses arrived to his grief, and no way to her content, who truly loved the sweet conversation and discourse of this nymph. To the fountain they then altogether took their way, the nymph setting herself so, as she might both see and touch the loved shepherdess, all the rest beholding this stranger with as much admiration as she did their mistress, thinking no difference between them in beauty, save that the new guest's fairness seemed more masculine, as fitted with her estate, yet full of grave, modest, and seemly bashfulness. Thus they beheld each other, the shepherdess passionately beholding Leonia in memory of her love, and the nymph amorously gazing on her in her own passions. [...]

[Veralinda discovers that she is a long-lost princess; Leonius then reveals to her his true gender.]

[...] Leonius in his man's habits, again came with more fear to Veralinda than before, to whom he spoke in this manner:

'Fairest princess, I hope your estate will not make you forget the estate you lived in love. I am the knight you loved as a knight; I am the man who, for fear you loved me not, to move your love made myself a woman, and the same man that loves if you cherish, else dies if you forsake.'

'I am, my lord,' said she, 'the woman that loves you as much, or more, if possible, than I did, having so many more bonds to tie me unto it. My life I owe you; I will pay it you by spending it in being yours, and now I know myself to be a princess, the freelier will I say this, being the fitter for you.'

Ben Jonson (1572–1637), poet and playwright

Posthumous son of a Protestant minister and the stepson of a bricklayer, Jonson was educated at Westminster school, served as a soldier in the Netherlands, and later returned to London, writing plays to support his wife, Anne, and their growing family. His successes on the stage – including *Volpone*, *The Alchemist*, and *Bartholomew Fair* – were matched by his successes at court, where he wrote verse epigrams for his many patrons, as well as masques for Queen Anne, and lyric verse.

9.7

From *The Forest* (1616)[1]

9.7.1 [Lyric] 10 ['And must I sing?']

And must I sing? What subject shall I choose?
Or whose great name in poets' heaven use,
For the more countenance to my active muse?

Hercules? Alas, his bones are yet sore
With his old earthly labours. T' exact more
Of his dull godhead were sin. I'll implore

Phoebus. No, tend thy cart still. Envious day[2]
Shall not give out that I have made thee stay,

[1] Published in *Works* (1616).
[2] *cart* Phoebus Apollo's sun-chariot.

And foundered thy hot team, to tune my lay.[3]

Nor will I beg of thee, lord of the vine,[4]
To raise my spirits with thy conjuring wine,
In the green circle of thy ivy twine.[5]

Pallas, nor thee I call on, mankind maid,[6]
That at thy birth mad'st the poor smith afraid,
Who with his axe thy father's midwife played.[7]

Go, cramp dull Mars, light Venus, when he snorts,[8]
Or with thy tribade trine invent new sports;[9]
Thou nor thy looseness with my making sorts.[10]

Let the old boy, your son, ply his old task,[11]
Turn the stale prologue to some painted masque;[12]
His absence in my verse is all I ask.

Hermes, the cheater, shall not mix with us,
Though he would steal his sisters' Pegasus[13]
And riffle him, or pawn his petasus.[14]

[3] *lay* song; *thy hot team*: Apollo (Glossary).

[4] *lord … vine* Bacchus (Glossary).

[5] *green … twine* Bacchus's traditional wreath.

[6] *mankind maid* referring to the masculine qualities of Pallas Athena (Minerva), as the goddess of wisdom and war; often depicted armed; *maid*: virgin.

[7] *That at thy birth … played* The *poor smith* is Vulcan, god of the forge. See Athena (Glossary).

[8] *cramp* squeeze tightly (usually said of punishment or torture); *light*: sexually promiscuous, unfaithful; *snorts*: snores.

[9] *tribade trine* literally, a tribadic (female same-sex) three-some; probably, the three Graces (Glossary).

[10] *looseness* licentiousness, lewdness, immodesty; *making*: poetic creation.

[11] *old boy* Cupid (Glossary).

[12] *turn* fashion artistically (here, said ironically); *masque*: spectacular court entertainment with elaborate costumes, scenery, music, and dancing; *painted*: brightly coloured, but also 'deceptive, false'.

[13] *his sisters' Pegasus* the fabled winged horse, Pegasus, lived with and was a favourite of the nine Muses (Hermes' sisters).

[14] *riffle* search thoroughly, taking whatever is valuable (presumably, Pegasus's ornamental bridle and other accoutrements with which he sometimes appears in contemporary illustrations); *petasus*: See Mercury (Glossary).

Nor all the ladies of the Thespian lake[15]
(Though they were crushed into one form) could make
A beauty of that merit, that should take

My muse up by commission: no, I bring
My own true fire. Now my thought takes wing,
And now an epode to deep ears I sing.[16]

9.8

From *The Underwood* (1640)[17]

9.8.1 Epigram 49: An Epigram on the Court Pucelle[18]

Does the court pucelle then so censure me,
And thinks I dare not her? Let the world see.
What though her chamber be the very pit
Where fight the prime cocks of the game, for wit?
And that as any are struck, her breath creates
New in their stead, out of the candidates?
What though with tribade lust she force a muse,[19]
And in an epicoene fury can write news[20]
Equal with that which for the best news goes,
As airy light, and as like wit as those?
What though she talk, and cannot once with them[21]
Make state, religion, bawdry, all a theme?
And as lip-thirsty, in each word's expense,
Doth labour with the phrase more than the sense?
What though she ride two mile on holidays

[15] *ladies … lake* the nine Muses (Glossary).

[16] *epode* i.e., the collection's next poem: a lyric of elevated style, on a serious subject.

[17] Published in *Works* (1640).

[18] *pucelle* whore; usually identified as Cecilia Bulstrode (1584–1609). Jonson's attack is surprising, since Bulstrode was a friend of Lucy, Countess of Bedford, one of Jonson's most supportive patrons.

[19] *tribade* adj., after the manner of a tribade (a woman who has sex with another woman); *force*: rape; also 'coerce [into giving Bulstrode poetic inspiration]'.

[20] *epicoene* someone with characteristics of both sexes; an hermaphrodite. Cf. Jonson's *Epicoene, Or The Silent Woman* (1609).

[21] *cannot once* sometimes emended to 'can at once'.

To church, as others do to feasts and plays,
To show their 'tires, to view and to be viewed?[22]
What though she be with velvet gowns endued,[23]
And spangled petticoats brought forth to eye,
As new rewards of her old secrecy?
What though she hath won on trust, as many do,
And that her truster fears her: must I too?
I never stood for any place: my wit
Thinks itself naught, though she should value it.
I am no statesman, and much less divine;
For bawdry, 'tis her language, and not mine.
Farthest I am from the idolatry
To stuffs and laces: those my man can buy.
And trust her I would least, that hath foreswore
In contract twice; what can she perjure more?
Indeed, her dressing some man might delight,
Her face there's none can like by candlelight.
Not he that should the body have for case
To his poor instrument, now out of grace.[24]
Shall I advise thee, pucelle? Steal away
From court, while yet thy fame hath some small day;
The wits will leave you, if they once perceive
You cling to lords, and lords, if them you leave
For sermoneers: of which now one, now other
They say you weekly invite with fits o' th' mother,[25]
And practise for a miracle; take heed,
This age would lend no faith to Darrel's deed,[26]
Or if it would, the court is the worst place,
Both for the mothers and the babes of grace;
For there the wicked in the chair of scorn
Will call it a bastard, when a prophet's born.

[22] *'tires* clothes; attire.

[23] *endued* endowed.

[24] *instrument* penis.

[25] *fits … mother* female somatic and psychological disorder, where virgins' or widows' sexual frustration made the womb (*mother*) malfunction in its hungry desire for sexual release.

[26] John *Darrel* (b. c. 1562, d. in or after 1607), Puritan preacher; imprisoned for his fake exorcisms in 1599.

Edmund Waller (1606–87)

For his biography, see Introduction to **8.16**.

9.9

From *Poems* (1645)

9.9.1 On the Friendship Betwixt Sacharissa and Amorett

Tell me, lovely, loving pair,
Why so kind, and so severe?
Why so careless of our care,
Only to prove yourselves so dear?

By this cunning change of hearts,
You the power of love control;
While the boy's deluded darts[1]
Can arrive at neither soul.

For in vain to either breast
Still beguiled love does come,
Where he finds a foreign guest,
Neither of your hearts at home.

Debtors thus with like design,
When they never mean to pay,
That they may the law decline,[2]
To some friend make all away.[3]

Not the silver doves that fly
Yoked in Cytherea's car;[4]
Not the wings that lift so high,
And convey her son so far,

[1] *the boy's* winged Cupid's (Glossary).
[2] *decline* avoid.
[3] *make all away* i.e., sign property over to a friend so that debtors cannot make claims against it.
[4] *doves … car* Venus's (*Cytherea's*) emblematic birds: they pull her chariot (*car*) through the heavens.

Are so lovely, sweet, and fair,
Or do more enable love;
Are so choicely matched a pair,
Or with more content do move.

9.10

A Copy of Verses Made by a Lady and Sent to Another Lady, with a Bracelet Made of Her Own Hair (1655)

'Copy of Verses' appears in John Cotgrave's *Wit's Interpretor, The English Parnassus* (1655), a multi-authored, heterogeneous collection of poetry and prose, aimed at elite readers and couched within a satire of the self-help books popular among the lower ranks of society, especially those eager to gain expertise in manners, writing, and rhetoric (Marotti 276). It is contained in Section 4, 'Apollo and Orpheus: Several Love-Songs, Epigrams, Drolleries, and Other Verses'.

Go, gentle wreath, and let her know,[1]
I love her when I say not so.
By my pains with thee she'll find
How oft she hath been in my mind.
To thy fabric hand and head
Jointly have contributed;
And whilst others speak her fair,[2]
'Tis I that have her to a hair.[3]
Go and be at her command,
For always thou wilt be at hand;
Warm the blood which from that part
Takes secret marches to her heart;
The endless circularity[4]
Will show love's perpetuity.
The subtle web, and secret twining,
Is like love with love combining.
Learn then by her pulse to know,
Whether she's in health or no;

1 *wreath* hair bracelet of the title.
2 *speak her fair* speak to her courteously.
3 *have her to a hair* know her with utmost precision.
4 *circularity* shape of the bracelet, but also circulation of the wearer's blood.

And convey news to me,
By some kind sympathy.[5]
  Tell her, then, that wearing thee,[6]
She's not without a part of me.

Andrew Marvell (1621–78), writer and politician

Supporter of the Protectorate, the Cambridge-educated Marvell became the long-serving MP for Hull in 1659. Writer of political satires, and supporter of religious toleration, parliamentary democracy, and civil liberty, Marvell is still best known for his lyric poetry, most published posthumously (1688). Marvell probably wrote the 97-stanza country-house poem 'Upon Appleton House' while he was tutor to Maria Fairfax, daughter of Thomas, Lord Fairfax (1612–71), general of the parliamentary army (1645–50).

Online Companion
From Marvell's 'Last Instructions to a Painter' (comp., c. 1667) and 'An Elegy upon the Death of My Lord Francis Villiers' (comp. after 1648).

9.11

From *Poems* (1681)

9.11.1 Upon Appleton House: To My Lord Fairfax

[Built on the lands (and partly out of the ruins) of the medieval Nun Appleton Priory, a Cistercian [Roman Catholic] convent, which were given to Fairfax's family at the dissolution of the monasteries (after 1542), Appleton House comes to embody aristocratic and Protestant values. Below, Marvell recounts the 1518 events involving William Fairfax, his promised bride Isabella Thwaites, and the nuns of Nun Appleton Priory, before the granting of the priory and its lands to the family.]

While with slow eyes we these survey,[1]
And on each pleasant footstep stay,
We opportunely may relate
The progress of this house's fate.

[5] *sympathy*   occult or supernatural connection.
[6] *thee*   in the original, 'me' (printer's error).

[1] Stanzas 11–35; *these*: the beauties of the house and grounds.

A nunnery first gave it birth.
(For virgin buildings oft brought forth);
And all that neighbour-ruin shows
The quarries whence this dwelling rose.

Near to this gloomy cloister's gates
There dwelt the blooming virgin Thwaites,
Fair beyond measure, and an heir
Which might deformity make fair.[2]
And oft she spent the summer suns
Discoursing with the subtle nuns.[3]
Whence in these words one to her weaved,
(As 'twere by chance) thoughts long conceived.

'Within this holy leisure we
Live innocently as you see.
These walls restrain the world without,
But hedge our liberty about.[4]
These bars enclose that wider den
Of those wild creatures, callèd men.
The cloister outward shuts its gates,
And, from us, locks on them the grates.[5]

'Here we, in shining armour white,[6]
Like virgin Amazons do fight.[7]
And our chaste lamps we hourly trim,
Lest the great bridegroom find them dim.[8]

[2] *an heir … fair* i.e., her great wealth would make even an ugly, indeed deformed, woman seem beautiful.

[3] *subtle* sly.

[4] *hedge* restrict; protect.

[5] *grates* the grilles through which cloistered nuns could speak with outsiders.

[6] *white* colour of Cistercian nuns' habits; emblematic colour of purity.

[7] *virgin Amazons* an oxymoron in the period, since the *virgin* symbolized pre-marital physical and spiritual purity, while the *Amazon* represented woman's monstrous aspects; *Amazons*: classical female warriors who had brief sexual liaisons with men to reproduce, but were usually lovers of their fellow Amazons.

[8] *our chaste lamps … dim* Mt. 25.1–13: The bridegroom (Christ) arrives late for the marriage feast, but finds awaiting him ten wise virgins, their lamps burning with the extra oil they have brought; the unprepared foolish virgins, who have left to find extra oil, are locked out of the feast. Believers must always be prepared, since no one knows the day or the time (of one's death, or the apocalypse).

Our orient breaths perfumèd are[9]
With incense of incessant prayer.
And holy-water of our tears[10]
Most strangely our complexion clears.

'Not tears of grief; but such as those
With which calm pleasure overflows;
Or pity, when we look on you
That live without this happy vow.
How should we grieve that must be seen
Each one a spouse, and each a queen;[11]
And can in heaven hence behold
Our brighter robes and crowns of gold?

'When we have prayèd all our beads,[12]
Someone the holy legend reads;[13]
While all the rest with needles paint
The face and graces of the saint.[14]
But what the linen can't receive
They in their lives do interweave.
This work the saints best represents;
That serves for altar's ornaments.

'But much it to our work would add
If here your hand, your face we had:
By it we would Our Lady touch;[15]
Yet thus she you resembles much.
Some of your features, as we sowed,[16]
Through ev'ry shrine should be bestow'd.

[9] *orient* fresh; also, 'eastern (exotic)'.

[10] *holy-water* for use in sacred rituals like baptism.

[11] *spouse* i.e., nuns were thought married to Christ.

[12] *beads* referring to the rosary, a devotion to Jesus's mother, the Virgin Mary, where a sequence of prayers is 'counted off' on a string of beads (like a necklace); condemned by Protestants as idolatrous and superstitious (cf. **n15**).

[13] *holy legend* saint's life; Protestants saw devotion to saints as another aspect of Roman Catholic idolatry.

[14] *with needles … saint* Nuns often produced liturgical textiles (e.g., altar coverings).

[15] *Our Lady* Virgin Mary. Protestants believed Roman Catholics made an idol of Mary, treating her as divine in her own right.

[16] *sowed* i.e., sewed (perhaps with visual pun on the insinuations the nun is 'sowing' or 'planting' in Isabella's mind).

And in one beauty we would take
Enough a thousand saints to make.

'And (for I dare not quench the fire
That me does for your good inspire)
'Twere sacrilege a man t'admit
To holy things, for heaven fit.
I see the angels in a crown
On you the lilies show'ring down:[17]
And round about you glory breaks,
That something more than human speaks.

'All beauty, when at such a height,
Is so already consecrate.[18]
Fairfax I know; and long ere this
Have marked the youth, and what he is.
But can he such a rival seem
For whom you heav'n should disesteem?
Ah, no! and 'twould more honour prove
He your *devoto* were, than love.[19]

'Here live belovèd, and obeyed:
Each one your sister, each your maid.
And, if our rule seem strictly penned,[20]
The rule itself to you shall bend.
Our abbess too, now far in age,[21]
Doth your succession near presage.
How soft the yoke on us would lie,
Might such fair hands as yours it tie!

'Your voice, the sweetest of the quire,[22]
Shall draw heav'n nearer, raise us higher.
And your example, if our head,
Will soon us to perfection lead.

17 *lilies* symbol of purity (a Marian flower).

18 *consecrate* consecrated.

19 devoto *were, than love* i.e., your worshipper rather than your lover.

20 Each religious order had requirements (*the rule*) governing members' behaviour. Protestants charged that the *rule* simply disguised monks' and nuns' horrific sins, particularly sexual ones. Cf. Bale, 'Votaries', *Online Companion.*

21 *abbess* head of a nunnery.

22 *quire* choir.

Those virtues to us all so dear,
Will straight grow sanctity when here:
And that, once sprung, increase so fast
Till miracles it work at last.

'Nor is our order yet so nice,[23]
Delight to banish as a vice.
Here pleasure piety doth meet;
One pèrfecting the other sweet.
So through the mortal fruit we boil
The sugar's uncorrupting oil:[24]
And that which perished while we pull,[25]
Is thus preservèd clear and full.

'For such indeed are all our arts;
Still handling nature's finest parts.
Flow'rs dress the altars; for the clothes,
The sea-born amber we compose;[26]
Balms for the grieved we draw; and pastes[27]
We mould, as baits for curious tastes.[28]
What need is here of man? unless
These as sweet sins we should confess.

'Each night among us to your side
Appoint a fresh and virgin bride;
Whom if Our Lord at midnight find,
Yet neither should be left behind.[29]
Where you may lie as chaste in bed,
As pearls together billeted.
All night embracing arm in arm,
Like crystal pure with cotton warm.

[23] *nice* strict.

[24] *So … oil* fruit, boiled down to a sweet reduction.

[25] *while we pull* i.e., when we plucked the fruit we destroyed it.

[26] *for … compose* i.e., for the altar cloths, we prepare a perfume from *sea-born amber* (i.e., ambergris, a wax-like substance found floating on tropical seas and in whale intestines; used in perfumes).

[27] *grieved* distressed; *draw*: prepare.

[28] *and … tastes* i.e., we makes pastries to tempt fastidious (*curious*) taste-buds; *baits*: refreshments; also 'enticements'.

[29] *Whom … behind* i.e., if they die in the night, both will go together to heaven.

'But what is this to all the store
Of joys you see, and may make more!
Try but a while, if you be wise:
The trial neither costs, nor ties.'
Now, Fairfax, seek her promised faith:
Religion that dispensèd hath,
Which she henceforward does begin;[30]
The nun's smooth tongue has sucked her in.[31]

Oft, though he knew it was in vain,
Yet would he valiantly complain.
'Is this that sanctity so great,
An art by which you finelier cheat?
Hypocrite witches, hence avaunt,
Who though in prison yet enchaunt!
Death only can such thieves make fast,
As rob though in the dungeon cast.[32]

'Were there but, when this house was made,
One stone that a just hand had laid,
It must have fall'n upon her head
Who first thee from thy faith misled.
And yet, how well soever meant,
With them 'twould soon grow fraudulent
For like themselves they alter all,
And vice infects the very wall.

'But sure those buildings last not long,
Founded by folly, kept by wrong.
I know what fruit their gardens yield,
When they it think by night concealed.
Fly from their vices. 'Tis thy 'state,[33]
Not thee, that they would consecrate.
Fly from their ruin. How I fear,
Though guiltless, lest thou perish there.'

[30] *Religion … begin* i.e., religion has annulled (*dispensèd*) Isabella's promise to marry William and thus allowed her to enter the convent as a novice (to *begin* her life there).

[31] *tongue* clearly glancing at cunnilingus; the 'tongue' was a symbol of 'female' sins: talkativeness, gossip-mongering, etc.

[32] *As rob though* i.e., who are able to steal even though [they are].

[33] *'state* estate, property.

What should he do? He would respect
Religion, but not right neglect,
For first religion taught him right,
And dazzled not but cleared his sight.
Sometimes resolved his sword he draws,
But reverenceth then the laws:
For justice still that courage led;
First from a judge, then soldier bred.[34]

Small honour would be in the storm.[35]
The court him grants the lawful form;
Which licensed either peace or force,
To hinder the unjust divorce.
Yet still the nuns his right debarred,
Standing upon their holy guard.
Ill-counselled women, do you know
Whom you resist, or what you do?

Is not this he whose offspring fierce
Shall fight through all the universe;
And with successive valour try
France, Poland, either Germany;[36]
Till one, as long since prophesied,
His horse through conquered Britain ride?[37]
Yet, against fate, his spouse they kept,
And the great race would intercept.[38]

Some to the breach against their foes
Their wooden saints in vain oppose.
Another bolder stands at push
With their old holy-water brush,
While the disjointed abbess threads
The jingling chain-shot of her beads.
But their loud'st cannon were their lungs;
And sharpest weapons were their tongues.

[34] William Fairfax's father was a *judge*, and his mother was descended from a famous *soldier*.

[35] *in the storm* in entering the nunnery by force.

[36] *France … Germany* the countries in which William and his descendants fought.

[37] *Till … ride?* Thomas, Lord Fairfax, or some yet unborn descendant of William.

[38] *Yet … intercept* by retaining Isabella the nuns defy fate, attempting to end the lineage (*race*) which her marriage to William is destined to perpetuate.

But, waving these aside like flies,
Young Fairfax through the wall does rise.
Then th'unfrequented vault appeared,
And superstitions vainly feared.
The relics false were set to view;[39]
Only the jewels there were true.
But truly bright and holy Thwaites
That weeping at the altar waits.

But the glad youth away her bears,
And to the nuns bequeaths her tears:
Who guiltily their prize bemoan,
Like gypsies that a child hath stol'n.
Thenceforth (as when th'enchantment ends
The castle vanishes or rends)
The wasting cloister with the rest
Was in one instant dispossessed.

At the demolishing, this seat
To Fairfax fell as by escheat.[40]
And what both nuns and founders willed
'Tis likely better thus fulfilled,
For if the virgin proved not theirs,
The cloister yet remainèd hers.
Though many a nun there made her vow,
'Twas no religious house till now.

Margaret Cavendish, Duchess of Newcastle (?1623–73), writer

Staunch royalist and maid of honour to Queen Henrietta Maria, Cavendish published *Poems and Fancies* and *Philosophical Fancies* in 1653, both of which display her lifelong interest in natural science. Later, she published plays; a miscellany of poetry, fiction, and autobiography (*Nature's Pictures*, 1656); and

[39] *relics* objects belonging to or bodily parts of a saint; objects of devotion in the Catholic tradition, of superstition and idolatry in the Protestant.

[40] *escheat* when an estate with no direct male heir reverts to the next closest male relative. The female 'line' of the nuns ends with the seizure of their abbey and its lands, and the male line of the Fairfax family takes over. Ironically, the nuns have tried to retain Isabella so they can enjoy her property, but she finally becomes the possessor of theirs.

a scientific utopian romance. Cavendish's plays and fiction acknowledge the oppression women faced within marriage in particular, often constructing fantasy versions of capable women acting in the public spheres of war and government.

Editions

Bowerbank, S. and S. Mendelson, ed., *Paper Bodies: A Margaret Cavendish Reader.* Peterborough, ON: Broadview Press, 2000.

Lilley, K., ed., 'Assaulted and Pursued Chastity.' *The Blazing World and Other Writings.* London: Penguin, 1994, 47–118.

Shaver, A., ed., *The Convent of Pleasure and Other Writings.* Baltimore: Johns Hopkins University Press, 1999.

9.12

From *Nature's Pictures* (1656)

9.12.1 Assaulted and Pursued Chastity

[The beautiful, virtuous, and intelligent Miseria cross-dresses to escape imprisonment and rape by a married prince. Surviving storms, shipwrecks, and New World encounters, Miseria (now called 'Travellia') is captured by pirates and sold to the Queen of Amity. Thinking Travellia a man, the queen falls in love with her. The King of Amour is at war with the queen, because she has rejected his love suit. The king makes the married prince, who has pursued Travellia throughout the narrative, commander of his forces.]

In the meanwhile the queen was not ignorant of their intentions, nor slack in her preparations, sending forth an army to meet them; but the queen herself had a war in her mind, as great as that in the field, where love as the general led her thoughts, but fear and doubt ofttimes made great disorder, and especially at that time; for Travellia, on whom she doted, was then sick, in which sickness she took more care to recover him, than to guard herself and kingdom; but the army she sent out was led by one of her chief noblemen, who marched on until he had view of the other army, and being both met, they set their armies in battle array.

[The prince wins this battle. On Travellia's advice, the queen consults her councillors, who advise her to go to the front lines to encourage her troops.]

'And this,' said she angrily to him,[1] 'was by your advice? For, had I not called a council, but had sent a general of my own choice, it would not have been put to a vote, for me in person to have gone; but had you had that love for me, as I have for you, I should have had better advice.' And with that [she] wept. 'Heaven knows,' said she, 'the greatest blow fortune can give me is to go and leave you behind me.'

He seeing her weep thus spoke: 'Beauty of your sex and nature's rarest piece, why should you cast your love so low upon a slave so poor as I, when kings their kingdoms hazard for your sake? And if your people knew, or did suspect your love to me, they would rebel and turn unto your enemy; besides, conquerors are feared and followed, where losing is a way to be despised, and trod into the earth with scorns. Alas, I am a creature mean[2] and poor, not worthy such a queen as you, and 'twere not wise to hazard all for me. Wherefore, go on, great Queen, and may you shine as glorious in your victories, as the brightest stars in heaven. May Pallas b[e] your guide and Mars, the god of war, fight your battles out. May Cupid give you ease, and Venus give delight; may Hymen give such nuptials as best befits your dignity; may fortune always smile, peace in your kingdom dwell.

And in each heart such loyal love may grow,
No disobedience may this kingdom know;
Age crown your life; and honour close your days:
Fame's trumpet loud to blow about your praise.'

She weeping said,

'No sound will pierce my ear or please my mind,
Like to those words you utter when they're kind.'

[Named the queen's heir, Travellia governs wisely. When the queen is taken prisoner, Travellia as the country's general wins a decisive victory. Under siege, the king of Amour asks Travellia to negotiate peace. Meanwhile, the queen laments her hopeless love for Travellia.]

'Oh, what a hell it is to love, and not be loved again! Nay, not only to love, but to love a slave, and he regards me not. Do I say "slave"? No, he is none that hath no slavish passion: then he is free,

And I am only bound to slavery
First to my passions, then to his tyranny.

1 *him* Travellia.
2 *mean* of low rank.

What shall I do, you gods above?
You punish me, and yet you make me love.
Do you delight still in a tortured mind?
Make you no sympathy in human kind?
Must all your works consist in contradiction?
Or do we nothing enjoy but fiction?
The mind is nothing but apprehension,[3]
'Tis not a thing, unless it hath dimension.
But, O you powerful gods, by your decree,
Can of nothing a something make to be:
Then make me something, grant me my delight,
Give me my lover, or destroy me quite.'

[Travellia works out a profitable treaty between the two kingdoms.]

[…] he[4] and the council, and the chief commanders went unto the palace of the king, where after some discourse, [he] was brought to the queen, who joyed more to see her Travellia than the victories they won, and after she had condoled with him for the loss of his father,[5] she congratulated him for the good success he had in the wars, and withal told him she must set at liberty his prisoner the prince,[6] for she had given him back unto the king, whereupon he presently gave orders for the prince to repair[7] to the court, and after she heard the relations of all their several actions and accidents, and had pleased herself with the variety of other discourses, she told them she would sit in a council to consider what was to be done as concerning the peace, and so dismissed them for that time, only she stayed Travellia, loving his company so well, she could not so easily part. But the king perceiving her affections, as being never pleased but when Travellia was with her, he grew so jealous that had not honour forbid him, having passed his word unto her they should all there be safe, otherwise he should not have let him live to have been his rival.

[The prince reveals Travellia's gender to the king, and that the queen is unaware of it. Messengers arrive with letters revealing the death of the prince's wife.]

[…] Travellia looking upon his[8] face as he was coming in amongst the

3 *apprehension* the faculty of understanding.
4 *he* i.e., Travellia.
5 Travellia's foster-father has recently died.
6 Travellia has earlier captured the prince in battle.
7 *repair* go.
8 *his* the prince's.

society, seeing the man she most did fear, she fell into a swound;[9] at which accident the queen being extremely afflicted, thinking it was done by some design wrought from the jealousy of the king, broke up the juncto[10] for that time, taking all the care she could for his recovery. But Travellia, being recovered out of her swound, yet was she sick in mind, though not in body, and kept her bed, as being very ill.

Whereupon the queen's suspicion was more increased, and [she] feared some poison had been given him; and with that conceit[11] could not endure to see the king.

The king being much troubled that the queen was more strict[12] to him than she was used to be, and perceiving that it was Travellia that was the cause, complained unto the prince, and angrily merrily said, 'Dispose of your mistress some way, for I am jealous,' (said he), 'although she is a woman.'

'Sir,' said the prince, 'I have as much reason to be jealous of the queen as you have of my mistress, setting her masculine habit aside.'

At last they did agree to discover her to the queen.

[…]

'Then, madam,' said he,[13] 'I must tell you, you are in love; and those you love, although there is a society of all excellencies, yet cannot return such love you desire; for you have placed your affection upon a woman, who hath concealed her sex, in taking the habit of a man, and might more confirm your mistake by the actions of a soldier. I know not (said the prince) how kind you have found her, but I have found her cruel,' then telling the story from the first time he saw her until that present.

When the queen had heard his relation, her colour came and went, moved by her mixed passions, anger and love: angry that she was deceived, yet still did love, as wishing she had been a man.

Then the prince began to move unto her the suit of the king, but she was so impatient and troubled in her mind, being crossed in her love, that she would hear nothing concerning love more at that time; which he perceiving, took his leave for the present, but as soon as he was gone,

> Tears from her eyes flowed out, as if they meant
> To make her there a watery monument;
> And her oppressèd heart such sighs sent forth,

[9] *swound* faint.
[10] *juncto* council.
[11] *conceit* notion.
[12] *strict* severe.
[13] *he* the prince.

Like gusts of wind that blow from south or north.
After this furious storm, a calm did rise,
Her spirits like a still, smooth water lies.
Then laying down her gentle head to rest,
Thus to the god of love her prayers addressed:
'Thou powerful god of love, that shoots from high,
One leaden arrow in my breast let fly,
To quench that scorching heat thou mad'st to burn,
Unless a woman to a man can turn.'
With that the god of love did pity take,
Quenched out the first, and did a new fire make;
Yet was it weak, as being made but new,
But being kindled, it much better grew.
At last, the flame got hold upon the king,
Which did much joy unto each kingdom bring.

After a sweet and refreshing sleep, she rose, and went to Travellia's chamber, and told her how she was discovered; then chiding her gently for not making herself known unto her: 'For,' said she, 'you have caused me many unquiet rests.'

But Travellia begged her pardon, telling her, it was the cause of her misfortunes that concealed her, and not out of any evil design she had to deceive her; then desired her assistance and help to secure her[self].

Whilst they were thus talking, the king and the prince came to see the sick person, to whom the queen with a smiling countenance said, she was a-courting her hard-hearted lover.

The king answered, that he hoped she would take pity on him, by what she had felt herself.

The queen told him that she was likelier to love him now than if she had never been a lover before: 'For,' said she, 'there is something pleasing in lovers' thoughts, be their fortunes never so adverse; and I believe (said she) the prince will say as much.'

'Madam,' said he, 'it is a pleasing pain, as being mixed with hopes and fears; but if our hopes do cease, all pleasure is gone, and nothing doth remain but pains of hell.'

'Then,' said the queen, 'your mistress were in a sad condition, if she loved you, as you seem to love her, you being a married man.'

'No,' said the prince, 'I am now a widower; but I doubt (said he) that doth advantage me in my mistress's affection.'

But when Travellia heard he was a widower, her heart did beat like to a feverish pulse, being moved with several passions, fearing it was not so, hoping it was so, joying if it were so, grieving that she ought not to wish it so.

But the queen asked the prince, how that he came to know of it. Whereupon he told her.

Said she, 'I have promised your mistress to protect her against your outrageous assaults; but since your suit is just, and your treaty civil, I will yield her to you, upon that condition you carry her not out of my kingdom; for since I cannot marry her, and so make her my husband, I will keep her if I can, and so make her my friend.'

With that, Travellia rises up in her bed, and bowed herself with a pleased countenance, giving the queen thanks.

Said the prince, 'You have given me as much as the gods could give, which is felicity.'

'Madam,' said the king, 'you have given me nothing.'

The queen, with blushes, answered, that if her council would agree, she would give him herself.

The king for joy kneeled down, and kissed her hand: 'Now I am like to the gods, they can but have their wish.'

Thus passing that day in pleasing discourses, the next day they caused their councils to meet, where they concluded the marriage of the king and queen; and that the queen should live with their king in the kingdom of Amour, and that her first son should be heir to the crown, and her second should be heir to the kingdom of Amity; but in case there were no sons, or but one, then daughters should inherit.

In the meantime, the prince, and his princess that was to be, should be viceroy, or rather she should rule; who was so beloved of the people, as if she had not only been a native born, but as if she had been born from the royal stock. But they thought it fit she should make herself known unto the army by word of mouth that she was a woman; otherwise they might think she was made away by a violent death, and that the report of being a woman was only a trick to deceive them, and from thence arise such a mutiny as might bring a ruin to both kingdoms.

When all was agreed, they prepared for the marriages.

In the meantime, Travellia goeth to the army, attended by the prince, where the king and queen came soon after, that the soldiers might see they were there, as witnesses of what she told them. And being all in a circle round about her, she being upon a place raised for that purpose, thus spoke:

'Noble friends, and valiant soldiers,

I am come here at this present to declare I am a woman, although I am habited[14] like a man, and perchance you may think it immodesty; but they that will judge charitably, will enquire the reason before they give their censure, for upright judges never give sentence before the party proves

[14] *habited* dressed.

guilty: wherefore I believe you will not condemn me, because necessity did enforce me to conceal my sex, to protect my honour; for as the love of soul and body is inseparable, so should the love of chastity, and the effeminate[15] sex; and who can love, and not share in danger? And since no danger ought to be avoided, nor life considered, in respect of their honours; and to guard that safe from enemies, no habit is to be denied;[16] for it is not the outward garments that can corrupt the honest mind, for modesty may clothe the soul of a naked body, and a sword becomes[17] a woman when it is used against the enemies of her honour; for though her strength be weak, yet she ought to show her will; and to die in the defence of honour is to live with noble fame; therefore neither camp, nor court, nor city, nor country, nor danger, nor habit, nor any worldly felicity must separate the love of chastity and our sex; for, as love is the sweetest, so it is the strongest of all passions; and true love proceeds from virtue, not from vice; wherefore it is to be followed by life, to be maintained till death; and if I have served my queen honestly, condemn not my modesty.'

Then bowing her head down low, first to the king and queen, then to the army.

Whereupon the army gave a shout, and cried out, 'Heaven bless you, of what sex soever you be.'

[…]

Then was there a declaration read to the army of the agreement of peace; and when it was read that that the prince should be viceroy in the kingdom of Amity, all the soldiers, as if they had been one voice, cried out 'Travellia shall be viceregency'; which was granted to pacify them. Whereupon there were acclamations of joy.

But the prince told his mistress, she should govern him.

She answered, that he should govern her, and she would govern the kingdom.

Then went the king and queen, the prince and Travellia, the nobles and the chief commanders, to celebrate their nuptials; where on the wedding day, the queen was adorned with a crown of diamonds, and hung about with rich jewels, yet her beauty did dim their lustre; but Travellia was only dressed in a white silk garment, which hung loosely about her, yet then:

> Her face did seem like to a glory bright,
> Where gods and goddesses did take delight;

[15] *effeminate* feminine.

[16] *And since no danger … denied* Many early modern Christian theologians would agree, but others rejected all justifications for cross-dressing.

[17] *becomes* is appropriate for.

And in her eyes, new worlds, you there might see
Love, flying cupids there as angels be;
And on her lips Venus enthronèd is,
Inviting duller lovers there to kiss;
Winged Mercury upon her tongue did sit,
Strewing out flowers of rhetoric and of wit;
Pallas did circle in each temple round,
Which with her wisdom, as a laurel crowned;
And in her cheeks sweet flowers for Love's poesies,
There Fates spun threads of lilies and of roses;[18]
And every loving smile, as if each were
A palace for the Graces to dwell there;
And chaste Diana on her snow white breast
There leaned her head, with pure thoughts to rest;
When viewed her neck, great Jove turned all to wonder,
In Love's soft showers melting without thunder;
The lesser gods on her white hands did lie,
Thinking each vein to be their azure sky;
Her charming circling arms made Mars to cease
All his fierce battles, for a love's soft peace;
And on our world's globe sat triumphing high,
Heaved there by Atlas up unto the sky;
And sweet-breathed Zephyrus did blow her name
Into the glorious trumpet of good fame.

[After their marriages, the king and queen govern the kingdom of Amour, and Travellia and the prince the kingdom of Amity.]

9.13

From *Plays Never Before Printed* (1668):
The Convent of Pleasure

[The play opens in the aftermath of the death of Lady Happy's father; two gentlemen fortune hunters delight in the sudden availability of the wealthy heiress.]

[18] *Lilies* and *roses* emblems of the Petrarchan mistress's perfect complexion.

9.13.1 Act 1, scene 2

Enter the Lady Happy, *and one of her attendants.*

Servant. Madam, you being young, handsome, rich, and virtuous, I hope you will not cast away those gifts of nature, fortune, and heaven, upon a person which cannot merit you?

Lady Happy. Let me tell you, that riches ought to be bestowed on such as are poor, and want[19] means to maintain themselves; and youth, on those that are old; beauty, on those that are ill-favoured; and virtue, on those that are vicious. So that if I should place my gifts rightly I must marry one that's poor, old, ill-favoured, and debauched.

Servant. Heaven forbid.

Lady Happy. Nay, heaven doth not only allow of it, but commands it; for we are commanded to give to those that want.[20]

Enter Madam Mediator *to the* Lady Happy.

Mediator. Surely, Madam, you do but talk, and intend not to go where you say.

Lady Happy. Yes, truly, my words and intentions go even together.

Mediator. But surely you will not encloister[21] yourself, as you say.

Lady Happy. Why, what is there in the public world that should invite me to live in it?

Mediator. More than if you should banish yourself from it.

Lady Happy. Put the case I should marry the best of men, if any best there be; yet would a married life have more crosses and sorrows than pleasure, freedom, or happiness. Nay, marriage to those that are virtuous is a greater restraint than a monastery. Or, should I take delight in admirers? They might gaze on my beauty and praise my wit, and I receive nothing from their eyes nor lips; for words vanish as soon as spoken, and sights are not substantial. Besides, I should lose more of my reputation by their visits than gain by their praises. Or, should I quit reputation and turn courtesan, there would be more lost in my health than gained by my lovers; I should find more pain than pleasure; besides, the troubles and frights I should be put to, with the quarrels and brouilleries[22] that jealous rivals

19 *want* lack.
20 *want* are impoverished.
21 *encloister* shut up in a cloister or convent.
22 *brouilleries* tiffs.

make, would be a torment to me; and 'tis only for the sake of men when women retire not. And since there is so much folly, vanity and falsehood in men, why should women trouble and vex themselves for their sake? – for retiredness bars the life from nothing else but men.

MEDIATOR. Oh yes, for those that encloister themselves bar themselves from all other worldly pleasures.

LADY HAPPY. The more fools they.

MEDIATOR. Will you call those fools that do it for the gods' sake?

LADY HAPPY. No, madam, it is not for the gods' sake, but for opinion's sake. For can any rational creature think or believe, the gods take delight in the creature's uneasy life? Or did they command or give leave to nature to make senses for no use or to cross, vex, and pain them? For what profit or pleasure can it be to the gods to have men or women wear coarse linen or rough woollen, or to flay their skin with hair-cloth, or to eat or saw through their flesh with cords? Or what profit or pleasure can it be to the gods to have men eat more fish than flesh or to fast? – unless the gods did feed on such meat themselves, for then, for fear the gods should want it, it were fit for men to abstain from it. The like for garments: for fear the gods should want fine clothes to adorn themselves, it were fit men should not wear them. Or what profit or pleasure can it be to the gods to have men to lie uneasily on the hard ground? – unless the gods and nature were at variance, strife, and wars, as if what is displeasing unto nature were pleasing to the gods, and to be enemies to her were to be friends to them.[23]

MEDIATOR. But being done for the gods' sake, it makes that which in nature seems to be bad, in divinity to be good.

LADY HAPPY. It cannot be good, if it be neither pleasure nor profit to the gods; neither do men anything for the gods' but their own sake.

MEDIATOR. But when the mind is not employed with vanities nor the senses with luxury, the mind is more free to offer its adorations, prayers, and praises to the gods.

LADY HAPPY. I believe the gods are better pleased with praises than fasting; but when the senses are dulled with abstinency, the body weakened with fasting, the spirits tired with watching,[24] the life made uneasy with pain, the soul can have but little will to worship: only

[23] *No, madam … them* referring to Catholic penitential practices aimed at mortifying the flesh, usually practised by nuns or monks, but sometimes by laypeople: self-inflicted pain (wearing a rough hair-shirt), self-mutilation, self-flagellation, fasting (abjuring meat), and sleeping on the ground. Rejecting fine clothes and adopting a simple habit were part of a nun's vow of poverty, chastity, and obedience.

[24] *watching* staying up all night to pray.

the imagination doth frighten it into active zeal, which devotion is rather forced than voluntary; so that their prayers rather flow out of their mouth than spring from their heart, like rain-water that runs through gutters, or like water that's forced up a hill by artificial pipes and cisterns. But those that pray not unto the gods, or praise them more in prosperity than adversity, more in pleasures than pains, more in liberty than restraint, deserve neither the happiness of ease, peace, freedom, plenty and tranquility in this world, nor the glory and blessedness of the next. And if the gods should take pleasure in nothing but in the torments of their creatures, and would not prefer those prayers that are offered with ease and delight, I should believe the gods were cruel. And what creature that had reason or rational understanding would serve cruel masters, when they might serve a kind mistress, or would forsake the service of their kind mistress to serve cruel masters? Wherefore, if the gods be cruel, I will serve nature. But the gods are bountiful, and give all that's good, and bid us freely please ourselves in that which is best for us. And that is best, what is most temperately used, and longest may be enjoyed, for excess doth waste itself and all it feeds upon.

MEDIATOR. In my opinion, your doctrine and your intention do not agree together.

LADY HAPPY. Why?

MEDIATOR. You intend to live encloistered and retired from the world.

LADY HAPPY. 'Tis true, but not from pleasures! For I intend to encloister myself from the world to enjoy pleasure, and not to bury myself from it; but to encloister myself from the encumbered cares and vexations, troubles, and perturbance of the world.

MEDIATOR. But if you encloister yourself, how will you enjoy the company of men, whose conversation is thought the greatest pleasure?

LADY HAPPY. Men are the only troublers of women, for they only[25] cross and oppose their sweet delights and peaceable life; they cause their pains, but not their pleasures. Wherefore those women that are poor, and have not means to buy delights and maintain pleasures, are only fit for men, for having not means to please themselves, they must serve only to please others. But those women, where fortune, nature, and the gods are joined to make them happy, were mad to live with men, who make the female sex their slaves. But I will not be so enslaved, but will live retired from their company. Wherefore, in order thereto, I will take so many noble persons of my own sex as my estate will plentifully maintain, such whose births are greater

[25] *only* alone.

than their fortunes, and are resolved to live a single life and vow virginity. With these I mean to live encloistered with all the delights and pleasures that are allowable and lawful. My cloister shall not be a cloister of restraint, but a place for freedom; not to vex the senses but to please them. [...]

[...]

Exeunt.

9.13.2 Act 2, scene 1

Enter MADAM MEDIATOR.

TAKE-PLEASURE. O Madam Mediator, we are all undone![26] The Lady Happy is encloistered.

MEDIATOR. Yes, gentlemen, the more is the pity.

ADVISER. Is there no hopes?

MEDIATOR. Faith, little.

FACIL. Let us see the clergy to persuade her out, for the good of the commonwealth.

MEDIATOR. Alas gentlemen! they can do no good, for she is not a votress to the gods but to nature.

COURTLY. If she be a votress to nature, you are the only person fit to be lady prioress;[27] and so by your power and authority you may give us leave to visit your nuns sometimes.

MEDIATOR. Not but at a grate,[28] unless in time of building, or when they are sick; but howsoever, the Lady Happy is lady prioress herself, and will admit none of the masculine sex, not so much as to a grate, for she will suffer no grates about the cloister; she has also women physicians, surgeons, and apothecaries, and she is the chief confessor[29] herself, and gives what indulgences or absolutions[30] she pleaseth. Also, her house, where she hath made her convent, is so big and convenient, and so strong, as it needs no addition or repair; besides, she has so much compass of ground within her walls as there is not only room and place enough for gardens, orchards, walks, groves, bowers, arbours, ponds, fountains, springs and the

26 *undone* ruined.

27 *lady prioress* head of a convent.

28 *grate* iron grille through which cloistered nuns could talk with visitors.

29 *chief confessor* the convent's priest: he would hear nuns' confessions.

30 *indulgence* remission of the punishment due even to forgiven sins; *absolution*: forgiveness for one's confessed sins.

like, but also conveniency for much provision, and hath women for every office and employment. For though she hath not above twenty ladies with her, yet she hath a numerous company of female servants, so as there is no occasion for men.

TAKE-PLEASURE. If there be so many women, there will be the more use for men. But pray, Madam Mediator, give me leave, rightly to understand you, by being more clearly informed: you say, the Lady Happy is become a votress to nature; and if she be a votress to nature, she must be a mistress to men.

MEDIATOR. By your favour, sir, she declares that she hath avoided the company of men by retirement, merely because she would enjoy the variety of pleasures which are in nature; of which, she says, men are obstructors; for, instead of increasing pleasure, they produce pain; and, instead of giving content, they increase trouble; instead of making the female sex happy, they make them miserable; for which, she hath banished the masculine company forever.

ADVISER. Her heretical opinions ought not to be suffered, nor her doctrine allowed; and she ought to be examined by a masculine synod, and punished with a severe husband, or tortured with a deboist[31] husband.

MEDIATOR. The best way, gentlemen, is to make your complaints, and put up a petition to the state, with your desires for a redress.[32]

COURTLY. Your counsel is good.

FACIL. We will follow it, and go presently about it.

Exeunt.

9.13.3 Act 2, scene 2

Enter the LADY HAPPY, *with her* LADIES*; as also* MADAM MEDIATOR.

LADY HAPPY. Ladies, give me leave to desire your confession, whether or no you repent your retirement.

LADIES. Most excellent lady, it were as probable a repentance could be in heaven amongst angels as amongst us.

LADY HAPPY. Now, Madam Mediator, let me ask you, do you condemn my act of retirement?

[31] *deboist* debauched (licentious). Adviser's language is that of the Spanish Inquisition (Catholic group that punished heretics on the Continent).

[32] *petition … redress* referring to Civil War petitions to Parliament for redress of various injustices (in one, maids and wives lament the war that steals away their men).

MEDIATOR. I approve of it with admiration and wonder, that one that is so young should be so wise.

LADY HAPPY. Now give me leave to inform you how I have ordered this our Convent of Pleasure. First, I have such things as are for our ease and conveniency; next, for pleasure and delight; as I have change of furniture for my house, according to the four seasons of the year, especially our chambers: as in the spring, our chambers are hung with silk-damask, and all other things suitable to it; and a great looking-glass in each chamber, that we may view ourselves and take pleasure in our own beauties, whilst they are fresh and young. Also, I have in each chamber a cupboard of such plate[33] as is useful, and whatsoever is to be used is there ready to be employed; also, I have all the floor strewed with sweet flowers. In the summer, I have all our chambers hung with taffeta, and all other things suitable to it, and a cupboard of purseline,[34] and of plate, and all the floor strewed everyday with green rushes or leaves, and cisterns placed near our beds-heads, wherein water may run out of small pipes made for that purpose. To invite repose in the autumn, all our chambers are hung with gilt leather, or franchipane;[35] also, beds and all other things suitable; and the rooms matted with very fine mats. In the winter, our chambers must be hung with tapestry, and our beds of velvet, lined with satin, and all things suitable to it, and all the floor spread over with Turkey carpets, and a cupboard of gilt plate; and all the wood for firing to be cypress and juniper; and all the lights to be perfumed wax. Also, the bedding and pillows are ordered according to each season: *viz.*, to be stuffed with feathers in the spring and autumn, and with down in the winter, but in the summer to be only quilts, either of silk or fine holland;[36] and our sheets, pillows, tablecloths, and towels, to be of pure fine holland, and every day clean. Also, the rooms we eat in, and the vessels we feed withal, I have according to each season; and the linen we use to our meat to be pure fine diaper and damask,[37] and to change it fresh every course of meat. As for our galleries, staircases, and passages, they shall be hung with various pictures; and, all along the wall of our gallery, as long as the summer lasts, do stand, upon pedestals, flowerpots, with various flowers; and in the winter orange trees; and

[33] *plate* special tableware and utensils, often made of precious metals.
[34] *purseline* porcelain.
[35] *franchipane* jasmine perfume (perhaps, here, fragrant jasmine branches?).
[36] *holland* prized linen.
[37] *diaper* linen fabric; *damask*: rich, embroidered silk.

my gardens to be kept curiously,[38] and flourish, in every season of all sorts of flowers, sweet herbs and fruits, and kept so as not to have a weed in it, and all the groves, wildernesses, bowers and arbours pruned, and kept free from dead boughs, branches or leaves; and all the ponds, rivulets, fountains, and springs, kept clear, pure and fresh. Also, we will have the choicest meats every season doth afford, and that everyday our meat be dressed[39] several ways, and our drink cooler or hotter according to the several seasons; and all our drinks fresh and pleasing. Change of garments are also provided, of the newest fashions for every season, and rich trimming; so as we may be accoutered properly, and according to our several pastimes; and our shifts[40] shall be of the finest and purest linen that can be bought or spun.

LADIES. None in this world can be happier.

LADY HAPPY. Now, ladies, let us go to our several pastimes, if you please.

Exeunt.

9.13.4 Act 2, scene 3

[...]

Enter MADAM MEDIATOR *to them.*

MEDIATOR. Ladies, do you hear the news?

LADY VIRTUE. What news?

MEDIATOR. Why, there is a great foreign princess arrived, hearing of the famous Convent of Pleasure, to be one of nature's devotees.

LADY AMOROUS. What manner of lady is she?

MEDIATOR. She is a princely brave woman, truly of a masculine presence.

LADY VIRTUE. But, Madam Mediator, do they live in such pleasure as you say? For they'll admit you, a widow, although not us, by reason we are wives.

MEDIATOR. In so much pleasure, as nature never knew before this convent was; and for my part, I had rather be one in the Convent of Pleasure than empress of the whole world; for every lady there enjoyeth as much pleasure as any absolute monarch can do, without the troubles and cares that wait on royalty. Besides, none can enjoy those pleasures they have, unless they live such a retired or retreated life, free from the world's vexations.

38 *curiously* carefully; artistically.

39 *dressed* prepared.

40 *shifts* undergarments.

[...]

Exeunt.

9.13.5 Act 2, scene 4

Enter MONSIEUR ADVISER, COURTLY, TAKE-PLEASURE, *and* FACIL.

COURTLY. Is there no hopes to get those ladies out of their convent?
ADVISER. No faith, unless we could set the convent on fire.
TAKE-PLEASURE. For Jupiter's sake, let us do it! Let's everyone carry a firebrand to fire it!
COURTLY. Yes, and smoke them out, as they do a swarm of bees.
FACIL. Let's go presently[41] about it.
ADVISER. Stay, there is a great princess there.
TAKE-PLEASURE. 'Tis true, but when that princess is gone, we will surely do it.
ADVISER. Yes, and be punished for our villainy.

[...]

TAKE-PLEASURE. Faith, let us resolve to put ourselves in women's apparel, and so by that means get into the convent.
ADVISER. We shall be discovered.
TAKE-PLEASURE. Who will discover us?
ADVISER. We shall discover ourselves.
TAKE-PLEASURE. We are not such fools as to betray ourselves.
ADVISER. We cannot avoid it, for, our very garb and behaviour, besides our voices, will discover us: for we are as untoward[42] to make curtsies in petticoats as women are to make legs[43] in breeches; and it will be as great a difficulty to raise our voices to a treble-sound as for women to press down their voices to a bass; besides, we shall never frame our eyes and mouths to such coy, dissembling looks, and pretty, simpering mopes[44] and smiles, as they do.
COURTLY. But we will go as strong, lusty country-wenches, that desire to serve them in inferior places and offices, as cook-maids, laundry-maids, dairy-maids, and the like.
FACIL. I do verily believe I could make an indifferent[45] cook-maid, but

[41] *presently* immediately.
[42] *untoward* incapable.
[43] *make legs* bow ceremonially.
[44] *mopes* sulky looks.
[45] *indifferent* satisfactory.

not a laundry nor a dairy-maid, for I cannot milk cows nor starch gorgets.[46] But I think I could make a pretty shift[47] to wash some of the ladies' night-linen.

TAKE-PLEASURE. But they employ women in all places in their gardens; and for brewing, baking and making all sorts of things; besides, some keep their swine, and twenty such like offices and employments there are which we should be very proper for.

FACIL. Oh yes, for keeping of swine belongs to men. Remember the prodigal son.[48]

ADVISER. Faith, for our prodigality we might be all swineherds.

COURTLY. Also we shall be proper for gardens, for we can dig, and set, and sow.

TAKE-PLEASURE. And we are proper for brewing.

ADVISER. We are more proper for drinking: for I can drink good beer or ale when 'tis brewed, but I could not brew such beer or ale as any man could drink.

FACIL. Come, come, we shall make a shift one way or other. Besides, we shall be very willing to learn, and be very diligent in our services, which will give good and great content; wherefore, let us go and put these designs into execution.

COURTLY. Content, content.

ADVISER. Nay, faith, let us not trouble ourselves for it, 'tis in vain.

Exeunt.

9.13.6 Act 3, scene 1

Enter the PRINCESS, *and the* LADY HAPPY, *with the rest of the ladies belonging to the convent.*

LADY HAPPY. Madam, your Highness has done me much honour to come from a splendid court to a retired convent.

PRINCESS. Sweet Lady Happy, there are many that have quit their crowns and power for a cloister of restraint; then well may I quit a court of troubles for a Convent of Pleasure; but the greatest pleasure I could receive were to have your friendship.

LADY HAPPY. I should be ungrateful should I not be not only your friend but humble servant.

[46] *gorget* kerchief for breast and neck.

[47] *make … shift* do a fairly good job.

[48] For the parable of the prodigal son, see Lk. 15.11–32.

PRINCESS. I desire you would be my mistress, and I your servant;[49] and upon this agreement of friendship I desire you will grant me one request.

LADY HAPPY. Anything that is in my power to grant.

PRINCESS. Why then, I observing in your several recreations, some of your ladies do accouter themselves in masculine habits[50] and act lovers' parts; I desire you will give me leave to be sometimes so accoutered and act the part of your loving servant.

LADY HAPPY. I shall never desire to have any other loving servant than yourself.

PRINCESS. Nor I any other loving mistress than yourself.

LADY HAPPY. More innocent lovers never can there be,
Than my most princely lover that's a she.

PRINCESS. Nor never convent did such pleasures give,
Where lovers with their mistresses may live.

Enter a LADY, *asking whether they will see the play.*

LADY. May it please your Highness, the play is ready to be acted.

The scene is opened, the PRINCESS *and* LADY HAPPY *sit down, and the play is acted within the scene; the* PRINCESS *and the* LADY HAPPY *being spectators.*

Enter one dressed like a man that speaks the prologue.

Noble spectators, you shall see tonight
A play, which though't be dull, yet's short to sight;
For since we cannot please your ears with wit,
We will not tire your limbs, long here to sit.

9.13.7 Act 3, scene 2

Enter two mean[51] WOMEN.

1 WOMAN. Oh, neighbour, well met. Where have you been?

2 WOMAN. I have been with my neighbour the cobbler's wife to comfort

49 *mistress* and *servant* conventional designations for female beloved and male lover.

50 *accouter* dress; *habits*: clothes (also, name of a nun's ritual garb: 'habit').

51 *mean* lower-class.

her for the loss of her husband, who is run away with Goody[52] Mettle, the tinker's wife.

1 WOMAN. I would to heaven my husband would run away with Goody Shred, the butcher's wife, for he lies all day drinking in an alehouse, like a drunken rogue as he is, and when he comes home, he beats me all black and blue, when I and my children are almost starved for want.

2 WOMAN. Truly, neighbour, so doth my husband; and spends not only what he gets, but what I earn with the sweat of my brows, the whilst my children cry for bread, and he drinks that away that should feed my small children, which are too young to work for themselves.

1 WOMAN. But I will go, and pull my husband out of the alehouse, or I'll break their lattice-windows down.

2 WOMAN. Come, I'll go and help, for my husband is there too. But we shall be both beaten by them.

1 WOMAN. I care not! For I will not suffer him to be drunk, and I and my children starve; I had better be dead.

Exeunt.

[...]

9.13.8 Act 3, scene 4

Enter two LADIES.

1 LADY. Why weep you, madam?

2 LADY. Have I not cause to weep when my husband hath played all his estate away at dice and cards, even to the clothes on his back?

1 LADY. I have as much cause to weep then as you, for though my husband hath not lost his estate at play, yet he hath spent it amongst his whores; and is not content to keep whores abroad, but in my house, under my roof, and they must rule as chief mistresses.

2 LADY. But my husband hath not only lost his own estate, but also my portion; and hath forced me with threats, to yield up my jointure,[53] so that I must beg for my living, for anything I know as yet.

1 LADY. If all married women were as unhappy as I, marriage were a curse.

2 LADY. No doubt of it.

Exeunt.

[52] *Goody* respectful title for lower-class women.

[53] *jointure* money settled by a husband on his wife when they marry, as security in case he died first.

9.13.9 Act 3, scene 5

Enter a Lady, *as almost distracted,*[54] *running about the stage, and her maid follows her.*

Lady. Oh! my child is dead, my child is dead, what shall I do, what shall I do?

Maid. You must have patience, madam.

Lady. Who can have patience to lose their only child? Who can? Oh I shall run mad, for I have no patience.

Runs off the stage. Exit Maid *after her.*

[...]

9.13.10 Act 3, scene 7

Enter a Lady *big with child, groaning as in labour, and a company of* Women *with her.*

Lady. Oh my back, my back will break, Oh! Oh! Oh!

1 Woman. Is the midwife sent for?

2 Woman. Yes, but she is with another lady.

Lady. Oh my back! Oh! Oh! Oh! Juno, give me some ease!

Exeunt.

9.13.11 Act 3, scene 8

Enter two ancient[55] Ladies.

1 Lady. I have brought my son into the world with great pains, bred him with tender care, much pains and great cost; and must he now be hanged for killing a man in a quarrel? When he should be a comfort and staff of my age, is he to be my age's affliction?

2 Lady. I confess it is a great affliction; but I have had as great; having had but two daughters, and them fair ones, though I say it, and might have matched them well: but one of them was got with child to my great disgrace; th'other run away with my butler,[56] not worth the droppings of his taps.

1 Lady. Who would desire children, since they come to such misfortunes?

Exeunt.

[54] *distracted* mad.

[55] *ancient* elderly.

[56] *butler* servant who dispensed the household's ale and wine.

9.13.12 Act 3, scene 9

Enter one WOMAN *meeting another.*

1 WOMAN. Is the midwife come? For my lady is in a strong labour!

2 WOMAN. No, she cannot come, for she hath been with a lady that hath been in strong labour these three days of a dead child, and 'tis thought she cannot be delivered.

Enter another WOMAN.

3 WOMAN. Come away! The midwife is come!

1 WOMAN. Is the lady delivered she was withal?

3 WOMAN. Yes, of life; for she could not be delivered, and so she died.

2 WOMAN. Pray, tell not our lady so, for the very fright of not being able to bring forth a child will kill her.

Exeunt.

9.13.13 Act 3, scene 10

Enter a GENTLEMAN *who meets a fair young* LADY.

GENTLEMAN. Madam, my lord desires you to command whatsoever you please, and it shall be obeyed.

LADY. I dare not command, but I humbly entreat, I may live quiet and free from his amours.

GENTLEMAN. He says he cannot live, and not love you.

LADY. But he may live, and not lie with me.

GENTLEMAN. He cannot be happy, unless he enjoy[57] you.

LADY. And I must be unhappy, if he should.

GENTLEMAN. He commanded me to tell you that he will part from his lady for your sake.

LADY. Heaven forbid, I should part man and wife.

GENTLEMAN. Lady, he will be divorced for your sake.

LADY. Heaven forbid I should be the cause of a divorce between a noble pair.

GENTLEMAN. You had best consent, for otherwise he will have you against your will.

LADY. I will send his lordship an answer tomorrow; pray him to give me so much time.

[57] *enjoy* have sex with.

GENTLEMAN. I shall, lady. [*Exit* GENTLEMAN.

LADY *sola*[58]

LADY. I must prevent my own ruin, and the sweet virtuous lady's,[59] by going into a nunnery; wherefore, I'll put myself into one tonight:
There will I live, and serve the gods on high,
And leave this wicked world and vanity.

Exeunt.

One enters and speaks the epilogue.

Marriage is a curse we find,
Especially to women kind:[60]
From the cobbler's wife we see,
To ladies, they unhappy be.

LADY HAPPY [*to the* PRINCESS]. Pray, servant, how do you like this play?

PRINCESS. My sweet mistress, I cannot in conscience approve of it; for though some few be unhappy in marriage, yet there are many more that are so happy as they would not change their condition.

LADY HAPPY. O servant, I fear you will become an apostate.[61]

PRINCESS. Not to you, sweet mistress.

Exeunt.

[...]

9.13.14 Act 4, scene 1

Enter LADY HAPPY *dressed as a shepherdess. She walks very melancholy, then speaks as to herself.*

My name is Happy, and so was my condition before I saw this princess; but now I am like to be the most unhappy maid alive. But why may not I love a woman with the same affection I could a man?
No, no, Nature is Nature, and still will be
The same she was from all eternity.

[58] Latin, 'alone'.

[59] *lady* the importunate lord's present wife.

[60] *women kind* either to 'womankind' or to 'kind women'.

[61] *apostate* someone who forsakes his or her religion.

Enter the PRINCESS *in masculine shepherd's clothes.*

PRINCESS. My dearest mistress, do you shun my company? Is your servant become an offence to your sight?

LADY HAPPY. No, servant! Your presence is more acceptable to me than the presence of our Goddess Nature, for which she, I fear, will punish me, for loving you more than I ought to love you.

PRINCESS. Can lovers love too much?

LADY HAPPY. Yes, if they love not well.

PRINCESS. Can any love be more virtuous, innocent, and harmless than ours?

LADY HAPPY. I hope not.

PRINCESS. Then let us please ourselves, as harmless lovers use[62] to do.

LADY HAPPY. How can harmless lovers please themselves?

PRINCESS. Why very well, as, to discourse, embrace and kiss, so mingle souls together.

LADY HAPPY. But innocent lovers do not use to kiss.

PRINCESS. Not any act more frequent amongst us women-kind; nay, it were a sin in friendship should not we kiss. Then let us not prove ourselves reprobates.

They embrace and kiss, and hold each other in their arms.

PRINCESS. These my embraces though of female kind,
May be as fervent as a masculine mind.

[After performing together in a pastoral tableau, the princess and Lady Happy vow to love each other.]

[…]

PRINCESS. May I live in your favour, and be possessed with your love and person, is the height of my ambitions.

LADY HAPPY. I can neither deny you my love nor person.

PRINCESS. In amorous pastoral verse we did not woo
As other pastoral lovers use to do.

LADY HAPPY. Which doth express, we shall more constant be,
And in a married life better agree.

PRINCESS. We shall agree, for we true love inherit,
Join as one body and soul, or heav'nly spirit.

62 *use* are accustomed to.

[...]

A wassail is carried about and syllabubs.[63]

Another SHEPHERD *speaks, or sings this that follows.*

Written by my Lord Duke.[64]

The jolly wassail now do bring,
With apples drowned in stronger ale,
And fresher syllabubs, and sing;
Then each to tell their lovesick tale,
So home by couples, and thus draw
Ourselves by holy Hymen's law.[65]

The scene vanishes.

Enter the PRINCESS *sola, and walks a turn or two in a musing posture, then views herself, and speaks.*

PRINCESS. What, have I on a petticoat? O Mars, thou god of war, pardon my sloth! But yet remember thou art a lover, and so am I; but you will say, my kingdom wants me, not only to rule, and govern it, but to defend it: But what is a kingdom in comparison of a beautiful mistress? Base thoughts fly off, for I will not go; did not only a kingdom, but the world want me.

Exeunt.

Enter the LADY HAPPY *sola, and melancholy, and after a short musing speaks.*

LADY HAPPY. O Nature, O you gods above,
Suffer me not to fall in love!
Oh, strike me dead here in this place
Rather than fall into disgrace!

[...]

Enter the PRINCESS.

PRINCESS. Come, my sweet mistress, shall we go to our sports and recreations?

63 *wassail* spiced ale; *syllabub*: sweetened alcoholic drink (with milk or cream).
64 *Lord Duke* Cavendish's husband, William, Duke of Newcastle.
65 *Hymen's law* law governing marriage. See Hymen (Glossary).

MEDIATOR. Beshrew me,[66] your Highness hath sported too much I fear.
PRINCESS. Why, Madam Mediator, say you so?
MEDIATOR. Because the Lady Happy looks not well: she is become pale and lean.
PRINCESS. Madam Mediator, your eyes are become dim with time; for my sweet mistress appears with greater splendour than the god of light.[67]
MEDIATOR. For all you are a great princess, give me leave to tell you,
I am not so old, nor yet so blind
But that I see you are too kind.
PRINCESS. Well, Madam Mediator, when we return from our recreations, I will ask your pardon, for saying, your eyes are dim, conditionally you will ask pardon for saying, my mistress looks not well.

Exeunt.

[...]

9.13.15 Act 5, scene 1

Enter the PRINCESS *and the* LADY HAPPY. *The* PRINCESS *is in a man's apparel as going to dance; they whisper sometime; then the* LADY HAPPY *takes a ribbon from her arm, and gives it to the* PRINCESS, *who gives her another in stead*[68] *of that, and kisses her hand. They go in and come presently out again with all the company to dance. The music plays. And after they have danced a little while, in comes* MADAM MEDIATOR *wringing her hands, and spreading her arms; and full of passion cries out.*

O ladies, ladies! You're all betrayed, undone, undone, for there is a man disguised in the convent. Search and you'll find it.

They all skip from each other, as afraid of each other; only the PRINCESS *and the* LADY HAPPY *stand still together.*

PRINCESS. You may make the search, Madam Mediator; but you will quit[69] me, I am sure.
MEDIATOR. By my faith but I will not, for you are most to be suspected.
PRINCESS. But you say, the man is disguised like a woman, and I am accoutred like a man.
MEDIATOR. Fiddle, faddle, that is nothing to the purpose.

66 *beshrew me* exclamation, 'The devil take me!'
67 *god of light* Apollo (Glossary).
68 *in stead* in place.
69 *quit* absolve.

Enter an AMBASSADOR *to the* PRINCE*; the* AMBASSADOR *kneels, the* PRINCE *bids him rise.*

PRINCE. What came you here for?

AMBASSADOR. May it please your Highness, the lords of your Council sent me to inform your Highness that your subjects are so discontented at your absence, that if your Highness do not return into your kingdom soon, they'll enter this kingdom, by reason they hear you are here; and some report as if your Highness were restrained as prisoner.

PRINCE. So I am, but not by the state, but by this fair lady, who must be your sovereigness.

The AMBASSADOR *kneels and kisses her hand.*

PRINCE. But since I am discovered, go from me to the councillors of this state, and inform them of my being here, as also the reason, and that I ask their leave I may marry this lady; otherwise, tell them I will have her by force of arms.

Exit AMBASSADOR.

[...]

9.13.16 Act 5, scene 3

Enter the PRINCE *as bridegroom, and the* LADY HAPPY *as bride, hand in hand under a canopy borne over their heads by men; the magistrates march before, then the hoboys,*[70] *and then the bridal-guests, as coming from the church, where they were married.*

All the company bids them joy; they thank them.

MEDIATOR. Although your Highness will not stay to feast with your guests, pray dance before you go.

PRINCE. We will both dance and feast before we go; come, madam, let us dance to please Madam Mediator.

The PRINCE *and* PRINCESS *dance.*

PRINCE. Now, noble friends, dance you; and the princess and I will rest ourselves.

[70] *hoboys* hautboy (early oboe) players.

After they have danced, the LADY HAPPY, *as now princess, speaks to the* LADY VIRTUE.

LADY HAPPY [*speaks to* LADY VIRTUE]. Lady Virtue, I perceive you keep Mimic[71] still.
LADY HAPPY [*to the* PRINCE]. Sir, this is the Mimic I told you of.
LADY HAPPY [*to* MIMIC]. Mimic, will you leave your lady and go with me?
MIMIC. I am a married man, and have married my lady's maid, Nan, and she will keep me at home do what I can; but you've now a mimic of your own, for the prince has imitated a woman.
LADY HAPPY. What, you rogue, do you call me a fool?[72]
MIMIC. Not I, please your Highness, unless all women be fools.
PRINCE. Is your wife a fool?
MIMIC. Man and wife, 'tis said, makes but one fool.[73]

[...]

Katherine Philips (1632–64), poet

After receiving an excellent education in her father's puritan household, Philips attended a boarding-school (c. 1640), where she probably met some of the women who figure prominently in her poetry; Mary Aubrey ('Rosania') was a fellow-student. Married in 1648 to James Philips, a fifty-four-year-old parliamentary colonel, Katherine retained her early royalist principles, and, although these initially made trouble for James, her connections aided him at the Restoration. During the early years of her marriage, she became the central poet in her circle, adopting the name 'Orinda,' under which guise she appears in many of her writings. Her verses for her husband ('Antenor') and her closest female friend Anne (née Lewis) Owen ('Lucasia') are among her most famous. Philips's marriage was marred by the death of her infant son Hector, but her daughter Katherine went on to marry herself and have sixteen children. Philips's poetry and her translation of Corneille's *Pompey* were highly praised, both before and in the wake of her untimely death by smallpox.

Editions

Thomas, Patrick, ed., *Collected Works of Katherine Philips*, Volume 1: The Poems. Stump Cross, Essex: Stump Cross Books, 1990.

71 *Mimic* a professional jester.
72 Lady Happy's last line.
73 In the wedding service, man and wife are said to comprise 'one body'.

9.14

From *Poems* (1667)[1]

9.14.1 Friendship's Mysteries: To my dearest Lucasia

Come, my Lucasia, since we see
  That miracles men's faith do move
By wonder and by prodigy,
  To the dull, angry world let's prove
  There's a religion in our love.[2]

For though we were designed t'agree,
  That fate no liberty destroys,
But our election is as free[3]
  As angels, who with greedy choice
  Are yet determined to their joys.[4]

Our hearts are doubled by their loss,
  Here mixture is addition grown;
We both diffuse, and both engross,[5]
  And we, whose minds are so much one,
  Never, yet ever, are alone.[6]

We court our own captivity
  Than thrones more great and innocent:[7]
'Twere banishment to be set free,
  Since we wear fetters whose intent
  Not bondage is, but ornament.

[1] Based on the 1667 versions, the following selections have been emended in places from *Works* (1990), ed. P. Thomas, above.

[2] Influenced by phrases from Donne's 'The Canonization' and 'The Good Morrow', highly erotic heterosexual love poems.

[3] *election* choice, but also, Calvinist 'election', where some are predestined for salvation, and others for damnation (raising obvious issues concerning free will).

[4] *As…joys* i.e., angels choose their bliss, even though they are also predestined to it.

[5] *engross* collect up (so as to gain or keep exclusive possession of), set up against its opposite 'diffuse'. Cf. Donne's contrast between 'breach' and 'expansion' in 'Valediction: Forbidding Mourning' (ll. 21–4).

[6] *And … alone* Cf. 'The Canonization' (ll. 24–5).

[7] *thrones* third of the nine orders of angels.

Divided joys are tedious found,
   And griefs united easier grow:
We are ourselves but by rebound,[8]
   And all our titles shuffled so,
   Both princes, and both subjects too.[9]

Our hearts are mutual victims laid,
   While they (such power in friendship lies)
Are altars, priests, and off'rings made,
   And each heart which thus kindly dies,[10]
   Grows deathless by the sacrifice.

9.14.2 Friendship in Emblem,[11] or, The Seal, to My Dearest Lucasia

The hearts thus intermixèd speak
A love that no bold shock can break;
For joined and growing, both in one,
Neither can be disturbed alone.

That means a mutual knowledge too;
For what is't either heart can do,
Which by its panting sentinel
It does not to the other tell?

That friendship hearts so much refines,
It nothing but itself designs:
The hearts are free from lower ends,
For each point to the other tends.

They flame, 'tis true, and several ways,
But still those flames do so much raise
That while to either they incline
They yet are noble and divine.

8 *rebound* returning.

9 Cf. Donne's 'The Sun Rising' (ll. 21–2).

10 *kindly* naturally, but also 'generously'.

11 *emblem* a symbolic picture with a motto (short explanatory phrase) and/ or explanatory verses. Wither's popular *Collection of Emblems* (1635) contains one of intertwined hearts on fire.

From smoke or hurt those flames are free,
From grossness or mortality:
The hearts (like Moses' bush presumed)[12]
Warmed and enlightened, not consumed.

The compasses that stand above[13]
Express this great immortal love;
For friends, like them, can prove this true,
They are, and yet they are not, two.

And in their posture is expressed
Friendship's exalted interest:
Each follows where the other leans,
And what each does, the other means.[14]

And as when one foot does stand fast,
And t'other circles seeks to cast,
The steady part does regulate
And make the wanderer's motion straight:

So friends are only two in this,
T'reclaim each other when they miss,
For whose'er will grossly fall,
Can never be a friend at all.[15]

And as that useful instrument
For even lines was ever meant,
So friendship from good angels springs,
To teach the world heroic things.

As these are found out in design
To rule and measure every line;
So friendship governs actions best,
Prescribing law to all the rest.[16]

[12] God appears to Moses in the form of a burning *bush*, which gives light and heat but is never consumed (Ex. 3.2–6).

[13] On the controversy concerning the compass as an image of clitoral as well as penile erection, see General Introduction, **n4**.

[14] *the* emended from 'this'.

[15] Stanzas 1–9 summarize Cicero's idealized *amicitia* (see 'Laelius', *Online Companion*).

[16] *law to* emended from 'unto'.

And as in nature nothing's set
So just as lines and numbers met,[17]
So compasses for these being made
Do friendship's harmony persuade.

And like to them, so friends may own
Extension, not division:
Their points, like bodies, separate,
But head, like souls, knows no such fate.

And as each part so well is knit
That their embraces ever fit,
So friends are such by destiny,
And no third can the place supply.

There needs no motto to the seal:[18]
But that we may the mind reveal
To the dull eye, it was thought fit
That 'friendship' only should be writ.

But as there are degrees of bliss,
So there's no friendship meant by this,
But such as will transmit to fame
Lucasia's and Orinda's name.

9.14.3 Rosania shadowed whilst Mrs Mary Aubrey [19 Sept. 1651]

If any could my dear Rosania hate,
They only should her character relate.
Truth shines so bright there, that an enemy
Would be a better orator than I.
Love stifles language, and I must confess,
I had said more, if I had loved less.
Yet the most critical who that face see,
Will ne'er suspect me of partiality.[19]
Others by time and by degrees persuade,

[17] *and* emended from 'in'.

[18] *seal* stamp affixed as a sign of agreement to a legal document; sign stamped into hot wax to seal a letter; *motto*: See **n11**.

[19] *me of* emended from 'a'.

But her first look doth every heart invade.
She hath a face so eminently bright,
Would make a lover of an anchorite.[20]
A face where conquest mixed with modesty
Are both completed in divinity.
Not her least glance but sets all hearts on fire,
And checks them if they should too much aspire.[21]
Such is the magic of her looks, the same
Beam doth both kindle and refine our flame.
If she doth smile, no painter e'er would take
Another rule, when he would mercy make.
And to her splendour heaven hath allowed,[22]
That not a posture can her beauty cloud:[23]
For if she frown, none but would fancy then
Justice descended here to punish men.
Her common looks I know not how to call
Any one grace, they are composed of all.
And if we mortals could the doctrine reach,
Her eyes have language, and her looks do teach.
Such is her whole frame, heaven does afford
Her not to be desired, but still adored.[24]
But as in palaces the outmost, worst[25]
Rooms entertain our wonder at the first;
But once within the presence chamber door,
We do despise whate'er we saw before:
So when you with her mind acquaintance get,
You'll hardly think upon the cabinet.
Her soul! that ray shot from the deity,
Doth still preserve its native purity;
Which earth can neither threaten, nor allure,
Nor by false joys defile it, or obscure.
Such innocence within her breast doth dwell,[26]
Angels themselves do only parallel.[27]
And should her whole sex to dissembling fall,

20 *anchorite* hermit vowed to enclosure and chastity.

21 *them if they* emended from 'it if it'.

22 *And … allowed* emended from 'And Heav'n to her such splendour hath allowed'.

23 *not a* emended from 'no one'.

24 *Such … adored* Missing from *Poems* (1667); supplied from *Works*, p. 118.

25 *But* emended from 'And'.

26 *Such … dwell* emended from 'The innocence which in her heart doth dwell'.

27 *do* emended from 'can'.

Here's one integrity redeems them all:
Transparent, clear, and will no words admit,
And all comparisons but slubber it.[28]
More gentle soft than is an evening show'r:[29]
And in that sweetness there is couched a pow'r,
Which scorning pride, doth think it very hard
If modesty should need so mean a guard.[30]
Her honour is protected by her eyes,
As the old flaming sword kept paradise.[31]
Such constancy, such[32] temper, truth and law,
Guides all her actions, that the world may draw
From her one soul the noblest president[33]
Of the most safe, wise, virtuous government.
She courts retirement, is herself alone,
Above a theatre, and beyond a throne.
So rich a soul, none can say properly
She hath, but is each noble quality.[34]
And as the highest element is clear
From all the tempests which disturb the air:
So she above the world and its rude noise,
Within a storm a quiet calm enjoys.[35]
She scorns the sullen trifles of the time,
But things transcendent do her thoughts sublime;[36]
Unlike those gallants which take far less care
To have their souls, than make their bodies fair,
Who (sick with too much leisure) time do pass
With these two books, pride, and a looking glass,
Plot to surprise men's hearts, their pow'r to try,
And call that love, which is dull vanity.[37]

[28] *And should her whole sex … but slubber it* Missing from *Poems* (1667); supplied from *Works*, pp. 118–19; *slubber*: disfigure.

[29] *gentle* emended from 'gently'.

[30] *If* emended from 'that'.

[31] God set a *flaming sword* at the entrance to Eden to prevent humanity from re-entering it after the Fall (Gen. 3.24).

[32] *such* emended from 'of'.

[33] *president* precedent.

[34] *She courts … noble quality* Missing from *Poems* (1667); supplied from *Works*, p. 119.

[35] *Within a storm* emended from 'Above our storms'.

[36] *She scorns … thoughts sublime* emended from 'Transcendent things her noble thoughts sublime, / Above the faults and trifles of the time'.

[37] *dull* emended from 'mere'.

But she, although the greatest murderer,
(For every glance commits a massacre)
Yet glories not that slaves her pow'r confess,
But wishes that her monarchy were less.
And if she love, it is not thrown away,
As many do, only to spend the day;
But hers is serious, and enough alone
To make all love become religion.
But to her friendships she so faithful is,[38]
That 'tis her only blot and prejudice:
For envy's self could never error see
Within that soul, 'bating her love to me.[39]
Now, as I must confess, the name of friend
To her that all the world doth comprehend,
Is a most wild ambition; so for me
To draw her picture is flat lunacy.
Oh! I must think the rest; for who can write
Or into words confine what's infinite?

9.14.4 To My Excellent Lucasia, On Our Friendship [17 July 1651]

I did not live until this time
  Crowned my felicity,
When I could say without a crime,
  I am not thine, but thee.

This carcass breathed, and walked, and slept,
  So that the world believed
There was a soul the motions kept,
  But they were all deceived.

For as a watch by art is wound
  To motion, such was mine:
But never had Orinda found
  A soul till she found thine;

Which now inspires, cures and supplies,
  And guides my darkened breast,

38 *friendships* emended from 'friendship'.
39 *'bating* abating.

For thou art all that I can prize,
  My joy, my life, my rest.

Nor bridegrooms nor crowned conqu'rour's mirth
  To mine compared can be:
They have but pieces of this earth,
  I've all the world in thee.

Then let our flame still light and shine
  (And no bold fear control),[40]
As innocent as our design,
  Immortal as our soul.

9.14.5 Injuria Amici[41]

Lovely apostate! what was my offence?[42]
Or am I punished for obedience?
Must thy strange rigour find as strange a time?
The act and season are an equal crime.
Of what thy most ingenious scorns could do,
Must I be subject and spectator too?
Or were the sufferings and sins too few
To be sustained by me, performed by you?
Unless (with Nero) your uncurbed desire
Be to survey the Rome you set on fire.[43]
While wounded for and by your power, I
At once your martyr and your prospect die.
This is my doom, and such a riddling fate
As all impossibles doth complicate:
For obligation here is injury,
Constancy crime, friendship a heresy;
And you appear so much on ruin bent,
Your own destruction gives you now content:
For our twin-spirits did so long agree,
You must undo yourself to ruin me.

[40] *bold* emended from 'false'.

[41] Latin, 'The wounding of a friend'. Probably addressed to Rosania (see Introduction to **9.14**) after her 'private marriage' in 1652, an action which Philips clearly found personally wounding (Thomas, p. 350).

[42] *apostate* one who abandons his or her religious faith.

[43] *Unless … fire* Emperor Nero (37–68 CE) watched while his order that whole sections of Rome be burned was carried out.

And, like some frantic goddess, you're inclined
To raze the temple where you were enshrined;[44]
And (what's the miracle of cruelty!)
Kill that which gave you immortality.
Whiles glorious friendship, whence your honour springs,
Lies gasping in the crowd of common things;
And I'm so odious, that for being kind
Doubled and studied murders are designed.
Thy sin's all paradox! for shouldst thou be
Thyself again, 'twould be severe to me;[45]
For thy repentance, coming now so late,
Would only change, and not relieve the fate.
So dangerous is the consequence of ill,
Thy least of crimes is to be cruel still;
For of thy smiles I should yet more complain,
If I should live to be betrayed again.
Live then (fair tyrant) in security,
From both my kindness and revenge be free;
While I, who to the swains had sung your fame,[46]
And taught each echo to repeat your name,[47]
Will now my private sorrows entertain,
To rocks and rivers (not to you) complain.[48]
And though before our union cherished me,
'Tis now my pleasure that we disagree;
For from my passion your last rigours grew,
And you kill me, because I worshipped you.
But my worst vows shall be your happiness,
And ne'er to be disturbed by my distress.[49]
And though it would my sacred flames pollute,
To make my heart a scorned prostitute;
Yet I'll adore the author of my death,
And kiss the hand that robs me of my breath.

44 *were* emended from 'are'.

45 *'twould* emended from 'th' wouldst'.

46 *swains* poet-shepherds in pastoral verse; *your*: emended from 'thy'.

47 *your* emended from 'thy'.

48 *you* emended from 'thee'.

49 *ne'er* never; emended from 'not'.

9.14.6 [6 April 1651. L'amitié:] To Mrs Mary Aubrey

Soul of my soul! my joy, my crown, my friend!
A name which all the rest doth comprehend;
How happy are we now, whose souls are grown,
By an incomparable mixture, One:
Whose well-acquainted minds are now as near
As love, or vows, or secrets can endear.[50]
I have no thought but what's to thee revealed,
Nor thou desire that is from me concealed.
Thy heart locks up my secrets richly set,
And my breast is thy private cabinet.
Thou shed'st no tear but what my moisture lent,
And if I sigh, it is thy breath is spent.
United thus, what horror can appear
Worthy our sorrow, anger, or our fear?
Let the dull world alone to talk and fight,
And with their vast ambitions nature fright;
Let them despise so innocent a flame,
While envy, pride and faction play their game:
But we by love sublimed so high shall rise,
To pity kings, and conquerors despise,
Since we that sacred union have engrost,[51]
Which they and all the factious world have lost.[52]

9.14.7 Orinda to Lucasia parting, October 1661. At London

Adieu, dear object of my love's excess,
And with thee all my hopes of happiness,
With the same fervent and unchangèd heart
Which did its whole self once to thee impart,
(And which, though fortune has so sorely bruised,
Would suffer more, to be from this excused)
I to resign thy dear converse submit,[53]
Since I can neither keep, nor merit it.
Thou hast too long to me confinèd been,
Who ruin am without, passion within.

[50] *secrets* emended from 'friendship'.
[51] *engrost* engrossed.
[52] *factious* emended from 'sullen'.
[53] *converse* conversation; perhaps also 'spiritual or mental communion'.

My mind is sunk below thy tenderness,
And my condition does deserve it less;
I'm so entangled and so lost a thing
By all the shocks my daily sorrows bring,
That would'st thou for thy old Orinda call,
Thou hardly could'st unravel her at all.
And should I thy clear fortunes interline
With the incessant miseries of mine?
No, no, I never loved at such a rate,
To tie thee to the rigours of my fate.
As from my obligations thou art free,
Sure thou shalt be so from my injury;
Though every other worthiness I miss,
Yet I'll at least be generous in this.
I'd rather perish without sigh or groan
Than thou shouldst be condemned to give me one;
Nay, in my soul I rather could allow
Friendship should be a sufferer than thou;
Go then, since my sad heart has set thee free,
Let all the loads and chains remain on me.
Though I be left the prey of sea and wind,
Thou, being happy, wilt in that be kind;
Nor shall I my undoing much deplore,[54]
Since thou art safe, whom I must value more.
Oh! may'st thou ever be so, and as free
From all ills else, as from my company;
And may the torments thou hast had from it,
Be all that heaven will to thy life permit;
And that they may thy virtue service do,
Mayest thou be able to forgive them too.
But though I must this sharp submission learn,
I cannot yet unwish thy dear concern.
Not one new comfort I expect to see,
I quit my joy, hope, life, and all but thee;
Nor seek I thence ought that may discompose
That mind where so serene a goodness grows.
I ask no inconvenient kindness now,
To move thy passion, or to cloud thy brow;
And thou wilt satisfy my boldest plea
By some few soft remembrances of me,

[54] *undoing* ruin.

Which may present thee with this candid thought,
I meant not all the troubles that I brought.
Own not what passion rules, and fate does crush,
But wish thou could'st have don't without a blush;[55]
And that I had been, ere it was too late,
Either more worthy, or more fortunate.
Ah, who can love the thing they cannot prize?
But thou may'st pity though thou dost despise.
Yet I should think that pity bought too dear,
If it should cost those precious eyes a tear.
  Oh, may no minute's trouble thee possess,
But to endear the next hour's happiness;
And may'st thou when thou art from me removed,
Be better pleased, but never worse beloved.
Oh, pardon me for pouring out my woes
In rhyme, now that I dare not do't in prose:
For I must lose whatever is called dear,
And thy assistance all that loss to bear,
And have more cause than ere I had before,
To fear that I shall never see thee more.

Edward Howard? (1624–1712), writer

Younger son of Thomas Howard, First Earl of Berkshire, Edward wrote a number of works, including stage tragedies, comedies, and heroic and lyric verse, none of which earned him popularity or respect, and almost all of which were savaged by the critics. 'Fricatrices: Or, A She upon a She' appears in *Poems and Essays, With a Paraphrase on Cicero's Laelius, or, Of Friendship* (1674). Although Wing's *Short Title Catalogue* attributes the volume to Howard, the writer's *DNB* entry does not mention it.

9.15

Fricatrices:[1] or, A She upon a She (1674)

Two females meeting, found a sportful way
Without man's help a tickling game to play.[2]

[55] *don't* 'done it'.

[1] *fricatrices* See **2.2.1 n10**.
[2] *tickling* sexual.

They cozened Venus, yet consented so,[3]
That something like it they resolved to do.
What Nature to their aid did next present,
We must suppose was short of their intent.
The fairest then lay down; the other strove
Manhood to act with female power and love.
Their nimble heat dissolved the active dew,[4]
Which from their pearls within its moisture drew.[5]
But soon their pleasures were deceived, to find
The one thing wanted to which both had mind:
Like vessels that no rigging want or gale,
Ply here and there for want of a top-sail.[6]
One said she was the woman; t'other swore
She ought to be the man, and she the whore.
Who upper lay, the under now would be;
But which should be the woman, can't agree:
At last, at their mistake they yield to smile,
And grant love's pleasures nothing can beguile.[7]
A man they wanted, and a man would have,
Since he the dildo has which Nature gave.

Jean Barrin (c. 1640–1718), vicar-general of the diocese of Nantes

Barrin's *Venus dans le Cloître, ou, La Religieuse en Chemise* (1683) has its origins in the classical whore's dialogue (e.g., Lucian's *Dialogues of the Courtesans*: see **7.31.1**) and its early modern descendants (e.g., Aretino's *Ragionamenti* (*Dialogues*), 1534; 1536). Although primarily concerned with heterosexual intercourse and transgressive heterosexual pleasures, Lucian's and Aretino's works also contain scenes of female same-sex sexual acts. Barrin's *Venus* and Aretino's *Dialogues* also originate in the same long tradition of anti-clerical satire.

Venus in the Cloister received its first English translation in 1683, very soon after its publication in French. Its second appeared in 1724 (second edn, 1725), produced by the prolific writer and translator Robert Samber

[3] *cozened* deceived.

[4] *dew* sexual emissions or lubrication.

[5] *pearls* unclear; seems to refer to the inner source of sexual lubrication.

[6] Although they have part of what they need to 'move forward' (like a ship with rigging and wind), they lack the most crucial element (the top or uppermost sail).

[7] *beguile* cheat.

(1682–c. 1745), and published by the notorious Edmund Curll (d. 1747), who also brought out such titles as *A Treatise of Flogging in Venereal Affairs* (1718) (containing Jacob's *Tractatus*: see **2.1**), *Eunuchism Displayed* (1718), and *The Pleasures of Coition* (1721). The publication of Samber's version partly led to Curll being convicted and fined in 1728 for corrupting public morals. In contrast, the earlier 1683 translation does not seem to have been censored or suppressed, and indeed Curll tried to use this fact in his own defence; however, the 1683 translation (from which the following extracts are taken) is not really any less explicit than Samber's.

Editions

Cope, Kevin L., ed., 'Venus in the Cloister' (1725), trans. R. Samber, *Eighteenth-Century British Erotica I*, 2.157–358.

9.16

From *Venus in the Cloister: Or, The Nun in Her Smock* (1683)

9.16.1 First Dialogue

Sister Agnes.[1] *Sister Angelica.*

[Sister Angelica enters Sister Agnes's room and finds her masturbating, leading to a frank conversation about friendship, love, and sex.]

ANGELICA. Ah, my dear […] I am wholly thine; and though Nature had produced me from the same blood, it could not have given me sentiments more tender than these I feel.[2] Allow me to embrace thee that our hearts may speak to one another in the midst[3] of our kisses.

AGNES. Ah, God! How thou graspest me in thy arms! Thou little thinkest I am naked in my smock![4] Ah! Thou hast set me all on a fire.

ANGELICA. Ah! How finely doth that vermilion, wherewith thou art at present animated, augment the lustre of thy beauty! Ah! How

[1] *Agnes* from the Latin, 'lamb', with a blasphemous glance at Christ's epithet *Agnus Dei* or 'the Lamb of God which taketh away the sin of the world' (Jn. 1.29).

[2] Samber: 'it could not have given me more tender sentiments than those I now perceive with such excess of pleasure'.

[3] Samber: 'midst' becomes 'tumult'.

[4] *smock* undergarment.

amiable does that brightness render thee which now sparkles in thy eyes![5] No, no, my pretty rogue, I will impart to thee my most secret acquisitions, and give thee a perfect idea of the conduct of a prudent nun. I do not speak of that austerity and scrupulous wisdom which is only nourished by fastings, and only covered with haircloths. There is another prudence, which all understanding persons make profession of following, and which has no small affinity to thy amorous nature.

AGNES. I of an amorous nature!? My physiognomy must certainly be very deceitful, or else you are not perfectly well acquainted with the rules of that science![6] There is nothing which touches me less than this passion, and for these three years that I have been a nun it has not given me the least disturbance.

ANGELICA. That I very much doubt, and am of the opinion, if thou wouldst speak with more sincerity[7] thou wouldst own that I have said nothing but what is true. How a maid of sixteen, of so quick a wit and so handsome a body as thine, should be cold and insensible? That I cannot persuade myself. All thy most careless actions have assured me of the contrary, and *That I know not what*[8] which I perceived through the keyhole of the door before I came into the room, makes me know that thou art a dissembler.

AGNES. Ah, Lord! Ah, Lord! I am undone!

ANGELICA. Go, thou silly creature![9] What shouldst thou apprehend[10] from me? Prithee, tell me: hast thou reason to be afraid of a friend? I told thee this with no other design than to make thee my confidante in several such-like cases of my own. Truly, a fine business it is,[11] but what the most scrupulous put in practice, and this is called in cloistral terms, 'The Amusement of the Young, and the Passion[12] of the Old'.

AGNES. But pray, what did you see then?

5 Samber inserts: 'How lovely! Must a young creature so accomplished be thus reserved?'

6 *the rules of that science* i.e., physiognomy (judging inner character by the face or body).

7 Samber's note on this passage reads: 'Recommending *sincerity*, we see, is much older than some of our modern malevolent would have it.'

8 Samber: 'Je ne sais quoi' (French, 'something that cannot be expressed').

9 *Go … creature* Samber: 'Indeed thou hast no reason to say so'.

10 *apprehend* fear.

11 *Truly … is!* Samber: 'Really these are pretty bagatelles [i.e., trifling sexual practices].'

12 *Passion* Samber: 'Pastime'.

ANGELICA. Thou weariest me with thy fooling! Dost thou not know that love banishes all fear, and that if we both mean to live in so perfect a correspondence,[13] as I desire we may, thou must hide nothing from me, and I must keep nothing secret from thee. Buss[14] me, my little heart! Considering thy perverseness,[15] a discipline[16] would be of good use to punish thee for the small return thou makest to the kindness one shows thee.[17] Good God, how soft and plump thou art! Ah! Thou art of a delicate shape! Let me –

AGNES. Ah! For heaven's sake, let me alone! I cannot recollect myself from this surprise! But in good earnest, what did you see?

ANGELICA. Dost thou not know, thou little fool, thou, what I might have seen? I saw thee in such a posture and action as, if thou pleas'st, I will serve thee in myself, wherein my hand shall at present[18] do thee the office which thy own awhile ago did so charitably render to another part of thy body. A very great crime, indeed, that I have discovered![19] It is but what my Lady Abbess[20] practices, as she herself says, in the most innocent diversions; it is but what the prioress[21] does not reject, but what the mistress of the novices[22] called 'The Ecstatic Intromission'.[23] Thou couldst not have believed that such holy souls could have been capable of employing themselves in such profane exercises? [...] After which[24] thou shalt be my confessor,[25] I will be thy penitent, and I protest thou I will as freely unbottom to thee my heart as if thou thyself feltest the purest motions of it.

AGNES. After so many words, I do not think I ought to doubt of your sincerity, wherefore I will not only tell you what you desire to know of me, but I shall even take a sensible pleasure in communicating to you my most secret thoughts and actions. It will be a general

13 *correspondence* agreement; harmony.

14 *Buss* Kiss.

15 *perverseness* i.e., her persistence in refusing to acknowledge her masturbation and sexual desires.

16 *discipline* whipping.

17 *to … thee* Samber: 'for the friendship I show thee'.

18 *at present* immediately.

19 *A … discovered* obviously, said teasingly or ironically.

20 *Lady Abbess* head of the convent.

21 *prioress* abbess's second-in-command.

22 *mistress … novices* in charge of probationer-nuns (who have not taken their final vows).

23 *intromission* sexual penetration.

24 *after which* i.e., after Agnes confesses her passions and actions to Angelica.

25 *confessor* priest who listens to and then absolves a penitent of his or her sins.

confession,[26] which I know you have no design to prevail of,[27] but the imparting whereof to you shall only serve to unite us to one another with a more strict and indissoluble bond.[28]

ANGELICA. It shall so, without doubt, my dear, and thou wilt afterwards find that there is nothing more delightful[29] in this world than to have a true friend, who can be the depository of our secrets, of our thoughts, and of our very afflictions. Ah, how easing and comfortable are the disclosings of one's mind in suchlike occasions! Speak then! Prithee, my dear,[30] speak! I will sit down by thee upon thy bed. 'Tis not necessary that thou dress thyself; the season allows to continue as thou art, methinks! Thou art so much the more lovely, and the more thou approachest the estate wherein nature brought thee into the world, the more charms and beauty dost thou appear with. Hug me, my dear Agnes, before thou beginnest, and confirm by thy kisses the mutual protestations we have interchanged of loving one another eternally. Ah, how pure and innocent are these kisses! Ah, how full of tenderness and sweetness! Ah, how they tickle me with delight![31] Hold a little, my pretty heart; I am all of a flame! These caresses have brought me into a panting condition! Ah God, how powerful is love! And what will become of me if mere kisses animate and transport me to such a pitch!

AGNES. It is indeed a very difficult matter to contain oneself within the bounds of one's duty when we in the least slacken the reins to that passion! Would you believe it, Angelica? These little wantonings,[32] which in the bottom[33] are nothing, have had a wonderful effect upon me? Ah, ah, ah, let me breathe a little! Methinks my heart is too much pent up at present! Ah, these sighs give me ease! I begin to have for you a new affection, and more strong and tender than before! I know not from whence this proceeds, for can mere kisses cause so much disorder in the soul? The truth is you are very dexterous in

[26] *general confession* i.e., of one's entire life (a requirement before a nun may take her final vows).

[27] *prevail of* take advantage of.

[28] *a … bond* Samber: 'the strictest and most indissoluble chains of friendship'.

[29] *delightful* Samber: 'sweet and agreeable'.

[30] *my dear* Samber: 'my minion' (sweetheart; also, a dependant who provides sexual services).

[31] *Ah … delight!* Samber: 'What excess of pleasure do they afford me!'

[32] *wantonings* amorous caresses.

[33] *in the bottom* i.e., in the final analysis. Although 'bottom' did not mean 'arse' until the end of the eighteenth century, 'bottom' did mean the 'genitals or genital region' as early as 1660 (Williams, 1.135).

your caresses, and all your ways are extraordinary engaging; for you so won upon me, that I am more yours than my own. [...]

[Agnes experiences pangs of conscience over her masturbation, which Angelica dispels by arguing for their innocence. Angelica asks Agnes about the extent of her self-inflicted injuries, aimed at punishing her sexually desiring flesh.]

AGNES. Alas! My zeal was indiscreet, and I fancied the more strokes that I gave, the more did I merit. My plump body and my youth rendered me insensible to the least lashes; so as at the end of this fair exercise, my backside was all of a flame. Nay, for ought I know I broke the flesh, and made a wound, for that I was wholly transported[34] when I outraged it so cruelly.

ANGELICA. My pretty, little dear! Prithee, let me see and search[35] it. I'll see what an ill-managed fervency is capable of.

AGNES. O Lord! Why, must I suffer this? What, you are then in earnest! I cannot endure it without confusion. Oh! Oh!

ANGELICA. Hey day,[36] to what purpose then was all my discourse, if thou art still withheld[37] by a silly bashfulness? What hurt is there in granting me my request?

AGNES. Indeed, indeed, I am to blame, and your curiosity is not to be found fault with; satisfy it according to thy desires.

ANGELICA. So, so, this beautiful face that's always veiled is now uncovered. Get thee on thy knees on thy bed, and duck down thy head a little that I may see the violence of thy blows. Ah, good Lord, how 'tis streaked! Methinks I see China taffetas,[38] or else the sky at sun-setting. You must needs be very devout at the mystery of flagellation,[39] since you scourge your buttocks at this rate![40]

AGNES. Well now, you have sufficiently contemplated this innocent outrage? Ah, Lord, what makes you grope there?! Ah, let it alone that it may recover its former complexion and get rid of that stranger of a colour. Pooh, what! Do you kiss it?

[34] *transported* excited beyond self-control.

[35] *search* examine closely.

[36] *Hey day* an expression of impatience.

[37] *withheld* restrained.

[38] *taffeta* light silk.

[39] *mystery* ordinance, rite, or sacrament; for flagellation as a female homoerotic sexual practice, see **2.1.4**.

[40] *since ... rate!* Samber adds: 'thus to illuminate one's thighs' (where *illuminate* refers punningly to adorning precious manuscripts with gold, silver, or illustrations).

ANGELICA. Lie still, my pretty rogue. Be not refractory. I have the most compassionate soul in the world; and as it is a work of mercy to comfort the afflicted,[41] 'tis my opinion that I cannot afford them too many caresses, for the worthily acquitting myself of that duty. Ah! This part of thy body is delicately well made! And what a lustre does it receive from its whiteness and plumpness! I perceive also another part[42] which is no less well-endowed by Nature: 'tis Nature itself.

AGNES. Prithee, take away thy hand from thence, if thou meanest not to cause there an inflammation which cannot easily be extinguished. I must needs own to thee my weakness: I am the most sensible[43] maiden that ever was, and what would not cause in others the least emotion often puts me all in disorder.

ANGELICA. What, then you are not of so cold a temper as thou wouldest have persuaded me at the beginning of the conversation! And I fancy thou wilt play thy part as well as anyone I know, when I have put thee into the hands of true, honest friars. [...] Come, cover your backside for fear thou should'st catch cold. Stay, let me kiss it once more, and again, and again.

[...]

[Angelica recounts Father de Rancourt's abandonment of his lover, an unnamed nun, to pursue the beautiful Sister Virginia. Virginia finally grants him sexual favours, but Rancourt's cast-off beloved decides to surprise them in the act and destroy the faithless priest's career. She and another nun watch the sexual encounter through a peep-hole.]

[ANGELICA *reporting the words of Virginia to Rancourt*]. [...] 'Cannot we remain in the terms we are under, pass together soft delightful moments and enjoy pleasures so much the more perfect as they are pure and innocent? If your happiness, as you say, does only depend on what I have most dear,[44] you can be happy but once, and I always miserable, since it is a thing which cannot be recovered. Believe me, let us love as a brother loves a sister and brother, and let us allow this love all the freedom that can be imagined, with exception to one alone.'[45]

AGNES. And what answer did the Jesuit make to all this?

41 *comfort ... afflicted* one of the traditional four works of corporal mercy recommended to all Christians.

42 *another part* Agnes's external genitalia (especially, her clitoris).

43 *sensible* sensitive.

44 *what ... dear* her virginity.

45 *one alone* vaginal penetration in heterosexual intercourse.

Angelica. During the discourse, he said not a word, but leaning with his head on one of his hands, he looked with eyes full of languishment on her who spoke to him. After which, taking her by the hand through the grate, he told her after a touching manner:

'Must we then change our method, and no longer love as before? Can you consent to this, Virginia? For my part, I can retrench nothing of my love, and the rules which you have newly prescribed to me, not to be received by a true lover.'

He exaggerated to her afterward, with so much heat, the excess of his flames, that he absolutely disconcerted her, and drew from her an oral promise of granting him within some few days what alone would render him perfectly happy. He then made her come nearer to the grate, and, having made her mount upon a pretty high stool, he conjured her to allow him at least to satisfy his sight, since he was barred all other liberty. She obeyed him after some resistance, and suffered[46] him time to see and grope the parts consecrated to chastity and continency. She, for her part, would also needs satisfy her eyes with the like curiosity. And the Jesuit,[47] who was not insensible,[48] easily found the means for her so doing; she obtained from him what she desired with more easiness than she granted his request. Then was the fatal moments of 'em both and what our spies desired; they contemplated with an extraordinary satisfaction the fine parts of the companion's body, which the Jesuit laid to view and felt and groped with transports of an enchanted[49] lover. Sometimes they admired one part, and sometimes another, according as the officious father turned and changed the situation of his mistress; so that when he considered the fore part, he exposed her breech[50] to the light, because her petticoats all round were lifted and tucked up above her middle.

Agnes. Methinks I am present at this spectacle, so naturally dost thou tell the story.

Angelica. At length, they terminated their wantonings, and our two sisters retired with a design to put a stop to these ill-managed amours and to hinder the effect of Virginia's promise. By a particular happiness for that poor innocent creature, the nun whom her rival had associated to her in the consideration of what had passed, had

46 *suffered* allowed.

47 *Jesuit* Samber: 'father'.

48 *not insensible* perhaps, he understands her needs, and experiences a similar arousal.

49 *enchanted* Samber: 'furious'.

50 *breech* backside.

> a very tender kindness[51] for her,[52] and endeavoured to find a bias[53] for ruining the Jesuit without injuring her she loved. She gave her to understand what she knew of her intrigues; assured her of doing nothing to her prejudice, provided she would promise her to break entirely off with that priest, and not have for the future the least communication with him. Virginia, extremely ashamed at what she heard, engaged herself to all that was desired, only earnestly begs the Jesuit's reputation may be saved, because it was impossible to wound the one without doing some damage to the other. She protested she would see him no more, and that the letter she was going to write to him never to return again, should be the last he should receive from her. These conditions were accepted by both, though with trouble. They embrace Virginia, of whom they were becoming enamoured, and said at parting that they would supply the father's place, and enter into a strict friendship with her.

[…]

Aphra Behn (?1640–1689), writer

Probably the daughter of a barber, Behn served as a royalist spy in Surinam and Antwerp. A member of Rochester's libertine poetic circle, and the lover of the notoriously bisexual, republican lawyer John Hoyle, Behn was a prolific dramatist, penning some nineteen plays (including *The Rover* (1677)) and collaborating on more. Her major works of poetry and prose include *Poems upon Several Occasions* (1684), *Love Letters between a Nobleman and His Sister* (1684; expanded, with seven editions by 1765) and the prose fiction *Oronooko* (1688).

Online Companion
From Behn's *The Amorous Prince* (1671).

[51] *kindness* Samber: 'friendship'.
[52] *her* Virginia.
[53] *bias* indirect way.

9.17

From *Poems upon Several Occasions* (1684)

9.17.1 To my Lady Morland at Tunbridge[1]

As when a conqu'rour does in triumph come,
And proudly leads the vanquished captives home,
The joyful people crowd in ev'ry street,
And with loud shouts of praise the victor greet;
While some whom chance or fortune kept away,
Desire at least the story of the day;
How brave the prince, how gay the chariot was,
How beautiful he looked, with what a grace;
Whether upon his head he plumes did wear;
Or if a wreath of bays adorned his hair:[2]
They hear 'tis wondrous fine, and long much more
To see the hero than they did before.
So when the marvels by report I knew,
Of how much beauty, Cloris, dwelt in you;
How many slaves your conqu'ring eyes had won,
And how the gazing crowd admiring throng:
I wished to see, and much a lover grew
Of so much beauty, though my rivals too.
I came and saw, and blest my destiny;
I found it just you should out-rival me.
'Twas at the altar, where more hearts were giv'n
To you that day, than were addressed to heav'n.
The rev'rend man whose age and mystery
Had rendered youth and beauty vanity,
By fatal chance casting his eyes your way,
Mistook the duller business of the day,
Forgot the gospel, and began to pray.
Whilst the enamoured crowd that near you pressed,
Receiving darts which none could e'er resist,
Neglected the mistake o'th' lovesick priest.
Ev'n my devotion, Cloris, you betrayed,

[1] *Lady Morland* Carola (1651–74), daughter of Sir Roger Harsnett; second wife of Samuel Morland, natural philosopher and diplomat (1625–95). Together they had two children before Carola's death (aged twenty-three) in 1674.

[2] *wreath of bays* laurel crown worn by victorious Roman generals.

And I to heaven no other petition made,
But that you might all other nymphs out-do
In cruelty as well as beauty too.
I called Amyntas 'faithless swain' before,[3]
But now I find 'tis just he should adore.
Not to love you, a wonder sure would be,
Greater than all his perjuries to me.
And whilst I blame him, I excuse him too;
Who would not venture heav'n to purchase you?
But charming Cloris, you too meanly prize
The more deserving glories of your eyes,
If you permit him on an amorous score,
To be your slave, who was my slave before.
He oft has fetters worn, and can with ease
Admit 'em or dismiss 'em when he please.
A virgin-heart you merit, that ne'er found
It could receive, till from your eyes, the wound;
A heart that nothing but your force can fear,
And own a soul as great as you are fair.

9.18

From *Lycidus* (1688)

9.18.1 To the fair Clarinda, who made love to me, imagined more than woman

Fair lovely maid, or if that title be
Too weak, too feminine for nobler thee,
Permit a name that more approaches truth:
And let me call thee 'lovely charming youth'.
This last will justify my soft complaint,[4]
While that may serve to lessen my constraint;
And without blushes I the youth pursue,
When so much beauteous woman is in view;
Against thy charms we struggle but in vain,
With thy deluding form thou giv'st us pain,

[3] *Amyntas* Jeffrey Boys, member of Gray's Inn, friend of Behn (M. Duffy, *Passionate Shepherdess* (London, 1989), p. 131). See Glossary.
[4] *complaint* lamentation.

While the bright nymph betrays us to the swain.[5]
In pity to our sex sure thou wert sent,
That we might love, and yet be innocent.
For sure no crime with thee we can commit,
Or if we should – thy form excuses it.
For who, that gathers fairest flowers believes
A snake lies hid beneath the fragrant leaves.[6]
Thou beauteous wonder of a different kind,
Soft Cloris with the dear Alexis joined;
Whene'er the manly part of thee would plead,
Thou tempts us with the image of the maid,
While we the noblest passions do extend
The love to Hermes, Aphrodite the friend.

9.19

From *Miscellany Poems upon Several Occasions* (1692)[7]

9.19.1 Verses designed by Mistress A. Behn, to be sent to a fair lady, that desired she would absent herself, to cure her love. Left unfinished

In vain to woods and deserts I retire,
To shun the lovely charmer I admire,
Where the soft breezes do but fan my fire!
In vain in grotto's dark unseen I lie,
Love pierces where the sun could never spy.
No place, no art his godhead can exclude,
The dear distemper reigns in solitude:[8]
Distance, alas, contributes to my grief;
No more, of what fond lovers call, 'relief'
Than to the wounded hind does sudden flight
From the chaste goddess's pursuing sight:[9]
When in the heart the fatal shaft remains,

[5] *nymph* lovely rural maiden; *swain*: country dweller; wooer.

[6] *snake* penis. In Behn's 'The Disappointment', Cloris touches Lysander's penis after his premature ejaculation, comparing it to a snake.

[7] Multi-authored volume.

[8] *distemper* bodily disorder (love was often figured as an illness).

[9] *Than … sight* Actaeon (Glossary); *hind*: female red deer.

And darts the venom through our bleeding veins.
If I resolve no longer to submit
Myself a wretched conquest to your wit,
More swift than fleeting shades, ten thousand charms
From your bright eyes that rebel thought disarms:
The more I struggl'd, to my grief I found
Myself in Cupid's chains more surely bound:
Like birds in nets, the more I strive, I find
  Myself the faster in the snare confined.

'Ephelia' (*fl.* 1670s and 1680s), writer and royalist

A still-unidentified London-based poet and playwright, 'Ephelia' had connections with the aristocracy and with a circle of famous male and female writers, including Katherine Philips, Anne Finch, and John Dryden. In *Female Poems on Several Occasions* the female speaker's relationship with her fickle male love Strephon and this relationship's conventional romantic trajectory, beginning in bliss and ending in male betrayal and abandonment, may have an autobiographical basis. The volume's other poems celebrate her platonic friendship with a man ('Phylocles') and her passionate friendships with women.

9.20

From Female Poems on Several Occasions
(1679; second edn 1682)

9.20.1 To the Beauteous Marina

Nature that had been long by art outdone,
Resolved a piece to frame
So beauteous that saucy art should own,
She was quite vanquished and o'erthrown:
And all her mended faces, after came.
In this resolve, your lovely self she made,
And, lavish of her graces,
Outdid herself, exhausted all her store
Of ev'ry sweet, till she could give no more,
Bankrupt forever, to all other faces.
In infancy all did the bud admire,

But when full blown, it raised our wonder higher,
And admiration grew into desire.

When with your sight the 'Change you bless,[1]
Or walk the open street,
A thousand tongues your praise express,
While dying eyes aloud confess,
You have a captive in each man you meet.
When bashful Clovis chanced to spy
Your killing face, with mine,
So much you charmed that shepherd's eye,
That my faint lights he did despise;
And looked as I my empire must resign:
Though his each look, I challenge as my due,
He scarce gave one; his eyes no motion knew;
But fixed as the dull earth, with wonder gazed on you.

9.20.2 To Clovis, desiring me to bring Him into Marina's Company

Charming insulter! sure you might have chose
Some easier way than this you now propose,
To try the boundless friendship I profess;
For if fate can, this task will make it less.
Clovis, believe; if anything there is
I can deny your merit, it is this:
If I had rocks of diamonds, mines of ore,
Engrossed the pearls upon the eastern-shore;
With as much joy, I'd lay 'em at your feet,
As youthful monarchs in new empires meet.
Could you be happy by my misery,
In any shape but this, I'd wretched be:
With every other wish I would comply,
But bright Marina's sight I must deny:
That gift's too prodigal; I'd rather part
With life itself, and give my bleeding heart:
For I with blushes own, that sacred fire
Once ruled my breast, degenerate to desire.
I thought it friendship; swore it should be so,

[1] *'Change* either the New Exchange (in the Strand) or the Royal Exchange (fashionable London shopping districts).

Yet 'spite of me, it would to passion grow.
When to this worthless heart, you did address,
With all the marks that passion could express;
On my soft neck your pensive head would lay,
And sigh, and vow, and kiss the hours away.
Your tears, and languished looks I did neglect,
And would not love, yet highly did respect;
Thought you the best of men, and counselled you,
To turn your passion into friendship too:
Told you, my heart was cruel Strephon's prize,
His devout, though neglected sacrifice:
Would often talk of sweet Marina's charms,
And oft'ner wish her lodged in your dear arms.
Ah, fatal wish! Ye gods! why should you mind
The foolish wishes made by woman-kind?
I every hour saw Strephon's love decay;
And Clovis more endeared me every day.
Why at so vast a rate should he oblige?
Or, why so soon should he remove his siege?
That hour that mine began, your love did end,
You took my counsel and became my friend:
And by those ties, did earnestly request,
That I would make Marina's heart your guest.
Oh, cruel task! You Destinies, am I
In my own ruin made a property?[2]
Yet want the pow'r the treason to deny?
Yes; though this piece of knotty friendship be
Hard in itself, and harder far to me;
I'll try, and in th'attempt such vigour show,
I'll make her yours, though fate itself say no:
I'll tell your merits in such soft, smooth strains,
Shall leave a thrilling pleasure in her veins;
And when my tongue no sweeter words can find,
I'll look, as there were ten times more behind.
Then speak again; nor leave her till I spy
She is enthralled, and loves as much as I.
Then I'll present you with this beauteous slave,
The greatest gift a lover ever gave:
And when you cannot wish happier to grow,
Then think with how much pain I made you so.

2 *property* accomplice.

9.20.3 To the Angry Eugenia

Incensèd fair one! If forgiveness be
Not in thy power to extend to me –
Which to believe were such an impious thought,
Heav'n scarce would pardon, though with tears 'twere sought –
Destroy at once the creature that you hate,
And wrack me not with a sad ling'ring fate.[3]
Yet ere I die, permit some small defence,
Not that I will pretend to innocence;
That were to think that you have been unjust,
Which let me perish when I once mistrust.
With all that rev'rence that a pious Jew
Would name Jehovah, I should speak of you.[4]
But I profanely named you in the ear
Of crowds unfit such sacred sounds to hear:
Yet what I said, if traced, you will find,
Though short of you, outdid all woman-kind.
My fault was too much zeal; this forced my tongue
To tell the worth it had adorèd long.
My life will witness this; for, madam, know,
I love too well to live and injure you.

Anne Killigrew (1660–85), poet and painter

Maid of honour to Mary of Modena, second wife of James, Duke of York, later James II, Killigrew was celebrated by her contemporaries as poet and ideal woman, particularly after her death from smallpox, which occasioned numerous eulogies emphasizing her virtue, beauty, and talents. *Poems*, her only published work, includes epigrams, occasional verse, and pastorals, appearing a year after her death, prefaced by laudatory commendatory poems, the most famous by Dryden. Of her paintings, few survive: her portrait of James II, long misattributed to the portraitist Sir Peter Lely (1618–80), and two self-portraits.

[3] *wrack* destroy (playing on 'rack', meaning 'torture').

[4] *With … you* 'Jehovah' replaced the incommunicable name of God, a name so holy that it could not be uttered.

9.21

From *Poems* (1686)

9.21.1 On a Picture Painted by Herself, Representing Two Nymphs of Diana's, One in a Posture to Hunt, the Other Bathing

We are Diana's virgin train,
Descended of no mortal strain;
Our bows and arrows are our goods,
Our palaces, the lofty woods;
The hills and dales, at early morn,
Resound and echo with our horn;
We chase the hind and fallow deer,
The wolf and boar both dread our spear;
In swiftness we outstrip the wind,
An eye and thought we leave behind;
We fauns and shaggy satyrs awe;
To sylvan pow'rs we give the law.[1]
Whatever does provoke our hate,
Our javelins strike, as sure as fate;
We bathe in springs to cleanse the soil
Contracted by our eager toil,[2]
In which we shine like glittering beams,
Or crystal in the crystal streams;
Though Venus we transcend in form,
No wanton flames our bosoms warm!
If you ask where such wights do dwell,[3]
In what blessed clime, that so excel?
The poets only that can tell.

Jane Barker (1652–1732), writer

Committed royalist, coterie poet, and successful professional writer, Barker was largely self-educated. Converting to Catholicism and travelling into exile with James II and his supporters, Barker returned to her home at Wilsthorpe in 1704, but spent her last five years in France. Barker's works range from Catholic religious dialogues to verse epistles, occasional poetry, political

[1] *sylvan* woodland.
[2] *contracted* attracted, drawn (upon ourselves).
[3] *wights* persons.

satire, and proto-feminist fiction. Her most famous work is the 'Galesia Trilogy', three volumes of prose fiction published between 1713 and 1726, including *Patchwork Screen* (1723). She never married.

9.22

From *Poetical Recreations*, Part I (1688)

9.22.1 On the Death of My Dear Friend and Play-fellow, Mrs E.D., Having Dreamed the Night before I Heard thereof, That I Had Lost a Pearl[1]

I dreamed I lost a pearl, and so it proved;
I lost a friend much above pearls beloved.[2]
A pearl perhaps adorns some outward part,
But friendship decks each corner of the heart.
Friendship's a gem, whose lustre does outshine
All that's below the heav'nly crystalline:[3]
Friendship is that mysterious thing alone,
Which can unite, and make two hearts but one;
It purifies our love, and makes it flow
I' th' clearest stream that's found in love below;
It sublimates the soul, and makes it move
Towards perfection and celestial love.
We had no by-designs, nor hoped to get
Each by the other place amongst the great;
Nor riches hoped, nor poverty we feared;
'Twas innocence in both, which both revered.
Witness this truth the Wilsthorpe fields, where we
So oft enjoyed a harmless luxury;
Where we indulged our easy appetites,
With pocket-apples, plums, and such delights.[4]
Then we contrived to spend the rest o'th' day,
In making chaplets, or at check-stone play;[5]

[1] Cf. Cicero's description of ideal friendship (*Laelius* (*Online Companion*)).
[2] See Mt. 13.45–6 (parable of the merchant and the pearl of great price).
[3] *heavenly crystalline* Spheres (Glossary).
[4] *pocket-apples* i.e., apples small enough to slip into a pocket.
[5] *chaplets* wildflower crowns; *check-stone*: children's game played with smooth, round pebbles.

When weary, we ourselves supinely laid
On beds of vi'lets under some cool shade,[6]
Where th' sun in vain strove to dart through his rays,
Whilst birds around us chanted forth their lays;[7]
Ev'n those we had bereavèd of their young,[8]
Would greet us with a querimonious song.[9]
Stay here, my muse, and of these let us learn,
The loss of our deceasèd friend to mourn.
Learn, did I say? alas, that cannot be:
We can teach clouds to weep, and winds to sigh at sea,
Teach brooks to murmur, rivers to re-flow,
We can add solitude to shades of yeaugh.[10]
Were turtles to be witness of our moan,[11]
They'd in compassion quite forget their own;
Nor shall hereafter Heraclitus be
Famed for his tears, but to my muse and me[12]
Fate shall give all that fame can comprehend.
Ah, poor repair for th' loss of such a friend!

9.23

From *A Patchwork Screen for the Ladies* (1723)[13]

9.23.1 The Unaccountable Wife

'This gentleman,' said Galesia, 'had married a young gentlewoman of distinction, against the consent of her friends; which she accomplished by

[6] *vi'lets* i.e., violets, a traditional symbol of faithfulness in love, associated with Venus.

[7] *lays* songs.

[8] *bereaved … young* by taking either their eggs to eat or their hatchlings to keep as pets.

[9] *querimonious* complaining.

[10] *yeaugh* yew-tree: often planted in churchyards (symbolizing grief).

[11] *turtles* i.e., turtle doves, believed to mate for life; emblems of faithful marriage.

[12] *Heraclitus* of Ephesus, pre-Socratic philosopher, famed for misanthropy and solitude; nicknamed 'the Weeping Philosopher'.

[13] *patchwork* hybrid piece of needlework (pieces of fabric sewn together to form one article), like Barker's heterogeneous volume (comprised of poetry, fiction, etc.). At one point in the volume, gentlewomen ask the work's main narrator, Galesia, to contribute patches to their screen, and they subsequently add her scraps of poetry and fiction.

the help of her mother's maid-servant. To say the truth, though her birth was very considerable, yet her person was not at all agreeable and her fortune but indifferent:[14] her parents, I suppose, thinking, that more than just enough to support her would but betray her to an unhappy marriage. In short, married she was to the foresaid young man, whose person was truly handsome; and with part of her fortune he placed himself in the army, bestowed another part in furnishing her a house, and so lived very decently; and notwithstanding her indifferent person, he had children by her, though they did not live long. Thus they made a pretty handsome shift[15] in the world, till a vile wretch, her servant, overturned all, as follows. This servant whether she was a creature of her master's before she came to her mistress is not known; but she became very fruitful, and had every year a child, pretending that she was privately married to an apprentice. Whether the wife knew the whole of the matter, or was imposed upon, is uncertain; but which way soever it was, she was extremely kind to this woman, to a degree unheard-of; became a perfect slave to her, and, as if she was the servant, instead of the mistress, did all the household-work, made the bed, cleaned the house, washed the dishes; nay, farther than so, got up in the morning, scoured the irons, made the fire, etc., leaving this vile strumpet[16] in bed with her husband, for they lay all three together every night. All this her friends knew, or at least suspected; but thought it complaisance, not choice in her; and that she considered her own imperfections and deformity; and therefore, was willing to take no notice of her husband's fancy in the embraces of this woman her servant.

But the sequel opens quite another scene. And now I come to that part of the story, where he came to my mother. His business was, to desire her to come to his wife, and endeavour to persuade her to part with this woman:

"For," said he, "she has already three children living, and God knows how many more she may have. Which indeed, madam," said he, "is a charge my little substance is not able to sustain; and I have been using all endeavours to persuade my wife to part with her, but cannot prevail. Wherefore I beg you, as a friend, relation, and her senior in years, to come, and lay before her the reasonableness of what I desire, and the ridiculousness of her proceeding."

"Good Heaven!" said my mother. "Can you think thus to bore my nose with a cushion? Can you imagine me so stupid as to believe your wife can persist in such a contradiction of nature? It is impossible a wife should oppose her husband's desire in parting with such a woman."

"Madam," replied he, "I beg you once more to be so good as to come to my wife, and then condemn me if I have advanced a falsehood."

14 *indifferent* middling; unimpressive.

15 *shift* method of living.

16 *strumpet* whore.

"Well," replied my mother, "I will come, though I doubt not but upon due inspection the whole will prove a farce composed amongst you, in which your wife is to act her part just as you between you think fit to teach her; which she, out of fear, or some other delusion, is to perform."

But he averred again and again that, without fraud or trick, the thing was as he said. In short, my mother went; and there she found the servant sitting in a handsome velvet chair, dressed up in very good laced linen, having clean gloves on her hands, and the wife washing the dishes. This sight put my mother into such a violent passion, that she had much ado to refrain from laying hands on her. However, she most vehemently chid the mistress, telling her that she offended God, disgraced her family, scandalized her neighbours, and was a shame to womankind.

All which she returned with virulent words. Amongst other things, she stood buff[17] in favour of that woman, saying that she had been not only a faithful servant, but the best of friends, and those that desired to remove such a friend from her, deserved not the name of friends, neither did she desire they should come into her house. All which she uttered with such an air of vehemency that there was no room left to doubt of the sincerity of her words; but that all proceeded from an interior thoroughly degenerated. All which my mother related to me with great amazement, but withal told me that she would have me go to her on the morrow, and with calm and friendly words, endeavour to persuade her to reason.

"For," said she, "I was in a passion at the disagreeable view; but you, who have naturally more patience than myself, pray put on the best resolutions you can to keep your temper, whatsoever provocations shall occur."

Thus instructed, thus resolved, I went next day, hoping that a night's repose would calm the storm my mother's anger might have raised. But when I came, I found it all the same. Though I took her apart, and with the utmost mildness persuaded her, and used the best reasons I could think on to enforce those persuasions, yet all was in vain.

And she said we all joined with her husband to make her miserable, by removing from her, the only friend she had in the world; and passionately swore by Him that made her, that if we combined to send the woman away, she would go with her.

"I would try that," replied I, "were I in your husband's place."

At which her passion redoubled, and she, with violent oaths, repeated her resolution; desiring that her friends would meddle with their own business, and let her alone to remain in quiet in her house, and not come to give her disturbance. After these uncouth compliments, I left her, carrying with me the greatest amazement possible.

[17] *buff* firm.

After this, the husband came to us, and asked if we did not find true what he had told us.

"Indeed," replied I, "true, and doubly true; such a truth as I believe never was in the world before, nor never will be again."

"In this case," said he, "what would you counsel me to do?"

"Truly," said my mother, "it is hard to advise; for to let the woman live there still is not proper, nor can your circumstances undergo the charge. And if your wife should do as she says and go with her, I should in some degree be accessory to the parting man and wife."

"I would venture," said I, "for when it comes to the push, I warrant her she will not go."

Hereupon the man said he would try; and accordingly, hired a place in a wagon to carry the creature into her own country; hoping, as I suppose, that his wife would have rested herself contented with him, when the woman had been gone; but instead thereof, she acted as she said, and went along with her.

This transaction was so extraordinary that everybody was amazed at it; and when they had been gone some time, there arose a murmuring amongst friends, neighbours and acquaintance, as if he had made his wife away; and when he told them the manner of her departure, they would not believe him, the thing in itself being so incredible.

But we will leave him to make his party good,[18] as well as he can, amidst the censure of his neighbours, the threats of her friends, and the ridicule of his acquaintance, and follow the travellers into the country whither they were gone.

They arrived safe at the woman's father's, where they found as kind a reception as a poor cottage could afford; and a very poor one it was, there being no light but what came in at the door, no food but from the hands of charity, nor fuel but what they pilfered from their neighbours' hedges.

Now what this unaccountable creature thought of this kind of being, is unknown, or what measures she and her companion thought to take, or what schemes they formed to themselves is not conceivable; but whatever they were, the discreet neighbourhood put a period[19] to their projects; for they got a warrant to have them before a justice, in order to prevent a parish charge; there being two children there already, which they had sent some time before; and now two helpless women being come, they knew not where the charge might light, and therefore proceeded as aforesaid.[20] It happened

[18] *make … good* justify his position.

[19] *period* end.

[20] *for they got … as aforesaid* Taxes or poor rates were assessed and levied at the parish level for the support of the poor, and there was always much anxiety in parishes when those without money or work moved into the district: it meant an inevitable increase

as the constable was conducting them to the justice, with a mob at their heels, that they passed by the house of a lady of quality,[21] who looking out of her window, saw in the midst of this throng, this unfortunate wife, whom she immediately knew to be the daughter of her friend, knew to be the child of an honourable family. It is impossible to describe what amazement seized her. She called out to the constable and other neighbours there, bidding them bring that gentlewoman to her, which they immediately did. This good lady, out of respect to her old friends, a worthy family, bid them discharge her, telling them that herself would be bound that she should be no parish charge; so took her into her house, treated her kindly, and offered her all she could do on such an occasion. For all which she returned the lady but cold thanks, and begged her ladyship's assistance to convey her to London along with the other woman, "who," she said, "was the truest friend in the world." The lady knowing nothing of her story, with much goodness provided for her departure, together with her companion. In this manner, loaden with disgrace, they came back to London, to her husband, from whom, no doubt, she found reproaches suitable to her folly.

Long it was not, ere[22] death made a true and substantial separation, by carrying the husband into the other world. Now was the time to make manifest, whether promises, flatteries or threatenings had made her act the foresaid scene. But it appeared all voluntary; for when he was dead, her friends and relations invited and persuaded her to leave that creature and her children, and come to live with them, suitable to her birth and education. But all in vain; she absolutely adhered to this woman and her children, to the last degree of folly, insomuch that being reduced to poverty, she begged in the streets to support them. At last, some friend of her family told the queen of the distressed way she was in, and in some degree, how it came to pass, that neither her dead husband nor her relations might be blameable. The queen, with much goodness, told her friend that if she would leave that woman, and go live with some relation, she would take care she should not want; and withal sent her five guineas,[23] as an earnest of a monthly pension; but notwithstanding, this infatuated creature refused the queen's favour, rather than part with this family. And so, for their support, begged in the streets, the remainder of her days.

"Sure," said the lady, "this poor creature was under some spell or enchantment, or she could never have persisted, in so strange a manner, to oppose her husband, and all her nearest friends, and even her sovereign."'

in these taxes. In 1662, legislation formalized the right of parishes to expel such new arrivals.

[21] *quality* high rank.

[22] *ere* before.

[23] *guinea* English gold coin of considerable value.

Catharine Trotter (?1674–1749), writer

Largely self-educated, Trotter published one novella, before turning to the drama. Her five plays – *Agnes de Castro* (1695), *Fatal Friendship* (1698), *Love at a Loss* (1700), *The Unhappy Penitent* (1701), and *The Revolution of Sweden* (1706) – all feature passionate yet rational heroines, who espouse the highest moral and ethical standards. Her other works are philosophical treatises in the Lockean tradition. She married the clergyman Patrick Cockburn in 1708, and spent time in parishes in Suffolk, London, and Northumberland.

9.24

From *Agnes de Castro* (1695)

[Princess Constantia and Agnes de Castro are the closest of friends. Prince Fernando, the princess's husband, has unfortunately fallen in love with Agnes and the prince's vengeful cast-off lover, Elvira, attempts to use this circumstance to cause dissension and hatred between the two women.]

9.24.1 Act 1, scene 2

[Constantia reveals to Agnes that she suspects Fernando's affections have been stolen away from her, and that he loves another.]

[…]

AGNES. Compose yourself, madam, I beg your Highness.
PRINCESS. That was a word of too much distance, Agnes,
Looks like the prince's cold indifference
In ceremonious respect disguised;
Leave it, I would believe I have thy heart,
The only comfort for the loss of his;
For you are both so equal dear to me,
So closely wove by fate to my fond breast,
That neither can be severed from my love,
Without unravelling this web of life.

[Elvira's servant, Bianca, brings a paper written by the prince detailing his anguish over his hopeless love for Agnes.]

PRINCESS. […] Doubly unhappy princess!
Agnes, my fears are true! All that I feared,

More than I feared, is true.
AGNES. It can't be: the prince is not so stupid
To love Elvira still; I heard indeed
He had awhile amused himself with her
Before your marriage, but what charms has she
To vie with those perfections all divine,
Which grace your body and adorn your soul?
PRINCESS. Ah! She who robs me of my husband's heart
Is all a charm, to plead for his excuse;
Young, beautiful, discreet, and chaste, as fair
By Nature formed to captive ev'ry heart.
My reason must approve the prince's choice,
For I myself prefer her to myself,
And love her too, as tenderly as he.
AGNES. Who can this angel be?
PRINCESS. Are there so many merit more than I,
Thou can'st not guess among 'em?
AGNES. Indeed I know not one deserves like you;
And therefore cannot guess.
PRINCESS. Have you so long been privy to my thoughts,
Yet know not her who is so dear to me?
Who with the prince shares my divided heart
So equally, I cannot tell myself
To which I have given most? Know you not her?
For if you know my friend, you know my rival.
AGNES. How very miserable must I be
When I'm reduced to wish you did not love me!
Those marks of that peculiar, dear affection,
Which ev'ry day your partial kindness gave,
Are witnesses which I would disbelieve;
Oh! Let me think your friendship was divided!
Tell me you have another, nearer friend,
For I had rather lose your love forever
Than be the wretched cause of your misfortune;
Rather be hated by you, than deserve it;
Oh, ease my cruel fears, and name some other!
PRINCESS. Too sure, alas, the prince does love thee, Agnes;
And I'm so vain to think that only thou
Could gain a heart to which I laid a claim.

[...]

AGNES. Heav'n strike 'em blind for the base treachery;[1]
Where shall I hide these curst, these guilty eyes?
They dare not look upon the injured princess,
Though she was all they took delight to see;
How could heav'n make so great a contradiction,
As in one person, friend and enemy!
PRINCESS. Thou art not my enemy; I know you love me.
AGNES. Yet I have robbed you of your dearest part,
Destroyed your soft tranquillity of soul,
And left you nothing but despair and sorrow;
I only have done this, ev'n I who love you;
I who to serve you would abandon life;
Oh! Can I say I am the curse of yours!
But all ill fortune flies from you with me;
And all the curse lights heavy on my head,
For we must part, forever, ever part.
PRINCESS. Part! Would you add to my unhappiness?
Be yet more cruel than my destiny?
Fate has deprived me but of half my blessing,
And you would tear the other half away,
To leave me sad, desolate, and comfortless?
AGNES. Alas! We ne'er shall meet in joy again,
This tender love must all be turned to hate.
PRINCESS. That thought was too injurious from a friend:
Thy only guilt is having too much merit,
For which 'twere most unjustly base to hate thee.

[...]

AGNES. Oh, wond'rous instance of a matchless goodness!
Gods! Is it just the prince enjoy this blessing,
Who knows not how to value the vast treasure?
PRINCESS. You are ungrateful to condemn the prince,
And I, for all I suffer, can't accuse him!
I know he struggled long against your charms,
And those efforts are more obliging far
Than if his inclinations were for me.
Love ruled by fate does ne'er consult our will,
But if we strive to love, it shows esteem;
And 'tis more kind to wish I had his heart,

[1] *'em* them: Agnes's eyes (praised in the prince's writings which Constantia has been reading aloud).

Than if he gave the prize unwillingly.
Why should I blame the prince for loving her?
Were reason, duty, honour, all against me,
I still should dote on him in spite of all:
The same strong destiny controls his heart,
And my fair rival's worth bounds my complaints.
There is no room for my resentment left,
Nor shall the prince perceive my inward grief;
You, only you, shall ease the wounds you made,
For thou wilt pity me, I know thou wilt,
Thou dear, thou less my rival than my friend.

[Prince Fernando enters, and responds to the charge that he loves Agnes.]

PRINCE [*to the* PRINCESS]. [...] Revenge your wrongs, but upon me alone;
This only criminal, unhappy wretch,
And share the guiltless cause of our misfortune.
PRINCESS. Fear not for Agnes, sir.
I love her, and her being dear to you
More strongly recommends her to my care;
For my repose depends so much on yours,
I must lose all my own, to rob you of it.
PRINCE. Too generous princess! But in spite of you,
You have revenged yourself with sharpest wounds,
Deep in that faithless breast which injured you.
This cruel kindness has undone your husband,
Thou miracle of virtue.

[Agnes's refusal to marry the courtier Alvaro, Elvira's evil brother, angers the king, Fernando's father. Her reputation in jeopardy and determined to leave the court, Agnes is persuaded to stay by Princess Constantia for their friendship's sake. When another forged letter convinces Constantia that Agnes has slept with Fernando, Constantia isolates herself from everyone, but then decides to see Agnes, and is waiting for her in the garden.]

9.24.2 Act 3, scene 2

[...]

PRINCESS. Tell her I will expect her here.

[*Exit* WOMAN.

'Twere most unjust to punish her unheard.
Thus far I owe to one that was my friend,

To one who, though ungrateful, still I love.
Something, methinks, pleads strongly for her truth,
Tells me she may be wronged and innocent;
Yet what should move Bianca to deceive me?
What interest could she have? What end in that?
No, no, 'tis plain:
Agnes is false, as false as she was true;
For she was true till by the prince seduced.
The prince! That name's enough for her excuse.
What virtue can be proof against his charms?
That irresistible, that god-like man;
Yet much she might have suffered, much for me,
For none could love more tenderly than I;
I found in her supposed fidelity
Full recompense for all I lost before.
My husband's want of love her love atoned.
This was a blow struck to the very heart;
There's now no remedy in nature left;
No, both shall see me quickly in my grave;
My death will make your loves more innocent,
Your guilt and my misfortunes in one tomb forever shall be laid.

[Elvira stabs Princess Constantia, thinking she is Agnes, who Constantia now knows is innocent of adultery with the prince.]

PRINCESS. Now let me die in peace, since heav'n allows
Me once to see thee, dearest, injured maid.
AGNES. Now let my soul be calm, die all my fears,
Since you, the object of my hopes, are kind:
Not ships in storms, not travellers benighted,
Amongst wild beasts, left in a lonely wood,
Can half express the anguish I have felt,
Deprived of you, my light, my guard, my all.
PRINCESS. Forgive me, child. Be all thy wrongs forgot,
Forever washed away in my life's blood.
AGNES. Better all womankind at once should perish
Than you, the sole perfection of the sex,
The greatest blessing of the whole creation.
PRINCESS. Say rather, the encumbrance of the Earth;
One who but lived for an unhappy plague[2]

[2] *for* as.

To the most noble, most divine of men;
Which heav'n, grown mild, most kindly does remove,
With this additional favour to my death:
That it preserves thy dearer envied life,
And in thy life, the prince's!

AGNES. Horrible mystery of life and death!
Oh, ease my trembling heart! What mean you, madam?

PRINCESS. Fear only for thyself, for I am well;
But, Agnes, thou hast many enemies.
The death I have received was meant for thee:
Elvira's black design, whose envy first
Contrived against thy fame and then thy life;
But by a happy error both are safe;
At once she gave the welcome deadly blow,
And with malicious boasting cleared thy virtue.

AGNES. Perish the sacrilegious, hellish hand!
Too fatally it wounded where it aimed,
And gave me double death in striking you.
Ah, cruel fate! Was there no other way
To make us friends but parting us forever?
Would I had rather died unjustified,
Contemned, and loathed by you and all the world!

PRINCESS. Be less transported; thy too moving grief[3]
Had almost forced from me a wish to live.

AGNES. Alas! my heedless sorrow had forgot
To call assistance for my dearest princess.

[*Going, the* PRINCESS *holds her.*

PRINCESS. It would be vain, for death has seized me all,
And if thou go'st, I ne'er shall see thee more.
These eyes will be shut up in lasting night.
Stay, and receive a dying friend's request;
Believe thou always hast been dear to me:
Ev'n when I feared thee false, I thought thee true,
And let this forgery excuse my fear.

[*Gives her a letter.*

Then, if thou'st ever bore me true affection,
Double it on the prince, my better part;
Entreat him to forgive me, for thy sake,
The troubles I unwillingly have caused him.
Be thou to young Fernando what I was;

[3] *transported* frantically emotional.

Speak of me to him. Don't forget thy friend;
Remember with my latest breath, I beg,[4]
I charge thee love the prince, I charge thee marry him.
My dear, I'm going. Heav'n receive my soul.

[*Dies.*

AGNES. Oh! She's gone, she's gone, and left me here!
But I shall overtake my dear, dear, mistress.
This poniard, purple with her precious blood –[5]
'Tis useless, grief has kindly done its work.

[*As she is going to kill herself, she falls in a swoon.*

[…]

9.24.3 Act 5, scene 1

[With Elvira driven mad and Alvaro's conspiracy defeated, Agnes decides to return home; she struggles to resist Prince Fernando's continued proposals].

PRINCE. No, dear Constantia, she upbraids me justly,[6]
Thy love deserved eternal gratitude,
Thy virtue should forever be remembered;
All these complaints and sighs of love for Agnes
Should burst in tears of lasting grief for thee.
I've judged, I have condemned myself already,
And willingly submit to your decree.
[*To* AGNES] You can effectually revenge the princess.
Go, madam, I deserve the harshest usage.
Go, though your cruelty will give me death,
Go boast that though you knew my love to you,
Stronger than reason, honour, or my virtue,
Yet your impartial justice was not bribed
To save a perjured and ungrateful man.
Agnes, farewell. Farewell to you and life,
For I will lose those blessings both at once;
No sooner shall you leave this hateful place
Than you shall hear your lover is no more.

AGNES. [*To herself*] Oh! How his words prevail upon my heart,
It melts, 'twill yield I fear. Why should it not?
Should he who for my freedom, fame, and life

[4] *latest* last.

[5] *poniard* dagger.

[6] The prince addresses his dead wife, whom Agnes (*she*) has just reminded him of.

Exposed his own receive his death from me?
Is treating thus the man my princess loved
The way to pay her memory respect?
And do I thus obey her dying charge?
[*To the* PRINCE] Brave prince, if I have pow'r you must not die.
That were a loss too great to be permitted
For nothing but a name, a puff of breath.
What, though my honour lie at stake, I'll stay;
Yet let convenient decency be kept.
I must not, dare not, entertain your passion.

[Alvaro tries to stab Prince Fernando: he avoids the blow, but Agnes is mortally wounded. Fernando kills Alvaro. Agnes encourages Fernando to live: the people and nation depend on him.]

PRINCE. All trifles to thy loss, thou brightest blessing!
Ah, art thou gone? Speak once again, my soul!
AGNES. How have you charmed my fleeting spirits back!
I felt unusual glowings at my heart,
It warmed and kindled into life again,
But death extinguishes the new-born fire.
Ah, lovely prince! Must I forever lose you?

[*Dies.*

[The king prevents Prince Fernando from committing suicide.]

9.25

From *A Collection of the Most Choice and Private Poems*[1]
(1699)

9.25.1 Chloe to Artimesa, 1700[2]

Madam,
While vulgar souls their vulgar loves pursue,
And in the common way themselves undo,
Impairing health and fame, and risking life,

[1] MS Collection. Reprinted by permission of the Brotherton Collection, Leeds University Library. See **6.2**.

[2] *Chloe* and *Artimes[i]a* common women's names in pastoral and lyric verse.

To be a mistress, or what's worse a wife;
We, whom a nicer taste has raised above[3]
The dang'rous folly of such slavish love,
Despise the sex, while in ourselves we find[4]
Pleasures for their gross senses too refined.[5]
Let brutish men made by their weakness vain,
Boast of the easy conquests they obtain;
Let the poor loving wretch do all she can
(And all won't please th'ungrateful tyrant, man).
We'll scorn the monster, and his mistress too,
And show the world what women ought to do.

Lady Mary Chudleigh (1656–1710)

For her biography, see Introduction to **8.30**.

9.26

From *Poems on Several Occasions* (1703)

9.26.1 Song: To Lerinda

Cease, dear Lerinda, cease admiring
  Why crowds and noise I disapprove;
Whate'er I see abroad is tiring;
  Oh, let us to some cell remove;[1]
Where all alone ourselves enjoying,
  Enriched with innocence and peace,
On noblest themes our thoughts employing,
  Let us our inward joys increase.
And still the happy taste pursuing,
  Raise our love and friendship higher,
And thus the sacred flames renewing,
  In ecstasies of bliss expire.[2]

[3] *nicer* more fastidious.
[4] *the sex* men.
[5] *gross* coarse.

[1] *cell* isolated, humble dwelling, often associated with the anchorite's/hermit's sacred retreat from the world.
[2] *expire* die.

9.26.2 Friendship[3]

Friendship is a bliss divine,
And does with radiant lustre shine:
But where can that blest pair be found
That are with equal fetters bound?
Whose hearts are one, whose souls combine,
And neither know or mine or thine;[4]
Who've but one joy, one grief, one love,
And by the selfsame dictates move;
Who've not a frailty unrevealed,
Nor yet a thought that is concealed;
Who freely one another blame,
And strive to raise each other's fame;
Who're always just, sincere, and kind,
By virtue, not by wealth, combined;
Whose friendship nothing can abate,
Nor poverty, nor adverse fate,
Nor death itself, for when above,
They'll never, never, cease to love,
But with a passion more refined,
Become one pure celestial mind.

9.26.3 The Choice: A Dialogue between Emilia and Marissa[5]

MARISSA. Virtue sure's th' only treasure,
Th' only solid lasting pleasure:
It does our souls, our thoughts refine,
And gives us joys almost divine.
It may a while obscured remain,
But soon its lustre will regain;
Like Phoebus chase the shades away,[6]
And bring again triumphant day:
Censures like clouds sometimes appear,
And keep its rays from shining clear,
But having reached meridian height,

[3] Cf. Cicero's representation of idealized *amicitia* (e.g., between true friends there are no secrets) ('Laelius', *Online Companion*).

[4] *or ... or* either ... or.

[5] *Marissa* Chudleigh's adopted name in some of her letters and poems; *Emilia*: unidentified.

[6] *Phoebus* the sun.

They fly before its conqu'ring light;
Before that light whose glorious blaze
Does trembling guilty souls amaze,
And from its dazzling seat on high
Disperses splendour through the sky.
Pale envy sickens at the sight,
And full of shame, and full of spite,
To the dark nether world returns,
And there, her disappointment mourns.
But oh! my dearest friend, I find
That malice still is left behind.
Alas! that Fury never sleeps,
But through the world still slyly creeps;
Each day a new disguise she takes,
Each day some diff'rent figure makes.
Like zeal and pity she appears,
And drowned in false dissembling tears,
Often the mask of friendship wears,
And with a show of love ensnares.
On me she's bent to wreak her spite,
And with her dire attacks affright:
From her to this recess I fled,
And here my life obscurely led,
Supposing she with crowds would stay,
Or with the great, the rich, the gay,
With the young, the fair, the wise,
And me, poor worthless me, despise;
But now too late, alas! I find
She will not, will not stay behind.

EMILIA. Since virtue's seated in her breast,
Marissa ne'er can be distressed.
Malice may you perhaps assail,
But never, never can prevail.
Fortune too may take her part,
Exert her strength, and show her art;
With these the vicious may combine,
And favour their unjust design;
But virtue will the shock sustain,
And you'll unvanquished still remain;
Your inward joys will be secure,
And you'll no loss, nor ill endure.

MARISSA. Virtue has, ever had, my love,

And still my choice, my guide shall prove;
To me shall still point out the way,
Until I reach eternal day,
That dear, that welcome, blissful shore
Where I shall never suffer more;
No more the toils of life sustain,
But live secure from sin and pain.
Hark! hark! I'm called! I'm called away!
I cannot, will not, longer stay:
My guardian angel see appear,
See! see! he cuts the yielding air:
Celestial music sweetly plays,
I hear! I hear seraphic lays!
Oh! the soft enchanting sound!
Nothing here's so charming found!
Adieu, vain world, vain world, adieu:
I come, ye blest! I come to you!
Fortune's gifts I ne'er could prize,
And now her trifles I despise.
If at my feet her bounties lay,
And crowns were scattered in my way,
I'd scorn 'em all, and onward go;
There's nothing tempting here below.

EMILIA. Oh! stay my friend! Oh! stay for me,
I still will your companion be!
My love to virtue, love to you,
Was ever strong, and ever true,
And still the same shall ever prove;
Nothing my fixed resolves shall move.
The sun may sooner cease to shine,
And it may freeze beneath the line;[7]
Mountains may sink, and plains may rise,
Beasts choose the seas, and fish the skies;
Birds their loved airy region leave,
And flatt'ring men no more deceive,
Than my Marissa shall e'er find
Emilia faithless or unkind.
Oh! do not then her suit disdain,
Oh! let her not implore in vain.
She longs, she longs with you to die;

[7] *line* equator.

Thus, hand in hand we'll upward fly;
Thus, thus, my best, my dearest friend,
Thus, thus embracing we'll ascend.
MARISSA. No, thou loved darling of my heart,
We'll never, never, never part.
Those virtues which our souls combine,
Shall ever in our union shine.
Together we'll lay down our clay,
Together throw the load away;
And bright as fire, and light as air,
To the superior world repair,
To glorious seats and realms divine,
Where love does in perfection shine;
Love undisguised, without alloy,
Noble, pure, and full of joy,
Sincere, and strong, and still the same,
One steady, bright, immortal flame.
There, there our friendship we'll improve,
Together taste the sweets of love;
Still in each other's bliss rejoice,
And prove one soul, one thought, one voice;
In nothing ever disagree,
Throughout a blest eternity.

Delarivier Manley (c. 1670–1724), writer

Author of scandalous prose fiction, drama, Tory propaganda, and fictionalized autobiography, Manley became notorious for her bigamous marriage; her flirtation with the son of her patron, Barbara, Duchess of Cleveland; her affair with the married John Tilly; and her 'live-in' relationship with the Tory printer John Barber. Her roman-à-clef *The New Atalantis* (2 vols, 1709) is a thinly veiled account of contemporary persons and events, satirizing the Whigs and their supporters. Popular and controversial, *Atalantis*' tales of sex and betrayal, with separately published keys identifying the characters, led to Manley's arrest and brief detention. For a full discussion of the work's political satire, the reader should consult Rosalind Ballaster's 1991 edition of *New Atalantis* (London: Pickering and Chatto).

9.27

From *The New Atalantis* (1709)[1]

[...]

ASTRAEA.[2] Does your ladyship's intelligence extend to the knowledge of those ladies (we know 'em to be such by their voices) who fill those three coaches that run along the gravel-road on the right hand of us? They laugh loud and incessantly. 'Tis certain they have neither the spleen nor vapours![3] Or for the present seem to have forgot 'em. Can any persons be more at their ease? Sure these seem to unknow[4] that there is a certain portion of misery and disappointments allotted to all men, which one time or other will assuredly overtake 'em. The very consideration is sufficient, in my opinion, to put a damp upon the serenest, much more a tumultuous joy.

INTELLIGENCE.[5] That is afflicting themselves unprofitably. Nothing ought to hinder a man from enjoying the present, no reflection of the future carry away his relish of the instant, if it be innocently employed. To one of right understanding it will certainly happen thus; provided he be free of bodily pains, which, notwithstanding the vain celebrated apathy of the Stoics,[6] none was ever found to be insensible of and, whoever has pretended to the contrary, must be as ridiculous as affected.

But to satisfy your Excellency, these ladies are of the new cabal,[7] a sect (however innocent in itself) that does not fail from meeting its share of censure from the world. Alas! What can they do? How

1 From Volume 2.

2 *Astraea* the virgin goddess of justice. In Ovid's *Metamorphoses* she is the last classical deity to abandon the Earth when humanity descends into the violence and depravity of the Iron Age. Occasionally identified as playwright and poet Aphra Behn, who adopted this name in some of her writings, Manley's Astraea more likely represents the conservative model of the early eighteenth-century woman writer: modest, chaste, and retired. See P. McDowell, *Women of Grub Street* (Oxford, 1998), pp. 234–5.

3 *spleen* and *vapours* psychosomatic disorders involving lassitude and melancholy; *vapours* was a specifically woman's illness.

4 *unknow* forget; be ignorant of (the fact that).

5 *Intelligence* Meaning both 'secret information and its discovery and dissemination' as well as 'the capacity to understand', Intelligence has long been identified as a 'stand-in' for Manley herself.

6 *Stoics* Greek philosophers who promoted indifference to the vicissitudes of fortune, pain, and death.

7 *cabal* clique (connotations: 'secrecy' and 'intrigue').

unfortunate are women? If they seek their diversion out of themselves and include the other sex, they must be criminal? If in themselves (as those of the new cabal), still they are criminal? (– though censurers must carry their imaginations a much greater length than I am able to do mine to explain this hypothesis with success). They pretend to find in these[8] the vices of old Rome[9] revived and quote you certain detestable authors[10] who (to amuse posterity) have introduced you lasting monuments of vice, which could only subsist in imagination and can, in reality, have no other foundation than what are to be found in the dreams of poets and the ill nature of those censurers, who will have no diversions innocent but what themselves advance!

Oh, how laudable, how extraordinary, how wonderful is the uncommon happiness of the cabal! They have wisely excluded that rapacious sex who, making a prey of the honour of ladies, find their greatest satisfaction (some few excepted) in boasting of their good fortune, the very chocolate-house[11] being witnesses of their self-love where, promiscuously among the known and unknown,[12] they expose the letters of the fair, explain the mysterious and refine upon the happy part, in their redundancy of vanity consulting nothing but what may feed the insatiable hydra![13]

The cabal run no such dangers, they have all the happiness in themselves! Two beautiful ladies joined in an excess of amity (no word is tender enough to express their new delight) innocently embrace! For how can they be guilty? They vow eternal tenderness, they exclude the men, and condition[14] that they will always do so. What irregularity can there be in this? 'Tis true, some things may be strained a little too far, and that causes reflections to be cast upon the rest. One of the fair could not defend herself from receiving an importunate visit from a person of the troublesome sex. The lady who was her favourite came unexpectedly at the same time

[8] *these* these women.

[9] *vices … Rome* sexual corruption and decadence were thought the most significant causes for Rome's fall.

[10] *detestable authors* any of the classical writers who focused on sexual vice and female same-sex intercourse (e.g., Lucian and Juvenal).

[11] *chocolate-house* where chocolate would be drunk as a beverage; like the coffee-house, an exclusively male space for discussing politics and exchanging gossip.

[12] *promiscuously … unknown* without restraint among both those of high and low rank.

[13] *hydra* many-headed monster; as one head was cut off, two more grew in its place; common symbol of scandal and rumour.

[14] *condition* contract; promise.

upon another. Armida heard her chair[15] set down in the hall and presently knew her voice, enquiring with precipitation[16] who was above? Having observed a common[17] coach at the gate without a livery, the lover became surprised to the last degree to see Armida's. She trembled! She turned pale! She conjured him to pass into her closet and consent to be concealed till the lady was gone! His curiosity made him as obliging as she could desire; he was no sooner withdrawn, but his fair rival entered the chamber enraged, her voice shrill, her tone inquisitive and menacing, the extremes of jealousy in her eyes and air:

'Where is this inconstant –, where is this ungrateful girl? What happy wretch is it upon whom you bestow my rites?[18] To whom do you deliver the possession of my kisses and embraces? Upon whom bestow that heart so invaluable and for which I have paid the equivalent? Come, let us see this monster to whom my happiness is sacrificed! Are you not sufficiently warned by the ruin of so many? Are you also eager to be exposed, to be undone, to be food for vanity, to fill the detestable creatures with vainglory! What recompense – ah, what satisfaction – can there be in any heart of theirs more than in mine? Have they more tenderness, more endearments? Their truth cannot come in comparison! Besides, they find their account in treachery and boasting, their pride is gratified, whilst our interest is in mutual secrecy, in natural justice and in mutual constancy.'

Such excursions as these have given occasion to the enemies of the cabal to refine, as much as they please, upon[19] the mysteries of it. There are, who[20] will not allow of innocency in any intimacies, detestable censurers who, after the manner of the Athenians, will not believe so great a man as Socrates (him whom the oracle delivered to be the wisest of all men) could see every hour the beauty of an Alcibiades without taxing his sensibility. How did they recriminate for his affection, for his cares, his tenderness to the lovely youth? How have they delivered him down to posterity as blameable for too guilty a passion for his beautiful pupil? Since then it is not in the fate of even so wise a man to avoid the censure of the busy and the bold, care ought to be taken by others (less fortified against occasion

15 *chair* sedan chair.
16 *precipitation* haste.
17 *common* public (for hire).
18 *rites* rights; also, perhaps, 'habitual expressions of love and sexual desire'.
19 *refine … upon* misrepresent.
20 *There are, who* i.e., There are those who.

of detraction) in declining such unaccountable intimacies to prevent the ill-natured world's refining upon their mysterious innocence.

The persons who passed us in those three coaches were returning from one of their private, I was going to say silent, meetings, but far be it from me to detract from any of the attributes of the sex. The Lady L— and her daughters[21] make four of the cabal. They have taken a little lodging about twelve furlongs from Angela in a place obscure and pleasant with a magazine[22] of good wine and necessary conveniences as to chambers of repose, a tolerable garden and the country in prospect. They wear away the indulgent happy hours according to their own taste. Their coaches and people (of whom they always take as few with them as possible) are left to wait at the convenient distance of a field in length, an easy walk to their bower of bliss.[23] The day and hour of their rendezvous is appointed beforehand; they meet, they caress, they swear inviolable secrecy and amity. The glass corroborates their endearments. They momently[24] exclude the men; fortify themselves in the precepts of virtue and chastity against all their detestable, undermining arts; arraign without pity or compassion those who have been so unfortunate as to fall into their snare; propagate their principles of exposing them without mercy; give rules to such of the cabal who are not married how to behave themselves to such who they think fit they should marry, no such weighty affair being to be accomplished without the mutual consent of the society, at the same time lamenting the custom of the world, that has made it convenient (nay, almost indispensable) for all ladies once to marry. To those that have husbands, they have other instructions, in which this is sure to be one: to reserve their heart, their tender amity, for their fair friend, an article in this well-bred, wilfully undistinguishing age which the husband seems to be rarely solicitous of.

Those who are in their opinion so happy as to be released from the imposing matrimonial fetters are thought the ornament of the cabal and by all most happy. They claim an ascendant, a right of governing, of admitting or extending; in both they are extremely nice,[25] with particular reserve to the constitution of the novice:

21 *The Lady L—* Margaret Sutton, Lady Lexington, wife of Robert, Second Baron Lexington (1661–1723); *her daughters*: Eleanora-Margaret and Bridget (Ballaster, p. 292).

22 *magazine* storehouse.

23 *bower of bliss* in Spenser's *Faerie Queene* (II.xii), a sensually inviting arbour, emblem of sexual corruption.

24 *momently* immediately.

25 *nice* exacting (in their standards).

they strictly examine her genius,[26] whether it have fitted her for the mysteries of the cabal, as if she may be rendered insensible on the side of Nature: Nature, who has the trick of making them dote on the opposite improving sex, for if her foible be found directed to what Nature inspires, she is unanimously excluded, and particular injunctions bestowed upon all members of this distinguishing society from admitting her to their bosom, or initiating her in the mysteries of their endearments.

Secrecy is also a material article. This they inviolably promise, nor is it the least part of the instruction given to a new bride, lest she let her husband into a mystery (however innocent) that may expose and ridicule the community as it happened in the case of the beautiful virgin Euphelia.[27] No sooner did she appear as attendant to the queen,[28] but all the eyes of all the circle were directed to her. The men adored, the ladies would have discovered something to destroy that adoration if it had been possible, except the Marchioness de Lerma[29] who, bold and masculine, loudly taxed these invidious spectators of ill-nature and malice. She took the fair maid into especial consideration, sheltered her under her distinguished protections and, in short, introduced her into the cabal, of which, they say, the marchioness was one of the first founders in Atalantis, having something so robust in her air and mien that the other sex would have certainly claimed her for one of theirs, if she had not thought fit to declare herself by her habit (alone) to be of the other, insomuch that I have often heard it lamented by the curious, who have taxed themselves of negligence, and were intimate with her lord, when living, that they did not desire him to explain upon that query.

Euphelia flourished under the shine of so great a favourite. The Marquis de los Minos[30] fell in love with her. There was nothing to obstruct his happiness but the Marchioness de Lerma's jealousy. Enraged to lose her beautiful pupil, she traversed her advancement all that lay in her power, but the honour of such a marriage being conspicuous on the young virgin's side, she was forced to give up the secrets of the cabal and sacrifice the marchioness's honour to preserve the opinion of her own.

26 *genius* governing spirit.

27 *Euphelia* Mrs Proud, one of Queen Anne's waiting gentlewomen (Ballard, p. 292).

28 *the queen* Queen Anne (reigned 1702–14).

29 *Marchioness de Lerma* Anne Charlotte, Lady Frescheville (née Vic); lady of the bedchamber to Queen Anne (from 1686); one of Anne's favourites (Ballaster, pp. 292–3).

30 *Marquis de los Minos* Henry Scott (1676–1730), First Earl Delorain, important Scottish nobleman (Ballaster, p. 293).

Some few such discoveries have happened to cast a taint upon the innocency of the cabal. How malicious is the world? Who would no[t] avoid their censure if it were possible? We must do justice to the endeavours of the witty Marchioness of Sandomire[31] when she used to mask her diversions in the habit of the other sex, and with her female favourite, Ianthe,[32] wander through the gallant quarter[33] of Atalantis in search of adventures. But what adventures? Good heaven! none that could in reality wound her chastity! Her virtue sacred to her lord and the marriage bed was preserved inviolable! For what could reflect back upon it with any prejudice in the little liberties she took with her own sex, whom she used to cajole with the affected seeming gallantry of the other, engage and carry them to the public gardens, and houses of entertainment with music and all diversions? These creatures of hire failed not to find their account in obliging the marchioness's and Ianthe's peculiar taste, by all the liberties that belonged to women of their loose character and indigence. Though I should look upon it as an excess of mortification were I the marchioness to see the corruption of the sex and to what extremes vice may step by step lead those who were born and probably educated in the road of innocence, it may be surely counted an inhuman curiosity and shows a height of courage more blameable than otherwise not to be dejected at the brutality, the degeneracy, of those of our own specie.[34]

The Viceroy of Peru's lady[35] has a more extensive taste, her circle admitting the eminent of both sexes. None can doubt of her condescension to the men, and, because she will leave nothing undiscovered or unattempted in the map of tenderness, she has encouraged the warbling Lindamira[36] (low as is her rank) to explain to her the *terra incognita*[37] of the cabal. Not one of 'em but think themselves honoured by a person of her distinction and agreeable merit. To complete their happiness they seem to wish (but I

[31] *Marchioness of Sandomire* either Lady Sandwich, wife of Edward Montagu, Third Earl of Sandwich (1670–1729); or Anne, Lady Popham (née Montagu) (Ballaster, p. 290).

[32] *Ianthe* Anne Gerard, Countess Macclesfield, divorced (1698) by her husband Charles Gerard, Second Earl of Macclesfield, on the grounds of adultery with Richard Savage, Earl Rivers (Ballaster, p. 293).

[33] *gallant quarter* district known to cater to amorous and sexual adventures.

[34] *specie* either 'gender' or 'class'.

[35] *The Viceroy of Peru's lady* Lucy Wharton (née Loftus) (1670–1718). Her husband Thomas, Marquis Wharton (1648–1715), was a member of the Whig Junto (Ballaster, pp. 278, 293).

[36] *Lindamira* Katherine Tofts, opera singer (?1680–1758) (Ballaster, p. 293).

[37] *terra incognita* Latin, 'the unknown land or country'.

doubt[38] it is in vain) that it were possible to exclude the other sex and engross her wholly to their own. But, alas! what hopes? Her heart, her eyes, her air, call for other approbations, the admiration of the men! In her alone that diffusive vanity is pardonable, is taking.[39] She undoubtedly knows herself born to a greater capacity of giving happiness than ought to fall to the share of one mortal and, therefore, in her just and equal distribution of beauty, she seems to leave none of her numerous favourites solid reason of complaint, that they are not in their turn considered as they deserve.

Anne (Kingsmill) Finch, Countess of Winchilsea (1661–1720), poet

Supporters of James II, Anne and her husband Heneage Finch (1657–1726), soldier and courtier, found their hopes for continued public careers dashed by the events of 1688. Retreating to the country estate of Heneage's cousin Charles, Fourth Earl of Winchilsea, and to the support of friends, most notably the Thanets and Thynnes, Anne and Heneage had a happy (albeit childless) marriage. In 1712, Heneage succeeded to the family title, and the following year Anne published *Miscellany Poems, on Several Occasions*, a volume of odes, love lyrics, verse epistles, and other poetic genres. Friend of the poets Anne Killigrew and Elizabeth Rowe, Finch's poetic reputation was high in her lifetime, and throughout the eighteenth century.

9.28

From *Anne Finch Folger MS: Miscellany Poems with Two Plays by Ardelia* (c. 1685–1702), pp. 48–9[1]

9.28.1 An Epistle from Ardelia to Mrs Randolph in Answer to Her Poem upon Her Verses[2]

Madam, till pow'rfully convinced by you,
I thought those praises never were their due,

[38] *doubt* suspect.
[39] *taking* attractive.

[1] Reproduced by permission of the Folger Shakespeare Library.
[2] *Ardelia* Finch's adopted name; *Mrs Randolph*: one of Finch's contemporaries and a poet; her commendatory poem appears at the beginning of Finch's autograph manuscript.

Which I had read, or heard bestowed by men
On women that have ventured on the pen.
But now must yield (persuaded by your style)
That Lesbian Sappho's might all hearts beguile.
The vanquished Pindar, now I must believe,
Might from Corinna's muse new laws receive,[3]
Since our own age is happily possessed
Of such a genius in a female breast,
As gives us faith for all those wonders told,
Producing new to justify the old.
Then we'll no more submit, but (in your name)
To poetry renew our ancient claim;
Through its retirement, we'll your worth pursue,
And lead it into public rule and view,
As the best monarchs, which the Romans made
Were forced to thrones from some beloved shade.[4]
Nor let it to your verse objected be
That it has stooped so low to find out me,
Since a mean subject greater skill requires
Than one which of itself high thoughts inspires.
And 'twas the Mantuan Poet's boasted praise,
Virgil's, who kings and heroes best could raise,
That if to lowly plains he did repair,
His song should make 'em worth a consul's care;
Thus, have you, madam, by your lines enhanced
My humble worth, and so, my fame advanced,
That wheresoe'er that panegyric's shown,[5]
It stands inferior only to your own;
And whilst Orinda's part you far transcend,[6]
I proudly bear that of her glorious friend,
Who though not equalling her lofty wit,
Th' occasion was, of what so well she writ.
Might I the parallel yet more improve,
And gain as high a station in your love,
Then should my pen (directed by my heart)

[3] *The … receive* *Corinna*, ancient Greek poet, won several poetry competitions against her famed contemporary, Pindar.

[4] *As … shade* e.g., Cincinnatus (fifth century BCE), appointed Roman general during a military emergency, left his plough, raised an army, defeated the foe, and then returned to his fields, all within fifteen days.

[5] *panegyric* poem of praise

[6] *Orinda* Katherine Philips's adopted name (see Introduction to **9.14**).

Make grateful nature speak the words of art,
Since friendship like devotion clears the mind,
Where every thought is heightened and refined.
Had Saul alone upon Mount Gilboa fell,
David had sung, but had not sung so well;
Described th'abandoned shield, and broken bow,
But to the love of Jonathan we owe
The love which that of women did surpass,
Of that sweet elegy, the mournful grace;
The brother Jonathan pierced deeper far
Than all the spears of that destructive war.[7]
Thus, may your valued kindness raise my sense,
Who can but treat you at your own expense,
Nor must, until I in that wish succeed,
E'er hope to write what's fit for you to read,
Since upon you it does alone depend
To make a poet, when you make a friend

Of Madam, etc.

9.29

From *Miscellany Poems* (1713)

9.29.1 Friendship between Ephelia and Ardelia[8]

EPHELIA. What friendship is, Ardelia, show.
ARDELIA. 'Tis to love as I love you.
EPHELIA. This account, so short (though kind)
Suits not my enquiring mind.
Therefore farther now repeat:
What is friendship when complete?
ARDELIA. 'Tis to share all joy and grief;
'Tis to lend all due relief
From the tongue, the heart, the hand;
'Tis to mortgage house and land;
For a friend be sold a slave;
'Tis to die upon a grave,
If a friend therein do lie.

[7] *Had Saul alone … war* 2 Sam. 1.19–27; cf. **8.30.1**.
[8] *Ephelia* unidentified.

EPHELIA. This indeed, though carried high,
This, though more than e'er was done
Underneath the rolling sun,
This has all been said before.
Can Ardelia say no more?
ARDELIA. Words indeed no more can show:
But 'tis to love as I love you.

9.30

From *Anne Finch Wellesley MS* (c. 1702–1719/20), pp. 92–3[9]

9.30.1 The White Mouse's Petition: To Lamira, the Right Honourable the Lady Ann Tufton, Now Countess of Salisbury[10]

With all respect and humble duty,
And passing every mouse in beauty,
With far more white than garden lilies
And eyes as bright as any Phyllis,[11]
I sue to wear Lamira's fetters,
And live the envy of my betters.
When I receive her soft caresses
And creeping near her lovely tresses,
Their glossy brown from my reflection
Shall gain more lustre and perfection.
And to her bosom if admitted
My colour there will be so fitted
That no distinction could discover
My station to a jealous lover.
Her hands whilst they're my food bestowing
A thousand graces will be showing,

[9] Reproduced by permission of the Wellesley College Library, Special Collections.

[10] *white mouse* The pet as a surrogate for and rival of the pining lover is a common trope in early modern love poetry, deriving from Catullus's 'Carmen 2'; it is envied for its physical closeness to the beloved. Cf. Sidney, Sonnets 59 and 83, *Astrophil and Stella* (1591); *Ann Tufton*: daughter of Finch's friend Catharine, Countess of Thanet. Finch wrote several poems for Anne, who married James Cecil, Earl of Salisbury in 1709.

[11] *Phyllis* common shepherdess's name in pastoral poetry.

And smiles enliven every feature
Whilst I engage her youthful nature
To mind my little tricks and fancies,
My active play and circling dances;
And if by a genteel behaviour
'Tis but my lot to gain her favour,
To her my life shall be devoted;
And I as her first captive noted
Shall fill a mighty place in story,
And share in that ambitious glory
To which so many hearts are growing,
Where loss of freedom shall be owing
To her whose chain my value raises
And makes me merit all your praises.

An Epistle from Signora F——a to a Lady (1727)

Epistle purports to be the address of the mezzo-soprano Faustina Bordoni (1700–81) to an unknown female beloved, and was a salvo in the spectacular feud between Bordoni and her operatic rival, Francesca Cuzzoni (1696–1778). From 1722 to 1728, Cuzzoni had sung all the lead roles with George Frederic Handel's Royal Academy opera company, and she had become enormously popular. However, Cuzzoni viewed Bordoni's arrival in the company in 1726 as a challenge to her position. Partly created by the press and company managers in order to increase ticket sales, and fuelled by each singer's faction enthusiastically applauding its favourite and heckling her opponent, the conflict came to blows during a 1727 performance. The fight between Bordoni and Cuzzoni was so spectacular that it was quickly satirized in prose pamphlets and John Gay's *The Beggar's Opera* (1728). While Bordoni had a successful career, later retiring to Venice to live with her husband and daughters, Cuzzoni's personal and professional prospects gradually diminished, and she finally died impoverished and in debt (I. Emerson, *Five Centuries of Women Singers* (Westport, 2005), pp. 59–76).

Editions

McGeary, Thomas, ed. and intro., 'Verse Epistles on Italian Opera Singers, 1724–1736', *Royal Musical Association Research Chronicle* 33 (2000): 29–88.

Norton, Rictor, ed. 'An Epistle from Signora F——a To a Lady (1727)', *Eighteenth-Century British Erotica II*, 5.179–88.

9.31

An Epistle from Signora F——a to a Lady (1727)[1]

Condemn not, madam, as I write in haste,[2]
My thoughts confused, or any word misplaced.
Of cens'ring tongues I scorn the little spite,
In wild disorder, as I love, I write.
In haste I write to ease your tortured mind,
Spite of your jealousy, I still am kind.
Unspotted as the sun, my love shall rise,
And soon dispel the fears that cloud your eyes.

Let others for dear scandal search the town,
Or with superior fancy choose a gown:
Others their heads with learned volumes fill,
Or boast of deeper science at quadrille:[3]
In the gay dance let other nymphs excel;
F——na's glory lies in loving well.
Of pleasure all the various modes I know,
In different degrees, its ebb and flow.
Ladies, unpractised in the art of love,
A living Aretin in me may prove.[4]
Propitious Venus, grant me power to give
Joy to fair ——, 'tis for her I live.[5]
Cease then to let your jealous fancy rove,
Nor give me such a cruel proof of love.
Am I in fault that crowds obsequious bend,
And rival beauties for my love contend?
That fierce Thalestris has attacked my heart?[6]

[1] Title page epigram: 'They do let heav'n see the pranks, / They dare not show their husbands' (*Othello* (3.3.216–17)). Place of publication is Venice (probably false); no publisher's name recorded.

[2] *madam* unidentified (and perhaps not a real person). Bordoni's faction was headed by Dorothy, Countess of Burlington and Lady Charlotte De La Warr (Delaware) (d. 1735) (Norton, *Eighteenth-Century British Erotica II*, 5.183). While the title 'madam' originally indicated a woman of high rank, it was increasingly applied to women of all classes.

[3] *quadrille* card game.

[4] *Aretin* Aretino (Glossary).

[5] The Folger Shakespeare Library copy identifies the 'fair —' as 'Stanly' (McGeary, p. 68).

[6] *Thalestris*, an Amazon queen, spent thirteen days having sex with Alexander the

Or gentle Chloe cast a milder dart?[7]
To fierce Thalestris I disdain to yield,
And gentle Chloe ne'er shall gain the field.
In vain she breathes her passion in my ear,
For when you speak I nothing else can hear:
In vain with transport to my feet she flew,
All joys are tasteless, but what come through you.
Before your fatal face I chanced to see,
No Cynic ever laughed at love like me.[8]
Inconstant as the wind, free as the air,
I ranged from man to man, from fair to fair.[9]
I roved about like the industrious bee,
First sucked the honey, then forsook the tree.
In Venus' combats I have spent the day,
Swiss-like, I fought on any side for pay.[10]
But now I love and your bewitching face
Has well avenged the cause of human race.
Do justice to yourself, review your charms,
Nor fear to see me in another's arms.
Have you not beauty equal to your youth?
Look in your glass, and then suspect my truth.
No passion tramontane in you I've found,[11]
By love and gratitude I'm doubly bound.
You first of all the British fair declared,
I sung unrivalled, e'er my voice you heard.
By sympathy you felt each charm, each grace,
And loved my person ere you saw my face.
Nor was I coy, or difficult to move,
When you revealed the story of your love.
With such pathetic mirth you played your part,

Great so that she could have a child by him. The FSL copy identifies Thalestris as 'Delaware' (Norton 5.183; McGeary, p. 68). See **n2**.

[7] *Chloe* common pastoral name. The FSL copy identifies Chloe as 'Hervey', perhaps John, Lord Hervey (1696–1743), well-known 'effeminate bisexual', but just as probably his wife, Mary (née Lepell), Lady Hervey (1699/1700–68), courtier and famed beauty (McGeary, p. 68).

[8] *Cynic* Greek philosophers infamous for their misanthropy and shameless indulgence in autoeroticism.

[9] *from man to man, from fair to fair* implying the speaker's bisexual love interests; *fair*: beloved woman.

[10] *Swiss-like* The Swiss were well-known mercenaries.

[11] *tramontane* literally, 'beyond the mountains'; thus, 'foreign, barbarous'.

You found an easy conquest of my heart.
I felt a thrilling joy, till then unknown,
And loved with ardour equal to your own.
Witness the transports of that happy day,
When melting in each other's arms we lay.[12]
With velvet kiss your humid lips I pressed.
And rode triumphant on your panting breast.[13]
Thus rode St George, thus fearless thrust his dart
Up to the head in the fell dragon's heart.[14]

In ecstasy you cried, 'What joys are these?
Not Durastanti's self so well could please.[15]
This is no sleepy husband's feeble mite,
The tasteless tribute of an ill-spent night.'

Such were our joys, Oh, could they always last!
But greatest pleasures are the soonest past.
Oh, did my power and will in concert move!
And were my strength but equal to my love!
Th'incredulous philosopher should see
Perpetual motion verified in me.[16]

John Hoadly (1711–76), poet and playwright

Educated at Cambridge (LLB, 1735), Hoadly was the son of the Bishop of Winchester. Ordained in 1735, apparently to reap the financial rewards of a career in the 'family business', Hoadly composed a number of plays, favouring music and spectacle, as well as biblical and classical themes; the best-known remains *The Contrast* (1731), featuring satiric portraits of contemporary writers. Some of his light verse, including the following poem, appeared in Dodsley's *Collection of Poems in Six Volumes* (1758).

[12] *melting* achieving orgasm.

[13] *rode* had sexual intercourse (with) (implication: the speaker is the active, perhaps penetrative, partner); the following image suggests that the speaker uses a dildo or her own hypertrophied clitoris. See Chapter 2, Introduction.

[14] *Thus … heart* St George, patron saint of England, slew a dragon (symbol of Satan); *dart*: spear (common euphemism for 'penis'); *fell*: mortally dangerous.

[15] Margherita *Durastanti* (*fl.* 1700–34), principal soprano at the Royal Academy opera company before the arrival of Cuzzoni; Durastanti played many different roles, but was not reportedly an exciting singer (Emerson, pp. 64, 70).

[16] A *perpetual motion* machine produces more energy than it consumes (an impossibility).

9.32

On the Friendship of Two Young Ladies (1730)[1]

Hail, beauteous pair, whom friendship binds
  In softest, yet in strongest ties,
Soft as the temper of your minds,
  Strong as the lustre of your eyes.

So Venus' doves in couples fly,[2]
  And friendly steer their equal course;
Whose feathers Cupid's shafts supply,
  And wing them with resistless force.

Thus as you move Love's tender flame,
  Like that of friendship, paler burns;
Both our divided passion claim,
  And friends and rivals prove by turns.

Then ease yourselves and bless mankind,
  Friendship so cursed no more pursue:
In wedlock's rosy bow'r you'll find
  The joys of love and friendship too.

William King (1685–1763), Oxford college head and minister

A lawyer by training, the Oxford-educated King never practised, spending his career in the Church and academia. Famed for his neo-Latin verse and pro-Tory Latin orations satirizing Whig corruption, King was a strident Jacobite, but finally accepted the legitimacy of the Hanoverian dynasty around 1761; some of his later verse praises George III and his effect on Britain. King's mock-heroic poem *The Toast* (2 vols, 1732; 4 vols, 1736) is an attack on Sir Thomas Smyth and his wife, Myra, former Countess of Newburgh, King's uncle and aunt, for defaulting on a substantial loan that King had made to them; the text is King's revenge for his ultimately unsuccessful twenty-year pursuit of restitution through the courts. However, *The Toast* is much more than a savage libel: its objects of satire include academic pedantry, literary critics, translators, Anglo-Irish political and

[1] 5.275.

[2] *doves* Venus's emblematic bird; drew her heavenly chariot; symbols of marital love and fidelity.

sexual corruption, and the Irish national character. Purporting to be Peregrine O'Donald's translation of the Swedish writer Frederick Scheffer's *Phoebus Noctivigator, seu Hermaphroditus* ('Phoebus, the Night-Wanderer, Or, The Hermaphrodite', a nonexistent work by an equally nonexistent writer and translator), *The Toast* is also a literary game, inviting the reader to identify the mythic personages of the poem with their contemporary real-life counterparts. The British Library copy concludes with one reader's list of these identifications. Scheffer's and King's 'learned' footnotes and appendices comprise some of the work's most vicious assaults on Myra, as well as an index of classical and contemporary beliefs about female homoerotic relationships, desires, and sexual acts.

9.33

From *The Toast*[1] (second edn, 1736)

[Apollo, Vulcan, and Mars are drinking toasts to all the beautiful women they know, from goddesses to mortals. Apollo suggests Myra, leading to laughter and mockery from his companions, especially Mars, Myra's husband. Apollo decides to visit Myra and see if his companions' monstrous representation of her is true. Looking in at her bedchamber window in the early morning, he sees her rise.]

9.33.1 Book 3

[. . .]

There he saw the huge mass tumble out of her bed;
Like Bellona's her stature, the Gorgon's her head;
Hollow eyes with a glare, like the eyn of an ox;[2]
And a forehead deep furrowed, and matted grey locks;
With a toothless wide mouth, and a beard on her chin,
And a yellow rough hide in the place of a skin;
Brawny shoulders upraised; cow udders; imp's teat;[3]
And a pair of bowed legs, which were set on splay feet.[4]

[1] Subtitle: 'An Epic Poem in Four Books'.

[2] *eyn* eye.

[3] *imp's teat* Witches were believed to possess a *teat* through which they fed their demonic familiars or *imps* (Satan in animal form). Cf. **n12–13**.

[4] *splay* flat.

With the figure the god was surprised and offended,
When he marked how these various defects were amended;
How her back was laid flat with an iron machine,[5]
And her breasts were laced down, with a sweet bag between[6]
How she shaded her eyes, and the squalid black beard[7]
Was so smoothly shaved off, scarce a bristle appeared;
How she cleared the old ruins, new plastered her face,
And applied red or white as it suited the place:
With a set of Watts' teeth, and a cap of Deard's hair,[8]
Like a virgin she bloomed, and at sixty seemed fair.

[…]

[…] a soul he espied
Full of envy, black malice, base leasing, and pride;[9]
Hypocritical, sordid, vainglorious, ingrate;
In her friendships most false, and relentless in hate.
He beheld, at one view, all the acts of her life;
How experienced a miss; how abandoned a wife![10]
That advancing in years, all her wants she supplied,
By an art which the famed Messalina ne'er tried.[11]
Though her gallants were few, nor not made to her mind;
Yet her joyance was full, if the Jewess was kind.[12]

[…]

5 *iron machine* corset stiffened with strips of steel.

6 *bag* perfumed sachet.

7 *shaded* darkened (by using cosmetics).

8 *Watts's teeth* false teeth made by the John Watts's company (*fl.* 1711); *Deard's hair*: wig.

9 *leasing* lying.

10 *abandoned* sexually unrestrained. King's note: His Latin 'original' calls Myra 'Libido Mascula', and King explains the phrase refers to Horace's sorceress Folia (Epode 5.42), who 'was a woman *masculae libidinis*, that is to say, she loved women in the same manner as men love them; she was a tribade' (pp. 116–17; misnumbered in the original 100–1).

11 *Messalina* wife of the Emperor Claudius; a by-word for insatiable licentiousness.

12 King's note: The 'Jewess' refers to 'the same person who in the second book is called […] "the little Dutch frow" and who hereafter is [called] "Myra's Imp"' (p. 117; misnumbered 101). In Book 2, p. 67, King describes the Frow as 'a Jewess and a dwarf', as well as 'the wife of one Traulus'. She 'gave Myra more pleasure than all the rest of her lovers and mistresses. She was therefore dignified with the title of "Chief of the Tribades or Lesbians".' The BL copy identifies the *Jewess* as Lady Allen, wife of Lord Viscount Allen (*Traulus*).

Thus dismissed the male gallants, in crawled her own imp
In a scaly small body, contorsed like a shrimp.
In a rapture she stroked it, and gave it the teat,
By the suction to raise sympathetical heat.
Then by Hecate she swore, 'she was sated with men,'
Sung a wanton Sapphoic, and stroked it again,[13]
And again, and the thrice she erected her rod:
(For the numbers in magic must always be odd.)
See the force of her spells mighty Circe's surpass,
And the beldams, which made Apuleius an ass![14]
See a reptile transformed to a shape near the human,
And the imp, that erst entered, resemble a woman![15]
Not a woman like those which the Musslemen use,[16]
Or the grandees of Britain for mistresses choose:[17]
The indelible mark on her forehead impressed,[18]
God's revenge, and old Shylock's cursed lineage confessed;[19]
With the locks of a Negress half-mingled with grey,
And a carcass ill-moulded of dirty red clay;
Clammy, livid, cold lips, with a crooked long nose;
And a skin full of spots from her head to her toes.[20]
Nor a daughter of Eve has a body so foul;[21]
Nor has Envy herself so envenomed a soul.
But to Myra most dear! Nor so fair in her sight,

[13] *Sapphoic* song in the manner and metre of Sappho. King's note: '[…] every witch is attended by an imp, who is called her familiar, and who assumes any shape to do her pleasure or service. As soon as the imp approaches her, the witch immediately gives it the breast. This is a ceremony which must be constantly observed. Without it, all her spells and incantations would be ineffectual' (p. 123; misnumbered 107).

[14] In Apuleius's *Golden Ass*, Lucius is turned into an ass through the intervention of a sorceress.

[15] King's note: '*Succuba* is a devil that assumes a woman's shape to lie with a man, or to lie with a woman when the act of tribadism is to be performed, as in this place. *Succuba* likewise signifies any notorious adulteress' (p. 124; misnumbered 108).

[16] *Musselmen* Muslims.

[17] *grandees* persons of high rank.

[18] *indelible mark* referring to the mark God places on Cain, the first fratricide (Gen. 4.15). In the Latin 'original', Myra's imp is called *Demonassa*, which King traces back to Lucian's 'Dialogues of the Courtesans', 'where we find a woman of […] the same uncouth appetites', supporting the view that Myra and the imp are engaged in 'the act of tribadism' (p. 125; misnumbered 109).

[19] *Shylock's cursed lineage* Jews.

[20] *skin … spots* sign of sexually transmitted disease.

[21] *daughter of Eve* human woman.

Was Anacthon or Cydno thus formed for delight:[22]
O ma vie, ma femme! What a shape, and a face![23]
Then impatient she rushed to a closer embrace.
Let the rest be untold! And thus ever forbear,
Lest thy numbers, O Scheffer, offend the chaste fair.
And do thou, O my Clara, this freedom excuse.[24]

[...]

When a pair of foul tribades I rudely unveil,
'Tis Charybdis I show you, 'tis Scylla's dog-tail.[25]

[...]

[Apollo, feeling that he has been deceived by poets' praise of Myra into making her a toast, decrees that no man should any longer praise his mistress unless that woman is first vetted by himself and the Muses; he also commands that Myra should be barred from intercourse with men, and confined to 'her kind'. As Venus makes clear below, she interprets 'her kind' to mean other women, not other hermaphrodites.]

[...]

22 King's note: 'Anacthon (or Anactorie) and Cydno were two of Sappho's mistresses. [...] Sappho was a famous tribade, as appears by the testimonies of all the old poets, but particularly from that beautiful ode (addressed to one of the ladies with whom she was in love) which Longinus has preserved, and which has ever been so highly esteemed by all the critics. But though she had acquired so much glory by her verses as to be styled "the Tenth Muse", yet she acknowledges that her love of the Lesbian women had destroyed her reputation. [...] As amorous and vicious as the Greeks were, yet they accounted this a most infamous passion. And there seems to have been a peculiar act of justice in the punishment of Sappho, who killed herself at last for the love of a man' (pp. 125–6; misumbered 109–10). See Introduction to **7.2–7.9**; see also **7.3.1** and **7.3.2**.

23 *O ma vie, ma femme!* French, 'O my life! My woman!' (probably an address to Clara; see **n24**). King's note: The 'original' Latin phrases, King notes, are too obscene for translation: 'That is, "I am all man."' In Lucian's 'Dialogues of the Courtesans' (see **7.31.1**), an 'impudent woman' uses this expression to indicate 'I have all the appetites and desires of a man, I am all over man.' French refugees living in Dublin also gave Myra the name '"Homesse" or "Homasse", "*quia tribas diffamata fuit*"' (i.e., because she was an infamous tribade) (p. 126; misnumbered 110).

24 *Clara* if a real person, she remains unidentified; apologies of this type, however, occur sporadically throughout the text.

25 *Charybdis* was a dangerous whirlpool in the straits of Messina, while *Scylla* was a sea monster in the same straits, with six heads and a group of yelping dogs at her tail. 'To be caught between Scylla and Charybdis' is 'to be trapped between two equally dangerous alternatives'.

And whereas maugre all the old creature's disguises,[26]
I discern her true form and unnatural vices;
'Tis my will, since to wayward amours she'd inclined,
She be only permitted to mix with her kind:
Though the Fates to a hundred should lengthen her span,
Let the matron no more be compressed by a man;
And whereas I foresee, that a mind so impure
Will incite the decrepit old dame to procure;
By the force of her spells, with a forward court air
And the semblance of virtue to ruin the fair.
By a special grace moved, I enjoin and command
You the tutelar gods, who bear sway in that land
All her actions to watch, all her witchcrafts to cross,
And to save other nymphs, as ye saved Lady R-sse.[27]

[Venus rebukes Apollo for his misogynist disgust with Myra's ageing face and body, but more particularly for meddling in the goddess's sphere of authority: sexuality and desire. She cannot cancel Apollo's decree, so she 'gets around it' by granting Myra a penis.]

9.33.2 Book 4

[...]

'If the women are bald or their tresses are grey;
Father Time and the Fates are in fault and not they.
Shall the want of a tooth, when a dame is well born,
Or perhaps a few wrinkles expose her to scorn?
You confess (and we know you surveyed ev'ry place)
She's young as your godship except in the face.
For the secrets we use to preserve complexion,
They are none of your drugs, nor create an infection;
Paints and lotions on all royal toilets are seen:[28]
Mark the court of young Lewis, and censure his queen.[29]
Should I make your decree, sir, a matter of quarrel;

26 *maugre* in spite of. Apollo speaks here.

27 Lady Ross's escape from being initiated into Myra's tribadic circle, King says, is well known in Dublin (p. 134; misnumbered 118).

28 *toilets* make-up tables.

29 *Young Lewis* Louis XV, King of France (1710–74), famous for his debauched private life.

While I speak it, my Myra should change to a laurel.[30]
Then your rhymers in dogg'rel her beauties would prize,
Proud to wear the bright locks, they are bid to despise.
But you know I love peace; nor my manners incline
To impertinent meddling, like you and your nine.[31]
Be the matron restrained, as your edict directs;
But allow me to make her more fit for her sex.[32]
Let her thus be erect [*Here she held out her fan*]
And be superinduced all the virtue of man![33]
Nor Priapus in action shall equal her fame;
Nor so oft shall Dan Chanticleer feather his dame.[34]
Let her passions be strong as her form is complete,
And her name of distinction be Friga the Great![35]
And, my Friga, to thee, ere revolve many years,
Shall the man most renowned of Ierne's new peers,[36]
In return for thy labours to honour his bed,
(Nor **** has done more to exalt a great head)[37]
In the plains of S—l—gan a monument raise,[38]
Where the centaurs and satyrs shall envy their praise.
What intends the quaint figure, few clerks shall divine,
But the tribades shall ken it an emblem of thine.'[39]

30 *change … laurel* 'Apollo and Daphne' (Glossary).

31 *your nine* the Muses (Glossary).

32 King's note: '[…] she was perfect male and female, and could exercise both sexes with equal ability' (p. 165).

33 *be superinduced* be given in addition; *virtue:* strength.

34 *Dan Chanticleer* in Chaucer's *Canterbury Tales*, a lustful rooster; *dan*: sir; *feather*: copulate with.

35 *frig* copulate with (or masturbate). King's note: Friga or Freya was 'the goddess of all impurities. She was worshipped in the shape of an hermaphrodite, and her statue represented both sexes […] When I call Friga the Venus of the Saxons, you must not from thence conclude that she was a beautiful person, but on the contrary, that she had strong, masculine features, with a great beard. For as such a person, even Venus herself was represented in all those places where she was worshipped as a hermaphrodite.' King's history of sex changes concludes by asserting that they do occur naturally, noting at least twenty changes of this kind (e.g., Sister Magdalena Mugnoz, expelled from her nunnery when she turned into a man, went on to rape and impregnate women) (pp. 166–7).

36 *Ierne* Ireland.

37 **** denoting a name that King wants to avoid even hinting at; unidentified.

38 *S—l—gan* 'Skylagan, a seat [place of residence] of Lord Allen's' (BL Library copy; see **n12**); *monument*: an obelisk erected by a gentleman who had enjoyed Myra's sexual favours; it is the 'symbol of old Myra's transformation' on account of its phallic shape (p. 168).

39 *ken* declare.

[…]

[Mars, hearing of his wife Myra's metamorphosis into a man, is enraged, and rushes off to confront her.]

[…]

Here alighting he entered androgyne's dome,[40]
Though a brazen-head swore that she was not at home.[41]
Nor recalled him a voice, as he mounted the stairs;
Though the treble squeaked thrice, 'Sir, my lady's at prayers.'
Nor abated his rage, when he reached the first floor:
But, without previous rap, he forced open the door;
And surprised (well-a-day!) the great Friga and Frow[42]
In a posture the Muse must not venture to show!
So uncommon, it 'scaped Peter Aretine's touch;[43]
Nor was practised before, but on Sappho's own couch.
Thus the warrior began: 'Pretty lambkins at play!
Lo, the fervour with which great hermaphrodites pray!'
The virago bounced up; and her impy bedight,[44]
Unabashed she advanced, thus upbraiding the knight:
'What intends this antique? What are you who presume[45]
To disturb my repose and intrude to my room?
Do you come here to rob or my manhood to try?
Or has Traulus prevailed on your knightship to spy?[46]
Boast the noble adventure; indulge your mad spleen;[47]
Bid your trumpeter sound the rare feats you have seen!
Say, to help the good wife, I have formed a new plan,
And, as thou art turned child, I am ripened to man;
That I double the favours, which now I bestow,
And create two cornutos, embracing one frow.'[48]

40 *he* Mars; *androgyne*: hermaphrodite.

41 *brazen-head* unabashed liar.

42 *Frow* Dutch, 'wife'; here, sexually available woman. Cf. **7.23.5 n24**.

43 *Peter Aretine* Aretino (Glossary).

44 *virago* mannish-woman; also, 'sexual athlete'; *impy*: See **n3**; *bedight*: arrayed (perhaps, 'wrapped up, covered').

45 *antique* relic; old-fashioned man.

46 *Traulus* See **n12**.

47 *spleen* violent ill-nature or irritable temper.

48 King's note: 'Here, the hermaphrodite boasts of the great benefit she had received by her metamorphosis, as being now in a condition to make two *cornutos* (meaning Sir Mars and Traulus) by embracing one wife. At the same time, she insinuates that she was able to do the work of a hundred men, and could in her own person, supply the

[Mars and Myra battle for mastery, the weapons involved being urine (which Myra spills on the floor to make Mars slip), fists, crockery, a sewing needle, a hot poker, and Mars's powdered wig. Thrown in her face, the last item blinds her. Captured and bound by Mars, Myra rejects his conditions for liberty (begging for her life, divorcing him, compensating his financial losses, ceasing her public slander of him and his lover, Molly).]

[…]

This enraged the chevalier; he changed his mild note,
And his eyes, while he spoke, were was red as his coat:
'Is it thus, when my offers are civil, you dare me?
Do you think at noon-day that your goblins can scare me?
Or submit or by Styx (here he drew the broad blade)[49]
Shall your manhood as smooth as a black eunuch's be made.'[50]
Friga heard him, and trembled: the same panic fear
Seized the imp in her hole; if the imp was still there!
As a bold British sailor, far distant the shore,
All the sea-gods defies, bids the elements roar;
But descends to his prayers, is confounded, aghast,
When he hears the dire order to cut down the mast:
So the mighty virago, whom naught could affright;[51]
Nor the duns of the day, nor the demons of night;[52]
Nor diseases, old age, nor a satire could move,
Nor the anger of Phoebus, nor the thunder of Jove
Was appalled at the sight of a rusty short sword,
And alas! was subdued by the force of one word.
'Me an eunuch!' she cries. And with suppliant hands,
But indignant submits to the victor's demands.

[…]

necessities of all the married women in Dublin' (p. 178); *cornutos*: horns (sign of the cuckold, a man sexually deceived by his wife).

49 *Or … or* Either … or.

50 *black eunuch* supervisor of Turkish seraglios (harems); completely castrated. See **4.3.3 n9**.

51 *virago* See **n44**.

52 *duns* demands of debt collectors.

Glossary

Achates the hero Aeneas's faithful friend; by-word for unquestioning loyalty.

Achilles in Homer's *Iliad*, legendary Greek warrior; son of the sea goddess, Thetis, and the mortal king Peleus; killer of the son of King Priam of Troy, Hector, most famous of the Trojan warriors. Thetis dressed Achilles in women's clothes and hid him among the daughters of the King of Lycomedes in a vain attempt to protect him from his prophesied death in the Trojan War.

Achilles and Patroclus The ancients and early moderns often saw the relationship between Achilles and his fellow Greek warrior Patroclus as an erotic one; the ancients disagreed over which of the two was the older *erastes* ('lover') and which the younger *eromenos* ('beloved'). Their relationship began when Patroclus, son of King Menoetius of Opus, accidentally killed Amphidamas, for which crime he fled to the court of King Peleus, there becoming the inseparable companion of Achilles, accompanying him to the siege of Troy. When Patroclus was killed by the Trojan hero Hector, Achilles (who had refused to fight on account of a dispute with King Agamemnon; the Greek general had seized for himself the beautiful Briseis, Achilles' concubine and spoil of war) re-entered the fray, finally killing Hector in revenge. Achilles' profound love and grief became proverbial, and the couple often occurs in classical and early modern lists of devoted male friends and lovers.

Actaeon ancient hunter who gazed upon the goddess Diana while she was bathing; she transformed him into a stag, and he was subsequently killed by his own hounds.

Admetus See *Hercules and Admetus*.

Aegina Jove assumed the shape of a flame to seduce this mortal woman.

Alcibiades famously handsome, and reputedly licentious, young Athenian; intimate friend of Socrates. In Plato's *Symposium* (216–23), Alcibiades details his failed seduction of Socrates, who spends the night in the same bed as Alcibiades without succumbing to sexual temptation. Plutarch details Alcibiades' bisexual propensities, and Socrates' love for Alcibiades as demonstrated in the philosopher's attentive guidance and education of the young man ('Life of Alcibiades', *Online Companion*). Early modern readers would also know of Socrates' reputation for being erotically attracted to beautiful youths, and certainly some assumed that Socrates and Alcibiades had been lovers.

Alcmena Jove seduced this mortal woman by transforming himself into her husband; he tripled a normal day's length to prolong his sexual enjoyment of her.

Alcon archer, reputedly so skilled that he shot and killed a snake that had his son in its coils without hurting him (Menalcas invites Mopsus to sing 'in praise of Alcon' (Virgil, 'Eclogue 5.11')).

Alexander and Hephaestion It was widely assumed that Alexander the Great (356–323 BCE), King of Macedon, and the famously beautiful Hephaestion (d. 324 BCE), his Macedonian general, were lovers. At Troy, Alexander laid a wreath on Achilles' tomb, Hephaestion on Patroclus's, signifying the erotic nature of the Macedonian pair's relationship. Alexander grieved terribly and publicly when Hephaestion died, commanding that his dead beloved be paid semi-divine honours.

Alexis young shepherd and scornful male beloved of the older shepherd Corydon in Virgil's 'Eclogue 2'.

Amyntas shepherd (in Virgil's *Eclogues*).

Antiope in the form of a satyr, Jove seduced this mortal woman.

Aphrodite See *Venus*.

Apollo Phoebus, god of the sun, poetry, music, and the liberal arts and sciences; famously beautiful; often pictured driving his sun chariot across the sky.

Apollo and Daphne When Apollo tried to rape the nymph Daphne, she fled. Praying to the gods for rescue, Daphne was transformed into a laurel tree, which became sacred to Apollo, and out of which was subsequently fashioned the crown awarded to conquering heroes and superlative poets.

Apollo and Hyacinthus The beautiful Greek youth Hyacinthus, native of Amyclae (near Sparta), was beloved of Apollo, who accidentally killed Hyacinthus during a discus-throwing contest; the discus was blown towards the boy by Apollo's jealous rival, Zephyrus, god of the west wind. Apollo transformed Hyacinthus's blood into the flower that still bears his name, with the figure AI inscribed thereon, Greek for 'alas'.

Aretino Pietro Aretino (1492–1556), Italian poet and satirist, composed a group of sonnets (*Sonetti Lussuriosi*) accompanying sixteen engravings depicting various sexual positions. In his *Ragionamenti* (Dialogues) (Part 1, 1534; Part 2, 1536), 'Dialogue 1.1' details nuns' same-sex intercourse, but focuses largely on their engagement in heterosexual vaginal and anal intercourse; Aretino was a by-word in England for the sexual licentiousness of Italy.

Ariadne daughter of King Minos of Crete. Betraying her father, she helped the Greek hero Theseus kill the Minotaur, the monster to which Minos fed tribute Athenian boys and girls. Although Theseus took her with him when they left Crete, he abandoned her. Coming upon the forlorn woman, Bacchus fell in love with her and later married her.

Athena also 'Pallas' and 'Minerva'; virgin goddess of wisdom and war; born fully formed out of the head of her father, Jove, split open by Vulcan, god of the forge or smithy.

Atlas one of the Titans, ancient demi-gods; condemned to bear eternally the world on his shoulders.

Atys/Attis See *Cybele.*

Bacchus also, 'Dionysus', god of wine and revelry; famously beautiful. Bacchus's female followers, the Bacchants or Maenads, were famous for being driven into sensual and sexual abandonment or ecstatic frenzy by the god.

Bellona goddess of war.

Briseis See *Achilles and Patroclus.*

Callisto virgin nymph and huntress-follower of Diana; Jove assumed the shape of a nymph or Diana herself to rape Callisto. Becoming pregnant, she was banished from Diana's company, giving birth to a boy who later became the great hunter Arcas. Juno transformed Callisto into a bear as punishment, but later Jove transformed both Callisto and Arcas into constellations, when Arcas was on the verge of killing his mother in her bear-shape.

Calypso beautiful nymph; in Homer's *Odyssey* imprisoned Ulysses on her island in a vain attempt to compel him to marry her.

Castor and Pollux the Gemini; in some myths they are the twin sons of Jove and the mortal woman, Leda; in others, only Pollux is Jove's son, while Castor is the son of Leda and her human husband, King Tyndareus of Sparta. As a result, some myths say that only Pollux was immortal, and, when Castor died, Jove granted Pollux's request that Castor be given half his immortality; they lived and died alternately, some writers say every day, others every six months. To celebrate their love, Jove transformed them into the constellation Gemini. Early modern images of the Gemini could be both platonic and erotic. Clothed, the Gemini often figured ideal male friendship and brotherly devotion; naked, they assumed homoerotic overtones, featuring in lists of male erotic couples, alongside Hercules and Hylas, Achilles and Patroclus, etc. (J. Kolve, *Telling Images* (Stanford, 2009), p. 136). For Castor and Pollux's sisters, Helen of Troy and Clytemnestra, see *Helen of Troy* and *Leda.*

centaurs half-man, half-horse creatures; Ovid describes their war against the Lapithae.

Ceres goddess of the harvest and fertility.

Charon ferryman; in his boat, he conveyed the souls of the dead across the River Styx to the classical underworld Hades (hell) or paradise Elysium, also called 'the Elysian fields.'

Circe sorceress; in Homer's *Odyssey* struck Ulysses' men with her wand, turning them into pigs, often allegorized as the transformation of the soul by bestial lust.

Corydon See *Alexis*.

Cupid god of love, son of Venus; famously beautiful; pictured as a winged boy, although as the embodiment of love and desire, he was also considered the eldest of the gods.

Cybele ancient mother-goddess, whose ritual worship involved ecstatic dancing and singing; the early moderns associated her with witchcraft. She loved Attis (Atys), a beautiful shepherd youth, and appointed him chief priest of her temple. When he violated his vow of chastity with the nymph Sangaris, Cybele drove him mad, and he castrated himself. Ever after, the priests of Cybele were castrated to ensure their celibacy and as a sign of their devotion.

Cyparissus beautiful boy beloved by Apollo and Zephyrus, god of the west wind, or Silvanus, a Roman forest god. When Cyparissus accidentally killed a stag which he loved, he pined away from grief; Apollo transformed him into the cypress tree, symbolizing sorrow.

Cytherea See *Venus*.

Daedalus artificer; created wings for himself and his son, Icarus, so they could escape imprisonment in Crete. Ignoring his father's advice, Icarus flew too near the sun, and when his waxen wings melted he fell into the sea and was drowned; Icarus became a common emblem of over-reaching pride.

Damon common shepherd's name in pastoral verse (goatherd in Virgil's *Eclogues*).

Damon and Pythias ancient emblems of ideal male friendship. Damon offered himself as a hostage for his friend, Pythias (condemned to death by the tyrant Dionysius I), so that Pythias could return to their shared home and make arrangements for his death. Dionysius mocked Damon's faith when it looked as though Pythias would not return, leaving Damon to die in his stead. When Pythias did return, Dionysius was so impressed that he freed both men, and sought to be their friend.

Danae Imprisoned in a tower by her father, King of Argos, in response to the prophecy that she would bear a son who would cause his death, Danae was impregnated by Jove in the form of a golden shower; she gave birth to the hero Perseus, who later accidentally killed his grandfather.

Daphne See *Apollo*.

Daphnis herdsman and legendary inventor of pastoral poetry; appears in Theocritus and Virgil (Virgil's 'Eclogue V' mourns Daphnis' death and celebrates his 'deification').

David and Jonathan The friendship of these Israelite warriors is described as 'wonderful, passing the love of women' (2 Sam. 1.26). Jonathan and his father, King Saul, died together in battle on Mount Horeb, occasioning David's famously beautiful elegy (2 Sam. 1.19–27).

Diana also 'Phoebe', 'Dictina', 'Cynthia', and 'Artemis'; goddess of the moon, virginity, and the hunt; often accompanied by her attendant virgin huntresses (her 'virgin train').

Dis See *Pluto.*

Echo See *Narcissus and Echo.*

Elysian Fields See *Charon.*

Elysium See *Charon.*

Endymion beautiful shepherd boy from Caria; falling asleep on Mount Latmos, he was spotted by Diana (the moon), who fell in love with him, causing to sleep forever so she could constantly gaze on his loved form. See *Diana.*

Epaminondas and Pelopidas famed classical warriors and an emblem of idealized male friendship; Pelopidas was the leader of the Sacred Band, and together the friends freed Thebes from the dominance of Sparta.

Europa daughter of the King of Tyre; kidnapped by Jove in the shape of a bull; resuming his shape, he seduced her; she gave birth to three sons.

Fates supernatural figures in charge of one's life-span: Lachesis appointed the length and nature of a life; Clotho spun the thread of life; and Atropos cut it (determined the moment of death).

Fauns and satyrs notoriously licentious, mythological creatures; often emblems of unrestrained lust; human from the waist up, but goat-like from the waist down; usually associated with Bacchus (Dionysus), the god of wine and revelry, and Pan, Faunus, and Silenus, divine patrons of rural life.

Furies Greek spirits of vengeance; pursued and drove mad those who violated important taboos, such as the murder of a parent or sibling.

Ganymede See *Jove and Ganymede.*

Gemini See *Castor and Pollux.*

Giants sons of Gaia (Earth) and Uranos (Heaven), who rebelled against Jove, but were defeated, struck down by his thunderbolts; Jove condemned them to terrible punishments in Hades.

Gorgon horrifically ugly monster; looking into its face would turn one to stone.

Graces also, the *Charites* or *Gratiae*; the three Graces (Aglaia, Euphrosyne, and Thalia) are daughters of Jove; Venus's semi-divine attendants, embodying beauty, charm, and grace; often depicted nude.

Hebe See *Jove and Ganymede.*

Hector See *Achilles and Patroclus.*

Hecuba wife to King Priam of Troy; driven to grief-driven madness when Troy was destroyed by the Greeks, her husband murdered by Achilles' son, herself taken by the Greeks, and her daughter Polyxena sacrificed on the tomb of Achilles, who had once sought to marry her.

Helen of Troy According to the most prevalent myth, Helen was the daughter of Leda and Jove, and she was born from the same egg as Pollux, while her half-siblings, Castor and Clytemnestra, were fathered by Leda's human husband, King Tyndareus of Sparta. Famed as the most beautiful woman in the world, some legends say she was the prize for Paris, prince of Troy, when he was called upon to judge the relative beauty of the goddesses Venus, Diana, and Juno (see *Paris*). In Homer, Helen is the wife of Menelaus, king of Sparta; she is seduced by Paris and carried off by him to Troy, thus triggering the Trojan War. See *Castor and Pollux* and *Leda*.

Heliogabalus Roman emperor (204–22 CE); famed for his sexual excesses and gender 'irregularities' of all kinds, including cross-dressing, polygamy, incest, same-sex sexual acts and relationships (his officer Hierocles was his favourite), as well as cruelty and indulgence in sybaritic luxury; murdered by his army.

Hercules also, 'Alcides' and 'Heracles'; ancient hero; son of Jove by the mortal woman, Alcmene; husband of the mortal women, Megara and Deianira; famous for his Twelve Labours and participation in the Argonaut expedition; made a god at his death, and given Hebe, goddess of youth, as his wife. Hercules's many love affairs, with both men and women, were well known.

Hercules and Admetus Hercules's dear friend Admetus, King of Pherae, had won a favour from the god Apollo in exchange for the kind treatment Apollo received at Admetus's hands when Apollo was exiled from heaven: the Fates greed that Admetus would be allowed to live forever if he could find someone else to die in his place when the time came. Admetus's wife, Alcestis, agreed to do so; Hercules descended into the Underworld and brought her back. Some myths link Hercules erotically with Admetus, some with Alcestis.

Hercules and Hylas Hercules's beloved boy, Hylas, was drowned when the nymphs, seeing his beauty, pulled him down under their spring to possess him; not knowing what had happened, Hercules grieved terribly, abandoning a heroic quest with Jason's Argonauts to go in search of his lost beloved. Cf. Martial, *Epigrams*, 6.68, where the boy Eutychus is drowned in this way and mourned over by his master and lover, Castricus.

Hercules and Omphale Omphale, Queen of Lydia, purchased Hercules, and freed him. Lovesick for her, he agreed to put on women's clothes and spin, while she put on his lion's skin and took up his weapons; emblem of masculine sovereignty overthrown by sexual passion.

Hermaphroditus dual-sexed son of Venus (Aphrodite) and Mercury (Hermes); refusing the love of the nymph Salmacis, Hermaphroditus's body was fused together with Salmacis's, in response to her desperate prayer to the gods; interpreted as accounting for the origin of hermaphrodites and individuals who loved both men and women.

Hermes See Mercury.

Hero and Leander a lovely priestess of Aphrodite/Venus at Sestos, Hero was the lover of Leander, a beautiful youth of Abydos, who would swim the Hellespont to visit her. During one crossing, he was drowned, and Hero committed suicide by leaping into the sea.

Hierocles See Heliogabalus.

Hippolytus son of Theseus and Hippolyte, Hippolytus virtuously rejected the sexual advances of his stepmother, Phaedra. Enraged, Phaedra accused Hippolytus of attempted rape, and Theseus, believing her, asked Neptune to punish him. Neptune caused Hippolytus' horses to trample him to death. Phaedra hanged herself.

Hyacinthus See *Apollo and Hyacinthus.*

Hylas See *Hercules and Hylas.*

Hymen Hymenaeus, a beautiful but low-born Athenian youth, who eventually became an emblem of marital felicity, and was deified; god of marriage.

Icarus See *Daedalus.*

Jason celebrated hero, founder and leader of the Argonauts, a group of hero-adventurers; son of Aeson, rightful King of Iolcos. Arriving to claim his father's throne from his usurping uncle, Jason was gazed upon for his beauty.

Jove also 'Jupiter' and 'Zeus'; king of the gods, and husband of Juno (Hera); often called 'the Thunderer'; notorious for his numerous adulterous relationships, particularly with mortal women.

Jove and Ganymede The beautiful boy, Ganymede, son of the King of Troy, was hunting (or tending his father's sheep) when Jove swept down in the form of an eagle and carried him off to Olympus to be his beloved and serve as the gods' cupbearer. Ganymede was granted immortal youth and beauty; his epithets include 'the Phygian', 'the Trojan boy', and the 'Idalian boy'. 'Ganymede' became a by-word for a boy kept to satisfy the sexual desires of his master; often represented as the object of Juno's hatred for usurping Jove's affection and the place of their daughter, Hebe (whose name means 'youth'), as the gods' cupbearer.

Juno queen of the gods, goddess of childbirth, and wife of Jove. Raging jealously at Jove's infidelities, she severely punished the hapless mortal women involved.

Jupiter See *Jove.*

Leander See *Hero.*

Leda wife of Tyndareus, King of Sparta. In the most popular version of the myth, Jove transformed himself into a swan and raped her, and she subsequently gave birth to an egg, out of which were born Pollux and Helen of Troy, while her two other children, Castor and Clytemnestra (later the wife and murderer of King Agamemnon of Mycenae), were fathered by her human husband, King Tyndareus of Sparta. See *Castor and Pollux* and *Helen of Troy.*

Lucrece also 'Lucretia'; wife of Tarquinius Collatinus; killed herself after she was raped by Sextus, son of the Roman king, Tarquinius Superbus, triggering a revolution that ended the Roman monarchy and introduced the Republic; by-word for female chastity and honour.

Lycidas shepherd-poet; appears in Virgil's 'Eclogue 9' (praises the verse of his fellow poet Menalcas) and Theocritus's 'Idyll 7' (called an excellent piper; involved in poetic contests with another respected poet, Simichidas); also, a beautiful, admired Roman youth (Horace, *Odes*, 1.4.19).

Mars god of war. See *Venus and Mars.*

Megara See *Hercules.*

Mercury also 'Hermes'; son of Jove (Zeus); messenger of the gods; often pictured with winged sandals, a petasus (winged cap) and caduceus (staff in the shape of intertwined serpents); famed for eloquence and persuasiveness; crafty and given to stealing the other gods' property. See *Hermaphroditus.*

Minerva See *Athena.*

Muses nine semi-divine female patrons of the liberal arts and sciences; attendants of Apollo.

Narcissus and Echo The nymph Echo fell in love with Narcissus, a beautiful youth, son of the river god Cephisus. He rejected her; she pined away and died, leaving only her voice behind. Described as coy, scornful, and proud, for rejecting not just Echo but all the young men and women who desired him, Narcissus was punished by falling hopelessly in love with own reflection; unable to look away from it, he starved to death; subsequently changed into the flower that bears his name.

Nero Roman emperor (reigned 54–68 CE); notorious for his sexual transgressions, such as seducing free-born boys. Wearing a bridal veil, and with all the accouterments of a Roman wedding, Nero married his freedman Doryphorus (sometimes called 'Pythagoras'), and assumed the 'passive' role in their sexual intercourse. As a man, Nero later married one of his male slaves, Sporus, after first having the youth castrated and dressed in bridal attire.

nymphs spirits of nature; semi-divine beings in the form of lovely women; often associated with particular natural settings (groves, caves, and springs, in particular).

Oenone See *Paris.*

Omphale See *Hercules and Omphale.*

Orestes See *Pylades.*

Orpheus and Eurydice famed singer and musician, son of Apollo and the muse Calliope; descending into the Underworld to reclaim his dead beloved, Eurydice, Orpheus sang and played so movingly for Pluto and Proserpine, the god and goddess of the Underworld, that Pluto granted Orpheus's wish for Eurydice to live again. Unfortunately he disobeyed Pluto's injunction not to look back at Eurydice while the pair ascended back to life, and Eurydice was lost to Orpheus forever.

Pallas See *Athena.*

Pan rural fertility god, usually having goat's horns, ears, and legs; patron of shepherds and herdsmen. Falling in love with the nymph Syrinx, daughter of the river god Ladon, he attempted to rape her; praying for rescue, she was transformed into a reed, out of which Pan subsequently made his pipes.

Paris son of King Priam of Troy; exposed as a baby on Mount Ida to prevent a prophecy from coming true: that he would be the instrument of his nation's destruction. Raised a shepherd, he later married Oenone, a nymph and healer. Wise and prudent, he was commanded to judge a contest between the goddesses Venus (Aphrodite), Juno (Hera), and Minerva (Athena), to decide which of them was the most beautiful (which deserved the golden apple marked 'for the loveliest'). Venus promised Paris the most beautiful woman in the world (Helen of Troy) as a reward, and he gave the judgement to her. Paris's seizing of Helen initiated the Trojan War; and led to him later being a symbol of rashness and sexual incontinence.

Pasiphae daughter of Helios (Sol, the sun), and wife of King Minos of Crete; satisfied her sexual desire for a bull by getting the artisan Daedalus to construct an artificial cow within which she climbed to be mounted by the bull; consequently, gave birth to the Minotaur, a monster, half-man, half-bull.

Patroclus See *Achilles and Patroclus.*

Peleus See *Achilles and Patroclus.*

Pelopidas See *Epaminondas and Pelopidas.*

Pelops son of King Tantalus of Phyrgia. Testing the omniscience of a visiting group of gods, Tantalus killed his son Pelops and served him as dinner. Most of the gods refused to eat, but the distracted Ceres (Demeter), goddess of the harvest, ate one of Pelops's shoulders. When Jove restored Pelops to life, he made the boy a replacement out of ivory.

Penelope wife of Ulysses, Greek hero and King of Ithaca; in Homer's *Odyssey* she waited twenty-three years for his return from Troy, resisting all the while her threatening and demanding suitors; common early modern archetype of wifely constancy and chastity.

Phaethon Apollo's son. Apollo rashly granted his wish to drive his father's sun-chariot; losing control of the fiery horses, Phaethon was killed by Jove (Zeus) to prevent the destruction of heaven and earth

Philomela, Tereus and Procne King Tereus of Thrace married Procne, daughter of King Pandion of Athens; Tereus invited Procne's sister, Philomela, to visit, and subsequently imprisoned and raped her, and cut out her tongue. Philomela wove her story into a tapestry that she smuggled to Procne; together, they killed Procne and Tereus's son, Itys, cooked and served him to his father; the gods prevented Tereus's retributive murder of the sisters, turning them all into birds; most famously, Philomela became a nightingale.

Phoebe See *Diana.*

Phoebus See *Apollo.*

Phoenix fabled Egyptian bird; lived on incense; immolating itself every five hundred years, on a pyre of cassia, nard, cinnamon bark and other sweet-smelling spices, it would rise newborn from its own ashes (Ovid, *Metamorphoses*, 15.391–430); emblem of eternal youth and resurrection; common symbol of Christ.

Pirithous and Theseus Perithous, King of the Lapithae, admired the reports of the hero-king Theseus's virtues so much that he decided to meet him on the field of battle and win his friendship. Meeting there, they immediately loved each other, embraced, and ended the conflict; emblem of ideal male friendship.

Plato and Socrates Greek philosophers; well known among the early moderns for their avocation of platonic pederastic love, but also for their strong erotic feelings for and relationships with boys; epigrams for the beautiful boy Aster (attributed to Plato) appeared in the *Greek Anthology*; Socrates acknowledged his erotic attraction to beautiful youths in *Charmides* (155c–e). Plato's dialogues *Phaedrus* and *Symposium*, featuring Socrates as interlocutor, treat Greek pederastic love at length.

Pluto also 'Dis'; god of the Underworld.

Pollux See *Castor.*

Priapus god of fertility, son of Venus and Bacchus. The deformed Priapus was exposed by his mother, but was rescued by shepherds; often depicted with an enormous erect phallus.

Proserpine also Proserpina; wife of Pluto, goddess of the Underworld.

Pylades and Orestes somewhat controversial ancient emblem of male friendship; Pylades, son of the King of Phocis, helped Orestes murder Orestes' mother Clytemnestra and her lover Aegisthus, to revenge their murder of Orestes' father, Agamemnon.

Pythagoras See *Nero.*

Pythias See *Damon.*

Sardanapulus last King of Assyria; reputed lover of men and women; enjoyed sitting cross-dressed among his concubines spinning wool; primary sexual relationships with his eunuchs.

Satyrs See *Fauns and satyrs.*

Semele daughter of King Cadmus of Thebes; asked her lover Jove to appear before her in his divine form; forced to do so because he had promised to grant her anything she asked, Jove consumed Semele with his divine fire, but he saved her unborn son, later the god Bacchus.

Semiramis wife of Ninus, King of Assyria; had sex with a horse. Her son, Ninyas, later killed her when she conceived an ungovernable passion for him.

Silvanus See *Cyparissus.*

Socrates See *Plato and Socrates*; *Alcibiades.*

Spheres In pre-Copernican astronomy, the Earth was surrounded by a set of nesting concentric spheres, each of which contained a heavenly body or bodies; the crystalline sphere was that of the unchanging stars, above which was the realm of the prime mover (God) and below which was a set of increasingly corrupt and mutable realities; the spheres' friction produced a divine music inaudible to people.

Sporus See *Nero.*

Styx See *Charon.*

Syrinx See *Pan.*

Tantalus King of Phrygia; punished for stealing the food of the gods and his treatment of Pelops, he was condemned to the Underworld, where he stood with water up to his chin that receded whenever he tried to drink, and fruit overhead that pulled back whenever he tried to eat. See *Pelops.*

Thetis See *Achilles and Patroclus.*

Thyrsis shepherd; engages in a singing contest with his fellow shepherd Corydon (Virgil, 'Eclogue 7'); laments the herdsman and legendary creator of bucolic poetry, Daphnis (Theocritus's 'Idyll 1').

Tiresias Transformed into a woman for seven years before resuming his male gender, as a woman, Tiresias married, and adjudicated Juno and Jove's dispute about who enjoyed the most pleasure in sexual intercourse: men or women. When Tiresias said 'Men', Juno struck him blind, but Jove gave him prophetic insight and long life.

Titus and Gysippius also 'Josip' and 'Josippus'; together, a popular emblem of ideal male friendship. Titus, son of a Roman senator, was desperately in love with the Athenian prince Gysippus's female beloved. Placing friendship above heterosexual love, Gysippus surrendered her to Titus, and later in the story claimed responsibility for a murder that Gysippus had been unjustly accused of, willing to sacrifice his own life for that of his friend.

Troilus famously handsome warrior, son of King Priam of Troy; one tradition says that Achilles loved Troilus and that he inadvertently killed the youth by the strength of his embraces.

Venus also 'Aphrodite' and 'Cytherea'; goddess of love, wife of Vulcan, the lame god of the forge or smithy. See *Hermaphroditus.*

Venus and Adonis Adonis, the famously beautiful mortal youth with whom Venus fell in love, died after being gored by a boar that he had been hunting.

Venus and Mars lovers. Venus's husband, Vulcan, trapped the adulterous pair under a net and then called all the gods in to laugh at them.

Vesta virgin goddess of the hearth.

Zephyrus See *Apollo and Hyacinthus.*

Works Cited

Andreadis, Harriette. 'Re-Configuring Early Modern Friendship: Katherine Philips and Homoerotic Desire.' *SEL* 46.3 (2006): 523–42.

—. *Sappho in Early Modern England: Female Same-Sex Literary Erotics, 1550–1714.* Chicago: University of Chicago Press, 2001.

Ashton, Robert, ed. *James I by His Contemporaries.* London: Hutchinson, 1969.

Bergeron, David M. *King James and Letters of Homoerotic Desire.* Iowa City: University of Iowa Press, 1999.

Borris, Kenneth, intro. and ed. *Same-Sex Desire in the English Renaissance: A Sourcebook of Texts, 1470–1650.* New York: Routledge, 2004.

— and George Rousseau, ed. *The Sciences of Homosexuality in Early Modern Europe.* London: Routledge, 2008.

Bray, Alan. *The Friend.* Chicago: University of Chicago Press, 2003.

—. 'Homosexuality and the Signs of Male Friendship in Elizabethan England.' *Queering the Renaissance.* Ed. Jonathan Goldberg. Durham, NC: Duke University Press, 1994, 40–61.

—. *Homosexuality in Renaissance England.* New York: Columbia University Press, 1995.

Bushnell, Rebecca W. *A Culture of Teaching: Early Modern Humanism in Theory and Practice.* Ithaca: Cornell University Press, 1996.

Cady, Joseph. '"Masculine Love," Renaissance Writing, and the "New Invention" of Homosexuality.' *Homosexuality in Renaissance and Enlightenment England.* Ed. Claude Summers. New York: Haworth, 1992, 9–40.

Crompton, Louis. *Homosexuality and Civilization.* Cambridge, MA: Belknap/Harvard University Press, 2003.

—. 'The Myth of Lesbian Impunity: Capital Laws from 1270–1791.' *Journal of Homosexuality* 61.1/2 (1980/81): 11–25.

Davidson, James. *The Greeks and Greek Love: A Radical Reappraisal of Homosexuality in Ancient Greece.* London: Weidenfeld & Nicolson, 2007.

DiGangi, Mario. *The Homoerotics of Early Modern Drama.* Cambridge: Cambridge University Press, 1997.

Donoghue, Emma. *Passions Between Women: British Lesbian Culture, 1668–1801.* New York: Harper, 1996.

Edelman, Lee. *Homographesis: Essays in Gay Literary and Cultural Theory.* New York: Routledge, 1994.

Elias, Richard. 'Political Satire in *Sodom*.' *SEL* 18.3 (1978): 423–38.

Frye, Susan. 'Sewing Connections: Elizabeth Tudor, Mary Stuart, Elizabeth Talbot, and Seventeenth-Century Anonymous Needleworkers.' *Maids and Mistresses, Cousins and Queens: Women's Alliances in Early Modern England.* Ed. S. Frye and K. Robertson. Oxford: Oxford University Press, 1999, 165–82.

Goldberg, Jonathan. *Sodometries: Renaissance Texts, Modern Sexualities.* Stanford: Stanford University Press, 1992.

Goldsmith, Netta Murray. *The Worst of Crimes: Homosexuality and the Law in Eighteenth-Century London.* Aldershot: Ashgate, 1998.

Gonda, Caroline and Chris Mounsey. 'Queer People: An Introduction.' *Queer People: Negotiations and Expressions of Homosexuality, 1700–1800.* Ed. Caroline Gonda and Chris Mounsey. Lewisburg: Bucknell University Press, 2007, 9–37.

Gordon, Peter and Denis Lawton. *Royal Education: Past, Present, and Future.* London: Taylor and Francis, 1999.

Gouws, J. 'Introduction.' *Nicholas Oldisworth's Manuscript (Bodleian MS. Don.c.24).* Tempe, AZ: RETS, 2009, xv–xl.

Green, David. *Sarah, Duchess of Marlborough.* London: Collins, 1967.

Gregg, Edward. *Queen Anne.* London: Routledge, 1980.

Grundy, Isobel. '"The Barbarous Character We Give Them": White Women Travellers Report on Other Races.' *SECC* 22 (1992): 73–86.

Haggerty, George E. *Men in Love: Masculinity and Sexuality in the Eighteenth Century.* New York: Columbia University Press, 1999.

—. 'Male Love and Friendship in the Eighteenth Century.' *Love, Sex, Intimacy and Friendship between Men, 1550–1800.* Ed. Katherine O'Donnell and Michael O'Rourke. New York: Palgrave, 2003, 70–81.

Halperin, David M. *How to Do the History of Homosexuality.* Chicago: University of Chicago Press, 2002.

—. 'Introduction: Among Men – History, Sexuality, and the Return of Affect.' *Love, Sex, Intimacy and Friendship between Men, 1550–1800.* Ed. Katherine O'Donnell and Michael O'Rourke. New York: Palgrave, 2003, 1–11.

Hamilton, Elizabeth. *William's Mary.* London: Hamish Hamilton, 1972.

Hammond, Paul. *Figuring Sex between Men from Shakespeare to Rochester.* Oxford: Clarendon, 2002.

Hanson, Ellis. 'Sodomy and Kingcraft in *Urania* and *Antony and Cleopatra*.' *Homosexuality in Renaissance and Enlightenment England.* Ed. C.J. Summers. New York: Haworth, 1992, 135–51.

Heffernan, Teresa. 'Feminism Against the East/West Divide: Lady Mary's "Turkish Embassy Letters".' *ECS* 33.2 (2000): 201–15.

Henderson, Judith Rice. 'Erasmus on the Art of Letter-Writing.' *Renaissance Eloquence*. Ed. J.J. Murphy. Berkeley: University of California Press, 1983, 331–55.

Herrup, Cynthia B. *A House in Gross Disorder: Sex, Law and the 2nd Earl of Castlehaven*. New York: Oxford University Press, 1999.

Holmes, Michael Morgan. 'The Love of Other Women: Rich Chains and Sweet Kisses.' *Aemilia Lanyer: Gender, Genre and the Canon*. Ed. Marshall Grossman. Lexington: University Press of Kentucky, 1998, 167–90.

Hunt, Margaret R. 'The Sapphic Strain: English Lesbians in the Long Eighteenth Century.' *Singlewomen in the European Past, 1250–1800*. Philadelphia: University of Pennsylvania Press, 1999. 270–96.

Klawitter, George. *The Enigmatic Narrator: The Voicing of Same-Sex Love in the Poetry of John Donne*. New York: Peter Lang, 1994.

—. 'Verse Letters to T.W. from John Donne: "By You My Love Is Sent".' *Homosexuality in Renaissance and Enlightenment England*. Ed. Claude J. Summers. New York: Haworth, 1992, 85–102.

Laqueur, Thomas W. *Solitary Sex: A Cultural History of Masturbation*. New York: Zone, 2004.

Levine, Laura. *Men in Women's Clothing: Anti-Theatricality and Effeminization, 1579–1642*. Cambridge: Cambridge University Press, 1994.

Marotti, Arthur F. *Manuscript, Print and the English Renaissance Lyric*. Ithaca: Cornell University Press, 1995.

McClain, Molly. 'Love, Friendship, and Power: Queen Mary II's Letters to Frances Apsley.' *Journal of British Studies* 47.3 (2008): 505–27.

McFarlane, Cameron. *The Sodomite in Fiction and Satire, 1660–1750*. New York: Columbia University Press, 1997.

McRae, Andrew. *Literature, Satire and the Early Stuart State*. Cambridge: Cambridge University Press, 2004.

Mendelson, Sara and Patricia Crawford. *Women in Early Modern England*. Oxford: Clarendon, 1998.

Norton, Rictor. *Mother Clap's Molly House: The Gay Subculture in England, 1700–1830*. London: Gay Men's Press, 1992.

—. *The Myth of the Modern Homosexual: Queer History and the Search for Cultural Unity*. London: Cassell, 1997.

—. comp., intro., and ed. *Eighteenth-Century British Erotica II*. Volume 5. London: Pickering and Chatto, 2004.

—. comp. and ed. *Homosexuality in Eighteenth-Century England: A Sourcebook*. <http:// rictornorton.co.uk/eighteen/>.

Orvis, David L. '"Lustful Jove and His Adulterous Child": Classical *Paiderastia* as Same- Sex Marriage in Marlowe's *Dido Queene of Carthage*.' *Performing*

Pedagogy in Early Modern England: Gender, Instruction, and Performance. Ed. Kathryn M. Moncrief and Kathryn R. McPherson. Burlington: Ashgate, 2011, 101–12.

Pittenger, Eizabeth. '"To Serve the Queere": Nicholas Udall, Master of Revels.' *Queering the Renaissance.* Ed. Jonathan Goldberg. Durham, NC: Duke University Press, 1994, 162–89.

Reynolds, Margaret. *The Sappho Companion.* London: Vintage, 2001.

Rollinson, David. 'Property, Ideology and Popular Culture in a Gloucestershire Village, 1660–1740.' *Past and Present* 93 (1981): 70–97.

Schleiner, Winfried. 'Intrigues of Hermaphrodites and the Intercourse of Science with Erotica.' *The Sciences of Homosexuality in Early Modern Europe.* Ed. Kenneth Borris and George Rousseau. London: Routledge, 2008, 245–53.

Sedgwick, Eve Kosofsky. *Epistemology of the Closet.* Berkeley: University of California Press, 1990.

Smith, Bruce R. *Homosexual Desire in Shakespeare's England: A Cultural Poetics.* Chicago: University of Chicago Press, 1991.

Staves, Susan. 'A Few Kind Words for the Fop.' *SEL* 22.3 (1982): 413–28.

Stewart, Alan. *Close Readers: Humanism and Sodomy in Early Modern England.* Princeton: Princeton University Press, 1997.

Still, Judith. 'Hospitable Harems? A European Woman and Oriental Spaces in the Enlightenment.' *Paragraph* 32.1 (2009): 87–109.

Traub, Valerie. *Desire and Anxiety: Circulations of Sexuality in Shakespearean Drama.* London: Routledge, 1992.

—. *The Renaissance of Lesbianism in Early Modern England.* Cambridge: Cambridge University Press, 2002.

Trumbach, Randolph. 'The Heterosexual Male in Eighteenth-Century London and His Queer Interactions.' *Love, Sex, Intimacy and Friendship between Men, 1550–1800.* Ed. Katherine O'Donnell and Michael O'Rourke. New York: Palgrave, 2003, 99–127.

—. 'The Birth of the Queen: Sodomy and the Emergence of Gender Equality in Modern Culture, 1660–1750.' *Gender and History in Western Europe.* Ed. R. Shoemaker and M. Vincent. London: Arnold, 1998, 161–73.

—. 'Sodomitical Subcultures, Sodomitical Roles, and the Gender Revolution of the Eighteenth Century.' *'Tis Nature's Fault: Unauthorized Sexuality During the Enlightenment.* Ed. R.P. Maccubbin. New York: Cambridge University Press, 1987, 109–21.

Turner, James Grantham. *Schooling Sex: Libertine Literature and Erotic Education in Italy, France, and England, 1534–1685.* Oxford: Clarendon, 2003.

Vitkus, Daniel J. 'Introduction.' *Three Turk Plays from Early Modern England.* New York: Columbia University Press, 2000, 1–53.

Wahl, Elizabeth Susan. *Invisible Relations: Representations of Female Intimacy in the Age of the Enlightenment.* Stanford: Stanford University Press, 1999.

Weitzman, Arthur J. 'Voyeurism and Aesthetics in the Turkish Bath: Lady Mary's School of Female Beauty.' *CLS* 39.4 (2002): 347–59.

Wunder, Amanda. 'Western Travellers, Eastern Antiquities, and the Image of the Turk in Early Modern Europe.' *Journal of Early Modern History* 7.1–2 (2003): 89–119.

Young, Michael B. *James VI and I and the History of Homosexuality*. London: Macmillan, 2000.

Index